F

166822

BARRICADES

BARRICADES

*The War of the Streets
in Revolutionary Paris,
1830–1848*

Jill Harsin

First published 2002 by PALGRAVE™
175 Fifth Avenue, New York, N.Y.10010 and
Houndmills, Basingstoke, Hampshire RG21 6XS.
Companies and representatives throughout the world.

PALGRAVE is the new global publishing imprint of St. Martin's Press
LLC Scholarly and Reference Division and Palgrave Publishers Ltd.
(formerly Macmillan Press Ltd.).

ISBN 0–312–29479–4 hardback

Library of Congress Cataloging-in-Publication Data

Harsin, Jill
Barricades : the war of the streets in revolutionary Paris, 1830–1848 / Jill
Harsin.
    p.   cm.
    Includes bibliographical references and index.
    ISBN 0–312–29479–4
    1. Paris (France)—History—1830–1848. 2. Republicanism—
France—Paris—History—19th century. 3. Revolutions—France—
Paris. 4. France—History—Louis Phillip, 1830–1848. I. Title.

DC733.H37 2002
944'.36063—dc21
                                                                    2001058802

A catalogue record for this book is available from the British Library.

Design by Letra Libre, Inc.

First edition: July 2002
10 9 8 7 6 5 4 3 2 1

Printed in the United States of America.

To my husband,
Briton Cooper Busch,
with all my love.

CONTENTS

Acknowledgements   ix

I. HONOR

1. Introduction: Montagnardism   3
2. The End of the Regime: Joseph Henry's *Préméditations*   20

II. INSURRECTION

3. The Failure of Moderate Republicanism   39
4. Preparing for Battle:
    The *Société des Droits de l'Homme et du Citoyen*   65
5. April 1834: La Guerre des Rues, I   84
6. The Republican Underground: The *Familles* and the *Saisons*   106
7. May 1839: La Guerre des Rues, II   124

III: ASSASSINATION

8. Fieschi's Infernal Machine   147
9. Alibaud, Meunier, and the Cult of Regicide   168
10. Republican Communists: The *Travailleurs Égalitaires*   188

IV: RECRIMINATION

11. Competitors and Mouchards   211
12. Captivity and Defiance: The Years of Mont-Saint-Michel   229

V: DEFEAT

13. Restaging the Revolution: February 1848   251
14. Living the Republic: The Provisional Government   275
15. "*Une mâle et sombre résignation*": The June Days   294
16. Epilogue: La Proscription   319

Notes   323
Selected Bibliography   391
Index   409

ACKNOWLEDGEMENTS

Working on this book has taken me on a joyous journey through nineteenth-century Paris. I would like to thank my colleagues at Colgate University, in the History department and elsewhere, for their stimulating presence, as well as several generations of students, whose questions have forced me to clarify my thoughts and presentation of events. My thanks also go to the Colgate University Library staff, and particularly Ellen Bolland, Ann Ackerson, and Faith Stivers of the Interlibrary Loan department, and David Baird of the Information Technology department. Finally, I owe many thanks to Amanda L. Johnson, my editor at Palgrave, for her kind and thoughtful help in putting this book into final form.

I am grateful to my parents for their unwavering support, and especially to my husband, Briton Busch, for reading the manuscript as I wrote it: there are great advantages (if insufficient shelf space) in having another historian in the house. Finally, three German Shepherds—Saxon, Gretchen, and Lili—have taught me that sometimes it is better to stop writing and go out for a walk.

NOTE ON TRANSLATIONS

All translations, except where otherwise noted, were done by the author.

PART I

✛✛✛✛✛✛

HONOR

Note on "Legal System and
Trad "under Orders"
p 51— 57

CHAPTER 1

INTRODUCTION: MONTAGNARDISM

IN JULY 1830, PARISIANS TOOK TO THE STREETS to overthrow Charles X, the last Bourbon monarch, and many Europeans feared they were on the brink of another great war. The victors of 1815—Great Britain, Prussia, Russia, and Austria—had pledged to maintain the peace for twenty years against a French resurgence; fulfilling that commitment, which many saw as synonymous with keeping the Bourbons on the throne, would have meant an invasion of one of the most powerful nations in Europe. The situation was taken in hand by the ruling classes in France, primarily by the liberal members of the Chamber of Deputies. They brought the revolution to an end in less than two weeks and recruited the duc d'Orléans to become king as Louis Philippe I (third in line anyway, as the head of the royal family that would succeed if the Bourbons were ever extinguished). He acted with moderation to consolidate his regime; the other powers soon extended diplomatic recognition to his government. The crisis was over.

The outpouring of relief that greeted the Orléans settlement stemmed from the magnitude of the wars that preceded it, only fifteen years in the past. The French Revolution had begun in 1789, with the bankruptcy of the government and the calling of the Estates-General. It had progressed rapidly, soon becoming an assault on the intellectual, political, and religious foundations of Europe. In 1792, a combined spirit of paranoia and missionary zeal had led to a declaration of war by the revolutionary ministers who had been forced upon the king. European governments, one after the other, joined the battle to liberate their fellow monarch from his countrymen. Louis XVI was overthrown and imprisoned in August 1792, in the midst of French defeats. The First Republic was founded in September, its reputation bloodied by the trial and execution of the king in January 1793. In the meantime, the republican constitution was suspended—indeed, it had never gone into effect—and there was instead a wartime dictatorship under the Committee of Public Safety. The Reign of Terror and the trial and execution of thousands of supposed internal enemies of France finally ended in 1794, as the Republic devoured its founders—Georges Danton guillotined in April, Maximilien Robespierre himself in July. A republic of sorts continued as the Directory, but was overthrown by Napoleon in 1799. Napoleon ruled as First Consul until he made himself Emperor of the French in 1804.

Throughout this internal turmoil the war continued, under different names, against different coalitions. In Europe it raged from Britain to Russia, toppling the Holy Roman Empire founded by Charlemagne, chasing the princelings of central Europe from their petty kingdoms, and kindling the spirit of patriotism in disunited Germany and Italy and the overrun territories of Poland and Spain. Napoleon surrendered in April, 1814 and was exiled in Elba, too close to the southern coast of France; he escaped and plunged Europe into renewed war during the Hundred Days. It ended, at last, with Napoleon's final defeat at Waterloo in June 1815.

The Congress of Vienna met in 1814 and 1815; the leaders attempted a settlement that would dampen the "revolutionary embers" that remained.[1] The new German Confederation had 35 states, loosely joined under the hereditary presidency of the Habsburg emperor—which meant, until 1848, the minister Clemens von Metternich, who imposed a regime of censorship and police surveillance. Italy was also left disunited, many of its *ancien régime* rulers kept in place or restored, including the Bourbons of the wretched Kingdom of Naples; Spain was given back its own unpopular Bourbon monarch. A reconstituted Poland was left under the control of Russia; Polish freedom fighters would rebel in 1830–31, in 1848, in 1863. The Quadruple Alliance, in the few years of its post-congress existence, sent troops against liberal uprisings in Italy and Spain.

The Vienna peacemakers accepted the one overriding fact of life in postwar Europe: France was still intact, still wealthy, still (even without Napoleon) a great power. They took away her empire—or rather, the empire had dissolved, in Napoleon's retreat from Russia in December 1812, in his defeat at the battle of Leipzig in October 1813. They attempted to provide barriers against renewed French aggression. The peoples of Belgium and Holland were consolidated into a short-lived kingdom on France's northeastern boundary. In the southeast, they enlarged Piedmont-Sardinia, nucleus of the future kingdom of Italy. The buffer zone was completed by a line of middling German states, including several little enclaves granted to Prussia.

The stability of France was further guaranteed by the Bourbon monarch Louis XVIII, the brother of Louis XVI; he had taken his title much earlier, upon the death in June 1795 of his nephew, known to the faithful as Louis XVII. The childless monarch was succeeded in 1824 by Charles X, the last of the three royal brothers. The Bourbon Restoration had not been untroubled—the Bonapartist Grenoble conspiracy of 1816, the underground *carbonari* conspiracies of 1821 and 1822, the assassination of Charles X's younger son, the duc de Berry, in 1820—and yet the new regime had mastered these expressions of discontent.[2] Indeed, the members of the Quadruple Alliance considered France stable enough to entrust with the expedition to crush the Spanish revolution in 1823; hence the consternation when Charles X was overthrown by Parisians at the barricades in July 1830, and the relief when Louis-Philippe restored order.

But if Europe had been saved from another war, France itself entered into a period of dramatic instability. The July Revolution had ended too swiftly; the emotions aroused had been crushed and left to simmer beneath the surface. Republicanism suddenly emerged as a challenge to the status quo: a revolutionary republicanism, one that defiantly embraced the discredited legacy of Robespierre and Marat and proclaimed its commitment to violence and terror. The work that follows is an examination of this phenomenon.

✤✤✤✤✤

Nineteenth-century French republicanism has been the subject of an extremely rich body of work. Most of it has focused on the moderate version that finally succeeded in the Third Republic, with the basis for that success variously defined as ideological/political,[3] cultural,[4] or economic.[5] A number of studies have examined the growth of the strong provincial republican movement whose interests did not always agree with those of the Parisians.[6] In his study of Edgar Quinet, François Furet drew attention to the internal divisions between *true* the liberal, individualistic republicanism of 1789 and the Jacobinism of 1793. The sudden reappearance of this violent strain after 1830, with none of the mitigating circumstances alleged for the Reign of Terror—no credible counterrevolution, neither foreign nor civil war[7]—was evidence of a genuine divide in the nineteenth-century movement, a split that could not be fully explained by external pressures. Georges Weill, whose major survey was long the standard work, had a deceptively simple explanation: the Parisian movement, he said, was characterized by the fact that "the young republicans loved the Convention."[8] And though there was a moderate, middle-class republicanism that existed in July Monarchy France as a whole—the bourgeois "circles" described by Maurice Agulhon, and the provincial organizations discussed by Pamela Pilbeam, for example[9]—the focus here is on what I have called *montagnardism*, defined as a Paris-centered movement (largely working class but with bourgeois allies and spokesmen) that looked back to the Reign of Terror for inspiration.[10]

The montagnard movement was characterized by three primary features. The first, and most obvious, was violence: violence not only in action but in ideology, a theoretical commitment to the revolutionary appropriation of the machinery of state as the chief means to transform the social and economic environment. The second feature was honor, bound up with a contemporary working-class definition of masculinity that shaped the behavior of those in the movement. Finally, there was a third aspect, in the romantic consciousness that guided the movement. This was a republicanism of excess and sacrifice, a republicanism that was fonder of its losses than of its victories.

Montagnard violence began with the following belief: in order to understand society, one had to comprehend the economic and social relations between classes and the manifestation of these relationships in the government. This was not an unusual assumption in this era; Karl Marx shared it, as did many of the utopian socialists. Thus the active republicans did not see the government as a neutral force, but rather as the repressive arm of the financial and commercial bourgeoisie who ruled. The Chamber, based on a restricted suffrage, passed laws that were designed to aid the propertied classes, just as judges, the partisan agents of the government that appointed them, invariably found for property owners.

The montagnard view of government as monolithic and undivided in its interests was grossly oversimplified. They were blind to the significance of purely local influences (of landlords over peasants, employers over workers) as well as of competing interests within the government itself (among regions, bureaucracies, constituencies, and ideologies). But their perception—whether right or wrong—guided their political strategy, which became concentrated on the single project of forcibly seizing the apparatus of the state and wielding its power to transform society. During the 1840s, the growing numbers of socialists developed an entirely different course of action from the same set of external factors, the same understanding of exploitation. The struggle to capture the bourgeois state was the main goal of the republican movement—and thus is the focus of this study—but it was not the only way of seeing and thinking and acting in the July Monarchy.[11]

In the beginning, some republicans were willing to take a less violent road. The moderate leaders of the *Société des Amis du Peuple* insisted that the 1830 revolution had ended the need for conspiracy, asserting that the "republican institutions" supposedly surrounding the new monarchy would include a free press and the right to assemble; they tested both in the early months of the regime, and were soon disillusioned by a series of heavy-handed prosecutions. The government passed harsh new legislation against the civil rights of association, speech, and the bearing of arms (in this place and time, a liberty staunchly defended by the Left). The new laws were coupled with abusive, excessive enforcement, as the government repeatedly wore down the activists with lengthy pre-trial detentions. The July Monarchy also developed a harsh penal system, culminating in the decision to sentence political prisoners to solitary confinement.

Though republicans faced an increasingly rigid government, their violence in this era cannot be fully explained by external repression. Within montagnardism was an unresolvable conflict between liberty and coercion, between individual heroics and conformity to group discipline—between, as Patrice Higonnet has recently described it, "private rights and public good."[12] Consider, for example, this position paper composed by the tailor Louis Quignot, one of the secondary leaders of the underground *Société des Saisons*, in 1839:

> It is uncontestable that after a revolution carried out to the profit of our ideas, a dictatorial power should be created, with the mission to direct the revolutionary movement. . . . The first care of this power should be to organize revolutionary forces, to stir up the enthusiasm of the people in favor of equality by every means, to suppress those enemies that the popular torrent did not engulf in the moment of combat. . . .

After the provisional dictatorship had been established and their enemies "suppressed," the next step would be the shifting of the tax burden from the poor to the rich; the new government would also confiscate the property of the crown and of "some great personnages." Even that would not be enough; it would be necessary to declare national bankruptcy, which would undoubtedly bring upon France a general European war. A triumvirate (preferable, he thought, to a single man as dictator) would be established to conduct the struggle for survival, in which all laws would be "suspended," until the vestiges of the old society were completely destroyed.[13]

This was less a plan than a curse, leaving France doomed, in the tailor's vision, to an endless vista of war and authoritarianism. His proposal looked forward to the notion of an elite vanguard and the dictatorship of the proletariat, a statist conception of revolution from above that would dominate the twentieth century; it looked backward to the revolutionary government of the Terror and Gracchus Babeuf's *acte insurrecteur.* But these new montagnards believed, as had Robespierre and his followers in the first revolution, that they were acting on behalf of freedom. In the words of the short-lived 1840 newspaper *L'Égalitaire,* the people had been "macerated by the bonds of servitude": "It is thus necessary, for liberty to see the light of day, that energetic men force [the people] . . . to manifest their most ardent desires."[14] The tension between liberty and compulsion would become unbearable during the Provisional Government of 1848, when universal manhood suffrage led away from the republic of montagnard dreams.

The rationale for violence guided its performance. In a pattern recently described by social anthropologist David Riches, political violence has three main functions. First, violent acts are both "instrumental" and "expressive." The most obvious purpose of a violent act is "tactical preemption"—to seize control of a military post or palace, to force government troops out of the capital. But violence also has the ability to "transform the social environment in a practical sense *and* strikingly dramatize important social ideas"—and it is likely that a violent act will give rise to many different impressions, from the anger of those in power to the realization, among potential recruits, of the possibility of resistance. Second, violence may serve as a vehicle for linking in political opposition people who otherwise have little to do with each other. Riches uses the example of different ethnic groups; in the Parisian context, violence allowed for political action across a divided labor market separated by different trades, by the generally small size of workshops, and by the still highly competitive journeymen's associations known as *compagnonnages.* Those who became involved in the republican movement saw themselves both as historical actors who carried on the tradition of the first great revolution, and increasingly as *prolétaires* who had common interests different from those of the bourgeoisie—and in this latter aspect, at least, there developed a sense of unity even among those who were not active republicans. Finally, Riches has suggested that violence is essentially a poor man's method, requiring little more than physical strength, "together with the knowledge that such strength effectively transforms the physical environment."[15] Montagnard republicans endowed violence with potency: "Before proletarians supported on their muskets," wrote Louis-Auguste Blanqui, "obstacles, resistances, impossibilities, all evaporate."[16]

Republican violence represented a controlled use of force. The various montagnard societies, notably the *Société des Droits de l'Homme et du Citoyen*, the *Société des Familles*, and the *Société des Saisons*, existed primarily to curb spontaneous outbursts; they stressed instead a highly disciplined deployment of an insurgent "army." Nor were they anarchists, attempting indiscriminate violence in order to destroy state authority altogether. "If we had the government, we would want it only on condition that it was strong, very strong," commented republican journalist Godefroy Cavaignac.[17]

But the performance of violent acts obviously begged the question of legitimacy. Republicans, as the initiators, stressed the prior aggression of the government, which promoted an economic system in which men could not protect their families from starvation. In so doing, they attempted to redefine the nature of violence, to persuade Parisians that a government that allowed its citizens to starve was itself committing a violent act. They publicized military overreactions or mistakes, notably the rue Transnonain affair in 1834 (see chapter 5). They cast their own struggle as a continuation of the first French Revolution—a contested legacy to be sure, but one that only the Legitimist minority would deny completely.

Another way of creating legitimacy, however, was to stress their own honorable behavior as combatants. An outnumbered, outgunned force against a large, well-armed body of troops, they exposed themselves to enemy fire in a manly fair fight. While their instrumental or practical purpose in each uprising was victory—street battles had been won in the past—they nevertheless also had an expressive function in their hopes of rallying greater public support (even in the course of the insurrection) and, at the very least, of winning hearts and minds in order to fight again another day. They consciously sought to create martyrs, men whose death or imprisonment for the cause provided a heroic face for the abstract demand for a Republic.

Recent theoretical examinations of gender as a cultural construction, subject to change over the course of time, have led to the recognition that gender is as central to our understanding of political, social, and economic systems as are the more traditional categories of class and race.[18] This approach has yielded many superb studies of women's lives and roles in society; yet too often, as Mark C. Carnes has noted, male attitudes and behavior have been simply assumed rather than examined.[19] A serious consideration of gender has been mostly absent from the history of the nineteenth-century republican movement, despite its prominence in the recent historiography of the French Revolution.[20] And yet republicanism in this era was noteworthy for its extraordinary male-centeredness, an attribute that is particularly striking when one compares republicans to the popular contemporary socialist sects (the Saint-Simonians, Fourierists, and Icarians, for example), who actively recruited women and moved issues involving family life and sexuality to the center of their concerns. The republicans, organized in male clubs and paramilitary groups, preoccupied with the seizure and manipulation of power, excluded women by definition. The republicanism of this era became intertwined with a particular vision of masculinity. This was both its weakness and its strength.

We do know some things about the men of this era. In his pioneering study, Peter Stearns described the creation of a new working-class masculine ethos in the nineteenth century, an aggressive, assertive maleness that reflected an attempt to defend status against the loss of property and skill.[21] Indeed, the working-class republicans represented a challenge to the hegemonic masculinity of the period: the spirit of the businessmen and the bosses, the middle-class respectability that placed a new emphasis on personal advancement and self-enrichment, a masculinity similar to what historians of the United States have described as the "masculine achiever" of early industrialization.[22]

But American and British models of middle-class masculine codes, thus far the most frequently studied, cannot simply be superimposed on the French bourgeoisie.[23] In the most thorough study of bourgeois masculinity in nineteenth-century France, Robert Nye begins with the continuing influence of the old regime. The bourgeoisie had engaged in a long struggle for social recognition, adopting a code of personal self-discipline and a strategy of economic, legal, marital, and reproductive choices that were followed over the course of several generations in order to elevate the family into the nobility. The nineteenth-century bourgeoisie, Nye argues, continued to function with a code of honor, based on virtue, that regulated their private and public lives. They became, in his words, a "'new aristocracy' of work, competence, and wealth," whose ideology stressed personal initiative and independence.[24]

Thus it could be argued that the moderate republicanism that shaped the Third Republic, with its stress on individualism, was not purely an economic or ideological choice, but rather represented an aspect of the bourgeois masculine code. Indeed, Nye has argued that after the French defeat in the Franco-Prussian War (1870–1871), republicans attempted to base their self-definition on honor, on their willingness to risk their lives in the defense of France. This ideal came to be embodied in the duel—the test of one man against another, both equal, both exhibiting "personal courage"—the numbers of which increased greatly by the end of the century. But the épée, the favored weapon, was largely a weapon of the upper classes; moreover, dueling was a very controlled form of violence, with elaborate rules that tended to exclude the masses.[25]

This argument can be extended by suggesting that working-class republicans also embraced a code of honor. Their battlefield was Paris; their ethos was founded on solidarity, not individualism. William Reddy, in his examination of the changing nineteenth-century workplace, has suggested that workers defended themselves from the disciplinary practices of employers through a mutual appeal to honor, whether expressed in the cohesion of sudden, spontaneous work stoppages or in secret labor organizations:

> From the laborer's point of view, as the nineteenth century wore on, the workplace became replete with military significance, something like a prisoner-of-war camp in which two contending disciplinary orders confront each other, one formal and explicit, enforced by the employer and his prison guards, one informal and implicit, with no reward or punishment other than the honor or shame before one's fellows resulting from courage or cowardice in the performance of work or in conflict with authority.[26]

As Joan Scott has noted, the nineteenth-century male worker, faced with increasing competition from women, implicitly came to define the working class as masculine, to discuss labor and political issues in terms of what was necessary for a male worker and head of a family.[27] A sense of honor and manhood—compounded of pride in work and skill, defiant resentment of upper-class privilege, nostalgia for the imagined great days of the Revolution—guided working-class republican behavior.

How unusual were republicans among the laboring classes? Historians have recognized a contradiction between French political sophistication and what was long described as economic backwardness. Today, most make two points: first, that while there were a number of highly developed industrial sectors even as early as the eighteenth century, France generally followed a different path to industrialization from that of Britain—a more gradual path, with a focus on her traditional strength in products of high quality—but one that revealed a steady increase in both the size of the economy and the standard of living; and second, that the lives and working conditions of French artisans were nevertheless dramatically transformed for the worse, less by the introduction of new machinery than by new workshop routines (payment by the piece, the use of unskilled labor, subcontracting, and the standardization of product lines) that served to devalue the workers' training and ability.[28] Thus

France retained a significant population of highly skilled, educated, and literate workers, who saw themselves as subject to increasing levels of exploitation and to the loss of control and autonomy in the workplace. In the early part of the century, moreover, this change was likely to have occurred in the course of their lifetimes.

In an insightful survey of recent literature, Lenard Berlanstein has made the distinction between those historians who believe that working-class activism was a product of laborers' experiences on the shop floor in disputes over discipline and de-skilling, on one hand, and those who have argued for the preeminence of political concerns.[29] The two views were not necessarily antagonistic. Workers involved in politics were not uninterested in economic and trade issues—quite the contrary, for as Tony Judt has noted, they believed that by capturing the government they could transform the social and economic environment.[30] Even those who take the "shop floor" approach in rejecting the notion of political causation implicitly note its impact: Gérard Noiriel, for example, regards the "sequence of rupture and breakdown" which characterizes French history as the obstacle that prevented the formation of a "genuine class."[31]

The group of active Paris republicans can be identified through the many previous studies of various rebellions and revolutions, based on lists which were themselves a record only of arrests and/or casualties. In terms of total numbers, there were perhaps several thousand committed activists—a minority, though a highly vocal and visible one, and a group whose propaganda and activities created a republican consciousness among the masses in February 1848. But they were very hard to count: the levels of commitment varied widely; activists dropped in and out of the movement; casualty and arrest lists frequently included innocent bystanders; and the excitement of insurrection called forth men who were not necessarily involved in the movement at all, even as genuine activists sometimes stayed home or were kept off the streets by imprisonment. But taken together, these studies suggest a broad consistency.[32]

Those involved in insurrection and revolution came from just a few trades. The construction industry, including both carpentry and stonemasonry, was active in numbers disproportionately larger than its total numbers in Paris—clear evidence of a strong, continuing link between urban insurgency and rural sensibilities, since many construction workers, like the memoirist Martin Nadaud, were seasonal migrants.[33] The building trade by its nature was more resistant than others to inroads from technological innovation. It was characterized by a strong tradition of journeymen's associations (through the *compagnonnage*), as well as division among the different trades on the building site. Moreover, the carpenters carried out two of the most famous strikes in the July Monarchy, their actions provoked by changes in the organization of work. The metal-working trades in both base and precious metals, in which new chemical and technological processes were transforming the workplace, also contributed a disproportionate number of combatants. Prominent as well were those from the furnishing and wood-working trades, both of which were experiencing changes as a result of the standardization of products and the hiring of unskilled and lesser-skilled workers, with sweatshop labor an increasingly common feature. Finally, the tailoring and shoemaking trades, particularly hard-hit by standardization and payment by the piece, also contributed disproportionate numbers to revolts.

According to Jacques Rougerie's study of the period from 1830 to 1845, wages in most trades remained stagnant. They went down for the metalcasters, bronze workers, gilders, and those in the textile and shoemaking trades. The pay for the various segments of the building industry, including masonry and carpentry, rose slightly. But at the same time the cost of living increased throughout the period, leading to a perceptible lowering of the standard of living in the first half of the century, even for those with steady or rising wages.[34] Participation in insurrection was not, as historians have long realized, a function of absolute misery, but rather an attempt to defend the status quo or even some relative ease.

The working-class men who became active republicans adopted a pattern of behavior that was meant to distinguish them from their fellows. First, republicans believed in a republic of virtue, embracing (or at least endorsing) a strict code of private morality. As many aspects of traditional plebeian behavior (brawling, public drunkenness, wife-beating) were "criminalized" in the nineteenth century, as employers tried to suppress the practice of "Mondays" (taking the day off) republicans sought to create an internalized discipline—a stern, almost dour creed of duty, sacrifice, and self-abnegation.[35] The following composition, "*Sur les devoirs de l'homme vraiment moral*," listed the desired attributes; handwritten and misspelled, it was found in the pocket of the would-be assassin Marius Darmès when he was arrested:

1. Love of the great principles of humanity and the disposition to make the sacrifice of his interests and his passions to them
2. Courage, that is to say, scorn for danger and love of work, patience [to bear] sorrows
3. Reflection, gravity, and prudence
4. Firmness and perseverance
5. Scorn for wealth, for places, for honors, and [unclear]
6. Modest, sober, and well-regulated life
7. Inviolable respect for the word sworn, the promise made
8. The willingness to forget personal injuries

9. Profound memory of the wrongs done to the masses

10. Moderation in the use of intoxicating drink

11. The habit of speaking little, and to the point

12. No desire to appear to shine and to impose oneself upon others

13. Self-control in gambling, love, anger, and the outpourings of the heart

14. Exquisite sensibility for the evils that weigh upon humanity.[36]

This list reflected a call to self-discipline—of desire, behavior, appetites, display—that in many respects resembled the bourgeois code of honor. Yet the republican code of virtue differed from bourgeois morality most notably in its explicit emphasis on that which transcended individual self-interest on behalf of the general good.

Second, republicans shared an insistence on physical courage. They were not alone in this: in July Monarchy Paris, the men of all classes seemed improbably brave, from the poorly armed workers who hazarded their lives for an ideal, to the shopkeepers who hastily donned their national guard uniforms when the drumbeat called them to action, to the king and princes and generals who rode on horseback through imperfectly pacified neighborhoods. Republican courage came to be defined around the principles of unity, fraternity, and self-sacrifice. In revolt, the republicans seized power rather than property; one of their standards was the code of *mort aux voleurs* (death to thieves), the summary execution of those who looted in the confusion of insurrection. (Only later, after the June Days, did some republicans repudiate this, arguing that the "fetishism" of the "cult of property" should not take precedence over human life.[37]) Their willingness to expose themselves to death or mutilation on the barricades was reinforced through the paramilitary *sections* of the underground groups; failure to appear on the streets when called meant a serious loss of face. They also placed themselves squarely in a tradition of forlorn hopes, and expected to lose before they finally won. "A republican, is virtue, perseverance; is devotion personified," according to an awkwardly worded 1836 pamphlet; "[he] is Leonidas dying at Thermopylae, at the head of his 300 Spartans; he is also the 72 heroes who defended during 48 hours the approaches of the Cloître Saint-Merry, from 60,000 men, and who . . . threw themselves onto bayonets to obtain a glorious death"[38]—a reference to the premier battle of the republican insurrection of 1832.

Third, montagnardism was unquestionably a working men's movement. Republicans valued physical strength as well as strength in union, stressing their own masculinity in contrast to that of the men of other classes; Michael Paul Driskel has noted the common juxtaposition, among popular July Monarchy cartoonists, of burly working-class men in opposition to the effete bourgeoisie.[39]

And in the tradition of the Great Revolution, they accepted the common dichotomy of men as active and public, and women as passive and domestic.

Politically active women joined the Saint-Simonians in the 1830s, later moving on to the Fourierists, Icarians, and other sectarians, who were attractive because of their willingness to address gender as well as the economy. The influence of these groups is reflected in the remarkable memoirs of Suzanne Voilquin, a working-class Saint-Simonian, and the writings of socialist Flora Tristan.[40] Even ordinary women, who had no thought of changing the world, could nonetheless appreciate the utopian socialists: "Before Icarian Communism appeared, our husbands were nearly all in secret societies . . . neglecting their work, spending all their money, always uneasy and upset, often arrested and prosecuted," wrote one working-class wife to communist leader Étienne Cabet in 1842, drawing a contrast with republicanism; but then her husband and his comrades had become Icarians, and "they take us with them to their meetings with their friends to discuss things."[41] Republicans had no use for women as comrades, excluded them from their underground societies, and covered their role in insurrection—for women built barricades, tended the wounded, and delivered cartridges—with a thick veil of silence. Ironically (and in a manner no doubt maddening to old montagnards) the new generation of Third Republic bourgeois republicans, as Judith Stone has noted, "always linked women and the working class," since "women's 'natural' subordination mirrored the condition of the entire working class."[42]

Finally, republicans were characterized by emulation.[43] They explicitly modeled themselves on Robespierre, Saint-Just, and Marat, whose violent ends attracted rather than deterred them, and often adopted a deliberate theatricality in rhetoric and action. (And because of the wealth of memoirs and histories of the Revolution, notes Elizabeth Eisenstein, "Robespierre, Saint-Just, Couthon, Marat, and the rest of the dead, were almost as alive in the France of the 1830s as those of their contemporaries who survived."[44]) A confrontation with the upper classes—imbued with power, wealth, influence—was fraught with anxiety for working-class men. Republicanism provided a sort of script for their public behavior, by borrowing from a period of revolution and war that, in memory at least, had seemed to offer greater scope for heroism, even for ordinary men.

The montagnards' deliberate, knowing re-enactment of the past leads to the third primary aspect of this movement, the romantic consciousness of republican activists. This is perhaps not a startling assertion: they lived in the Romantic age. But it is meant here in the more precise definition of Northrup Frye (by way of Hayden White): romanticism as "fundamentally a drama of self-identification symbolized by the hero's transcendence of the world of experience, his victory over it, and his final liberation from it."[45] The other classic emplotments (tragedy, comedy, and satire) allow at best only a partial or temporary victory in the face of unalterable conditions. Only the romantic consciousness admits the possibility of human activity as sufficiently potent to change the world, and that is what republicans believed they could do. This world-view made them unusual among their fellows.

Many contemporaries noted the prevailing sense among workers of being trapped in a situation that would not improve. *Le Travail*, a Lyon journal that defined itself as "communist," suggested that in order to understand the difficulties of a man's life one had to look to his household, his "private life": "How much resignation is necessary to support a life without glory, without hope." A man serves a painful term in the army, where he is little more than cannon fodder; he returns home to marriage and the responsibility of fatherhood: "His privations grow, but he feels some satisfaction in his spouse and his children." But then he loses his job and "goes from door to door" for work; his children cry out in hunger. Finally he is reduced to begging; perhaps he is disgraced by an arrest. But "times change," and the economy recovers; he finds a job: "Worn by distress, aged before his time, bent under the weight of the humiliations to which he has been forced to submit, he no longer has even the semblance of happiness." He ends his days in an asylum, assigned a mattress still warm from the man who occupied it before him.[46] This was the life of a man: soldiering, marriage, work, "some" pleasure in his family, bouts of unemployment that undermined his patriarchal function, and death.

Unless he lived for the Republic. Recent studies by Mary Jo Maynes and others on nineteenth-century working-class autobiographies have provided a theoretical understanding of the ways in which individuals told stories about themselves and made sense of their world.[47] Republicans lived, in an emotional and intellectual sense, within the context of the Great Revolution. Just moments before his execution, it was clear from his remarks that the would-be regicide Marius Darmès had come to terms with death by placing himself in the Year II. He held out his hands to his jailers, insisting that they take note of the fact that he was not trembling. He made explicit reference to one of the few celebrities who had died badly: "I'm not going to die like the DuBarry." (And in his memory all was conflated, the republican victims as well as those who had been victimized by republicans.)[48] The men of the July Monarchy adopted many of the symbols of the revolutionary period of half a century before: the phrygian cap, the color red; the *Marseillaise*, the *Chant du Départ*, *Ça ira* and other revolutionary and Napoleonic songs; the title "citizen"; the calling of meetings *en permanence;* the division of the *Société des Droits de l'Homme et du Citoyen* into neighborhood-based "sections." The beginning of the Second Republic would see an intensified revival—a new *Père Duchêne* (several of them), a new *L'Ami du peuple,* a new call for Robespierre's Declaration of the Rights of Man and the Citizen, even the continued use of the term *Gironde* to attack moderates. This represented not an irrational, anachronistic attempt to relive the past, but rather a deliberate strategy based on their understanding of the world. They borrowed symbols that were familiar to them, which carried with them a certain prestige, as a means of defining their activities.

Those who became republicans found it possible to cope with their situation by making it concrete and comprehensible, by transforming it into a conflict over physical control of the capital, into—as both generals and militants called it—*la guerre des rues.* Republicanism gave its followers, marooned in a dull postscript of an era, a chance to relive the Great Revolution; as they lost authority in the workplace they might gain it, momentarily, in the streets. "In Paris there are fortresses by the hundreds, by the thousands, as many as the imagination can dream," wrote Louis-Auguste Blanqui, many years later:

> One's fancy creates them with streets, as language creates words with the letters of the alphabet. It is a question of choosing, in any quarter whatever, by chance or according to one's caprice, a perimeter (formed of a series of streets) in any figure—triangle, square, rectangle, hexagon, etc. One closes with barricades the streets that end on the border. One occupies the streets on the perimeter of this front, and there is the fortress.[49]

The city thus became, at least in fantasy, a battleground for winning glory as their fathers and grandfathers had done. That this method did not work— witness the conservative results of revolution in 1830—was easily explained by "betrayal," a constant republican trope: betrayal by former allies, by bourgeois politicians, by comrades who were undercover agents or who got cold feet.

For some men, of course, the underground movement was a mere distraction, a rite of young manhood; they gathered in cafés, perhaps swore an oath to overthrow the government. Many became terrified at their own temerity and hastily withdrew. For the true montagnards, republicanism was all-encompassing, providing importance and excitement to those whose lives would otherwise have had little of either. Republicans refused to see themselves as passive victims of forces beyond their control. They embraced sacrifice and suffering, elements of life that were intrinsic to the harsh, uncertain, and rapidly changing conditions of their era. But such privations acquired new meaning, if seen through the prism of revolutionary struggle.

Above all, republicans saw themselves as historical actors; and this study is conceived as the narrative of their acts. The choice of the narrative form, however, has certain implications. Lawrence Stone defines a narrative as "the organization of material in a chronologically sequential order, and the focusing of the content into a single coherent story, albeit with subplots"; further, the narrative is "descriptive rather than analytical," with the "central focus" on "man not circumstances," on the "particular and specific rather than the collective and statistical."[50] No historian today would consciously adopt the great metanarratives of the nineteenth century—history as the rise of liberal democracy, or the coming to power of the proletariat.[51] Yet Robert Berkhofer has suggested that historians think (and must think) narratively at some level, must see the past "as a combined or unified flow of events organized narratively," and thus susceptible to being understood and written.[52]

Narrative brings with it an apparent transparency, a sense that one is seeing history "as it really happened"; the more skillfully written the work, the more complete is the illusion. And yet narrative, as Hayden White has noted, is not neutral; it is, rather, a form "with distinct ideological and even specifically political implications."[53] Narrative history imposes coherence upon the chaos of real life, and the narrative form, in rather insidious fashion, repels criticism. While individual facts can be verified, the relationship imposed on those facts by the narrative frame cannot be.[54] As Lynn Hunt has expressed it, "History is better defined as an ongoing tension between stories that have been told and stories that might be told."[55] Most important, a narrative form, in its focus upon character and action, implicitly explains historical events as a matter of human agency and desire: things happen because real people do them, think them, will them into being.

The narrative form as a choice for this work mirrors the republican consciousness, allowing their actions to emerge in bold relief against the structural limitations of their situation. Republicanism in this era can only be captured in terms of the activities of the ordinary men who lived and breathed the revolution: those who got themselves fired for haranguing their fellow workers, who stayed up late making cartridges, who built barricades and were killed behind them, who schemed to get their hands on a gun so they could shoot the king. The July Monarchy republicans, who suffered numerous defeats, did not expect to succeed in their lifetimes. Speakers at the 1845 funeral of *La Réforme* editor Godefroy Cavaignac, who died young of tuberculosis, expressed this sense of entrapment in an age that was both too late and too soon:

> To fight, always to fight, obscurely, patiently, and not against Europe in arms, not at the head of a quivering nation and to the acclamations of a million men, but against discouragement and disgust, under the weight of defeat and in the midst of universal silence . . . this is the zenith of heroism.[56]

They saw their generation as transitional figures, caught between what had been and what would be. They were denied both the glory of the first republican martyrs and the peace and plenty of their successors. Republicans might win no immediate victory; they might achieve no personal gain; but they had faith that they made a difference in the ultimate outcome. They believed they could change the world; and finally, the world changed.

CHAPTER 2

THE END OF THE REGIME: JOSEPH HENRY'S *PRÉMÉDITATIONS*

Seeing that it is necessary to die,
Let us examine the route, the point of departure and the end.
Would I not have done better, about eighteen years ago, to have killed my
adulterous wife and her lover?

(*From the* Préméditation *of Joseph Henry.*[1])

JOSEPH HENRY BURST ONTO THE PUBLIC SCENE in July 1846 when he became the seventh—and, as it turned out, the last—to make a serious attempt against the lives of King Louis-Philippe or his sons, but that was not what made him important. What mattered about Joseph Henry was that he tried to put down on paper the anguish of being a man and an artisan in nineteenth-century France. The resulting manuscripts—obsessive, barely literate, written in a stream-of-consciousness that often veered into unintelligibility—nevertheless provide a window into the mind of an "ordinary" man: a man forced to prove his worth repeatedly in the self-consciously competitive arena of laissez-faire capitalism; a man whose aspirations lay only in achieving some degree of material comfort and personal happiness; and finally, a man who was a foil for the republican character that will be discussed in these pages. Henry was an artisan who had risen to the rank of master-manufacturer and employer. Then everything fell apart: his marriage was a disaster, he barely knew his children, and his business was about to go under.

Artisans who wrote—those who occupied the "nights of labor," as Jacques Rancière has termed it, those hours stolen from sleep after a day of work—were driven by a need to remake their world, through poetry or prose, through cheap brochures or painfully composed letters to a newspaper.[2] Adolphe Boyer, a typographer, committed suicide after the failure of his socialist tract, which he had gone into debt to publish.[3] His death gave rise to a campaign by the elite against worker-authors, who faced emotional isolation and physical exhaustion, as they cheated themselves of companionship and sleep.[4] Henry's own rest had been disturbed for nearly six years: "The three first years I could almost not sleep at all, and what astonishes me, for two years I have slept too much." But such sleep was troubled and ennervating: "I am less fatigued when I go to bed than when I get up."[5] And, a month before his attempt: "My God, my head does not burst at so many sorrows, how much is it necessary to suffer, and how many times is it necessary to die? My God, I can no longer sleep when I go to bed, and I can no longer wake up when I sleep." So he stayed up late, writing, his light burning into the night.[6]

In the last few months before his attempt he wrote compulsively, first the *Lettre à M. de Lamartine*, addressed to the poet, historian, and Deputy Alphonse de Lamartine (Henry had read his *Jocelyn* and *l'Ange déchu*, and believed him a kindred spirit), and then the *Préméditation*. He had begun the *Lettre* on approximately 25 April 1846—significantly, nine days after the assassination attempt by Pierre Lecomte—and finished it on "31 May 1846, 10 P.M."[7] His *Préméditation* was completed on the day of his assassination attempt on 29 July, "at the moment of leaving."[8] Both were narratives, interspersed with philosophical meditations, that attempted to explain the sequence of events that had led him to the impasse of July 1846. The *Préméditation*, a private journal, began with his musings about killing his adulterous wife. The *Lettre* presented the public face of his dilemma: "Here is the situation of my business, my assets are 65,000 francs, and my liabilities are 28,000 francs, on which 28,000 I have 26,500 francs to pay at the end of next September, in paying this sum my establishment will belong to me, and if I cannot I will be lost."[9] In his own mind the sexual humiliation of his broken marriage was inextricably linked with—indeed, had caused—commercial failure.

Joseph Henry was 51 years old, a national guard who had stood duty at the Tuileries barely a month before his attempt. Born in Haute-Saône to a peasant mother and artisan father, he had accompanied his parents to Paris in 1811, at the age of 16. His father, a worker in polished or stainless steel, had taught his son the trade, and they had briefly prospered by manufacturing equipment for the army. The market had dried up suddenly in 1814, about the time when both parents had died. Left on his own, Henry had decided to become a master, not out of ambition but rather by an "accident in my nature." Frequent migraines incapacitated him, often causing him to lose as much as two days of work per week; by establishing himself and taking an apprentice, he could work when he was able and profit, on his bad days, from the apprentice's labor. And there was another overwhelming advantage, in that a mastership would allow him to unleash his creativity: "I would be more free and less a machine, being able to submit [myself] to diverse things, the articles of my taste; because I suffered from being a worker, a daily machine . . . to make 6 pieces, 12, 30, 100, at so much the piece, the dozen, or the day; always to repeat the same thing, for me, was to suffer, inasmuch as God had endowed me like my father with an innovative spirit."[10]

The inspiration and excitement that republicans found in insurrection was achieved by Henry in his work. He had switched his specialty into a more artistic direction, making jewelry, ornaments, and *objets d'art*. He had risen through his own efforts to the rank of respected businessman, a *fabricant d'objets de fantaisie*, as he described himself; his factory, which had employed as many as 25 men, was down to 17 at the time of his arrest.[11] But Henry had many beginnings and endings, many starts and stops; in his writings he moved through his life with little regard for time and order, as one thing reminded him of another.

Thus he began his life story at the age of 24, when after painful economies he had been able to establish himself in a small shop. He had acquired a wife, a pretty woman of 19 who brought him virtually nothing as a dowry but whom he had believed to be "animated with honest sentiments." He had managed to keep her with him for eight years, but only with much mental anguish and many "hypocritical handshakes" with her lovers. He had designed and produced the goods; she had taken his products around to other merchants, and her frequent trips out of the shop had given her many opportunities for infidelity: "I clearly recognize today that if I had had the happiness to have a virtuous woman to second me I would today have fifteen to twenty thousand francs in secured income." Honor and prosperity, happiness and capital, were thus intertwined. She had not understood that success required self-sacrifice: "the words, future, virtue, probity were for her devoid of sense."[12]

Finally she had engaged in flagrant adultery. Henry had offered to pardon her; but he had wanted to kill her, and had even planned how he would do it (a hunting trip, a loaded gun, his early unexpected return to find the lovers in bed, a double homicide, acquittal as an outraged husband). But it would have been "calculated, premeditated," not a spontaneous act of passion; he would have been forced ever after to live with remorse ("Did I do well or badly?").[13] She left him, after eight years of marriage and two children; he had seen "Madame Henry" five times since then, each time pregnant with another man's child, a constant and repeated reminder of his humiliation.[14] His business fell apart: "Sorrow had paralyzed my courage."[15] Everything he owned had been sold off, and he was reduced to working alone out of his chamber.[16]

Nevertheless, Henry slowly built himself back up again. Neither a widower nor a single man, he had decided to acquire a mistress, and had made a proposal to a young woman whose chief attraction, it seemed, was that she already lived in his building. Louise Antoinette Chevalier recalled the rocky beginning of their relationship: "I had entered his home on a Sunday, I had not yet had any intimate relations with him; and the morning of the next day, Monday, when we got up, he informed me that he was [in debt] for 5,000 francs. I reproached him for having hidden this circumstance from me, telling him that if I had known it, I wouldn't have moved in with him." He agreed; that was why he had not told her.[17]

Chevalier had not been in love, and had moreover been forced to endure Henry's frequent monologues about world peace (to be achieved by a universal religion and language and a home for *invalides civiles*, or workers exhausted by a lifetime of labor) and the urgency of informing Louis-Philippe of his insights so the king could bring about the "Golden Age." "As much as possible I avoided these conversations, which bored me," recalled Chevalier. They lived together for six years, when she finally confronted him: "I told him it wasn't fair that I continue thus to work during all my youth for nothing and without ensuring myself for the future." He had given her a share in the business. Their personal relationship had fallen apart when he found her in bed with an actor from one of the neighborhood theaters. She continued to work in his shop.[18]

Before this calamity, however, Chevalier and Henry had moved to larger quarters on the rue de Limoges, where she met Caroline Lemaury, also in an irregular union.[19] In about 1840, Henry was introduced to Lemaury's lover, a certain M. Lelarge, a wealthy retired lawyer. Lelarge, impressed with Henry's products, proposed a bargain: he would lend Henry money—the sum of 25,000 francs—to expand his shop, and Henry in turn would take in his 28-year-old "goddaughter" Lemaury to teach her the business.[20]

Henry saw this offer as the chance of a lifetime, but because of his nerves and his headaches and his anxiety over his *maison* (the women mocked his use of this pretentious term), he asked for a liberal credit arrangement: he wanted the loan for a period of ten years, during which he would pay interest but would not be asked for repayment of the principle. Henry spent the 25,000 francs before he had it, using as down payment the 7,500 francs he had painfully managed to save on his own: "On his word I began my expansion, I ordered a rolling mill, a grinder, a balance wheel, a polisher, etc., to rent premises three times more [than the size of his current shop], to subscribe to agreements, finally to do as if I had the 25,000 francs." Then Lelarge brought him the money—only 7,500 francs, ironically—and refused to give it over until Henry signed a note that the sum was payable on demand. Having begun the expansion, Henry could not turn back.[21]

Lelarge never brought him the promised amount as a whole, but rather only in bits and pieces, and never enough at one time ("He brought me 3,000 francs when I had 4,000 to pay"[22]). He never had sufficient funds to get past the threshold of immediate expenses, and having incurred the initial obligations he began borrowing from others, then had to borrow yet again to pay off previous creditors, building a mountain of debt that was about to bury him. The judicial investigation of his books revealed that his total obligation was 100,000 francs, while his assets totaled a little less than half that; in 1841, before he had begun borrowing, his assets had amounted to 11,072 francs with almost no encumbrances.[23] (His own assessment of his debts and assets, at the beginning of the *Lettre*, was wildly off.)

Henry soon came to suspect that Lemaury controlled her lover's stingy disbursement of the cash; moreover she filled the *atelier* with "intrigues," constantly seeking to undermine his authority. He soon decided that it was Lemaury's ambition to bankrupt him so her lover could buy the business for her; then she would dominate Henry as her *contre-maître* (foreman).[24] In the meantime, his losses mounted because of what he called *coulage*, or the enforced idleness of his workers, for he could not buy the raw materials necessary to employ them: "I did not want to send away my workers accustomed to my specialty, that would have been to ruin myself even sooner."[25]

At one point Henry believed he had found an ally in the person of Lelarge's widowed mother, who promised him 25,000 francs in one lump sum if he would send Caroline Lemaury away. Instead, he found himself embroiled in a quarrel between mother and son; a conference among the three of them ended in rancor. Mme. Lelarge, in parting, gave Henry 10,000 francs. But this was not good enough: "I had then 11,000 francs to pay to diverse suppliers whom I put off from Saturday to Saturday, for more than two months; I returned to my establishment with the 10,000 francs that I immediately gave to my suppliers, I then owed 1,000 francs and found myself still without money and my credit was sagging."[26]

In an attempt to wrest control of his premises from Lemaury, Henry invited his spinster sister to live with him. She was a disappointment, unable to learn his ways and too timid to exert authority.[27] Henry felt even more isolated and alone. Aside from his useless sister, his only brother was long gone, having left for Buenos Aires more than 16 years earlier. (Henry believed he was dead, "also a victim of intrigues."[28]) His older son Charles was serving with the army in Algeria and his younger son Frédéric worked in the shop.[29] Frédéric spoke of an austere, distant childhood; Henry noted that both sons took after their "miserable mother."[30]

But his sister's arrival had at least caused Lemaury, feeling herself displaced, to leave, "because he did everything in his power to show me that he desired I not remain with him." Not surprisingly, Lemaury had found him difficult: obsessive, inclined to brood, subject to extremely violent headaches that brought the shop to a complete halt, and given to the frequent lectures ("of universal peace and the means he found to assure it") that had driven Chevalier to distraction.[31] If she was aware that he considered her a "demon female,"[32] she gave no sign of it.

The departure of Lemaury had brought about a crisis between Henry and Lelarge, and they discussed the repayment of the enormous sum, now up to 80,000 francs, that had been eaten up by the business. (Said Henry: "Now that I have a *maison* four times stronger, I am four times poorer, and always notes [of creditors] that prevent me from sleeping."[33]) The fault rested with Lelarge, who had not given him 25,000 francs in a lump sum, as he had promised. Since Lelarge had broken his word, Henry attempted to bargain, asking him for three years, untroubled by interest payments, to repay the loan: "I will be tranquil, I would belong to myself, I could work, I will go little by little, the interest each year instead of giving it to you will augment my liquid capital *[fonds de roulement]*."[34] But Lelarge was now strapped himself; he too had made a bad marriage, to a wealthy woman who had left him and taken her dowry with her. Devastated by the refusal, Henry became unable to work; his business declined further.[35]

Then in early 1845, two surprising deaths occurred: Lelarge, on 4 February; and Henry's long-lost wife, who died of the complications of syphilis on 22 February.[36] The death of his wife suddenly opened up the possibility of remarriage. He developed an odd and persistent preoccupation with marrying a "little hunchback," or some other woman who had been "disgraced by nature"; he even wrote letters to notaries and orthopedists in Paris to ask for referrals to infirm but wealthy women.[37] But rich hunchbacks were not so readily available as he had imagined; what he really needed, in any case, was the prosperous widow of a merchant or manufacturer (*commerçant* or *fabricant*) who was accustomed to business, with a fortune in the range of 20,000 to 30,000 francs, and a willingness to take over the shop. Somehow, Henry was introduced to two women "who had supposedly 20 to 25,000 francs and after loss of time in visits (always *coulage* [idleness] in my absence) in reality they had only 10,000 francs it was enough if I were not in the position that I am, what a pity."[38]

Henry also had to deal directly with Mme. Lelarge, who was attempting to wind up her late son's affairs. He decided to write her a letter explaining his situation, but found the composition of the missive to be extremely painful:

> As I had all my people [*mon monde*] to direct, I could write only a little from time to time and more after 10 P.M. . . . the torments of the day prevent me from having a sure hand, for example some worker tells me that he's finished and asks me what he's going to do, and often not having anything to give him to do that is lacking, I make him do what there's already a lot of, and almost always the profit that the half of my workers makes me balances the *coulage* of the other half.[39]

But in the end, his proposal to Mme. Lelarge was that she reduce the amount he owed her to 25,000 francs and give him 18 months, interest-free, to pay. She agreed to a reduction (from 86,000 to 25,000), so long as he paid it within a year; if he failed, the debt would revert to the original sum.[40] That was not good enough. As October 1846 loomed (when the 25,000 francs fell due), he angrily regretted her lack of generosity. He needed two year-end sales periods ("like harvests to a farmer") to make a success, and she had given him only one; she had not acted "grandly generously," was molded "of a very hard egoism."[41]

Were Henry's torments visible in the workshop? Surely, as a master, he would have managed to put up a strong front. But the investigators instead discovered that his workers knew all the details of Henry's sorrows, of his wife, her lovers, the Lelarges. He had confided in all of them ("if one can call that a confidence," remarked one of his workers, aware of Henry's compulsive chatter), and he had, moreover, threatened suicide so frequently that no one took it seriously.[42] His workers generally tried to avoid him, but there was one day of the week when they could not. Philippe Petit, who had been working for Henry for nearly two years, described what payday was like:

> He spoke to us often, especially Saturday, payday, of the bad situation of his affairs and his pecuniary embarrassments; he returned to it always, to such a point that he wearied us and we sought the occasion to avoid his confidences. . . . In the month of January, he asked us to let him keep back a third of our pay, that he would reimburse towards the end of the year, the most active period of his sales.[43]

Thus he was in debt even to his own workers. When he did not distress them with gloomy financial predictions he bored them with his talk of the *invalides civiles*, universal peace, a single language, his desire to turn all swords into plowshares (or rather, as one of his more prosaic confidants expressed it, "to melt down all muskets, sabers and daggers into agricultural implements").[44] In 1847, only 30,000 Parisian workers were employed in workshops of more than 20; Henry had managed, on the strength of his own skill, to build such an establishment not once but twice.[45] Yet his employees believed that Henry was not in command of his business, nor was he fit for "commercial affairs": "He would have been an excellent *chef d'atelier*," a foreman or a chief in a small shop, but he was not meant to be the chief of a large establishment.[46]

Henry's attempt against the king, apparently so senseless, nevertheless struck a chord with many contemporaries. Society was in the process of being transformed by capitalism, fostered by the policies of Louis-Philippe and the financiers and businessmen who dominated the regime. By any measure, productivity and wealth increased dramatically during the July Monarchy. Steam engines (Henry passionately desired one for himself) rose in number from 625 in 1830 to nearly 5,000 in 1847, productivity in mining and metallurgy doubled, and textiles remained a powerful sector of the economy. But the wealth was not equally distributed, nor was the labor; politicians debated economic legislation with regard to the needs of industrial expansion, ignoring the well-being of workers.[47] Though the government prosecutor stressed Henry's personal failings, others were quick to see broader social significance in his assassination attempt, regarding it as an implicit critique of the ruthlessness of the reigning free-market ideology. The socialist newspaper *La Démocratie pacifique* suggested that Henry, facing economic annihilation, had determined not to go quietly: "Joseph Henry wanted to attract on his sufferings the attention of the public powers, because he could not understand how a man fortunately gifted, eager for the progress of his art, could arrive by a constant and passionate work only at the abyss."[48]

In discussions of nineteenth-century capitalism, historians have tended to dwell upon the undoubted agonies of the *prolétaires*. Workers found themselves transformed from skilled artisans to mere "hands"; journeymen and apprentices could not expect the paternalistic care they had once experienced (or so it was believed) from masters.[49] Machinery and the division of labor made certain crafts obsolete or so devalued them that their practitioners starved; highly trained workers often found themselves in competition with the unskilled. Division of labor, payment by the piece, and subcontracting were taking over those trades that remained; the subcontractors (*marchandeurs*) absorbed an excess of the profits, and they did not teach the craft to the cheap labor they hired to undercut skilled artisans. Workers experienced speed-ups and increased work discipline, even as they were subjected to crippling periods of unemployment.[50]

But what of the masters themselves, who were forced to swim in an ever-rougher industrial tide or sink into the proletariat? The leading socialists, including Louis Blanc, Victor Considérant of the Fourierists, Etienne Cabet, and the Buchezian school represented by the workers' newspaper *L'Atelier,* had developed nearly identical analyses of the likely future. If capitalist competition continued unchecked, money, property, and production would be in the hands of fewer and fewer individuals. Big capitalists had the resources to devour small ones, and they did so every day: witness the notorious Laffitte and Caillard case, in which two large transport companies had colluded to lower their rates below cost until a small competitor went bankrupt. The great mass of the bourgeoisie, dispossessed of what they had by this inexorable concentration of wealth, would collapse into the proletariat. And the process would inevitably lead to war; Great Britain, the bastion of capitalism, supported her productivity by the forcible seizure of colonies and trade.[51]

Republicanism in this era called upon workers to overthrow their capitalist oppressors. But all of the major theorists of pre-1848 French socialism preached class cooperation instead of class warfare, pitching their appeal as much to the bourgeoisie as to the working classes, and urging both groups to realize that they were equally victims of a wretched system. Victor Considérant predicted that the ultimate outcome would be "the progressive destruction of small and medium-sized property, small and medium-sized industry, small and medium-sized commerce, under the weight of big property, under the colossal wheels of big industry and big commerce."[52] And many economists, socialists as well as apologists for the bourgeois, pro-capitalist *juste milieu,* frequently dwelled on the burdens of the employers—their worries about their payrolls and taxes, competition with their fellows, the stress of managing workers who had once been their equals.

In 1833, during the era of the first great wave of workers' coalitions and strikes, the typographer Jules Leroux (brother of Pierre, founder of the *Globe*) discussed the lonely struggle of the artisan-master: "Far from coming to his aid, from the moment that his position, though only impaired, is known by his colleagues, they redouble their competition, they cause all credit to flee from him; they force him to sell out, and this man returns frequently into our [the workers'] midst."[53] Henry eagerly embraced this general critique. The rugged nature of capitalist competition, its "egoism," ensured that his collapse would be welcomed by his competitors ("when a man falls one destroys him again by saying, that makes one less").[54] He was not entirely fair in this regard: his fellow manufacturers, laborers who had risen in the world as he had, were willing to tide him over occasionally. He had made it through the month of April 1846 with a loan from François Fontaine, who had worked for him twenty years earlier.[55] But as the size of the businesses grew, they slipped from the grasp of artisans like himself and Fontaine.

Henry paid wages by the day rather than by the piece, which gave rise to his workers' frequent preference for idleness (evident from his own writings and from other testimony), and despite the fact that in many trades piecework was becoming more common precisely as a means of increasing productivity. He used both men and women, whose wages ranged from 2 francs to 5.5 francs per day.[56] But despite his extensive use of unskilled labor, a practice that undercut wages, he seems not to have been an abusive master, particularly when considered within the contemporary climate. The workers' journal *L'Atelier* (foreshadowing Michel Foucault and Erving Goffman) complained of "this tendency to transform *ateliers* into barracks and prisons, by the introduction of severe regulations, whose least inconvenience is to wound the dignity of the workers." Masters formulated regulations "with no other rule than their own caprice, their whim [*bon plaisir*], their interest or their fear." Some workshops were as silent as penitentiaries; in others, the often unavoidable defects of workmanship were hit with stiff fines, "a new way of diminishing salaries."[57]

Henry, in contrast, had tried to be a benevolent master who cared for his workers: "I was good, sensitive, humane, upright"; he had kept a dying worker on the payroll for over a year, hired the man's widow as his cook, and taken her brother as apprentice.[58] Hoping to be regarded as progressive and scientific, he had joined the *Société des Inventeurs*.[59] Though he never spoke, he said he "went there sometimes to be *au courant* of discoveries, to see if others had been inspired by the same ideas that I had."[60] And despite his reticence in the *Inventeurs*, he frequently claimed to his workers that he had found a new way to produce aventurine glass, that he had designed new "atmospheric machines" to replace steam engines.[61]

Henry was not, of course, the only self-made man in the nineteenth century. Denis Poulot, the entrepreneur/inventor who wrote a book about the character and behavior of workers, represented a successful version of Henry's story. Born in 1832, also in Haute Saône, Poulot received from his bourgeois family a more extensive education than Henry's. Poulot entered the *atelier* of his older brother at the age of 15, where he learned the business. At the age of 20, he became the foreman of another establishment, and at the

age of 25, in association with his brother-in-law, he founded his own shop
with a small inheritance. The brother-in-law had managed the business end;
Poulot, more like Henry, had managed the manufacture, instituting new
methods in order to free himself from the so-called "*sublimes*," the skilled but
rebellious workers in his industry. As Alain Cottereau has shown in his study
of Poulot's book, much of the impetus for innovation in the nineteenth-century *atelier* was an attempt, in Poulot's words, "to diminish the free will of the
worker"; each technological labor-saving change had to undergo a struggle
with labor.[62] Thus even a born captain of industry had to contest every inch
of terrain with those under him.

Henry's own difficulties as a master, largely the result of his timidity,
were compounded by his inability to turn out anything less than excellent. *La
Démocratie pacifique* suggested that Henry was a victim of the new tendency
toward low-quality mass production. A perfectionist, he sometimes spent
"five or six nights" finishing an item; sadly, the products over which he labored were items of "fashion," embraced and then rejected in a matter of
weeks. One of his oldest friends said Henry "was perhaps the premier worker
in Paris for steel," and added that he was a man "who manufactured too well
for commerce."[63]

But his major problem was credit, one of the essential demands of socialists in the 1840s. Considérant referred to "financial feudalism," and Louis
Blanc noted that banks "lend only to the rich," while P. J. Proudhon championed the idea of a peoples' bank to make loans to small businesses.[64] David
Landes has noted that credit was "immobilized" in the 1840s, being largely
tied up in the railroad boom.[65] Henry was not alone in seeing his business collapse in 1846 for lack of funds. And Henry had jumped at Lelarge's offer because even small loans were unavailable; a recent study of credit in France has
suggested that an unmet demand in the credit market was in loans of the one
thousand to five thousand-franc range.[66]

Henry brought a human dimension to this fundamental economic problem of the era. In one of his lengthy digressions he relived an event in his own
life; suppose, he said, that a manufacturer is about to go bankrupt, and so he
makes an appeal to *capitalistes*:

> He encounters men who know only figures, and who would risk a stock mar-
> ket coup [*coup de bourse*] rather than risk sustaining or propagating an indus-
> try. He shows his products, one does not deign to examine them.... He
> speaks the language of the *atelier*, he trembles, he has an awkward bearing;

what he says of his obstacles appears imaginary; he lacks aplomb, and one turns his back on him. . . . He is not rich enough to lend [to].[67]

Henry had groped his way to an indictment of the *laissez-faire, laissez-passer* attitude of the regime, and like many he believed that too much wealth was being absorbed by the non-productive few—the *capitalistes*—who played the market, rather than by those who actually did the work and produced the goods.[68] The influx of capital and the transformation of trades had been occurring during his lifetime and that of his contemporary J. E. Bédé, a chair-maker involved in the numerous labor troubles of 1820. Bédé had arrived in Paris in 1812 and, like Henry, had observed the rapid evolution of his trade, with the standardization of products and the growing use of unskilled labor. He had also noted the important distinction between the "old" and the "new" masters. The old masters were the men like Henry, artisans of their crafts, who worked alongside their men and acted as *chefs d'atelier*. The new were the large *marchands-fabricants* who reduced their employees to "hands," transforming the trade to piecework and using unskilled and even sweated outwork to produce in mass quantities at low cost. Rather than supervise the workers themselves they hired *contre-maîtres* or foremen; and these foremen, as Bédé noted, were often the old masters, the "ruined masters," who had been bankrupted by the more efficient competition.[69]

Many of those who knew him thought that Henry would do better to work by himself, with perhaps an apprentice or two, in a small shop where he could focus on production rather than management. One long-time friend advised him to gather together his creditors and make arrangements with them; perhaps he would have to give up his establishment, but he would then be free to "do as he had done at the time of his beginning, work on his own account."[70] But Henry could not resign himself to being a laborer, not now in his fifties; his "nature" and experiences had unfitted him for any turning back: "There is more than 25 years that I [have] command[ed] and at least 20 years that my body is no longer broken to daily manual work; I would earn only enough to eat and I would bring my industry to enrich men beneath me [in skill] and who would mock me, I would be exposed to hear the workers beside me say, there is a man who had a good hand and did not know how to play it."[71] The prosecutors of course saw all this as "vanity": *Procureur-Général* Hébert expressed the scorn of the *juste-milieu* for such failures: "Henry, who was a simple worker and who should always have remained a simple worker, Henry pushed by an exaggerated confidence in himself, always wanted to elevate himself to the status of inventor and the rank of manufacturer."[72]

Some of Henry's fears obviously did stem from pride. But the Peers who judged his case in the *Cour des Pairs*, members of the *haute bourgeoisie* and nobility, were insulated from the harsh equation in which old age equaled impoverishment: "If I were ten years younger I would not have done it [attempted the assassination]; but seeing myself soon reduced, by age and especially by the trembling of my hands, to being no longer able to work, I wanted to finish with my misfortunes."[73] (The stonemason Martin Nadaud recounted an almost identical lament from his own father, 11,000 francs in debt as a result of a failed business venture: "'If I were younger I would get out of this more easily, but in three or four years no one will want me on the building site.'"[74])

In the few months before his attack on the king, Henry was depending on new loans to pay off old ones and was in debt to all of his workers for one-third of their wages. The big crash (repaying Mme. Lelarge before the sum reverted to the full 86,000 francs) was to come in October.[75] What pushed him over the edge was Pierre Lecomte, the penultimate would-be assassin of Louis-Philippe. The Lecomte attempt occurred on 16 April 1846, ending a period of nearly five years of relative peace for the king. Joseph Henry, uninterested in current events, pored over Lecomte's case in the newspapers, according to his workers, and he saw several affinities between himself and his immediate predecessor.[76]

Pierre Lecomte was a 48-year-old retired soldier and forest guard, who had served with distinction in the 1823 Spanish campaign and as a volunteer in the Greek struggle for independence. In 1829, back in France, he had successfully petitioned the then-duc d'Orléans for a position; his last posting had been in the royal domains of Fontainebleau.[77] His quarrelsome nature had led him to quit the forestry service in 1844 over an imagined insult.[78] After retiring, Lecomte had demanded to have his pension paid all at once, in a lump sum.[79] The idea of getting a lump sum instead of an annual amount became, said prosecutor Franck-Carré, "a sort of *idée fixe* of which the absurdity escaped him." He had finally written three letters directly to the king in September and October 1844: "I was far from suspecting that the vengeance your administrative chiefs have heaped on me could reach as far as Your Majesty."[80] Convinced that Louis-Philippe had seen his letters and personally denied his request, he had decided to kill him. At 4 A.M. on 16 April 1846, he positioned himself in the park at Fontainebleau for the king's afternoon drive. After waiting all day, even building himself a shooting platform behind a convenient wall, Lecomte finally left in frustration. He had walked only a short distance when he heard the horses coming down the path. He ran back to the wall, which put him only a little over four meters from his target, and jumped onto the platform. It shifted under his feet, causing him to miss. The fringe of the *charabanc* was singed; the cloth, draped only ten centimeters above the king's head, was pierced in several places, and the gun's wadding was found in the carriage, on the skirts of the queen.[81]

Lecomte was found guilty and executed on 8 June 1846. In his losing battle against the death penalty, his attorney had asked that Lecomte be spared the full rigor of the law, on the grounds of his previous military service; he was not the leader of a seditious group, and he would inspire no one, not even a "fanatic," to follow in his footsteps.[82] But he had inspired Joseph Henry.

Henry had decided to kill himself: "I could in cold blood, without feverishness, with my two pistols put the barrel of one on the right temple and the other below the ribs aiming in the direction of the heart, and with attention, reflection and very slowly, with precision press at the same time the two triggers at once and with the same nervous movement and then it's finished."[83] But he was concerned that suicide would lead to his eternal damnation. The Lecomte attempt had given him a brainstorm: by "shooting at" the king (at trial, Henry insisted that he had not tried to kill him) he would accomplish his own death without sin; simultaneously, he believed, the fact that he had committed a crime to get the death penalty would lead to the abolition of capital punishment, another of his reforming obsessions.[84] He was fearful of what would come after the shooting ("to risk first of all to be stoned or massacred, failing that, to be arrested and treated as a *misérable*, to be garroted, imprisoned, to await the judgment and interrogations . . . all the time of the trial to be abominated and then to make the journey to go to my death and then to mount the steps [of the scaffold] . . ."[85]) But he had steeled himself to it. Afterward, the abbé Grivel, the confessor of prisoners before the *Cour des Pairs* (the Chamber of Peers, constituted as a court for high crimes), had explained that to commit a crime in order to receive the death penalty, as he had done, was a "demi-suicide," and therefore sinful; this had thrown Henry, in his own words, into a mental "labyrinth."[86]

Henry saw an ironic twist in the fact that he and his misanthropic predecessor Lecomte could easily have changed places, that Lecomte would have been better suited to the current economic environment, "and if in my position I had had the character of Lecomte (although I do not desire it, I prefer my own), I would be rich, I would have been harsher to the workers and those who surrounded me, which would have profited me, and all my domestic sorrows, the first cause of my misfortunes, would not perhaps have happened."[87]

But Henry also identified with Lecomte's middle-aged hopelessness and restricted horizons. Neither of them had much to look forward to, and their best
years—Lecomte's heroic military career, Henry's glorious creation of a large
establishment—were behind them. Nor were their professions so different; for
Henry, like most of his contemporaries, saw capitalism as war:

> I am no more a bad administrator than the general who would be surrounded,
> blocked his communications intercepted, and in order to extend his provisions,
> to conserve his troops and his position as well as his honor, expecting and hop-
> ing for aid, he allows the distribution of a half-ration, then a third, and this
> third causes to begin the partial desertion of his troops, he fears to be ruined
> abandoned he sees that soon his provisions will be gone that he will be forced to
> reduce the rations again, he knows that if he can hold on he will be saved, he
> has some abilities and some hope, he has already acquired some renown, he
> wants to maintain himself he harangues and remoralizes his troops . . . he
> knows that it is you *M. le spéculateur* who could furnish him the provisions. . . .
> He tells you that he was surrounded because a particular general was not there
> at the agreed hour to protect him so he could march ahead, he causes you to in-
> spect his troops and gear . . . you find that he does badly, you say, why this, why
> that, you look you examine, you see some soldiers lounging around you see oth-
> ers who are playing various games to kill the time. . . . You turn your back on
> him without saluting and you go to dine. . . . The general weakens more and
> more, his troops desert little by little, the enemy realizes he is at the bottom,
> one orders him to surrender, he blows his brains out.[88]

Henry added, as if explanation were necessary, that in this "allusion" he
was the beleaguered general, *M. le spéculateur* was the capitalist lender, the soldiers who deserted were his workers.[89] Also to be noted was the general who
"was not there at the agreed hour" (with 25,000 francs) and the soldiers
"lounging around," "playing various games to kill the time," testimony to the
fact that he was not in command of his shop. Henry lived in an era that required entrepreneurs, risk-takers, those able to live with uncertainty and by
their wits; trouble and debt had caused him to lose his nerve.[90]

In the last days before the attempt Henry was still hoping to extricate himself
in some other way. On the very day of buying his pistols he spotted a hunchback who seemed prosperous; his clumsy efforts to contrive an introduction
were rebuffed by her disgusted male companion.[91] He placed a newspaper ad-

vertisement for a wife in the first week of July, under the name *Revuasa*, a re-versal of *à sauver* (to be saved). His new effort led to a briskly practical inter-view with an attractive woman with whom he could not come to terms, and thus the closing of the avenue of marriage.[92]

The choice of Louis-Philippe as target ensured that Henry would get the death penalty without actually having to kill someone; but there were other reasons as well. Henry held the government responsible, as republicans and so-cialists did, for the general welfare of the population. The existence of poverty and misery in old age, the harshness of capitalism, were issues with which the king and his ministers should concern themselves. The carpenter Agricole Perdiguier, elected to the new republican assembly in 1848, would attack the prevailing governmental aloofness: "Workers suffer, workers despair, workers die of hunger, and you believe there is nothing to do; that governments should remain indifferent before such calamities! You think that does not concern them!"[93] "You don't know what's going on in your household," Henry wrote more simply to the king.[94] But the king had ignored him. Henry's letter to Louis-Philippe, just before the Lecomte attempt, had been answered by a sec-retary, its cordiality of the sort offered to "a man that one believes crazy or that one only considers as an atom." The king may have dismissed him as an "atom," a nothing, but he was "not microscopic," and he existed.[95]

Though he did not carry it out, Henry had a fantasy of destruction. He would buy large sandstone pots, telling the curious that he had invented a new way to make cider. Then, the day having arrived when he could no longer meet his obligations, "I would englobe in my sandstone pots more than 30,000 francs in merchandise, putting in some precious tools, so that they would not go into the hands of those who would say, how, with such processes, he did not make a fortune, there is something behind that (yes, fate), I add still some water and a sufficient quantity of nitric acid so that in four hours all would be corroded and reduced to zero."[96]

Just like Joseph Henry.

On 29 July 1846, at 7:35 P.M., Henry was in the Tuileries garden for the public concert in celebration of the July Revolution. The king and several members of the royal family made their appearance on a palace balcony as the orchestra struck up the *Marseillaise*. Henry fired two shots quickly in succes-sion; several birds on the cornice started up in fright. "He missed him!" shouted several high-spirited young men. Louis-Philippe's personal courage was in evidence for one last time, as he was observed standing his ground on the balcony and pointing out the assassin's location. Henry was grabbed al-most immediately by a *sergent de ville* and several other men standing near him in the densely packed crowd. Trembling, obviously frightened, he threw his pistols to the ground and shouted, "It's not me!"—and then, "I want to die, I did it to die."[97] Because Henry was an obvious lunatic he was sentenced not to death but to life at hard labor (a sentence always heard with amusement by workers with a sense of irony)—not long, as it turned out, for he was liberated after February 1848 as a political prisoner of the former regime. Shortly after that he was seen badgering Albert, the only *prolétaire* in the Provisional Government, who was in charge of the relief fund for former political detainees. It was reported that Albert gave him 1,000 francs.[98]

Henry illustrates some of the difficulties faced during the period by ordinary men, even those with considerable talent. For work, above all, was a defining element in the construction of a masculine identity, a source of identification and worth: "talk about the quality of work," as Michael Sonenscher has noted of journeymen, "was also talk about the quality of the individual."[99] Henry, an excellent master craftsman, had stepped beyond that level to the rank of *fabricant*. He failed, and people—the women in his shop, the workers who discussed him behind his back, even the neighbors who had witnessed the vicissitudes of his love life—were talking about him. He turned his anger inward rather than outward; he repressed his rage for years, and then he exploded. Flailing in a society that obliged men to prove themselves every day, trapped by economic realities beyond his control, repeatedly humiliated by the women in his life, he hacked out a tortured path to self-destruction. But the anti-monarchical channel taken by his anger was not haphazard. Montagnard republicans turned their anger outward; the avenues of protest they chose will be the subject of the chapters that follow.

PART II

++++++

INSURRECTION

CHAPTER 3

THE FAILURE OF
MODERATE REPUBLICANISM

THE JULY REVOLUTION OF 1830 WAS STUNNINGLY SWIFT, a matter of days instead of years. On Monday, 26 July, King Charles X issued the four *ordonnances*, a bold attempt to subvert the constitution and increase royal power. By late Thursday morning, he had lost control of Paris; by Saturday, the duc d'Orléans had accepted an invitation from the Chamber of Deputies to become Lieutenant General of the kingdom. On Monday, 2 August—just a week after the *ordonnances* had appeared—Charles X abdicated on behalf of his grandson. On 7 August, the Chamber approved a hasty revision of the constitution. And on Monday, 9 August, a mere two weeks after it all began, the duc d'Orléans was installed as Louis-Philippe I, King of the French.[1]

Republicans were not happy, but there were too few of them to affect the outcome. "We ceded only because we were not in force," said republican journalist Godefroy Cavaignac.[2] Nevertheless, the leading moderate republicans, all of them members of the educated middle classes—physicians, lawyers, *hommes de lettres*—were willing to tolerate a throne genuinely "surrounded by republican institutions," according to the popular formula. The July Monarchy soon disappointed expectations, first with a contrived political trial, the *Procès des Dix-Neuf*, and then with a series of judicial attacks against the free press, the right of association, and the *Société des Amis du Peuple*. By 5–6 June 1832, violent montagnardism had emerged, and active Parisian republicanism had become a largely working-class movement.

There were significant economic problems in the background of the 1830 revolution, acute in the period from 1827 to 1832; the years were marked by harvest failures, food shortages, and increases in the cost of living. These agricultural difficulties made worse the recession in the industrial economy, leading to an upsurge in the number of bankruptcies, a sharp rise in unemployment, and the lowering of wages in several important industries. During the unusually cold winter of 1828–1829, up to a quarter of Paris residents had depended on bread cards, which entitled them to cheap loaves.[3] Yet the revolution was a political adjustment rather than an economic upheaval; the economic forces that drove it were not in the streets but in a struggle of the elites, and the regime that emerged—despite the continuing strength of the nobility—was called, with reason, the bourgeois monarchy.

The revolution began within the government itself. On 16 March 1830, by a vote of 221 to 181, the members of the liberal opposition in the Chamber of Deputies deliberately challenged the king by requesting that he change his council, which was headed by the reactionary Prince Jules de Polignac. Rather than concede, the king dissolved the chamber. New elections in June led to results even more lopsided; the opposition was now at least 270 votes strong, with only about 145 firmly for the Polignac ministry.[4] In early July, after a very brief campaign, French forces seized Algiers. The initial conquest was easy; pacification would become the chief foreign military burden of the Orléans regime. But for the moment, it seemed that colonial success might embolden Charles X to use article 14 of the Charter, which allowed the monarch to issue *ordonnances* for "the security of the state," and thus effectively to assume dictatorial powers.

These premonitions were fulfilled on Monday, 26 July 1830, with the publication of the four *ordonnances*. The new regulation on the press prohibited newspapers from publishing without government authorization, renewable every three months and revocable at will. The already narrow voting rights (based on the payment of taxes) were further restricted to landowners, by a disqualification of the sorts of taxes paid by wealthy businessmen. Of the remaining voters, only the top one-quarter would elect deputies directly. The other two decrees dissolved the new Chamber and called for elections in September.[5] If the *ordonnances* had stood, the monarchy would have been able effectively to muzzle a critical press and manipulate elections. To the liberal opposition, such a regime would have meant dominance by the old nobility and clergy.

July was the first of what would become an astonishing series of revolutions and unsuccessful rebellions. The National Guard of Paris, dissolved by Charles X after many of them had shouted against his ministry during an 1827 review, spontaneously began to appear on the streets to mediate between combatants and troops. Among the insurgents, ordinary working people predominated, with little to guide them except the energetic journalists' protest, drafted by Adolphe Thiers of *Le National* and read out on the streets by angry printshop workers (their livelihoods threatened) on Tuesday, 27 July. Those who fought, according to David Pinkney, were mostly respectable artisans and skilled workers. The construction and wood-working trades, including masons, carpenters, joiners, cabinetmakers, and locksmiths, were overrepresented, according to their total numbers in Paris. There were relatively few students. Pinkney suggested that the principle leadership was provided by veterans of the empire, an impression shared by physician F. Poumiès de la Siboutie, who set out with his medical kit on the second day of the fighting and noted "uniforms of all branches [of the service], of all epochs, of the Republic, the Empire, worn by old soldiers or retired officers." The dead numbered 496 civilians and 150 soldiers.[6]

But the insurgents were not republicans. Edgar Leon Newman has shown that the working classes of 1830 spurned the republican students and journalists who tried so desperately to enlist them. Instead, they had learned to trust the liberal opposition leaders of the Restoration, bound to them by a shared anticlericalism that was nourished with cheap reissues of Enlightenment classics.[7] They followed these same leaders in 1830, to the amazement even of liberals; *Le National* editor Armand Carrel was frankly surprised that working people concerned themselves with the constitutional questions that agitated the political classes: "Everywhere in the streets men without coats, shirtsleeves rolled up, armed with muskets, and running to the defense of the barricades, said: 'We want our Deputies; our Deputies know what we need, and the king doesn't.'"[8] The duc d'Orléans' oldest son later remembered the appeal of a wounded combatant: "'Prince,' he said to me, his eyes haggard and his hair bristling, 'time presses. It is necessary to save the fatherland! Your father at our head, your father king, and we will finish with the emigrés and the Jesuits!'"[9]

The new regime was created by the wealthy opposition, those who embraced economic expansion, limited government, and secularism. The kingmaker was Jacques Laffitte, a carpenter's son and self-made banker, who had been completely won over by Orléans' easy manner at their first meeting in 1814. He was the financial backer of the aggressive *Le National*, founded in January 1830 by Adolphe Thiers, François Mignet, and Armand Carrel, and at this period the only frankly Orléanist journal. Thiers and Mignet had written two of the

earliest histories of the French Revolution; Carrel was a former soldier and author of an extended parallel between the Stuart and Bourbon restorations. All
four men dreamed of a French 1688, with the duc d'Orléans in the role of
William of Orange.[10]

At the moment of interregnum—on Thursday night (29 July), when
Charles X's troops had lost control of the capital but before a settlement had
been reached—Laffitte boldly decided to draft the wavering Orléans, torn between ambition and fealty, and Thiers and Mignet produced the following
placard:

> Charles X can never return to Paris: he has shed the blood of the people.
>
> A republic would expose us to horrible divisions: it would involve us in
> hostilities with Europe.
>
> The Duc d'Orléans is a prince devoted to the cause of the revolution.
>
> The Duc d'Orléans has never fought against us.
>
> The Duc d'Orléans was at Jemappes.
>
> The Duc d'Orléans is a citizen king.
>
> The Duc d'Orléans has carried the tricolor flag under the enemy's fire;
> the Duc d'Orléans can alone carry it again. We will have no other flag.
>
> The Duc d'Orléans does not declare himself. He waits for the expression
> of our wishes. Let us proclaim those wishes, and he will accept the Charter, as
> we have always understood and desired it. It is from the French people that
> he will hold his crown.[11]

This declaration was hastily printed and posted throughout the city by
early Friday morning. As a journalist himself, the socialist Louis Blanc admired the power, if not the sentiments, of the document: it repeated the name
of their candidate to people who were largely unfamiliar with him, and it associated him with revolutionary glory and the beloved tricolor flag, banished for
the white Bourbon fleur-de-lis during the 15 years of the Restoration.[12] (On
28 July, the insurgents had briefly raised the tricolor at both the Hôtel de Ville
and Notre-Dame, the big bells ringing in the cathedral to draw the attention
of the city; attorney and future liberal opposition leader Odilon Barrot was
surprised at the depth of his own emotion at the sight.[13]) While it embraced
the revolution, moreover, the proclamation also broke definitively with legitimacy and implied a contractual monarchy. It raised and disposed of republicanism by evoking the specter of foreign invasion, only 15 years in France's
past. And by no means least, it circulated the term "citizen king."

The duc d'Orléans was then 56. A lieutenant general in the revolutionary
armies, present at the victory of Valmy in 1792, he had fled France in April 1793,

shortly after his father, Philippe Égalité, had voted as a member of the Convention for the death of Louis XVI. In November 1793, Égalité's execution made his oldest son the new duc d'Orléans, but in exile, and shadowed by his father's act. During the 1790s he traveled to Sweden, Norway, Finland, the Germanies, and the United States. Later he returned to Great Britain, where the British government granted him a modest pension. With him throughout this difficult period of exile was his sister and greatest lifelong confidante, Adélaïde, who never married. In 1808 Orléans traveled to Sicily, held by the Neapolitan Bourbon Ferdinand IV with the help of Great Britain, and soon married Marie-Amélie, the daughter of Ferdinand and Queen Marie-Caroline, a sister of Marie-Antoinette. Eventually they had ten children, eight of whom—five sons and three daughters—would survive into adulthood, and enjoyed a marriage that was never tainted by scandal. In contrast to the *ancien régime* court of the Bourbons, the new king would project an image of bourgeois domesticity.

But the duc d'Orléans was also one of the richest men in France, the fortune of his house founded by the younger brother of Louis XIV. He and his sister Adélaïde had received the largest single benefit from the 1825 Indemnity Act for lands seized during the revolution. Guy Antonetti's biography of Louis-Philippe skillfully illuminates the century-long tension between the Bourbons and the aspiring Orléans family, the casual slights inflicted by the older branch upon the younger; Orléans had been scarred, moreover, by years of impoverished exile.[14] During the Restoration he had courted popularity, most recently in May 1830, with a magnificent fête for his brother-in-law the King of Naples, when he had opened the Palais Royal grounds to the city (a near-disaster, for the crowd had grown unruly and set fire to the garden chairs).[15] Now the suspected ambitions of Philippe Égalité, so evident in the early years of the first revolution, were about to be realized by his son.

Approximately 80 members of the Chamber of Deputies met at the Palais Bourbon on 30 July (Friday) from 12:30 to 6:00 P.M., in a momentous assembly that effectively established a new dynasty before the old one was completely vanquished, largely through the skillful stage-managing of Laffitte. After taking over the presidency of the irregular session, Laffitte used the republican threat to further the Orléanist cause, frightening the deputies with the prospect of continuing disorder and a new Reign of Terror. These manipulations eventually resulted in the decision to offer the lieutenant generalcy to Orléans, in what would prove to be a very brief interlude before the new monarchy.[16]

The relatively few republicans, mostly students and young professionals, attempted to seize control of the rapidly evolving situation. On Friday, 30 July, at their headquarters at the Lointier restaurant, they founded the *Société des*

Amis du Peuple.[17] Though the Orléans solution had support even here, the majority wanted a republic.[18] And they had great hopes for Lafayette, the "hero of Two Worlds" and *carbonari* conspirator from the early 1820s, who on Thursday had taken over the spontaneously re-forming National Guard.[19] As the deputies moved toward a new dynasty on Friday afternoon, the republicans delivered a manifesto to Lafayette at the Hôtel de Ville. The republican delegation included Joseph Guinard, Jules Bastide, Charles Teste, Dr. Ulysse Trélat, and Jean-Louis Hubert—all educated bourgeois republicans, most of them *carbonari* veterans, and the core of the new *Amis du Peuple*. Their petition represented the first decisive action taken by the Left as a group; significantly, as moderates, they demanded not a republic but a national referendum and popular consent to the form of the new government:

> The people, yesterday [29 July], reconquered their sacred rights at the cost of their blood. The most precious of these rights is that of choosing its government freely. . . . There exists a *provisional* representation of the nation. Let it remain until the wishes of the majority of the French can be known.[20]

The notary Hubert (who carried the proclamation on the end of his bayonet) read the address and followed it with a brief speech in which he urged Lafayette to assume provisional power until the nation could be consulted. Lafayette had avoided a direct answer, launching instead into reminiscences about the first revolution. Nevertheless, he had sent liberal attorney Odilon Barrot with a message to the rump Chamber of Deputies, warning against the "precipitation" with which they seemed to be disposing of the crown and demanding that "one stipulate beforehand some guarantees for the nation."[21] Fearing that Lafayette might be wavering toward a republic, the deputies in turn hastily drafted a request to Orléans: "The meeting of the Deputies currently in Paris beseeches his Royal Highness the duc d'Orléans to come to the capital to exercise the functions of Lieutenant General, and expresses to him the wish to retain the national flag."[22] Despite the additional promise of "guarantees"—but only for the "full and entire execution of the Charter"—republicans harshly criticized the address for its obsequious tone.[23]

But Laffitte was now confident of the outcome; the duc d'Orléans, in response to his urgent summons, walked to the city late Friday night from his chateau in Neuilly (the streets, full of barricades and debris, were virtually impassable) and settled himself at the Palais Royal. On Saturday morning the deputies' delegation delivered their cringing invitation. After a becomingly modest hesitation Orléans assented. His reply was printed in 10,000 copies and distributed through the streets. The 91 deputies then in Paris responded with another proclamation, an attempt to appease the Hôtel de Ville crowd with the addition of specific guarantees: the election of national guard officers, the jury for press offenses, a promise of local government.[24] As the two placards blanketed the city, republican agitation increased, expressing itself in a blizzard of posters. On 30 July, from the Lointier restaurant, a warning was issued against the theft of the revolution by wealthy men who had done none of the fighting.[25] On 31 July a more specific proclamation duplicated the deputies' demands and added several others: an end to the hereditary peerage; an end to Catholicism as the state religion; "entire liberty" of the press; and universal manhood suffrage.[26]

While republicans wrote and posted, the duc d'Orléans triumphed on Saturday morning with a single bold stroke: a visit to the republican headquarters in the Hôtel de Ville. An exchange of messages with Lafayette had led him to believe that his reception would not be openly hostile.[27] The hastily-assembled deputies accompanied the prince across the city to his destination. Liberal Auguste Bérard, who feared an assassination attempt, found the procession painful because of the "excessive heat," the difficulty of getting over the barricades, and the "fraternizing" of the prince ("a little too much in my opinion") with the workers who ran up to shake his hand. François Guizot was also disturbed by the crowd that pressed around them "without violence but without respect": "Shouts and questions of all sorts emerged at each instant from this crush; they pointed out to each other the duc d'Orléans: 'Who is the gentleman on the horse? Is it a general? Is it a Prince?'—'I hope,' said a woman to a man who gave her his arm, 'that it's not another Bourbon.'"[28]

The victorious Laffitte later recalled the festive atmosphere—drums, shouts, *gamins* running back and forth, tricolor flags everywhere. But as they neared the Hôtel de Ville, "the enthusiasm appeared to extinguish itself completely." There were audible cries of *A bas* [down with] *les Bourbons! A bas le duc d'Orléans!* They walked up the steps in silence, armed men lining the staircase.[29] Once inside there was more awkwardness; then, recalled Laffitte, "Suddenly, I do not know how, there surged forth a great tricolor flag. . . . [Lafayette and Orléans] seized it and went toward the windows to salute the people." In one of the most famous moments of the revolution, the two men embraced and draped themselves in the flag, finally eliciting the desired shouts of approval.[30]

But Orléans left without promising any reforms. That night, in the offices of the *National*, Thiers suggested to the unhappy republican leaders that the duc d'Orléans desired a meeting—a deception exposed by the prince's obvious surprise when they arrived. The conversation covered a number of issues without resolving them: the humiliating treaties of 1815; the status of the peerage; and a national referendum on a new constitution. The discussion ended in mutual dissatisfaction.[31]

Thus Lafayette felt obliged to try as well, and he asked the young republicans around him to draft a list of demands for him to present to the new lieutenant general. Orléans received him warmly. While both agreed that a republican government was unsuited to France, Lafayette insisted that the country needed "a popular throne surrounded by republican institutions." The prince asserted that such was his desire; however, he could not make changes without the consent of the chambers. Lafayette, who would have preferred written guarantees, nevertheless believed they had understood each other as gentlemen.[32]

For republicans, this inconclusive meeting later became the pivotal episode of the revolution, as the origin of the *programme de l'Hôtel de Ville*. The list of demands brought by Lafayette was first published in early 1831 by journalist Armand Marrast:

1. National sovereignty recognized at the beginning of the constitution as the fundamental basis of government.
2. No hereditary peerage.
3. Complete renewal of the magistracy.
4. Municipal and communal elections on the basis of the broadest possible suffrage; no tax requirement for eligibility for office.
5. Election of all inferior magistracies.
6. Reforms of several of the specific provisions of the privileges and monopolies that paralyze industry, etc.(sic)
7. All of this *adopted provisionally, to be submitted to the sanction of the nation, alone capable of imposing the system of government that will suit it.*[33]

These demands were the essence of moderate political republicanism at the beginning of the July Monarchy. The ideas behind the awkward sixth provision, the only reference to economic or social reform, suggested if anything a *laissez-faire* demand to liberate the economy from restrictive legislation; by contrast, the socialist ideas of many members of the *Amis du Peuple* would soon cause rifts within the movement. But it was the last article of the program, the insistence upon the consent of the governed, that later led to attacks on the legitimacy of the regime.

Within the next few days, Louis-Philippe consolidated his authority and the deputies established the new settlement, which was completed on 7 August. The legislative session opened at 9:30 A.M.; it would be adjourned at 7

P.M. The deputies swiftly rejected both a constitutional convention and a national referendum, the core republican demands. Another republican defeat came with attorney André Dupin's strong defense of the present magistracy; judges, he noted with woeful inaccuracy, were "strangers to politics."[34] Within hours the deputies provided France with a revised constitution and a new dynasty. (This was the same group, republicans cynically noted, who spent "entire months voting a law on river fishing."[35]) "We succeeded in setting aside all delay, all vain debate," recalled François Guizot with satisfaction; "in two sessions, the Charter was modified; in eight days, the revolution was closed and the government established."[36] *Communism couldn't have been faster!*

Republicans would soon describe the democratic process that should have been followed. Auguste Fabre, co-founder with his brother Victorin of *La Tribune*, claimed that republicans had wanted Lafayette as provisional president, along with a constitutional convention. The republicans had tried to persuade Lafayette to accept the burden of such powers until the nation had been consulted, but Lafayette had been overtaken by events.[37] While most republicans had envisioned a similar process, not all of them had insisted on Lafayette as provisional head of state. Some had suggested the rump Chamber of Deputies in the role, others even the duc d'Orléans himself.[38] Ironically, as many republicans acknowledged, the Orléanist monarchy would probably have been the nation's choice. But in the absence of a referendum, republicans soon labeled the regime a usurpation, an *escamotage* or "snatching" of the popular triumph.

For a very brief moment, the new King Louis-Philippe I attempted to court popular favor. He accepted the title "King of the French," borrowed from the 1791 constitution, as opposed to the traditional "King of France and Navarre"; in his first official decrees he personally suppressed the archaic formulas and references to "faithful subjects." He stood on his balcony and sang the *Marseillaise* with the crowds; one of his first acts as monarch was to provide a pension for Rouget de l'Isle, its elderly composer.[39] His manners were refreshingly informal in comparison to the Bourbons, including "*les shake-hands*" *anglicism!* with commoners.[40] His advisors even briefly considered a plan for a parade "review" of "the armed Paris population," "these citizen-workers, artisans, students, artists, and other citizens of all professions," the report rather awkwardly continued, "who conquered liberty in shedding or offering to shed their patriotic blood to wash the tomb of despotism!" But cooler heads among the king's council prevailed.[41] The king, moreover, became increasingly less eager to remember, much less celebrate, the popular origins of his throne.

In his swift progress to the right of the political spectrum, Louis-Philippe replaced Laffitte as first minister in March 1831 with another wealthy banker,

Casimir Périer. Laffitte and Périer represented the liberal and conservative tendencies, respectively, of the governing class, but both were comfortable within the new regime. Within the next eighteen months, the Périer ministry completed the unfinished business of revolution, most of it legislation started under Laffitte. The national guard law of 22 March 1831 established the principle that service was "universal and permanent" for all Frenchmen from 20 to 60, if they did not belong to the army and other exempted occupations; workers were excused when their "lack of resources" made regular service a burden.[42] The new suffrage law of 19 April 1831 reduced tax requirements and lowered the ages for voting and holding office, but still left France with an electorate of only about 250,000, out of a population of 35,000,000.[43] Most members of the Paris National Guard did not qualify; thus, as Louis Girard has noted, the monarchy's security was heavily dependent on men without full political rights.[44] Finally, on 29 December 1831, the hereditary peerage made way for an upper chamber composed of life peers, chosen by the king from among men of distinction, drawn from strictly defined categories.[45] It would continue to be a conservative body; the lower chamber, given the restricted suffrage, also tended to represent the prosperous and powerful. The revolutionary settlement was complete.

The revolution of 1830 was, then, a victory for the wealthy elite; the few constitutional adjustments left intact the exclusion of the vast majority, including most of the July combatants, from the political body. The beneficiaries of the revolution—wealthy members of the bourgeoisie and pragmatic members of the aristocracy—referred to themselves as the *juste milieu*. As a class of "notables," they shared an increasingly oligarchical entrenchment in the power of the state, as officeholders, as *fonctionnaires*, and often as both at the same time; in the 1846 Chamber, 40 percent of the deputies were also public functionaries, and thus automatic votes (if they wished to keep their lucrative positions) for the ministry.[46]

The guiding philosophy of Orléanism, according to historian Jean Touchard, emerged from the blending of two liberal political tendencies during the Restoration. The Doctrinaires saw themselves as holding the middle ground between the *ancien régime* and democracy; the chambers, representing not the citizenry but financial "interests," were to be reserved for those with property and wealth. The Liberals, most prominently exemplified by Benjamin Constant, gave pre-eminence to the liberty of the individual and, in political terms, believed in ministerial responsibility to the chambers, a decentralized government, freedom of religion, and a king who reigned but did not rule. Their preference for a smaller and more limited government generally caused them to oppose an active foreign policy.[47] In practice, the devotion to individual liberty allowed Orléanists to foster a *laissez-faire* economic program that benefited the already affluent.

Republicans were hostile to the bland foreign policy of Louis-Philippe, which they denounced as cowardly. They regarded the concept of the *juste milieu*, the supposed function of holding the middle, as no more than a mask for bourgeois domination. But the key to understanding republicanism during the July Monarchy lies in its failure to embrace liberalism, in spite of many shared values, including the civil liberties of speech, press, assembly, and conscience. Liberal economic theory separated the two ideologies, for July Monarchy republicanism was increasingly imbued with socialist ideas. The other major difference lay in liberalism's wariness about the uses of government; republicans hoped to wield the power of a strong centralized state. Finally, the moderate, non-violent republican movement was discredited early in the regime, both by its own failure to seize control of events in 1830 and by the government offensive against it.

✣ ✣ ✣ ✣ ✣

Having lost the battle for the Republic, the new *Société des Amis du Peuple* shifted their aims to the preservation of basic civil rights, especially of assembly and press. Throughout the group's existence they would actively insist upon publicity, attempting to republicanize fellow Parisians through open meetings and inexpensive brochures, though in the end their most important field of combat proved to be the courtroom. The *Amis* had a bourgeois, educated leadership, and shared members with a number of other early leftist (though not necessarily republican) middle-class groups, such as the *Société pour la Défense de la Liberté de la Presse patriote*, which provided legal expenses and subsidies for struggling provincial papers, or the *Association libre pour l'Education du Peuple*, which offered public courses that enrolled some 2,500 working-class adults.[48]

Unlike the other groups, however, the *Société des Amis du Peuple* moved steadily leftward. Philippe Buchez, leader of a Saint-Simonian splinter group and an advocate of worker association, was influential in shifting the *Amis* away from economic liberalism. In the 1840s, he became one of the proponents of Christian socialism and the inspiration behind the workers' journal *L'Atelier*.[49] *Carbonari* veteran Dr. Ulysse Trélat, a noted alienist and future minister in 1848, was president of the society during much of its first year.[50] François-Vincent Raspail was a respected scientist who eventually devoted most of his time to a free clinic for the poor. He was the author of a popular book of home remedies (1843) and an admirer of Jean-Paul Marat.[51]

Behind the scenes was the venerable conspirator Philippe Buonarroti, an Italian aristocrat who had dedicated himself to the French Revolution. In 1828, his reputation had been explosively revived with his *La Conspiration pour l'Égalité*, an account of the 1796 Babeuf conspiracy in which he had participated (and the inspiration for many montagnard political ideas). Buonarroti was befriended by the socialist aristocrat and deputy René Voyer d'Argenson, who supported him financially until his death in 1837. But his chief contact in the *Amis* was probably Charles Teste, a founding member and radical writer with whom he had been in correspondence for many years. (Ironically, his older brother, the cabinet minister Jean-Baptiste Teste of the 1847 Teste-Cubières corruption scandal, probably did more to undermine the regime.)[52] The three men were important in broadening the purely political focus of the early July Monarchy into social and economic issues.

Finally, the *Amis du Peuple* included many future montagnard leaders. In 1830, the professional revolutionary Louis-Auguste Blanqui was a law student and reporter for the Saint-Simonian *Globe*. Early in 1831, he founded his first group, a student association that demanded "the destruction of the University" as an "odious monopoly" of knowledge.[53] Most influential among the young republicans was journalist Godefroy Cavaignac, a leader of the *Amis* and of the successor *Société des Droits de l'Homme et du Citoyen*. Like Blanqui the son of a *conventionnel* (a member of the revolutionary Convention of 1792–95), Cavaignac was a *carbonari* veteran and would later be one of the founders of the newspaper *La Réforme* in 1843. He was the older brother of the future general Eugène Cavaignac, who would crush the insurgents in the June Days of 1848.

In early September, the *Amis* began regular meetings in the large Pellier Hall in Montmartre, arguing that article 291 of the Penal Code, which prohibited groups of over twenty people from meeting regularly without police authorization, had been nullified by the revolution.[54] The right of free assembly had been one of those "republican institutions" set aside for later consideration during the hasty consolidation of the regime, but the new government soon began to have second thoughts. On 25 September, Interior Minister François Guizot denounced the *Amis du Peuple* as one of those societies "where all things are called into question" at every moment: "It is the government, the distribution of fortunes and properties, that one agitates in these societies." That evening the group was expelled from their meeting place.[55] The official story held that the neighbors, "the merchants and small manufacturers," had finally had enough; seeing their "commerce paralysed," "the tranquillity of their quarter incessantly troubled," they had taken matters into their own hands. In contrast, the republican version blamed the police for surrounding their hall with hired troublemakers, whose threats had forced them to leave. The group would continue to meet in various locations but always, from this moment on, under threat of harassment.[56]

After several minor skirmishes, the government's first major assault on the group was the *Procès des Dix-Neuf* (Trial of the Nineteen). For republicans, this case provided their first major opportunity to manipulate the courtroom to their own advantage, their strategy possible only because of the judicial reforms of the first revolution. French trials under the old regime had been conducted according to the fundamental *Ordonnance* of 1670, which had codified an inquisitorial process. Professional judges read the written evidence—the depositions of suspects and witnesses (assembled in closed session by investigating magistrates), and *mémoires* from the defense—and issued a verdict based on this material, according to strict rules of evidence. This secret procedure had been opened up in the course of the revolution through the adoption of the jury system and oral arguments, confirmed in the *Code d'Instruction criminelle* of 1808.[57]

under the Napoleonic Code?

An element of the 1670 procedure survived in the preliminary investigation by the *juge d'instruction*, who continued to possess many intangible advantages. The suspect was not allowed to have a lawyer present, nor was he told of the charges or evidence against him, unless the examining magistrate chose to reveal this information.[58] In the *Procès des Dix-Neuf*, an unusual number of defendants and witnesses complained that their written depositions (used against them in trial) did not conform to what they had said to the examining magistrate; Dr. Ulysse Trélat told of questions so complex that one needed "great power of concentration," as well as practice in debate, in order not to be tripped up. Because of the ease with which their words could be manipulated, many republicans refused to give pretrial depositions. The underground *Société des Familles*, founded by Blanqui in 1834, formally prohibited its members from speaking to the *juge d'instruction*.[59]

Nevertheless, the judiciary could exert pressure by holding a defendant in custody for lengthy periods before filing formal charges. The law required only that a defendant be questioned before the end of 24 hours. Republicans complained that this formality was often fulfilled merely by asking the arrested individual his name. Months would then pass before further interrogation, a particular source of frustration for working men whose families were dependent on their income.[60] In 1833, the *Procureur-Général* of Paris frankly acknowledged the value of constant harassment through frequent police searches, whether followed by arrest or not: "It takes from them all their courage."[61]

Although the pretrial procedures remained similar to those of the old regime, the trial itself had been transformed through the revolutionary innovation of the jury, including both a jury of judgment and a *jury d'accusa-tion*, or grand jury, to bring indictments. The latter was replaced, during the Empire, by a panel of judges called the *chambre des mises en accusation*, or in-dictment chamber; the mighty weapon of prosecution, then, was entirely in the hands of appointed government officials.[62] On the other hand, the power of juries in assessing penalties was dramatically increased by the law of 28 April 1832. This major legislation reduced the number of capital crimes, abolished branding and mutilation, and allowed juries to consider "extenuating circumstances" that would lead to a reduction of the penalty—this last measure designed to end acquittals by jurors who found the pre-scribed penalties too harsh. The number of jurors necessary to convict varied from 7 to 9 (out of 12) between 1830 and 1848; the jury list was se-lected each year from among the electors, or eligible voters, by the ap-pointed departmental prefect, who had the power to weed out enemies of the regime. Political suspects nevertheless preferred the *Cours d'Assises*, with a jury, to the *Tribunal de police correctionnelle*, where a panel of magistrates is-sued the verdict; even though the possible sentences were less severe in the lower court, the conviction was more certain.[63]

The presiding magistrate or *président* had considerable power: to direct the debates, to summon new witnesses, to order the reading of pretrial depositions when they conflicted with oral testimony.[64] Immediately after the reading of the indictment, the presiding magistrate conducted an interrogation of the defen-dant, often in the manner of a prosecutor.[65] Until 1881, the *président* finished the case by a summary of the evidence which, because of an "unconscious esprit de corps," frequently amounted to a second summation for the prosecution.[66] The nature of the judicial hierarchy—a part of the government bureaucracy—further skewed the entire procedure. It was possible to move back and forth between the "seated" magistracy, or the judges' bench, and the "standing" magistracy, or prosecutorial bench; judges had permanent tenure, but prosecutors might ad-vance through the ranks—or perhaps, from the provinces to Paris—more quickly. In both branches there was a strong incentive for junior members to defer to the opinions of their superiors; as Benjamin Martin has remarked, they were not seen, by "themselves or by outsiders, as an independent judiciary."[67]

In the courtroom, attorneys and defendants deliberately portrayed them-selves as Davids against multiple Goliaths. The defense attorney's chief oppor-tunity to sway the jury was through his pleading (*plaidoyer*) at the end, delivered after the prosecutor's summation (*réquisitoire*); thus, much depended on his persuasiveness and oratorical skill. Many of the frequent political defen-dants—Cavaignac, Raspail, Blanqui—also developed a reputation for public speaking, and often played to a full house. In addition, their words were frequently immortalized in one of the republican trial brochures, cheap pamphlets that highlighted lawyers' *plaidoiries* and defendants' statements, omitting much extraneous testimony in order to provide a clear narrative. When the cases involved press offenses, the brochures included reprints of the offending articles—permissible because the prosecutors had to read them into the record as evidence—and thus provided even wider circulation for the original material. Finally, the republican trial pamphlets included a generous sampling of audience reaction, always at the expense of the government.

The *Procès des Dix-Neuf*, the first judicial tournament of the regime, concerned the street disturbances of 20–22 December 1830 during the *Procès des Ministres*, the trial of four of Charles X's ministers (those, including the hated Polignac, who were unlucky enough to get caught). When it was announced that the ministers had been sentenced to life imprisonment instead of death there had been minor riots, in which the government had professed to see a conspiracy to overturn the new regime; hence the extraordinary exaggeration of the charges against the protesters, which could conceivably have resulted in death sentences. Most saw in this case a preemptive strike against the republican leadership; the nineteen defendants included republican notables Cavaignac, Trélat, Joseph Guinard, and the two Garnier-Pagès brothers, the elder Étienne (age 28), soon to be a republican deputy, and Louis, age 20, a future member of the Provisional Government in 1848. And the trial was meant to be impressive, with 96 witnesses for the prosecution (*témoins à charge*) and 84 witnesses for the defense (*témoins à décharge*). But sheer volume could not make a case.

The first part of the indictment centered around the student radical Jules Sambuc, author of a pamphlet published in December 1830. In labored metaphors he noted that the men of the older generation were building the future, but "it is we who have to live in it"; if his generation destroyed the edifice, "it is because up to now the architects have not acknowledged the slightest obligation to consult the taste of the young tenants."[68] He had read this brochure to a group of ten fellow students on 9 December 1830. His *Société*, "definitively constituted" on 11 or 12 December, had lasted only until the beginning of January, with a total membership of 32.[69] This was dangerous stuff indeed, but the prosecution was even more interested in Sambuc's private diary which was, to his acute embarrassment, read out in court and published in the newspapers.

Sambuc's journal provided an intimate look into post-July exuberance, a period of heated meetings and events rushing by too rapidly for detailed recording. On December 19, Sambuc wrote: "Interview with Captain [of the National Guard] Cavaignac; meeting at his home. Opinions shared; nothing fixed, nothing certain. It is believed that the Napoleonists will attack tomorrow; should they be allowed to do so or be stopped?" On December 21: "Recruited some fifteen first-rate individuals; brought them to the home of Antoine to fraternize with us; distribution of lists." And then on December 22: "Judgment of the ministers, meetings, scuffles, trips to the Bastille, 1 franc, return, speeches in various places, at the École de Médecine, at the École Polytechnique; went to the *estaminet hollandais*, the crisis is abating, useless efforts."[70] The prosecutor had apparently found this sinister enough to bring to trial, despite the inclusion of personal banalities (one franc per trip). Sambuc's associates, similarly menacing, included Pierre-Louis Chapparre, a 21-year-old pharmacy student, who had been captured with the following note in his pocket: "Six students have been arrested and imprisoned. It is necessary to know who they are, where they are, and see what is best to do. Pass it on."[71]

The second part of the case focused on the second and third batteries of the national guard artillery, commanded by Guinard and Cavaignac, which included many members of the *Amis du Peuple*. The six guards on trial were charged with having conspired to turn over their artillery to the people in the December disturbances. The prosecution's evidence was fragmentary: at the time of the troubles the members of the *Amis du Peuple* "held themselves apart, and mysteriously"; they "ceased their conversations when someone approached them"; there had been dinner table talk of the Republic; defendant Edouard Chauvin had been seen at the grille of the Louvre, with "shabbily-dressed individuals," and another *artilleur* had had a "nocturnal rendezvous" under the Pont-des-Arts. As the prosecutor promised, after reciting the other bits of doubtful hearsay that made up the government's brief, "it is in appreciating the totality of these general facts" that the case could be fully understood.[72]

But the hearsay did not wear any better in open court. A certain Fourchon, a witness in the matter of turning over the cannons to the people, said that he only knew what he had been told by M. Leclerc; Leclerc himself, testifying immediately after, reported that it was "A grenadier, I don't know which one, in effect [who] reported these words to me, not as having heard them himself, but having them from a third person."[73] Other evidence, suggesting the defendants' involvement in midnight meetings under the bridges, or talking through the gates with tattered men, completely fell apart and was rightly held up to ridicule by the defense.

The last phase of the case was the most unfocused part of the trial, involving several men who were supposed to have encouraged the people to revolt. Most of the witnesses in this loosely related group were called against Jean-François Danton, a 28-year-old editor of *La Tribune* and one of the founders of the *Amis du Peuple* (though not related to "*Danton le conventionnel*").[74] The proprietor of the Sorbonne café asserted that his billiard room had become the hangout of "young men who do not dissimulate their intention of working for the overthrow of the government," but he could not remember Danton as having been among them.[75] A cabriolet driver testified that on 20 December he had picked up an individual who "appeared to be a provocateur of troubles"; the subversive passenger was not Danton or indeed any of the other nineteen.[76] A lodginghouse keeper had heard the following words: "Robespierre and Marat were honest patriots; Christ himself was an excellent patriot, for he was the first to preach equality." He did not know who had said it; he was only sure that it was not Danton, whom he had never seen until this moment in the courtroom.[77] Finally, a cafekeeper recognized Danton as having criticized the light sentences given Charles X's ministers; he rather spoiled the effect by adding casually that "everybody said that in the *faubourg*." (With some prompting, he recalled that he himself had declared that "If the faubourg Saint-Marceau turns out, the faubourg Saint-Antoine will follow.")[78] As a final blow to the case, the police *commissaire* was reluctantly forced to admit on the stand that the information against Danton and another "co-conspirator" came from the reports of a police informer, a certain "Joanny, aka Ceratti."[79]

The defendants were universally acquitted. But despite its absurdities, the case had irrevocably altered the political landscape. The monarchy had clumsily declared war on moderate republican leaders, most of whom had hoped to support the new regime. This trial ended all good will; now the moderates were discredited and the montagnard faction strengthened, and there was, in the words of attorney and journalist F. Rittiez, "an uncrossable barrier" between the monarchy and its republican opponents. As relentless government prosecutions constrained the rights of assembly and press, moderates were forced either to drop out of the movement or follow the extremists into more flagrant illegality.[80] Rittiez knew from experience; he was one of the dropouts.

Even before the triumphant *Procès des Dix-Neuf*, the *Amis du Peuple* had decided to diversify their activities. In February 1831, they determined upon a strategy of written propaganda; without renouncing "in any way the right of the [Society] to meet in public sessions," they voted to create a publishing committee. Its members selected articles written by the membership but disclaimed responsibility for the content, asserting that the committee merely shepherded the pamphlets through production.[81] After the government threatened their printer (legally responsible for anonymous publications), committee members initialed each article, though insisting that this did not imply authorship.[82] The *Amis du Peuple* were soon visible primarily through brochures and the trials provoked by them, both of which drew heavily upon the skills of educated members.

The *Procès des Quinze* involved the fifteen members of the publishing committee. Arrests began in the summer of 1831 for a trial finally held in January 1832, when the *Amis* unveiled a twofold defense strategy. First, they proclaimed the joint complicity of all society members in the publications, the course undertaken in advance; second, they attempted to prove that what was said in the incendiary brochures was factually true, a method that would allow them to turn the trial back onto the government.[83] The most provocative of their pamphlets, on the demonstrations in June 1831, charged that the police had deliberately incited the disturbances and had spread false rumors of pillage in an attempt to rouse the bourgeois national guards against the people.[84] Thus defendant Anthony Thouret asked that the presiding magistrate question one witness "to learn if a citizen was not murdered in front of his eyes, rue Mauconseil"—an inflammatory reference to the death of one of the demonstrators. Attorney Dupont was able to go even further with the next witness, Symon: "We have caused the witness to be called to prove the truth of a fact: last 15 June, a lawyer, M. Duverger, finding himself at the prefecture of police, chatted with one of the high-level chiefs. He asked how the police could publish placards to the effect that shops had been pillaged, when that information was false. The high-level employee answered: 'If the people don't pillage shops, the police will cause some to be pillaged.' M. Duverger reported these words to M. Symon who will testify to them"[85]—not that there was much left to say. The jury deliberated for just under three hours, returning with acquittals. The celebration was extinguished when the court immediately handed down sentences for seditious remarks made in the course of the trial, including fifteen months for Raspail and one year for Blanqui (his first sentence). Shouted the youthful Thouret, who received six months: "We still have bullets!"[86] But the government tactic of going after the publishing committees took its toll, as numerous republicans found their health worn down by long pretrial detentions and their courage diminished by uncertainty—for juries occasionally convicted.[87]

The *Amis du Peuple* also endured two important trials on the basis of article 291 of the Penal Code, as they continued their efforts to gather in large public sessions. They were mostly unsuccessful, with the police tracking them from one location to another and bullying potential landlords. Prefect of Police Henri-Joseph Gisquet had no doubt about the stakes of the contest: "What was especially important was to disperse this agglomeration of capable and enterprising men ... to take from them the means of speaking to the masses ... and finally to reduce these proud enemies to their proportions, to the shameful role of obscure conspirators!"[88] The last important trial was in December 1832, when 19 leaders of the group were tried for violation of the association law. The case resulted in universal acquittals, but also in a formal judicial dissolution of the *Amis*.[89] But by the time this case came to court, the educated, gradualist republicanism of the *Amis* had given way to montagnard extremism, its debut to be marked by the insurrection of 5–6 June 1832.

The 1832 uprising, brought vividly to life by Victor Hugo in *Les Misérables*, was preceded by months of destabilizing events. Parisian activists emotionally embraced the heroic, ill-fated Lyon uprising of November 1831.[90] The legitimist threat was represented by the abortive rue des Prouvaires conspiracy of February 1832 and by the duchesse de Berry, who arrived secretly in France in May 1832 to rouse Provence and the Vendée on behalf of her son, Charles X's only grandson, the pretender Henri V. Berry was finally captured in November; in an unchivalrous act that embarrassed even the Orléanists, the government held the pregnant widow captive until she gave birth the following spring. She was forced to confess to a "secret marriage," and eventually to produce a bridegroom from the ranks of the minor Italian nobility.[91]

The spring of 1832 also saw Paris ravaged by a Europe-wide outbreak of cholera, which ended with a death toll of 18,402 in the city. The statistics verified what everyone already knew, that the poor neighborhoods were particularly devastated by the disease.[92] In response to the crisis, Prefect of Police Gisquet published a well-meant but remarkably clumsy declaration that the government was *not* poisoning public wells, though he acknowledged that evildoers had spread such a rumor and might even, to gain credit for it, have thrown suspicious matter into them—a convoluted revelation that contributed to several ugly scenes of mob violence. A contemporary noted that after the proclamation "men of the people" posted themselves in the streets, "suspecting and believing they saw poisoners everywhere."[93] Dr. Poumiès recalled a crowd gathered around a speaker who proclaimed "that cholera was a pretext invented to disembarrass [society] of poor people, that doctors and pharmacists were the chosen *exécuteurs* of the government, that the public fountains were all poisoned, etc."[94]

The epidemic soon claimed two famous victims. Casimir Périer fell sick on 5 April and died on 16 May; the government drifted through his illness, and after him there were a series of colorless ministers and unstable coalitions until Louis-Philippe settled on Guizot in 1840. In late May the *National* began to include daily bulletins about the health of General Maximilien Lamarque, who died on 2 June, one of the last links with that "glorious generation" of the revolution.[95]

Périer was given a grand state funeral; it was decided that Lamarque's funeral would demonstrate the strength of the opposition. On 5 June the *National*, by now an openly republican newspaper, published the order of the procession (as it would publish a similar order in February 1848, precipitating the revolution), inviting Deputies, national guards in uniform, foreign refugees, and the *décorés de juillet* to participate.[96] According to historian Louis Blanc, the *Société des Amis du Peuple* had decided to hold themselves in readiness for any "collision" that might develop. On the morning of 5 June, law and medical students joined the assembled *Amis* along the route; many of the young men provocatively had daggers and pistols half-visible under their coats.[97]

Gisquet posted the uniformed *sergents de ville* along the route, and throughout the morning there were skirmishes (or as republicans told it, the *sergents de ville* engaged in attacks on peaceful working men). When the procession reached the Place de la Bastille, the crowd cheered the sudden appearance of a group of 60 *polytechniciens*, out of breath and disheveled after escaping over the walls of the elite École Polytechnique.[98] At almost the same time there arrived an unidentified column of about 400 to 600 men, "rather poorly dressed and threatening," "with sinister faces, for the most part with sleeves rolled up, armed with large clubs," who joined the cortège. Blanc asserted that soldiers, including officers, approached the students and assured them of their willingness to "fraternize."[99]

At about 3:30 P.M., the head of the convoy reached the speakers' platform on the right bank of the Pont d'Austerlitz, where the eulogies were to be spoken. After a number of brief tributes, Lafayette was brought to the podium by popular demand. As he was speaking, there were rumors that he was about to proclaim the republic and establish a provisional government. Several men, members of the shadowy *Association gauloise*, suddenly shoved him into a carriage bound for the Hôtel de Ville; Lafayette kept his head sufficiently to escape from his escort and make his way home. A detachment of 200 dragoons was seen to be heading toward the Pont d'Austerlitz; Prefect Gisquet had summoned them, concerned about the passage of the coffin over the bridge.[100] Suddenly, there appeared the spectre that republicans later blamed for their defeat: a cadaverous man with a ghastly white face, dressed in black, riding on horseback through the crowd and carrying a red flag on which was written *Liberté ou la mort!*—an embodiment and reminder of the horrors of the Year II.[101]

But the episode that later caused the most debate concerned the detachment of dragoons. Blanc praised them for their self-control under a barrage of stones; at least two were wounded before several deputies interposed themselves between the soldiers and the people.[102] But the dragoons had already sent to their nearby barracks for help; the second group of 200, led by the colonel of the regiment, had barely left their quarters when they came under a fire that killed six men and seriously wounded the colonel and lieutenant colonel. In the sudden leaderless confusion, the second column apparently galloped straight into a group of "inoffensive citizens," those who had neither thrown rocks nor fired. A number of national guards—including Charles Jeanne, who would become the archetypal montagnard hero of this day—now joined the side of the rebels. At the same time there was an attempt to hijack Lamarque's coffin and take it to the Panthéon. The municipal guard cavalry, waiting on the other side of the river, secured his remains with the loss of one killed and several wounded, and put him on the road to his final resting place.[103]

The authorities were now confronted with a far more aggressive insurrection than the one that had triumphed in 1830. In under two hours the center of Paris was taken; more than 4,000 muskets and rifles were seized from barracks, guard posts, and gunshops. But on the government's side, the Paris garrison at 18,000 men included nearly twice as many soldiers as Charles X had had at his disposal.[104] The police forces, the *sergents de ville* and the Municipal Guard, took back the Ile de la Cité and the Châtelet on the Right Bank in short order; within hours the Left Bank was once again under control. And the government also had the citizen-soldiers of the National Guard, the symbols of the regime, who were soon out in force.[105] Later that night Louis-Philippe, who like Charles X in 1830 had been at Saint-Cloud, arrived at the Tuileries.[106] (Some hoped he would be less bold: Besson, a carpenter, was arrested in the middle of the night with a glue pot and brush, pasting up a placard entitled "Flight of Louis-Philippe."[107])

By midnight, the insurgents were entrenched in only a few pockets in the east, and the mopping-up began in the early morning hours of 6 June. The hotly contested passage du Saumon was taken before dawn. The large barricade that closed off the faubourg Saint-Antoine was taken in mid-morning, finally falling after an artillery barrage. Whenever possible the national guards marched with the troops, providing political cover; for the same reason Marshal Lobau, as their commandant, was in overall command.[108] The *élan* was now entirely with the government forces, as the last few bands of rebels were quickly cut off and defeated.

At noon General Tiburce Sébastiani was ready to take the last enclave of revolt, the Right Bank area around the Saint-Méry church, when suddenly all action was halted for nearly two hours. The delay was caused by Louis-Philippe, who rode through the city to the cheers of the Paris crowd. The king was urged to take some precautions for his safety; his answer was widely reported: "I have an excellent *cuirasse*, my five sons."[109]

Finally, Sébastiani was given permission to finish. Most of the barricades of the rue Saint-Martin were barely manned, abandoned as their defenders retreated; Sébastiani's troops were met with gunfire from windows, as well as paving stones, tiles, logs and boards dropped from the roofs: "The soldiers penetrated [the buildings], killed all who defended themselves and conducted [prisoners] to the [nearby] Hôtel de Ville . . . they fought in the stairways, in the apartments; but everywhere the advantage remained with our soldiers." Those who could not escape by way of roofs or alleys ended up inside a large, several-sided barricade that closed off the intersection of Saint-Martin and Saint-Méry; it took the artillery to end their resistance. "From the moment the gunfire ceased, the inhabitants of all the *quartiers* that we had just passed through showed themselves in the streets," reported Sébastiani; "they accepted us with cries of *Vive le Roi! vive la liberté!*, showing us their joy at the success we had just obtained and their indignation at the *attentat* that had troubled the tranquillity of the capital for two days."[110]

The total cost of the insurrection was high: for the National Guard, 18 dead, 104 wounded; for the regular army, 32 dead, 170 wounded; for the Municipal Guard, 20 dead, 52 wounded. There was no way to determine the total insurgent casualties, though contemporary estimates put the number at from 80 to 100 dead, with 200 to 300 wounded.[111] Of the slightly more than 200 identified insurgents, 34 percent were "petty bourgeois," predominantly shopkeepers and clerks; but 66 percent were workers, with construction workers accounting for nearly a third.[112] After peace was restored, the police conducted house-to-house searches, their efforts yielding nearly 3,000 muskets and rifles as well as quantities of sabers, épées, pistols, and daggers.[113] With over 1,500 prisoners in the city jails, the king's ministry recommended that the capital be placed in a state of siege, under military courts—a dreadful political blunder, the more remarkable since Charles X had taken the same step in 1830.[114]

The danger of hasty military justice was clearly evident in one of the first cases tried, that of the young painter Michel Geoffroy, who was convicted as the bearer of the notorious red flag and sentenced to death. His attorney Odilon Barrot appealed the case to the *Cour de Cassation*, which met on 29 June and declared the state of siege to be in violation of the Charter. Geoffroy was sent before the *Cour d'Assises* and his "natural judges" for retrial, where he received a shorter sentence for his other rebellious activities.[115] (The real flag-bearer was found a few weeks later, and sentenced to only a month in prison because of his obvious mental instability.[116])

The cases of individual insurgents went forward throughout the rest of the year. A total of 82 people were convicted by juries in the *Cours d'Assises*, of whom 7 were sentenced to death; all 7 death penalties were commuted to "deportation," which in practice meant a prison term in one of the state fortresses.[117] The two most famous capital cases involved Cuny and Lepage, on whose behalf the fledgling *Société des Droits de l'Homme et du Citoyen* threatened an armed rescue. Lepage, a 24-year-old porter in the markets, was accused of having taken a shopkeeper's iron door-bar (for which he had left a deposit) to rip up paving stones for a barricade. The jury found him guilty only of one of the charges, that of "inciting citizens to arm themselves"; upon hearing the death sentence the startled jurors immediately drafted a petition for mercy. (Years later, *La Réforme* reported his death in 1843, impoverished, mentally ill, and consumptive from his captivity in the prison of Mont-Saint-Michel.)[118] Cuny, a cook, claimed that the stolen weapon in his possession had been forced on him and denied that he had fired it. Upon hearing his death sentence he shouted *Vive la République!*, making his case a *cause célèbre*; the *National* asserted that his would be the regime's first execution for "political beliefs." His lawyer Adolphe Crémieux, future member of the Provisional Government of 1848, successfully solicited Louis-Philippe for clemency: "King of the barricades of July, pardon the barricades of June."[119]

The other death sentences seemed equally random. Pierre-Joseph Lecouvreur, a 44-year-old stonemason, had rushed home from the cortège, shouting to his wife as he entered the house: "Quickly! quickly! hurry up, give me the you-know-what!" He exited shortly with two sacks of about 1,500 homemade cartridges. (His defense was that a "stranger" had left the sacks, their contents unknown to him, in his apartment that morning.) He was one of the neighborhood republicans, and only the day before had harangued a local gardener, making him listen to passages from a brochure about Robespierre.[120] The

other four men sentenced to death—three of them for the battle in the Passage du Saumon—also had their sentences commuted, and after they helped to
fight the fire at Mont-Saint-Michel in late 1834 they were amnestied, after
only two years in prison.[121]

While few workers had considered themselves republican in 1830, many of
those now on trial were explicitly republican in sentiment and montagnard in
their theatricality. The tailor Prosper, a 30-year-old *décoré de juillet*, had gone to
his local mayoralty to protest. There he had encountered a bourgeois national
guard: "'What,' he said to me, 'you're fighting against the government, you
who founded it?' 'I didn't found it,' I said; 'and when I spilled my blood in the
Three Days, if someone would have shouted in front of me *vive le duc d'Orléans*
I would have shot him as a traitor.'" He was sentenced to ten years, after delivering a lengthy speech, later published, to the jury.[122] F. Petel, a printer who
worked for the *Tribune*, fought at the Passage du Saumon, and he and his two
companions in arms, Joseph and Casimir Roussel, each received five years in
prison. They began a series of "seditious cries" ("*Vive la république! Death to
tyrants! We will see you at the barricades!*") and were threatened with additional
punishment. As their lawyers attempted to repair the situation, each spoke separately. Said Joseph Roussel: "I shouted *vive la République* because I was upset";
Petel: "I shouted *vive la République* because I'm a republican"; and finally,
Casimir Roussel: "I wasn't a republican and now I am!"[123]

The most compelling narrative was that of the battle of the Cloître-Saint-
Méry, which provided republicans with their first montagnard martyr in the
worker Charles Jeanne. The mutation of this final military episode into legend
is evident in the account by Louis Blanc, only a few years after the fact, as he
described the insurgents down to their last hundred cartridges:

> Thus, in the heart of a city with more than a million of inhabitants, in the
> most populous quarter of Paris, and in the open light of day, sixty citizens
> were seen utterly defying the government, keeping its army in check, parley-
> ing, and giving battle. . . . An old man, with a bald head and grey beard, fell
> dead just within the barricade, at the moment when, elevating a tricoloured
> flag, he was calling upon his comrades to make some grand, desperate ef-
> fort. . . . One of the combatants complained of hunger, and asked for provi-
> sions: "Provisions!" exclaimed Jeanne: "it is now three o'clock; at four o'clock
> we shall all be dead."[124]

The trial of Saint-Méry finally began in late October. Virtually all 22 of
the defendants denied their guilt; they claimed that they had been trapped on
the wrong side of the barricades, menaced by insurgents, even forced to take

up a gun and shoot. In stark contrast were Jeanne's frank avowals. As a national guard, he had attended Lamarque's funeral unarmed, when he and his colleagues had suddenly been stampeded by the dragoons. Convinced that the government had deliberately sent troops against its opponents, he had rushed home to build barricades for self-defense—just as he had done in July, when the former government had also launched an assault against its own people.[125]

Jeanne acknowledged his actions with a bravado that even his opponents could admire, particularly given his physical frailty; Gisquet recalled that "under a spindly physique and suffering in appearance, he unveiled an inflexible character."[126] He was particularly insistent upon the honor of himself and his men, protesting (when a witness suggested that he had been firing from a protected position), "I always presented my breast to the bullets of the enemy." He and his men had retreated only when they ran out of cartridges—"without that we would have remained."[127] And for the same reason he disputed the number of his troops, insisting that they had been overwhelmingly outnumbered. The porter of no. 30 Saint-Méry, their headquarters, estimated about 300 insurgents, as did the National Guard Claris. Jeanne asserted that there had been no more than 110; he received unexpected support for the lower number from Gisquet.[128] The neighbors (battered by constant shouts of *vive la république!*, endless choruses of patriotic songs) nevertheless praised Jeanne for his restraint. Mme. Gravelle, a jeweler, recalled that "They shouted '*qui vive?*' [who goes there?] It was necessary to answer '*Citizens!*'" Still, what she most feared was property damage, and Jeanne had kindly agreed not to shoot from her windows.[129] Another woman in no. 30 reported that "These gentlemen announced to me that the provisional government *m'indemniserait.*" And according to the surgeon Dalvigny, who spent the night of 5–6 June tending the wounded: "I advanced to the barricade, the sentinel shouted '*Qui vive!*' and took aim; Jeanne threw himself on him, raised the weapon, and said: 'Poor creature! One does not fire on an unarmed man!'"[130]

Jeanne's defense had been prefigured as early as 10 June in *Le National* by Armand Carrel, who had stated unequivocally that the dragoons had provoked the insurrection by charging into an unarmed crowd. The task for Jeanne's attorney Alexandre Marie (future member of the Provisional Government in 1848) was to show why he had acted, and to provide some mitigating circumstances that might lighten his penalty—a difficult burden, in that Marie addressed a jury that was essentially supportive of the troops.[131] (Early in the trial, when a witness claimed that soldiers had fired on civilians, one of the jurors had spoken up: "That's an error."[132]) Thus Marie had to stress that he was merely trying to explore the perceptions of his client, who had genuinely believed himself attacked, and he called as witnesses many obviously bourgeois guards who had shared Jeanne's impression. Delair, an attorney, had suddenly been confronted with galloping cavalry: "There was a lot of exaltation among the national guards who had also been charged, each shouted 'To arms!' . . . I was strongly moved. Two national guards had just been wounded beside me." Another witness had seen the dragoons suddenly increase their speed to a gallop, "and divided up firing right and left with pistols. We fell back onto the bridge screaming, as you can well imagine." Thibaudot, a manufacturer, stated that "the general sentiment was that it was a surprise, and that one had been attacked by the troops."[133] Marie had shifted the focus of the trial away from Jeanne, so much so that it became necessary to call the officers of the dragoons, who spoke of being pelted with rocks, even assaulted by gunfire. *Chef d'escadron* Desolliers emotionally denied that he and his men had fired even a single shot.[134]

The verdict was delivered on 31 October 1832; 15 of the 22 were acquitted. Jeanne was sentenced to deportation, which meant incarceration for life in the fortress of Mont-Saint-Michel.[135] At first he continued his militancy, organizing a protest against prison conditions.[136] But soon he became ill; from the Bicêtre prison hospital in Paris, where he lived in April 1834, he wrote to the *National* to protest that he had not requested his transfer, that he was not—as vicious rumor had it—exchanging "revelations" for favors.[137] Olivier Dufresne, the inspector-general of prisons, confirmed that it was the authorities who had made the decision to move him, and he provided one of the last descriptions of Jeanne: "I found him [in his cell] in bed, having beside him two crutches without which he could not walk, and victim of a continual trembling, the result of the bad treatment he had experienced at Mont-Saint-Michel." Dufresne asserted that since his stay in Bicêtre he had made steady progress; he deplored Jeanne's tendency to exaggerate his hardships, which his own improving health belied. Charles Jeanne died of tuberculosis in 1837.[138]

Moderate bourgeois republicanism had been defeated in Paris. It would experience a brief revival in 1839 and 1840, in the campaign to extend the suffrage; it would dominate the early months of the Second Republic; it would triumph in the Third. But for the moment the montagnards led the movement, insistent on blood and martyrdom, and consumed with violent fantasies of power.

CHAPTER 4

PREPARING FOR BATTLE: THE *SOCIÉTÉ DES DROITS DE L'HOMME ET DU CITOYEN*

"MON PÈRE, THE FATHERLAND HAS CALLED ME," wrote Étienne-Denis Gallay, a 21-year-old jeweler, on the eve of the 1834 insurrection; "duty commands me to obey and defend our rights, I must not remain deaf to the appeal of our brave citizens and I glory in marching in their ranks; if I succumb it will be in defending my country gloriously if we triumph I will have even greater pleasure in seeing you again, in case of difficulties receive my last embrace." Afterward, when the police searched his bare little fifth-floor chamber, they found an affectionate letter from his father, warning him against filling his sister's head with "your nonsense of revolution"; a stack of Étienne Cabet's republican paper *Le Populaire;* and 800 homemade cartridges. A member of the republican *Société des Droits de l'Homme et du Citoyen* (SDHC), of the *section* named *Abolition de la propriété mal acquise* (Abolition of Wrongfully Acquired Property), Gallay spent the night on guard duty at a barricade in the rue Beaubourg. He was killed the following morning when the troops took the street.[1]

The SDHC emerged as a workers' annex to the dying *Société des Amis du Peuple.* Throughout the early months of 1832, republican leaders conducted a drive to organize workers, grouping them in small neighborhood *sections* in order to take advantage of the loophole in article 291, which required police authorization only for groups of more than 20.[2] The new society quickly evolved into a paramilitary group; its elite were the *hommes d'action,* the self-selected avant-garde who were to begin the attack against the government. By 1834 the organization had between three and four thousand members in 163 *sections*.[3] As the rest of this chapter will indicate, it is impossible to determine the effective size because of the constant turnover in membership, the varying levels of individual commitment, and the tendency of *section* leaders to inflate their own numbers. Though undoubtedly smaller than imagined, however, the *Société des Droits de l'Homme et du Citoyen* became the most important of the republican associations of the July Monarchy.

The responsibility for organizing the sections fell to Auguste Caunes, a writer and publisher whose republicanism had been intensified with the death of his only son in the failed *Amis* expedition, in October 1830, to establish a Belgian Republic. He announced the group's definitive organization in an *ordre du jour* of 29 August 1832, and he attempted to push the *Amis* leftward with the pressure of these newly recruited working-class members.[4] In Caunes' opinion the *Amis* lacked "energy," was without "sufficiently pronounced opinions," and was dominated by "Girondins"; he proposed as the new credo Robespierre's Declaration of the Rights of Man, submitted to the Convention in 1793 and rejected by even that body as too extreme.[5]

The SDHC *Réglement* divided the group into sections of between 10 and 20 members; when a group reached 20, half would split off to form a new section. Each section would decide individually when to meet, with meetings to last for at least two hours. Each section had a *chef*, or president, a *sous-chef* (vice-president), and three *quinturions;* the term of office and manner of voting was left up to the individual section. The president made certain that discussions did not stray from relevant topics, the *sous-chef* took charge in his absence, and each of the *quinturions* managed four or five *sectionnaires*, notifying them of special meetings and (though this was not stated openly in the rules) conducting them in battle. Candidates for membership were to be voted upon by their individual sections; two negative votes were sufficient to deny. New members were required to make a formal adherence to Robespierre's Declaration, and anyone found guilty of unrepublican conduct was expelled from the society and denounced to its members. Those able to pay contributed money for the purchase of republican brochures; the main business of the weekly meetings was the reading and discussion of these "patriotic writings."[6] Each group of twenty chose a colorful and often provocative name: *Marat, Couthon, Saint-Just, Robespierre, Chute des Girondins* (Fall of the Girondins), *Quatre-vingt-treize* ('93), several *Montagnards* or *Montagnes, Jacobins, Guerre aux Châteaux* (War on the Palaces), *Paix aux Chaumières* (Peace to the Cottages), *Babeuf, Buonarroti, Incorruptible, Mort aux tyrans, 5 et 6 Juin, des Piques* (Pikes),

Tocsin, Barricade Méry, Insurrection de Lyon, 21 Janvier (the date of the execution of Louis XVI), and *Louvel* (assassin of the duc de Berry).[7]

The government's first court challenge to the new group came in April 1833. The indictment charged that the sections were not independent entities but rather parts of a large whole, and thus in violation of article 291. Four of the seven defendants, all *chefs de série* with authority over several sections, were found guilty, and the society was formally dissolved (a decision ignored for another year).[8]

In the course of this trial defendant Simon Petitjean, a lawyer, asserted that the SDHC had only the rather benign purpose of "political education." The society archives, composed of membership lists (seized at the homes of the leaders throughout 1833 and early 1834) seemed to belie his peaceful characterization. Section chief Pinel, for example, boasted of his most distinguished members: "sentenced to a 1,000-franc fine and six months in prison"; "pure patriot, arrested last June [1832]"; "his father served a sentence for written threats to King Philippe."[9] The register from the section *Souveraineté* jumbled personal qualities with equipment: "Michel (chief), rue Quincampoix 11, reflective, saber, musket, cartridge pouch; Honoré, painter, rue de Bièvre 37, courageous, *décoré de juillet*, pistol and saber; Casimir, tailor, rue de l'Arbre-sec 47, courageous, bold, saber, musket, cartridge pouch"—and so on, for a total of 13. The roster of the section *Washington* revealed that its 19 members had 322 cartridges among them.[10]

Several chiefs explicitly assessed the likely fighting qualities of their members. For example: "a little young, doesn't lack courage, but one doesn't know to what point he would hold in combat." Another member was described as "a man who is being molded; one should scarcely count on him yet." And finally: "has already fought; can be counted upon," and "having already served, can be useful in combat, has a lot of sangfroid." Bernard Pornin, who supervised several sections, reported that the clerk Benjamin Ennery, the chief of *Travailleurs*, was "full of ability, an energetic man, excellent patriot ready to march"; Jean-Baptiste Roques, clerk, was described as "lukewarm, but he would march with the section"; of Henri Jallon, porter and third quinturion: "He lost his leg in June; he is ready to begin again for the republican cause."[11]

The registers, in short, did not suggest a society devoted to peaceful propaganda, and it soon became apparent that a militant force had been created in the heart of the *Amis du Peuple*. The new activists publicly expressed their dissatisfaction with the old leadership's moderation in April 1833, at the time of the trial.[12] In the early summer of that year many *Amis* members, especially those from the middle classes, simply dropped out. The rest joined the new *sections*, adding to an internal split between moderates who favored propaganda, as the *Amis* had done, and radicals who wanted action.[13]

The divisions soon became apparent in the *Procès des Vingt-Sept*, or Trial of the Twenty-Seven. The case lasted an unusually long 11 days, from 11 to 22 December 1833, and included more than 100 hundred witnesses and 12 defense lawyers. The government charged that the SDHC had plotted an insurrection for the third anniversary of the July Revolution. Nothing much had happened on the day in question, but the non-event, as the prosecutor explained to the jury, was no barrier to trial: conspiring to overturn the government was a crime in itself, according to the recently revised law, whether or not any action had followed.[14] It was a flimsy case. Charges against 11 of the defendants were dropped at the end of the testimony, and the remaining 16 were acquitted on 55 separate counts after a deliberation of only two hours. The only sentences, imposed by the panel of judges, were suspensions of three of the defense attorneys for insults to the prosecuting attorney and an excessive three years in prison for SDHC activist Jean-Jacques Vignerte, who shouted from the courtroom audience, "You lie, *misérable*"—twice—at the beleaguered prosecutor.[15]

But while the case fell apart in the courtroom, there was formidable documentary evidence, obtained from ransacking the homes of the leaders, that provided a glimpse of the crisis within the group. The *Comité Raspail* were the moderates (insulted as the "Gironde") who favored propaganda. The *Comité Lebon* (after law student Napoléon Lebon, oddly not included as one of the *Vingt-Sept*), or the self-styled "Mountain," stressed direct action. Their two competing position statements, presented in the indictment, showed a serious philosophical divide within the group that finally ended with the expulsion of the moderates and the victory of the montagnards.

The Raspail group called for doctrinal tolerance. The most important goal now was "to bring back the bourgeoisie to the place where they were in July 1830," before numerous riots had frightened them; eventually, when both the middle and working classes had been inculcated with republican ideas, the SDHC would provide leadership for another mass revolution. The *Comité Lebon*, on the other hand, opposed compromise on matters of principle; they stressed the need for a revolutionary vanguard to precipitate an insurrection, as well as for a social and economic, rather than purely political, agenda.[16]

These differences—they would follow the organization throughout its existence, in various forms—had paralyzed the group. On 21 July 1833, Théophile Guillard de Kersausie, an aristocrat and former cavalry officer (and eventual freedom fighter, in Naples in 1848), had attempted a truce between the two factions in anticipation of the July festivities. He called for the selection of a temporary *Comité d'Action*, a provisional leadership consisting of six members each from the Raspail and Lebon wings. There would be no "personal" attacks in that period, and the election of a permanent governing committee would be adjourned to 1 August. Kersausie did not disavow the proposed truce. His lawyer, J. F. Dupont, claimed that it had merely been a proposal to unify rather than a "resolution" to act against the government; that interpretation was unconvincing, especially given the militant tone of the document.[17]

The failed rapprochement had forced the leadership struggle into the open, with the publication of two separate *ordres du jour* to the membership. The Lebon montagnard wing directed the *sectionnaires* to remain *en permanence*, or in continuous session, from Saturday 27 July to Monday 29 July, and to obey the orders that would be sent them.[18] Raspail, fearing that the police wanted to provoke a "collision" in order to destroy the group for good, issued a proclamation that was in direct contradiction to the Lebon group's order of *permanence*:

> Tomorrow the *sectionnaires* should content themselves with going forth as simple citizens, and joining their wishes to those of the patriot portion of the National Guard; they will have to be careful of *agents provocateurs*. . . . If ever, and even if tomorrow, the ENTIRE people, by unforeseen chance, impose other obligations [i.e., if the people rise up], each of us, as in 1830, should hear only the inspirations of his conscience.[19]

On 30 July, Raspail resigned from office in the group, thus acknowledging a montagnard victory.[20] On 19 August, all remaining officers resigned their positions, calling for new elections and urging that the old committees not be re-elected, given the dissension between them; indeed, in a clear indication of the leftward trend of the organization, they urged the membership to elect *prolétaires*, in order to avoid further "writers' quarrels."[21]

The new *Comité central* of 11 members was unveiled in October 1833, along with a controversial new program. Though nothing changed at the section level, the deliberately egalitarian structure, with a number of *chefs de série* of equal status within the group, was replaced by a pyramidal chain of command with the *Comité central* at the top, *commissaires d'arrondissement* directly below them, followed by *commissaires de quartier*, and finally by the chiefs of the sections. The members of the Central Committee, elected by the sections, were to be renewed by one-third every three months, with re-election allowed. The tighter structure was meant to provide unified leadership and quick action in potential crises; moreover, only the committee could now speak or publish in the name of the group. The committee was also given the power to expel entire sections for political deviation, as when they rid themselves of *des Victoires* for Bonapartist tendencies.[22] Finally, the new committee engaged in an aggressive effort to set up a nationwide organization. Attempts to recruit soldiers had some success in Dijon, Marseille, and Lunéville, but the second city of the SDHC was clearly Lyon, visited by Cavaignac in April and December 1833.[23]

The new committee issued a manifesto in October 1833, calling for sweeping reforms: universal manhood suffrage and greater local government; free public education; and public credit to allow workers to start their own businesses. They also called for a more equal sharing of the labor and rewards in society, the vagueness of this provision a clear indication of continuing rifts over economic and social policy. In terms of political action, they enshrined the right and "duty" of insurrection, and thus acknowledged a goal beyond propaganda.[24] The Central Committee concluded by signing their names, most of them familiar from the *Amis*, including socialist Deputy Voyer d'Argenson, Guinard, medical student Camille Berryer-Fontaine, Lebon, Vignerte, Cavaignac, Kersausie, Deputy Audry de Puyraveau, Dr. Arthur Beaumont, and the lesser-known Desjardins and Titot.[25] In January 1834, the latter two were replaced by Dr. Adrien Recurt and the *prolétaire* François Delente.[26] But public attention was captured by the committee's formal endorsement of Robespierre's Declaration of the Rights of Man and the Citizen.

The Orléanist *Journal des Débats* responded to the manifesto with ridicule, certain that "in the little world of the *Société des Droits de l'Homme*" this "pompous hodgepodge of bad metaphysics" must have caused great excitement.[27] But their attacks soon gave way to pleased speculation about the thundering silence of the *National*: was there a schism among republicans? Armand Carrel eventually published a lengthy response on behalf of *l'Association républicaine de la liberté de la presse*, a moderate, largely middle-class group which decided not to support the new direction. Carrel's earliest public statement accompanied the manifesto, which he finally printed in the *National* at the end of October. He praised the SDHC as a restraining force among the proletariat, whom they shielded "from the provocations of the police and the force of their own ardor." But Carrel regarded Robespierre as an unnecessary distraction. The ministerial and opposition journals had "fixed" upon his name, "to accuse the republican party *en masse* of wanting . . . the re-establishment of the scaffolds and the Terror."[28]

The battle over Robespierre's declaration soon made evident the split within the group, between moderates and montagnards, over the broad issue of social welfare. *Le Messager* attempted a dispassionate commentary: "According to Robespierre, society should not abandon its members to themselves, delivering them up to their own forces without aid, by assuring only their liberty: it should raise them, instruct them, ameliorate [their conditions], procure them labor and means of existence, when they cannot work"[29]—a program in stark opposition to the laissez-faire philosophy that individuals had no responsibility to each other, nor the government any obligation to ensure the well-being of its citizens.

Among republicans, the debate over the Robespierrist vision of social justice was largely argued in terms of two specific issues: taxation, and the role of the state. Carrel represented the view of moderate republicans, who rejected the goal of economic equality. He opposed a progressive income tax on the grounds (as many economists had argued) that it would impoverish the wealthy; moreover it would not distinguish between inherited and earned wealth, between the idle and the hard-working rich. He did agree, however, that the state relied too heavily on indirect sales taxes that were disproportionately harder on the poor, and stressed the need for workers to gain political rights in order to defend themselves.[30] In contrast, Albert Laponneraye's frequently reprinted commentary on the Declaration of the Rights of Man indicated the consensus of the montagnard wing. Laponneraye argued that property was not a "natural" right but rather one defined by the law, which could thus regulate or expropriate it, restrict or extinguish inheritance. He suggested a limited assault on property through a progressive income tax, collected only on income that was "excessive"; the surtax on the wealthy would allow the government to do away entirely with regressive indirect or sales taxes. More controversially, he argued that the progressive tax would "insensibly" cause inequality to disappear, would "level conditions" between rich and poor.[31]

As for the role of the state, the moderate Carrel shared the liberal belief in a limited government. In contrast, the social proposals of the republican Left centered around major initiatives to be carried out by some powerful future republican state. In February 1834, Jean-Jacques Vignerte articulated an explicit defense of political action as the necessary starting point for social and economic change; his statement reflected the essential vision of the montagnard wing. The wealthy, wrote Vignerte, had passed laws to protect property but not labor: "Because the wealthy, after having exploited [workers] in the guise of owners, manufacturers, and businessmen, suddenly change costume and present themselves under the usurped titles of *Peers, Deputies, and Administrators of the Public Weal.*" In Vignerte's plan (foreshadowing Louis Blanc), revolution would establish a republican state that would then assist workers in

the formation of producers' associations; thus they, and not the capitalist spec-
ulators and bosses, would get the full benefit of their labor.[32]

In the fall of 1833, a small propaganda commission was created within the
SDHC to deal specifically with labor issues; its membership included Lebon,
Vignerte, Berryer-Fontaine, Recurt, and journalist Marc Dufraisse.[33] Republican interest in labor organization had recently been awakened by the rise of
working-class activism. The summer and fall of 1833 had seen numerous work
stoppages and "coalitions" throughout the country; in Paris the movement
began with the tailors, soon followed by stonecutters, bakers, locksmiths, and
mechanics. Workers within the same trade, often torn apart by feuding fraternal organizations, began to unite. In September 1833, five thousand carpenters of two *compagnonnages* (traditional journeymen's associations, which often
split trades internally) united to demand a four franc daily minimum wage.
Also in September, the three organizations that had divided the tailors joined
together; they were soon found to have a direct link with the SDHC in the
person of Grignon, the chief "motor" of the tailors' coalition.[34]

The 22 members of the Propaganda Commission issued an *ordre du jour*
of 24 November 1833, which acknowledged the impressive efforts of workers
on their own behalf; they made an attempt, ultimately unsuccessful, to organize sections by trade. On 8 December they were arrested.[35] At their trial in late
April 1834 (they were in custody during the insurrection), Lebon, Berryer-
Fontaine, and Vignerte insisted that they alone (and not their working-class
colleagues) composed the Propaganda Commission and were responsible for
all its actions. Lebon and Vignerte also denied any efforts to organize illegal
trade coalitions; they had attempted instead to encourage "political association" among workers, inspired by Deputy Voyer d'Argenson (who had urged
workers not to waste their efforts "to claim a miserable augmentation of
salary" when there was greater benefit to be gained by changing society itself).[36] Both Lebon and Vignerte believed in worker "coalitions"; their denial
was merely a part of their unsuccessful defense strategy, as they protested their
appearance before a correctional tribunal (which handled labor cases) instead
of the *Cour d'Assises* and a jury.[37]

In its short life, the commission had given rise to a number of proposals.
The shoemaker Efrahem, a commission member, authored a plan by which all
workers' groups would be linked in a single organization powerful enough to
support strikes: when one trade engaged in a work stoppage, the others would
tide them over.[38] The tailor Grignon wrote a pamphlet outlining a plan for association and ending with an assertion of the primacy of political power: "It is
less the masters for whom we work than the laws of our country that prevent

the amelioration of our status. . . . Let us not forget that the rich alone make the laws, and that we cannot definitively free ourselves from the yoke of misery except in exercising, as they do, our rights as citizens."[39] In Grignon's coalition trial, Claveau, the attorney for the masters, found his ideas self-evidently absurd; in their "delirium" the workers had dared to suggest "that soon man will no longer be exploited by man. *Insensés!* Will there not eternally be manufacturers, workers, and wages?"[40]

Looking back in 1840, journalist Théophile Thoré mourned this lost era of social republicanism, recalling the lively doctrinal quarrels between the old guard and the "militant youth." But Vignerte and Lebon had been forced into exile; Blanqui, though socialist himself, had organized his post-SDHC societies entirely around insurrection, neglecting education and propaganda. Thoré criticized the *National*, the one remaining bastion in the late 1830s, for having ignored worker issues. (*La Réforme*, founded in 1843, would attempt to fill this gap.) But the several years of neglect, according to Thoré, had caused republicans to lose the working classes to socialism and even communism.[41]

In the meantime, the SDHC remained split between those who wanted direct action and their increasingly cautious leaders, who feared that the government was trying to provoke a showdown. Controversy came to be centered on the *permanence*, or the calling of members into continuous session. This act most obviously had the purpose of gathering *sectionnaires* for battle, but the SDHC Central Committee used it in other ways as well—to appease hotheads impatient with inaction, to discipline the sections, and to remove members from the scene of police provocation. There were only five such convocations. The first had occurred in late 1832, ordered by Kersausie to prevent the executions of the June insurgents Cuny and Lepage; the second had been ordered in July 1833 by the Lebon wing, and became the pretext for the *Procès des Vingt-Sept.*[42]

The final *permanence* occurred on 11 and 12 April 1834, just before the insurrection. The third and fourth convocations were called in early and mid-February 1834, for the Dulong funeral and the Bourse demonstrations. At the end of January 1834, General (and Deputy) Thomas Bugeaud had challenged republican Deputy Dulong to a duel, after a parliamentary debate had degenerated into a shouting match: Bugeaud had had the ungallant task of imprisoning the duchesse de Berry during her illicit pregnancy, and Dulong tactlessly reminded him of it. But their duel soon took on political overtones. Dulong was widely rumored to be the illegitimate son of Jacques Dupont de l'Eure, the republican first minister of justice in the July Monarchy, and he was seconded by George Lafayette, son of the General. Bugeaud was seconded by General de Rumigny, Louis-Philippe's aide-de-camp. In the event, Bugeaud fatally wounded Dulong with a shot in the head.[43] The *National*, along with even liberal monarchists like Odilon Barrot, believed Bugeaud's refusal to settle the episode short of a duel was the result of an Orléanist conspiracy, a blunt attempt to send a message to the Left.[44] During Dulong's funeral, the sections were commanded to remain *en permanence* and then, as in the previous July, were ordered to stand down: "The Committee engages you, as you withdraw, to make no demonstration; be certain that [the Committee] will always direct you well, and that it will strike with you when a favorable occasion presents itself."[45]

Unfortunately for the Central Committee, another serious matter arose almost immediately with the new law on *crieurs publics*. *Crieurs*, or newshawks, shouted out headlines and additional commentary in a sort of crude propaganda that was available even to the illiterate. The law of 10 December 1830, one of the gains of the revolution, required only that the hawker deposit a copy of his pamphlet or newspaper with the local *commissaire*, who was then required by law to hand over a permit to sell. In late 1833, Prefect of Police Gisquet ordered *commissaires* to refuse the authorizations if the material seemed inflammatory; many *crieurs* were arrested, only to be released when they proved that permits had been refused them.[46] The most famous *crieur* was François Delente, a leather worker, elected in early 1834 to the Central Committee; his clashes with the police finally ended in late November 1833 in the *Cour de Cassation*, which found in his favor.[47] Though consistently defeated in the courts, the prefect had nevertheless achieved his purpose of harassment: "What one wants at any price," wrote the *National*, "is to break the sole means of communication that still exists between a very numerous portion of the population and the independent press."[48]

On 16 February 1834 a new law went into effect, granting local authorities broad powers to withdraw or withhold the authorization to sell.[49] In response, *Le Bon Sens*, *Le Populaire*, and Auguste Blanqui's short-lived *Liberateur* announced that these papers would be hawked on Sunday, 24 February, on the Place de la Bourse. The confrontation resulted in skirmishes for several hours, finally brought to a conclusion by the arrival of the mounted police.[50] The *permanence* called in advance of these troubles led to the arrest of several entire sections (40 men in the Café des Deux Portes alone) in police sweeps. The following day warrants were issued for another 73 chiefs and *sectionnaires;* many of them were still in prison awaiting possible charges by the time of the April insurrection, two months later.[51] Once again the rank and file expressed impatience with the Central Committee, their anger increased on this occasion by the pointless sacrifice of so many men. Many decided to join the new *Société d'Action.*

Kersausie had formed the *Société d'Action* in late 1833 from among the "most energetic" SDHC members.[52] According to the overheated description of one of Gisquet's agents, "This corps will be constantly in movement. With neither regular nor irregular meetings, with a single sign, a password, it will be able to leap onto the public square unexpectedly to give birth to a riot, then disappear; such will be its mission." The *Société d'Action* held only "reviews," of which members were given verbal notice by their chiefs. During such convocations they walked silently down a given street, two by two or three by three, proving their obedience to an invisible leader watching from a distance. They agreed to fight without question when the order came.[53]

Kersausie's initiative had not met with universal approval within the Central Committee. An *ordre du jour* of 24 November 1833 warned against schismatic tendencies within the sections, urging members not to "renew the deadly dissensions from which we have had to suffer so much," and adding that "it is important, in our position, to submit all the forces of the party to a single direction."[54] A reprimand advised Kersausie "that the title of *chef du Comité d'action* [sic] had been conferred upon him by a common accord only for the military direction of the sections in the case of a war in the streets, and not to form a rival society in the heart of the *Société des Droits de l'Homme.*" Angered, Kersausie resigned from the Central Committee late in 1833, and from the society itself in February 1834.[55]

But Kersausie's group had already forced the parent society into a more aggressive stance. Early in 1834, the Central Committee asked the sections to collect funds for "armaments" and to pledge their obedience "to all the orders of the Central Committee, as the sole condition of the success of a future armed enterprise."[56] Meant to appease the militants, this directive had the effect of frightening away moderates and thus made some kind of "action" more likely. The Central Committee at the same time tried to shield itself from an imprudence by the upstart splinter group. An *ordre du jour* of 5 February 1834 from Cavaignac ordered *sectionnaires* to choose within eight days between the *Société d'Action* and the SDHC.[57] But the separation came a little late. Voyer d'Argenson and Audry de Puyraveau, both deputies and virtually the last remnants of the link with respectable republicanism, had resigned from the SDHC on 3 February.[58]

Alain Faure's analysis of known SDHC members reveals that 75 percent were workers, with an average age of 26; they were younger in the eleventh *arrondissement*, where students were in the majority. Among the workers, the building trades accounted for 14 percent, with metal workers at 12.9 percent and the clothing trade at 11.1 percent, all of them familiar groups in insurrections. There was also an unusually strong contingent (20 percent) of leather workers.[59] But any statistical analysis must also take into account the softness of many commitments. After the April 1834 insurrection, a large section of the SDHC archives, found piecemeal before this, were discovered in Sainte-Pélagie prison, concealed there by the group's imprisoned secretary, Berryer-Fontaine. *Juges d'instruction*, or examining magistrates, questioned all those listed on the rosters.[60] These men of course had a great interest in not incriminating themselves; nevertheless, the flat responses of the rank and file illustrate the clashes that must often have occurred between dedicated activists and those average workers who joined out of simple curiosity.

One of the first questions asked of the men was why they had joined the group. Many men had attended for pragmatic reasons. Denis Quetin, a hawker of Cabet's *Le Populaire*, went to sell his newspapers; a member of the section *Cordeliers* had been told that it was a society "to procure jobs for those who have none."[61] A German from Baden believed the meetings would be a place to learn French; so did a medical student from Belgrade.[62] The cook Alphonse Fournier had quite specific economic goals, including control of each trade by an elected assembly of workers: "This association would fix the price of wages, which would not be less for a head cook than 75 to 80 francs, and for a roaster [*rotissier*] 60 to 70 francs per month."[63]

Others were more fixed on politics. A member of *Travailleurs* wanted "complete liberty of the press, and no electoral monopoly," adding, "I am not, I assure you, a man of anarchy, and I could say that in various circumstances I have been treated as a Girondin and Fayettist because of my moderation."[64] A member of *Cincinnatus* claimed that they had frequently discussed the violated *programme de l'Hôtel de Ville*.[65] Another member of *Travailleurs*, listed on the roster as "energetic and capable," indignantly declared that he had given "no proofs of energy and capacity," for he had only attended two sessions. He had considered the society too undisciplined: he had hoped to find a *Chambre de députés en petit* (underlined by the questioner), but had left "when I saw that we only chatted among ourselves as friends."[66]

While none admitted directly that the group was preparing itself for battle, many had quit out of fear that it might be. Louis Crevin had belonged to *Marcus Brutus* for only three weeks and left because it took too much time: "I saw that it occupied itself too actively with politics, my wife observed to me that I could be compromised in remaining longer, and if I had been arrested, I would have left her in great difficulties with the three children we had at the time." When asked if he had ever been told to provide himself with weapons and ammunition, he answered carefully that he had heard of this "in an indirect way from a *sectionnaire* whose name I don't recall," that "it was one of the things that made me reflect; I saw there was nothing good to be gained from that."[67] Laurent Pommery, a 21-year-old jewelry engraver, joined because he thought it was a philanthropic group; when he learned otherwise he wanted to get out immediately but did not, "fearing to pass for a coward."[68] A young clerk in *Dévouement social* had believed that the society would ameliorate the condition of workers: "It was said in the section that they wanted to arrive at the Republic by discourse and reasoning, however the committee had required a list of all the members in the section with the indication of those who had weapons."[69] Jacques Leclerc of *Marcus Brutus* "had heard some speeches which hadn't pleased me in the section to which I belonged; there were some young men who spoke of the Republic and that displeased me, I didn't want to remain among them."[70] *Vengeurs/Socrates* lost Charles Lepreux, a coachman: "I didn't see any projects formed against the government, but . . . I wouldn't have wanted to find myself dragged into collisions, where in spite of myself I would have been obliged to play a role."[71]

The regulations required that at least a portion of each meeting be devoted to the discussion of Robespierre's declaration and recent brochures, and many cited this rule to suggest the essential harmlessness of the group. A number of men also claimed that the educational sessions had not been particularly useful; remarked a visitor to the section *Torrijos*, "It was said that it was for the instruction of the people and that we read the works of M. Cabet; the following day I reflected that this could lead me to nothing and I didn't return."[72] This section, named after General José Torrijos, the martyr to the Spanish liberal cause, was a puzzle to some of its members, and one admitted that he did not quite understand the name: "A man of about 35 came to the section, he appeared very exalted in his discourse, and he read a brochure where the name Torrijos was found, he spoke with a lot of fire and this is what made us take the name for the section."[73]

The investigators were particularly suspicious of the weekly collections. Most of the members acknowledged the practice—a sou at the end of every meeting, according to a member of *Mucius Scaevola*—and asserted that the money was spent on pamphlets and brochures, on charity for political prisoners, and on such mundane items as drinks and paper for the sessions.[74] A member of *Vengeurs/Socrates* stated more forcefully that it was never a question of ammunition: "On the contrary one always said to us that it wasn't by force that one could make reforms, but by propaganda; and by propaganda we understood that it was necessary to make efforts to draw men away from debauchery and lead them to virtue."[75] A member of *Barricades* claimed that any such talk of revolt would have been "repulsed, because we met to instruct ourselves and not to conspire."[76]

But others acknowledged that the collection of money was not so innocent. The tailor Claude Prévost, the chief of *Jean-Jacques Rousseau*, agreed that the collections at first were destined for brochures. But toward the end of February 1834, "the society no longer finding any printer, the *chef de quartier* declared to us that the collections would have as their object to provide for political detainees and to buy ammunition."[77] Jacques Leclerc of *Marcus Brutus* claimed that the Central Committee had sent an agent to suggest that they lay in a store of cartridges: "He said it was necessary to prepare because soon a *coup* would explode against the government"; this proposition, added Leclerc, "was rather well-received."[78] A member of *Torrijos* recalled that "a young man came to the section, to propose that we make a collection to procure arms and ammunition, he said that already in his section which so far as I can recall was *Léonidas*, he had made this proposition; in my section it was repulsed and this young man was even accused of being a police agent, he was even followed [but] one of the members of our section assured [us] that he knew him and it had no other result."[79]

The questioners discovered that the destruction of several sections through *permanences* was a source of considerable anger. A member of *21 Janvier* complained that his entire group had been arrested by the local *commissaire*, though they had merely been drinking and talking.[80] Most of *Barra* and *Cincinnatus* had been arrested at the Café des Deux Portes on the boulevard Saint-Denis on 25 February; detained in prison for three months, they had missed the April insurrection.[81] Alphonse Fournier of *Phocion/Lycurgue* was *en permanence* during the Bourse troubles. They were visited by "a tall man, acting a little suspiciously, with a mustache," who told them to wait for orders. When they learned of the mass arrests at the Café des Deux Portes, they decided to go home, "when on the rue Jean-Jacques Rousseau we encountered two sections that were going [to the café] with the intention of rescuing [those arrested] and who urged us to accompany them; there was a little hesitation among several of us, but when they treated us like cowards we decided to follow the others. We arrived to see them taken away by the Municipal Guard and we distanced ourselves, without saying or doing anything."[82]

Some members described the *permanence* as a way of keeping the peace. A quinturion of *Travailleurs* suggested that the motive was "precisely to distance ardent men from the theater of troubles, and it often resulted that they prevented public tranquillity from being troubled."[83] A member of *Mort aux Tyrans* echoed this view more emphatically: "Every time there were troubles, we were always *en permanence* in our section, but it was not to take part in the troubles, it was on the contrary to restrain those among us who, having drunk a glass of wine, would have been able sometimes to allow themselves to be led; moreover we feared the provocations of the police and being thus gathered, we mutually prevented each other from going to these actions."[84]

But others were certain, as indeed the government was, that the sections gathered in readiness for possible combat. A member of *Marcus Brutus* said it had been "understood" that they would act if the orders came.[85] A *sectionnaire* from *Cimber* recalled that nothing had been said of fighting, "but it is very certain that it was only for that [purpose], so I never went."[86] A former section chief testified that the reason for the *permanence* was to "sustain the *Société d'Action*," and a member of *Marcus Brutus* agreed that the purpose of this group was to "march ahead of the *Société des Droits de l'Homme*."[87] And many of the more temperate members, already uneasy about the special convocations, had been alarmed by the aggressiveness of the new group. Jean Chapuis, a 20-year old shoemaker of *Montagnards,* said that the *Société d'Action* "aroused discontent," even as it remained something of a mystery. Charles Mugnier, arrested just after the Bourse riots, had quit because of the heavy recruiting for the *Société d'Action*, which was "conspiratorial, and departed in that way from the views of the section, which only wanted propaganda." Claude Billon, age 20, had heard that the *Société d'Action* was composed of "a thousand men divided by threes, fours, and fives," adding, "I think that [the *Société d'Action*] was to act by means of riots; the day of Dulong's burial it was to act, but I believe the *Société des Droits de l'Homme* had prevented it."[88]

The preparations for insurrection had begun in earnest in March, according to Prefect Gisquet:

> The language, the steps taken, the recommendations of the principle members of the committee; the mystery with which they sought to surround themselves; the care that several took to go out only at night, and to change their names; the semi-confidences made to their intimate friends; the cartridges distributed, and the order given to the sections to furnish a complete list of their men with information on their character, courage, and state of their weapons, gave me the conviction that the revolt was irrevocably fixed for the epoch when the law on societies would be promulgated [10 April].[89]

Gisquet believed that there were about 1,000 to 1,200 men of action, all prepared for instant mobilization. Rittiez, in contrast, suggested that the insurrection did not have as much manpower as supposed: the SDHC had perhaps 1,500 men, not all of them fighters; the *Société d'Action* had no more than 400 to 500, the number also claimed by Kersausie; and the radical foreign refugee community counted between 200 and 300 men.[90]

In the days leading up to insurrection, Gisquet redoubled his searches.[91] On 9 March the section chief of *Purs républicains* was found with a box of 678 cartridges and 243 balls. He admitted that he had received them from *commissaire* of the ninth *arrondissement* Henri Leconte, who deposited supplies in a small room on the rue Saint-Honoré; the police doggedly recovered the remainder from the latrines, where they had been dumped after a tip-off.[92] On 23 March Hubert Tassin, a 20-year-old jeweler and chief of *Thermopyles*, was caught with 629 lead balls and a packet of 14 cartridges.[93] Alexandre Yvon, the *commissaire* of the fourth *arrondissement*, was found on 17 March with 102 cartridges, 4 *livres* of gunpowder, and 25 *livres* of lead. On 26 March the police carried away 34 packets of cartridges from a certain Belissant, who said he had received them two weeks earlier from his section chief, Gautier of the *Quatre-Sergens*, "and that one should soon use them to attack the Government and fire on the National Guard."[94] All these seizures, claimed the eventual indictment, proved that the SDHC had conspired; but they also revealed the extent to which the police of Paris had undercut the society by capturing its meager stores.

Minister of the Interior Adolphe Thiers would later announce in the Chamber of Deputies that the government had known all, seen all ("Then why didn't you stop it?" shouted a heckler).[95] He and Gisquet worked closely together, with Gisquet favoring massive preventive arrests. But Thiers and the rest of the cabinet, meeting on 11 April, had decided that rounding up large numbers of men before the uprising would simply allow them to escape conviction once again. The frustrated Gisquet issued 150 more warrants anyway, to be executed on 12 April; he received Thiers' authorization just before sending out his agents, and in a flurry of last-minute arrests removed many additional men from the fray.[96]

By the time of the insurrection, a total of 129 "influential" *sectionnaires* had already been jailed, including almost all of the present or past members of the Central Committee.[97] Lebon and Berryer-Fontaine, arrested in early December, were awaiting trial for their involvement in the Propaganda Commission. Vignerte had been in prison since the *Procès des Vingt-Sept* in December, when he had been sentenced for disturbing the courtroom. Deputies Audry de Puyraveau and Voyer d'Argenson were off the committee, too prominent to arrest but also unlikely to be on the streets. The *crieur* François Delente had been in prison since late February.[98] Joseph Guinard, considered one of the military specialists, was arrested on Saturday, 12 April, at 5 A.M. *La Tribune* editor Armand Marrast, warned that the police had staked out his offices, left Paris on the twelfth, finally to be picked up on 20 April. Godefroy Cavaignac was not captured until 24 April.[99]

Even as these arrests continued, all eyes turned to Lyon. In February, an eight-day work stoppage had provided a powerful demonstration of solidarity. Afterward, a number of strike leaders were taken into custody; their trial was set for early April. On 9 April, the Lyon SDHC ordered its workers to come to the courthouse unarmed; if the government provoked a confrontation, they would retreat to specified positions for instructions. It was a dangerous course, as Robert Bezucha has noted, for they had few weapons and their strategy left them no protection against "provocation," either from the police or from hotheads on their own side. The resulting battle lasted six bloody days.[100]

The first news from Lyon arrived in Paris on 10 April; the capital spent 11 and 12 April in suspense, the story disrupted by the breakdown of the semaphore telegraph system. The twelfth of April was the day of decisive victory for the government, when the army crushed the suburbs of La Guillotière and Vaise as well as the insurgent center of the city.[101] But the *Tribune* on 13 April reported that the Lyonnais rebels were in control, that other towns and entire military regiments were rising up in revolt throughout France; its editorial was a clear provocation to take to the streets.[102]

Kersausie had been on the move all week, conducting "partial reviews" and sleeping under a different roof every night. Gisquet had allowed him free rein, using him to smoke out the activists. According to one of his undercover agents, "he exhorted all his men to do their duty, telling them that it wasn't up to him to take the initiative but to the *Société des Droits de l'Homme*; if [the SDHC] was bold enough it would act, but if not, there would be nothing on Sunday the thirteenth [and] he didn't want to sacrifice his men uselessly, certain they would be massacred." He further told them to "be at their posts" on Sunday; the word would be given "only in public."[103]

Alphonse Fournier of *Phocion/Lycurgue* had joined the *Société d'Action* on Wednesday, 9 April, and was summoned to a review the next day. The men passed before Kersausie silently, by twos and threes.[104] Pierre Pichonnier heard Kersausie promise "that we would attack the following Sunday, that it was necessary to get the *commissaires d'arrondissement* to force the Central Committee . . . to join itself that day to the *Société d'Action*."[105] At the meeting of *Phocion/Lycurgue* on Friday, 11 April, *sectionnaire* Louis Herbert announced "that the *Société d'Action* would begin the movement on Sunday 13 April, from 3 to 4 P.M."; chief Eugene Candre distributed cartridges.[106] But this meeting was stormy, for they also learned, apparently for the first time, of the resignations of the two deputies Voyer d'Argenson and Audry de Puyraveau. The resulting confusion was mirrored in Fournier's recollections:

> That [news] excited a great deal of discontent; the section was divided and wanted to dissolve itself; it had already been told to opt between the *Société des Droits de l'Homme* and the *Société d'Action*. . . . There were a lot of complaints against this [Central] Committee that did not work very well; some wanted to join the *Société d'Action*, others wanted to wait.

On Saturday, 12 April, the section met at the same café at about 10 P.M. Recalled Fournier: "We were two sections and in great number, about 60. There was standing room only, the Committee hadn't yet given any order."[107] Xavier Sauriac, author of *Le Catéchisme républicain*, made a heated appeal, saying (according to a police report) "that there was still time to act but there was not an instant to lose"; the meeting must choose a chief: "He said that the [Central] Committee had abandoned us, that it was necessary to march without it, that the members of the Committee were afraid for their skins, they were cowards, they kept us inside; that it was necessary to name workers for chiefs and not aristocrats, men we didn't know; that it was necessary to bypass the orders of the Committee, to meet Sunday on the boulevards from 2 P.M. to 3 P.M. and to commence if we were strong enough."[108] It was finally decided that on the following day, Sunday, the *sectionnaires* would make their way to the streets Saint-Martin and Saint-Denis.

They counted on a large initial gathering and a show of force by the vanguard. Kersausie's order of the day, sent to his chiefs by way of his "aides-de-camp," stressed the importance of setting an example:

> [In order] to engage the people to participate in the insurrection, the members of the societies should disperse themselves widely [and] begin to form barricades; from the moment they see the workers come to join them, and when the number of those [workers] helping them surpasses their own, they should abandon [the barricade] to begin another one a little farther on, and in this manner seize all the streets and fire on the troops without ever showing themselves in great number.[109]

Finally, it was Sunday the thirteenth. The men of action were at their posts by early afternoon. Kersausie went from place to place, counting their numbers and giving orders to their chiefs; the password was *Mort aux tyrans.* Placards were ready, and it was rumored that Voyer d'Argenson and Audry de Puyraveau would stroll the boulevards, allowing themselves to be seen.[110] The final signal to move was to come from Kersausie directly, and Gisquet, who had finally issued the warrant for his arrest, was unable to put his hands on him.[111]

Suddenly, one of his agents came through with a location. *Officier de paix* Pierre Tranchard, who knew Kersausie by sight, hurried to the boulevard Saint-Martin with 20 men in plainclothes. "I saw there several groups, in which I remarked several men that I had already seen in the streets," recalled Tranchard; "then I saw a *cabriolet* going slowly, from which Kersausie presented himself to the several groups."[112] Tranchard and his men leaped on him, making the arrest at 3:30 P.M. and quickly hustling him out of sight. He was taken to the Conciergerie prison, where he was in custody by 4 P.M.[113] At the moment of his arrest Kersausie called for help, shouting for his followers to save him: "Republicans, here! I'm Captain Kersausie!" No one was brave enough. A 50-year-old merchant, who followed this curious spectacle for some time, saw indecision: "The crowd was very considerable and I heard a lot of colloquies among the young men who held forth with nasty remarks about the government and appeared to take an interest in the accused, but no one dared to make an attempt."[114]

There were enough men present to spread the news of this last-minute arrest, which came as the culmination of so many others. The "demoralization," according to Gisquet's agent, was complete; there was no one capable of inspiring similar confidence as a leader. "Each took counsel of himself," with many deciding to go home and wait for a better day: "The little placards posted everywhere, announcing that the workers had proclaimed the republic in Lyon, had for a moment raised the courage of the republicans and made them think that the people could turn in their favor." Instead the "people," for the most part, would stand by and look on; but the forlorn struggle was already engaged.[115]

CHAPTER 5

APRIL 1834:
LA GUERRE DES RUES, I

THE UPRISING OF APRIL 1834 WAS THE FIRST planned insurrection, different in character from 1830 and 1832. The militants of the *Société des Droits de l'Homme et du Citoyen* (SDHC) were self-conscious about their role as the avant-garde, and awkwardly attempted to stir the masses with republican rhetoric and signs. They forced passersby to work with them, even if it meant laying only a single paving stone on a barricade. They asserted control of the neighborhoods, set up patrols and sentinels, and requisitioned supplies from local stores, in an attempt to establish an alternative authority. They made great efforts to capture the hearts and minds of the masses, and they were absurdly confident of victory. But the whole exercise failed miserably, even (as the next uprising would show) as a learning experience.

The struggle was far more severe in Lyon, where it became a 6-day pitched battle with over five hundred casualties.[1] In Paris, the death toll included only 16 on the side of the government, and 53 civilians and insurgents; the fighting lasted less than a day, from late Sunday afternoon to early Monday morning.[2] The revolt became an ironic defeat for republicans even in symbolic terms, for the boldness of the attack was soon overwhelmed in public perception by the murder of 12 innocent civilians by soldiers, an event which came to be known as the massacre of the rue Transnonain. In July, Honoré Daumier published a lithograph of the scene, dominated by a dead man in a nightdress who has fallen onto the body of a child, the image of a peaceful citizen suddenly violated in his home.[3] Alexandre Ledru-Rollin, a rising radical lawyer who represented the brother of one of the victims, soon published an inexpensive pamphlet, which required a second edition only three weeks later. It consisted largely of interviews with the survivors, the simple recollections of ordinary people in their own words; he thus made available to the public the poignant details that would otherwise have been left in judicial files.[4] But while the rue Transnonain became an enduring reproach to the government, it also denied the insurrection a heroic martyr in the mold of Charles Jeanne. Instead, the rising was symbolized by noncombatants who were explicitly victims.

The insurrection began on the Right Bank on Sunday, 13 April. The *hommes d'action* had slowly congregated on the streets Saint-Denis and Saint-Martin. According to local resident Jeanne Colas, there were relatively few of them at the start; their numbers only began to swell, perhaps to as many as 150, by late afternoon: "The street was encumbered, one continually heard cries—Republic or Death!"[5] At about 4 P.M., a shopkeeper on the rue Beaubourg remarked many suspicious strangers in the quarter, "with long hair and long beards," walking in small groups through the streets. Two men suddenly brought out the "republican banner"; one of them fired a gun as the signal to begin, and the groups began to shout *Vive la République! vivent les Lyonnais! à bas Philippe!*[6] One man read out a proclamation (which no one could hear) and various placards were posted on the walls, both printed and crudely handwritten ("It is finally broken, this too-long chain of humiliating tyrannies, infamous perfidies, criminal betrayals!" began one example).[7]

A man in an *Invalides* uniform (from the Hôtel des Invalides, for wounded veterans), was heard to admonish the individual who had fired the opening shot: "You're too soon!"[8] The *Invalide* nevertheless began taking charge, organizing barricade-builders and posting sentinels.[9] Others dismantled the street lights to ensure the cover of darkness after sunset. The *gamins* enthusiastically lent themselves to this hooliganism. The elderly Jean-Baptiste Laselve attempted to stop a boy of about 13 who was cutting the cords of the street lights and letting them smash to the ground. The *gamin* insolently threatened him with his bayonet; Laselve went after him with his crutch, and turned in the captured bayonet to the local national guard post.[10]

Barricades soon began to appear. From the cafés, several of which were forced open to serve as headquarters, the *sectionnaires* took empty barrels. From other shops they seized the iron rods that barred the doors, which they used to pry up paving stones. Passing coaches and wagons were intercepted, the horses unharnessed, the vehicles overturned. Local resident Imbert Rolot estimated that 40 to 50 people, many of them *gamins*, worked on the formidable barricade on the corner of Montmorency and Transnonain.[11] Sunday strollers were pressed into labor: retired cavalry officer Jean-Baptiste Dupont, age 68 and on his way home from mass, was made to lay a few stones. (He immediately wrote to the prefect of the Seine to express his loyalty for the government, identifying himself as *ancien garde française, un des vainqueurs de la Bastille le 14 juillet 1789*.)[12] Bertrand Brunet was allowed through because he was accompanied by his small son, while 18-year-old Adolphe Donval, an apprentice brushmaker, was stopped on the rue Michel-le-Comte and forced to work all night: "They told me that if I didn't want to work they would shoot me."[13]

Other groups conducted house-to-house searches for weapons: a total of 185 muskets and rifles, 37 sabres, and 40-odd pistols were taken from 104 buildings, many of them from national guards.[14] Such seizures brought guards and insurgents face to face: the *sectionnaires* explained "that they wanted to reconquer their rights," that they were "for liberty," or that they belonged to the SDHC and "fought because of the law that prevented associations."[15] Two men invaded the home of a national guard on the rue de Montmorency, "and the oldest stuck his pistol or musket into M. Boivin's neck, until his wife brought down the [national guard] musket and gave it to them."[16] A national guard on the rue Saint-Méry, visited by three men, recalled that "I sought to appease them, telling them that what they wanted to do could only harm everybody, but they answered that it wasn't reasoning they wanted, but weapons."[17]

The chalked message "*armes rendues*" (weapons given up) began to appear on many buildings whose inhabitants had yielded their swords and guns. On the rue Beaubourg, Alphonse Garnier, section chief of *Prise du Louvre*, provided receipts, to be redeemed at the mayoralty on the following day—when the rebels would presumably be in possession of the city.[18] Gunshops were especially rich targets. Louis Remé, an *armurier* on the rue Beaubourg, lost his entire stock to a gang of 20 raiders; at his insistence, the insurgents stationed a sentinel at his door so he would not be troubled again.[19] In contrast, the large Lepage shop on the rue Bourg l'Abbé was saved because the 6th Legion sensibly established a post there.[20]

As the insurrection was crushed elsewhere, the affected quarter on the Right Bank, a warren of narrow streets lined with buildings of several stories, gradually became isolated. The porter Pierre Roussel of No. 27 Beaubourg stayed up all night with the *Victimes du Champs-de-Mars* who had taken over his lodge, bringing them food and candles. They discussed whether or not to carry paving stones into the building for throwing; there was also a spirited debate about pouring boiling oil on the troops, a plan which foundered for lack of both oil and something to boil it in. In their excitement, Roussel said, "they left my lodge and the alleyway from time to time, to go fire some shots from the barricade; but they fired haphazardly." They confidently expected reinforcements from *Marat* and *Saint-Just*, even from soldiers of the line who had been won to their cause. But by 4 A.M., with no sign of help, they became angry, swearing vengeance against those who had led them into "political societies."[21] Their barricade, composed largely of barrels, paving stones, and furniture, was one of the strongest in the area, reaching the second story of the surrounding buildings and commanded by Nicolas Pruvost the *invalide*. Like Transnonain, it too would be the site of a massacre, but a massacre that no one would remember.[22]

The Left Bank action, dominated by students rather than workers, was considerably less violent. The barricades were also less impressive, most consisting of overturned coaches that only partly blocked the streets; the builders, who started in the early evening, had lacked the time to pull up paving stones and scavenge the neighborhoods. The subsequent investigation suggested two principle causes for the relative mildness of the struggle. First, there were fewer insurgents, their numbers cut dramatically by several Sunday arrests, including the capture of 62 men at the Café des Sept Billards. And second, many of the streets were longer and broader, allowing the troops more mobility and speed. Military activity in the early hours was thus far more extensive.[23]

The events began at Madame Millet's Hôtel Saint Dominique, a café and boarding house on the rue Saint-Jacques, where many young men suddenly dropped in at 5:30 P.M. She became nervous and asked them to leave, "but they told me my *maison* was public and they had the right to stay; I believe they had come to receive orders." While she was feeding her boarders, additional "strangers" disrupted their dinner: "One of them said let's go to the Café des Progrès and the Café Suisse and then they all left . . . [my boarders] left upon the arrival of several men they called *sectionnaires*."[24] The action then moved to the Café des Progrès on the rue Sainte Hyacinthe, from which a horde of young men suddenly burst onto the street at 7 P.M., shouting "To arms!"[25] A local concierge reported the first gunfire at about 8 P.M.[26]

But while there was much talk and noise, there was little action. The single exception was the killing of National Guard Captain Edmund Baillot, the only son of a prominent deputy. At about 8:30, Baillot led his four-man mounted detachment down the narrow rue d'Enfer and was struck by a shot that came suddenly out of the darkness.[27] At almost the same time, Captain François Henrion of the 5th Light Infantry started his patrol down the same street from the opposite direction; he stopped and read the legal *sommations* to the rebels, ordering them to disperse or face military action: "They answered that they would rather die." He ordered them again, in the name of the law: "They answered that they no longer recognized any law, that they were going to make the laws. As I advanced toward them, they also cried, '*Vive la République, vive la ligne!*'" Henrion heard several shots, which he later took to be those that had killed Baillot. By the time he reached the barricade, everyone had fled.[28] An eyewitness described the assailants as a band of about 30 men, most "with a language that suggests a good education."[29]

Nothing of significance happened on the Left Bank after Baillot's death; most insurgents, finding themselves outnumbered by the forces of order, dumped their incriminating weaponry and made their way home. A porter on the rue Saint-Jacques was confronted by four men at 9 P.M., "one armed with a musket, the two others each with a sabre and the fourth with a pair of epaulettes; they left these objects with me saying that they were followed very closely and could no longer keep these arms in their possession without danger."[30] The Left Bank insurrection was virtually over by late Sunday night. On Monday at dawn, a military patrol found the streets already full of ragpickers working through the debris.[31]

On the Right Bank, the barricade builders were granted an entire evening to work, interrupted only by sporadic and undermanned efforts on the part of the police.[32] The *chef de barricade* of the rue Transnonain was overheard rallying his men: "Tomorrow the government wants to destroy us, let's raise the barricades 20 feet high."[33] In the grand old republican tradition, there was also much talk of "avenging" the newly dead.[34] Some, on the other hand, found their enthusiasm waning. The *homme d'action* Alphonse Fournier had spent all day Sunday *en permanence* with his section *Phocion/Lycurgue*. At 6 P.M. they were sent into battle, and Fournier joined a group in the rue Beaubourg who had just overturned several vehicles. "The men at these barricades told us that we mustn't remain there doing nothing, so we ripped up some paving stones; we put them under, in, and on the omnibus," he said, sounding slightly disgruntled. At about 10:30 P.M., cold and still weaponless ("we'd asked for them everywhere without success"), he left the field of combat.[35] Ironically, the faint-hearted Fournier was among those eventually tried before the *Cour des Pairs*.

The authorities prepared to end the insurrection at first light. The government had available to them approximately 35,000 regular troops in Paris and

1,450 municipal guards (military veterans who policed the city); 5,000 national guards had been summoned to duty. Men from the three services converged simultaneously on the quarter, now cut off from the rest of the city.[36] There were two civilian massacres on the Right Bank on the morning of the fourteenth, but the first deaths, on the rue Beaubourg, passed virtually unnoticed.[37]

The rue Beaubourg had been heavily invested from the beginning. The police counted eight formidable barricades within a short distance, most of them at intersections, with the barricade at No. 26 blocking both Beaubourg and the rue des Menestriers.[38] The elderly porter of No. 26, Nicolas Blondeau, had spent Sunday afternoon at Père Lachaise cemetery with his daughter Charlotte. When he returned he found the insurgents in command of his building, "going and coming in the courtyard and posting guards at the barricade and in front of the door."[39] In the course of the night, No. 26 became both a refuge and a stronghold. Alexis Lelievre, of the city's night patrol, arrested by insurgents as a "police spy," was taken to Blondeau's lodge and remanded to the custody of the *gardiens de la barricade*.[40] There as well were Anselme Ribier, an apprentice (and at 13, the youngest person to die in the insurrection); an unidentified German with a head wound; and 18-year-old Jean Adolphe Marino, who had spent Sunday evening dancing and then found himself unable to get through the streets. Also in the lodge for a time were Joseph and Eugenie Bremont, accompanied by their friend Breliniat. The Bremonts made a fearful journey home in the early morning hours, past barricades and rebel sentries. Breliniat, who stayed at No. 26, was killed there.[41]

In the morning, the troops swept through the rue Beaubourg swiftly and unexpectedly; many insurgents fled into the porter's lodge, with soldiers close on their heels.[42] Nicholas Blondeau's other daughter, Jeanne, saw two armed men enter their building and fire on the troops from a window. She attempted to stop them, "for fear that what did happen to us, would happen." Almost immediately, the troops invaded: "I saw that the first to enter the lodge was a municipal guard holding something in his hand that I think was a saber; he shouted in entering, 'Give up, give up.' . . . All I can recall is that the troops entered pêle-mêle."[43]

The investigation eventually listed ten killed and three wounded in No. 26.[44] Of these, four were insurgents, including an unidentified man with cartridges and a dagger. The body of *Francfort* member Augustin Thomas was covered with thick homemade paper armor. His employer described him as a good worker but said that his friends had rendered him "fanatic," that for some weeks he had been "exalted."[45] Marino, Ribier, and Charlotte Blondeau, all killed, were clearly non-combatants, and the remaining three victims were of uncertain status. Thus the Beaubourg incident remained muddy, both in reality and public perception.

It was No. 12 rue Transnonain that instead became the symbol of the insurrection. The streets Transnonain and Montmorency were at right angles to each other, and on each of two corners was a large building, each one with a front on both streets. One of the corner buildings was Number 12, primarily residential, but with several small shops on the ground floor and a neighborhood theater occupying much of the third and fourth floors. Théophile Lemire's café filled the ground floor of the other building, 19 rue de Montmorency. Because it had public exits on both streets, the insurgents seized it as their headquarters and built a large several-sided barricade to close off the intersection. The *chef de barricade* was Adolphe Buzelin. Lemire described him as dressed in black with a red sash, and belligerent: "He entered my shop and ordered me, with threats, to allow no one else to enter or leave; he had me in his sights while he gave this order and forbade me to leave my shop, which I wanted to abandon." Lemire spent the rest of the night hovering in the back, fetching drinks when ordered.[46]

In anticipation of the planned attack at dawn, *chef de bataillon* Louis Montigny of the 8th regiment of the regular army had been ordered just before midnight to destroy the barricades in the Saint-Martin quarter. With two local guides, he and his men had marched into complete darkness. At some cost (a total of three dead, including one insurgent), he took the Transnonain barricade and one other, but then left them virtually intact; he had brought neither picks nor axes to level them.[47] Lemire, in his kitchen, had only a confused impression of this attack. At the first sound of gunfire the insurgents had rushed outside, only to charge back a few moments later in some "disorder," bringing with them two of their own who had been wounded and a third, shot in the neck, who soon died. This encounter subdued the group until about 4 A.M.; then they began to make noise again, dramatically swearing vengeance.[48]

The offensive began at dawn on the morning of the fourteenth. The troops first took the barricades on the periphery, forcing the fighters into the central hive of narrow streets, and coming at rue Transnonain from several directions.[49] After firing at the troops, the outnumbered insurgents fled. The soldiers of the 35th regiment stopped to dismantle the barricade. A national guard marching with them went into Lemire's wineshop for a glass of water and observed a dead man laid out on a table. "A man who was in shirtsleeves at the counter [said] that he had nothing left, they had taken everything," he recalled; "to hear him tell it, he was the *marchand de vin*." The man doing the honors was *chef de barricade* Buzelin.[50]

Suddenly, sniper fire struck Captain Alfred Dupont-Degault and imperial veteran Captain Paul-François Rey.[51] Witnesses believed that the shots came from the second, third, or fifth floor of 12 rue Transnonain. The soldiers fired back. Colonel Adolphe de Tarlé stopped the random shooting and made the decision to pursue the snipers into the building.

Lieutenant Jacques Aufray of the *sapeurs-pompiers* (the Paris firefighters) and his 25 men were ordered to break down the doors. The entry took approximately ten minutes. He and his men hit dead ends—two shops that had no outlet into the upper stories—before they found the main vestibule. The tension grew; as the soldiers waited outside, the seriously wounded Dupont-Degault and the lifeless body of Captain Rey were carried past them. "The soldiers appeared to be in a great hurry to penetrate into this building and in effect they threw themselves in impetuously after the opening of the door," recalled Aufray, "but I affirm that they weren't in any way commanded to commit acts of *rigueur*, on the contrary I heard the officers and particularly the colonel near whom I was standing for a moment engage them not to fire." But Aufray's testimony seemed to contradict the orders admitted even by the officers. Colonel de Tarlé acknowledged later that he had told his men to lay "a heavy hand" on the insurgents found inside. And according to *chef de bataillon* Armand de Gibon of the 35th, he had been ordered by the colonel "to break down the doors and not to give any quarter."[52]

The building had six stories (five upper floors plus the ground floor, or *rez de chaussée*). The porter, the elderly widow Pajot, lived on the ground floor but had spent the night in Antoine Bouton's apartment on the top floor, along with many of her neighbors. At 5 A.M. they were cheered by the sound of gunfire; the former soldier Bouton had remarked that "it was the troops taking the barricades, for which he as well as we were very glad."[53] Soon they heard the firemen breaking into the building, an event whose implications they did not comprehend. But there was little time for thought. The events in No. 12 happened within the space of a few minutes, and those on the top floor were convinced they were about to be rescued even as their neighbors below were dying.

The third floor was inhabited by Louis Lamy and his wife, jewelers who also directed the theater (which encompassed much of the third and fourth floors), in which a number of the tenants had sheltered. With them were two of their apprentices and Mme. Lamy's mother; the actor Adolphe Guittard, engaged to Lamy's sister; and Edme Daubigny, his wife, and her mother. Mme. Daubigny remembered saying, when she heard the hatchets against the outside doors, "It's the Line; we're saved."[54] She and her husband went downstairs, along with the actor Guittard, to let them in. Daubigny, a 36-year-old former building painter crippled by attacks of paralysis, made his way painfully, saying that the troops were "saviors." Mme. Daubigny, in advance of the two men, pulled the latch just as the firemen broke through, and she heard an order to shoot.[55] Lamy, who had run up to the fifth floor to get the key from the porter, dashed back down in time to see Daubigny, "shot through the heart," fall dead at the bottom of the stairway, along with Guittard. Mme. Daubigny, left standing amidst the broken glass from the porter's lodge, fled back to the third floor ("in my trouble," she later said, "I didn't pay attention to M. Guittard"). She soon returned to attempt her husband's rescue but was stopped on the second-floor landing by Annette Besson, an employee in the paper shop, who revived her with eau de cologne; ordered away by the soldiers, she went back to the theater.[56]

Corporal Joseph Planche was the first to reach the second floor, and he was suddenly shot in the elbow. His vision was obscured by gunsmoke, but he described the man who had wounded him as young and dark: "My comrades who were just behind me fired immediately on him and I saw him fall." But who had shot Planche, and with what? No weapon was found in the Poirier-Bonneville apartment, where he claimed the shot had originated. Ledru-Rollin suggested that he was probably hit accidentally by one of his comrades, perhaps by a ricochet; the soldiers behind him had fired more than thirty bullets in the hallway.[57] Nevertheless, his injury convinced the others that insurgents were hidden in the building.

This second floor apartment and workshop was shared by Mme. Rosalie Bonneville, 65, and Jean-François Breffort, 58, her business partner for the past ten years. Also there were her niece, Annette Besson, and young Pierre Delarivière, an acquaintance of Jean-François' son Louis Breffort, who lived on the top floor. Delarivière clerked for a lawyer in Versailles and was in Paris on business. He had come a day early for the museums, but had returned to the building in the early evening, "very pale and preoccupied with the dangers he had run." He was unable to stay with Louis, as he had hoped, because of Louis' overnight guest, prostitute Annette Vacher.[58]

These four had hidden themselves in one of the inner rooms, and young Delarivière, who might have fit Corporal Planche's description, had stayed well back—this according to Mme. Bonneville, the only survivor. It was her partner Breffort who opened the workshop door, with the shout "I'm a friend of Order!" A moment later he staggered over to Mme. Bonneville, astonished: "I've been killed." Remembered Bonneville, "I cannot say with precision all that happened around me, while M. Breffort was in my arms. I saw my niece and M. Delarivière dragged in at my feet." Her efforts to protect Breffort left five bayonet wounds in her hands.[59] Her niece Annette had comforted Mme. Daubigny on the stairs only moments earlier. Now one of the soldiers plunged his bayonet into her neck just below her jaw, and freed it by firing a shot, at point-blank range, that sent bits of her skull flying through the air; De Gibon described her as "having half her face shot away." Delarivière, killed last in the back room, was also shot at point-blank range, and his head and back bore the marks of multiple bayonets.[60] Breffort, caught in the fusillade at the doorway, died early the next morning of his bayonet wounds; none of the gunshots had hit him. "He was known for his attachment to public order and the government," recalled Mme. Bonneville, "and he had openly expressed his satisfaction at the news that the insurrection had expired in Lyon."[61]

Throughout the building, women courageously became the mediators. The door to the Hordesseaux apartment, also on the second floor, was broken down by a "furious" soldier with red hair who shouted at them, "another man, he'll have to die like the others." Hordesseaux's wife and two daughters threw themselves in front of him, begging the soldier for mercy. After searching the apartment, he left: "I won't do as the others, I don't want to kill without knowing."[62]

Next came the theater. When soldiers broke into the fourth floor balcony, the women appeared on the small stage and called out to them. Mme. Lamy advised them that her husband was a national guard: "I told them my husband is here but don't kill him." Jeanne Doyen, her mother, conducted the soldiers through a search of the premises: "As I was trembling they told me not to be afraid, they didn't want women."[63] Lamy showed himself. The soldiers left, but one of them, missing an officer, suddenly returned: "'You'd better find my corporal for me; if you don't we'll do with you what we've done to the others.'" Lamy threw down his candle and ran to his friend Archimede Closmenil, a stonemason on the fifth floor. Closmenil was already gone: he had heard the slaughter in the other apartments on the fifth, and when the soldiers came he climbed through his window and leaped onto the roof of the building next door. Mme. Closmenil showed Lamy the escape route just used by her husband, and he also survived.[64]

On the fourth floor, the Lepères had taken refuge with the Robiquets, along with each family's apprentice. Pierre Robiquet, assuming the soldiers were searching for weapons, had placed his national guard musket in plain sight. The women hurried to open the door: "More than 20 entered, taking aim at us. An officer or soldier lifted [the barrels of] their muskets with his saber, saying *No Women*."[65] At that moment Robiquet, who came into the front room behind them, was bayoneted in the heart. The apprentice Adèle Couban said that Robiquet had tried to quiet the soldiers for the sake of his pregnant wife; Lepère "was driven by the soldiers into the back room where they killed him by firing upon him and piercing him with several bayonet thrusts." Robiquet's young male apprentice was hiding under the bed, and Adèle and the two wives were spared, "inasmuch said the soldiers that it was necessary to preserve the women for their children."[66] Jean Lepère was found by his new widow, his body cut and bleeding, Robiquet's musket tumbled at his feet. She and Mme. Robiquet were "desperate." She remembered that some of the soldiers took their hands, saying, "you are unfortunate but so are we; we had to obey our orders."[67]

There came, finally, the fifth floor. In addition to the Closmenils, there were two other lodgings, inhabited by Louis Breffort, the son of the dying Jean-François on the second floor below, and by Antoine Bouton. Breffort had shared his bed that night, as he often did, with Annette Vacher. He had a neighborhood reputation of being "a little bit republican," largely because of his long hair and goatee; but these were likely the harmless affectations of the poet and painter he claimed to be.[68] (Ledru-Rollin later saw the walls of his room, on which he had painted "little scenes of martyrdom, the punishments of Hell, diabolical tortures," clearly in imitation of Jacques Callot, a seventeenth-century painter much admired by the romantics.[69])

Ledru-Rollin found Vacher with little trouble; the prosecutors never questioned her at all, even though her testimony disproved the semi-official version of the massacre. According to Vacher, she and Louis were getting dressed when she went out onto the landing to investigate the noises in the stairwell. A soldier fired at her and she rushed back, urging Louis to escape by way of the roof. He instead opened the door and invited the soldiers to search the room: "A soldier aimed, Louis fell with his face against the floor, he uttered a long cry, Ah! . . . The soldier gave him two or three blows on the head with the butt of his musket, then turned him on his back to assure himself that he was truly dead."[70] Later Mme. Pajot, the porter, saw Breffort's body lying partially dressed at the foot of his bed and Annette in disarray, her dress unfastened, hunting for her stockings, which were later found in the sheets.[71] She managed to slip out of the building, but her account was important, because the authorities later decided that it must have been Louis Breffort who had fired on the troops in the street that morning.

The largest group of tenants, a total of 16, had gathered in the fifth floor lodgings shared by Bouton, the housepainter and retired soldier, and the jeweler Pierre Thierry. This flat was nothing more than a long, narrow room with a single window that overlooked the rue de Montmorency. In the apartment were Louise Godefroy and her infant from next door; M. and Mme. Hû and their five-year-old son; the porter Mme. Pajot and her son, François Loisillon; her sister Séraphine Brunaux, her son Baptiste, and her 13-year-old grandson Francisque; Bouton's cousin Huguette; Mme. Marrast and Annette Bourgeot, who shared an apartment and worked as housemaids for different tenants; and Joseph Certeaux, the 13-year-old apprentice of Daubigny, who had just been killed at the entrance. As Mme. Hû remembered, "We were packed together, one on top of the other."[72] Just before the invasion of the troops into the building, three of the women—Brunaux, Marrast, and Bourgeaud—left to go to a lower floor for milk, thus increasing the proportion of men in the room.[73]

Louis-Marin Hû, 46, was the proprietor of a furniture store on the ground floor. He had responded to the raising of the barricades that Sunday afternoon by putting his accounts in order. "Devoted to the government," as his brother later described him, he had joined the National Guard, purchased a musket, and proudly had engraved on it the number of his legion. On Sunday afternoon, a neighbor had observed Hû at his window, calling out to the insurgents to respect private property. The Hû family was joined in the early evening by Mme. Godefroy and her child. Her apartment, in the building next door, had windows in every room, and she believed she would be safer in No. 12. At about 11 P.M. the five of them—the three adults and two children—had joined the group in Bouton's fifth-floor apartment. They had fallen into a restless half-sleep when the fighting resumed. "At daybreak the noise recommenced, the gunshots once again could be heard, they were pulling up the paving stones, the insurgents were calling back and forth to each other," recalled Mme. Hû; "Terror seized us again."[74]

Daubigny's apprentice, Joseph Certeaux, ran down the stairs when the soldiers broke in; he rushed back with the news that Daubigny and Guittard had just been killed, "which M. Hû did not want to believe."[75] When the soldiers arrived, Mme. Godefroy was fearful of opening the door, but Hû reassured her: "We're families in here." The soldiers thrust her roughly behind them into the hallway.[76] Hû, who had followed her to the door with his son in his arms, said—and this was repeated by everyone who survived in that room, in more or less the same words—"Come in, my friends, my brothers, we're families here, I have a brother serving under the colors in Algeria." The first volley struck him, the porter's son Loisillon, and Thierry. According to Mme. Hû, "[The soldiers] were maddened, they cried out to each other, but I couldn't understand their shouts."[77] Baptiste Brunaux kicked open a cupboard and leaped into it, and at the same moment Mme. Hû grabbed her wounded child from her dead husband's arms and fell backwards into the same small closet. The apprentice Joseph was hidden under the bed and escaped harm.[78] One of the soldiers said,

"That bastard is still moving," and he bayoneted the porter's son Loisillon, age 20, in the neck. At that moment they spotted 52-year-old Bouton under the table; he shouted, "Comrades, I served in the 35th!"—ironically the very regiment now before him—and he was bayoneted repeatedly by the soldiers who had expended all their fire, until several others arrived and finished him off with bullets. Bouton's murder, coming several seconds after the initial attack, was the one that continued to haunt the survivors. Mme. Hû recalled "the stifled cries of this poor man as well as the noise caused by the bayonets that cut through his clothing and penetrated his body." Several months later, Mme. Pajot described it to Ledru-Rollin: "I heard the bayonet blows that they *rammed* into his body; it was *frou . . . frou . . .* like the blade of a knife that one agitated in the straw stuffing of a chair."[79] By this time the air was black with smoke; an officer just arrived at the scene ordered his men to stop. Mme. Pajot grabbed him by his lapels: "No pity, no mercy; kill me!" She had borne 13 children, all dead except for François Loisillon, her youngest, whom she had just seen finished off with a bayonet to the throat. "Good woman," said the officer, "we won't hurt you."[80]

A total of 12 people were killed in No. 12.[81] Had anyone fired from the windows, the supposed reason for the invasion? A total of 19 witnesses were prepared to say that they had seen gunfire from No. 12.[82] But the search for weapons in the building turned up only five rifles or muskets, a sabre, and Lamy's pair of old stage-prop pistols.[83] Of the five guns, one had belonged to Jean-François Breffort and was in no condition to fire; the Robiquet musket was unloaded and unfired; Hordesseaux, a national guard, had the unfired third musket as well as the sabre; Daubigny and Hû, both killed, had unfired national guard muskets in their apartments. Jean-Charles Hû, summoned shortly after the shooting, examined the hands and faces of all the dead men found with his brother on the fifth floor, including young Louis Breffort, and found no traces of powder.[84]

A neighbor in a nearby street who watched from his attic (with more than passing interest, since he was related to the Lamys) said that he saw a shot fired from the fifth floor, describing it in such a way as to suggest that it was from the distinctively arched window of Louis Breffort. There was also a fifth-floor window accessible from the public staircase, but no debris was found in the hall or stairwell, no discarded cartridges, abandoned weapons, or anything else that might have indicated the presence of insurgents.[85] No weapon was found in

Louis Breffort's room, and Annette Vacher's testimony, taken only by Ledru-Rollin, clearly exculpated him; but for lack of someone better, Breffort was labeled the most likely culprit. The investigators did not put too much urgency into the search for Vacher, even after Ledru-Rollin sent them her address.[86] The answer to the mystery probably lay in the apartment of Henry Raoul, a former national guard and veteran of Wagram. Many of the most precise recollections—a puff of smoke, or the agitation of a blind—placed the shot at the second or third story. Raoul claimed that in the moments of brief calm that had followed the taking of the barricade there had suddenly been a shot *into* his third-floor apartment, breaking the glass and disturbing the blinds.[87]

There were plenty of snipers in the area. Sergeant-Major Claude Mestre of the 54th, the regiment that occupied the building when the out-of-control 35th was ordered away, believed that the soldiers had indeed been fired upon, but from the wineshop across the street. National Guard Captain Jacques Lanquetin had wanted to invade "that wineshop building where I had seen the individuals who had fired on us go back inside." And Sublieutenant Jean Redel of the 35th believed that Captain Rey had been shot from a cellar below the street level, even though he was also convinced that No. 12 sheltered several insurgents.[88] The possibility that Rey had been killed by a shot from below gained more credence with a medical report indicating that the bullet had an upward trajectory.[89] However, the majority of the soldiers were convinced that the shot that killed their captain had come from above, evidenced by their spontaneous fusillade against the building. Indeed, the *commissaire* later reported that the window frames of the Breffort/Bonneville residence on the second floor and those of Louis Breffort on the fifth had been shattered by bullets.[90]

The soldiers who entered the building were in a highly emotional state. According to 13-year-old apprentice Edmond Fredricy, "They were very animated. They said there were republicans here."[91] Annette Bourgeot, who left Bouton's apartment just moments before the entry of the troops, was in her own lodgings: "I opened [the door] without hesitation, and I suddenly found myself in the midst of several bayonets. They were furious and said they didn't want women but were looking for men."[92] A corporal of the *sapeurs-pompiers* noted that their officers made efforts to contain them, but the soldiers were "very animated," repeating that their captain had just been killed.[93] According to several witnesses, another detachment of the 35th dragged two or three prisoners out of the Lemire wineshop who were "immediately shot" in the street, though unarmed.[94]

The invading soldiers generally expressed the view that they had not overstepped the bounds, because of the threat to their own lives. Sergeant Jean

Bernand claimed to have seen a dangerous houseful of insurgents, including "a man who had a saber in his hand and was gesticulating" in Bouton's room on the fifth floor, where no saber was found.[95] Lieutenant Simon admitted that some of the soldiers had become maddened by battle, but he denied that excessive force was used: "I neither struck nor personally saw anyone struck; I did see in a chamber on the third, where an old woman was huddled against the wall, a soldier striking or disposed to strike her with a bayonet; I stopped him."[96] But Simon, like the others, seemed engaged in self-deception:

> When this [ground floor] door was opened, I penetrated into the room with the soldiers, and the men who were encountered there [Guittard and the semi-paralyzed Daubigny, both unarmed], opposing some resistance, were struck. At the second floor the door was broken down, a woman and a young man were killed. I don't know it if was by my soldiers or from outside, before our arrival. We went then to the third floor, where a man and some women opened the doors voluntarily [the Lamy or possibly the Hordesseaux apartment]; no harm was done to them. We found other men hidden in the rooms of the upper floors where they were gathered. The soldiers thought that these men who were gathered together and hidden, and who refused to open their doors, were seditious and designated them as such.[97]

Some months later, in September, *chef de bataillon* Armand de Gibon made the following deposition, not to save himself—for no soldiers were prosecuted in this incident—but to justify what had happened:

> The order to break down the doors and enter the building No. 12, rue Transnonain, was given only because it was certain to us and to all who were present that someone had fired, several times, from the building in question, which appeared to us clearly to be at the disposal of the insurgents; the order to give no quarter was given, that is to say, *to shoot whoever resisted or who was presumed to be in a state of hostility to us* [emphasis added]. I insist particularly on this point, that in our eyes the building contained only enemies and we did not suppose that inoffensive inhabitants would still remain in a building, serving as a refuge to the insurgents, that should later be submitted to the laws of war. . . .
>
> Finally, I observe that the building in question was the first in which our soldiers penetrated; our soldiers were exasperated and it would not have been possible to contain their furor [since they were] sure that they were dealing with enemies. Lieutenant Simon, who received the order to penetrate into the building, came to tell me at the moment he left that a woman had been killed by gunfire that was certainly not meant for her [Annette Besson]. Lieutenant Simon was personally very afflicted by this misfortune. Sergeant-Major Plante

also told me that he had seen this woman fall to the ground, he had returned and picked her up to see if there was still time to help her. The misfortune I have just noted, the only one we knew of at the time, sufficed to change our orders and when later the men of our regiment penetrated the buildings occupied by the insurgents, *we contented ourselves with taking prisoner even those who appeared to have taken an active part in the revolt* [emphasis added].[98]

Six years later, prefect of police Gisquet claimed that the soldiers had "excuses" for their actions: the shot or shots from the building; the residents' unwillingness to open their doors, which forced the soldiers to break them down and "authorized [the soldiers] to regard as insurgents the persons found in the apartments"; and the "desire for vengeance" on the part of the troops, after everything they had suffered.[99] Ledru-Rollin, in contrast, suggested that the killings were part of a pattern, that the soldiers had been ordered to show no mercy; those who had killed Lepère and Robiquet on the fourth floor had said as much to the victims' wives.[100] But though there was considerable brutality and even murder in carrying out arrests elsewhere, what had happened at No. 12 was fundamentally different; and there would be no retribution.

It was at least clear why Transnonain, and not Beaubourg, endured as a symbol. The Beaubourg victims were largely unknown to each other, and included both insurgents and noncombatants. The account by Jeanne Blondeau, who lost her sister, proved that several men had fired from the building. And Blondeau also provided significant testimony of the good conduct of the troops, noting that they attempted several times to get her to safety, "which gives me the conviction that if my sister was a victim it's because in firing they weren't able to see that there was a woman there." She believed it must have been the same with the child, Ribier.[101] In contrast, the people of the rue Transnonain were friends, and grieved for their neighbors as well as for themselves. They were all clearly noncombatants, in spite of the effort to pin the blame on Louis Breffort. When a government brochure (supposedly written by a lieutenant of the 35th) suggested that the inhabitants themselves were at fault, there was an immediate response in the form of a joint letter, including tenants from numbers 11–14, affirming that the details of the massacre as published by the *National*, the *Messager* and several other leftist newspapers were correct.[102]

Perhaps most importantly, there was one survivor determined to present the case before the court of public opinion. Charles Breffort, the brother of Jean-François and uncle of Louis, arrived on the scene almost immediately. The physician who provided the death certificates remembered that he had insisted on being present at all the autopsies, and "even invited me to establish

that certain wounds had been caused by gunshots at point-blank range."[103]
Several days later, Breffort sent a letter to the *National* with some of the earliest details of the killings. His brother, an "old man with white hair," had been
mortally wounded with bayonet thrusts; the *demoiselle* Besson had been shot
"at point-blank range"; Delarivière had been shot from so close that his
clothes caught fire. Breffort also hired an ambitious and energetic attorney,
and within a few months was able to refer readers to the brochure produced by
"my lawyer, M. Ledru-Rollin."[104]

By 6:30 in the morning, on the day of the massacre, the young princes d'Orléans, age 24, and Nemours, 20, were in the heart of barricade country, re-
viewing the troops and braving potential snipers.[105] A few hours later, at
mid-morning, the authorities began to mop up the last remnants of revolt. Arrest reports showed 76 men captured in the quarter in possession of bullets,
cartridges, and other incriminating items, and an additional 39 swept up by
the soldiers and national guards after the fighting was over, including 11
stonemasons who were pulled out of their rooming house. The *commissaire* reported frankly that these last arrests were unwarranted, but he nevertheless
kept the men in custody: "In releasing them I would have had the air of blaming the conduct of the troops, who have had enough to suffer from the inhabitants and their adherents."[106]

The insurgents were melting away and disposing of their weapons—dump-
ing them in courtyards, on roofs, in latrines. Once rid of their guns, they mingled with the crowds who thronged the streets as soon as the shooting stopped.
Nicolas Pruvost the *invalide*, one of the most conspicuous of the combatants,
was arrested in a fourth-floor room on the rue Beaubourg, trying to pass himself
off as one of the tenants. He denied any participation in the revolt, alleging
merely an old soldier's curiosity to see the fighting, and he soon wrote a letter
from prison to the *National*, complaining that he had been framed. Much later,
after the February revolution of 1848, he would write a letter to a newspaper
signing himself *Pruvost dit l'Invalide, chef des barricades de Transnonain*.[107]

Of those individuals captured on the scene many were, like Pruvost,
SDHC members. Sweeps of buildings on the rue Beaubourg netted Denfer,
first quinturion of *Francfort*; Lacombe from the *Procès des Vingt-Sept*; Renard,
first quinturion of *Fleurus*; Sans of *des Gracques*; Laureau, the chief of *Léonidas*,
along with one of his *sectionnaires*; Perdon of *Barricades Méry*. There were also
Delaqui, of *Sidney*, Billon, a quinturion of *Barricades Méry*, and Caillet of the
Victimes du Champs-des-Mars, all three of whom would be tried before the *Cour*

des Pairs. Other sections who had members arrested were *Liberté de la Presse, 5 et 6 Juin, Guerre aux Châteaux, Abolition des impôts indirects, Amis de la vertu, Prise du Louvre,* and *Vengeurs/Socrates.*[108] But the turnout, as everyone realized, was minimal. Prosper Beaudot, a drop-out from *Mirabeau,* reported an encounter on Monday with his former *sous-chef:* "I joked with him saying he was turning his back on the *quartier* where he should be; but he told me there was no counting on anyone, that there were only three men per barricade."[109]

The *Messager* reported a huge crowd at the Paris morgue on 15 April, which had required the cavalry to keep order.[110] Among the dead was 17-year-old Charles Bernier; his mother said that her son was a steady worker, never got into trouble, and never touched alcohol. On Sunday, the insurgents "got him drunk" and he staggered home, badly wounded, unable to say how or where.[111] The mother of Pierre Pretot admitted that her son had been "exalted" by the reading of republican brochures; he had Cabet's inflammatory *La Révolution de 1830,* and the authorities found in his room a letter from Joseph Guinard containing "anarchist and republican principles." He was captured on 14 April, escaped from his escort, and threw himself off a bridge; it was reported that he had been finished off by gunfire while in the water. The controversy over his death made his corpse a particular attraction.[112] One of the noncombatants who was trapped in the fighting was Jean Schosseler, a 33-year-old husband and father. When he failed to return home, his wife inquired after him at the prefecture and the morgue, without success. Then she went to the Hôtel-Dieu, "where I learned that in the *salle des morts* there was an individual who had not yet been identified, and in the cadaver that was presented to me I recognized my husband."[113]

Municipal Guard Pierre Crétigny saw one of the last insurgents on the rue Beaubourg, who defiantly planted a flag on one of the barricades and then took deliberate aim at him: "I riposted immediately with a shot that made him fall to the ground, then advancing, I seized the flag which flew above the barricade." The flag was a tricolor but with a broad red band in the center, across which was written in gold letters, *Révolution républicaine, Société des Droits de l'Homme.* The prosecutor read of the flag in several depositions and wanted it as evidence for the case, but the municipal and national guards on the scene had cut it into small pieces, sharing it among themselves as a "souvenir of the events of April."[114]

This insurrection finished the SDHC. The leadership was in custody or in flight, and the rank and file were disheartened by heavy-handed policing. The *National* reported 1,156 initial arrests. As of September, 736 prisoners had been released, but 420 remained in prisons in Lyon and Paris, still in suspense over whether or not they would be indicted; the archival lists suggest that the *National*'s figures were low.[115] When the trial began in May 1835, many of the defendants had been in prison for at least thirteen months, and the proceedings would take an additional seven.

The stress of these lengthy detentions in crowded prisons led to self-destructive quarrels over doctrine, notably the controversy surrounding the death of Lafayette in May 1834. Armand Carrel published a warm eulogy in the *National*.[116] But from the city jails came reports of a fight between the left wing, who staged a festive celebration of his death, and the moderates who were offended. The *Journal de Paris* soon received a letter from brothers Jean-Jacques and Benjamin Vignerte, who denied that the prisoners had quarreled: "The radicals remain and will always remain united, in spite of all these maneuvers [by the press]. *They have never seen in Lafayette anything but an enemy of the people, a representative of the bourgeois aristocracy and a deplorable hindrance to social reform* [their emphasis]." This letter was followed by another with 86 signatures, which asserted that "the immense majority" of Sainte-Pélagie inmates had supported the revelry at Lafayette's death.[117]

The debate over Lafayette, which was a proxy for the battle between moderates and montagnards, dated from the previous year. In 1833, the unknown 20-year-old Émile Gigault had published the *Vie Politique*, a vicious attack on Lafayette's entire public life. Many leading republicans had been offended by its tone, even though Gigault merely said openly what many had thought privately: that in July 1830 Lafayette had sold out the republic, either through stupidity or anti-democratic tendencies. Armand Carrel published a severe review of the *Vie Politique*, and the workers' paper *Le Bon Sens* expressed distaste for his youthful dogmatism. The position of editor Armand Marrast was delicate, for the *Tribune* usually recognized no enemies on the left; thus when Marrast denounced the pamphlet he felt it necessary to add an attack on the general, calling Lafayette's behavior in 1830 not "a mistake, but a crime."[118] This statement in turn deeply offended the Lyon republicans. Writing of the *National*'s troubled relationship with the *Tribune*, Carrel privately assured Lyon journalist Anselme Petetin that Marrast had taken "many steps toward us," obscured by his need to conciliate the extremists. Marrast, he added, had even been challenged to a duel "by one of these maddened imbeciles who found that it was not enough to treat Lafayette as a great criminal!"[119]

Late September 1834 brought news of a major riot in Sainte-Pélagie, a full-fledged confrontation between the prisoners and a squad of municipal guards.[120] It was followed by a public letter from 44 politicals:

Some hundreds of men have been packed here together for six months; workers for the most part and with the impossibility of working, they are dying of
hunger, or are [having their health] impaired by the unhealthy and insufficient
food that the establishment furnishes them. The families they support are also
suffering from misery; two poor children [of prisoners] have succumbed.[121]

The troubles continued through the fall and winter months. A letter in late
October from those transferred to the Force prison complained that their mothers and wives were humiliated by overzealous searches when they visited.[122] In
early November, another joint letter from the Force enclosed a moldy sample of
their daily bread: "We are almost all workers, in iniquitous *prévention* [in custody, awaiting possible charges] for seven or eight months."[123] Jacques Imbert,
of the newspaper *Le Peuple souverain*, was transferred to the Force and thrown
into an airless cell. He announced a hunger strike, to the death if necessary.[124]
On 21 January 1835, the inmates noisily celebrated the 42nd anniversary of the
execution of Louis XVI. Only Armand Carrel refused to participate; attacked as
an "aristocrat," he had to be rescued by the guards.[125] But finally, in the winter
of 1834–35, the trial was at last in sight.

The *Procès d'avril*, or *procès monstre*, would eventually involve 121 defendants from 9 cities (42 from Paris, 59 from Lyon).[126] They were tried by the
Chamber of Peers, sitting as the *Cour des Pairs*—essentially a stacked jury, as
defendants did not fail to point out, composed of the wealthy elite and politically far more conservative than the men they judged.[127] At the beginning, in
May 1835, the rival Paris and Lyon leaders quarreled over strategy. The
Parisians wanted to stage a "republican congress," calling as defenders a number of leading republicans to join them in an exposition of the doctrine. The
court said no; the Parisians then refused to participate.[128] The Lyonnais, in
contrast, wanted to attend the courtroom debates and contest them. In a
highly visible sign of disarray, the Paris contingent finally issued a public
anathema against their erring brothers who went to court, declaring them
"dropped from the title of our comrades and from republican fraternity."[129]
Twenty-nine of the Paris leaders, including Cavaignac, Guinard, and Lebon,
dramatically escaped from Sainte-Pélagie prison in July 1835 (they tunneled
into a neighboring courtyard) and went into exile.[130] This flight, which occasioned further discord, was so damaging politically that many believed the
prefect of police must have contrived it.[131]

After the sentencing of the Lyon defendants (the cases pertaining to each
city were heard separately), the court entered into its lengthy autumn recess,
convening again on 19 November. In the meantime, Chancellor Pasquier and

a small group of peers investigated the Fieschi assassination attempt, which occurred on 28 July. The trial of the Parisians—or rather, those few who had not escaped—did not begin until 11 January 1836. The only remaining members of the Central Committee were Dr. Arthur Beaumont, who delivered an impassioned denunciation of the government, and then said nothing else; Kersausie, who refused to say anything at all; and Dr. Adrien Recurt, who actually put up a defense, arguing that the criminal actions of the Central Committee had come before or after his time on that body.[132]

The witnesses against the Central Committee were, for the most part, young working-class *sectionnaires*, who were questioned on the basic issues of ammunition and orders of *permanence*. Many had forgotten the details. On the second day, the *Procureur-Général* complained that there was "a system adopted by the witnesses no longer to recall what they declared in the *instruction*"; he began to read aloud some of the original depositions, now nearly two years old.[133] An example had to be made. When Nicolas Minot, a 22-year-old basket maker, claimed with great vehemence to remember nothing and accompanied his remarks "with gestures and unsuitable expressions," he was put under arrest on the spot. Later he was released on the grounds that he had been drunk when he came before the court.[134]

The *Procès d'avril* had finally come down to this: intimidated workers who were openly mocked by the court and the press. One of the chief witnesses against Left Bank defendant Joseph Mathon was "the woman Bolle," who refused to speak: "Someone told me that if I said something, I would be killed." In view of her silence (according to the *Gazette des Tribunaux*, "the old concierge encloses herself in the long streamers of her old bonnet, puts her old hands under her old shawl and no longer responds"), both her depositions were read. The first, full of her excited volubility in the immediate aftermath of the revolt, was damaging to Mathon; the second was considerably less so.[135] On the other hand, Victor Crevat was doomed by the testimony of the numerous street porters he had hired to deliver cartridges to his men.[136] But the escape of the star defendants had virtually ended public interest in the case. Bavoux, in defending his client Eugene Candre, sounded a note of exhaustion: "This fatigue, moreover, is shared by everyone, judges, lawyers, defendants, and the public, in the midst of whose indifference these proceedings are expiring."[137]

The Peers began to deliberate on 20 January 1836. Only Recurt occasioned some discussion; the lack of written evidence against him, and perhaps the fact that he had contested the charges instead of attacking the court, worked in his favor, and he was acquitted.[138] The penalties were most severe for Beaumont and Kersausie, who received deportation (i.e., life imprisonment in a fortress); the other Paris defendants received lesser but still substantial sentences. Kersausie was granted his request to be incarcerated in Brest, near his family; he was put on his honor to travel to the prison and turn himself in, which he did, in only a few days.[139]

There was to be yet one final disaster for republicans at the end of these dismal two years. It began to unfold when *Le Bon Sens* criticized Émile de Girardin's new "mass" paper, *La Presse*. Girardin was regarded as someone who cared little for the working classes to whom he was attempting to appeal. He was personally wealthy, and thus able to support his losses while he drove out the competition. He stopped *Le Bon Sens* by charging them with defamation. The *National* attacked him for the use of that law against another newspaper. Girardin chose to respond not with another lawsuit but rather by challenging Armand Carrel to a duel, and he mortally wounded him.[140]

Convinced from the start that he was dying, Carrel made his friends promise to carry him directly to the cemetery: "No priest, no church." A fairly quiet day passed, followed by a sleepless, agitated night. On the next day he was bled three times. He lost his sight but did not realize it, continuing to ask for candles and struggling against delirium: "Several times . . . he felt himself to be off the subject, and he cried out: 'These cursed doctors have taken so much blood that I am losing my reason!'" In the middle of the second night he began to demand a bath, because he had always believed ("like Napoleon") in its calming effects. But his thoughts continued to drift from one thing to another: Madrid, where he had gone in 1823 to fight with the Spanish rebels; an old friend who had died in a duel; and Foy, Manuel, and Benjamin Constant, the liberal heroes of the Restoration. Finally his friends prepared his bath, assured by the doctor that it would make no difference. He had scarcely been lifted into it when he began to choke: "Replaced on his bed, he felt life escape him."[141] Carrel's funeral attracted 10,000 mourners. Annual commemorations at his gravesite would continue through the rest of the regime; shortly after the revolution of 1848, a special ceremony to render homage to him, as one of the precursors of the new republic, would be attended by Émile de Girardin.[142]

The planned insurrection had failed. Two years, and more, were lost in judicial proceedings and petty disputes. Carrel, the leading voice of moderation, was eventually replaced by Armand Marrast of the old *Tribune*. As chief editor during the 1840s, he surprisingly took the *National* in a cautious, narrowly political direction. Montagnardism itself moved decisively to the left, into the arena of social reorganization and economic redistribution, becoming a hybrid form of communist republican-socialism that would not survive 1848.

CHAPTER 6

THE REPUBLICAN UNDERGROUND: THE *FAMILLES* AND THE *SAISONS*

THE OATH TO THE *SOCIÉTÉ DES FAMILLES*, a successor to the SDHC, included the following passage:

> Our tyrants have forbidden us the press and association; therefore it is our duty to join together with more perseverance than ever, and to fill the void of the press by spoken propaganda. . . . Later, when the hour has sounded, we will take up arms to overturn a government that has betrayed the country. Will you be with us that day? . . . When the signal of combat is given, are you resolved to die, weapons in hand, for the cause of humanity?[1]

At least two elements of this vow were noteworthy. First, the emphasis on press and association served as an essential link to the *Société des Amis du Peuple* and the SDHC, and thus connected this new secret society to the republican tradition. Second, the stress on personal sacrifice, even to the death, was the essential difference between July Monarchy republicanism and such rivals as communism and socialism, whose followers expected to enjoy their victories. Republicans, in contrast, stressed a code of honor and sacrifice: loyalty to comrades, fortitude to stand in the breach, the willingness to die for the sake of the whole. What this oath also made clear, however, was the dramatic transformation of the legal climate. Republican opposition was driven underground, and the new societies exchanged the goal of open debate for rigid orthodoxy and unquestioning obedience.

The attack on political rights began with the association law of April 1834, a blunt instrument that required all clubs to obtain police permission no matter how often they met, or how large the group, or whatever their purpose.[2] After this came the famous September Laws of 1835, made possible by public revulsion over the Fieschi assassination attempt; they codified the actions taken in the *Procès d'avril*. If a defendant refused to appear in the courtroom, the presiding magistrate could now legally have him brought by force or, alternatively, continue the trial in his absence. The presiding magistrate was given the power to remove from the courtroom any defendant who caused "tumult" or "put an obstacle to the free course of justice." The jury majority required for conviction was reduced from eight to seven out of twelve. (As a safeguard, the panel of magistrates was given the right to annul a guilty verdict when they believed it to be in error.) The law also regularized the long-standing practice in regard to deportation, stating explicitly that the sentence would be served in prison.[3]

The press provisions of the September Laws caused considerably more controversy and were subjected to attacks even from supporters of the monarchy, including André Dupin, president of the Chamber of Deputies, and the respected Pierre Royer-Collard.[4] One of the guarantees of the July Revolution—one of the "republican institutions"—had been the promise of a free press, with offenses to be brought before a jury. But since 1830, journalists had often been tried on elastic and ambiguous charges, such as "affront to the king," or "inciting to hatred and contempt of the Government."[5] In January 1832, the Périer ministry had even begun the policy of pretrial detention of editors and journalists; Odilon Barrot had argued the journalists' case and won a rare judicial victory, ending the practice.[6]

The September Law not only toughened the press regime but redefined certain offenses as *attentats à la sûreté de l'État*, or crimes to be brought before the *Cour des Pairs* (instead of a jury), and for which the ultimate penalty might be death. These included newspaper articles that could be regarded as inciting the assassination of the monarch, the changing of the government or the order of succession to the throne, or the arming of citizens against the government (the wording from articles 86 and 87 of the Penal Code)—and regardless of whether or not their published "provocations" had been followed by any actions, on the part of anyone.[7] In addition, caricatures, engravings, and drawings were declared subject to prior censorship, and could not be published without permission from the departmental prefect or, in Paris, from an official in the Ministry of the Interior.[8]

As Irene Collins has shown, journals were now also bedeviled with a number of smaller changes in the law. The amount that could be levied against them in fines was doubled; the common practice (especially among cash-poor republican or working-class papers) of paying fines with public subscriptions was outlawed. (Raspail's *Réformateur* went out of business in November 1835, as the result of three convictions and heavy fines within ten days, along with the imprisonment of most of his editors.) *Caution* money (a required cash deposit) was increased (from 24,000 francs to 100,000 francs for national papers that appeared more than twice a week, for example). Journals were required to publish immediately all announcements sent to them by government officials. The *gérant*, or responsible editor (who would serve time in prison if the paper were convicted), was subjected to certain conditions: he was to provide one-third of the *caution* (thus restricting available candidates); he was under the obligation to reveal the author of any article brought to trial; and he could not sign the newspaper (as legally required for publication) while in prison.[9]

The most conspicuous victim of the new climate was the strident *Tribune*. Late in the evening of 13 April 1834, the offices were invaded, their contents placed under seal, and the printer, Auguste Mie, deprived of his printer's certificate (*brevet*). Armand Marrast escaped this first round-up but was eventually included in the *procès monstre* as one of the defendants, on the grounds of the "coincidence" between the insurrection and what the *Tribune* had published.[10] The *National* maintained a steady drumbeat of bulletins on developments in the case: Marrast's arrest on 21 April; the arrest of the *metteur en pages* on 26 April, apparently to force him to name the authors of various articles; on 4 May, the report that Marrast was still being held in isolation; and so on, through July.[11] The *Tribune* began to publish again on 11 August 1834, beginning with a discussion of the Transnonain affair.[12] By May 1835 it was gone, having collapsed financially; Louis-Philippe's government had taken it to court 111 times, securing 20 convictions and fines which represented a total of 157,630 francs and 49 years in prison; it alone had accounted for nearly one-fifth of the 520 press cases in Paris by the end of 1834. Gisquet saw the departure of this "flag of the insurrection" as significant: "the death of this newspaper . . . revealed the exhaustion of the violent party that had sustained it."[13]

But unquestionably the most important of all the new laws concerned the right to bear arms. It was passed immediately after the April insurrection and was to become one of the most important weapons in the government's arsenal against the underground movement—perhaps the most significant of all post-April legislation (even including the September Laws) in its effects.[14] It was passed quickly, with little discussion, and was formally promulgated by the king on 24 May 1834.

Several sections of the new law filled gaps in existing legislation. Before this, even men taken in the midst of the barricades could not be convicted unless it was proved that they were connected to an *attentat*, that is, to a planned attempt to overturn the government. Article 5 allowed for the punishment of anyone "who will have brought" either hidden or obvious weapons or ammunition into an insurrection. Article 9 provided punishment for those who built barricades, hindered the gathering of the armed forces with either physical force or threats, or "provoked" the gathering of insurgents by means of orders, proclamations, flags, or other signs. The purpose of these provisions was to allow for the prosecution of the specific acts alone, without having to link them to some larger conspiracy. And Article 7 gave a brief nod to the Transnonain affair by punishing with hard labor any individual who invaded a domicile, thus creating a situation in which soldiers might become involved.[15]

But it was the peacetime use of this law that was to be the most significant, providing something of a charter for police harassment by criminalizing the mere possession of weapons and ammunition. The new law gave prosecutors two options in such cases: an individual could be charged with conspiracy to overthrow the state, for which his amassing of weapons and cartridges would be evidence; or, if this more serious charge could not be sustained, he could now be tried simply for possession. A prosecutor could also try an individual twice for the same seizure of weapons or cartridges: it was not unusual for those acquitted in conspiracy cases in the *Cour d'Assises* to be sent to the *Tribunal de police correctionnelle*, where they were convicted of the lesser charge.[16]

The legal right to bear arms in France had previously been linked to citizenship and equality, a fact that gave this law an added impact. An *ordonnance* of 18 July 1716 (prompted by the large numbers of weapons acquired by civilians during the War of the Spanish Succession) had prohibited the *porte des armes*, except for nobles, gentlemen living nobly, proprietors, those in the liberal professions, the bourgeoisie of the cities, and officers of royal justice. The abolition of privileges on 4 August 1789 temporarily gave to all men the right to bear arms; just over two weeks later, a decree of 20 August prohibited weapons to vagabonds and masterless men [*gens sans aveu*]. Subsequently, Article 34 of the Penal Code had established that only a court of law could deprive someone of the right to carry weapons. A police ordinance of 1806 required Parisians who wished to carry pistols for self-defense to obtain permits.[17]

Article 2 of the new law prohibited the unauthorized manufacture, sale, and distribution of gunpowder, as well as the possession of more than 2 kilograms of *poudre de chasse* (gunpowder for hunting), and prohibited the possession of any quantity of powder defined as *poudre de guerre*. Article 3 prohibited the manufacture and sale of *armes de guerre*, which the state reserved for itself (they distributed these weapons to their troops and national guards), and also prohibited the possession of a "depot" of any kind of weapons whatsoever.

These offenses were to be brought before a panel of magistrates in the *Tribunal de police correctionnelle* rather than a jury; the sentences would be lighter than if they had gone to the *Cour d'Assises*, but a guilty verdict was more certain.[18]

A number of pragmatic concerns were raised in the course of the debates. One deputy wondered how people could be prevented from buying saltpeter, sulfur, and charcoal, and combining them together; the making of gunpowder was "no longer an occult science." Then there was the issue of what exactly constituted a "depot" of weapons: those who lived in isolated rural areas might not feel safe with only "one or two *fusils de chasse*." Hunters also complained about the small amount of gunpowder that could be kept on hand.[19] The justice minister asserted that the *ordonnance* of 1816 was still in force, which required all possessors of *armes de guerre* to leave them at the mayoralty; in 1832, the administration decided to keep all national guard muskets in central depots. Lafayette protested this decision, asserting that it would reduce the National Guard to a "*landwehr*," a troop meant for the defense of territory, "and neglect the right of the people to remain armed for the defense of their liberties." Apparently the Paris Guards agreed with him, for many (and insurgents counted on this) kept their government-issued muskets at home.[20]

But the most compelling arguments, in retrospect, concerned issues of civil rights. If a "depot" was left undefined, suggested a dissenting deputy, the police or courts would define it, potentially in arbitrary fashion. Further, he warned that these provisions of the new law would have unintended consequences against individual privacy: "This vote implies the right of search and domiciliary visit . . . you are about to decide, that in order to find weapons or under the pretext of searching for them, all the habitations of France will be opened before the police, and that there is no longer an inviolable refuge in the domestic foyer."[21] This prediction was correct: republicans in the future would find their homes ransacked, themselves convicted in correctional courts for the sake of a few cartridges, and left to cool their heels for short but dispiriting jail terms. Arrest for possession would become the most common offense charged against republicans, a sort of fallback (because they always had ammunition) if nothing else could be found against them.

It was in this changed legal environment that the *Société des Familles* emerged from the remnants of the SDHC. Its creators were Louis-Auguste Blanqui and the relatively obscure republican publisher Hadot-Desages.[22] It burst dramatically onto the public scene through the midnight revelations of Théodore

Pepin, co-conspirator in the Fieschi assassination attempt, made just hours before his dawn execution on 19 February 1836. Pepin asserted that he had been received into a new group, led by "very dangerous" men whose goal was to overthrow the government.[23] His statement, made in the shadow of the guillotine, took on the trusted status of a deathbed confession.

Pepin's revelations also seemed to corroborate several significant police discoveries of the same period. A smuggled letter from Sainte-Pélagie escapee Victor Crevat to another prisoner hinted at a new organization: "The patriots seek each other out, tell each other their troubles and hopes; all have confidence in the future; a great number prepare themselves by the purchase of weapons. . . ." Crevat went on to speak of a "manifesto," and the pressing need to resolve "the departmental and foreign question."[24] A raid at the home of wealthy activist Armand Barbès on the day of the Fieschi attempt resulted in the seizure of recruitment guidelines for the new group. Every prospective new member was to be investigated in regard to his "morality, sobriety, discretion, and energy"; to be admitted, "one must have reached one's majority, enjoy a good reputation, conduct oneself well, be able to justify one's means of existence [a precaution against police spies], and be endowed with the greatest discretion."[25]

The *Familles* was thought to have perhaps 1,000 to 1,200 men in early 1836 (undoubtedly an overestimate), while the subsequent *Saisons* was perceived as somewhat smaller; because of their secrecy, necessary under the new association law, neither society had much impact beyond its own members.[26] The rules of both the *Familles* and the *Saisons* prohibited paper trails that could be used against them: no lists of sections, no *ordres du jour*; no pamphlets or brochures; the members were to say nothing of the society in the courtroom. The *Familles* were forbidden to assemble in public places, whether in cafés or in the flamboyant street "reviews" made familiar by the *Société d'Action*. The section chiefs were supposed to maintain regular individual contact with their men, summoning them verbally for relatively infrequent meetings, usually in a private home; the sections consisted of 6 to 12 men at most. Members were required to keep a supply of gunpowder and bullets; weapons were promised for the day of combat. Undercover police spy Lucien Delahodde described a hierarchical but rather vague structure, culminating in the *agent révolutionnaire* (a term taken from Babeuf). The *agents* themselves supposedly reported to a secret committee of powerful men, who would make themselves known on the day of insurrection. But the three *agents révolutionnaires*—accurately rumored to be Louis-Auguste Blanqui, Armand Barbès, and Martin-Bernard—were themselves the committee; there was no one above them.[27]

Louis-Auguste Blanqui, born in 1805, the son of a *conventionnel* and a member of the educated bourgeoisie, first became widely known through the striking speech in the *Procès des Quinze* that had kept him in prison during June 1832. He became a professional revolutionary and was eventually famous for his endurance, spending a total of nearly 34 years in prison. The police described Blanqui in 1839 as spare, slight, and ascetic, with a "sardonic" air; he drank no wine, was careless of his appearance.[28] An unsympathetic though shrewd observer described him in 1848, after the revolution: "He spoke slowly, in an abrupt and dry voice. . . . With neither brilliance nor élan, but in the manner of presenting facts, with a meticulous and continuous care to incite anger and bitterness in the unlettered masses of his listeners. The people were always the victims: always one imprisoned them, always one oppressed them, always one slaughtered them."[29] Even a former associate, Alexandre Raisant, described him in 1848 as "very *égoïste*, without sympathy, living uniquely by his head, playing with men as if they were tokens."[30]

Armand Barbès was born in 1810 in Guadeloupe, the son of a lapsed priest. The ultimate revelation of the secret had shattered his family, a tragedy which gave a romantic aura to the already dashing Barbès, who was wealthy and unemployed except for his political ventures. His activities had begun with his membership in the SDHC as chief of the *Montagnards* section. After the failed insurrection in 1839, he remained incarcerated until February 1848.[31] He was loved because of his chivalric bravery, and would be revered because of his sufferings in prison.

The least known was Martin-Bernard, born in 1808, a printer and one of the educated elite of working men. In 1833 he joined both the SDHC and the *Société libre typographique*, and soon made a name for himself as an artisan-propagandist. He was brought into the *Familles* by journalist Fulgence Girard, a longtime friend to Blanqui and Barbès. Before his death in 1883, he would serve in legislatures in both the Second and Third Republics.[32]

Their respective characters were well captured by the *procureur-général* in 1839, when he described Blanqui as the intellectual, Barbès as the "man of action," and Martin-Bernard as the recruiter, constantly talking, visiting, persuading, cajoling: "We do not fear to affirm that the shadowy organization of this redoubtable band is due principally to [Martin-Bernard]."[33] But their fame was largely in the future. Now, at the beginning of their careers, none of the three yet had sufficient reputation to be credible as the prominent men of the Central Committee.

The authorities occasionally obtained glimpses of this society. The soldier Joseph Grison came forward after the Meunier assassination attempt. He had joined the *Familles* in the fall of 1835 while working as a printer, invited by a fellow worker "whose name"—in time-honored fashion—"I no longer recall today." He had been blindfolded and sworn to the oath. Then his political instruction began:

> They commenced by explaining the goal of the society, which was to achieve a moral revolution by means of propaganda; failing that, a material revolution by force of arms when the order was given. Then it was a question of the griefs against the current government, in the number of which were enumerated the king's forgetting of the promises made in July 1830; the lack of education for the people; the unjust apportionment of the taxes; the vengeance owed to the victims of Lyon and Paris.

Grison was ordered never to answer the questions of a *juge d'instruction*. He was to maintain a supply of gunpowder and, if possible, to procure a weapon. Finally, he pledged "not to descend onto the public streets except when the Committee (which will make itself known) has given the order by a proclamation signed by all the members composing it, who will put themselves at the head of the insurrection." He belonged until November 1836, when he joined the army.[34]

The program of the *Familles* reflected the social republicanism of the SDHC Propaganda Commission, emphasizing the concept of class warfare and the division of society into rich and poor, but explicitly going no further than demands for the "right to existence," political participation, and free public education. These views were evident in the "political questions" of the *Familles* initiation ceremony (the new member was provided with both questions and answers):

> Q. What do you think of the current government? A. It is a traitor to the people and the country.
> Q. In whose interest does it function? A. In the interest of a small number of the privileged.
> Q. Who are the aristocrats of today? A. They are the money men, the bankers, the merchants, the monopolists, the large proprietors, the speculators, in a word all the exploiters who fatten themselves at the expense of the people.
> Q. By what right do they govern? A. By force.
> Q. What is the dominant vice in society? A. Egoism.
> Q. What takes the place of honor, probity, and virtue? A. Money.
> Q. Which men are esteemed in the world? A. The rich and powerful.

Q. Which men are scorned, persecuted, and put outside the law? A. The poor and weak.

Q. What do you think of the city tolls, the taxes on salt and drink? A. They are odious taxes, destined to oppress the people while sparing the rich.

Q. Who are the people? A. The people are the totality of those who work.

Q. How are the people treated by the law? A. They are treated as slaves.

Q. What is the fate of the proletarian under the government of the wealthy? A. His fate is similar to that of the serf and the negro; his life is only a long tissue of misery, fatigue, and suffering.

Q. What is the goal that should serve as a basis for society? A. Equality.

Q. What should be the rights of the citizen in a well-regulated country? A. The right to existence, the right to free education, the right to participation in government.

Q. What are his duties? A. His duties are devotion towards society and fraternity towards his fellow citizens.

Q. Is it necessary to make a political revolution or a social revolution? A. It is necessary to make a social revolution.[35]

This catechism was replaced in the *Société des Saisons* by another list of questions, of which a copy was found in 1838 in Barbès' handwriting. The tone of the *Saisons* oath was more violent and babouvist (after Gracchus Babeuf, leader of the 1796 communist Conspiracy of the Equals), and called for a revolutionary dictatorship, a purge of the governing classes, and a more serious and far-reaching "social revolution":

> 3. Who are the aristocrats now? The aristocracy of birth was destroyed in July 1830; now the aristocrats are the wealthy, who constitute an aristocracy as devouring as the first.
>
> 4. Must one be content with overthrowing the Monarchy? One must destroy all aristocracies and privileges whatsoever; otherwise one has done nothing. . . .
>
> 7. What are the duties of each citizen? Obedience to the general will, devotion to the *patrie*, and fraternity towards each member of the nation. . . .
>
> 10. Are those who have rights without fulfilling duties, as the aristocrats of today, part of the people? They should not be a part of the people; they are to the social body what cancer is to the human body. The first condition of the return of the body to health, is the excision of the cancer; the first condition of the return of the social body to a just state, is the annihilation of the aristocracy. . . .
>
> 13. Immediately after the revolution, can the people govern itself? The social state being gangrened, heroic remedies are necessary to achieve a healthy state; the people will have need for some time of a revolutionary power.[36]

The "right to existence" was by now understood as requiring some redistribution of wealth: progressive income taxes, limitations on property use, even seizures of certain kinds of property. The only means of transition to a republican state was revolution, followed by dictatorship (a babouvist *Comité insurrecteur*, a committee of public safety, a provisional government): a temporary ruling group to educate the masses and take the brutal but necessary step of exterminating the old ruling class, without which action the people would slump back into their ingrained habits of obedience. "The day after the insurrection the People will be on the public square, without work and without bread," intoned the November 1839 manifesto of the *Société démocratique française*, a London refugee group, in a potent montagnard evocation of chaos and paranoia: "Commerce . . . will be annihilated. . . . Many of the rich, all the nobles and the ex-great functionaries, will seek to save themselves in flight; the most fanatic, however, will certainly remain in France, to try to carry out a counter-revolution; ambitious intriguers, and these are the most greatly to be feared, because they assume any mask, will try to take power." A provisional government was essential, but "the great majority of the people could be mistaken in their choice of men," and so the "Republicans, the authors of the insurrection," would need immediately to proclaim a slate of leaders. The provisional government would last for "the time necessary to prepare the masses to accept our ideas."[37]

The most important judicial exposure of the *Familles* involved the clandestine gunpowder factory in No. 113 rue de l'Oursine (or Lourcine), at the deserted end of a desolate street. It first came to police attention in March 1836 through an informant's tip. Young men, correctly identified by the neighbors as middle-class students disguised in working-class *blouses* and *casquettes*, came to the premises at all hours. Every other night, a tall man in a long coat (believed to be Martin-Bernard) carried parcels away from the building. *Commissaire* Michel Yon and his officers captured five men inside, including Eustache Beaufour, a former Rouen textile manufacturer and Saint-Simonian, who had rented the building in February 1836. The police also found 150 *livres* of gunpowder, raw materials and powder in different stages of preparation, and a fully equipped lab.[38] They soon found another republican warehouse on the rue Dauphine, with material sufficient to make about 200,000 cartridges, though far fewer than that were finished.[39] These initial arrests gave rise to many others. When the police raided Barbès's apartment in early March, unexpectedly they caught Blanqui with him. Yon and Blanqui had a brief struggle over the papers in the latter's pocket before Blanqui stuffed them in his mouth and swallowed, saying "Go look for them."[40]

Unfortunately, Barbès was in possession of a notebook belonging to medical student and leading *sociétaire* Eugène Lamieussens, with the heading *Société des Familles* and several membership rosters, including actual names and their corresponding *noms de guerre*.[41] The lists provided several hundred men to be investigated, of whom many were eventually brought to trial, 43 as defendants and others as witnesses. (The defendant Alexandre Raisant wanted to know why he was one of the unlucky ones: "Were the names put in a sack, to be drawn at random, like a game of lotto?"[42]) Blanqui claimed that the Lamieussens lists were nothing more than the subscribers to his short-lived 1834 newspaper, the *Liberateur*. It was pointed out to him that many of the so-called subscribers had peculiar notations after their names ("4 pist., 12 sabr., two hatchets, can furn. some powder," for example). Blanqui blandly explained that he was always on the lookout for antique weaponry, including hatchets and battle axes, as props for the studio of his artist-wife.[43]

The rue de l'Oursine case, first trumpeted as a major plot to overthrow the government, rather fizzled out, downgraded from the *Cour d'Assises* to the Correctional Tribunal. The original conspiracy charge was dropped; most of the defendants were accused of violating the association law, several with illegal possession of gunpowder, Barbès and Blanqui with resisting arrest, and two other defendants with maintaining a primary school without authorization, lending a touch of incoherence to the proceedings.[44] The evidence for conspiracy—the lists, the *Familles* initiation formula found on one of those arrested, the two "factories"—was at least as strong as that in many earlier conspiracy cases. The reduction in charges reflected a different approach, now possible because of the new association and ammunition laws: convictions, even with shorter sentences, would keep troublemakers out of circulation for dispiriting lengths of time. The trial resulted in guilty verdicts for 40 men, with sentences ranging from one month, to one year (for Barbès), to two years (for Blanqui, Beaufour, and the building's caretaker, Adrien Robert). Blanqui and Barbès were liberated in the mass political amnesty of May 1837.[45] After their release they joined Martin-Bernard, who had avoided conviction, to restructure the group into the *Société des Saisons*.

In the meantime, the August trial was closely followed, in September 1836, by arrests for the other major *Familles* case. This episode started with the death of Canlay, veteran of 1832 (he had lost an arm) and a former hawker of *Le Bon Sens*. About five hundred people had gathered to follow the long and provocative route (according to the prosecution) of his convoy. There were cartridge distributions (364 cartridges were later found by a ragpicker), a collection for burial expenses (allegedly destined for gunpowder), and a commemoration at the would-be regicide Alibaud's tomb. The graveside eulogy made repeated references to the Republic.[46]

Before the funeral, the former *Familles* member and *révélateur* Grison had been convoked *en permanence* to the Jardin des Plantes, where—apparently to everyone's surprise—there gathered an unexpectedly good turnout of about 150. Each man was given ten cartridges. They were eventually to proceed to Sainte-Pélagie prison, where they would liberate Barbès and Blanqui. In the meantime, they were told to wait for "final orders" and the arrival of additional sections; men began to drift away, and after an hour only eight of them were left.[47]

Grison's revelations came months later. Just after the funeral, the police captured one of the sections. At 3 A.M. on 1 September, *Commissaire* Yon, accompanied by several agents (including *officier de paix* Tranchard, who knew many republicans by sight) went to the third floor apartment of Clément-Charles Leprestre-Dubocage, on the impasse Saint-Sébastian. Yon knocked on the door: "Someone opened up, and immediately I was hit; I called for help and the brawl began; they raised daggers against us." The 11 men inside were soon overpowered. "Someone threw me on the bed," recalled Dubos, one of those captured, "and with a dagger at my throat said: 'If you move you're dead.'" Yon seized 13 daggers, along with 440 pistol cartridges, 400 musket cartridges, and 471 recently cast balls. He noted that the single chamber was adorned with "republican emblems" as well as lithographs of the April defendants. The hand-decorated red-and-yellow mantelpiece, with a liberty bonnet surmounting two crossed bundles of battle axes, was exhibited in the trial.[48] The testimony of the neighbors revealed meetings every Saturday and Sunday night, during which the *sectionnaires* read aloud and sang republican songs "in low voices."[49]

The leader of this small band was copper-worker Leprestre-Dubocage, born in 1815. His former employer noted that he was "a little excessive" (*un peu exagéré*) and had stirred up some "discords" in the shop, which had led to his dismissal. According to Dubocage, he had attended the Canlay funeral only because a "headache" had incapacitated him for work. That evening, he had invited some friends to his apartment to help with his hobby: "It amused me to make cartridges, it was my passion; I spent my salary on it." The many daggers had been used for dining.[50] All of his co-defendants followed Dubocage's lead in minimizing the events of the evening. One of the defense attorneys, the republican J.-A. Plocque, suggested that the young men were merely indulging in the "mania of the day." Continued Plocque, "It probably made them feel good to tell everyone,

'During the night of 31 August to 1 September I was with ten resolute men, we were *en permanence*, we waited for orders, we were to march at the first signal.' This is how [a young man] gives himself some depth, some importance."[51]

The loose ends of the case gave further insight into the organization. While awaiting trial, Dubocage wrote a letter from prison to fellow *sociétaire* Alphonse Grimault. Grimault "must have seen in the papers" that he had been arrested; Dubocage continued: "We spent the night waiting for orders which were to be, I think, for the morning of the first of this month." He described the raid, bragging a little of the police brutality he had endured, and then gave Grimault some instructions, revealing the fragile sorts of connections that held this group together:

> You must warn a certain Chauvet who lives at rue du Pont-aux-Choux no 13, in a furnished room [*garni*]. Show him this letter so he'll believe it; there must be no delay. Tell him to hide everything he has at home. Then tell him to go find Perrodin who works for Bouvaist and that he should tell him to go to Hennin, rue Transnonain, to see if he's arrested, and if he isn't to go see all the dispersed men in order to rally them and I'll send someone to give him orders.[52]

After this case, the *Familles* simply faded from view, to be resurrected with a much tighter organization as the *Société des Saisons*. In the meantime, the police went after known activists for ammunition and weapons possession.[53] The leaders had learned their lesson from the gunpowder factory experience. Now the well-to-do members—Barbès, Raisant, some of the students—distributed money to working class *sectionnaires*, who bought powder in small quantities and made it up into cartridges. Many thus found themselves subject to arrest, as they were caught storing, fabricating, or carrying large quantities of matériel.[54]

As a result, the gunpowder cases tended to be large, involving anti-association charges as well. Thirty-three men were tried in March 1837, including Benjamin Flotte, former SDHC member and future disciple of Blanqui. A search of his room revealed a great deal of gunpowder (which he claimed to need for his "health") and a handwritten tribute to the would-be assassin Alibaud. Among his co-defendants was Jules Delarue, who swallowed a list when the police arrived, engaging in such a struggle that he began to bleed at the nose; the agents seized his copy of the *Oeuvres de Saint-Just*. Co-defendant Jean-Baptiste Deligny had traced republican emblems on the tools in his shop; his boss had fired him because other workers complained that he constantly talked politics.[55] Louis Raban was an engraver who ran a charity for the relief of political prisoners; the police believed much of the charity money was spent

on ammunition. He was arrested in his home along with several friends, surrounded by scissors and paper. He said that he liked to keep his hands busy
while he was talking, casually cutting pieces into whatever forms came into his
head; his paper-cutting fantasies all happened to be in the shape of cartridges,
a coincidence made more interesting by the fact that he had 10,300 recently
cast bullets in his back room.[56]

Against this background, the *Société des Saisons* began to take shape in the
summer of 1837. It has been suggested that the *Saisons* was a more solidly
working-class group than the *Familles*, which had included many students and
soldiers, but the origin for that assertion was apparently the controversial
Taschereau document.[57] Given the lack of membership lists, as well as the difficulty in counting committed members, it is impossible to determine with any
accuracy the composition of either group. Government prosecutors saw the
Familles and the *Saisons* as essentially the same, dispersed and then pulled back
together. They were probably correct in asserting that the transformation had
occurred because of the need to tighten discipline. The *Saisons* consisted, on
the lowest level, of 6-man sections known as "Weeks" (*Semaines*), each led by a
"Sunday" (*Dimanche*); four Weeks formed a "Month" (*Mois*), led by a "July"
(*Juillet*), for a total of 29 men; three Months formed a "Season" (*Saison*), each
under a chief called a "Spring" (*Printemps*), for a total of 88 men; and four Seasons formed a "Year" (*Année*), under an *Agent révolutionnaire*, for a total of 353
men. There were only three revolutionary agents, their names rumored
among the members: Blanqui, Barbès, and Martin-Bernard. Above them was
the mythical "Executive Council" (*Conseil exécutif*) of powerful men who would
reveal themselves on the day of insurrection. The printer Pierre Nouguès confirmed the widespread belief in the topmost rank: "I heard it said by the most
lowly of the association, by the young men and workers, that there was an executive council that would declare itself at the moment of combat."[58]

Mathieu Viot, a 28-year-old cook, had been recruited into the *Familles* by a
law student in late 1835 or early 1836. He and five others had met almost every
month in the home of a bookseller: "We talked politics; we especially occupied
ourselves with events of the day. It was said that when the society was strong
enough, we would attack the government, and would wait two or three years if
necessary; others, more in a hurry, spoke of attacking immediately; but this
opinion was not general." After the rue de l'Oursine arrests, his section had
fallen apart.[59] At the end of 1837, Viot had been approached by Jean, a
concierge, who had the use of a vacant apartment for meetings. His new section
seemed to be full of water carriers, and was often visited by the indefatigable
Martin-Bernard: "There was mention of an attack, and I heard Martin-Bernard

say that weapons would not be lacking when we had need of them, and that the committee would show itself then." He had attended for only six months, during the winter of 1837–1838.[60] He had, however, brought other cooks into the society, effectively creating a professional cadre. (Pierre Nibaut, the proprietor of the Café de Foy in the Palais-Royal, on the day of insurrection found himself deserted by his entire staff of chefs and busboys.[61])

The cook Joseph Pons, age 23, had been recruited by Viot in late 1837 or early 1838: "He informed me that he was part of a secret society whose members met in cafés, and proposed to have me admitted." Pons had been inducted by wealthy *sociétaire* Alexandre Raisant, who informed him afterward that he had just pledged to fight for the republic. He and his section gathered about every two weeks, "sometimes in one place, sometimes in another, particularly [in the café owned by the *sociétaire*] Charles." "In general we spoke a great deal about organizing and coming to agreement on the overthrowing of the government," recalled Pons; "it was always a question of fighting." Pons had been a *Dimanche*, over a section composed of six tailors, and he had reported directly to Martin-Bernard.[62]

Despite the basic continuity, there were some significant differences in the new group. The *Saisons* ended the isolation that had put so much pressure on each section chief, instead holding irregular meetings of entire Months or even Seasons in cafés. The senior chiefs came to these meetings (Martin-Bernard was the most active) and delivered exhortations to the troops. The *Saisons* also staged "general reviews" in the streets. Since the members were told that any such review might result in an order to take up arms, the exercise served to count the men who would be likely to turn out for battle. *Juillet* Alexandre Quarré, a cook recruited by Viot, stated that "[the sections] were organized on a footing of the completely passive obedience of inferiors to superiors"; he compared the group to the army.[63]

Though Blanqui and Barbès had been liberated by the May 1837 amnesty, they had left the daily business in the hands of Martin-Bernard. Barbès remained at his family estate in Carcassonne. Blanqui, forbidden to reside in Paris, lived in the little town of Gency near Pontoise, in Seine-et-Oise. He made frequent trips to the capital, always precipitated, as the villagers recalled, by letters informing him of a sick relative. In January 1839, a police agent who had Blanqui under surveillance in Paris suggested that he "seeks very actively to reorganize something," indicated by his frequent meetings with Martin-Bernard.[64]

Blanqui was under considerable pressure from the most militant of the *sociétaires* to launch an attack. The government seemed vulnerable, after a months-long cabinet crisis and the apparent inability of the king, even after new elections in March, to form a stable ministry. The police believed that the insurrection had finally been set for Sunday, 5 May; the Springs, or *Printemps*, were ordered to assemble their men for a "strict review" (*revue de rigueur*), and the groups were in position from midday. But at 1 P.M. the committee sent word that it was "satisfied with the zeal of the revolutionary army" and sent them home. Blanqui had pulled back, believing the following Sunday more favorable. A new regiment was moving into Paris that week; the transition would cause some confusion, and the troops would not know the terrain. In addition, the opening of the Champs de Mars races on 12 May would likely occupy many of the city's officials.[65]

Barbès, who had attended a meeting on 4 May convoked by the hatter Benoît Ferrari, perhaps also contributed to the delay. He had asked many questions "on the subject of their opinion of the timeliness of the attack, on their relations with the proletariat outside the association, on the dispositions of the working class." Apparently not entirely satisfied, Barbès had announced (according to police informants) that he wanted further consultation with the *Dimanches*, and had asked the same questions at a large convocation on Monday, 6 May.[66] On Tuesday, 7 May, there was another meeting of Sundays and Julys, in which the various chiefs reported "nearly 400" combatants: "Barbès then made a speech in which he announced that the society was on the verge of gathering the fruits of its labor and that soon the patriots 'would have nothing more to do than to rest in the shadow of their laurels.'"[67]

Joseph Pons did not attend this meeting, alarmed by the rumors. Several days later he encountered Quarré, who reproached him, saying that "if I had gone, I would have seen Barbès and Blanqui; I don't recall [he added carefully] that he told me what one did at this session." A few days before 12 May, the building painter Thébaut told Pons that "things are getting hot."[68] In the meantime the *Montagnards*, an extremist splinter group, had been on alert as of 1 May: "The plan of attack has been communicated with details," reported the police agent; "it consists of descending into the streets, calling the population to arms, and setting fire to properties."[69]

It was now only a matter of time. Antoine Lechaudé, a farmer and the barber of the hamlet of Gency, saw Blanqui heading home on 8 May; he had gone to Paris several days earlier, as the villagers had been told, to see an ailing sister. Lechaudé had stopped the following day to see if he wanted a shave but was not allowed in. He had assumed that Blanqui was being visited by "some strange person who did not wish to be seen by anyone," as had frequently occurred. The pharmacist in Pontoise, who doubled as the ticket agent for the coach, reported that Blanqui had arrived at 6 A.M. on Friday, 10 May for the trip to Paris.[70]

The *sectionnaires* were convoked for Sunday; on the body of Eugène Maréchal the police later found a small scrap of paper written in the hand of Barbès: "Marchand de vin/Rue Saint-Martin no. 10/2 heures 1/2."[71] The leaders attempted to put the police off the track by announcing late on Saturday, 11 May, that the insurrection was going to be postponed again; several undercover agents had arrived at the prefecture late that night with the news. Prefect Gabriel Delessert (who had replaced Gisquet in 1836) later claimed, on the contrary, that he had received certain confirmation that the attack would occur on the following day. He had taken no obvious precautions because he did not wish to disturb the city and fatigue the troops. He believed—correctly, as it turned out—that he had sufficient municipal guard forces to hold out for several hours until the Paris garrison could be mobilized.[72]

The *sectionnaires* gathered, as ordered, on Sunday the twelfth. That afternoon, cafés throughout the Right Bank, in the terrain of the two previous insurgencies of 1832 and 1834, found their business better than usual. Boniface Lecuze, on the corner of the rue Saint-Martin and the rue aux Ours, reported that at 1 P.M. some 20 or 30 young men had suddenly arrived and "established themselves"—some "playing cards, others going and coming, others banging on the counter or walking up and down the street in front of my establishment." At 3 P.M. he was abruptly deserted as they "hurled themselves" outside; a dozen of them returned later to build a barricade with his tables and stools. Louis Bernier, on the corner of the rue aux Ours and rue Quincampoix, had taken note of the many strangers who had dropped in at 2 P.M.: "They were not of the same trade and yet they were fraternizing together." Puzzled by this, he had kept his ears open as he moved through the hall to serve them; various remarks about "finishing today" so they would not lose their jobs led him to conclude that it was something related to a workers' coalition. Suddenly, a newcomer stuck his head in the bar: "'Come quickly, it's time!'" His customers jumped up to follow "like a flight of pigeons," leaving opened bottles and unfinished drinks as they rushed into the street. And finally, café-keeper François Regnard on the rue Bourg l'Abbé—the starting point of the insurrection—was patronized by a small but mysterious group of well-dressed strangers who kept looking out the door. Suddenly, they all surged outside to meet several men who had just pulled up in a coach, shouting, "'Now's the time, come quickly!'"[73]

Blanqui had kept his troops in the area for more than an hour, as he scouted the somnolent government buildings in the center of the city. He returned to this café on the rue Bourg l'Abbé, where several of the secondary leaders were gathered, and his decision to proceed had triggered the series of alerts. Local residents heard excited shouts of "To Arms!" from young men running through the narrow streets, as the *sectionnaires* spread the word. At least two informants rushed for the prefecture of police.[74] The insurrection of 12 May 1839 had begun.

CHAPTER 7

MAY 1839:
LA GUERRE DES RUES, II

INSURRECTION WAS THE CLIMAX OF UNDERGROUND ACTIVITY, the goal to which all the meetings, *permanences*, reviews, and clandestine manufacture of cartridges were directed. But there was a tension between the self-assertive violence of a small vanguard and obedience to the popular will. To overcome this, republicans envisioned the insurgency as a moment when the people would rise as one, stirred by revolutionary rhetoric and the willingness of the avant-garde to expose themselves to the first bullets of their oppressors: expressive violence would become instrumental through the force of example. Montagnard republicans distinguished between a genuine revolution of the whole, and what they referred to as the *émeute* or *coup de main*—an isolated attempt by a small band to impose their will on the nation. The government always used these pejorative terms, of course; but nothing was worse for insurgents than to realize for themselves that no one followed them, that they were regarded with horror by the people they were attempting to liberate, that they were in fact guilty of placing their particular wills above the general will. Nothing was worse than an *émeute*.

The *Société des Saisons* insurrection of Sunday, 12 May 1839, was thoroughly planned: its army organized in *sections*, the ammunition provided beforehand, the leaders designated in advance. The *sectionnaires* had become accustomed to frequent reviews, any one of which might end in a call to arms, and they had been sworn to obedience. Their plans were aided by Paris geography. The Hôtel de Ville and the traditional insurgent *quartier* of Saint-Martin and Transnonain were within minutes of each other. The insurgents would also seize the nearby prefecture and the *mairies* of the sixth and seventh *arrondissements*, thus crippling the police and local national guards. In this secure central area, they would be impregnable; Parisians would rally to their side, and the republic would be proclaimed.[1]

It began to go wrong almost immediately.

The insurrection started on the Right Bank, on the rue Bourg l'Abbé (near the rue Saint-Martin), the location chosen because of the large Lepage weapons shop. The insurgents broke through the massive wooden shutters and hurled themselves inside, then threw hunting rifles and pistols out the windows to their comrades, in an operation that lasted for perhaps half an hour; Alphonse Lepage reported a loss of 310 rifles and 100 pairs of pistols.[2] On the same street lived Georges Meillard, a young Swiss jeweler who was one of the military leaders of the *Saisons;* as the Lepage shop was being emptied, he brought down from his apartment a heavy trunk full of cartridges. On the nearby rue Quincampoix, Barbès had left another trunk with his acquaintance, Mme. Roux; in her absence he broke down her door and carried it to the street. The *sectionnaires* were excited, singing the *Chant du Départ* and the *Marseillaise* and shouting revolutionary slogans; several fired into the air, at which Barbès "appeared vexed," according to a witness, and ordered them to stop.[3] Soon they rushed back to the Lepage shop and Blanqui.

But despite the impression of swiftness, it had been a slow start. The insurrection was supposed to resemble a whirlwind, sweeping all before it and engulfing Paris in a contagion of enthusiasm. But the initial pillaging had taken too long. Many *sectionnaires* were also discouraged by the visibly poor turnout. Printer Pierre Nouguès counted "300 soldiers"; another witness described "40 men" clustered around the Meillard trunk, with "200–300 men" in and around the Lepage shop.[4] Police spy Lucien Delahodde believed there were 500 to 600, of whom 300 at most took up arms, and Blanqui biographer Maurice Dommanget summarized the other estimates, which were as low as 150 to 200. Dommanget also cited an unpublished account by Blanqui ally Dr. Louis Lacambre (he thought there were 1,200 men, of whom more than half soon slipped away), who provided a grim description of the early moments: "Blanqui sought to give orders, to stop the desertions. . . . Everybody shouted. Everybody wanted to command, no one to obey. . . . Barbès accused Blanqui of having allowed everyone to leave, Blanqui accused Barbès of having discouraged everyone because of his slowness."[5] *Juillet* Alexandre Quarré told much the same story: "When I arrived, the rifles had already been distributed: it was a *pêle-mêle* and complete confusion, and it was easy to see that all principle of discipline was lacking in the gathering."[6] Nouguès recalled that several of the men had approached Martin-Bernard and demanded the names of the *conseil exécutif*, the powerful, prominent leaders who were to reveal themselves on the day of revolution. Martin-Bernard's answer (as Barbès and Blanqui quarreled in the background) could not have been satisfactory: "There's no council; we're the council."[7] The disgruntled band set off.

The Paris garrison usually hovered at around 30,000 men, but the key to its effectiveness was rapid deployment. "I have noted," later wrote General de Rumigny in his action report, "that one must strike quickly and strongly in the first moments, because discouragement spreads swiftly among [the *émeutiers*]."[8] On this occasion, the Line troops were fully active within a few hours, with some 650 infantry and 80 cavalry placed at Prefect Gabriel Delessert's disposition; additional companies left the Place du Carrousel headquarters between 6 P.M. and 7 P.M. But the Municipal Guard had essentially won the battle before the Line and national guard units could be fully mobilized; between 4 P.M. and 5:30 P.M., close to 150 men, in 5 separate foot and cavalry detachments, had been sent into the heart of the insurrection.[9]

Most of the *sectionnaires* initially headed toward the river. A 45-minute siege at the Châtelet post—manned by only 8 municipal guards and their commander—resulted in the death of Étienne-Martial Jubelin, a cook at the Café de Foy, and one of the military leaders.[10] Jean Fournier was the man who had first raised the tricolor above Notre-Dame in 1830 (he was a roofer, until a fall cost him his leg). He led a band of about 20 men in an attack on the Leyde weapons shop on the quay, obtaining 45 rifles and 27 pairs of pistols. They built barricades on the rue Planche-Mibray, blocking a major route to the Hôtel de Ville. A brief encounter with Municipal Guard Lieutenant Claude Ladroite's men had resulted in the deaths of two guards, and the bloodied *casque* of one of them soon decorated the main barricade. Several municipal guard detachments joined to drive the insurgents away. The death toll in the area was six (including the *jambe de bois* or "wooden leg" Fournier), and evenly divided between the two sides.[11]

The most significant of these early targets, because of its proximity to the prefecture of police, was the Palais de Justice. It was manned by 24 men of the 21st infantry of the Line, most of them young and inexperienced. Lieutenant Pierre Drouineau, warned in advance, had taken no precautions until the insurgents actually appeared on the horizon—60 of them, according to Corporal Martin Grossman; only "about 30," according to a civilian eyewitness. Drouineau refused Grossman's request that the men be allowed to load their weapons, no doubt mindful of the political and legal dangers of shooting into a crowd.[12]

This band had an obvious leader, a tall man in an unusually short dark frock coat who was later believed to have been Armand Barbès. Drouineau bravely went forward to speak to him; the insurgent chief told him to surrender his weapons, and Drouineau laconically replied, "Rather die!" In the version of events subsequently adopted by the prosecution, the *chef des insurgés* then shot Drouineau at point-blank range and gave the signal to attack.[13] But there would in fact be considerable debate, not only on the issue of whether Barbès was the chief (he almost certainly was) but—more significantly—on whether or not it was the chief who had actually shot Drouineau, a deed which Barbès emphatically denied.

A total of six soldiers were killed, three of whom died instantly; four others were wounded. The survivors on both sides fled, except for a few of the attackers who hastily looted the post. Moments later, the municipal guards arrived from the nearby prefecture of police, surrounding the area and firing on those still present. "They didn't know where to run," said a local resident who chased eight *sectionnaires* out of the alley beside his building.[14] Pierre Bonnefond, a cook with Jubelin at the Café de Foy, was captured in another alleyway, bleeding profusely and trying to hide his gun.[15] On the Left Bank, a café keeper on the rue de la Tannerie (near the present-day Boulevard Auguste-Blanqui) spotted a group of insurgents, "who appeared to be then in a rout," charging down his street. When one of them tossed a rifle he picked it up, noting that it appeared new and was loaded: "I scarcely held it than a man passing near me ripped it from my hands."[16] What was left of the band attacked the prefecture of police, but according to *Commissaire* Alexandre Vassal, there was not much of a battle: "Seven or eight of the boldest men fired on the Prefecture. . . . The Municipal Guard fired, we also fired, and the insurgents dispersed."[17]

Next came the attack, of great symbolic importance, on the Hôtel de Ville. It was protected only by a sleepy national guard post in front, with most of the eleven men on duty still dining in local cafés; the commander, Captain François Drouot, had no ammunition for those few who had ambled back. When Drouot was warned by a passing patrol of imminent attack, he had the call (*rappel*) beaten to summon additional men.[18] Most fled at the news of the Palais de Justice massacre. One guard frankly admitted his panic: "Towards 4 P.M. at the moment when I came off sentinel duty someone came to tell us that many people were coming and were going to kill us. I escaped . . . I only saw from afar a crowd of armed men." Louis Saugrin, in contrast, had rushed to the post: "I asked [Drouot] what we were going to do, he answered, we're going to defend ourselves, a soldier dies and does not surrender. I asked if he had any cartridges, he said no."[19]

Between 3:30 P.M. and 4 P.M. the armed group approached—30 to 40, according to the local *commissaire* and two of the guards, or 60 to 80, according to Saugrin—firing their weapons in the air and shouting "We want the Republic!" Captain Drouot bravely approached the band, saying "that he had accepted a position and would die there." One of the insurgents came forward to shake his hand. But the tenuous peace was broken when the crowd suddenly surged into the post. Guard Thomas Farjas was threatened: "'*Canaille*,' said a little man with a short nose and a bearded chin, 'you've made us suffer a long time, now it's your turn.'" Several others more reassuringly shouted "*Vive la Garde nationale.*" But Drouot was roughed up despite this, as he and fellow guard Joseph Devignon were dragged for some distance by the crowd. Devignon, rescued along the way, inquired that evening after his shaken captain: "[Drouot] told me that they had wanted to make him kneel and shoot him and that they had ripped off his epaulettes, his saber, his shako," before he had managed to escape. Jean Sadoul had merely been forced to give up his musket but added, "for two days I was sick with the vexation of having given up my weapon."[20]

At some point in the proceedings Barbès stood on the steps of the Hôtel de Ville—no one even attempted to enter the building—and finally read the Insurrectional Act, the "Executive Council" proclamation long promised to the *sectionnaires* on the day of revolution:

To arms, citizens!
The fatal hour has sounded for the oppressors.
The cowardly tyrant of the Tuileries laughs at the hunger which tears at the entrails of the people, but his crimes have reached their peak; they are finally going to receive their punishment. . . .

More and similar rhetoric followed. Republicans were advised to "strike and exterminate without pity the vile satellites, the willing accomplices of tyranny," but also to "hold out your hand to these soldiers, who come from out of your midst, who will not turn against you any parricidal weapons." The *Acte* (it went virtually unheard, but a copy was found in the Lepage shop) ended with an odd anticlimax, an assurance that proclamations and a decree of the "provisional government" were "in press." The designated military commanders were Blanqui as "commander in chief," along with Barbès, Martin-Bernard, Quignot, Meillard, and Nétré, the "commanders of divisions of the Republican Army." The members of the provisional government—the elusive *Conseil exécutif*—were Barbès, Voyer d'Argenson, Auguste Blanqui, Lamennais, Martin-

Bernard, Dubosc, and Laponneraye.[21] The investigation cleared Voyer d'Argenson, the socialist aristocrat; Lamennais, the priest and Christian socialist; and Laponneraye, recently convicted of a press offense. Prosper-Richard Dubosc, *Saisons* member and veteran of an ammunition case, formally denied having anything to do with the insurrection. The workers Jean Netré and Georges Meillard, wounded in the course of the day, managed to escape into exile; tailor Louis Quignot was sentenced to fifteen years.[22] And as for their conquest, it yielded an armory of only 40 muskets. Farjas noted a spontaneous exchange: those with Lepage hunting rifles replaced them with the national guard service models, those with pistols took the discarded rifles, and those with nothing grabbed up what was left.[23] At 4:45 P.M. the Municipal Guard retook the post, and at 6 P.M. General Trézel and his troops secured the area for the night.[24]

Barbès and Blanqui probably went directly to the Saint-Martin area, since neither was seen at the next two attacks. Instead, it was the Italian Benoît Ferrari, a political refugee and leader of the large contingent of hatters within the *Saisons*, who led the main group to the Marché Saint-Jean post in the seventh *arrondissement*, just to the north and east of the Hôtel de Ville.[25] Paris military plans listed it as one of the weak posts, incapable of defending itself; evacuation orders went out at 4 P.M., just too late to save it.[26] Sergeant Denis Girard of the 28th Line regiment and his 11 men had only a few minutes' warning from Antoine Morsaline, a passing tripe-seller. Girard ordered his men to take up arms; before they could load their weapons, according to one of the survivors, they saw an armed mass heading their way, shouting "Long live the Republic!" and demanding their surrender. Girard ordered his men to present bayonets. He, his corporal Alexis Henriet, and several soldiers estimated the band at three to four hundred, while two local residents saw no more than half that number. Girard noted that at least 50 to 60 had service muskets, an indication that many of the attackers were likely veterans of the Palais de Justice or the Hôtel de Ville.[27]

Sergeant Girard went forward and was immediately swallowed up by the crowd, who warned him that "blood was going to flow" unless he surrendered. They shouted at the soldiers to give up their weapons; one of the rank and file called back a refusal. The attackers fired suddenly and without warning. Several soldiers dropped immediately: "The insurgents rushed forward at the same time against the [remaining] soldiers who defended their weapons," recalled teacher Louis Riquier, "and one of them who had already been shot, had his head cracked open with a hatchet blow from one of the insurgents."[28] Of the 12 men on duty, 4 were killed and 3 were wounded.[29]

Sergeant Girard was cut off from his men but saw them fall, including the man whose head was laid open with a hatchet. He was forced to his knees, a rifle barrel against his chest, when someone intervened: "But Gentlemen, they are French as you are, leave them their lives"; the insurgent who had been about to kill the sergeant raised his gun. Girard had made his way to the fringes of the crowd when he was seized from behind by a dark, bearded man, whom he later recognized as the leader Ferrari. (The next time he saw Ferrari was on a slab in the *salle des morts* of the Hôtel-Dieu.) Ferrari ordered him to march with them or die. One of his men protested ("we have the weapons, let him go"); then a bourgeois intervened: "Yes, leave him, I'll answer for him." The second good samaritan, local resident Napoléon Josset, later took Girard back to his barracks.[30]

The remaining soldiers had fled into the post, pursued by the most furious of their assailants. Tripe-seller Morsaline spoke to a man with an axe and pistols stuck in his belt: "There are enough of you to take the weapons from these soldiers, without murdering them like this." The aggressor backed away.[31] "When I saw my comrades fall," admitted one of the soldiers, "I placed my musket against the wall and said to the one who approached me, to take it."[32] Printer Pierre Nouguès later recalled that he had knelt by one of the wounded soldiers "and I asked him if he wanted to get even with us, seeking to persuade him that we deplored the necessity in which we found ourselves. This *malheureux* died in pardoning us"—a rather more touching version of the scene than other testimony suggested.[33] But one small band led by Jean Dubourdieu, a member of the extremist *Montagnard* splinter group, had indeed carried a wounded soldier to a nearby physician; his good deed allowed several witnesses to get a clear look at him, and he was sentenced to ten years.[34] The attackers departed precipitously, leaving not even a token force. At 5:30 P.M. *Commissaire* Charles Loyeux found the post in a shambles: a corpse extended on the camp bed, placed there by several of the rescuers, along with sacks, shakos, and cartridge pouches, all liberally covered with blood.[35]

Ferrari next led his excited band to the *mairie* of the seventh *arrondissement* on the rue des Francs-Bourgeois, manned that day by 20 national guards who had muskets but no ammunition; the mayor told them to hide their guns in the latrines. When Ferrari realized that the national guards were not going to resist, "he seemed to give the order to suspend all assaults," and about 100 insurgents entered the courtyard, with the rest, perhaps 100 more, remaining in the street.[36] "They fired some shots in the air," recalled mayor's Deputy Jacques Levaillain, "and shouted, '*Vive la République*, down with the tyrant; the people have died of hunger for too long; down with the tyrant, this is his last day; liberty or death'; and other similar things." National Guard Prosper Thibault recalled that "they said they did not want to spill any blood, that their cause was ours." Several of the group attempted to fraternize, approaching the guards to shake their hands.[37]

Ferrari promised they would come to no harm if they gave up their weapons. But the appearance of the band was not reassuring: one of those who kept his rifle constantly trained on them, remembered the mayor, had "red trousers and a face speckled with blood"; another had a "repulsive face" and a contusion on his nose, and was "dirty and badly-dressed." One man carried an axe, which seemed to be matted with blood and hair. And indeed, they described what had just occurred: "They told us that blood was going to flow, they were going to sacrifice us though we were fathers of families, they had just killed several soldiers, they were very sorry but it was for the good cause. . . ."[38]

The post had a depot of more than 150 service muskets, hidden and under lock and key. A search soon turned up the 20 in the latrines; in a bold lie the mayor told them there were no more, and the group fell into bickering. Lieutenant Levasseur heard arguments over whether or not to kill anyone. Some were angrily shouting, "'there must be blood, pay with blood, no concessions, there have always been too many.'" A tall man with a grizzled beard said "there were too many concessions, it was necessary to finish it, they had been deceived too often, blood was necessary."[39] The drummers (two were killed, two wounded within the next hour, in beating the *rappel*) suddenly found themselves menaced. The man with the axe became their unlikely protector: "I'll kill anyone who touches the drummers; we don't want to do any harm, we only want weapons. We've suffered a long time, we're workers, things must change." Finally, indecisively, they departed, leaving the floor splattered with drops of blood.[40]

Most headed toward the sixth *mairie*, on the rue Saint-Martin; controlling the mayoralty building would allow them to dominate the traditional insurgent quarter. There they joined a substantial number of men who had remained in the area all afternoon. A café employee had heard the first rumors about the sacking of the Lepage shop when "40 or 50 armed insurgents" entered his café, forcing him to serve them: "Some paid, others didn't, they remained thus during about an hour going and coming and drinking."[41] By late afternoon the locals noted a renewed invasion. An armed band with two drummers arrived at about 4:30 P.M., its size estimated at anywhere from 150 to 400; some sheared off to build barricades or go house-to-house for weapons. A resident of the rue Transnonain spotted a group at 5 P.M., preceded by two "scouts" and a drummer. He described the chief of the band as short; otherwise, the description (black hair and beard, short black frock coat, broad chest, a "very energetic" countenance) fit Barbès. The leader was making speeches, urging "unity" as they marched, punctuating his remarks with an épée; his rifle was slung across his back in a bandolier.[42]

The most important barricade in the area was at the entrance of the rue Greneta, a small street which linked the two large parallel throughways of Saint-Martin and Saint-Denis. Its strategic purposes were to keep the government troops from using Greneta as a passageway and to threaten the nearby sixth *mairie*, just a few yards away. The construction had begun at about 4:30 P.M. according to Boniface Samson, the bartender in Duval's café on the corner, who had unwillingly contributed tables and stools, as well as wine and eau-de-vie.[43] Later the insurgents had turned the café into an improvised field hospital, and he estimated that 45 to 50 had received rudimentary first aid; three corpses were left inside. According to the investigating *commissaire*, "There existed in the establishment of M. Samson a frightening disorder, and a great quantity of blood spread onto the pavement of the street. . . ."[44]

Because of the presence of Barbès, Blanqui, and Martin-Bernard, the Greneta battle later came to be regarded as decisive. The mayoralty building had been reinforced shortly after 4 P.M. by Lieutenant Jean-Pierre Leblond and 20 municipals. At approximately 4:45 P.M., a large group of insurgents joined those already at the barricade. Lieutenant Leblond, with nearly half of his men escorting a national guard drummer, withdrew into the *mairie*, with about 30 national guards who had reported in response to the *rappel*. The insurgents held the street unchallenged for more than half an hour but did not move directly against the mayoralty. At about 5:20 P.M., Leblond's lookouts reported the arrival of Lieutenant Émile Tisserand with 44 men. Leblond and a number of the national guards, having slipped out the back, joined Tisserand's attack against the barricade, and the two sides engaged in a brisk exchange of fire for perhaps 45 minutes.[45]

Lieutenant (soon to be Captain) Tisserand had left the barracks on the rue Saint-Martin at 5:10 P.M. At first he found himself surrounded by a "dense but inoffensive" crowd who told him to turn back, "saying that my detachment was too weak and I would inevitably be cut to pieces." National Guard Jules Pelletier had joined his troop: "I placed myself behind him. We hugged both sides of the street, extending ourselves along the buildings; having arrived near the barricade, we came under the fire of the insurgents at point-blank range; several municipal guards were wounded." Sublieutenant François Cauche saw four insurgents fall in the initial exchange. Tisserand finally ordered his men into the courtyard to regroup.[46]

Tisserand's version of the events that followed put himself in a heroic light (a view echoed by all the eyewitnesses). Armed with his épée, he had led his men against the barricade at attack speed, ordering them "to give no quarter to those who had weapons in hand." The insurgents, Tisserand recalled,

> . . . received me with a rolling fire, at point-blank range; one of them, placed at the right angle of the barricade, fired at me at point-blank range; when I found myself upon him, [he attempted] a gunshot to the head. He missed me in his precipitation; I ran him through with an épée and saw him fall a few steps away. I leaped onto the barricade, but at this moment a second insurgent who was going to fire, who was knee to the ground, placed his rifle barrel on my chest; I was nimble enough to run him through with my épée. This unfortunate one in falling convulsively seized my legs and dragged me in his fall; my shako was crushed under us.[47]

The battle of Greneta soon took on great emotional significance for republicans because Barbès fell there—not killed, as it was later discovered, but left unconscious and bleeding from a head wound, a sight that demoralized those few who had not fled. Though Blanqui refused to discuss the events publicly, his lawyer Dupont later published his account. In the final moments the barricade had been defended by "no more than a dozen of us," Blanqui had said; and the first exchange "had reduced the number of combatants to seven or eight." As for Barbès, "We believed to have left in the hands of our adversaries only the body of a hero."[48] But somehow in the confusion Barbès had picked himself up and escaped, wandering through the cordoned area for several hours until arrested by Lieutenant Leblond. Barbès gave his name as Paul Durocher; Leblond soon recognized him from the rue de l'Oursine trial: "Immediately he said: 'Kill me, I'm lost!'" To Captain Michel Godquin of the 6th Legion, Barbès said that "he was done for [*un homme perdu*], and showing me his head wound he told me the bullet had merely grazed the skin, that he regretted it had not hit him two inches more to the right. . . ."[49]

Another casualty was the tall and blond Florentz (Fritz) Austen, age 23, a Polish bootmaker born in Danzig, Prussia, who was found unconscious at the foot of the barricade. A youthful veteran of the Polish insurrection of 1831, Austen had lived in France since 1836. The authorities believed him to be associated with radical German refugee groups in Paris. Austen denied membership in any society and claimed that he had found himself in the rue Greneta merely "by chance."[50] After Austen was convicted, he wrote two letters and hid them so clumsily that the authorities believed them to have been written, for some obscure reason, to be found. One, to another bootmaker, provided a vivid account of the Greneta battle: "I rushed with my rifle against the enemies when I saw Barbès fall, and hoped to defend our barricade; but it was too late, the municipal guard advances, I see the comrades retreat." Lieutenant Tisserand had seen a man to the right of him shoot and miss, then take aim again. His account coincided with that of Austen, who claimed he had tried to shoot the commander but missed, hitting instead a rank-and-file guard behind him, who collapsed to the ground. "Immediately I load my rifle in the heat of combat, I take aim, but it is too late . . . as quickly as I take aim, someone [Tisserand] plunges the épée into my chest. I turn around and I see nothing but dead and wounded lying around me."[51]

Tisserand had killed Émile Maréchal by running him through; his account of the victim's convulsive death grip around his knees later caused a visible response in the courtroom.[52] Maréchal had been in his early twenties, an upwardly mobile engineer. His friend Eugène Moulines claimed he had been a great admirer of the priest Lamennais, author of the popular *Paroles d'un Croyant*, and had learned passages of the book by heart. "He declaimed them with fire . . . he put himself in a fury when one contradicted him on these occasions," remembered Moulines; "I recall also that he established parallels between Moses, Jesus Christ and Lamennais." But he was also a great partisan of Barbès, and wanted equality and the return of the republic of 1793.[53]

Maréchal left behind a young laundress, Élise Mennesson, with whom he had a child. The police found a sad, nagging letter from her, written at the end of March: "I'm not giving you any news of your daughter, since you're scarcely interested in whether she is ill or well."[54] Afterward, Élise came to the Hôpital Saint-Louis to look for him; when she recognized his body she went into shock, trembling uncontrollably.[55] She was the chief mourner at his funeral; her mother went with her, "in order not to leave her alone." The following day, her stepfather forced her out of the house. Élise told the authorities she knew nothing of Maréchal's politics; but then her mother, naively trusting in authority, confessed that her daughter had sworn vengeance: "I know that she says the republicans are her brothers. She has abjured Catholicism to take up the pretended religion of Châtel [a republican church]. In a word my daughter, if she's not taken from these societies, will finish by turning very bad."[56] Élise was put under arrest as a result of her mother's revelations. The police learned that she had spoken wildly, adopting Charlotte Corday as her model (an oddly popular figure, though she had killed the republican Marat); she vowed to assassinate the king. She was given shelter by Mme. Laponneraye, the mother of the republican journalist.[57]

Night slowly extinguished the revolt. National Guard André Brulé was caught up in a crowd of 60 disillusioned men in the early evening: "The individuals I was with said that if their society put out they would be at least 1,500, but it didn't put out."[58] A national guard on his way to the *mairie* was stopped by a gang variously numbered by witnesses at 8 to 40 men, who began to rough him up: "You're going to slaughter your brothers! When your brothers are devoting themselves to the happiness of all!" His fumbled explanation about answering the *rappel* fell on deaf ears, and he was saved only by a neighbor who appealed to fair play: "What the devil, don't kill a man you've just disarmed, leave him be."[59] A bourgeois on the rue Mondétour was attacked at 7:30 P.M. by a band of ten men who demanded his gun and informed him that "We want to purge the nation this evening."[60] Louis-François Dantan, a 26-year-old mechanic and one of the *Saisons* commanders, was mortally wounded in a minor engagement on the rue Pastourelle at 6:30 P.M.[61] National Guard Ledoux of the 3rd Legion was killed nearby on the rue Tiquetonne, shot as his detachment advanced on the barricade and its 20 defenders. Sergeant Anselme Boyer rushed to Ledoux and spoke to him; receiving no answer, "I raised him up, and seeing the blood flow in abundance from his stomach, I saw he was a dead man."[62]

By this time the chiefs were gone: dead (Jubelin), wounded (Meillard, Netré, Dantan, Barbès), or vanished (Blanqui, Martin-Bernard). The only one left was Benoît Ferrari, who had led the way at the Marché Saint-Jean and the seventh *mairie*, and who now commanded on the rue Saint-Denis. This street, one of the main thoroughfares, was heavily barricaded; insurgents also took to the buildings, conducting a "war of the windows" against soldiers slowed by the obstructions in the street. A particularly bothersome barricade was at the corner of Aubry-le-Boucher and Saint-Denis, about three feet high and composed of stalls from the nearby market, disconcertingly still piled with baskets of eggs and vegetables. Though it looked abandoned, its defenders fired from the cover of nearby corners and buildings.[63] Another difficult barricade was at the junction of Saint-Denis and Greneta, composed of tables from a nearby café with an overturned omnibus on top of the pile. Wedged between the spokes of a wheel was a stick to which was affixed a scrap of red cloth.[64]

The arrival of the soldiers was signaled by the sound of their "heavy and prolonged" march; insurgents tossed their guns as they ran.[65] A detachment from the 53rd regiment of the Line under Colonel Ballon arrived between 7 P.M. and 7:30 P.M., taking the pile of produce. As they marched against the red-flag barricade the insurgents abandoned it, once again taking to the side streets; a sergeant was mortally wounded by a shot from an alley. From the opposite direction came General de Lascours and a combined Line and national guard detachment. After a fierce exchange of fire, the troops finally captured the street.[66]

In the course of the fighting Marie Guillateaux, who lived just off the rue Saint-Denis, realized that several insurgents had entered her building: "While shots were still being fired, I heard an individual climbing the stairs who appeared to be suffering; he knocked at my door, I asked who was there, he answered that he was wounded." She took him in. It was the 19-year-old locksmith Nicolas Lionnet, only hours away from death. "It appears that in the trouble this young man caused me," she continued, "I forgot to close my door; because soon I heard noise, I turned and saw several armed individuals, one of them drunk; he asked me if I would care to receive a wounded man." She was too intimidated to refuse. The casualty was dark, in his late thirties, with a wound in his right arm and a hole in his chest; she was later told that his name was Ferrari. One of the men attempted to cut off the sleeve of his jacket. She could not understand Ferrari's faint protest, but the other man reassured him: "'Be tranquil, I'm a tailor, I'll sew it up again.'" Ferrari and Lionnet were later taken to the pharmacy, then to the home of the local physician, and finally to their last stop at the Hôtel-Dieu.[67]

Dr. François Robertet had already told the insurgents on his street to bring him all the wounded, on both sides. His first patient was a young man who had been shot in the back. Robertet asked no questions, but was told that "the troops were beginning to be repulsed and the insurgents were beginning to have the upper hand." Soon a group brought Antoine Fombertaux, father of Eugène (who had been recently imprisoned as one of the publishers of the underground newspaper *Le Moniteur républicain*). Both men were later able to make their way home. The dying Ferrari and Lionnet were carried to Robertet's clinic after the last exchange of fire. Lionnet said that he had fought alongside 80 insurgents. Ferrari "made difficulties" about identifying himself; though mortally wounded, he "showed himself to be very exalted. He was armed with a freshly-sharpened dagger; he said that he was happy to die for the cause he had embraced, adding that he had fought by the bayonet and had wounded several people."[68]

Soon the combatants could be seen in flight, leaping from roof to roof or climbing over courtyard walls. The last battle occurred at the barricade in the cul-de-sac Saint-Magloire; it had been built in the late afternoon by a dozen men, in the courtyard shared by two transport businesses, and was constructed from their various equipages. The bourgeois Julien Garnot had observed them from his window through the afternoon and evening: "Before the shooting they traveled up and down and stood guard. . . . Some said, 'we don't have any chiefs, who wants to command?' Another in a black *casquette* and very well-dressed in a black coat said: 'whoever isn't disposed to fight, let him lay down his weapons and withdraw'; he recommended not to murder anyone, not to kill the national guards and to fire only on the troops." Garnot also recalled another whom he would recognize "among a thousand," a shabby little man with no socks and a red cap: "He was at least 40 years old and all in rags, the other insurgents had the air of not wanting to go with him."[69] The cul-de-sac was finally taken after 9 P.M.; its defenders had exchanged fire with the troops for nearly three hours.[70]

By late evening it was over. The government crisis ended when the reliable Marshal Soult formed a cabinet.[71] At 10 P.M. the soldiers were promised a double ration of wine, the cavalry horses a double ration of oats. At 10:30 P.M. it was reported that "free circulation" had been restored to all parts of the city; at 11 P.M. the military command ordered half the troops back to their barracks. At 3 A.M., commanding officers were authorized to retire, leaving their seconds in charge. At daybreak the young princes Orléans, Nemours, and Joinville, accompanied by Marshal Gérard and General Pajol, rode through the streets; later that day the king and all five of his sons reviewed the troops.[72]

Monday saw several feeble attempts to revive the revolt, but the city was quickly put back in order, the paving stones replaced. The Gérard plan, named after its creator Marshal Gérard, the commander of the Paris National Guard from 1838 to 1842, was soon unveiled. As described by historian Louis Girard, it placed a heavy initial burden on the National Guard, who were to hold their neighborhoods until the Line troops could be concentrated to crush the insurrection. The plan was pronounced successful against the worker demonstrations of 1840, but it would not receive a real test until February 1848.[73]

The death toll was slightly higher than in 1834, claiming about 25 to 30 more lives than the earlier insurrection. A total of 28 defenders of the government were killed, most of them from the Line regiments; 60 were wounded. Civilian deaths numbered around 66, including 5 women. Of these, 27 could be identified as innocent bystanders, while 12 were definitely insurgents and 3 were probables; there was too little information to determine the status of the rest.[74] In calculations based on the 323 individuals, both dead and arrested, for whom there was information, Claude Latta found that an overwhelming 87 percent of them were from the working classes.[75]

Many innocent victims died without realizing that an insurrection had started. Alcindor Leclers, a 20-year-old grocery clerk who lived near the Marché Saint-Jean, heard noise and went to his doorstep, where he was shot in the head.[76] Alphonse Élu, a porcelain painter, was out for a Sunday of pleasure; as he and his friends passed near the Châtelet, he was shot through the heart and fell dead.[77] François Wilmot, a housepainter, was stripping wall-paper in an apartment on the rue Dauphine, overlooking the Palais de Justice. At the sound of the disturbances he and his comrade Claude Jacquet both put their heads out the window. Jacquet felt "something shave my neck," and he turned back to see Wilmot fall dead to the floor, shot in the eye.[78] Minette Wolff, an 18-year-old shawlmaker, occupied a fifth-floor apartment on the rue Quincampoix. While rushing to get inside, she was hit in the head by a stray bullet and killed instantly.[79]

In the aftermath, the police received a number of reports from nervous Parisians. A certain Maugé, a porter on the rue Portefoin, was said by his neighbors and tenants to be "a very bad character and a very exalted republi-can": "[Maugé] did not, they say, take part, weapons in hand, in the insurrec-tion of 12 and 13 May, but we are assured in effect that during these two days he drank continually with the makers of the sedition [factieux]."[80] On 20 May, a woman reported fragments of a conversation she had overheard on the street among five young men, which included the phrases "faubourg Saint-Antoine" and "ten thousand men," with apparent references to seizing "all the posts at the same time" and blowing them up; the new attempt was to take place in a month.[81] The coachman L. Millot denounced his acquaintance Amant, a printer, who had tried to entice him into battle by boasting of "four or five hundred men" who would overturn the government and capture the prefec-tures: "In this short conversation," Millot recalled, "he trembled like a leaf."[82]

From the murky world of police spies, an undercover agent reported a con-versation with the cook Napoléon Bazin, last seen at the Greneta barricade and believed dead. Undaunted, Bazin had confided future plans for an insurrection "in a month, five weeks at most"; his group had been assured of full cooperation by the faubourg Saint-Antoine and the Montagnards: "Thus we have nothing to fear, we have a weapons depot all ready, but this time whenever we take a post we'll have to burn it"—apparently to be the only innovation in strategy.[83] Much early police speculation involved Blanqui, who had disappeared during the evening of 12 May. The famous split between Blanqui and Barbès, a fixture of subsequent decades, received perhaps its earliest recounting in a scrap of an in-formant's note to the prefect of police, which described a quarrel in the heat of battle: "[Blanqui] having realized shortly after the beginning of combat that the enterprise had failed, said to his friend Barbès, chief like himself, that he in-tended to withdraw; Barbès said he was free to, but he [himself] would remain to the end."[84] The questions about Blanqui's role would fester through the 1840s, surfacing in 1848 with the Taschereau document. In the 1850s, republican pris-oners would be divided into two camps, of Barbès and of Blanqui.[85]

Nearly 700 men were held while their cases were investigated, to be released only after some weeks or months in custody.[86] Blanqui was not arrested until October, just as he was about to flee to Switzerland; he was tried before the *Cour des Pairs* in January, along with 33 others.[87] To Barbès, of course, went the glory of a battlefield capture. Martin-Bernard, the third member of the Executive Council, was at liberty until 21 June, when the police discovered him in hiding in a room behind a bakery; he had whiled away his seclusion by drafting a new oath for a post-insurrection society.[88] He and Barbès were tried with 17 others in June and July. The defendants were indicted under the usual articles 87, 88, 89, and 91 of the Penal Code—with attempts to destroy or change the government, to incite citizens to arm themselves against the government, or to incite civil war—and Barbès and the ditchdigger Jean-Antoine Mialon were additionally accused of the murders of Lieutenant Drouineau and Maréchal des Logis Jonas, respectively, the latter deliberately gunned down from ambush.[89]

In contrast to the party celebrities who had attempted the "republican congress" in 1835, the men of the two trials of 1839 made a poor showing: a parade of unknowns who claimed, one after the other, that they had been unwilling participants caught up by insurgent masses, rifles thrust into their unready hands. ("We fought, that is to say they, for the Republic," stumbled one of them, when asked his motives.[90]) In the first trial only Barbès attempted a political demonstration, in taking full responsibility for the insurrection in his opening statement:

> I declare that on 12 May at 3 P.M., all of these citizens [his co-defendants] were unaware of our project to attack your government . . . that I made the signal, put weapons in their hands, and gave them the order to march. . . . I declare that I took part; and that I fought against your troops. . . .

There was a great deal in this speech to irritate the *Cour des Pairs* ("your government," "your troops") and even perhaps some of his fellow *sociétaires*, who might have preferred not to think of themselves as helpless pawns. But Barbès firmly denied that he had killed Lieutenant Drouineau at the Palais de Justice, "an act of which I am neither guilty nor capable [*ni coupable ni capable*]."[91] Despite seriously conflicting eyewitness testimony, both Barbès and Mialon were convicted of murder and sentenced to death. Barbès' impending execution resulted in a silent march to the Luxembourg by over a thousand students and workers, which had the effect of hardening conservative resolve.[92] But Louis-Philippe always preferred mercy, and in this instance Victor Hugo provided him with an excuse for it, in a four-line poem that mingled the recent death of the king's daughter, Marie, with the birth of his first grandson: "Mercy once more! Mercy in the name of the tomb! Mercy in the name of the cradle!" He commuted the penalty to life imprisonment on 14 July 1839.[93]

The second part of the case began on 13 January 1840, a dismal mopping-up of 33 obscure defendants whose cases had been too weak for the first round—with the exception, of course, of the recently captured Blanqui. As Barbès had done before him, Blanqui wished to make an opening statement, and he chose an implicit defense of Barbès's action at the Palais de Justice:

> Thirty men were standing in battle order; the insurgents, in the number of 30 to 40 poorly armed individuals, had arrived at the [Palais de Justice] without firing a single shot. . . . It has been said that the soldiers did not have their weapons loaded; but how could the insurgents have known that?[94]

The Peers did not like his speech, but even for republicans it was a miserable failure, with the undesired effect of stirring indignation anew about events seven months in the past. His lawyer Dupont felt compelled to publish an explanation after the trial. Blanqui would have preferred to take full responsibility for the insurrection, but Barbès had preempted him.[95] Nor could Blanqui mount a defense. In his closing argument, the prosecutor Franck-Carré had played upon the controversy in republican ranks: Barbès had been with his men to the last, while Blanqui, the mastermind, had avoided the worst consequences of what he had himself set in motion: "When the defeated insurrection tries its last and perilous efforts, the chief has disappeared."[96]

Dupont had been forced to renounce the *plaidoirie:* if he had pointed to the weakness of the case against his client, to the virtual absence of witnesses who could place him on the scene, then he would merely have strengthened Franck-Carré's unsubtle accusations of cowardice and betrayal. "You know," he had told Blanqui, "since your defeat of 12 May, numerous accusations have been directed against you by your conquered partisans. Shouts of treason have been raised against you." Dupont did not believe any of these slanders; moreover, both Barbès and Martin-Bernard had assured him that Blanqui had acted bravely: "they charged me to shake your hand if I came to see you again." Blanqui, concerned for his reputation and certain to be convicted anyway, had approved his lawyer's decision.[97] His death sentence led to no demonstrations. Since the other capital condemnations of Barbès and Mialon (both additionally convicted of murder) had been commuted, it was generally assumed that

Blanqui would receive royal clemency as well. On 1 February 1840, Blanqui's sentence was revised to life imprisonment.[98]

Blanqui continued to be beset with accusations of desertion, but he also aroused intense devotion. In 1849, when he was at the beginning of yet another lengthy prison term—he would be released only in 1859—his supporters published a pamphlet about the *Saisons* insurrection. Could the men who had since become his loudest critics—Martin-Bernard, Netré, Quignot—provide proof that they had remained on the field of battle until the bitter end? As a "general," Blanqui had had special responsibility for observing the enemy and adjusting his strategy. But he had also served as a soldier; his defenders had seen him at the barricades of Greneta and Saint-Magloire, "and when he was obliged to abandon the terrain like so many others, we could tell you where he threw his musket."[99]

Despite the failure of the insurrection, Blanqui continued to believe it possible to take power by taking Paris. He believed that "revolutions . . . are made by men," evidence of his commitment to the potential of human agency; the difference between success and failure lay in effective planning.[100] In 1868–69, he wrote his *Instructions pour une prise d'armes*, a brief essay about the 1848 June Days which was not published until after his death. It marked the culmination of his experience in waging what he referred to as *la guerre des rues*; but also, paradoxically—though this was not his intent—showed the impossibility of planning such ventures in advance:

> The essential thing, is to organize. No more of these tumultuous uprisings, of 10,000 isolated heads, acting at random, in disorder, with no thought of unity, each in his corner and according to his fantasy! No more of these barricades here, there, and everywhere, which waste time, encumber streets, hinder traffic circulation, as necessary to one party as to the other. No useless races, *tohu-bohu*, clamor! Minutes and steps are equally precious.

What he prescribed for the insurgency was an essentially military structure based on battalions, companies, and divisions, each unit with its own "officers" and distinguishing color, signified by ribbons.[101] The officers, chosen in advance, would impose discipline on the insurgents who rushed to the fight: "To engage them to silence and calm, to address a brief allocution to them. . . . To invite all those who have served in the army or belonged to the National

Guard to step out from the ranks and present themselves in front of the line."
(In assuming silent ranks of expectant combatants—"ten thousand" of them—
had he forgotten the chaos thirty years earlier on the rue Bourg l'Abbé?)
Those designated for any level of command would be put in charge of their
men, and "lieutenants" and "sergeants" would receive on the spot a printed
sheet of instructions explaining "the organization of the popular army and the
diverse measures to take."[102]

Then they would distribute ribbons and flags, and administer the oath
that pledged all combatants to remain in the field until the republic was won.
Blanqui also included a sample proclamation to soldiers, appealing to them in
class terms and stressing the scorn shown them by their officers.[103] The next
step was to distribute arms, the weapons presumably acquired, as always, by
raiding weapons shops and military posts. As the first units moved to their assigned stations, they would "organize" (or perhaps engulf, as countless 1839
defendants complained) those volunteers they found along the way. A committee of *sûreté publique* would have as its task "to thwart the plots of the police
and the maneuvers of counterrevolutionaries."[104]

The barricades, their placement determined by the commander-in-chief,
would remain in communication with each other, republican soldiers shifting
from one location to another as dictated by the requirements of defense. Nor
would they be built haphazardly as before, mere "unformed heaps of paving
stones, intermixed with vehicles on the flank, with beams and planks."[105] Instead Blanqui's ideal barricade was complicated, a two-part construction consisting of a rampart and back wall [*contregarde*], approximately six meters
apart, each three meters in height. Blanqui calculated, given the average
street width, that a typical barricade would require 9,186 paving stones—or
put another way, one would have to dig up approximately 48 meters of the
road. The detachment in charge of construction would report with sacks of
plaster (for the stones were not simply to be piled, as usual), as well as "wheel-
barrows, hand carts, levers, pikes, spades, pickaxes, hammers, cold chisels,
trowels, buckets, troughs." The revolutionary army could avoid having to
stagger through the city under its burden of tools by requisitioning the supplies from local merchants.[106]

The barricade was to serve as "barrier" rather than battlefield, for the
true *poste de combat* was the window—as the victors of 1830 had fought:
"From the moment [the enemy] attempts to pass, one must shoot to the ut-
most, overwhelm him with rocks and paving stones from the tops of buildings," as well as "bottles full of water, even furniture, for lack of other

projectiles."[107] As soon as the street barricade was completed, they would create what Blanqui called "lateral barricades," by cutting through the walls of all the attached houses on both sides of the street; he recommended they cut through the first and topmost floors, to give themselves two separate routes. (Blanqui's idea was not new; such interior breakthroughs had been reported in June 1848.[108]) Doors, or shelves in stores, could be turned into shields for windows or balconies simply by cutting small notch holes to shoot through.[109] And, writing in the post-Haussmann era, Blanqui saw the spacious sewers as new terrain to be contested: subterranean barricades would be necessary to prevent troops from mining the streets.[110]

Blanqui's recommendations were hardly practical; indeed, he seemed to wish for nothing so much as a professional army and a corps of engineers (a recent edition has stressed the utopian quality of his tract). But he nevertheless revealed longstanding frustrations with *la guerre des rues* as it was practiced, and he criticized the individualism of previous efforts:

> Five, ten, twenty, thirty, fifty men, having come together by chance, the majority unarmed, begin to overturn vehicles, lift and pile paving stones to bar the public roads, sometimes in the middle of streets, more often at their intersection. . . . All of that is done with neither concert nor direction, according to individual whim.

Eventually a few barricades, "higher, stronger, better built," would attract a concentration of defenders; but even these barricades might not be (and indeed, probably were not) built at strategic locations.[111] Even a formidable barricade was not likely to be well-defended: "The soldiers [insurgents] do what comes into their head. They remain, they leave, they return, according to their *bon plaisir.* At night, they go to bed." The men of such barricades were generally without chiefs, without news, and without a grand strategy: "Of what is going on elsewhere one knows nothing and cares less."[112] (Wrote Norbert Truquin, a participant in the June Days: "The combatants went home at night and returned to the barricades at break of day; they had no chiefs; each fought according to his own whim."[113]) Instead of taking the fight to the enemy, they were more than likely to be in the nearest café, listening "peacefully to the cannons and fusillades" elsewhere in the city as their brothers were cut down. With this "system," defeat was all but inevitable: "It arrives in the end in the person of two or three regiments who fall upon the barricade and destroy the few defenders. The entire battle is

only the monotonous repetition of this invariable maneuver. While the insurgents smoke their pipes behind their heap of paving stones, the enemy
brings all his forces successively on one point, then on a second, a third, a
fourth, and he thus exterminates the insurrection *en détail.*"[114]

Could *la guerre des rues* be won by men, or did a successful revolution wait
upon the evolution of impersonal socioeconomic forces? Blanqui believed it
could be won; he bet his life on it.

PART III

✝✝✝✝✝✝

ASSASSINATION

CHAPTER 8

FIESCHI'S INFERNAL MACHINE

BETWEEN 1834 AND 1839, THE FAILURES OF the republican movement, on the streets and in the courtroom, left something of a vacuum. It was filled, briefly and clumsily, by the assassins. The would-be regicides, though mostly republican in sentiment, were on the margins of republican groups, or even outside them altogether; the personal motives that drove them to violence were merely shaped by political unrest, without being caused by it. Republicans despised the actors (with one striking exception) but, in the absence of a major underground society, hesitantly applauded their acts.

The era of assassinations began on 28 July 1835 with Joseph Fieschi's deployment of his "infernal machine," a multi-barreled weapon that left 18 dead and 22 seriously wounded, including government luminaries and ordinary bystanders.[1] The occasion was the king's annual review of the Paris National Guard, held on the anniversary of the revolution that had put him in power. Louis-Philippe rode on horseback through the streets of Paris; his itinerary was published in advance.

It was noon when the king and his entourage, including his sons Orléans, Nemours, and Joinville, reached the Boulevard du Temple. Suddenly there was a terrible explosion—"like a ragged platoon fire," according to one of the military men present—and the street was filled with the dead and dying.[2] Men and horses dropped immediately, and in the vivid words of a witness there was suddenly "a void around the king."[3] Napoleonic war hero Marshal Mortier and his horse lay in a bloody heap on the pavement. Lieutenant-Colonel Rieussec of the 8th Legion was killed instantly. Colonel Raffet, *commandant* of the Gendarmerie, turned as if to give orders and fell to the ground; he died several hours later. The crowd panicked, rushing in all directions. The billiard room and garden of the nearby Café Turc became a makeshift morgue.[4]

The king and his sons galloped across the scene of destruction; Joinville remembered that they "counted themselves" as the review continued, determining which of their party were gone.[5] Later Louis-Philippe realized he had been struck by a spent ball, hard enough to cause a serious bruise on the side of his head.[6] Nevertheless, he continued for two additional hours along the original route; as planned, he reviewed the national guards as they filed before him on the Place Vendôme. Only at 5 P.M., nearly five hours later, did Louis-Philippe finally go home to the Tuileries.[7]

Immediately after the attack, everyone on the boulevard du Temple noted the thick black smoke rolling out of the third floor window of Number 50. The next moments were chaotic. Police agents rushed the building, leaping over fences and onto roofs, and scrambling over walls to get into the courtyard. The national guards broke down the main entrance and arrested most of the plainclothes policemen and many of the tenants.[8] On the third floor, Antoine Boucharet of the *Sûreté* kicked down the suspect door, and within the next few minutes at least 20 men from the police and national guards crowded into the tiny apartment.[9]

The flat from which the shots were fired consisted of four small rooms, one overlooking the boulevard and two overlooking the back courtyard and roof of the building next door. It was sparsely furnished and had the air of a hastily deserted lair, complete with a fire burning in the fireplace despite the heat of the day, a smoldering log in the center of the room, and masses of smoke. At the window were the remnants of the weapon, composed of 25 gun barrels anchored to a wooden frame, the barrels supported in circular channels carved in the wood.[10] The walls bore the marks of bloody handprints and projectiles, as if the machine had expelled bullets into the chamber as well as outside. There was a pool of blood on the floor and a blood trail into the small kitchen whose window gave onto the court, out of which hung a blood-stained rope nailed to the sill.[11]

The assassin had used the rope to swing onto the jutting roof of Number 52 next door, and several on the scene actually saw him sliding down the last few feet.[12] Fieschi was close to capture. In his daring escape he knocked a flowerpot to the ground, into the midst of the growing crowd below.[13] He climbed through a kitchen window and encountered the widow Gommès, who began to scream; when he wiped the blood from his eyes she recognized him as a neighbor. Fieschi exited her front door and was arrested on the stairs.[14]

The machine had blown apart in Fieschi's face, tearing the skin and muscles from his jaw and badly fracturing his skull. Nevertheless, he underwent his first interrogation immediately, responding largely in gestures. Asked how many were involved in the conspiracy, he held up one finger; asked who had ordered the attempt, he thumped his chest.[15] He was soon taken by coach back to his building to be formally identified by neighbors, who knew him as Joseph Gérard. At 6 P.M. he was moved to the Conciergerie prison, where the questioning had to be suspended several times when he grew faint or was bled by the physicians. All he would say was that his name was Joseph Gérard and that he had a wife and son in Lodève. By the next morning he was extremely depressed, answering in mournful fragments ("I'm a *misérable*").[16] The mystery was solved by Olivier Dufresne, *inspecteur-général* of the prisons of the Seine, who believed he had seen him in the company of National Guard Colonel Gustave Ladvocat. Gisquet invited Ladvocat to the prefecture on 2 August and brought the two men together. The culprit experienced "a great moral weakening, sobbing profusely and admitting that his name was Fieschi."[17]

Fieschi was Corsican. This fact alone requires consideration, because of Corsica's link with Napoleon, its custom of vendetta, and above all its Mediterranean sense of honor. Honor was both status and virtue: those of high station were born with it, those in the lowest or criminal classes had no chance for it, but for those in the middling ranks, behavior—integrity, morality in one's dealings with others—was what mattered.[18] And it was in the middling ranks where disputes over honor were most likely, precisely because honor could be lost. Fieschi, very conscious of his background and past deeds, was largely motivated throughout this affair by an attempt to regain his honor. His choice to validate himself through political action suggests the importance of republicanism in the working-class imagination, even among those with scant political conviction.

The records showed that Fieschi was born in Murato in 1790 to a landless, impoverished family. His father Louis Fieschi, member of a band that had raided Bastia under the brigand Martin Pietri, had died in Embrun prison, sentenced in 1809 to ten years for theft. Eric Hobsbawm has redefined much brigandage as a form of primitive political rebellion; the French struggle to "civilize" Corsica and bring it under administrative control perhaps allows this interpretation in the case of Fieschi's father. Of his sons, the oldest, Thomas, was a soldier who died in the battle of Wagram; the youngest brother Antoine, mute from birth, was reportedly virtuous and hard-working.[19]

Most remarkable had been the middle son, Joseph, who like his father had spent his youth as a shepherd. The wars had allowed him a field of action and opportunity; an inquiry among his old comrades-in-arms revealed that he was marked by "a certain spirit of intrigue and a great boldness of execution." In 1808, he joined a Corsican regiment and was sent to Naples, then to Russia. In 1812 he held the rank of sergeant, and attracted the favorable notice of Comte Gustave de Damas, an *aide-de-camp* to Marshal Soult. When his corps was disbanded in 1814, he returned to Corsica. In September 1815, Fieschi joined King Joachim Murat, Napoleon's brother-in-law and the former king of Naples, in an ill-fated attempt to retake his kingdom. The restored Bourbon king Ferdinand IV deported Fieschi and the others to France, executing only Murat, in October 1815.[20]

Like Napoleon, Fieschi had found himself adrift when the wars were over; he returned home with neither possessions nor prospects. He stole a mule and sold it, escaping trial only with the intervention of the more respectable members of his clan; he would later claim that he had merely appropriated his rightful share of the paternal inheritance. But when he took a steer from a neighbor he was sentenced, in August 1816, to ten years, to be served in the prison where his father had died. In Embrun, Fieschi's hard work and good conduct made him foreman of the prison-factory, and this post had allowed him to meet a fellow inmate in the women's section, Laurence Petit. He was freed in September 1826, and as an ex-convict under *surveillance* he was refused permission to return to Corsica. Instead he went to Lyon, Petit's home. Petit (who used her maiden name) returned there in April 1829 to live with Fieschi, though her husband François Abot was inconveniently still alive.[21]

Shortly after the July Revolution, Fieschi came to Paris, now styling himself a political prisoner—as opposed to common criminal—of the previous regime. He used his various military contacts to get himself incorporated into a regiment of *sous-officiers sédentaires*, a group assigned to guard public buildings and act as a reserve force.[22] In the meantime, Abot had died in January 1830, and Laurence Petit followed Fieschi to Paris. At the end of 1831, her 14-year-old daughter by her first marriage, Virginie Lassave, known as Nina, came to live with them. A serious childhood skin disease had deprived Nina of three fingers of her right hand as well as an eye.[23]

At some point Fieschi violated his lover's daughter; then he continued a clandestine "affair" with her, to which her mother long remained blind. "She admitted to me that she belonged to Fieschi," according to one of Nina's friends, "and she told me more than once that it was her mother's doing."[24] In January 1834, Petit finally got her daughter into the Salpêtrière asylum, classified as indigent and infirm. Nina and her mother then ceased to have any contact. As Fieschi's relationship with Petit unraveled in the course of that year, his liaison with Nina became overt, even as he continued to live with Laurence. Fieschi later described the unsavory relationship to the *Cour des Pairs:* "She was my mistress, this was a child that I raised and to whom I gave my principles."[25]

But this was in the future. At the end of 1830, Fieschi and Laurence were the concierges of a building on the rue de Buffon. One of their tenants was Jacques de Caunes, civil engineer for the city of Paris (and non-republican brother of SDHC organizer Auguste), who hired Petit as his housekeeper. In the pattern that he would repeat later, Fieschi became fiercely, obsequiously devoted to Caunes, engendering in turn a sense of obligation. In November 1831, Caunes got Fieschi a position as guard of the small Croulebarbe mill, which gave him a daily stipend of two francs. Caunes had tried to put Fieschi in the way of further opportunities by introducing him to his friend and former student Gustave Ladvocat, a member of the Chamber of Deputies, a national guard colonel, and a former officer in Napoleon's Imperial Guard. The two shared a devotion to the Emperor; Ladvocat would later claim that Fieschi ran errands and did "important services" for him during the numerous riots of 1831. As for Caunes, Petit and Fieschi had courageously cared for him during the cholera epidemic of 1832 ("Simply put, I owe him my life," said Caunes).[26]

In October 1831, Fieschi addressed a petition to the *commission des condamnés politiques* (the commission for political prisoners of the previous regime), claiming that he had served ten years in Embrun for the 1816 Bonapartist Grenoble conspiracy. He produced two phony certificates attesting to that fact, and was awarded a pension of 550 francs a year.[27] He was also employed occasionally by Prefect of Police Baude, recommended to him as a "likely man" by Comte de Damas, who had met him in Russia; Fieschi also attempted to use his connections to obtain a permanent position under Gisquet. Ladvocat was too uneasy about him to become his sponsor, and Caunes and Ladvocat later broke off relations with him in 1834, when his pension fraud was discovered; but both men also attempted unsuccessfully to intervene in his behalf when he was threatened with prosecution for it.[28]

Through 1832 and 1833, Fieschi lived by a variety of expedients. He tried to make himself a weaver again, the trade he had learned in prison; he gave lessons in the bayonet. The president of the political prisoner commission offered to find him a job, but Fieschi frankly told him that he was not interested in working, "that he was fatigued by the Russian campaign, [and] he wanted a pension of three or four francs a day." He became enraged when his request for more money was refused. Early in 1834, Caunes gave him a position as *chef d'atelier* of a resurfacing project in Arcueil, which involved the responsibility for managing a dozen men and handling a considerable amount of money.[29]

Then things began to fall apart. Laurence left Fieschi in the early summer of 1834. The neighbors were not surprised, having heard the screams and gunshots that preceded the rupture, and they were also aware of the situation with Nina; Fieschi, in fact, had told everyone that Nina was merely Petit's adopted daughter, as if to mitigate the affair.[30] Laurence claimed that their relationship had ended in June, but the porter in her new lodgings stated that Fieschi "came and went"; according to Fieschi, "I almost always slept there." It was not until November 1834 that Fieschi was finally denied entry to her apartment.[31] They parted on very bad terms, with Petit stating later that she was "inconsolable, to have shared her bed with such a monster." He too was angry, convinced that he was the aggrieved one: she had taken all their miserable possessions, the "fruits of his labor," and left him on the street.[32]

The rift with Petit shamed him. Indeed, he had been unceremoniously expelled from her bed because she controlled the purse strings. And by the end of the year, other troubles were coming to a head. In August 1834, Fieschi's position in the reserve officer corps was revoked because he failed to report even for the modest services required.[33] In October he lost the Arcueil supervisor's job when Caunes discovered that he had been gambling with the payroll. "I've lost all honor with you," Caunes remembered him as saying, throwing up his arms; "You won't see me again." Rather than "compromise" Fieschi, Caunes dissolved the entire crew, and a few days later rehired all the other workers.[34]

It was also in October that Fieschi's lies about his "political" imprisonment finally caught up with him. He had been under investigation for the better part of the year on suspicion of defrauding the government; at the time he attempted the king's life there was an arrest warrant outstanding against him, issued in April.[35] In the meantime, Fieschi's negligence as watchman for the Croulebarbe mill came under municipal investigation, and in January 1835 this position too was taken away, and with it his last regular source of income. With the loss of Petit and the mill, he lacked even a roof over his head.[36]

Laurence Petit was described by the prosecutor as still beautiful though of a certain age (38), but her life had failed to live up to its promising debut. An ambitious governess, she had married her much-older employer, the customs officer Louis Lassave, with whom she had two children. After his early death she had married the businessman Abot, and their efforts to make a fortune had led to a fraudulent bankruptcy and the prison sentence at Embrun. Her relationship with Fieschi was complicated by class: "I lowered myself to raise him to my level; he did not know how to profit by it."[37]

In the months before the attempt, Fieschi had tried to reconcile with her. Laurence told the *juge d'instruction* that Fieschi had "come to see me once or twice to make scenes": "Having lived with him I could not show him the door, but I was with him as with a stranger."[38] At the beginning of May 1835 she agreed to a meeting arranged by a third party. Fieschi was angered when she came escorted by her new lover Claude-Maurice Bourseau, a republican stalwart and leader of a Sainte-Pélagie prison riot. Nevertheless he asked her to come back to him, offering 200 francs as inducement. When she refused, he continued to send letters by way of a Mme. Dècle, to whom Laurence finally declared, "Madame, Fieschi has importuned me for a long time. . . . Tell him I'm in a building where there's a *commissaire de police*; if he returns I'll have him arrested." Fieschi sent word that if she went to the police he would have her killed by his Corsican compatriots. Laurence was so frightened that Bourseau started to accompany her to and from work.[39]

By early 1835 Fieschi was penniless. He turned first to sponging off his acquaintances, using his phony political-prisoner status as a calling card. His co-conspirator Pierre Morey put him up from November 1834 to January 1835, when Morey's mistress insisted he leave.[40] He stayed briefly with Morey's nephew, until the latter caught him with Nina in his room: "I had lent a small lodging to Fieschi, but not to make that use of it."[41] Then he spent a few days with Théodore Pepin, his other co-conspirator, and finally in March, with a loan from Morey, he rented the place on the boulevard du Temple. He worked for a few weeks, but during the final three months Fieschi was living on handouts from the other two.[42] He was now deeply in debt, primarily to Morey, and the debt was not one that would be demanded in money: for it was Morey who was the zealot, the driving force and inspiration behind the attempt, who suddenly had found himself in possession of a lethal weapon—Fieschi—and a plan.

Pierre Morey was a 61-year-old saddler with a republican past. He had been arrested but not indicted in 1816, on suspicion of having plotted the assassination of the Bourbons. He had been tried and acquitted for the murder of an Austrian soldier during the postwar allied occupation. In 1817, he left Dijon for Paris, abandoning his wife and living with Anne Mouchet. (His lawyer J. F. Dupont would retell these stories: the Austrian soldier was attempting to rape a French woman; Morey had fled an immoral wife.[43]) During the wars he had served in both the artillery and a regiment of hussars. His participation in the 1830 revolution had won him the July decoration. He had come to know Fieschi in 1831 when the two had been neighbors.[44]

Fieschi traced the invention of the infernal machine to his time with Morey:

> One day I said to myself, if you were in a fortress with 300 men, and an epidemic carried off half of them, could you not defend yourself with just a few people? I then had the idea to make this machine that would employ 90 muskets lined up

in rows. . . . I then explained the machine to Morey and he said: "that could be
used for Louis-Philippe."[45]

Morey had taken Fieschi's drawing to Théodore Pepin, a prosperous 35-
year-old grocer and chief of his SDHC *section Romme*. The three of them met
over lunch. Several days later Pepin asked Fieschi for a cost estimate of the
project, and Fieschi suggested a sum of five hundred francs, "counting all the
rent, the other expenses, some furnishings for me, such as a rough pallet to
rest on, etc." Pepin balked at the price, but he and the financially strapped
Morey finally agreed to share it. Morey rented the apartment, while Pepin
paid for the materials and supported Fieschi, who was allowed to supply himself at his grocery.[46] "It was the three of us together," recalled Fieschi later,
"with no bends in the road."[47]

Two other men were also eventually brought to trial. The most marginally involved was Tell Bescher, who at Morey's behest had lent his *livret* (a worker's
record, carried from job to job) and obtained for Fieschi's escape a passport in
his own name. Bescher, a former member of the *section Marat*, was told by
Morey only "that it was a question of helping out an unfortunate man in difficulty," and he was acquitted by the Peers.[48]

The other minor defendant was Victor Boireau, a 25-year-old tinsmith.
He had been arrested at the Café des Deux Portes in February 1834 with
many other *sectionnaires* and had remained in prison through the April insurrection.[49] While inside, Boireau had met fellow political Isidore Janot, the
nephew of Caunes, and through him had met Fieschi. Boireau had lent Fieschi
a drill; he had been smart enough to drop some knowing hints around Pepin,
who then assumed he was fully in on the plot.[50] Boireau's revelations did much
to confirm Pepin's participation, which provided the strongest support for a
link with the SDHC.

Fieschi was a swaggering man of action, Morey an intense and brooding
fanatic; but what of Pepin the grocer? He was a minor figure in republican circles, a member of *l'Union de Juillet* and a vice president of the *Société pour l'Instruction du Peuple*, knowing many people without being well-known himself.[51]
In court Pepin downplayed his republicanism, though pressed hard by *Procureur-Général* Martin du Nord. He admitted his membership in the SDHC
but contrived to make it sound something like the Chamber of Commerce: "I
belonged a very short time [to a section] entirely composed of established

men, all manufacturers [*industriels*] for the most part." Had he not been chief of his section? "I was never legally named *chef de section*. I filled the position two, three, perhaps four times, in place of the true chief, during a trip he took. He was a merchant-manufacturer."[52]

Pepin was known to be generous on behalf of political prisoners and their families. He had lent Cavaignac five hundred francs, and on occasion he had subsidized *Le Pilori*, a small republican newspaper.[53] His ledger also contained a page with two entries, one for 150 francs to "Bescher" and one for 68.50 francs, which was listed as "wood and rent." This matched the 218.50 francs "received" entry in Fieschi's own account book.[54] Pepin was able to come up with no convincing explanation for this, suggesting only that it could have been possible that he might have received a request for a loan from Fieschi, and would have jotted it down to reflect upon it—but then would not have paid it when the time came, having discovered what manner of man Fieschi was (this tortured phrasing a pale reflection of his own).[55] His general demeanor on the stand, his dithering about such simple matters as whether he knew Morey well or not so well (or what "well" might mean), his stubborn insistence that he had known Fieschi only under the name of Bescher (despite the irrelevance of this issue), and especially his tendency to come up with answers in a conditional mode—all of this finally roused *Procureur-Général* Martin du Nord: "I am not asking you if it would be possible that such and such was the case. I am asking you to search your memory."[56] (Later, when Martin had wrenched from him a definite admission of something, "This is no longer a probability, a hypothesis, it is a certainty for you?"[57])

But most things remained merely "possible" for Pepin, who thus tried to avoid facing the consequences of what he himself had set in motion. It was "possible" that Morey had been part of his SDHC section; it was "possible" that Morey had told him that "Bescher's" real name was Fieschi (he "admit[ted] the hypothesis"), but it was not a French name and he would not have remembered it.[58] He recalled no conversation with Fieschi about the purchase of gun barrels, "however it's possible they were discussed."[59] Pepin insisted that they had never talked about the machine; that was an "error." In countering Fieschi's testimony he used the term "error" repeatedly (becoming as fond of it as he was of "possible"), until Chancellor Pasquier finally pointed out that all these declarations by Fieschi, if false, would be not errors, but "the most serious lie[s] one could tell."[60]

Pepin's most troubling aspect for republicans was his relationship with party leader Godefroy Cavaignac. The attempt occurred only two weeks after the great Sainte-Pélagie escape, and Fieschi was convinced that the party leaders, warned by Pepin of his machine, had wanted to be free to take over the insurrection that would follow the death of the king. Morey's republican defender Dupont passed along Cavaignac's sworn word that he had had no advance knowledge.[61] But as usual for Pepin, the Cavaignac matter was finally left ambiguous. He admitted that during his trips to Sainte Pélagie to see Henri Leconte, a prisoner from the April uprising, he had also seen Cavaignac and Guinard "two or three times," but had not spoken to them. Pressed by Dupont in the courtroom, he suggested that perhaps he had seen them only in passing: "It's possible I saw [them] from the window."[62] Pepin for a long time denied Fieschi's testimony that he had written to Cavaignac; later he agreed "that it was not impossible" that he had done so.[63] In his February 17 confession (the day after he had been sentenced to death), Pepin admitted that he had once asked Cavaignac outright for guns, when Fieschi had briefly floated the idea of invading the Jardin-du-Roi barracks, killing everyone who got in the way, and seizing their armory: "I said to Fieschi, to hold him back and avoid a misfortune, that I could speak to some patriots, and notably to Cavaignac, and ask for some weapons." The incident sounded typical of Pepin: frightened by Fieschi's plan, he had merely thought of diverting the scheme instead of stopping it cold. Cavaignac had wanted nothing to do with it. In his final confession at 12:45 A.M. on the day of his death, Pepin stated that he had told Cavaignac enough to have allowed him to conjecture the assassination conspiracy, had he chosen to, thus leaving the matter unsettled.[64]

How did such a man, so readily intimidated by Fieschi, travel so easily among the republican elite? Oddly, Pepin was the only one of the three who had achieved some prior celebrity. As a national guard captain during the June 1832 insurrection, he had been one of the first defendants tried under the military courts. The large barricade that had blocked the entrance to the faubourg Saint-Antoine had been outside the building that housed his shop and home, and he had been accused of having fired on the troops from his windows.[65] Pepin had denied the charges: "I swear on my honor, on the heads of my poor children, on the love I have for my country, on my twelve years of honorable commercial dealings." The most troubling part of his case, however, had been the fact that all the arresting officers had noted that Pepin's hands were blackened and smelled, as if with gunpowder—as if he had fired a weapon. In 1832, Pepin had tried several explanations: "In the obscurity I could have put my hands in black dye. It is also possible that I could have grabbed a bayonet, a gun barrel, a cartridge pouch, and I could thus have blackened my hands with powder." And later, in a debate with another witness, he stated that if his hands were dirty—it was possible they were dirty—"it could have resulted from a fall, during the argument with the soldiers and the National Guard."[66] In the end his defense, bolstered by the testimony of fellow guards as to his character and devotion to the regime, was accepted by a majority of six out of the seven military judges. His attorney Alexandre Marie (also the attorney for Charles Jeanne) argued that 1832 had given Pepin "an unfortunate celebrity" in republican circles that was not warranted by "his limited intelligence, his timid character."[67] Police informant Adolphe Chenu suggested that Pepin's involvement in the Fieschi plot was an attempt to prove himself to his fellow republicans, who had taunted him for his courtroom protestations of loyalty to the king.[68]

With the agreement among these three men, the plan was set in motion. In March Fieschi moved into the residence on the probable parade route. The building was full of tenants—two cafés, a pastry merchant with a stall just outside the door, a gravestone-maker and his mistress, an actor, an elderly widow, respectable families and irregular unions—and he occupied an apartment on the third floor, accessible only by a public staircase.[69] He had no furnishings, but explained to his skeptical concierge that his "wife" was soon coming from the provinces with their worldly goods. Toward the end of May, he began bringing in the wooden frame for the machine, piece by piece. The concierge's wife, Julie Salmon, had caught him; he told her he was going to make a workbench and become a mechanic: "I have not however seen any tools," she reported.[70]

Two weeks before 28 July Fieschi bargained for the gun barrels, insisting that the ironmonger Bury throw in a pistol to seal the transaction. (Morey had urged him to get a gun so he could commit suicide if captured; later he gave it to Boireau.)[71] On Saturday 25 July, Fieschi arrived at the ironmonger's with a new trunk. Bury's nephew served him, at Fieschi's insistence making out the receipt (destined for Pepin) for 7.50 francs per barrel, instead of the actual price of 6 francs—no harm in making a little on the side, except that the discrepancy confirmed the existence of a conspiracy, since a lone assassin would have had no reason to falsify his bills.[72] Fieschi hired a coach to take the sealed trunk to a wineshop, then hired a porter to take it the rest of the way so that no single individual would know his entire route.[73] This was Fieschi's riskiest moment, and he resorted to the story he had established earlier. To the ever-vigilant Julie Salmon, who noted the apparent heaviness of the trunk (it required both himself and the porter to lift it): "Here's the advance guard; my wife sent this on ahead of her." He also ran into Étienne Travault, the *marchand de vin* on the first floor: "M. Travault, here's that trunk I told you about."[74]

Soon Fieschi had enlisted the services of his unwitting neighbors. He borrowed from the concierge an auger and a hammer ("that he has not yet given back"). Étienne Paul, the billiard maker, lent him a saw and a mallet ("It was, he said, to saw a plank"). The billiard-maker's brother lent him another saw ("I believe I recall he said it was to make small notches").[75] On the weekend before the attempt, Fieschi filled the building with the sound of hammering.[76]

But most of the neighbors were distracted from these odd doings by the procession of young women who came to his door, known as "the one-eyed girl," the "girl in mourning," and the "girl in the rose-colored hat." Opinion was divided on the subject of which one was Gerard's "hen," and some held out for all three.[77] The most recent addition to the trio, the "girl in the rose-colored hat," was Marguerite Daurat, who had arrived from Lyon in early July with hopes of becoming a *femme de chambre*, bringing only 40 francs and a letter of introduction to Nina from her brother, Amédée Lassave. Nina had introduced her to Fieschi in early July, and he had busied himself with finding her a job.[78]

The woman in black was Annette Bocquin, the abandoned *grisette* of the student (and Caunes' nephew) Isidore Janot. Janot, summoned home to the provinces and afraid that his working-class lover might enter a bordello, had asked Fieschi to take care of her. Fieschi spied on her first; when he determined that she had not been promiscuous, he gave her shelter in his new apartment, where she had remained for about a month. Fieschi claimed that he had "respected" her while she lived in his home, regarding her as a "sacred deposit" from his friend.[79]

And then, of course, there was Nina, the "one-eyed girl" who came every Sunday, each time bringing a dress, some undergarments, a handkerchief, a pair of earrings. He had variously told people that Nina was his "laundress" and "his laundress' daughter"—an apt metaphor, probably an unconscious one.[80] Nina had regarded Fieschi's new apartment as an escape from the Salpêtrière, and had told a friend that she would soon be living with "her lover, a Corsican named Joseph Fieschi."[81]

In the last days before the king's review, simmering tensions had burst out among the three conspirators. On Friday, 24 July, there was a particularly uncomfortable conference under the Pont d'Austerlitz, in which they settled their financial accounts. The budget was complicated. There was the bill for the gunbarrels which Fieschi would pick up the following day (for 7.50 francs apiece). Fieschi had taken many items from Pepin's grocery without paying. Morey had borrowed 50 francs from Pepin, but he had given Fieschi money to buy the trunk, as well as other sums at various times. Pepin and Morey haggled over all of this, going back and forth about what had been spent for this and that, until finally Fieschi angrily stood up: "I don't want it to be said that you keep me." Fieschi was sensitive about the unmanly implication that he was unable to support himself—not sensitive enough, it appeared, to get a real job, but distinctly uncomfortable about being "kept" by two men. A day or two later, Pepin asked Fieschi to confirm the sums Morey claimed to have advanced.[82]

Fieschi's contempt for these transactions went to the heart of why he disliked Pepin—and he had come to dislike him intensely. Morey's concern with money was forgivable, for he had a spendthrift mistress; but prosperous Pepin, in the face of the glorious action they were about to commit, was fretting over small change. In addition, Pepin, an "aristocrat" in spirit, had offered him a number of minor slights.[83] There was Pepin's unwillingness to be seen in his company (for example, his failure, when Fieschi had crashed a dinner party, to acknowledge him); and there was his stinginess in small things, such as not offering him a drink when he came by. On only one occasion had Pepin bought him a meal, and it was taken in a cheap café: "I am not a man of money . . . nor a gourmand for good dinners. . . ."—but still. On another occasion Fieschi had encountered Pepin in the company of a young bourgeois: "Pepin gave me a handshake, calling me, according to his habit, *mon brave*." He did not introduce him. And Fieschi had seen Pepin with other men, "that he called *mon brave, mon brave citoyen*"—Pepin's manner, as he had come to realize, with men he considered beneath him.[84]

At last the attempt was only hours away. On Monday evening Fieschi told the concierge that his "uncle" was with him and gave orders that they were not to be disturbed. Uncle Morey was loading the machine, and he and Fieschi worked steadily from 5 P.M. to 9 P.M. Then Morey took a last look around, and reminded Fieschi of his promise to kill himself if something went wrong. Otherwise, Morey would be waiting for him with Bescher's passport. The two men went for one last drink.[85]

After Morey left, Fieschi socialized with the regulars at the neighboring Café des Mille Colonnes. Victor Boireau came to see him at 11 P.M.; Pepin had asked him to ride in his place past the building that day, pausing at the Café Turc so Fieschi could aim the machine. Fieschi had used ordinary traffic for the purpose, but he was angry because of the principle of the thing, the fact that Pepin had not done his "part," as Morey had by loading the barrels. Boireau swore his devotion to the plan; nevertheless, he had already told a friend, who had told his father, who had reported it to the police. The next morning Fieschi saw him lurking in the vicinity with several other young men. Boireau ran up to him: "We're all ready . . . we'll be at our post."[86]

Fieschi spent the morning of 28 July disposing of his trunk, into which he packed all his possessions. He informed the concierge that he was sending some things to his wife, and he and a street porter set off.[87] Fieschi returned from this errand and was still outside the building shortly before the cortège arrived, when he spoke to a neighbor hurrying to get a good spot: "I was near him, he said to me: 'You're going to see your King?'"[88] Finally the moment was at hand. Louis-Philippe's party felt some relief as they passed the new Ambigu Theater, the area ransacked by Gisquet's men after Boireau's indiscretion had reached the police. They did not realize that it was the old Ambigu they had to worry about, the one near the Café Turc.[89]

Fieschi finally raised the window blinds, placing his work apron over the gun barrels to conceal them. Now he felt "ennui," and reflected that he was about to create a "tragedy," to kill generals who had fought under Napoleon. But he was bound by honor. Morey and Pepin had invested a great deal of money in the project, and if he failed it would look as if he had led them on just to get a roof over his head: "I would have been treated as a coward and swindler, in spite of the fact that I had received only about 40 francs outside of expenses." He lit the charge.[90]

Fieschi remembered only snatches of what happened next. The major blow that ripped the flesh from his face rocked him backwards, and he smeared the wall with his blood.[91] He descended the rope, a feat he did not remember well; an elderly woman watching the courtyard saw him emerge from his kitchen window in a "whirlwind" of smoke.[92] He recalled the men who had arrested him, remembered being slugged by a national guard; he had a memory of being in the coach on his way to the Conciergerie, and of thinking, as they traveled across the Pont Louis-Philippe, that if they threw him into the river he would certainly drown.[93]

Nina had promised Fieschi to stay away from the king's review, but she came anyway. She was near the boulevard du Temple when she encountered the periphery of an agitated crowd:

> I immediately had a frightful presentiment. . . . People there showed me the window from which the shots had been fired, and I recognized Fieschi's chamber. They also told me that the assassin had been killed himself by some gun barrels that had burst open in the room. For an instant my head was swimming; Fieschi was my only support, for my mother had long since abandoned me.[94]

Nina lingered in the area, until suddenly struck by the thought that she might be recognized. She rushed back to the Salpêtrière, "bathed in sweat"; a fellow inmate noted that "she trembled so strongly she could not unfasten her bonnet." She shredded Fieschi's letters and fled, spending the night with Annette Bocquin.[95] Fieschi had told her to go to Morey or Pepin if she ever needed help, but Pepin was not at home and Mme. Pepin received her coldly. At noon the next day Nina went to Morey, who feigned ignorance until she burst into tears. They agreed to meet several hours later at the barrière du Trône.[96]

Morey bought Nina dinner but was in a state of considerable irritation, referring to Fieschi as an "imbecile" and a "braggart." "I urged Fieschi to be sure to load his pistol," he told her, "and he was to blow his brains out." Nina expressed regret over the many deaths, noting that Marshal Mortier was said to be a good man; Morey responded that Mortier was *canaille* like all the rest. Their conversation had continued in this pleasant vein for some time, drawing attention from other diners: the *garçon* recalled that the many national guards in the restaurant were laughing "to see a young girl with an old man."[97]

By this time Morey had not only Nina but Fieschi's trunk on his hands, so he decided to dump both loose ends in an apartment. He rented a small chamber for Nina and promised her 60 francs; she would go to Lyon and dispose of the trunk and its contents there, where the police were not looking for it.[98] On Thursday, the morning of 30 July, Morey and a street porter arrived with the trunk, and that evening he and Nina sorted through the contents. It contained odds and ends, some of Nina's clothing, ten volumes of Cicero, and most significantly, Fieschi's green notebook with comments on the conspiracy. Morey promised to burn it but instead threw it into the latrine in his building, grossly underestimating the thoroughness of the police.[99] Morey must have believed he had covered his tracks; besides, as one of the usual suspects, he had already been picked up and released on the very night of the attempt—one of several blunders in the case.[100]

The police had received an indirect warning. Victor Boireau had been visibly excited on the eve of the king's review, alarming his co-worker Suireau, whose father was in the National Guard. Boireau had suggested that his father stay away from the Ambigu Theater. That evening Suireau *père* rushed to the police. *Commissaire* Dyonnet described him as extremely agitated, stammering about an infernal machine: "He told me . . . that this machine was made by an escapee from hard labor [a *bagne*] or by an ex-convict, a very ingenious man, who had been promised a lot of money. M. Suireau added that he presumed it was a question of barrels of gunpowder installed in someplace subterranean." The *commissaire* was not very alarmed; he did not see why putting barrels in a basement would require an "ingenious" mechanic, and Suireau later admitted that the notion of an underground explosion was only a guess on his part.[101]

By the following morning, Gisquet had searched the area around the Ambigu, but the odd juxtaposition of an "able mechanic" and a crude explosion had struck him as well. And Gisquet had naturally concentrated his efforts on the below-ground areas of the boulevard Saint-Martin (site of the new Ambigu) instead of the upper floors of the boulevard du Temple (site of the old). The police also looked for Boireau, who spent the day on the streets waiting for the revolution to start. That evening, Boireau threw the pistol Fieschi had given him into the river, and at 8 P.M. he was arrested and confronted with the still-nameless assassin; the two pretended not to know each other.[102]

The subsequent investigation relied on shoe leather. The trunk was the starting point, for Fieschi's neighbors had seen him take it away on the morning of the attempt. The street porter had carried it to the rue Vendôme, where Fieschi had dismissed him and picked up a cabriolet (his usual pattern of breaking his journey). They soon found the coachman, who had unloaded the trunk at the door of a café. The café keeper had seen Fieschi put the trunk on his back and head for the rue Saint-Victor.[103] By 30 July, the police had knocked on every door in the vicinity. Their efforts finally bore fruit when someone remembered a trunk being taken away from the home of the marble cutter Nolland, who confirmed that the trunk had been left with him by someone he had known several years earlier, who had lived on the rue Croulebarbe. The man—whose name he had forgotten—had told him to give the trunk only to himself, if he should return, or to another old acquaintance, Pierre Morey. On the morning of 30 July, Morey had arrived with a porter to take it away.[104]

On 31 July, at 11:45 P.M., Morey's home became the target of a full-fledged police and judicial descent. He claimed not to remember his activities of the previous day. He knew nothing of the trunk; he had no idea who had left it for him, and he could not recall what he had done with it. When asked if he knew someone on the rue Croulebarbe, Morey tried to throw them off track: "I only knew a launderer who is no longer there, whose name I don't recall; he was there with his mother." Nolland did not remember the launderer or his mother, but remembered someone else, who had "a daughter deprived of one eye." Questioning throughout the old neighborhood elicited the name of "Fieschi," who had lived with a certain Mme. Petit, who had a daughter with one eye.[105]

On Sunday, 2 August, Nolland was taken from prison to walk the streets in search of Morey's porter. He soon recognized Guillaume Dubromet, who could only pinpoint the general vicinity; after several intensive searches of the wrong buildings, the police finally found Nina, who immediately produced a suicide note.[106] ("You are asked not to look for Nina anymore, she will no longer exist after this night; she leaves in her chamber the *thing* which was deposited with her; this is what comes of abandoning her so quickly. Adieu, after my death let happen what may."[107]) After some initial reluctance, Nina began to talk.

On 5 August Pepin's name came into the case, from Nina and from a tailor who had delivered some clothing for Fieschi to Pepin's grocery. On the day of the attempt, Pepin had gone underground; he was not captured until 28 August, when he tried to return home in disguise. That same evening he was taken from jail for a search of the cesspool and privies of his establishment, and the confusion attending this operation allowed him to escape.[108] The police questioned Mme. Pepin, arrested with her husband. She was not acquainted with anyone named Morey, Fieschi, or Gérard. She knew of no one-eyed girl. Naturally she had no memory of anything to do with the SDHC, Cavaignac, or visits to Sainte-Pélagie: "My husband and I discussed our commerce and very little else"—a rather grim portrait of the marriage, but convenient under the circumstances.[109] Gisquet picked up Pepin's traces from an undercover agent. The prefect led the expedition to the nearby town of Lagny, and on the early morning of 22 September he captured Pepin in a farmhouse. He had on him 940 francs and the *Oeuvres de Saint-Just.*[110]

The peers finished with the *Procès d'avril;* the public became eager to move on to this next trial, the first of the great assassination cases, which promised so much more entertainment than the dreary final chapter of 1834. Fieschi, in the meantime, enjoyed himself immensely. He had a large room in the Conciergerie, with his choice of food and wine; he played cards with his guards. The abbé Grivel, the prison confessor, recalled that "he made himself completely comfortable," and was gracious, in his way, to visitors. He corresponded extensively, signing his letters *"le regisside Fieschi."* With his blessing, Nina sold autographed drawings of him.[111]

His star turn before the Peers finally came in February 1836. Fieschi was represented by fellow Corsican Patorni, along with prominent Parisian attorneys Parquin and L. A. Chaix d'Est-Ange. These three mostly confined themselves to dramatic *plaidoyers* at the end, making few objections; indeed, the prosecutor's case was largely shaped by Fieschi's revelations. Considerably more active were the republican attorneys J. F. Dupont, for Morey, and Philippe Dupin and Alexandre Marie, for Pepin, who attacked Fieschi's version whenever possible. The charges against Bescher were soon tacitly, though not officially, dropped. Boireau avoided death by disavowing his republicanism.[112]

Morey, very ill since his stay in prison, spoke in such a feeble tone that the clerk had to repeat his answers to the court; he, like the flustered Pepin, based his defense on denial.[113] But Fieschi told everything, perhaps because he became firmly convinced that Morey had attempted to kill him by loading several of the barrels in such a way as to explode in his face.[114] (Morey had told Nina that Fieschi must have been wounded by the barrels he had loaded himself.[115]) Still, Fieschi resented Morey's supposed sabotage far less than Pepin's condescension: "Morey is good, Morey is generous. He would have given me the shirt off his back."[116]

During the trial Fieschi clearly embraced his celebrity status, assumed that the slightest details about himself would interest the court, and entered into numerous narcissistic rambles about his thoughts, emotions, and habits. His authoritarian personality—manifested in a zeal for taking orders, as a subordinate in the hierarchy—had once led him to become a model prisoner and foreman in the prison factory. Now it revealed itself in his subaltern attachment to Colonel Gaspard Ladvocat, upon whom he fawned in the courtroom. In 1831, as Ladvocat's *homme de confiance*, Fieschi had attempted to make himself indispensable, warning Ladvocat of various imaginary murder plots being laid against him and vowing *protection de Corse*. "As a man, I would have marched before you and braved the cannons," he boasted. "You well know that without me you would not exist today."[117] Then Fieschi recalled at length the moment when he had recognized Ladvocat, in command of the 8th Legion outside his building, which had caused him to jostle the machine; thus Ladvocat had "saved the life of the king and the princes, civil war in our country, and perhaps today Cossack batteries would be on the borders of the Rhine. . . . I ask *M. le Président* to question M. Ladvocat on my other generous traits."[118]

Fieschi's witnesses included the doctor who had amputated two of his fingers after the explosion, to testify that Fieschi had kept his reason. The former inspector of Embrun prison remembered him as a good weaver and a good foreman. Baude, the former prefect of police, said that Fieschi had fallen into "bad hands": "I believe that if he had been otherwise surrounded he would have been able to render even brilliant services to his country."[119] But roughly half of Fieschi's witnesses were there to speak about the misdeeds of Laurence Petit; for example, Firmin Salis, a medical student who had been one of Petit's boarders: "Fieschi often said . . . that it was he who had paid for the furnishings, and consequently his wife should not treat him as she did." (Fieschi: "If the woman Petit had not refused me a mattress or two, I would not have needed to demand asylum.") Another of Fieschi's witnesses was the furniture dealer Lopinet: "Is it me or the woman Petit who bought the furnishings and paid for them?"[120] But

Fieschi only became truly bitter when confronted with his successor Bourseau, for whom he had only one question: "I would like him to say if the shirt he is wearing is his or mine; if the sheets he sleeps on were not put there by me; if the bed, the chairs, and the furniture he uses, were not earned by the sweat of my brow. If the woman Petit had given me a mattress, I wouldn't have gone to those others, and I wouldn't be here today before you."[121] Fieschi had been building up to this, his resentment having escaped him in earlier remarks as he had constantly, obsessively, returned to Petit. Chancellor Pasquier closed off the discussion of this issue, but when Petit came to the stand she insisted on proving her purchase of their property, for which she had brought the receipts: "I left Fieschi a bed, some chairs, everything a bachelor needs; if I had had 20,000 francs I wouldn't have given him any more."[122]

The *plaidoiries* of the defense attorneys were worthy of the grandeur of the audience. The Corsican Patorni, the first to speak on behalf of Fieschi, named three culprits: the government, which had chewed Fieschi up and spit him out; the "woman Petit," "the origin of his misfortune," who had the effrontery to come beautifully dressed to the courtroom, "and preceded by this athletic man that she has not feared to render the possessor of the bed and clothing of Fieschi"; and Prefect of Police Gisquet, who had known there was danger, and yet allowed the review to continue. Dupont stressed the honorable conduct of his client Morey; the accusations against him came from a man guilty of theft and incest. Parquin, who spoke next for Fieschi, portrayed him as a tempest-tossed son of the revolution, born under the wrong star. Philippe Dupin went next for Pepin, in a "brilliant improvisation"; many of the peers congratulated him afterward. Chaix-d'Est-Ange, speaking last for Fieschi, plunged them directly into the Russian campaign, detailing the wounded Sergeant Fieschi's heroic leadership of a small band of men after their commander was killed; Fieschi had won both a decoration and a scar.[123]

Fieschi was so moved by this last pleading that he needed time to compose himself before he made his own final speech. The court recessed briefly; when Fieschi came back, it was in the persona of a soldier ("you have my service record"), one of the blunt, rough-spoken men who had made the empire. He told of the campaign in Sicily, his imprisonment on Malta, his escape to rejoin the army in time for Russia. And then, despite all that, he was sent to prison: "You will not find a man who conducted himself as well as I in this prison, and yet I did not obtain my [parole]! I did ten years. . . ."[124] The verdict came down on 16 February 1836. Bescher, as expected, was acquitted. Boireau was sentenced to 20 years (he was amnestied in 1840). Fieschi, Morey, and Pepin were sentenced to death, with Fieschi to endure the penalty of parricide—to go veiled and barefoot to the place of execution. Pepin died first, then Morey; finally Fieschi mounted the scaffold, "took on the attitude of an orator, and in an assured voice cried: 'I'm going to appear before God! I have spoken the truth. I die content. I have rendered a service to my country in signaling my accomplices. . . . I regret my victims more than my life.'"[125]

On his last day, Fieschi was granted the company of Nina, who occupied herself with embroidery.[126] Surprisingly, Laurence wrote to ask if he would like to see "his old friend." Fieschi proudly declined; he hoped she would be happy, and he was pleased to reflect that he had never hit her, "because if you had left me the mattress that belonged to the two of us together, I would be free today."[127]

There were a number of postscripts. Fieschi's head went to a doctor at Bicêtre hospital who was known for "important work" on the brain.[128] On the eve of his execution, Pepin made several confessions to Chancellor Pasquier about revolutionary groups, providing the foundation for the next cycle of republican trials.[129] Nina obtained a position at the Café de la Renaissance, her duties confined to showing herself, elegantly dressed, to the crowds who flocked there for several weeks.[130] The national guard review on the anniversary of the *Trois Glorieuses* became a recurring nightmare, suspended in 1836, reestablished in 1837, and suspended again; the last was held in 1840.[131] In 1837, the obscure mechanic Champion attempted to follow in Fieschi's footsteps. The police learned of him through a series of anonymous letters, and discovered him with his own infernal machine: a little model, less than a foot tall, with three rows of barrels. Depressed and drinking heavily over the difficulties involved in transforming his design into a workable weapon, he had become indiscreet. Champion committed suicide in his jail cell, tying his cravat to the bars of his window and pushing away the cot.[132]

Mme. Pepin was granted a marital separation in December 1835 to protect her dowry; she continued to visit Pepin in prison.[133] Afterward, she kept up the grocery and grieved for her husband, often going to his grave accompanied by Minor Christophe Leconte, the younger brother of the late Henri Leconte, the April defendant whom Pepin had visited in prison. In 1837, Minor was arrested for decorating Pepin's grave, accompanied by the latter's daughter and his nephew, Prosper Magny. (Magny had had the task of recovering the body for the family, and had become ill when one of the executioners, reaching into the basket, had thrust the bloody stump into his face: "Is this the head of your uncle?"[134]) Leconte and Magny also sent out invitations to a memorial service for "Citizen Pepin, decapitated by the Thermidorians, Year 44 of the Republic," to be held at the republican Église française; this event was cancelled by the police.[135]

In 1839, Leconte married the considerably older Mme. Pepin and became a grocer; they had at least one son. Shortly after the marriage, Leconte was sentenced to five years for his role in printing the communist newspaper *l'Homme libre*; he was mildly active in the club movement in 1848, and was forced to flee the country after the *coup d'état* in 1851. Leconte resurfaced in 1871 during the Commune; born in 1813, he would then have been 58. He belonged to the National Guard that defended Paris against Thiers' Versailles army, and disappeared from the records after the Bloody Week.[136]

CHAPTER 9

ALIBAUD, MEUNIER, AND THE CULT OF REGICIDE

THE NEXT TWO ASSAULTS AGAINST THE KING OCCURRED in June and December 1836. They were carried out by Louis Alibaud, age 26, and François Meunier, age 23, both of them unemployed, socially isolated clerks. Each man, despite heavy debts to the landlord and boarding house, had compulsively spent himself into impoverishment in the days before his attempt. Each man acted alone.

The similarities ended there. Alibaud was an idealistic dreamer, a survivor of at least one ostentatious suicide attempt, who finally elevated his self-absorption onto a national stage. He became one of the pantheon of martyrs; his trial and execution gave rise to a mild sort of cult, marked by devotional poetry and graveside visitations by admirers (the police called them *alibauriennes*).[1] Meunier was the most ardent worshipper at this altar: strange, out of step with his surroundings—a "nullity," as not a few of his acquaintances referred to him—he was the more disturbing because of the very blankness of his personality.

Alibaud's attempt occurred only a few months after Fieschi's execution, and he was embraced more eagerly because of the differences between them. Fieschi fired from ambush; Alibaud was only a few feet from the king's carriage, thus exposing himself to death or capture. Fieschi had unleashed his machine into a crowd, while Alibaud chose one of the king's routine trips to Neuilly, when the area around the Tuileries was virtually deserted. In stark opposition to Fieschi's bloodbath, no one was hurt by Alibaud—the king escaping merely because he nodded to the national guards on duty outside the palace, just as the bullet slammed into the carriage behind his head.[2] And there were personal distinctions as well: Fieschi's short stature, stockiness, and animal vitality compared to Alibaud's height, slenderness, and fine dark eyes; the sordidness of Fieschi's private life in contrast to the solitary celibacy of Alibaud, who was thus free to become the object of romantic fantasies. Fieschi had introduced the practice of regicide, in a manner both crude and repugnant. Alibaud, through the sheer force of his personality, made regicide attractive. For a brief period in the late 1830s, it became the dominant external manifestation of republicanism.

Alibaud's attempt occurred just outside the Tuileries on 25 June 1836. He made no attempt to flee. He carried a dagger (for himself, when the deed was done). He was identified immediately by gunsmith Louis Devisme, a national guard sergeant on duty at the palace, who manufactured *canne-fusils* (cane-muskets), slender enough to be hidden under a coat. He had given Alibaud several to sell, and to his horror recognized both him and the weapon.[3] "No one will understand me," Alibaud told his captors; "no one believes in devotion to profound convictions in this century of egoism and venality. . . . I have only one regret: it is that I did not succeed. When a man does what I have done, he makes the sacrifice of his life in advance." When asked if he had accomplices: "The chief of this conspiracy, is my head, and the followers, are my arms."[4] Thus from the start he set the tone of his public performances: dedicated, didactic—and just a bit tedious. It is not at all certain that Alibaud said everything that was reported in the newspapers; he repudiated all his supposed ruminations on Fieschi, whose cell he briefly occupied.[5] His significance, instead, lay in his image, a joint creation of Alibaud and his devoted fans.

Alibaud was born in 1810 in Nîmes. His father, once a coachman, by 1836 had become an innkeeper. Alibaud was intelligent and had a good hand; his parents had intended him for a respectable career as a clerk and copyist, until he suddenly joined the army in 1829. He was stationed in Paris during the July Revolution but deserted, willing neither to fight for Charles X nor to join the rebels against his comrades. He left the army in January 1834, accepting a clerkship with the telegraph administration only to quit almost immediately, finding the job too dull. He attempted several other pursuits without success. When his parents moved to Perpignan he went with them, studying Spanish and bookkeeping to fit himself for business in the region.[6]

Alibaud soon was caught up in the events in Catalonia, as Polish and Italian refugees and French republicans rushed to defend the liberal cause.[7] Many of the volunteers passed through the town and stayed at his father's inn, and he was persuaded that his military experience would win him a prominent position; on

5 September 1835, he left for radical Barcelona.[8] He arrived during one of the quietest interludes of the war. He returned to Perpignan on 20 October, now fixed, by some strange process of substitution, on the murder of Louis-Philippe.[9]

Alibaud left for Paris with 250 francs from his parents, arriving on 17 November 1835 with fewer than 100 francs left. He stayed in a lodging house until January 1836, living off his remaining money and nursing his obsession. He was melancholy and depressed; the manager of his hotel had to talk him out of suicide.[10] His only friend during this period was Léonce Fraisse, the 20-year-old younger brother of one of his former classmates, who still retained a schoolboy's admiration for a charismatic upperclassman. Together they discussed the works of Saint-Just, especially popular among younger republicans because of his socialist ideas (the Ventôse law of March 1794) and his early, glorious death; among Alibaud's last few possessions was a copy of his collected works.[11]

Alibaud lived off Fraisse until he found a position with the wholesale wine merchant Antoine Batiza. Fellow employee Jean-Baptiste Manoury said that Alibaud had made no secret of his republicanism: "One day, I believe I said that Fieschi was a villain, and [Alibaud] told me I was an imbecile, I didn't know what I said." Batiza soon fired him.[12] Alibaud had already decided to quit, for the long hours of business had prevented him from stalking Louis-Philippe: "The good weather was approaching, I thought the king would go outside more often; I desired to find an employment in which I would be more free, in order to be able to follow him."[13]

On 25 May he moved to his last lodgings. Unemployed, he spent much of his time in the local Café Allemand, where he smoked and played billiards. He claimed that he would have money by the end of the month, relying on this fiction for his room and board, his drinks and tobacco. Just before the attempt, he sold his Spanish dictionary for 23 sous, which comprised his entire fortune at the time of the shooting.[14] On 25 June his rent was due, a fact that probably forced his hand. He read the papers in a nearby café, lunched at his *pension*, and went to the palace, his gun under his coat. Then, as he said in his trial, "You know the rest."[15]

Disturbed by Alibaud's favorable public image, the prosecution put great emphasis on the fact that he had acquired his weapon by an act of petty larceny: he had presented himself to the gunsmith Devisme as a traveling salesman, and then had reported one *canne-fusil* stolen. But this circumstance also seemed to prove that Alibaud had acted in isolation, since deception had been his only means of getting a weapon; the search for accomplices ended in a series of dead ends.[16] The prosecution moved swiftly to the trial phase: Alibaud's impact was the more remarkable in that he burst onto the scene on 25 June and was executed on 11 July, all in a little over two weeks. His lawyer Charles Ledru, one of the most famous defense attorneys in France, protested the indecent haste of the case.[17] But the trial, if precipitate and brief, was nevertheless both elegant and linear, without the messy digressions that had marked the Fieschi case.

Alibaud's defense was based on his character. Café owner François Dubois said he had had "the advantage of knowing [the gentleman]" because Alibaud had dined at his establishment. Young Léonce Fraisse defended him passionately, saying that "one can be an honest man, and have had a moment of error," the last word immediately raising the hackles of the peers. Gervais Corbières, a republican manufacturer in Perpignan, described the circumstances in which he had had the *honor* to know Alibaud, and the transcript duly noted his emphasis on the word "honor," as well as the "slight murmurs" in the court.[18]

The trial record was full of hints for whoever would wish to assume the principle rôle in some future *attentat:* Alibaud's answers were "strong and assured"; he sometimes raised his voice for emphasis ("For whom was [this dagger] intended? *For me*"); he "smiled bitterly" at some of the passages in the indictment.[19] The account of Alibaud's attempt to read his own written defense provided quite explicit stage directions:

> Alibaud: Regicide is the right of the man who can obtain justice only by his own hands. (Violent murmurs from the banks of the peerage.)
>
> The President ([Pasquier], after having scanned the assembly): I cannot allow you to continue such language. Sit down.
>
> Alibaud, with emotion: You are demanding my head, it is my right to defend it! (He remains standing, fixing his gaze on the face of the president. The gendarmes take Alibaud by the arms and force him to sit down). . . .
>
> Alibaud: Do not believe, Gentlemen, that I glory in being placed among the regicides, for such a title is not to be envied; it is a cruel necessity that I had to undergo! To kill one's fellow man is an act against nature; one must feel irresistibly pushed to have the courage to commit it. . . .
>
> (For some moments a muffled murmur has been heard on the banks of the peers; at this moment it almost drowns out the voice of the accused). . . .
>
> Alibaud: The corruption of those who wish to govern others, is the greatest scourge of humanity! (Sharp and ardent interruptions.)[20]

The prosecution portrayed Alibaud as a drifter who had been unable to hold down a job, corrupted by leftist malcontents in Barcelona. *Procureur-Général* Nicolas Martin du Nord went after his honor, accusing him of stealing not only the *canne-fusil* but money from his parents: "Let us say it, since the facts prove it, before becoming a miserable villain, Alibaud was a contemptible and vile man!"[21] In response, Charles Ledru crafted an eloquent defense from

Alibaud's brief memoir: "I belong to a poor family, and consequently honest and upright." On his mother's side was an uncle who had served under Napoleon. Alibaud recounted only one event from the life of his father; it echoed the old regime, was reminiscent of the episode of Voltaire beaten by the lackeys of the chevalier de Rohan:

> My father was a carter and coachman. He had the misfortune, in one of his voyages, to be robbed on the highway; the rope that held the possessions of the travellers was cut, and a trunk and a portmanteau were stolen. The owners of the stolen effects were opulent, they demanded an exorbitant sum; my father, not being able to pay a sum so considerable, was put in prison; these barbarous men kept him there. . . . [22]

Alibaud was sentenced to death as a *parricide*, for the attempted murder of his symbolic father. He refused to ask for clemency; though inclined to commute the penalty, Louis-Philippe allowed his ministers to overrule him.[23] Alibaud's one concern, on the Sunday before his death, was that the government would drug his food and drink with something that would take from him the "appearance of courage." He was reassured by the abbé Grivel, whose consolations (though not religious ministrations) he had come to accept.[24] On Monday, 11 July, he was awakened at 4 A.M.; he shuddered when the executioner ran his hand under his chin after trimming his hair and beard. As he left the Luxembourg prison, Alibaud shouted in defiance: "Yes, I die for the Republic. I repeat that I had no accomplices; I deny everything that the *Procureur-Général* said about my private life, my habits and my morals; I am as pure as Brutus and Sand; like them I wanted freedom for my country!"[25] He arrived at the scaffold at 4:55 A.M., his head draped in the required black veil. During the reading of his sentence he shouted, "I die for liberty!" Strapped to the plank, his neck under the blade, Alibaud looked up one last time: "*Adieu, mes braves! adieu! vive la liberté!*"[26]

Only a few weeks later, the police arrested two 17-year-old clockmakers, Fontelle and Oursel. Oursel's frequent boasts about killing the king had led his co-workers to report him to the police. He confessed freely, admitting that he had plotted an assassination with his comrade Fontelle, inspired by Alibaud's example. On 24 July they bought knives ("daggers") in preparation for the annual national guard review, when they would make a mad rush against the king. When there was no review—it would have been the first anniversary of the Fieschi attempt—they had agreed to wait for another opportunity.[27]

Oursel admitted to several motives. He did not like royalty, and he was angry about the state of siege back in 1832. The previous February, he had petitioned to get his father a position as *valet de pied* to Louis-Philippe, but nothing had come of it; if he killed the king, his ambition was to be *valet de chambre* to the First Consul (if there was one). He attributed his principles to the books Fontelle had lent him. Fontelle hesitantly confirmed all Oursel had said; a better worker, he had allowed himself to be led astray by his more adventurous friend. But Fontelle took considerable pride in his self-education. He had read the works of Saint-Just, Robespierre, Desmoulins, Marat's *Les Chaînes d'esclavage*—250 volumes in all; and as for newspapers, though *Le Bon Sens* was the journal aimed at the working classes, he himself "had the habit of reading and understanding *Le National*."[28]

Once the two teenagers were in custody, the police realized that they were the very individuals described in a recent anonymous letter, which told of two young men who had boasted loudly about their plans to kill the king, and included a description: "The taller could be more than five feet. He has very black hair, a big nose, big lips and pimples on his face. I forgot to say that the taller is a little bandy-legged."[29] Those last two sentences should have tipped them off (one could imagine the giggling). But the letter was made part of the indictment, and it was thus a thunderbolt when, just before the trial began, Oursel announced that he himself had written it to set up his own arrest ("I wanted to make a name for myself"), a claim verified by a handwriting expert. Oursel had also carefully prepared for a trial, with his own original poetry (on the defects of Louis-Philippe) and a memoir entitled *Ma vie écrite par moi-même*, which presented him as a brooding romantic hero. *Avocat-Général* Plougoulm solemnly read a portion of the manuscript in court, bearing on Oursel's unrequited love for a young woman: "The more I found her resistant, the more it seemed to me that I loved her; there was nothing I would not have given to possess her . . . in my passion I went so far as to say that I would willingly relieve myself of life. Do not, [my friend] said to me, die without being useful to your country"—the very words, claimed the prosecutor, of Alibaud: "Alibaud said: 'Before dying, be useful to your country.'" The two young men were acquitted. The *Gazette des Tribunaux* treated them as two "*gamins*," who had been "seduced by the idea of a sudden celebrity, and [had not calculated] the extent of their actions."[30]

Meunier's attempt occurred several months later, on 27 December 1836. The occasion was the opening of the Chamber of Deputies, attended by the king and his three oldest sons, the duc d'Orléans, the duc de Nemours, and the prince de Joinville. As the royal party left the Tuileries, Louis-Philippe leaned far out of his slow-moving carriage to acknowledge his national guard escort. Meunier, standing in the crowd, took aim; the man next to him grabbed his arm as he fired. The bullet entered the carriage and shattered the glass window, a few fragments slightly cutting the princes. Louis-Philippe was untouched. The carriage continued on its way and the king opened the Chamber of Deputies as scheduled.[31]

Meunier was seized almost instantly by the palace guards. On his way to the post there were shouts of "*Vive le Roi!*," to which he, in a state of desperate bravado, responded "*Mort au Roi!*"; and then, "Someone will get him." According to one of the guards, "He said that he feared nothing; that eight days ago he quit his job to do it."[32] But while Meunier did not deny his guilt, he refused to give his name. He remained unidentified until the next day, when his uncle Etienne Barré came to claim him, having recognized his description from the newspapers—not an impossible task, given his flat feet, broken canine teeth, and corpulence.[33] Meunier claimed that he had acted alone; that he had been bent on this action since 1830; that he was motivated solely by hatred for the Orléans family, stemming from the baleful effect on France of the Mississippi Bubble, a financial disaster during the regency of the duc d'Orléans in 1720.[34]

Meunier's vision of himself as another Alibaud explicitly appeared during his trip to the Conciergerie prison, under the escort of police *commissaire* Louis Marut de l'Ombre. In a state of stupid excitement, Meunier claimed to be "Number 2"—a member of a group of forty people who had drawn lots to determine the order in which each would try to kill the king. According to Marut:

> We left the Tuileries in a carriage, the assassin, two municipal guards, and I; we kept the most profound silence up to the Quai de l'École, near the Pont-Neuf, where the guard who was beside me, at the back of the vehicle, made aloud the reflection that passersby must think it was hot in our vehicle; at this, Meunier began to laugh and said: "They certainly wouldn't want to be in my place"; after that, [he said], "one must taste a little of everything." On [the guard's] observation that the guillotine was not a very tasty morsel, Meunier answered, still laughing: "When one's beard is cut with that razor, one doesn't come back a second time. . . ." Some moments after, the same guard asked [Meunier] if he was not part of a society; he answered that he was. Asked how many members composed this society, he answered: "Forty persons." The guard then asked him what number he had; he responded, "Number 2. . . ." I

should add that having arrived at the court of the Conciergerie, and having descended from the vehicle, [Meunier] said to me: "Don't believe what I just told you; our society doesn't exist; I just wanted a laugh."[35]

It was vivid, this account: the closed carriage, the garrulous guard, Meunier's evident relish for shopworn gallows humor. The tale, as Meunier told it, also served to link him with Alibaud, his predecessor as "Number 1." The prosecution reluctantly abandoned this trail, unable to find evidence of a regicidal society (not for lack of trying); after the coach ride, Meunier steadfastly denied membership in any group.[36]

The assassination lottery was an urban legend of the mid-1830s.[37] The experience of Jean Redarès, a young medical student briefly charged in Meunier's case, showed how seriously the story was taken by the authorities. Redarès, who witnessed Meunier's attempt, soon returned to his home in the provinces and boasted about life in the big city, discussing the lottery as if he knew of it firsthand. His rural neighbors informed the local police. Redarès backpedaled furiously: "Finding himself one day in a café . . . he had heard several young men, whom he did not know, talking among themselves; one [said] 19, another 32, another 35 individuals were numbered to fire on the king, that Alibaud had been the first and Meunier the second. . . . These young men, he added, themselves spoke as having hearsay, and not as having a personal knowledge."[38] The lottery story was always at least one step removed from its source.

Its persistence, however, illustrated an attempt to assimilate the act of regicide into revolutionary practices, for there was an inherent conflict between assassination and insurgency. Revolutionaries functioned in groups, their very numbers proof that they represented the people. Assassination, in contrast, was a solitary killing, an "egoist" seizure of initiative, in opposition to the revolutionary culture of fraternity and solidarity. Through the mechanism of the lottery, the assassin was bound to the will of a collective, and therefore excused from the charge of self-aggrandizement.

Alibaud had consciously attempted to rehabilitate the image of the assassin, laying stress upon the sacrifice and self-immolation required of the man who pulled the trigger: "I did not want to fall living into the hands of my enemies; I would have wanted to take from my success only a glorious and popular death. . . . I had, in regard to Philippe I, the same right as that which Brutus used against Caesar."[39] But Alibaud also insisted that he had acted alone, a position that put him at odds with the group discipline increasingly required of the revolutionary. The lottery story had to be grafted onto him afterward; his proud solitude was transformed into a refusal to betray his (nonexistent) comrades.

Meunier at first wanted to see himself as Alibaud's successor, another solitary hero prepared to give his life for the republic. The erosion, under pressure, of Meunier's self-image, combined with the government's desire for a conspiracy, eventually led to the concoction of a truly absurd tale that nevertheless was put in all seriousness before the *Cour des Pairs.*

Like Alibaud, Meunier was an only child; his parents had separated when he was five or six, the result of the failure of their small inn. His father had become a coachman; when his drinking cost him this position as well, he became a street porter.[40] Meunier and his mother had been taken in by his uncle Barré, who found him "docile and timid," but unable to settle down; Meunier's apprenticeships as music printer and hatmaker had ended when he left his masters without warning to wander the countryside.[41] He had found some stability in the school of Joseph Simonet, where he had been a boarding student. Simonet had pitied him because of "his badly formed fingers, his flat feet, the lack of development of his stature and intellectual faculties," and recalled that "when someone dared him to do something, however dangerous it was, he did not fail to do it . . . one could say that sometimes his mind went astray."[42] After two years, Meunier had again simply disappeared, soon turning up penniless in Haute Vienne. By this time, in 1833, Barré had started a saddlery business; he gave up on teaching Meunier a trade and employed him as clerk and errand boy.[43] But Meunier became restless again and left his uncle, compiling between 1833 and 1836 a depressing employment record as clerk in other businesses, where he was invariably fired for incompetence.[44]

Meunier's personal history thus revealed an insignificant man, who had made but a poor impression on his acquaintances and was seemingly interested in little but eating and drinking to excess. (Several weeks before the assassination attempt, Meunier became so intoxicated that he collapsed on the street—at ten o'clock in the morning—and had to be carried away on a stretcher.[45]) Several months before the attempt he had challenged a distillery clerk to a duel over a trivial exchange of words. Their seconds had persuaded the two men to abandon the affair; he had unloaded his pistol by firing it, and had been slightly wounded by the recoil.[46] For Meunier, as for Fontelle and Oursel, republican regicide offered a much-needed path to manhood.

The prosecution soon zeroed in on Meunier's love of wagering, the fact that he would do virtually anything—eat an enormous cheese, spend the night outside in winter—on a bet. Eugène Desenclos, a fellow clerk, confirmed the prosecution's belief in his malleability: "He is a man who could be made to do anything, precisely by daring him; that was the distinctive trait of his character."[47] A man who could be made to do anything? Desenclos's examples turned out to be prodigies of eating, performed at single sittings. But the indictment would stress this sense of *amour-propre* that would not allow him to walk away from a dare as striking evidence that he was someone's pawn. From the beginning, they looked for those who had challenged him to kill the king.

The prosecution was particularly interested in Meunier's apparent epileptic seizure (or excessive drunkenness, according to his doctor) in the spring of 1836, while he was working for his cousin Charles Lavaux. It had taken five men in the shop to hold him down; he had shouted, "Philippe, if you have some accounts to settle with God, hurry; because I have been sent from Hell to assassinate you!!!" The following morning his comrades had made a joke of it ("I've been sent from Hell!") and everybody had laughed—except Meunier.[48] The *Procureur-Général* Franck-Carré also did not think it funny, regarding this outburst as proof that someone had pressured Meunier to do something he did not want to do. This view of him was advantageous to the regime: as a helpless stooge, he would inspire none of the admiration that still swirled about the lonely figure of Alibaud.[49]

Why did Meunier attempt the life of the king? In contrast to the conspiracy scenario that Franck-Carré would eventually present to the *Cour des Pairs*, the real reason was probably much more complicated: he did it because he was broke, in debt, without prospects, and at odds with both his uncle and cousin, the last two men who had been willing to employ him. Alibaud provided a desirable model, both for acting out such despair and for winning renown. And as testimony would reveal, Meunier had long been mesmerized by tales of Roman assassins, whose fame had lived in history.

The prosecution traced his last week in exhaustive detail, perhaps driven by a sort of fascination with his aimless, ambitionless existence, so alien to the industrious ethos of the era. The investigation revealed Meunier's intense isolation, and the absence of any strong loyalties even to the family that kept him afloat. He lacked intellectual conviction, according to a fellow clerk, and "was always of the opinion of the newspaper he had just read."[50] In the tumultuous early days of the regime, a family friend had pulled Meunier out of a riot, lectured him, and unloaded his gun. "[Meunier] let him do it," recalled an acquaintance who had been present at the scene, "because he is a man who can easily be made to hear reason"; but when the older man left, Meunier's comrades had persuaded him to rejoin the demonstration.[51] Thus he was one of the *lumpen*, or rabble, doubly dangerous because of his literacy: pliant, susceptible to the radical press, a potential foot soldier in any upheaval.

In the last few months before the attempt, Meunier had worked for his cousin Lavaux's saddlery business and had lived nearby, in a furnished room in a

hotel/café kept by François Jacquet. His fellow clerks and the barroom habitués
had become his entire social world, providing an environment of spurious con-
viviality that Mme. Jacquet mercilessly laid bare: "I never knew any friends of
his, nor any relations; I never saw anyone come to get him, and I never saw him
with anyone except the clerks of M. Lavaux."[52] She further noted that though
Meunier was the "plaything" of her café, he had no true friends: "The people
who frequent our establishment are in general businessmen . . . who know Meunier only as a young man whom they sometimes see in the café, but with
whom they have no conversation because of his nullity." Others confirmed this
view: "This young man did everything the others wanted and served them so to
speak as a puppet"; "he was only a kind of fool, to whom no one paid attention"; he was "a man of limited intelligence, whom everybody mocked"; he was
"a type of buffoon who committed all sorts of acts of folly."[53]

His job was thus the source of his social life; in the week before the attempt,
Meunier abruptly quit after a minor argument with his cousin Lavaux. He was
deeply in debt—he owed his landlords 100 francs for his rent and bar bill—and
he sold his clothes, amassing about 70 francs. He spent the next several days
drinking, and by the time he attempted the king's life he was down to 100 sous.[54]

After his arrest, Meunier was subjected to an extraordinary 22 interrogations by Chancellor Étienne Pasquier and Duc Élie Decazes. The lengthy investigation was not required by the facts of the case, which were simple and
never in dispute, but rather was aimed at the discovery of who was behind him.
The questioning soon turned on the definition of "accomplice." The investigation had clearly revealed that there were no accomplices in the normal
sense, for he had provided his own weapon by stealing it from his cousin, and
he had been alone on the parade route—but in a spiritual sense? The pressure
was increased during the sixth interrogation by allowing Meunier's mother
and aunt to persuade him to "tell the truth":

> Pasquier: . . . Yield to their tears and prayers, make known to the law the men
> who incited you to commit the crime.
> Meunier: I persist in saying that I had no accomplices, no one gave me bad
> counsel.[55]

As Pasquier continued to apply emotional pressure ("You know how unhappy your mother is"), Meunier became desperate: "I swear to you . . . that if
I had any accomplices I would denounce them."[56] But doubt had been planted
in Meunier's own mind after 27 days of near-isolation and the constant harp-
ing on one theme: "I don't know what to tell you; I don't know what pushed

me toward this horrible project; I could not prevent myself. . . . I have questioned myself, and I still don't know what compelled me."[57] The interrogations had elicited no new facts for days; Meunier became more confused, Pasquier more implacable: "There was no one who knew the advantage that one could take of you by daring you to do something, who would have said to you that you would never have the courage to kill the king?"[58] By now Meunier had begun to feel a sense of grievance. During his convulsive attack in the shop he had said he was going to kill the king; why had no one tried to help him? Suddenly, after over a month in custody, Meunier requested an audience. He had finally found his way to the story the authorities wanted to hear.

His confession took him back to December 1835, when he, his cousin Charles Lavaux, and his friend Isidore Lacaze had all been clerks in Barré's saddlery business, and the three of them had been ordered to make a year-end, after-hours inventory of the stock. Meunier showed something of a gift for narration, describing the warm stove around which they gathered, the vat in which they heated the wine, the intimacy brought on by late hours and lack of supervision. One evening, they had begun to talk about the many republican prisoners. One of Meunier's companions had suggested that the death of the king might result in their release, and then the other one had proposed a lottery to kill him. Three pieces of paper had been rolled into balls, one with a piece of bread hidden inside. Then each drew from a hat, Meunier drawing first, and the choice fell upon him:

> Then I said: "Then I'm the one who should do the deed," and I began to laugh. I didn't think it would go any farther, nor the others either; because neither Lavaux nor Lacaze nor I ever spoke of it again. Since then, this idea has always pursued me; it has prevented me from sleeping, and at the home of my uncle as elsewhere, I did not feel well except when I was alone; all my thoughts were directed to it; I dreamed of it even when I slept.[59]

Meunier began by letting both his friends off the hook, but then he changed his mind: "When I said that Lacaze and Lavaux took as a joke the drawing of lots . . . that was just my supposition."[60] The next day he asked for another hearing: "When I said yesterday that after the drawing of lots I laughed, and didn't think it would go any further, nor the others either, I was motivated only by the desire to ease the position of Lavaux and Lacaze, because I would be sorry to get them in trouble."[61] The story got better as Meunier had time to think about it, undoubtedly buoyed by the favorable reception from Decazes and Pasquier. Perhaps, after all, they had spoken of the lottery again: "I think they might well have spoken to me about it when I was drunk; this is an idea that came to me." Decazes was sympathetic: "Did they not often amuse themselves by getting you drunk?"—this to a man whose one real distinction was his constant overindulgence.[62]

The preposterousness of the case against Lavaux and Lacaze resulted in their acquittals. Their defense revealed clearly that Meunier had long been enamoured of glory and, especially after Alibaud, had come to associate it with assassination. Lavaux's attorney, Alexandre Ledru-Rollin, called as a witness François Thousery, a teacher at the Simonet boarding school where Meunier had stayed as a teenager. The insensitive Thousery recalled that Meunier had once expressed a desire to enter the military:

> But, as I often mocked his big feet and the way he walked, I cried out, "You, a soldier! You're a big baby. Where would you put yourself? In the infantry? You couldn't march on foot. In the cavalry? You'd make a handsome cavalier." To which [Meunier] responded, "Laugh, if you want. Everyone takes me for an imbecile, but if I wanted to, I'd be a man, and I'll make them see later on."

Then Meunier, thumbing through a child's history book, had spoken of the republics of Sparta, Greece, and Rome; he had suddenly exclaimed that Louvel, the assassin of the duc de Berry, should have saved his dagger for Louis-Philippe.[63] The teacher's testimony reinforced the pattern that Ledru-Rollin had elicited from other witnesses as well: Meunier had often spoken of regicide, the republic, and the desire to make himself known.

And indeed, in clear relief at the end of the trial was Meunier's hunger for fame. He had immediately disavowed his first explanation to *Commissaire* Marut de l'Ombre only to have recourse to it later, as Pasquier pressed him for an explanation. When, and how, had he drawn lots before?—with his two friends, of course; even Lavaux and Lacaze agreed that they had held "lotteries" for the last bit of bread or wine. If (despite their denials) they had facetiously drawn lots to kill the king, it was likely Meunier who suggested it, since the others had never shown the slightest interest in politics. Meunier, in contrast, had often entered into political rants, talking of the republic and denouncing the Orléans family, usually when he was drunk.[64] Isidore Lacaze suggested that he wanted above all to become famous: "Meunier, when he spoke of the need to make himself illustrious, often said to me that if he hadn't had deformed feet he would have engaged himself [in the army] or done something like that."[65]

Caught in the act, Meunier had to be found guilty. But his embrace of the unheroic role of victim had made him a favorite of the prosecution; Franck-Carré was pleased to tell the court that the king had already decided to commute his death sentence to deportation. Shortly after the trial, Meunier died in exile in New Orleans.[66]

The era of assassination had now begun in earnest; it took center stage in large measure because the republicans had been completely stymied in the streets. But regicide caused an angry split within the ranks. Working-class republicans were, for the most part, craftsmen in honorable work. The assassins were mostly disreputable: unemployed or unemployable, casual laborers, domestic servants. Many republicans never became reconciled to regicide as a tactic. Others were willing to defend assassination on ethical grounds, though they did not encourage it. A very small contingent, around *Le Moniteur républicain*, embraced regicide and actively sought to promote it, as more sparing of lives than insurrection. The king was the "keystone of the arch": remove him, and the rest—the aristocracy of money and birth, the bureaucracy, all sources of power—would come tumbling down. It was a theory that social republicans regarded as hopelessly naive.

Even before Fieschi, the July Monarchy had witnessed several attempts. The November 1832 *coup de pistolet*, a shot taken at the king as he rode on horseback to open the Chamber of Deputies, was never solved, the suspect Louis Bergeron acquitted in the *Cour d'Assises*.[67] The pace soon accelerated. From the autumn of 1834 to the summer of 1835, a total of seven assassination projects were foiled by the police.[68] Gisquet, who was replaced in the fall of 1836 by Gabriel Delessert, later claimed that he had wanted to leave the prefecture largely because of his constant anxiety over repeated attempts.[69] Minister of Interior Appolinaire d'Argout insisted upon the cancellation of the 1836 national guard review because he did not want the king "to come, at a fixed day and hour, to plant himself like a target before the shots of these *misérables* who want to sacrifice their lives for the immortality of regicide."[70]

The defense of assassination began with the classical tradition of tyrannicide, revived during the revolution and empire. Schoolboys learned that Brutus had purged Rome of the Tarquins while another Brutus, "the last of the Romans," had attempted to save the Republic by killing Caesar: "and one wants a young man with a head vulcanized by this education to transform himself all of a sudden into a man of the *juste milieu*," wrote a concerned bourgeois.[71] Morey's defender, J.F. Dupont, had unfavorably contrasted Fieschi, who fired from cover and had an escape prepared, with the archetypal Roman assassin who risked his own life—thus unconsciously prefiguring the respect that would be extended to Alibaud.[72]

In 1836, former Propaganda Commission member Marc Dufraisse, disturbed that Fieschi was being used to blacken the SDHC, suggested that even this attempt could be rehabilitated.[73] First, Fieschi's act was moral because it had a "revolutionary goal," in the elimination of Louis-Philippe. But Fieschi himself was to be regarded as "infamous," the "salaried instrument" of a conspiracy, who had then betrayed his comrades. Pepin could be seen as a sincere republican whose family concerns had made him cowardly. Dufraisse's homage to Morey, the "old *prolétaire*," was to become the dominant refrain among those who could stomach this attempt:

> This heroic old man, so sublime in the act he prepared, so sublime in the courtroom debates, so impassive to the last moment . . . this old man so eloquent in his silence and unwavering taciturnity; this old man died without having received a word of consolation from the stupid mob that surrounded him . . . Morey! Morey was sublime from the beginning of the drama to the end.[74]

Beyond individual apologias, the most dramatic innovation was Alibaud's vision of the assassin as primary victim of his own act. This concept received perhaps its fullest expression in the following anonymous poem, printed by the clandestine *Imprimerie de la République* and sent to Paris officials:

> When at last all smile at the tranquil despot,
> From the midst of this crowd in sterile despair,
> One day there comes a man, tired of bemoaning his fate in silence,
> A man with a heart of iron, a hand strong and sure,
> Looking with scorn at death and torture,
> Who says to the tyrant: You will die!
>
> He needs courage . . . Oh! To strike from behind,
> The enemy that he would like to throw into the dust,
> Sword in hand, in the light of day, in honest combat;
> To hear the vile mob surrounding his execution,
> Stupidly blacken his noble sacrifice
> By calling it a cowardly assassination.[75]

A similar interpretation was provided in journalist Henri Dourille's *Histoire de la Conspiration du Général Malet,* published near the end of the assassination cycle. Malet had been imprisoned as a member of the regicidal Philadelphians. In December 1812, armed with forged documents, he escaped from prison and presented himself to government officials in Paris as the successor to Napoleon—who, he claimed, had just been killed in Russia. Malet had planned to have Napoleon assassinated on his way back, the event which Dourille moved to center stage. Malet had expected no reward for himself except the satisfaction of giving France a republic; he had anticipated that he would be murdered by the emperor's entourage. (When asked who was behind him in his attempt, Malet replied, "everybody, if I had succeeded.")[76] Thus Dourille's call was to the assassin's special, sacrificial martyrdom.

The rationale for assassination was proclaimed most explicitly in *Le Moniteur républicain*, a clandestine newspaper that began to appear in late 1837.[77] The issues were left in stacks in alleys and doorways, available to anyone who cared to pick them up, and copies were also addressed to top officials.[78] (The government gave the sheet a wider publicity than its authors could ever have hoped, through the extensive reprinting of the articles in the *Rapport* of the 1839 insurrection.) The icon of the newspaper was a proletarian Lady Liberty, armed with a musket and seated on a barricade, with the words "*Unité, Égalité, Fraternité*" on her right, and on her left, "*Prudence, Courage, Persévérance.*" "Unity" in place of liberty (now frequently associated with laissez-faire "egoism") was reflective of the increased emphasis on group discipline. Yet, in contrast to the rigorous conformity required by societies, the call for assassination was a demand for spectacular individual action: "Each of you is placed on an immense stage, where so many Brutuses and Alibauds have already left the legacy of their memory to all the centuries of the world, in immolating or seeking to immolate tyranny."[79]

The precursor to the *Moniteur républicain* was a series of provocative *affiches* posted on city walls. The first of these incendiary placards, in April 1837, reminded readers of the *escamotage* of 1830; the second, a few days later, attacked the monarchy for "having reddened the scaffolds with the blood of the most ardent defenders of liberty" (Alibaud, Fieschi, Pepin and Morey). It concluded: "The hour of vengeance has arrived; let us strike constantly to establish fraternity among people."[80]

The third of the *affiches*, titled "*Ordre du jour: Phalanges démocratiques*," was the troublesome link in the chain. The authors regretted that failed insurrections had driven devoted republicans to try assassination:

> Aside from all that is praiseworthy in their project, there is no true success to be hoped for; because it is not enough to kill the tyrant, one must also annihilate the tyranny. One could not and still cannot obtain this double result except by means of the union of all republicans: more than ever, union is strength. So the committee, impressed by the insufficiency or the danger of isolated attacks, reserves expressly to itself by article 9 the direction of the blows that the society

should strike to attain the *double result*. It has stated that no *sectionnaire* can attempt anything against the tyranny or the tyrant without a formal order.[81]

This was the voice of underground orthodoxy. Prosecutors, perhaps blinded by the ferocity of the language, did not seem to notice that this placard was a direct and rather desperate order to *end* assassinations, which were doing the party no good. The authors of the piece—"the committee"—were politically unable to condemn assassination outright, but they tried to assert their authority (by "article 9"), and formally promised a new insurrection.[82] The next *ordre du jour*, posted at the end of April, revealed the series back on its regicidal path, extolling the September Massacres that had "purified" the blood of the people.[83]

The first *Moniteur républicain* (dated 3 Frimaire Year XLVI) appeared in November 1837. The prospectus proclaimed the newspaper's purpose as the destruction of the government of "7 August 1830."[84] In the fourth issue, which appeared in February 1838, they gently separated themselves from the old SDHC by describing Robespierre as praiseworthy, but too moderate. Instead, they put forward Saint-Just, Collot d'Herbois (the mass executioner of counterrevolutionaries by cannonfire, in Lyon) and Billaud-Varennes (a vocal supporter of the September Massacres).[85]

The authors began the fifth issue, in April 1838, with an explicit demand for regicide: "Why, in the presence . . . of the strong men of '93, are we so miserably weak?" It was essential to exterminate "Louis-Philippe and his line; we will prove the necessity for this in our next issue." The sixth issue, of May 1838, included the promised "proof" in an article headed by aphorisms (all appropriately Roman and bloody-minded) from Billaud-Varennes, Saint-Just, and Alibaud.[86] Given the impossibility of insurrection, since the regime was so well-defended by its soldiers and its money, "there is only a single resource to employ, regicide, tyrannicide, murder, as one would want to qualify this heroic action." Regicide was frugal: "To cite only one or two facts, if Brutus had dispatched Octavius and Anthony at the same time as Caesar, civil war would not have torn the Roman Republic."[87] And how much better if all the relatives of Louis XVI, including the younger branch, had been wiped out 45 years earlier, if in the "great days of the popular societies" they had killed Louis-Philippe instead of each other. But most significantly, if belatedly, this article concluded with a direct challenge to the *Phalanges démocratiques* and Blanqui's new *Société des Saisons:*

> . . . it is premature to occupy oneself with disciplining the democratic ranks, with preparing weapons and ammunition for combat; there is only a single

means to finish promptly and economically with tyranny; it is to knock off the head of the tyrant; in consequence we invite all republicans . . . to take counsel only of their courage and especially of prudence.[88]

After numbers seven and eight, the *Moniteur républicain* was suddenly replaced, in August 1838, with a prospectus for *L'Homme libre* (the title from one of Gracchus Babeuf's publications), which changed the focus from regicide to communism. The second issue appeared on 4 September 1838, calling for equality in living conditions, and the third issue on 18 September, with an attack on inheritance. But finally it was over: the publishers (including Minor Leconte, married to Pepin's widow) were caught in the act of printing the fourth issue, a call to put the theories of the protocommunist Babeuf into practice.[89]

As the *Phalanges démocratiques* placard had indicated, there was dissension within the ranks; the leaders of the *Familles* and *Saisons* were opposed to *Le Moniteur républicain*, and had apparently applied sufficient pressure to bring about the shift to *L'Homme libre* and a focus on economic issues.[90] The Taschereau document (a confession found in the Ministry of the Interior after the 1848 revolution, controversially attributed to Blanqui) blamed the *Moniteur républicain* on the "subaltern agitators," the dissidents who were "jealous" of the leaders of the new *Saisons*. The police spy Delahodde similarly attributed the newspapers to "undisciplined spirits."[91] Altogether the evidence is murky, but clearly the outright regicides were an extremist fringe.

Several raids at the end of September 1838 ended the nearly year-long run. In one apartment the police caught Antoine and Eugène Fombertaux, father and son, along with Leconte and the printer Jean-Baptiste Guillemin, their hands stained with ink and the print run in progress. Fombertaux *père* was released, and would participate in the 1839 insurrection. This was the fourth political arrest for Fombertaux *fils*, age 20, who had begun his political career in 1836 with a threatening letter to the king. Guillemin, the printer, was a veteran of the Lyon insurrection. This series of arrests took care of *L'Homme libre*. At the same time, the police raided a different apartment on the rue de la Tonnellerie, where they found remnants of a printing operation and old copies of *Le Moniteur républicain*. Zacharie Seigneurgens, a former SDHC member, was able to escape. Claude Boudin, a hosier long known to the authorities for his underground activities, was captured.[92]

Included in this case was the 18-year-old carpenter Pierre Aubertin. After the initial arrests the police received a letter, apparently tossed over the wall into the courtyard of the prefecture, that spoke of forthcoming issues of a revived *Moniteur républicain*. To their surprise, the return address on the envelope was real, and they found Aubertin. He immediately claimed that he was "Number 2." Aubertin was in possession of six red cockades, a home-made gallows from which he had suspended a plaster bust of Louis-Philippe, and an original regicidal poem ("Death to Philippe, Death to the cowardly tyrant/Let us strike down this villain, he dares to defy us./He is an *infâme*, he has betrayed his oaths," etc.). He had pistols; he had taken his principles from the works of Marat and Robespierre (thus revealing himself somewhat behind the most advanced opinion); he had written the letter himself. Aubertin admitted in court that he had no connection with the newspaper and had merely hoped to throw the police off track. A juror intervened, suggesting that he had been motivated by "the desire to figure in a political case"; Aubertin eagerly agreed, clearing the way for his ultimate acquittal as yet another foolish young victim of the "regicidal monomania." The jury deliberated for six hours, a period regarded by the *Gazette des Tribunaux* as unusually long; Aubertin's co-defendants were each sentenced to five years in prison.[93]

The ninth issue of the *Moniteur républicain* appeared four days after this trial. Three men were arrested almost immediately, notably Henri-Stanislas Vilcoq, a member of the *Société des Familles*. The court was particularly outraged by Vilcoq's article "Aux Pairs de France," which suggested that republicans should kill peers, since the king was too well-protected. Asked about his invocation of Alibaud: "I don't know if you know it, but the praise of Alibaud is in many mouths; it's the opinion of many men who aren't even republicans." He received an unusually harsh sentence of eight years.[94]

The final *Moniteur républicain* trial occurred in October 1841, with the capture of the fugitive Seigneurgens. Much time had passed; none of the witnesses could remember him. Before his acquittal, however, Seigneurgens defended himself in a lengthy speech (later published as a brochure, at his own expense). He almost certainly had been involved with the newspaper—he refused to confirm or deny—but he had since become a communist. He criticized *Le Moniteur républicain* because it called merely for killing the king; it had not considered what government would follow him, nor had it discussed the redistribution of property.[95]

Seigneurgens was not unusual. By the 1840s, many working men had repudiated republican violence as a dead end. The newspaper *L'Atelier*, written by a remarkable group of socialist artisans, explicitly rejected the classical archetypes, describing Brutus, for example, as part of a corrupt Roman aristocracy who killed Caesar for personal gain.[96] Communism and socialism would make great inroads into republican ranks in the 1840s, in no small part because of the failure of the last great insurrection in 1839.

But regicide, while it lasted, was an overtly theatrical mode, a point almost instinctively grasped by the young clockmaker Fontelle, who claimed he had acted "to play a comedy; how many times must I tell you? Each evening one hisses the authors at the Comédie Française. So: at this moment I'm being treated like them."[97] Fontelle and Oursel, and Aubertin as well, were indeed engaged in comedy, as was the pathetically vicious Meunier. Fieschi, for all his bluster, never managed anything more than a bizarre twist on the bedroom farce, torn between mother and daughter and finally thrown into the arms of the conspirators Pepin and Morey. Only Alibaud could play tragedy.

CHAPTER 10

REPUBLICAN COMMUNISTS: THE *TRAVAILLEURS ÉGALITAIRES*

AFTER THE NEXT MAJOR ASSASSINATION ATTEMPT, the investigators found in the possession of the would-be assassin the following oath, of a group called the *Travailleurs Égalitaires* (Egalitarian Workers):

> Before going any further, swear to reveal nothing of what is going to happen here. . . . Listen with confidence and without fear; you are with republican communists, and thus you are about to begin life in the era of equality. They will be your brothers if you are faithful to your oath, but you will be forever lost if you betray them. . . . Once the oath is taken, your life belongs to us.[1]

Republicanism fragmented in the 1840s into a number of small sects, many of them influenced by socialist or communist ideas; the most visible and coherent of these sectarian groups was the *Travailleurs Égalitaires*. The undated preamble of their written rules claimed that they had long existed by means of "oral tradition," but the leadership and origins would remain obscure, despite two extensive investigations. Member Napoléon Mallet stated that he had been initiated before May 1839 by Quignot of the *Saisons*, an indication that the Egalitarian Workers were a smaller, more extremist annex to the larger body. At some point they had adopted communism; an undated memorandum titled "Profession of faith of the new direction" called for the "community of goods," to be achieved by a popular dictatorship that would "destroy the obstacles" and "level the path" to the new equality. The members

were warned to avoid those "pretended democrats who want only political reform without touching the foundations of society."[2]

The group was dictatorial. Discussion, it was asserted, was "forever
closed" on the manner of selecting the leadership. Even more bluntly, power
came from above, not below: "the agents are the representatives of the Committee, and not the representatives of those that the Committee directs." Anyone who did not like that, "if there are any," had the right to refuse the oath,
but was bound to obey once the oath was taken. At the bottom of the hierarchy were *métiers*, composed each of seven "citizens" and led by an *ouvrier*. Four
métiers made up an *atelier*, and the chief of an *atelier* was a *contre-maître*, or
foreman. Two *ateliers* made up a *fabrique*, or factory, and the leader of a factory
was a *commis* (clerk); up to this level, the officers were to be elected by majority
vote. At the top of these pyramids were "divisional directors," appointed from
above, who controlled units formed of no more than four factories, or 224
men. At the apex of the group was the "committee" which had the "sovereign
direction" of the association: "*The composition of the committee is unknown to all
the Travailleurs Égalitaires, except for the divisional directors;* at the moment of the
attack, and only then, the committee will reveal itself to the entire organization, and march at the head of citizens convoked to fight." The committee's
instructions were to be conveyed directly to the divisional directors and "revolutionary agents," two overlapping positions. There was also a separate hierarchy of censors, one per *atelier*, who were to serve as the recipients of
denunciations of the "conduct or morality" of individual members.[3]

The rules of the *Travailleurs Égalitaires* were characterized by their emphasis on discipline and blind obedience; by a marked distrust of their own
membership, borne of long experience with police spies; and by their openly
communist goals. The rules also had very little to do with the informal way in
which they actually functioned. Nevertheless, the group was linked to two separate assassination attempts. The first was carried out by Marius Darmès, the
purest of the regicides: a genuine fanatic ready to die for his ideals, and un-
tainted, as Alibaud had been, by self-indulgent posturing. François Quenisset,
in contrast, was an apolitical opportunist who acted almost by accident. Both
attentats resulted in investigations that illuminated the back-alley montagnardism of the era.

The Darmès attempt occurred on 15 October 1840, at six o'clock in the
evening on the Quai des Tuileries. The king was on his way to his palace at

Saint-Cloud; the would-be assassin, partially concealed by a lamppost, knelt
and fired. A cloud of thick black smoke momentarily obscured the scene.
Louis-Philippe had been lucky again: the carbine aimed at him was over-
charged with powder and blew apart in the shooter's hand. After the carriage
sped away, all attention focused on the assassin. He was Ennemond Marius
Darmès, age 43, born in Marseilles in the year V (1797), resident in Paris since
1810. His hand shattered, he was in a state of fury ("I had him! I was sure of
my aim!")[4] "We made him enter the post," said one of the palace guards, "and
there he cried that he 'was a conspirator, that the king was a tyrant and he
wanted to kill him. . . .' He took it up again: 'I greatly regret not having killed
him'; then looking at his hand he said: 'It is I who took the shot.'"[5]

It was soon discovered that Darmès had been stirred to murderous action
by the extraordinary political tensions of 1840: the renewal of worker coalitions; a cluster of suffrage reform banquets during the summer; the foreign
policy crisis in the Middle East; and even Louis Napoleon's second ludicrous
coup, at Boulogne in August. Darmès' attempt, coming on top of these issues,
would precipitate the formation of the Soult-Guizot ministry (on 29 October
1840) that would last until the end of the monarchy.

The prosecution did not believe he had acted alone. *Procureur-Général*
Franck-Carré's stirring indictment claimed that Darmès had been "flattered,"
"perverted," "exalted" to the point of madness by the men of the secret societies, who had played upon his misplaced desire for glory.[6] The prosecution
soon had under serious investigation a number of underground activists, all
known or suspected Darmès associates; but none of the eyewitnesses could
place any of them on the scene.[7] Moreover, Darmès repeatedly insisted upon
his own agency, rejecting the charge that he was a *"fanatique exploité"*: "I read
all the newspapers, and then I adopted my solution."[8] Though he identified
himself as a "conspirator" in his first interrogation, he later explained that he
had "conspired" only with his personal "Revolutionary Tribunal"—which consisted of "Mably, Jean-Jacques Rousseau, and me."[9]

Nevertheless, the government finally brought charges against two other
men. One of his co-defendants was Valentin Duclos, the 44-year-old owner-
driver of a small coach business, started from his savings as a domestic servant.
A member of the SDHC, Duclos had been driven from the National Guard because of his suspected participation in the June insurrection. When the police
searched his apartment they found numerous republican newspapers and pamphlets, a liberty cap, various measures of gunpowder, and packages of ball cartridges (51 packets of 10 cartridges each, 50 of 15, and smaller sets, for a total of
1,295). It was believed that he distributed cartridges as he drove through the

city; he and Darmès were known to have been frequent companions in wineshops, including the café of co-defendant Claude Considère.[10] But with Darmès's refusal to implicate him, Duclos (represented by Charles Ledru, who had defended Alibaud) was acquitted of conspiracy; brought before a lower court, he received the maximum two years for possession of ammunition.[11]

The other man on trial was Claude Considère, age 33, who had a small café managed by his wife. A police informant provided a list of known communists who patronized his establishment. Darmès and Duclos had been present on one occasion when the conversation had turned to "the abolition of money."[12] Considère also had a criminal record, as the most determined of a band of seven who in early 1832 had attempted to burn down Notre Dame cathedral as a signal for insurrection. He had given his profession then as *émeutier*, or rioter ("I was still young, and I had the scent of gunpowder in my head"), and had served five years in prison, from 1832 to 1837. After his release Considère had married Rosalie Deganne, the daughter of his former co-conspirator, and they had two small children.[13]

But Considère also had a powerful friend. His main income came from his position as cashier in the banking house of Jacques Laffitte. During the *Trois Glorieuses*, Considère on his own initiative had guarded the Laffitte establishment, the very embodiment of the revolutionary prohibition against looting. Laffitte, who learned his identity only at the time of the Notre Dame trial, sent him money in prison and then provided him with a job. Jean-Charles Pannié, the head cashier, stated firmly that "[Considère] is an honest man, and he has the entire confidence of the House." Laffitte himself wrote a strong testimonial.[14] Considère, like Duclos, was acquitted.

The prosecution would have preferred a conspiracy, with Darmès as a simple-minded "machine" manipulated by the familiar "agents of disorder." Darmès could have saved his life if he had been willing to play the role. Instead the government was faced, as in the Alibaud case, with a determined, self-motivated assassin. Darmès would not allow himself to be molded into another Meunier, and he mounted the scaffold alone.

Shortly after the attempt, police *commissaire* Alexandre Vassal investigated Darmès' residence at 43 rue du Paradis-Poissonnière. He had lived for the past few months in a closet (2.5 meters long by 1.9 meters wide) off the entryway; even the proprietor said that his room was "scarcely habitable." The tiny low-ceilinged chamber was divided by a high uneven step that ran along its entire length. One had to bend over to enter the space, as if entering a cavern, to get past the step; his one window looked onto a dark interior courtyard. His walls were crawling with vermin.[15]

His impoverishment was of recent vintage. Over the course of fifteen years, Darmès had slipped from a life of relative ease as a servant in great households, his downward slide accompanied by an increasing political extremism.[16] In 1829, he had been dismissed for incivility, in an early indication of his ultimate path. But with his new wife, a fellow servant, he had taken up another good position with the treasurer of the Invalides. The two of them would change employment several times in the next few years, each time dropping slightly in status. At the end of 1834, after service in a wealthy bourgeois home, the couple became the porters of 33 rue du Faubourg-Poissonnière, a situation that lasted until May 1838, when the childless marriage was ruptured by his improvidence.[17] In an effort to get rich quick he had attempted to play the stock market, dropping all six thousand francs of his own savings, his mother's five thousand francs inherited from her second husband, and his wife's dowry. He had also begun to attend political meetings—coming home "very exalted," according to his wife, from reading and political discussions: "He spoke of Russia, peace, war, the Republic; but of the Republic only when he was very angry, because he knew that made me tremble."[18]

He soon moved to the rue Hauteville and brought his widowed mother with him, giving her so little money that she finally was obliged to seek other shelter.[19] Twice a week he served as an extra waiter at dinner parties, a remnant of his years in service. After about nine months, he moved to a sixth-floor chamber on the rue de Trevise, but was asked to leave when he exposed himself to several women in the building.[20] Throughout this period he earned his living as a freelance scrubber/polisher, but had begun to lose clients because of his obsession with politics and his growing personal carelessness. One employer recalled his "disgusting filthiness," and his tendency to read her newspapers instead of working. Mme. Grébin had been taken aback by "the monomania he had to link everything to politics and to talk about it incessantly." He had flared up at Mme. Marchand, complaining of "the difficulty one had in earning one's living when there were, he said, so many rich people who did not put themselves to the trouble."[21] His last few employers had decided to dismiss him entirely; aside from everything else, items—bed and table linen, bottles of wine—had gone missing at their homes, and he had rifled their boxes and drawers.[22] By the time Darmès was evicted from the rue de Trevise, his only regular client was an insurance company, and it is likely he would have lost this job too had not the office boy protected him: "He claimed that those who had, should give to those who had not; and he had pushed things so far, that if not for his extreme misery I would have told my employers and had him sent away."[23] And then he had moved into the hole in the rue du Paradis-Poissonnière.

Darmès' serving life, spent in semi-public noble establishments and palatial private homes, must have provided many opportunities for developing an instinctive and visceral hatred of inequality; the luxury, idleness, and calm assumption of privilege angered many who were even less intimately acquainted with the wealthy.[24] There were indications that Darmès had been insufficiently humble: his dismissal for talking back and his rants to various clients bore clear evidence of class consciousness. But despite his misery and *ressentiment*, Darmès had not been irrevocably bent upon assassination. Victor Fassola, a cobbler, was teaching him the trade in the afternoons: "He came to my new lodgings and confided to me his miserable situation. He earned, he said, only 20 sous [1 franc] a day and didn't make enough to live on."[25] But he had little knack for the métier, and his impatience had taken its usual political turn. He told Fassola that he was a communist, only to meet with a sharp rebuff: "I said to him that didn't make good sense, and this system was made only for the street bums [traînards des rues] and the idle."[26]

His impoverished surroundings had forced him to live much of his life away from home. Many cafés knew him as a troublemaker, and all described him as "exalted," insistent on talking politics at every opportunity. One *garçon* remembered a constant theme: "His conversations always turned on the community . . . he said there should be no rich men, no men who exploited others, and that all should work four or five hours a day."[27] Café keeper François Bergeret recalled his efforts to engage in political debate, "but either he was told to be quiet, or no one answered him, because he inspired confidence in no one." Jean Raulet had finally banned him from his establishment.[28] Moreover, Darmès, too poor to buy journals himself, had complained rather offensively about the selection provided by the wineshops. He read only *Le National;* the other papers, he said, had "sold out to the established order."[29]

Darmès was uncompromising: others should recognize truths to be self-evident, and if he did not get instant agreement he closed the discussion. "At the time of the workers' assemblies," according to an acquaintance, "he said that the hours of labor should be limited . . . I remarked to him that one could not limit the intelligence of a man and could not prevent from working those who desired to do so. To [my remarks], he answered that we could not understand each other."[30] To his former concierge on the rue de Trévise, he had asserted that the rich should give their surplus to the poor: "I observed to him, that would be convenient for the lazy and I added: 'so, if I work and you do nothing, then I should give you the fruit of my labors?' He did not know what to say and left me, laughing."[31] But Darmès must often have felt himself the only sane man in a land of fools, as he repeatedly heard the self-serving sentiments of the bourgeois *juste milieu* coming from the mouths of workers.

In his last few months, Darmès divested himself of non-political acquaintances and sold or pawned most of his clothing. (He kept his respectable blue frock coat for formal occasions, including a suffrage banquet and—most solemn and formal of all—the assassination attempt.)[32] His remaining personal keepsakes, the cheap reproductions that allowed threadbare revolutionaries to create domestic shrines, were inventoried by *Commissaire* Vassal. In addition to a statuette of Rousseau he had three prints, including a portrait of the Biblical Judith who had beheaded King Holofernes to save her people, and a scene from the life of Lycurgus, the seventh-century B.C. Spartan lawgiver, in this era regarded as a social reformer brought down by aristocrats.[33] He had a bronze medallion of Armand Carrel of the *National*.[34] He also had over 50 volumes and brochures, some borrowed, some bought, some stolen. Among them were selections from the Abbé Mably's history of France; volumes two through five of *Les Siècles de Louis XIV et de Louis XV*; the *Lettres de M. Burke* on the French Revolution; works by Voltaire, Lafontaine, and Corneille; the trial proceedings of the 1839 defendants; the abbé Pillot's popular socialist pamphlet, *Ni chateaux ni chaumières*. He also had a number of things—one volume of the *Code Napoléon*, a manual from the *École militaire*—that suggested a reading man's simple greed for the printed page; he hoarded these books even as he sold off his clothing.[35]

His voluminous papers included about fifty references from masters who had employed him, many with noble insignia, but no longer relevant to the person (grimy, malodorous, unkempt) that he had become.[36] But most interesting to the investigators were multiple copies, in his own hand, of Robespierre's last speech before the Convention, Louis Napoleon's 1836 proclamation at Strasbourg, and aphorisms from Saint-Just. "At each catastrophe I wrote," he said, adding, "I wrote alone; no one knew anything about it"—and thus each new iniquity would find him closeted in his room, retracing the words of the great men who had preceded him.[37]

He also wrote original compositions, often using his middle name of Marius and adopting the rhetorical style of the Year II. He had declaimed to one of the insurance company clerks a poem about the death of Alibaud.[38] His "Discour d'un homme du people," dated August 1839, began with the supposition that he had just killed Louis-Philippe, and indicated the extent to which his mind had been preoccupied with regicide and martyrdom: "Gentlemen, I do not want to defend myself," it began; "you are the strongest, consequently able to rain down upon me all the tortures and inquisitions; only, I would like to explain myself to you for a second, if you have the patience. You will not fail to say that I am an exploited fanatic; I will prove to you the contrary, I am the man independent of all secret societies and factions." He claimed to follow in the footsteps of "Socrates, Plato, Lycurgus." The July Monarchy had dishonored Frenchmen abroad and oppressed them at home; thus, assassination was justified.[39]

Darmès was proud of his compositions, and though they seemed jumbled together from clandestine broadsheets and *ordres du jour,* he claimed that he wrote from inspiration. Even in speaking he expressed himself in a shorthand of ready-made images; the *procureur-général* complained that Darmès answered questions with "scraps of phrases" that had been "textually extracted from his writings."[40] Here, for example, is the interrogation of the day after the attempt:

[*Juge d'instruction*] Desmortiers: How did you form your convictions?

Darmès: From the totality of circumstances. If I had killed the tyrant, we would have conquered the universe and all the despots.

Desmortiers: What means did you have for that?

Darmès: The head of Philippe, fallen to the ground.

Desmortiers: The head of Louis-Philippe would not have given you the means to conquer the universe.

Darmès: We would have given liberty to all peoples, who would have helped us, and I think that all France would have risen up in an instant. We would have broken the treaty of 15 July, the lion of Waterloo, and given liberty to all people. . . .

Desmortiers: You said just a moment ago that you acted with the goal of conquering the universe; you were not alone for such an enterprise?

Darmès: You don't see the position of things! I would have had with me all of France. . . .

Desmortiers: Supposing you had killed the king, what would you have done the following day?

Darmès: I would have done nothing, because I expected that men avid for rewards would have made me suffer the fate of Jacques Clément. France would have acted then.[41]

Jacques Clément, assassin of Henri III, had been brutally murdered by the king's bodyguard; Darmès also expected no reward. His statement that "I would have had with me all of France" was a direct quotation from Henri

Dourille's *Histoire de la Conspiration du Général Malet*—and Darmès had this pamphlet in his pocket when he fired. The "lion of Waterloo" was the victory statue erected in Belgium by the "Holy Alliance" of 1815; Louis Napoleon had used the image in his 1836 "Proclamation to the French Soldiers," a copy of which Darmès had in his possession.[42] The treaty of "15 July" (1840) referred to the recent crisis in the Middle East in which France had once again been humiliated by the victors of 1815, as they united to defend the crumbling Ottoman Empire from France's Egyptian ally, Mehemet Ali.[43]

The epic tone that "Marius" affected with his inquisitors was not his normal way of speaking, but one that he used for the public sphere of politics; it was the style of his "declamations," his meditations and poetry, the speeches he hoped someday to deliver. The prosecutors blamed him for his "excessive vanity," his insistence upon his own will: "He poses always as a political man," complained prosecutor Franck-Carré, "whose reason has been matured by profound reflections on events and their causes."[44] But apparently he did not adopt this same tone with members of the working classes, speaking instead in far more direct terms of the benefits of communism. Antoine L'Hoste, one of his occasional employers, remembered that Darmès had once bragged that "We have adopted a new mode of propagandizing, it is to speak to old women of Jesus Christ, to workers of their exploitation by masters, to the poor of the harshness of the rich, finally to each in such a manner as to flatter their passions."[45] For all his trouble, Darmès claimed only a single "proselyte," a certain Benoît, who worked in a print shop. Benoît's supervisor demurred: "I know Benoît very well. . . . He laughs at everything and took great pleasure in allowing Darmès to believe that he had led him to profess his opinions."[46] His efforts had thus met with universal derision even from workers themselves.

Nevertheless, the events of the summer and early fall had led Darmès to believe that France was on the verge of revolution. Suffrage reform banquets were held throughout the country, beginning in 1839. By the summer of 1840, Paris banquets had begun to include the working classes, who found the entry price of 40 sous (or 2 francs) within their means—even Darmès, for whom 40 sous represented two days of labor. Darmès had attended the Châtillon banquet on 31 August—the largest such event, with reportedly more than six thousand participants, and set within a grassy amphitheater. Among the speakers, Edouard Degouves-Denuncques of the *National*, linking the recent treaty with that of 1815, asserted that France would not have been insulted by the treaty of 15 July "if the interests of national honor rested in better hands." (Reported the *National*, "for several minutes more than 5,000 citizens made the air ring with the cries: 'Down with the treaties of 1815!'")[47] The *National* praised the good order and pacific intentions of the banqueteers. But however peaceful the event, however clear the object of suffrage reform—it was not clear to Darmès, who must have believed himself in the midst of like-minded souls who would welcome his act, who took all too literally the exaggerated rhetoric that was customary even among moderates.

The summer and fall of 1840 had also witnessed numerous workers' coalition meetings: the tailors in June, followed by shoemakers, carpenters, stonemasons, cabinetmakers, locksmiths, and others. The number of legal pursuits against workers more than doubled in 1840 over the previous year.[48] Darmès had attended the gatherings held in the faubourg Saint-Antoine and the suburbs; on one occasion, stirred by a fiery speech, he became enraged at a worker who criticized it: "Darmès replied to me that I was not French, and that I should be sent out of France." But Darmès, the former "parasite" of the upper classes, also encountered bias from artisans and journeymen; this same demonstrator told him that it was only "workers who belong to *ateliers* here." Perhaps such scorn had driven him to his failed effort at cobbling.[49]

In the immediate aftermath of the coalition meetings, Darmès had been excited and talkative. Victor Fassola reported that he "spoke with a lot of exaltation of these gatherings"—so much so, that Fassola had once refused to let him inside the shop.[50] But then, suddenly, Darmès had become withdrawn, "taciturn and distracted."[51] During the last week before the attempt, he went several times to the Place de la Concorde to plan his shot.[52] In the last few days, his neighbors heard him shouting out the words of the *Marseillaise* in his room.[53]

Darmès spent the morning of 15 October at the insurance office where he scrubbed, even borrowing one of their desks to copy the rules of the *Travailleurs Égalitaires*.[54] He went to the palace, where he learned that the king would be leaving that evening for Saint-Cloud. He then went home, changed from his scrubber's garb to his clean blue frock coat, and left shortly after 1 P.M. Darmès told several stories before finally stating that he had gone to Considère's café to pay a debt (1.25 francs), then returned home for his gun.[55] This odd side trip, which took him all the way to the heights of Montmartre, led the prosecution to believe that Considère must have armed him; but they were unable to prove it, nor were they able to determine where Darmès had obtained his weapon.

In the courtroom, the prosecution resorted to the hoary device of testimony by prison guards to prove that he had accomplices. Darmès challenged their accuracy. He had not said "I was not alone" on the day of the attempt, but rather "I am not alone," a reference to the millions of Frenchmen behind

him: "I told them: 'I am not alone,' and not 'I was not alone on the place de la
Concorde.'" They claimed that Darmès had blamed Louis-Philippe for violating the laws of the Charter, to which he replied, "I did not say *the laws of the
Charter*, but *the program of the Hôtel de Ville*."[56] He was careful to avoid being
tripped up, refusing to answer certain questions and repeatedly referring the
court to his written depositions; he also requested a copy of each day's proceedings.[57]

It was clear that Darmès was entangled on some level with the underground movement. He may well have brushed up against some of the important men of the second rank, and put in a word or two at tavern conferences.
Franck-Carré noted his extensive document collection, including several
copies of the *Règlement*. Most of all, it was a matter of his speech: "It is the very
language of the clubs that he constantly spoke before justice."[58] But those indications did not make a conspiracy.

Darmès's act was an assertion of his own existence, of a life that was about
to be extinguished by misery. His future would have been a gradual descent
into despair, as he sold or pawned the remnants of his prosperous past, cadged
drinks, borrowed a few sous for the odd bowl of soup. Only his fanaticism
burned brightly, and even when he was sentenced to death he made no effort
to save himself with revelations about the underground. He was executed on
31 May 1841, having refused to request a pardon. Troops kept far back those
who had come to watch his last moments; nevertheless, he could be heard
shouting, "*A bas tyrans!*" and "*Vive la France! mort à ses ennemis!*" as his sentence was read on the scaffold. He made a speech before he died; his words
were not recorded.[59] Early in the investigation, one of his interrogators had
berated him on the grounds that his act, if successful, would have thrown the
country into chaos, the people into despair: France under Louis-Philippe was
perfectly tranquil. "You see it as tranquil," Darmès had replied; "I see it inside
a volcano."[60]

The next would-be regicide was less sublime. The Quenisset attempt of 13
September 1841 occurred during a regimental parade, and was directed
against three of the princes: the duc d'Orléans, the duc de Nemours, and especially the duc d'Aumale, just back from Algeria as colonel of the 17th Light Infantry. ("It appears that I begin to count for something," reportedly
commented 19-year-old Aumale, the fourth of Louis-Philippe's five sons.)[61]

François Quenisset had been on the parade route for some minutes, waving a big straw hat and shouting, "*A bas le duc d'Aumale! mort au Prince!*", causing one witness to think that "this man was an imbecile or drunk."[62] When the regiment appeared, Quenisset reached under his jacket, pulled out a gun, and fired. The single shot smashed through the eye of Lieutenant-Colonel Levaillant's horse; the animal fell to its knees.[63] The brothers displayed their father's characteristic coolness under fire, as they immediately calmed the soldiers. Their bravery provoked cheers of "*Vive le Roi! vivent les princes!*"[64]

Quenisset was almost immediately seized by members of the crowd. The police and municipal guards who took him into custody were obliged to defend their prisoner, "because he could have been killed by the people who threw themselves on him."[65] Quenisset, half-dragged, half-carried, shouted, "I'm the guilty one! Kill me! Don't make me suffer!"[66] Shortly thereafter he was placed in a coach. "Scarcely inside the vehicle, this man became terrible and very difficult to hold," reported one of his guards; "the efforts of four men were scarcely sufficient; he was like a Hercules."[67] Several of the arresting officers believed he was searching the faces of the crowd for rescuers; when no one came forward, he was completely overtaken by rage.[68] The prosecutors were eventually able to get convictions against twelve of the seventeen men brought to trial for this attempt, most of them members of the *Travailleurs Égalitaires*.

François Quenisset was a 27-year-old sawyer from Haute Saône who had been in Paris since November 1837. He lived with a laundress, Caroline Leplâtre, with whom he had a two-month-old daughter. He had been using the assumed name of Nicolas Papart because he was a fugitive from military prison. In his few years as Papart, he had already managed to earn a six-month sentence for knifing someone in a bar.[69] After two days in custody, Quenisset confessed, asserting that he had been forced to commit his attempt by the *Travailleurs Égalitaires*. He asked for protection for his wife and child from the vengeance of the group.

Perhaps inspired by the Meunier defense, he presented a version of the event that reduced his role to that of a trigger man manipulated by ruthless conspirators:

> I was like a machine that one sets into operation. . . . Considering the position in which I found myself, a deserter for four years, these men had no trouble winning me over. . . . I went into [the society] like a sheep, in the hope of changing my position, which was insupportable, because I expected every evening to find two gendarmes at my door.[70]

Quenisset claimed he had been set onto his regicidal path while in prison for his assault conviction. There he had met Joseph Mathieu d'Épinal from the *Procès d'avril*, Auguste Prioul of the *Travailleurs Égalitaires*, and several others ("these were my first relations with republicans").[71] His new friends had devoted themselves to his conversion: "They talked to me continually of their republican doctrines." Finally, Mathieu had pronounced Quenisset "a man of action on whom one could rely; they could make great sacrifices for me, because I could be very useful to them; but they must not fail me, because I would not fail them."[72] The last remark was perhaps an editorial addition, for he did indeed believe they had failed him, and he took his revenge in his revelations.

Quenisset had left prison and lived quietly for about ten months, until he had a chance encounter with Prioul and his friend Antoine Boggio, just six weeks before the attempt.[73] The two men told him of a secret society, which led to an appointment the following Monday at the establishment of the *marchand de vin* Jean-Baptiste Colombier on the rue Traversière-Saint-Antoine. Quenisset arrived with a fellow sawyer, Jean Boucheron, and found there virtually all of his future co-defendants:

> When we had each drunk a bottle, or 3/4 of a liter, Auguste [Petit] closed the door of the chamber in which we were all rather cramped, and he gave us a sermon. He said: "Citizens, you should realize that we're very badly governed, that tyrants hold the reins of the state; only the police and the lawyers earn any money. . . . I declare to you that I and my fellow citizens are revolutionaries, not those revolutionaries who want the bad, but rather those who want the good, for all workers; because I declare to you that we're Egalitarian Workers. Some of us here understand what this phrase Egalitarian Workers means, but others don't. I'm going to make you understand in a very few words. It's this: after bringing down the throne, we'll form national workshops, mutual schools, and other establishments of the same type.

The national workshops were to provide guaranteed work for eight hours a day, at a wage fixed by law; the schools were to be universal and free of charge. They all drank to the prospect, and the newcomers agreed to join. They went upstairs, into the apartment of Launois, known as the Chasseur:

> I went up with Boucheron; the Chasseur blindfolded me on the landing and he brought me into the room. Napoleon [Bazin], in a sonorous voice [*faisant la voix sonore*], said to me, as well as to Boucheron, "Citizen, what do you think of the present government? Do you think we're badly governed?" I answered yes. He said: "You know that we're revolutionaries; you'll raise your

hand and swear by your head that you'll despoil yourself of your goods and
your fortune, and you'll leave your wife and children if you have any, and
you'll be in the street at the first shout of alarm; you'll fight without counting
the number of your enemies. You swear? Pay attention to what you say, for it's
by your head. . . ." Before uncovering my eyes, the one who had made the
sermon told me that my wife and children, if I had any, ran the same risk as I,
if I revealed a word of what he had just told me; that I [must] guard well the
secret from my wife.

And that was that; from then on he had made it a habit to drop in every morning at Colombier's bar to fraternize.[74]

There was reluctant confirmation among the other co-defendants of this
particular evening of initiation, most notably by fellow sawyer Boucheron:

I allowed myself to be brought along; we went together to Colombier's
wineshop; there I found 7 or 8 people I didn't know. One of them said the
government was egotistical, commerce wasn't good, the workers were in bad
shape, and if I wanted to enter into the society, I would no longer need to
work when I was forty years old, because I would be taken care of; I accepted.
Someone asked me, who governs us? I answered that it was M. Philippe.
"No," answered the one who had spoken; "it's the bourgeoisie."

Boucheron added unnecessarily that "I didn't understand all they told me,
and I don't remember it. They blindfolded my eyes, made me get down on my
knees, and I swore to follow them everywhere."[75] The porter Giraud Pradel
had not understood what was happening until he was taken into the room,
blindfolded: "I realized, according to their language, that they wanted to overthrow the government; I swore what they wanted me to."[76] Antoine Boggio,
Napoléon Mallet, Auguste Petit, and Jean-Baptiste Colombier acknowledged
the existence of the group and the night of initiation.[77]

But if the group was real, did it follow that Quenisset had been manipulated by them? Certainly he presented a coherent and persuasive account of his
seduction: befriended in prison, accosted outside, enticed into taking an oath
that put the lives of his wife and daughter in jeopardy. His tale had the additional advantage of following the narrative long favored by prosecutors. Yet
Quenisset's past history and personal character seemed to belie such a passive
role. He was turbulent, having been sentenced to three years of hard labor in a
military prison for assaulting his corporal. His concierge regarded him as "violent and hot-tempered." A local tavern owner admitted that he was too frightened to collect the money Quenisset owed him. A number of his neighbors also

said they were afraid of him, and he was known by his fellow tenants as a man who beat his wife. The woman with whom he had lived for four years would admit to only one beating, when she had refused to give him money, and she also excused his recent conviction for assault by saying that "someone had provoked him" in a café.[78]

Quenisset combined his explosively savage character with feral cunning, exploiting the few chances that came his way. He had escaped from the army prison when lightning struck his dormitory.[79] The *Travailleurs Égalitaires* had been thrown in his path and he had bullied his way into the group (that was not how he told it, but his co-defendants had a different story). He also had a touch of paranoia that led him to believe he was being shadowed. Ironically, after insisting upon joining the *Travailleurs* he became genuinely afraid of them, impressed despite himself with the death threats in the oath. He believed there were powerful forces behind the group: he had seen "well-dressed" men at Colombier's café, shaking hands and speaking "to the most important men who were there." He claimed that he had been confronted by a man who corresponded directly with "the Committee," who had warned him over a drink that some of the other members were suspicious of him, adding, "you know that if you revealed something you would risk your life." And Quenisset believed he had been followed home on the night of his initiation by a stranger who kept about 40 paces behind him, which meant that they knew where he lived.[80]

During his pretrial interrogations, Quenisset had let slip his true motive for joining the society. The only part of his story that was flatly contradicted by the others concerned his initiation. Boggio claimed that Quenisset had not been entrapped into entering the group, as he said, but had urgently solicited his induction: "Quenisset demanded to be received immediately. . . . When I was asked if I could answer for him, I said I couldn't, because I had only known him three weeks, and I can't even answer for myself." Auguste Petit remembered it the same way: "He affected to have great sentiments, took out a knife in the wineshop we had entered, made scratches in his chest and threw it away, saying, 'It doesn't cut [deeply] enough.'"[81]

Quenisset had asked his father to obtain from his local mayor a certificate stating that he was his father's sole support and excusing him from the army on that account. Even if such a certificate had been granted, it would not have eliminated his military prison sentence. But he had taken that into account, asserting that if he had obtained the certificate, "my intention was to carry it myself to the Prefecture of Police, and to obtain my pardon by denouncing all those people."[82] In other words, Quenisset had decided that it might be profitable to be a police spy; his membership in the society gave him something of value to trade. By the time the mayor had refused the petition, he was already bound by his oath. Then, unable to go to the police, fearful of some distant "committee," he had believed himself compelled to fire the shot. Perhaps the greatest irony of this strange case was that in the end the *Travailleurs Égalitaires* did bear some responsibility for the attempt.

Nevertheless, the shooting itself was completely random. Quenisset did not have a permanent job, and depended on getting to the Place de Grève early enough to be hired as a day laborer. On Monday, 13 September, he failed to find work. He then wandered through the morning, aimless except for his steady drinking, until he chanced upon fellow *sociétaire* Boggio, who warned him of a "convocation" at Colombier's, called because of the regimental parade.[83] He found everything in ferment. Jean Jarrasse spoke wildly of seizing the guns of the regiment; others were earnestly debating whether or not to stage an assault. Quenisset attempted to question Louis Dufour, who was distributing two cartridges apiece to all the workers in the vicinity. Dufour told him "'that it was a question of a revolution; that it was a question of stopping the 17th Light and disarming them.'" Quenisset claimed that Dufour had given cartridges to "50 or 60 workers," with only a single dissent raised by a communist shoemaker, Louis-Eugène Couturat, who believed they were not yet ready for revolution; they needed another two weeks of organizing to pull it off.[84]

Quenisset then encountered Just Brazier, who gave him two loaded pistols and helped him hide them under his shirt.[85] After leaving Brazier, Quenisset walked the streets, looking for *sociétaires;* he went after his friend Boucheron who, like him, was "disquieted and exalted like a desperate man." He and Boucheron drank "a glass" together, and then they had breakfast, also undoubtedly well-lubricated, on credit. Quenisset gave Boucheron one of the pistols, adding a bit more gunpowder because he was sweating so badly, from alcohol and excitement, that he had dampened it.[86] Finally they heard the approach of the regiment: "I encountered [Boggio], and I said, 'You aren't attacking then?' He was reconnoitering, that is to say he ran from one side to the other to assemble his people." Boggio directed him to the other side of the street, where he spotted some of the members of his cell: "They began to shout: 'Long live the 17th! Down with Louis-Philippe! Down with Guizot! Down with the royal family and the Princes!'"[87] Quenisset had believed that "perhaps 60, perhaps more" would fire at the same time: "My intention was to do as a lot of others, to fire on the cortège that passed."[88]

Different parts of Quenisset's story were repeated in other testimonies. Quenisset had come to get Boucheron at his workshop: "He told me . . . that

there was something going on that day and we risked getting ourselves murdered if we didn't go." Boucheron also confirmed the events in Colombier's
café, while Colombier agreed that several *sociétaires* had organized the
demonstration there ("They were to shout, 'Down with the one! Down with
the other!'").[89]

Auguste Petit, the group orator, admitted that he was in on the early planning, having dropped in as usual "for a drop" at Colombier's: "We were about
8 or 9 [in number] when it was decided that a demonstration would be made
and each would arm himself for his own defense. No weapons were distributed, because it was only a question of a demonstration, and so, in this case,
each should arm himself as he wanted."[90] Others had been informed immediately. Just Brazier, who provided Quenisset with his pistols, was shaken awake
by Jarrasse.[91] Mallet, who had loitered indecisively in the neighborhood, went
to the parade route and "walked up and down on the sidewalk" before leaving,
well ahead of the appearance of the regiment. "I showed myself," he said, "in
the faubourg Saint-Antoine, so no one would hurt me"—i.e., he feared retalia-
tion for not keeping his oath.[92] Auguste Petit also suffered from nervous indecision. After borrowing a gun he fled back to his room, threw the gun on his
bed, probably stealing looks at it, and paced the floor. He ventured out an
hour later without the pistol. He had seen Quenisset ("he was in a sweat"), and
he fled when he heard the shot.[93]

Extensive corroboration of Quenisset's story was provided by Marin
Savelle, the terrified fellow worker who was dragged through several bars in
Quenisset's drunken wake. Finally they had arrived in Colombier's front
room: "Then [Quenisset] made me enter the room in back, where there were
10 or 12 persons who were as if in a conspiracy; I can't recall what was said.
There were 2 or 3 who said 'I'm going to go get so-and-so; [or] I'm going to
get a comrade,' and in effect [Quenisset] went to get *le grand Boucheron.*"
Savelle was left in the back room, pressed against the wall, too frightened to
leave; he was liberated only when Quenisset and Boucheron returned. Savelle
then attempted an escape, going into the alley as if to relieve himself, "but
[Quenisset] called me and made me come back in." Now "there were only
two or three people in the room; one of them put two cartridges in my hand
and gave two to [Quenisset]." Soon Savelle managed to bolt, "very relieved to
be thus delivered."[94]

Much of what had occurred was standard for republicans: the sharing of
cartridges, the discussion of weapons, the test of loyalty. Each man could decide whether or not to bring a pistol or dagger half-concealed under his shirt,

and it was undoubtedly more a matter of virile posturing than a real expectation of using a weapon. The testimony of the others clearly revealed Quenisset's dreadful misunderstanding, aggravated by his drunkenness, of what was really occurring; for he had mistaken the ritual demonstrations of solidarity for action, truly believing himself on the brink of battle. The carpenter Just Brazier, who had provided Quenisset with a gun (as a matter of republican courtesy) was roundly condemned for it. Colombier overheard the conversations of his customers to that effect: "They were sawyers, at the counter, who said: 'This imbecile who went and gave a pistol to that animal—he should have known he would make a bad use of it, a fool like that!'"[95]

The *Journal des Débats* believed it probable that Quenisset had acted on his own, but argued that the *Travailleurs Égalitaires*, engaged in a permanent conspiracy, were responsible nonetheless.[96] This foreshadowed the course taken by the prosecution. Still, the concept of a "permanent conspiracy" was difficult to take seriously in regard to this group. Quenisset, for example, had recounted the story of a high-level meeting at Mme. Poilroux's café in August (reluctantly confirmed by Auguste Petit), which involved Mallet and Launois the Chasseur and several others, including a certain Martin, "revolutionary agent for the communists of the faubourg Saint-Marceau." Petit had given another speech on this occasion: "We're composed of three fractions, the *Égalitaires*, the *Réformistes*, and the Communists; these three fractions are equally revolutionary, but they act in isolation and don't communicate with each other, and they're destroyed one after the other." They had then drawn lots to select "revolutionary agents" to bring together the sects; someone had also suggested that they take up a collection, "and putting in only 10 sous, if there were 300 of us, would make 150 francs, with which we could manufacture powder and bullets." And with that, "we settled up the four litres of wine we had drunk," and went home separately.[97]

The comic pathos of the meeting stemmed from the disproportion between their goals and means (the small-scale manufacture of powder and bullets, when they were facing a well-armed garrison and a government accustomed to insurrection). Adding to the futility was the fact that nothing about these meetings was secret, their very efforts to blend into the background calling attention to them. The 18-year-old *garçon* had observed them with great interest, noting that "they had the precaution to go out by twos and by threes, at more than a quarter-hour intervals." He had warned Mme. Poil-roux that the men were leaving without paying, but she was not concerned: "'Let them go; we know the Chasseur, he's good here.'"[98]

The government got its convictions in the case, including a controversial one against *Journal du Peuple* editor Auguste Dupoty. He was sentenced to five years under the September Laws on the vague charge of "moral complicity." In his panic at being arrested, the Chasseur had written to the *Journal du Peuple* to ask them to publicize his case, which the government took as a direct "link" to the conspirators; the discovery that Colombier subscribed to the paper for his café provided further "evidence."[99] Dupoty had attacked the government in his paper; the *Travailleurs* had carried out an actual *attentat*. Dupoty, who knew none of the men involved, was nevertheless the author of the offending articles and *gérant* of the newspaper, and was thus treated as their accomplice.[100] The *procureur-général's* ingenious argument against him, obviously an attempt to stifle the press, took more of the prosecutor's time than did the presentation of the case against Quenisset. There was great outrage among journalists over Dupoty's conviction, in part because it deprived the editor of trial by jury (one of the guarantees of the July Revolution) and brought him before the political body of the peers. The uproar over his situation obscured the fact that much the same argument—one might call it the charge of unwitting complicity—was being used against the others. If the case against Dupoty in effect rendered him responsible for violent acts committed without his knowledge or participation, the workers in Colombier's bar were also deemed guilty by virtue of the fact that their association with Quenisset had rendered them legally responsible for whatever he chose to do.

But prosecuting Dupoty offered the government an opportunity to remove a thorn from its side. Dupoty was one of the leaders of the electoral reform movement of 1838–1841, and the *Journal du Peuple* had become the movement's leading newspaper. Suffrage reform and its defeat, ably discussed in a series of articles by A. Gourvitch, marked the beginning of the Guizot ministry's fatal resistance to change.[101] This reform movement began as a petition drive to get the vote for all national guards; many were excluded from the suffrage, though called upon to defend the regime. The government became seriously worried only with the development of reform committees within individual legions. In addition, national guard banquets began to take on a reformist tone, particularly in the after-dinner toasts.[102] The reform movement provided a focus for worker demands as well as bourgeois leadership: though the expanded suffrage would likely not have included them, both Darmès and Duclos were found with reform petitions, as was café keeper Colombier.[103] Dupoty himself participated in a number of the banquets; he had made one of the toasts at the Châtillon banquet on 31 August 1840, which Darmès also attended.[104] He was a major figure in the reform campaign but was not—at least not until the Quenisset case—a name to reckon with. He was small enough to bring to trial, but important enough in the movement to make his prosecution a chilling blow.

The abbé Grivel, who had found something sympathetic about all the previous would-be assassins, was appalled by Quenisset, seeing him as something of a brute—physically powerful, with the "lungs of Stentor," given to excesses of all kinds; he admitted to an initial feeling of "repugnance."[105] But Quenisset had eventually shown regret, which—along with his confession—had allowed for the commutation of his sentence. Before he was deported, Queen Marie-Amélie busied herself about legitimating Quenisset's union with his mistress, and the little family set off together for New Orleans. There was disagreement about his ultimate fate. In late 1842, Quenisset wrote to Prefect of Police Gabriel Delessert, making reference to the "frightful misfortune" that had befallen him, but reporting that he and his wife had just become the parents of a new son, whom they had named "Gabriel" in the prefect's honor. Grivel stated that Quenisset had soon died of a fever; but the *Populaire* reported, about two years after his departure, that he had just been arrested for murder.[106] As an intemperate, wife-beating drunk—as well as a snitch—Quenisset had finally brought discredit upon regicide as a tactic.

Contemporaries had scoffed at the idea of bringing down the dynasty by killing a prince: Louis-Philippe, they pointed out, had five healthy sons and two grandsons. Yet within a year, a royal prince was lost, and the dynasty was mortally wounded. The duc d'Orléans, the popular heir to the throne, was killed on 13 July 1842. In leaping from his carriage, he tripped; his head smashed onto the paving stones. Louis-Philippe watched at the deathbed until the end, finally overcome with anguish: "If it were only me, instead of him!"[107]

This was a stunning political blow: the popular Orléans, well-known for his liberalism, had been the hope of the future. Now the king's heir was Orléans' four-year-old son, the Comte de Paris. Louis-Philippe was determined to have his second son, Nemours, designated as future regent. Nemours was known to be as conservative as his father, while the child's mother Hélène, the other potential choice, was liberal. After a noisy debate in the chamber, Nemours was confirmed.[108]

But personal grief was to shadow the aging king, creating a sense of melancholy that pervaded the final years of the monarchy. In 1847, Horace Vernet was commissioned for an equestrian portrait of Louis-Philippe and the princes, a painting meant to express the continuing vitality of the regime. The king, who took a close interest in this work, insisted on the inclusion of all five sons: at the king's right hand is the duc d'Orléans.[109]

PART IV

✛✛✛✛✛✛

RECRIMINATION

CHAPTER 11

COMPETITORS AND MOUCHARDS

"THE REVOLUTIONARY WORKER HAS PLACED HIS MUSKET in a secret redoubt," proclaimed the workers' journal *L'Atelier* in 1844; "he has thrown his last cartridges into the river, and the *ordres du jour* of the insurrectional society, save for a single example for history, have been fed to the fire by his own hands."[1] Republicans had won the battle for the working classes by 1848—the shape of *la guerre des rues* in February would prove that—yet in the 1840s, they seemed paradoxically in decline. They had no method: insurrection was impossible after 1839, the great secret societies were gone, and regicide was in disrepute. They had difficulty as well in carving out a distinct niche. As for political change, the half-loaf of suffrage expansion championed by radicals and the dynastic opposition promised a safer, less-sacrificial path. In social reform they had been outpaced by socialists, who offered an extended critique of the capitalist system and non-violent methods of remaking the world. In a blistering 1843 attack, Fourierist Victor Considérant asserted that the republicans had only one idea in their arsenal, the substitution of an elected head of state for a hereditary one; in the "matter of social and progressive ideas," he added, the republican party was "lighter in baggage than the government itself."[2] The *National* responded to such assaults in an important December 1844 editorial:

> All sectarians [Fourierists] have claimed that social reforms could be accomplished without politics; that they were practical with any form whatsoever of government. From that flow two consequences equally disastrous in our eyes: the first is that in following this route one must necessarily cause the people to become completely uninterested in politics; the second is that when people

are absorbed in the *unique* thought of well-being, the sentiments of abnegation and devotion so necessary to the grandeur of our nation are weakened, if
not destroyed.[3]

From this passage came two major points. First, the challenge for republicans in the 1840s was largely to preserve and defend the political arena as a legitimate site of engagement; they continued to insist that no meaningful
economic and social transformation could be achieved without a prior conquest of the state. Second, to reach that goal republicans believed that bloodshed would be necessary; the *National's* call for "abnegation and devotion"
meant nothing less than that. What follows is an attempt to situate the republican movement in relationship to its new competitors—the working-class associations, socialists, and communists.

Working-class groups, which included mutual aid associations, journeymen's
compagnonnages, and workers' "coalitions," or nascent trade unions, stressed
bread-and-butter issues. Many working men intent on improvements in wages
and conditions found 1830s-style republicanism to be irrelevant, compromising, and old-fashioned; the new generation of labor leaders often went out of
their way to deny any interest in politics. And yet the legal inequities suffered
by workers, clearly a product of their lack of power within the system, brought
many of them back full circle to the essential republican concern with politics.
    The old trade corporations had been abolished, in the name of economic
liberty, by the Le Chapelier Laws of 1791. "Citizens of the same profession"
were no longer able to meet and deliberate together; "coalitions" of workers
for a common purpose were forbidden; collective labor actions, or strikes,
were defined as "seditious crowds [*attroupements*]." The law of 22 Germinal
Year II prohibited masters, in their turn, from forming coalitions for the purpose of lowering wages in a given trade, a provision reproduced in article 414
of the Penal Code.[4] But while workers were forbidden to form unions, employer associations existed in the form of *chambres syndicales;* these organizations, composed of the masters of each trade, had been founded under the
empire as a means of regulating local conditions. Further, the masters were
not liable if they formed coalitions for purposes other than lowering wages—
and even a masters' coalition to lower wages was not necessarily illegal, in the
opinion of legal commentators Chauveau and Hélie, unless it was done "*unjustly and arbitrarily.*"[5] Masters were in any event unlikely to be prosecuted. In

a case involving a wallpaper workers' strike in 1840, the workers' attorney, Emmanuel Arago, clearly established that the masters' group not only had fixed the cost of labor but had even pressured a few recalcitrant fellow masters to lower wages. The appeals court responded merely by reducing the prison sentence of the strike leader.[6]

The prohibitions for workers, repeated in article 415 of the Penal Code, left them in a considerably more restrictive environment. It was forbidden "to cause all work to cease at the same time, to forbid work in a [particular] *atelier*, to prevent [workers] from going [to work] or remaining before or after certain hours, and in general to suspend, prevent, or raise the price of, work." Violation was punished by imprisonment for terms of between a month and three years, and for the *moteurs* or leaders of the coalition, with from two to five years. (The master's punishment, were he ever to be convicted, ranged from six days to one month.)[7] The legal inequities were frequently compounded by overt contempt. An article of the Civil Code, upheld by a *Cour de Cassation* decision of 1827, affirmed that the master was to be believed on his word alone in all work-related disputes with his employees.[8] Labor activists were denied the political-prisoner status they claimed, and were locked up with common criminals.[9] And workers were of course regarded as unfit for political participation. Shortly after the revolution, President of the Chamber André Dupin bluntly expressed the view of the *juste milieu*: "It is franker sometimes to say to the masses: 'You understand nothing.'"[10]

The July Revolution was followed by a period of unrest, caused in large part by disappointed expectations.[11] The 1840s were marked by renewed labor troubles, beginning with the series of mass walkouts in the summer and fall of 1840; contemporary estimates of those on strike ranged from a low of 30,000 to a high of 100,000.[12] In addition to disputes over wages and hours, the most significant issues were *marchandage* and the *livret. Marchandage* meant subcontracting, an agreement by which the *marchandeur* or *tâcheron* contracted to perform a particular task for a fixed sum; he recruited and paid his own labor force, and his profit came from lowering wages. It was a clear and obvious form of exploitation, and not merely because of the low pay. The young and unskilled were set to work at simple, repetitive tasks that failed to teach them their trade, "such that [wrote a carpenter] after having worked several days on a piece of wood, they are astonished to see what place it occupies in such and such a part of the carpentry."[13] The famous *compagnon* Agricol Perdiguier, a joiner himself, attacked the process for transforming men into "machines" who made the same things repetitively and were unable to craft an entire product from start to finish.[14] The practice was also a means by which workers might set up as subcontractors and acquire enough capital to go into business for themselves; even the striking carpenters of 1845 acknowledged as much.[15] But the attitude toward *marchandage* was largely negative, and workers, in opposing it, took a collectivist rather than an individualist approach.

The other major grievance was the *livret*, established by the law of 22 Germinal Year IX (1801). Every worker was required to deposit his *livret* (record of employment) with his master, and most were convinced, despite constant denials, that employers had ways of signaling troublemakers by means of agreed-upon signs. *L'Atelier* criticized the *livret* for its inconvenience in certain trades, such as tailoring and shoemaking, where changes of masters were frequent; for its indignity, in that no other class was treated to this kind of surveillance; for the master's ability to withhold the document in order to discourage a worker from leaving; and even for the cost of the *livret* itself, which amounted to a hidden tax applicable only to workers.[16]

The most famous collective action of the decade in Paris was the carpenters' strike of 1845.[17] The construction industry was not threatened by technological inroads, and the pay was generally good. It was characterized by a strong *compagnnonage* tradition, by a clear division of trades on the building site, and by the presence of many transient or seasonal laborers. Construction workers were stalwarts of insurrection in Paris.[18] In 1845, the carpenters demanded an end to *marchandage* and a raise in the day's pay from a four-franc minimum to five francs, in an agreement binding for ten years. French law did not allow for the fixing of wages, but informal *tarifs*, or local uniform rates, existed throughout France. Further, the carpenters referred back to the successful strike of 1833, when masters had agreed to end *marchandage* and had accepted the four-franc daily minimum for the next decade.[19] The masters now asserted that the 1833 agreement had been merely "optional" rather than obligatory, and that *marchandage* had never been prohibited. They denied that binding agreements could be established at all, a more extreme *laissez-faire* position than they had hitherto taken.[20]

The strike leader Jean Vincent began the contest on 17 May 1845, when he appeared before the masters. His proposals were flatly rejected. François Saint-Salvi, the president of the *chambre syndicale*, later explained that the masters had acted in order to preserve "a free contract"; moreover, the present masters could not bind the future: "if in the following year the salary is higher, so much the better for you." Between four and five thousand of the approximately six thousand carpenters in Paris went on strike on 9 June, in an unusual joint effort by two rival journeymen's organizations, the *Compagnons du devoir* (Vincent's group), and the *Renards de liberté*, along with many who were unaffiliated.[21]

L'ALLOCUTION (28 Juillet 1830.)

Polignac a mis la broche, y n'mangera pas l'roti enfans? veillez au grain, soignez les pénitens! du bon coin! tel et roid, d'hauteur ?!
Et quand nous aurons secoué le panier aus ordures, si la france nous doit plus qu'elle ne peut payer, nous lui ferons credit nom d. D...

Figure 1   Nicolas-Toussain Charlet, "The Speech," 1830. With permission of the
John Hay Library, Brown University.

Figure 2   Delaporte, "The 27th of July—The First Victim," 1830. With permission of the Bibliothèque nationale de France, Paris, Cabinet des Estampes.

Figure 3   Hippolyte Bellangé, "Revolution of 1830 (29 July): Forming Barricades," 1830. With permission of the Bibliothèque nationale de France, Paris, Cabinet des Estampes.

Figure 4 Nicolas-Toussaint Charlet, "29 July 1830: He Stole!" 1830. With permission of the Bibliothèque nationale de France, Paris, Cabinet des Estampes.

Figure 5   Jean Ignace Isidore Gerard Grandville, "Resurrection of Censorship: And it rose again the third day after its death," 1832. With permission of the Santa Barbara Museum of Art.

LES SAUVEURS DE LA FRANCE.

above   Figure 6   Henry Monnier, "The Saviors of France," 1831. With permission of the Santa Barbara Museum of Art.

right   Figure 7   Honoré Daumier, "Rue Transnonain, le 15 avril, 1834." Courtesy of the S. P. Avery Collection, Miriam and Ira D. Wallach Division of Art, Prints and Lithographs, The New York Public Library, Astor, Lenox, and Tilden Foundations.

Figure 8   Charles Joseph Travies, "Hercule vainqueur," 1834. With permission of the Santa Barbara Museum of Art.

Figure 9   Nicolas-Toussaint Charlet, "A Man of the People," 1841. With permission of the John Hay Library, Brown University.

BARRICADE IN THE RUE ST. MARTIN.

left Figure 10 "Barricade in the rue St. Martin," 1848. With permission of the Illustrated London News Group.

above Figure 11 "The Slaughter at the Hotel of the Ministry of Foreign Affairs." With permission of the Illustrated London News Group.

BEHIND THE BARRICADE.—DRAWN BY GAVARNI.

Figure 12   Gavarni, "Behind the Barricade," 1848. With permission of the Illustrated London News Group.

INTERIOR OF A PARIS CLUB.

Figure 13 "Interior of a Paris Club," 1848. With permission of the Illustrated London News Group.

INTERIOR OF A CHAMBER.—A FAMILY OF INSURGENTS PROTECTING A BARRICADE IN THE RUE DU FAUBOURG ST. ANTOINE.

Figure 14 "Interior of a Chamber—a family of insurgents protecting a barricade in the rue du Faubourg St. Antoine." With permission of the Illustrated London News Group.

Figure 15 "Insurgent Prisoners at Paris receiving Relief from their Families." With permission of the Illustrated London News Group.

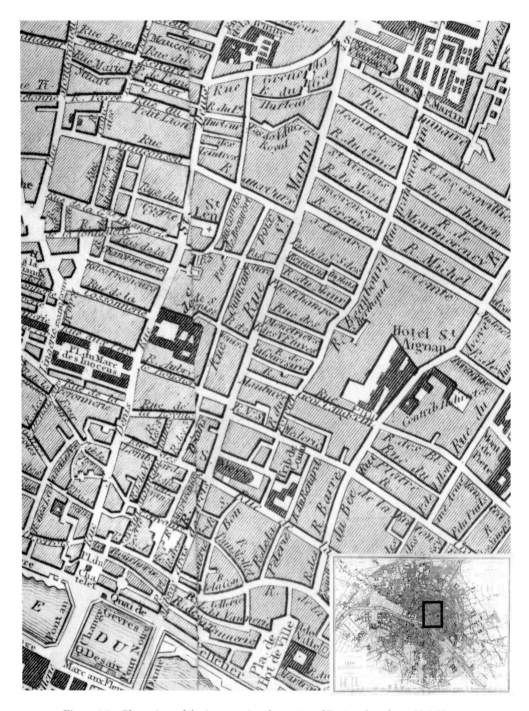

Figure 16 Close view of the insurrectional *quartier* of Paris; taken from SDUK, "Eastern Division of Paris," 1849. Property of the author.

The government soon intervened on the side of the masters. On 10 June, two of the strikers were arrested; their lawyers were refused access to them for over a month.[22] On 17 July, the police raided the *Mère* of the *Compagnons du devoir* (the inn that served as their operational base), seizing the strike fund and taking the innkeepers into custody.[23] *L'Atelier* pointed to the class-based nature of the government: "Is it not the masters who choose the functionaries of the government, who in their turn delegate authority? And are not the Prefect of Police and the *Procureur du Roi* agents of the bourgeoisie?"[24]

Throughout the dispute, both sides attempted to rally a broader public. Social novelist Eugène Sue published a calculation of the average carpenter's expenses, proving the need for a raise.[25] Strike leader Vincent asserted that "WE ARE NOT POLITICAL MEN"—indeed, they obtained the services of legitimist Antoine Berryer as their attorney, to remove any taint of republicanism—and wrote of the "forced unemployment" of most carpenters during at least five months of every winter, as well as the general rise in prices that had devalued their wages.[26] A letter from the *chambre syndicale* challenged their claims of distress, asserting accurately that carpenters were the best paid of all building workers. A worker had the right to demand a raise (and to go someplace else if he failed to get it), but not a fixed minimum. Complaining of the tyranny of the *compagnonnages*, 172 masters issued a joint statement in July that they would sign "no sort of compromise with the workers"—a collective agreement, as pointed out by *La Démocratie pacifique*.[27] (The masters, it should be noted, had also predicted that the sky would fall in 1833, and in much the same terms.[28])

By August, the employers clearly wanted the stoppage to end. President Saint-Salvi suddenly asserted that the *chambre syndicale* had no jurisdiction over wages. *La Démocratie pacifique* saw this as a surrender, slyly remarking that each master, upon "recovering his liberty" in the matter of paying his workers, would individually hasten to accept the new *tarif*. The masters had escaped the principle of collective bargaining, the ban on *marchandage*, and the ten-year agreement.[29]

But the ending of the strike did not prevent the coalition trial from going forward in August 1845. Several masters testified that their workers had been threatened and harassed by *compagnons*. The presiding magistrate Salmon, part of the panel that would decide the verdict, lectured the defendants on the virtues of free competition. Defense witness M. Ravot, a wood merchant, testified that four master carpenters, angry because several workers were attempting to go into business together, had pressured him not to sell to the upstarts.[30] (*La Démocratie pacifique* dryly reported, in a similar instance involving sawyers, that masters and government seemed to forget their devotion to the principle of free competition when workers struck out on their own.[31]) In his closing statement, the prosecutor considered it likely that the 1833 "arrangement" had been merely voluntary; otherwise, "it would be immoral and could never be invoked before a court of law." He finished with a by-now customary scolding of the workers for their tyranny: "You threatened the masters, you envy them; do you not make their existence intolerable? Is your lot not preferable to theirs? Does not the law give you, on a thousand occasions, a privileged situation?" The tribunal condemned Vincent to three years and the others to lesser sentences, with five acquittals. In November, *La Démocratie pacifique* reported that virtually all of the entrepreneurs had adhered to the demands of the workers.[32]

Socialism placed its primary emphasis on standard-of-living issues; it was, in the words of one exponent, "neither violent nor passionate."[33] It also had considerable intellectual appeal, providing a comprehensive explanation for the forces that were changing the workplace and a clear vision of the future. Among the major publications of the movement were Louis Blanc's *Organisation du Travail* in 1839, Flora Tristan's *Union ouvrière* in 1843, and (though just as influential for communism) P.-J. Proudhon's *Qu'est-ce que la propriété?* in 1840. The common thread among the varieties of socialism in this period was the belief in some form of workers' association. Such association plans, as William Sewell has noted, dated from the beginning of the monarchy. *L'Artisan*, a short-lived newspaper (August-October 1830), called for workers to pool their funds in order to create cooperative workshops; a similar project was put forward by Philippe Buchez in his newspaper *L'Européen* at the end of 1831.[34] The private ownership of the means of production would be replaced with joint ownership by workers, who would share in both the profits and the direction of the enterprise. While some republicans held such beliefs—the SDHC Propaganda Commission, for example—the republican movement of the 1830s had been focused largely on the revolutionary process. But by the 1840s, most republicans had adopted association in some form as a goal.[35] Many went further: according to one of the workers' journals that flourished after the revolution of 1848, "he who is not socialist is not republican."[36]

Louis Blanc's *Organisation du Travail* put forward a plan that required strong governmental intervention, and was thus extremely compatible with a future republican state. Blanc believed that associations started by the working classes alone would suffer from undercapitalization, so he looked to the state to create *ateliers sociaux*. The government would run the workshops for the first year; then the members would elect the leadership from among themselves. Every year the net profit would be divided into three shares: the first was to be split equally among the workers; the second, to be used for support of the elderly and infirm, as well as industries in crisis; the third, to be reinvested in tools and equipment.[37] Blanc's plan avoided harsh expropriations: social workshops, more productive because workers reaped the benefits of their labor, would gradually win out against private enterprise.[38] The state would manage the transition to a socialist economy by buying up collapsing businesses; by assuring financial resources and credit; by controlling or purchasing the central institutions—banks, railroads, canals—of the economy; and by regulating prices and exchange rather than allowing blind market forces to do so.[39] By 1848, Blanc's version of state socialism had won over many rank-and-file republicans.

Still, despite many shared ideas, socialism was perceived as distinct from republicanism.[40] First, socialists generally rejected the violence of the revolutionary tradition. They counted instead on a gentle, relatively painless economic evolution from the capitalist to the socialist state, relying on persuasion, education, and the gradual narrowing of the private sphere. Second, socialists of this pre-Marxist era rejected class warfare in favor of class harmony between workers and the bourgeoisie, who suffered equally, though in different ways, from the wretched system of free competition. Socialist rhetoric was quite different in tone from the standard republican attacks on bourgeois exploiters. Third, socialists rejected republican self-denial, favoring a vision of peace, prosperity, and fulfillment. In contrast to the communist position, which emphasized the achievement of material equality through the massive redistribution of goods, socialists accepted the existence of unequal rewards and obligations, for association would unleash productivity and provide plenty for all.

Republicans also had to come to terms in the 1840s with the revolutionary communists, or Babouvists—less a matter, in this case, of competing with an attractive ideology than of being tarred with the same brush. Like republicans, the Babouvist communists (inspired by Gracchus Babeuf's Conspiracy of the Equals in 1796, revived in 1828 by Buonarroti's *La Conspiration de l'Égalité*) still believed in insurrection, a vanguard of combatants, and a revolutionary dictatorship, a "provisional government" that would establish the basis for the new regime. Again like republicans, Babouvist communists believed in the need to take control of the machinery of state—in the communist case, in order to carry out their massive program of equalizing living standards. And it

was equal distribution of wealth that was the focus of their economic attention, in contrast to the socialist and republican emphasis on organizing the
means of production.[41]

Communists were also unlike republicans in their insistence upon the possibility of immediate fulfillment. Republicans found communists lacking in ideal-
ism, their desires "egoist": "All their theories finally are enclosed in the narrow
circle of physical needs." And the communists, in the *National*'s view, seemed entirely uninterested in political freedoms, "the extension of civic rights," as an end
in themselves.[42] Contemporary critic Théophile Thoré charged that communists were willing to sacrifice liberty for equality, while Sewell has noted the
"shadowy nightmare" within Babouvism of an authoritarian state.[43]

Some extreme varieties of communism took an odd path through the
Bible. While many republicans maintained the anticlericalism of the Jacobins
(the dying Armand Carrel's "no church, no priest"), republicanism also became inflected with Christianity. Albert Laponneraye, for example, linked
Jesus, Rousseau, and Robespierre as three "inseparable" names in the service
of humanity, with the first and last sharing a similar martyrdom; a post-1848
newspaper called *La Montagne* referred to Christ as "the first of the republicans."[44] Social Catholicism, or Christian Socialism, had started in the July
Monarchy with the priest Felicité de Lamennais, whose enormously popular
Paroles d'un Croyant presented Jesus as a friend to the poor; his famous address
to soldiers, written under the influence of the rue Transnonain incident, urged
them to disobedience when their orders were immoral.[45] Others went well beyond Lamennais to a justification of murder and regicide. Abbé Alphonse-
Louis Constant, tried in 1841 for *La Bible de la Liberté*, argued that the
violence of capitalism justified the physical force necessary to overthrow it.[46]
Abbé Jean-Jacques Pillot left the Catholic Church to form his own French
church, eventually arriving at a materialist, or atheist, communism. In his popular 1840 pamphlet, *Ni Chateaux ni Chaumières* (in Darmès' possession when
he fired at Louis-Philippe), he offered a justification of regicide: "When a nation finds itself under the yoke of a man who claims to have the right to govern
in spite of them, it has the right, at any moment, to attack him, surprise him,
and annihilate him without any legal proceedings."[47]

The single fundamental basis of 1840s communism was the abolition of
private property. Beyond that, its supporters fragmented into a number of different sects, the largest of which was also the most atypical.[48] Cabet's Icarians
(from *Voyage en Icarie*, 1840), intended to retain marriage and the family, united
by love rather than money; they preserved a belief in religion, though Cabet's
own religious writings (proving that Christ was a communist) were superfi-

cial.[49] In addition, Cabet shared with socialists a commitment to non-violent change: the transition to communism would be accomplished through a peaceful reduction of the private sector by means of a progressive income tax, the organization of labor, the education of the next generation, and the abolition of inheritance.[50] But Cabet himself seemed increasingly uncertain. In 1845 he approved the possibility of a mass revolution (as opposed to a minority *blanquiste* uprising), to be followed by a "provisional government" or dictatorship. Christopher Johnson has suggested that Cabet's attempted colony in Texas, his "escape" to Icaria, was a result of his growing dilemma. Ledru-Rollin and *La Réforme* had publicly rejected communism, and thus any union of the Left, in the fall of 1845. Cabet, who had come to recognize the irreconcilable differences between working class and bourgeoisie, could not suddenly champion class warfare after having spent years in denouncing the violence of others.[51]

The various materialist communists, in contrast, were defiantly revolutionary and often atheist. They were initially grouped around *L'Humanitaire*, which appeared twice in 1841 before succumbing to financial difficulties, doctrinal squabbles, and the arrest of most of the founders. Nevertheless, they had issued a powerful prospectus, described as "monstrous," "cynical," "disgusting"—and this from other communists.[52] *L'Humanitaire* called for the redistribution of land, the abolition of inheritance, and the immediate confiscation of property belonging to enemies of the revolution and those enriched by government service. In addition (taken directly from Babeuf's *Acte insurrecteur*), they called for the seizure of the homes of the wealthy and their instant occupation by the poor. (The short-lived newspaper *L'Égalitaire* defended this last provision, noting that the wealthy would be left with "their share" of their former homes.)[53] *L'Humanitaire*'s prospectus also proclaimed the abolition of marriage, the family, and cities. All these provisions, laid out rather baldly, were explained in Théodore Dézamy's *Code de la Communauté* of 1842, which envisioned a sort of anti-Icarie and became the primary text of materialist communism.[54]

Dézamy called for a division of the population into communes of equal size, to end the gulf between city-dwellers and peasants. Rural isolation would be avoided by "fraternization" among the settlements, as they exchanged goods and hosted festivals.[55] Cities were the origin of corruption because they were dominated by the wealthy—aristocrats, big capitalists, rich merchants—who built great palaces for luxury and display, engendering feelings of envy and greed. The rich also attracted to themselves a horde of unproductive flatterers, from domestic servants, to painters and poets (leading to a degeneration of the arts), to prostitutes and thieves.[56] After having "deeply reflected," Dézamy decided "provisionally" that each of the communes in the new system should be composed of ten thousand people. The peoples' palace in the center of each community, surrounded by a magnificent garden, would house cafés, theaters, a library, and shops.[57]

In discussing the family, Dézamy (who attempted to gain political cover by starting with the sexual arrangements in Plato's *Republic*) called for the abolition of individual marriage (the "parceled out" marriage or *mariage morcelé*, in his terms). Children would be scientifically raised in common; every adult, both male and female, would have a separate apartment, their couplings regulated by love rather than law. Since the "Equals" would spend most of their time in public spaces, they would require only three rooms each, including a bed chamber, a study, and a "small laboratory" that would also serve as a woodshed (the furnishings were described in considerable detail). The sexes would be fully equal, and "marital domination" would become a thing of the past.[58]

Did the materialist communists really envision themselves in communes of ten thousand, their children in dormitories? Were the males in the group prepared to accept full equality for women? One suspects that the rank and file might have been willing to keep the same old domestic arrangements in return for a greater share of economic prosperity. But what distinguished the Babouvists, what made them compatible with republicans despite all their differences, was the fact that they still believed in revolution.

The best expression of the Babouvist commitment to action appeared in a remarkable collective letter of 1840. The more than 50 signers included Louis Guéret and the cook Chaubard, revolutionary agents in the post-May *Nouvelles Saisons;* Auguste Petit and Louis-Eugène Couturat, both from the *Travailleurs Égalitaires* and soon to be caught up in the Quenisset affair; Louis-Charles Dutilloy, one of the organizers of the Belleville Banquet; and Celestin Parent, involved in two *Société des Familles* cases. All had attended the Belleville banquet on 1 July 1840, which served as a landmark for communists throughout the decade: a mass gathering, never to be repeated, of more than a thousand sympathizers, presided over by the Abbé Pillot.[59] The letter, occasioned by the negative coverage given the banquet in the republican *Journal du Peuple,* took the form of an attack on the "so-called" democratic press, which was mired in "the false and interminable route of purely political progress." Suffrage reformers, for example, did not understand that the worker was not free to cast his ballot unless he also cast off his economic dependence. Moreover, the original revolution had revealed "two salient facts" to those who could see them: "on the one hand the revolutionary lever, on the other the lack of foresight of the insurgents of '92, who did not have a new social organization to substitute for the one [they destroyed]." The communist activists differentiated themselves both from the "purely political" thinkers who had no social blueprint for the future, and from dreamers—the socialists—who had no understanding of the use of the "revolutionary lever."[60] The faith in insurrection was the principle reason why communism and republicanism could cooperate, and why so many self-identified communists joined the *Nouvelles Saisons*.

In contrast to its competitors, republicanism in the 1840s was virtually invisible. The moribund-from-birth *Nouvelles Saisons* kept no records and issued no brochures. The practice in the courtroom was to deny everything. The most detailed accounts of the movement came from Lucien Delahodde and Adolphe Chenu, both of whom were unmasked in 1848 as *mouchards*, or police spies—untrustworthy witnesses by definition, since both had joined republican societies and then betrayed their comrades-in-arms. Nevertheless, their memoirs (both published in 1850) were consistent with each other and with other sources.

Lucien Delahodde became a spy in 1838. In his letter of application, discovered in the police archives after the revolution, he admitted frankly that he had been unable to make a living as a journalist and wished to join the undercover police. His credentials were good (membership in the SDHC, as well as a trial for a press offense) and he was accepted.[61] But Delahodde wished to be regarded as more than a mere purveyor of information. In his memoirs he portrayed himself as a true collaborator to Prefect Delessert, as his advisor on the destruction of the movement.[62]

Adolphe Chenu, in contrast, admitted nothing, though he acknowledged that he had come under suspicion (unjustly, he said) after the February revolution. Chenu's political involvement had begun with his presence at Lamarque's funeral; caught up in the insurgency, he had spent several months in Sainte-Pélagie prison, where he became acquainted with many republicans. He came to trial in October 1832; the *Gazette des Tribunaux* described the 15-year-old Chenu and his four co-defendants as typical *gamins* of Paris, and all were acquitted.[63] He claimed to have participated in the uprisings of both 1834 and 1839; in between, he had joined and then fled from the army, returning to Paris to work as a shoemaker. According to Marc Caussidière, prefect of police under the provisional government of 1848, Chenu admitted privately that he had become a *mouchard* because the police had threatened to have him arrested for desertion.[64]

Both Chenu and Delahodde were active after the May insurrection, precisely the period that is most obscure. The creation of the *Nouvelles Saisons*, according to Delahodde, was undertaken by a "provisional" committee of journalists, including Napoléon Gallois and Richard-Prosper Dubosc (the latter named in the *Saisons* proclamation), who had rallied those *sectionnaires* still at liberty after 1839.[65] Delahodde quietly worked his way into the leadership ranks by playing against the stereotype of the *mouchard:* "[Some secret agents] are convinced that it is necessary constantly to roll one's eyes, make faces, and expectorate Montagnard phrases to stir the patriots; to each his own manner; this was not mine." When the new group decided to resurrect the SDHC *ordres du jour,* suppressed under the *Familles* and *Saisons,* Delahodde lent his apartment for the printing. According to Delahodde, the bulletins served as ideological lessons for the rank-and-file; they also reassuringly suggested the existence of a large organization under central direction. The new *ordres du jour* were handed out at monthly intervals to four *agents révolutionnaires,* who convoked the membership to various cafés. They posted sentinels, ordered wine, laid out card games: "In case of an alert everyone would begin to play, talking heatedly of indifferent matters." Finally, when all was safe, the *agent révolutionnaire* placed the party bulletin inside a newspaper and read it aloud; discussion of the doctrine was forbidden.[66] Delahodde became an *agent révolutionnaire* upon the retirement, early in 1842, of the communist cook Chaubard.[67]

The provisional committee soon turned over the direction of the group to journalist Henri Dourille—not a name to reckon with, but devoted and eager. The *Journal du Peuple* subsidized him with a job, and he soon gained some measure of fame as the author of the regicidal *Histoire de la Conspiration du Général Malet.* Delahodde thought he brought more "zeal" than "true capacity" to the job; moreover, he was notoriously indiscreet.[68] But he worked hard at recruitment, and in the words of one of his new members, Alexis Fougeray of the Quenisset case, "the workers of the faubourg had a great confidence in him because he was well-dressed, he always had a good coat."[69] But by the end of 1842, Dourille was increasingly under fire, reproached for his carelessness in allowing the police to find a list of *sociétaires* in a minor association case. Finally he quit, to work for a railroad company.[70] The *Nouvelle Saisons* fell into the hands of the four revolutionary agents; Delahodde would write the new *ordres du jour,* with the police receiving copies before the *sectionnaires.*[71]

But the *Nouvelles Saisons* was less a group than a collection of fragments; the different sects, most of them communists, included the *Travailleurs Égalitaires.* Some historians, drawing upon Girod de l'Ain's *Rapport* in the Darmès case, have suggested that the *Travailleurs Égalitaires* and the *Nouvelles Saisons* were the same organization; certainly the usual suspects turned up among the leadership of both.[72] But neither Chenu nor Delahodde thought the two groups were identical, and it is probably closer to the truth to suggest that the societies of the 1840s were fluid, held together only by personal bonds and the leadership of tested chiefs. As the Quenisset case revealed, there were frequent attempts to knit together the different "nuances," to establish working alliances among neighborhood sections. But the numbers were small. Cabet contrasted the popularity of Icarianism with the isolation of the other sects: the entire band of *Humanitaires* had been arrested in 1841, making a total of 19, while the *Travailleurs Égalitaires* "are 10, 20, 30, 40."[73]

Chenu, unaware of the shuffling of the upper ranks, described his younger, simpler self as a true believer: "I took my functions seriously and I executed with the most scrupulous exactitude the orders transmitted to me by the committee. It was then that I allied myself with Albert, who liked my zeal."[74] (Albert, or Alexandre Martin, was the famous working-class member of the Provisional Government in 1848.) But then Chenu was arrested and convicted in the rue Pastourelle affair, a pivotal episode in his personal political journey. He was set up, probably (as he believed) by Louis Guéret, a communist later revealed as an occasional informant, who left a sack of ammunition in his home just before a police raid.[75] In prison, he was snubbed by bourgeois republicans; and though he failed to mention it, he was undoubtedly found out as a military deserter.[76] Chenu's inclusion in the amnesty of October 1844, after less than half of his two-year sentence, was likely the beginning of his career as a police spy. In early 1845, Chenu made contact with Albert, a certain Boivin, and several others, including poet and doormatmaker Pierre Leroux (not the socialist philosopher), whom Delahodde also mentioned. (Leroux had presented himself as the chief of the faubourg Saint-Martin and had talked his way into the leadership.)[77] Albert's own stature was now greatly enhanced, for he had aligned himself with *La Réforme* (as the representative of working men) and thus with the leading old republicans.

The accidental death of the duc d'Orléans in the summer of 1842 put the long-term survival of the regime in doubt. About 40 republican veterans from the early regime (with Delahodde also in attendance) met and decided to overthrow the monarchy when the king died. Ferdinand Flocon, future editor of *La Réforme*, proposed a sort of un-society, by which those present would merely hold themselves in readiness as "the General Staff of a corps of revolutionary initiative."[78] This group became the nucleus of *La Réforme*, founded in 1843 as an assertive alternative to the increasingly moderate *National*. Godefroy Cavaignac, back from exile, was editor until his death in 1845, when it was taken over by co-editor Ferdinand Flocon. The journal provided great visibility for Deputy Ledru-Rollin, one of its financial backers. Editor Armand Marrast of the *National* kept the older newspaper away from the underground movement, preferring instead to build bridges to the opposition in the Chamber of Deputies. In contrast, the *Réforme* maintained an activist network. Marc Caussidière, a veteran of 1834, traveled through the countryside making personal connections with provincial republicans (and also selling a pleasantly surprising number of subscriptions, his ostensible purpose). Delahodde himself, regularly employed by the satirical *Charivari*, also had contacts among the editors.[79]

By the mid-1840s, Delahodde, responsible for the *ordres du jour,* took it upon himself to become the *endormeur,* the man who lulled the revolutionaries to sleep. Under Dourille, the orders had appeared regularly, in Robespierrist language, and all with the same three ideas: "propaganda, energy, hope for the near future." Delahodde's themes were prudence and patience. The *ordre du jour* of the rue Pastourelle case bore out his claim, consisting of a dull attack on the royal family and this soporific conclusion: "The path you follow is dark, but the sun is at the end. Let your steps be prudent and your words discreet; reflect: treason lies in wait for you, provocation is at your side. Thwart them by an energetic patience and indefatigable vigilance."[80]

Chenu soon found his *sectionnaires* becoming restive, impatient; they spoke of forming a *société d'action.* Even Albert was "received badly" by them, as one of the *aristos* of the *Réforme*, and the group began spinning off into various sects. Meetings continued, "but rather to drink and sing than to work seriously at conspiracy."[81] The questionable Guéret left to sell socialist books in the provinces, while Frédéric Dutertre—later revealed as a police informant—lost a compromising letter and was forced out.[82] The organization was entirely in the hands of Delahodde and Boivin for several months, until the latter quietly gave way to his enterprising lieutenant, Albert.[83]

The narratives of both Chenu and Delahodde provided the backdrop for the critical trial, in 1847, of the *Communistes matérialistes,* in which eleven defendants were alleged to have committed a string of thefts in order to finance the production of incendiary devices for a future revolution. This was not the only case of the late 1840s that involved the underground (nor was it even the only incendiary bomb case). But it was striking and unusual because of the prosecution's care in compiling the personal histories of the defendants, which had been shaped by the combined impacts of the republican, communist, and labor movements.[84]

The case of the Materialist Communists began on 16 January 1847, when Jean-Louis Crouzet, a 29-year-old metalcaster, was caught mid-robbery in the wealthy rue Saint-Honoré. He seemed an ordinary and practiced thief, in possession of all the tools of the trade. He betrayed his accomplice, Eugène Gannay, who was arrested with him. As they were being escorted to the prefecture, Gannay suddenly pulled out a pistol and shot himself in the head. On the following day, Prefect Delessert announced that many veteran *sociétaires* had recently formed a new group called the materialists. Four men—the suicide Gannay, Crouzet, Louis-Joseph Chabanne, and Charles-Claude Gautier—had carried out roughly a dozen thefts. They had pawned all the property and put the proceeds (they claimed) into a common fund, with which they had planned to purchase explosives. These men were guilty, convicted on their own confessions and other evidence. Chenu asserted that they were genuine communists who had rationalized their way to theft.[85] Republican outrage, however, was focused on the decision to prosecute eight other men—who had committed no thefts at all—on the grounds that their political sympathies had made them inactive partners in the conspiracy.

Of the thieves, Charles-Claude Gautier, a 30-year-old shoemaker, claimed a long involvement in republican politics. At the age of 16 he had been introduced into the SDHC by the newshawker Delente, a member of the Central Committee, "and he had been especially fanaticized (*fanatisé*) by the speeches of a certain Simon, water-carrier." He had joined both the *Familles* and the *Saisons*. After becoming involved in the 1840s labor coalitions, Gautier's first arrest had been in connection with the newspaper *L'Humanitaire*. In February 1846, he had been brought into the materialists by Léonard Delhongues, also known as Henri Blanchard, a Belgian shoemaker who had served eighteen months for weapons possession. Gautier had read Cabet, Dézamy, and the abbé Constant; he had been led astray primarily by Proudhon's writings on property: "He posed as a principle that property as it is organized, is a theft to the prejudice of humanity. . . . Imbued with these principles, I was led to think that theft is justified, when, like me, one does not apply the product to enrich oneself personally, but wants to use it to arrive at the end of what the materialists propose, social regeneration."[86]

The thief Louis-Joseph Chabanne, a 36-year-old shoemaker, dated his political awakening to his residence in a boarding house filled with republicans, including Fritz Austen, veteran of the 12 May insurrection. In April 1840, he had served a brief jail term for possession of a bayonet. In 1843 he had joined the *Travailleurs Égalitaires*, which had fallen apart by the end of that year. Chabanne had then ceased all revolutionary activity until entering the materialists, but throughout this period had subscribed to Cabet's *Le Populaire*.

The metalcaster Jean-Louis Crouzet, whose arrest had started the case, had become a communist several years earlier, when a coworker had given him

Cabet's *Le Populaire* and Dézamy's *Code de la Communauté.* As a new convert, he had been introduced to co-defendant Antoine Dejob, also a metalcaster. Through the efforts of Dejob's friend and co-defendant François Gibot, a 27-year-old *compagnon* carpenter, Crouzet had been thoroughly inculcated with the principles of communism: "They maintained that everything is bad in the current organization, that it was necessary to reorganize society on another basis, to suppress partial property [owned by individuals], the partial family."[87]

The eight non-thieves on trial were all avowed communists. Shoemaker Pierre-Joseph Javelot, investigated and released in May 1839, had a handwritten notebook titled *Philosophie et Chansons*, in which he had copied things that pleased him (for example, part of Constant's *La Bible de la Liberté*, something on the agrarian law). He also had some gun cotton, an explosive substance made of cotton treated with nitric and sulfuric acids, and instructions for making more. He had recently attended a banquet to celebrate Louis XVI's execution. Javelot denied that he was a *communiste matérialiste*, declaring that he was only one of the "republican communists who don't want to rush things," adopting the odd-sounding designation also used by the *Travailleurs Égalitaires.*[88]

François Gibot, the *compagnon* carpenter (who was working in the Franche-Comté at the time of the thefts), was said to be the brains of the group; knowledgeable about social theories, he had recently abandoned the Icarians for the materialists. Before leaving Paris, he had given a book on "military pyrotechnics" to Dejob. (Dejob had studied the book, according to Crouzet and Gautier, even reading passages to them aloud.) Gibot was one of the self-improving variety of workers, though his interests tended toward explosives; he had attended a course in physics and chemistry at the Conservatoire des Arts et Métiers. When arrested in the provinces, he was found with flasks of various acids.

The most prominent defendant was the prosperous Jean Coffineau, owner of a café and lodging house and entrepreneur in the construction industry. Coffineau claimed he had tried to "moralize and educate" the workers who came to his café: "What did I get out of that? They went to get drunk somewhere else." He regularly purchased large quantities of communist brochures, which he sold at a discount. He had also tried his hand at writing; the police seized manuscript notes for a work to be titled *Foundation of the Right of Equality:* "There are only snares, only murder, everywhere," he had written; "a handful of great thieves and millions of their victims. Inheritance is an immoral act; inheritance is an involuntary theft; inheritance leads inevitably to murder." Coffineau had been one of the founders of the notorious *L'Humanitaire*, and then of the 1845 working-class newspaper *La Fraternité*. Recently, he had become a shareholder in *La Réforme*. Coffineau later blamed the government for entrapment: "Individuals that some of us had known as workers having turned to theft for a living, fell into the hands of the police and the police used them to organize the so-called conspiracy which would present us to society as monsters."[89]

The materialists had been merely a talking group, nourishing their grievances with speeches, songs, and poetry. (Their anthem was the *Nouvelle Marseillaise:* "So that man has no more masters/And is finally sure of his rights,/With the guts of the last of the priests,/Let us strangle the last of the kings"—not much worse, in truth, than the real *Marseillaise.*[90]) Then had come a critical meeting in July 1846. Javelot, inspired by a newspaper serial about a revolt in fourteenth-century Picardy, had allegedly convoked the gathering to lay down concrete plans for insurrection. They had listened to a discourse on the necessity of ending the rights of property and heredity. Everyone being in agreement, the talk had quickly turned, as Javelot had wished, to methods. "It was no longer riots, barricades, gunfire," summarized the prosecutor, "but the destructive means furnished by physics and chemistry."[91]

The plan was to set off bombs simultaneously in different parts of Paris, overloading the police, the fire brigades, and the troops. Then the conspirators would begin the attack and carry out a "Saint-Barthélemy," defined by them as the massacre of all top officials. "This project raised some objections," according to Crouzet, on the grounds of practicality. Nevertheless, the group had approved the plan, and had decided upon theft as a means of amassing the necessary funds to purchase explosives—they believed three thousand francs would do it—"for the liberation and happiness of humanity."[92]

Gannay, Gautier, Chabanne, and Crouzet committed about a dozen quite ordinary thefts, until Gannay, "enterprising and audacious," began experimenting, nearly burning up his chamber in the process. Sufficiently encouraged by the results, Gannay proposed a new direction: they would use explosions, even before the revolution, as a diversion for theft. He suggested a wealthy grain merchant in Coulomniers, whose home could be incinerated while they robbed his business; nothing came of this. Crouzet provided the next target, which was suggested by a certain Lebrun, an impoverished peddler who briefed several members of the group on the wholesale liquor merchant Michaux, of Belleville. Gannay pulled out at the last minute when he became suspicious of Lebrun—correctly, as it turned out, for the peddler was working for the police, who had staked out Michaux's property.

In the end, the eight communists were each sentenced to between seven and five years of prison, with the lightest sentences—three years to Crouzet and Chabanne, two years to Gautier—going to the three thieves. The *Gazette des Tribunaux* found the *communistes matérialistes* a pitiful spectacle; the workers attempted to express themselves "in a sort of jargon of which they do not understand a great deal, and which is unintelligible for the public."[93] *La Réforme* made the inevitable, telling comparison with the Teste-Cubières affair, a notorious case that unfolded simultaneously in the summer of 1847. Former Minister of Public Works Jean-Baptiste Teste had taken a substantial bribe in 1842 to arrange a mining concession. Of the three principals involved, all members of the wealthy and powerful elite, two were punished only with a fine and *dégradation civique* (the loss of certain civil rights), while Teste, "who had soiled the highest functions of the state," received a sentence of three years, in stark contrast to Coffineau's seven. Teste was also punished with a fine of 94,000 francs—the size of his bribe.[94]

In the last months of the monarchy, the somnolence of the mid-1840s gave way to a more highly charged atmosphere, stirred by the banquet campaign for suffrage reform that finally provoked the revolution. Chenu and Delahodde both believed that the republican movement had begun to revive a little earlier, in 1846; Caussidière of *La Réforme* also believed that the societies began to reorganize themselves in 1846, "spoke of muskets" (though not, as it later appeared, procuring them), and attempted to overcome their differences.[95] Chenu pinpointed the materialist affair as a watershed event, stirring considerable anger within the ranks and opening up the possibility, once again, of a single powerful society; the *Réforme* committee gave Albert responsibility for the *rapprochement* of the various fragments.[96] Chenu would be forced to flee France in late 1847 because of his involvement in the *procès des bombes*, a case in which he was too obviously an *agent provocateur*. He would come under suspicion after the revolution, as would Delahodde, whose voluminous reports were found in the archives of the prefecture and who was confronted, in a notorious meeting, by his erstwhile comrades.[97]

But even their untrustworthy narratives made clear the extent to which working-class republicans had become indistinguishable from socialists and communists. The middle-class moderates who would dominate the Provisional Government in 1848 spoke a different language, had a different vision; their emphasis on political reform would be regarded as woefully insufficient by their followers. Moderate republicanism would become the mainstream of the movement, victorious finally in the Third Republic. But the old republicans could dream, and they did—triumphantly in February, tragically in June.

CHAPTER 12

CAPTIVITY AND DEFIANCE: THE YEARS OF MONT-SAINT-MICHEL

THE OATH OF A POST-*SAISONS* SOCIETY, a fleeting effort to rebuild upon the debris left by the last insurrection, included the following passage: "Our brothers are dead, the victims of tyranny: the glorious task of avenging them and continuing their work is reserved to us.... Do you feel in yourself the courage to withstand prison in order to fulfill your duties as a citizen?"[1] It was a foreshadowing, more perceptive than was realized by the young student who wrote it, of the future agony of the republican movement.

The image of republicanism would shift decisively in the 1840s, from active insurgency on the streets to passive suffering in captivity; it was the era of the republican as *l'enfermé*.[2] An SDHC *ordre du jour* had distinguished two modes of serving the cause, "whether our comrades fall in mid-career by the bullets of the aristocracy or by the sufferings of the dungeon."[3] But the prison terms of the early regime had often been cut short by royal clemency. Those captured in the May 1839 insurrection, no doubt expecting a continuation of the same pattern, displayed a noisy bravado in the early stages of their captivity. The printer Pierre Nouguès, in the depot of the prefecture, recalled that they drank a riotous toast to the "memory of the heroic defenders of the barricade Saint-Méry!" Fritz Austen was there too, his shirt open so his comrades could see his scars, toasting "our brothers dead at the barricade Greneta!"[4] But in the 1840s, the sentences would stretch into years, into lifetimes. In 1847, *La*

Réforme recalled those who, "conquered in the street, continued their resistance in the dungeons, and rather than recant, resigned themselves, and resign themselves still, to the tortures of a slow and pitiless agony."[5] The incarcerated leaders of the movement, released by the February Revolution, would return to Paris pale, enfeebled, and older than their years, blinking in the sunlight of their sudden resurrection.

Early in the regime, the premier prison for republicans was Sainte-Pélagie in Paris—rebellious, angry, and bursting at the seams. (A journalist on trial in 1832 gave his address in court as "Sainte-Pélagie, where all the energetic men are."[6]) Its population had swelled to 800 just after the June 1832 uprising, and the inmates developed the nightly tradition of the "evening prayer": a performance of the *Chant du Départ* and the *Parisienne*, a remembrance of those who fell in the *Trois Glorieuses*, a recital of the regime's broken promises, and a solemn rendition of the *Marseillaise* as they knelt in a circle.[7] The authorities occasionally thrust particularly stubborn politicals among common criminals; one of Blanqui's first public statements was an 1831 protest, full of rather strenuous sarcasm, against the imprisonment of himself and four other students with the thieves in the Force prison.[8]

But prisons, once disorderly and promiscuous, were substantially transformed in the nineteenth century. An influential interpretation has described the purpose of the prison—like that of the insane asylum and the factory—as a matter of reshaping the individual, disciplining him into a productive and industrious worker for capitalist society.[9] The American penitentiary became the favored model: absolute silence combined with work and prayer were the essential ingredients, juggled according to the method of Philadelphia (solitary confinement both day and night) or Auburn (solitary confinement only at night). The Pentonville prison in Britain, arranged according to the Philadelphia system, opened to much admiration in 1842, its record soon marred by cases of insanity.[10]

In France, the debate was led by Alexis de Tocqueville and Gustave de Beaumont, whose research in the United States and Europe, published in 1833, was followed by serious efforts to transform the French penal system. The July Monarchy was unable to pass the necessary laws to establish a penitentiary regime, though serious attempts were made in 1840, 1843–1844, and 1846; the law finally passed in 1847 was too late to take effect.[11] In the face of legislative inaction the administration, as Gordon Wright has noted, began to develop the system of "cellular isolation" by administrative fiat. In 1836, Interior Minister Adrien de Gasparin ordered that all new or remodeled departmental prisons be built with the new cells.[12]

Soon these changes were extended to political prisons. The Gasparin de-cree of 1839 provided a new discipline for the national *maisons centrales*, in-cluding the prohibition of alcohol and tobacco, the suppression of the prison canteen, and the rule of absolute silence.[13] The medieval structure of Mont-Saint-Michel, established as a state prison under the empire, received a new interior regime on 13 March 1840. The director was allowed a fairly broad range of punishments: he could control or prohibit all reading matter, he could limit or prohibit visits and correspondence, he could suppress the daily walk. The director also had the power to send prisoners to the *cachot*, or dun-geon, to put them in chains, and to condemn them, for as long as he wished, to bread and water.[14]

A political crime was defined in France as a "crime of opinion," the com-mission of which involved no personal interest or gain; political prisoners in-sisted upon this legal distinction, which preserved their honor.[15] Solitary confinement, instituted as a means of rehabilitation, was initially motivated by humanitarian concerns, and thus was likely to win support on the left. But were political prisoners to be "rehabilitated" from their opinions? Moreover, French leftists came to regard the solitary system as nothing else than *carcere duro*, the "hard time" of the notorious Habsburg Spielberg prison, imported into France for political dissenters.[16]

Spielberg was well known during the July Monarchy through Silvio Pel-lico's *Le Mie Prigioni*. Pellico was an intellectual; because of alleged carbonarist ties, he had been sentenced in 1820 to life in the grim prison, a damaged struc-ture near the site of Austerlitz. After his release in 1830 his memoirs, pub-lished in 1833, became an enormous European success, with five French editions alone in the first year.[17] Pellico was disliked by many republicans be-cause of his religiosity; the mistaken report of his death in 1841 gave rise to decidedly mixed tributes. The *National* was critical of his "profoundly ascetic spirit," and would have preferred more outrage about political injustice; aside from his memoirs, his writings had scarcely attained the level of mediocrity. Pellico—who was not dead after all—could not have been pleased with the premature obituary.[18]

Nor was the *National* entirely fair. Pellico vividly presented his readers with indelible images of *carcere duro*: chains, terrible food, hard surfaces, in-different medical attention, and the single daily hour of exercise, which the weakened prisoners could scarcely enjoy. One of the most debilitating as-pects was the lack of mental stimulation: the removal of his books in 1824, a policy of increasing "rigor" directed from Vienna, had rendered the next few years a dull blur.[19] As conditions deteriorated in the 1820s, the prisoners

were confined two to a cell to care for each other. Pellico's cellmate was
Pietro Maroncelli, whose leg, inflamed and irritated by the leg iron, went
untreated until it was too late for anything but amputation.[20] After Pellico
learned of a fellow prisoner who had killed himself by beating his head
against the wall, his wretchedness tempted him to do the same: "I wished I
had not heard of it; for I could not, do what I would, banish the temptation
to imitate him." Then he had coughed up blood, which caused him to believe he was blessedly close to a natural death.[21] He and Maroncelli were released in August 1830.

Another memoirist was the Frenchman Alexandre Andryane, incarcerated in Spielberg from 1823 to 1832. As a student in Geneva in 1820,
Andryane had met Babeuf's co-conspirator Philippe Buonarroti, living in impoverished and seditious exile. He had allowed himself to be swept away by
the romance of underground politics and had joined one of Buonarroti's elaborate international organizations which existed largely on paper, conspiratorial fantasies which he spun, recalled a more sober Andryane years later, "like a
spider in his web."[22] In December 1822, about to leave for a tour of Italy,
Andryane was induced by Buonarroti to deliver some papers to fellow *sociétaires*. They included the usual semi-masonic formulas and messages in
code—gibberish, as Andryane now regarded it, at which he barely glanced.[23]
In January 1823, he was arrested in the Habsburg territory of Milan. When
the cell door closed behind him, "my courage abandoned me all of a
sudden . . . I felt nothing more than an indefinable need to see the light of
day, only a horrible temptation"—Pellico's temptation—"to break my skull
against the walls of my dungeon."[24] He was sentenced to death, commuted to
life imprisonment in Spielberg.

Andryane soon found a few consolations. The prison guard Schiller, in his
sixties and a former soldier in Napoleon's Grand Army, was kind. Andryane
was also relieved to have access to books, and he made firm resolutions to set
himself a disciplined course of study, "to render myself capable of some great
work, of one of these works that never die."[25] Soon one of the guards passed
him a note from Pellico and Maroncelli; when the prisoners were deprived of
their books, in 1824, Pellico suggested that they read each other's compositions.[26] Andryane began his literary work; after an official inspection, the
guard Schiller informed them that he had burned all the "cursed papers" before they could be punished: "I have in my life supported many trials, but no
misfortune, no disaster . . . struck me with as much force and left me for a
longer time a prey to sorrow and despondency, than the loss of this work on

which I had founded so many hopes."[27] Finally Schiller retired, contriving before he left to smuggle Andryane a little German dictionary. Andryane conceived the maniacal task of scratching the dictionary into the stone walls with a nail, destroying each page as he finished it.[28]

Andryane was mostly deprived of news from the outside, with only spare summaries of letters, until he was informed of the death of his father. He was also given a legal accounting of what had once been a considerable inheritance (now greatly diminished by "lost lawsuits, burned properties"), and was a little ashamed when he realized how much that distant wealth had been a secret source of consolation.[29] He was soon faced with a progressive loss of vision, the result of poor diet and harsh conditions; because of his eyes he was given permission to stay outside longer, only to discover himself no longer capable of responding to nature. Andryane was released in 1832, and published his memoirs five years later.[30]

Throughout the 1840s, republicans attempted to make Mont-Saint-Michel the equal of Spielberg in the French popular imagination. The raw materials were promising. Mont-Saint-Michel was a medieval fortress built into a rock; the oubliettes, or dungeons, were claustrophobically pressed under tons of mountain. It was located on a desolate part of the coast of Brittany, subject to frequent fogs and chilling mists. At high tide, the prison was cut off from the mainland; at low tide it was surrounded by a god-forsaken shore. The small village consisted largely of fisherfolk who wanted no trouble with the government.[31]

Both Pellico and Andryane were men of letters who had dabbled in conspiracy. Theirs was an imprisonment informed by an acute self-awareness of their condition—certainly no less harsh for that, but a captivity that offered at least the promise of creative transformation. What would be the fate, in the same circumstances, of working men—perhaps literate, but without a broad background of reading and study, without the prospect of literary work in view? France would soon find out, with the insurgents of 1839.

As Victor Brombert has noted, prison literature in the Romantic era soon developed standard tropes:

> . . . the sordid cell and the hospitable cell, the cruelty of the jailers (but also the presence of the "good" jailer), glimpses of the landscape and of the sky, the contrast between the ugliness of the "inside" and the supposed splendor

of the surrounding scenery, prisons within the prison (the image of the iron mask), the insanity of the captive, the inscriptions in the stone, the symbolism of the wall as an invitation to transcendence.[32]

To all of these literary images should be added another: the terrifying awareness of physical and intellectual deterioration. Former soldier Sebastian Commissaire, a republican prisoner during the Second Empire, described himself at the age of 32, after nearly five years in prison: "What saddens me, is not to have white hair, but rather to see it thinning on my skull with a frightening rapidity. . . . I had a tooth pulled and I have three others rotted. Add to that some beginnings of wrinkles at the outer angles of my eyes, on each side of the nose and mouth, and you would have an idea of the ravages to which time and prison have subjected my poor self."[33] The noted economist and Deputy Adolphe Blanqui remembered his younger brother Louis-Auguste as a "pretty little blond child, who began his studies under M. Massin with the sons of the French aristocratic elite, and carried off all the prizes from them." After 1848, estranged from his brother, Adolphe wrote sorrowfully "of the emaciated face of the prisoner of State."[34] And Martin-Bernard was also shocked by a brother—his younger brother whom he had not seen for five years, once an admiring schoolboy, now an adult and equal: "This complete moral and physical transformation, accomplished during the time that I remained solitary, inert and immobile, threw me into an inexpressible stupor. It seemed to me an entirely new revelation of my position."[35]

But this was a rare moment in the work of Martin-Bernard, who made himself the chief memoirist of the prisoners of Mont-Saint-Michel; for even as he adopted the standard topoi of prison literature, he wrote an intensely political and largely impersonal narrative. He exhibited the expected emotions in regard to nature and friendship, the predictable attacks on injustice and arbitrary power, but of his feelings, nothing—or almost nothing. (Commissaire was more frank: he wanted freedom, a family, a woman: "Sometimes I felt on my lips a sort of itching sensation which would have made me embrace the air if this had not been senseless."[36]) Martin-Bernard avoided such weaknesses. A change for the worse, an unprovoked punishment, an unexpected favor: he presented all of them as political issues, to which it was incumbent upon him to respond correctly, as a prisoner of war. In his memoirs he elaborated a masculine ideal of stoicism and endurance. He also exhibited an interesting form of denial, a refusal to see himself as victim: aside from occasional moments of collapse (reported by others, not by himself), he had in his own eyes merely transformed his struggle from active to passive resistance.

While most of those convicted in the first May trial went to Doullens prison near Amiens, Martin-Bernard started for Mont-Saint-Michel in a group which included Barbès, the lathe-worker Delsade, and the Polish bootmaker Austen; they arrived on 17 July 1839.[37] His cell was tiny, the floor considerably below the doorsill, with only a cot, a table, a chair, and a covered chamberpot as furnishings. It overlooked the shoreline, upon which he gazed for his first few hours: "Its doleful and silent surface seemed to reflect the state of my soul. A picturesque and animated landscape would have dulled my heart, distracting me from a melancholy that I savored with voluptuous pleasure."[38]

Despite solitary confinement, the four prisoners were able to communicate, shouting from the windows and chimneys and passing messages in ways that no prisoner would ever divulge. Martin-Bernard later referred to these early months, the fall and winter of 1839 before the others arrived, as the "mythic age" of their captivity. He was perhaps still intrigued by the novelty of his situation, and he took up again his studies of the classics; he and Barbès spoke to each other in Latin, of "Moses and Jesus, Greece and Rome with their poetry and history, Homer and Virgil, Alexander, Hannibal, Caesar. . . ."[39] For sensual deprivations, his mind "had substituted, by a marvelous compensation, an inexhaustible power of reverie." He had terrible headaches, the result of little exercise and fresh air; he suffered from bad food and vermin. But he tried to find reasons for cheer: "A soldier of equality, I said to myself, can and should accustom himself to all types of nourishment. As to the vermin, it will not survive the first frosts."[40]

Martin-Bernard's cell was below those of the workers Delsade and Austen. His conversations with them, "although of a less philosophical order than those we had with Barbès, were nonetheless for them and me a great alleviation to the boredom of our solitude."[41] An educated working man, he was caught between the wealthy bourgeois Barbès, for whom he felt deference, and his simpler companions whom he judged—Delsade as an "*enfant du peuple*," Austen as a naive Polish freedom-fighter. Unfortunately, Austen's French was poor and his cell the most distant: "Our conversations with him were a true travail, which we were often obliged to abandon with the sorrow of not being understood."[42]

In October 1839, they were joined by three prisoners from the *Moniteur républicain* case. In December six more prisoners arrived, three from the Paris *Cours d'Assises*, and three transfers from Doullens, for a total of thirteen. In early February 1840, there arrived seven new prisoners from the second *Saisons* trial, including Blanqui.[43] The printer Jean-Baptiste Guillemin was among the most important of the newcomers; his wife, who moved to the local village, became a valuable conduit for news and messages.[44] Through her, they were astonished by another contact from the outside: Fulgence Girard, once a student with Blanqui in Paris, now a respectable lawyer and journalist. Barbès wrote that Girard's letter was "the drop of water in the desert." Blanqui echoed the same emotion: "It was like a renaissance of the world; a resurrection from my tomb. . . . One ends by believing that everywhere are jailers, keys, 100-foot high walls, functionaries who prowl around you like devouring lions."[45]

With the growing numbers, fault lines began to appear. Martin-Bernard emphasized the differences resulting from education. The workers, barely indoctrinated into republicanism, were "younger, more impetuous, less experienced in the true situation of things . . . [and] supported with a trembling impatience this odious prison regime."[46] Among the most impatient were Louis Roudil, an umbrella maker, and Noël Martin (Martin-Noël), a box maker. Both were 19; neither was a republican—at least in the beginning—and both had become involved in the May insurrection by chance. Martin-Noël had been in line for the *Folies dramatiques* when he learned of the fighting— "more amusing than the theater"—and had left to find it.[47] Roudil had been captured weapon in hand; he claimed that "15 men" had made him take up a rifle "for liberty": "You have to fight, or you're going to die: that's what they said to me." (In the trial he admitted the rifle had not been forced on him: "It was offered to me and I took it.") He had fired only once, by accident and into the air.[48] Both he and Martin-Noël had been sentenced to five years.

The two became fast friends in Doullens. When Martin-Noël organized a general protest in which all the inmates vandalized their cells, both he and Roudil were transferred in January 1840 to Mont-Saint-Michel. Further disobedience got them sent to the *cachots* for punishment, where they were roughly handled on the orders of the hated head jailer Turgot.[49] In reporting this event Fulgence Girard, like Martin-Bernard, underlined the distinction between the educated leaders and the "children of the people," accustomed to noise and activity: "They found neither the memories of erudition, nor the preoccupations of study, nor the philosophical contemplation of the future. . . . The resignation of the first days evanesced in the feverish anxieties of a mortal ennui. . . . A growing exaltation invaded their ideas."[50]

The worst catastrophe of early 1840 involved Fritz Austen. Delsade, his closest neighbor, reported hours of absolute silence broken by irrational shouting. On 14 February, Delsade heard "a fall that seemed extraordinary"; Austen had stabbed himself in the chest, just missing his heart.[51] (The prisoner

Boichot, in 1854, also remembered the unmistakable thump of a would-be suicide in the next cell, followed by "the swift steps of the sentinel, the comings
and goings of the guards, the groans of a man being taken away."[52]) Austen
was merely moved to another chamber where he continued in isolation, the
authorities suspicious that his insanity might be feigned. Blanqui, who was
next to him for six months, reported that he was tormented by the belief that
his father and brother were imprisoned in the room below. On 20 September
1840, Austen was finally taken to an asylum.[53]

The fall and winter of 1840–41 marked a low point. Girard received only
a single lethargic letter from Martin-Bernard, a half-hearted apology for not
writing, which he blamed on "extenuating circumstances." Girard soon realized the toll taken by depression and despondency.[54] (Martin-Bernard would
not acknowledge such periods of weakness, but Sebastian Commissaire was
more frank. "1858 was hard for me," Commissaire wrote of his ninth year,
"weakened by a long detention, physically and morally ill, the least annoyance
vibrated throughout my body and rendered me somber. I had an attack of mis-
anthropy."[55] And Marc Caussidière recalled Doullens: "One has moments of
disgust for life that are insupportable."[56])

In January 1841, Blanqui was informed of his wife's death. In early February the administration finally allowed him to see his mother and sister, who
had been engaged for some months in tedious negotiations with the bureaucracy.[57] Jean Herbulet, a 29-year-old cabinetmaker sentenced to ten years,
broke down and asked for a pardon. Because of his weakness, the others ceased
to communicate with him.[58] In February and March 1841, the fortress received two additional contingents from Doullens, all rebellious and impatient:
the cook Benjamin Flotte and Joseph Mathieu d'Épinal (imprisoned on
weapons and ammunition charges), locksmith Alexandre Thomas and law student Pierre Beraud (bombmakers), Aloysius Huber ("infernal machine" attempt in 1837), and Nougnès, Jean-Maurice Bordon, Constant Hubert,
Charles Élie, and Émile Pétremann, convicts of 1839. The last three shouted
"*Vive la République!* Down with Louis-Philippe!" as they arrived.[59]

In mid-April 1841, Delsade opened all the doors in his corridor with an
old scrap of wire, and between the 9 P.M. and midnight rounds, Martin-
Bernard, Barbès, and Louis Quignot from the *Saisons* gathered in his cell. On
the fourth evening (17 April) they were caught.[60] Girard reported, though
Martin-Bernard did not, that it was Joseph Hendrick (from 1839) who turned
them in. Apparently his decision to inform had its twisted roots in a quarrel
with Guillemin and Vilcoq (from the *Moniteur républicain*), and in rumors of an
amnesty. Those events triggered Girard's decision to go public.[61]

Blanqui biographer Maurice Dommanget, who examined the prison records in the departmental archives, summarized the director's rather frantic April 1841 report to the minister of the interior. He believed that Guillemin's wife had smuggled in picklocks, knives, and other small tools; he feared the inmates were planning an escape. He reported that at least nine men (including Blanqui, Barbès, and Martin-Bernard) were somehow in constant communication. Pressured by the local subprefect, he finally decided to put interior bars on the windows that would extend a considerable distance into the cells and deprive prisoners of their view.[62] On the day following his capture in Delsade's cell, Martin-Bernard was informed that while these "repairs" were being made to his chamber he would be placed "provisionally, and for a few days only," in the *loges*, along with a dozen of the others.[63]

Martin-Bernard had not yet encountered the *loges*: small wooden cages built onto the top of the fortress, buffeted by all winds, ventilated and lit only by a narrow window crisscrossed with a thick iron mesh. Freezing in winter, they became "ovens" in the summer, as the sun beat down on the slate roofs. In the doors of their *loges* were small windows; on 21 May, the guards inserted plugs of wood while each man was on his walk. Barbès refused to re-enter his cell. Martin-Bernard, taking advantage of the arrival of his dinner, burst out the door and stood beside him. The head jailer Turgot, saber in hand, arrived at the head of 15 guards, and "immediately we were thrown to the ground, ground up, crushed."[64] Half their attackers fell upon Barbès, pulling him by his feet down "the granite steps on which his head rebounded at each step," as Martin-Bernard recalled. He himself was dragged to the end of the corridor, where he was confronted by 20 soldiers: "I resolved to speak, first of all to prove that although chained, republicans did not tremble before the furors of force, and especially . . . in order to let our position be known to the public."[65] His speech was cut short by the order to take him to the dungeons.

Martin-Bernard's descent into the bowels of Mont-Saint-Michel took him past old funeral vaults and *oubliettes*. He finally emerged into the circular cave of the *cachots noirs*, greeted by the voice of Barbès; Delsade would soon follow. The guards pulled off his clothes and gave him the rough costume of the place, then forced him into the coffin-like hole cut out of the rock.[66] An 1843 article in *La Réforme*, quoting an anonymous source, referred to the *cachots* as "veritable subterranean tombs" infested with rats and insects, dampness oozing from the walls. The prisoners were unable to stand, nor could they lie fully extended; they talked through the night to combat their insomnia.[67]

On the following day (22 May 1841), Benjamin Flotte joined them, his legs chained. The attack on Barbès and Martin-Bernard had led to a general uproar. Flotte had questioned the director, Theurier, about their fate, and for his impudence he had been attacked by ten guards. They "rolled him like a ball down 80 granite steps," according to a republican pamphlet, "then made him walk back up again, holding him by the collar and overwhelming him with kicks, punches, and blows with the flats of their sabers."[68] As the protest continued, some prisoners were sent to the *cachots*, others to the *loges*. Aloysius Huber was beaten in his cell; Martin-Noël was chained again.[69] "Soon I saw my chamber invaded by 20 guards at the head of which was Turgot, saber in hand, fury in his eyes," later wrote the student Beraud. "They seized me and put me in irons, at the wrists and ankles." Turgot tightened the cuffs until he drew blood ("I felt my bones crushed"); just before Beraud fainted, one of the guards took away his eyeglasses.[70]

Another victim was Jean Bordon, who was put in chains ("These *misérables* have the ability to put us in irons at will," wrote Blanqui.[71]) Bordon, at 18 the youngest of the 1839 defendants, had claimed that insurgents had forced him to put cartridges in his pocket, and he had feared to empty them out in the darkness because he might drop his money. His employers gave him an alibi for all of 12 May.[72] He had been sentenced to five years, to be served with republican zealots with whom he had little in common. Girard suggested that the events of this day precipitated Bordon's insanity: enclosed "in one of these species of caskets," unable to move because of the weight of his new irons, hearing day and night "only sobs or the noise of chains," he developed a "profound horror" of life and wanted to die.[73]

Martin-Bernard, in the *cachot noir*, was as yet unaware of these aboveground troubles. He must have been profoundly depressed; according to his memoirs, he and his comrades were triumphant, recalling the victims of past ages and singing songs of the revolution. Finally, in June, they were led back up into warmth and light: "More than ever, I believed in the truth of our holy doctrines of equality and progress."[74] By August all the prisoners had returned to their cells to find them altered for the worse—the doors reinforced and the chambers encumbered by the protruding new double bars, which denied them the view of the shoreline.[75]

Girard had already witnessed the "moral annihilation" of the prisoners in late 1840, manifested by an extreme lethargy; this phase was succeeded by "an unhealthy agitation," stimulated by the new grievances.[76] On 7 September 1841, Roudil damaged his new bars. On 11 September, Huber attempted a harebrained escape in broad daylight, going down the wall by means of a rope fashioned from bed linens; he was captured almost immediately. On the night of the twelfth, they sang the *Marseillaise* and the *Chant du Départ*. On 14 September, Élie, Herbulet, and Delsade were sent to the *cachots* for "vociferations and threats"; in a general protest many prisoners shouted "Down with Spielberg! Down with the butchers! Down with the iron cages!" On 18 October, Flotte, Pétremann, Quignot, and Martin-Noël ripped out their bars and were sent to the *cachots*, along with Beraud and several others. At the end of six days the prison physician ordered Pétremann, freezing and covered with lice, to be withdrawn.[77] Blanqui, in mourning for his wife and suffering from fever, back pains, and a "tumor" on his ear, predicted disaster: "for my part, I no longer have much of anything to care about, nor much to fear; I no longer hold to life, it is a burden to me, that which remains will not last long, and I would wish only to exchange it for something. My companions, who are neither so ill nor so resigned as I . . . are also tired of suffering, and prefer to engage in a decisive struggle."[78]

Outside, the fall of 1841 saw the beginning, in earnest, of the republican campaign against solitary confinement. Fulgence Girard began to speak out, and Barbès' sister and brother-in-law filed a legal complaint against the prison director and conferred with prominent members of the Paris bar. The resulting *consultation* argued that French law had established the principle of detention in common. According to Article 20 of the Penal Code, those sentenced to detention "*will be in communication with persons placed in the interior of the place of detention or with those outside*" (their italics). Cellular detention (solitary confinement) and even chains and irons were authorized (by article 614) only in narrow circumstances, specifically if a prisoner threatened, insulted, or used violence against a guard or his fellow prisoners. The very fact that "sequestration" could be imposed as punishment meant that it was an "exceptional state" that could not be transformed into a standard condition; thus the solitary regime at Mont-Saint-Michel was illegal.[79] Inspector-General Charles Lucas, a known opponent of continuous solitary confinement (he favored confinement only at night), arrived on 26 October; hopes were dashed by his unsympathetic impassivity. The immediate response to all these efforts, as Blanqui wrote Girard, was that things got worse.[80]

Toward the end of November 1841, there was another case of insanity—Jean Charles, the innkeeper who had hosted *Saisons* meetings and sheltered Martin-Bernard after the insurrection. In an attempt to restore his senses, the director allowed Martin-Bernard to see him. The visit began well; Charles recognized him and spoke sensibly, "when, all of a sudden, and without any transition, he began to tell me of all the strange hallucinations which are the essence of insanity."[81] On 5 December, Charles was transferred to the nearest asylum. The mental breakdown of the young Bordon, apparent for some time, also became acute in December, but rather than admit to another case so soon, the director put him in a chamber with Constant Hubert and Flotte. Bordon was left to recover himself (he died fighting in February 1848).[82] At the end of 1841, the Quenisset case brought four new prisoners.[83]

The increasing public criticism, as well as negative reports by Inspector-General Lucas and the subprefect, led to the transfer of Director Theurier and his replacement by Firmin Bonnet, who took over on 28 December.[84] But Bonnet was a victim of bad timing: Blanqui, Barbès, Martin-Bernard, and Constant Hubert had decided to escape (Alexandre Thomas, due to be released on 27 May, would assist but not accompany them). The earliest favorable dates, according to the phases of the moon, were 4 to 15 February, when the sky would be dark. They would gather in Hubert's cell, which opened onto the ramp that led to a solid horizontal platform, to which they would lower themselves by rope; once there they would descend the steep vertical wall a further 80 feet to the base of the rock. In awe of their famous but aging leaders, Thomas and Hubert climbed down their chimneys on the cold January nights to work on the cells of Blanqui and Martin-Bernard, one and two stories below Hubert. They left thin sections of wall that could easily be broken through at the last minute, and hid the stones and debris in their mattresses. Hubert cut through the bars of his window, sawing during high winds because of the noise. Because a mass escape was impossible, Martin-Bernard convinced himself that they were acting appropriately; once outside, they would be free to publicize the conditions of their comrades.[85] On 16 January, Bonnet made an optimistic report to the subprefect of Avranches and decided to visit his ailing wife, leaving the prison in the hands of subordinates.[86]

Finally the preparations were complete, and they began to watch the weather. On 10 February the lanterns outside were overcast by a dense fog. After the midnight round, each escapee began his journey to Hubert's chamber. Martin-Bernard found the climb up the chimney nearly impossible, and he reached the opening "dripping with a cold sweat."[87] Once assembled, they took away the bars of Hubert's window and descended 40 feet to the platform, using a rope smuggled in by Blanqui's mother. They arrived on the platform at about 3 A.M., to discover that the sky was now dangerously clear. Pierre Beraud, Alexandre Thomas, and Jean Dubourdieu were out on the platform with them, to hold the rope (attached to a hoist) as they went over. Barbès descended first. There was silence, then a sudden jolt. They heard a sentinel's shout, followed by soldiers rushing out of the post: "We saw their weapons shine in the darkness." The escape was over.[88]

As they later learned, on the wall, about 30 feet above ground, was a support for the hoist used to lift supplies into the prison. Barbès, hitting this obstruction in the dark, lost his footing, became disoriented, and hit the ground hard—bloodied and bruised, but without broken bones. The event was sparsely reported by the republican journals, which had little information, and not at all in the *Moniteur*.[89]

Every captive dreamed of flight. In 1835, the prisoner Edouard Colombat broke through a hollow-sounding section and discovered a sealed, forgotten chamber. The chamber had an outside wall; every night he worked on it in darkness, and finally, having arranged things with a friend who brought a boat, he took advantage of high tide and made his escape—one of the few to outwit Mont-Saint-Michel. He started a small hostel on Jersey, where he provided a first haven to other refugees.[90] In 1836, the inmates attempted a mass escape from Doullens. After overpowering the guards they climbed down the walls, using their knotted sheets. The improvised cords broke and several escapees were seriously hurt.[91] In 1840, the prisoners at Doullens began digging a tunnel, but were defeated by its collapse and the impossibility of disposing of the dirt.[92] And then there was Sébastien Commissaire, alternately consoled and tormented by dreams of flight: "I fought for the Republic, I was alone on a barricade surrounded on all sides; all the other combatants were dead or gone and when the troops arrived to take me prisoner, I made an effort and elevated myself into the air to the great astonishment of the soldiers." But he also suffered nightmares of being smothered and paralyzed, usually by a hideous old woman who sat on his chest and tried to wring his neck.[93]

It was too late for his career, but Director Bonnet immediately sent the guilty prisoners to the *loges*. Dommanget's examination of the prison archives revealed a continuing series of incidents. On 19 February, Beraud ripped out the outer mesh of his window and threw it to the ground below; on the twentieth he was sent to the *loges*, along with four others who protested his fate. On the evening of the twenty-first, Élie and Roudil were sent to the *loges* after threatening the guards. Aloysius Huber and Nouguès,

in the *loges* already, broke their windows; they were put in irons and restricted to bread and water. On the evening of 23 February, François
Bézenac attempted to hang himself; saved by the guard on duty, "he declares he will do it again," and began a hunger strike. On 3 March, several
events took place: Charles Godard barricaded himself in his chamber and
demolished his bars; Flotte broke through the floor of his cell; Martin-Noël
broke his bed and kicked one of the guards. Blanqui abruptly joined the agitation on the night of 4–5 March, in protest against the noise of the nightly
rounds. When the jailers entered his room he pelted them with chunks of
firewood. On the following morning he was taken to the *loges* again, with
the increased discipline in use since 20 February: bread and water, neither
bedding nor straw, a mattress made of oakum and vermin. By mid-March
the *loges* housed 16 of the 29 politicals. Director Bonnet was forced out because the subprefect believed that a more "energetic" director was
needed.[94] The replacement, Leblanc, arrived in March 1842, and began by
adding two weeks in the *loges* for all prisoners already there. Nevertheless,
claimed Martin-Bernard, they were united in "holy solidarity, which was
not only a duty for us, but still more in conformity to our clearly-
understood interests."[95]

By the end of May 1842, most of the prisoners were in the *loges* on bread
and water, a subsequently famous ordeal that lasted 66 days.[96] For Martin-
Bernard this was a period of cold war, during which they struggled to maintain
an "impassivity," to avoid anger or emotion. At the same time they had to fight
against what he refused to call despondency, though he admitted that all were
tormented by what Barbès termed "*cogitations*," meaning "this order of ideas
which implant themselves in spite of yourself in your mind."[97] Commissaire
was as usual more explicit. In February 1856 he became obsessed with what
might have been, if only he had been prevented from leaving his native Lyon:
"What I mean, is that if I had had the misfortune simply to break a leg on the
day when I desired to leave, my ideas probably would have changed during the
time necessary to recover, and it is likely I would not be here. I would be married, the father of several children."[98]

But there was another kind of escape. By the early summer of 1842,
Barbès was seriously ill—coughing blood, unable to speak, barely able to
breathe. In late July, Director Leblanc finally summoned a physician. The
prisoner's sister and Girard made urgent and public pleas to get him transferred to the south, and Inspector-General Louis Moreau-Christophe finally ordered him sent to the prison in Nîmes.[99] Barbès fought against

removal, backed only by Martin-Bernard. He insisted that he would be cured, or not, at the Mont as well as anywhere else: "I have asked for nothing from the administration, I do not want to ask it for anything. My role is to remain absolutely passive."[100] The transfer occurred in January 1843. Four years later he demanded to be returned to his comrades on the grounds that his health was restored; he did not wish his continued presence in the kinder southern climate to be described someday as a favor from the regime.[101]

By early 1844, Blanqui too was suffering from consumption. Less resigned than Barbès, he demanded an outside specialist and asked Fulgence Girard to publicize his case. On 11 March it was decided to transfer him to Tours, where he finally arrived at the end of April. In December 1844, so critically ill that death seemed imminent, Blanqui was liberated from the rest of his sentence: the government wanted to avoid the embarrassment of having him die in custody.[102]

By this point, the events at Mont-Saint-Michel and other prisons had become widely known to the public. The *National* had started the campaign in the fall of 1839 with a series of individual health reports.[103] Louis Raban in Doullens, with rheumatic disorders and lung troubles, was no longer able to walk; Aloysius Huber had decided to starve himself.[104] Jacob Steuble, Huber's co-conspirator, had cut his throat; on the very next day the young medical student Martial Dussoubs was placed in the cell where Steuble had died.[105] In October they reported Austen's mental breakdown.[106] Girard's public letters began in 1841, providing more detailed information than the spare government bulletins.

In 1843, the new republican newspaper *La Réforme* began to add its voice. In September they reported on Aloysius Huber, who was judged too ill to be moved—the determination made by the working-class driver of the prison vehicle, to the shame of the authorities. In October there was word that Claude Boudin (from the *Moniteur républicain*) had gone insane, that Jarasse (from the Quenisset case) had attempted suicide.[107] The *National* reported that Jarasse had poisoned himself with verdigris; guards had found him rolling on the floor of his cell, and had managed to revive him only after six hours of agony. The *National* also reported that Emile Pétremann had consumption and was "pale like a spectre, his skull entirely bare," and that Huber had just spent two months in the *cachot*.[108] Both newspapers published a letter from two physicians who reported bluntly that Huber would die without removal to a hospital.[109] The *Réforme* and the *National* had further bulletins in November and

December as Huber was transferred; added the *Réforme*, "He has the haggard eyes and impassive features of a man who has long been tortured."[110] In November 1843, both the *National* and the *Réforme* provided an overall assessment, recapitulating the deaths, the cases of insanity, the transfers for reasons of health.[111] Two days later, in another lengthy piece, the *Réforme* noted that each exposé was the excuse for "new vengeances" against the prisoners: "But today why should we recoil before the truth? The excesses of the government have reached their limits: almost all the prisoners are either dying, or crazy, or dead."[112]

On 2 May 1844, the *National* triumphantly reported that even Alexis de Tocqueville, a supporter of solitary confinement, had finally felt obliged to denounce the excesses of Mont-Saint-Michel.[113] Tocqueville's surprising comment was made during a parliamentary debate over yet another new penitentiary law.[114] In presenting the bill, which he had largely drafted, Tocqueville had frankly acknowledged the problems of the Philadelphia system; based on a religious ethic of penitence, it had imposed *"rigueurs inutiles"* that were omitted in his proposal. The new French system would be based on "separation" rather than "isolation"; the proposed regime allowed for limited visitation from the outside. If separation drove a few people into insanity, even that was still preferable to the evils of the old system.[115]

In the course of the debate, Tocqueville had become increasingly irritated by references to Mont-Saint-Michel. Finally he addressed the subject, making a distinction between the "regime" and the penalties. The "regime" was pleasant: "Each detainee at Mont-Saint-Michel is enclosed in a vast cell which is well-situated and well-ventilated. There he receives nourishment, heat, and light in sufficient, even abundant, quantities. Moreover he is not forced to work; each day he can leave his cell, or rather his chamber, for two hours, with the prisoner of his choice." But Tocqueville acknowledged that the disciplinary penalties—the *cachots*, the *loges*, the extended periods on bread and water—were harsh. The minister of the interior had taken steps to end such abuses; the problems had been "exaggerated" in any case; and Tocqueville expressed anger that the press had continued to use Mont-Saint-Michel as an argument against the proposed law: "Mont-Saint-Michel has nothing to do with this."[116] The law failed, but two important points had emerged from this debate. One was Tocqueville's acknowledgement, however grudging, of the abuses at Mont-Saint-Michel. The other was his insistence that the interior regulations of prisons were to be decided by legislators rather than bureaucrats in the penal administration.[117]

At first, however, it seemed that nothing had changed. The newspapers continued their campaign, by now struggling to escape from stereotypes made banal by repetition. In May 1844, the *Réforme* listed (again) the old tales of abuse: "Let us repeat that Barbès was dragged by his hair and beard, that Delsade was struck with a sword, that there is not a single political prisoner on which the jailers have not put their hands."[118] The *National* provided a detailed update on the health of Blanqui, who had just been moved to the hospital in Tours.[119] In June 1844, the *Réforme* reported that Vilcoq was in danger of going blind, and Jacques Jouves had just died of consumption at Doullens.[120] The *National* reported that ten other politicals were suffering from the same illness.[121] "Huber cannot make a movement without spitting blood," wrote Etienne Cabet, communist editor of *Le Populaire;* "although only 30 years old and endowed with a vigorous constitution, his legs are so emaciated, the dorsal spine so affected, his natural strength so wasted, that for a long time he has not been able to leave his bed."[122]

In October 1844, the king issued a general amnesty for 59 political prisoners.[123] The *Réforme* soon noted that 40 of the men had been nearly at the end of their sentences; moreover, they had received not "amnesty" but rather a series of individual *grâces*. The distinction was significant. Amnesty wiped out the conviction, while *grâce* merely shortened the prison time; *surveillance* and the civil penalties of the original sentence (the inability to be a juror, guardian, or elector, for example) would stand. The *Réforme* further reported that 35 politicals remained in prison, most notably 13 men from 1839; 8 from the Queniset attempt; Aloysius Huber; and Louis-Napoléon Bonaparte.[124] An 1845 pamphlet, a summary of previously published information, noted darkly that the authorities had recently managed to sever the tenuous links between inside and outside: who could say what was happening to the remaining few?[125]

But in fact, for Martin-Bernard and the others, there had been an unexpected, bittersweet conclusion. In late July, the prisoners were informed that the cell doors of the political quarter would henceforth be open from 6 A.M. to nightfall, allowing them to communicate freely. Their solitary confinement had lasted just over five years, from 17 July 1839 to 28 July 1844; Martin-Bernard recalled the triumph with which they greeted each other: "What mattered the damages our bodies had undergone!" They assessed the ravages frankly: rheumatism, gastric pains, respiratory difficulties, "cerebral congestions," baldness, white hair: only a few had escaped such obvious badges of courage, the hardy Martin-Bernard among them. They set themselves a course of exercise, using the corridors for running and leaping, the bars for building strength.[126]

They had several months of this comparative freedom until late October 1844, when they were informed of their imminent departure. Doullens, their new destination, had its own formidable reputation, but Martin-Bernard's last years there were "fraternal," even pastoral. They cultivated a garden, growing strawberries and gooseberries as well as roses, carnations, dahlias, and tulips; the tailor Quignot from the *Saisons* landscaped patterns from the different varieties. They celebrated two banquets every year to which they all contributed financially, on 14 July and on 10 August, the overthrow of Louis XVI.[127]

When the February Revolution occurred in 1848, it found Blanqui still in Tours, just acquitted in a trumped-up conspiracy case; he had foiled the government by clinging to life.[128] He rushed to Paris. "Among my companions," he would write, only a few months later, "who has drunk as deeply as I at the cup of anguish? During a year, the agony of a beloved wife being extinguished far from me in despair, and then for four entire years, an eternal tête-à-tête, in the solitude of my cell, with the phantom of she who was no more."[129] He would be in prison again in three months, this time for more than ten years.

Many years later, in exile, Barbès received a letter from a self-described *homme du peuple* in one of Napoléon III's prisons, who had been in the crowd on the day that Barbès had left Nîmes:

> A friendly word, a handshake, that was all I had of you. But that was enough for me and I have kept it. . . . In February 1848, an immense crowd was pressed before the central prison of Nîmes. I was there. A man, or rather a martyr, came out; he had a pale face, head held high, black and abundant hair, a tall and thin physique, a proud and precipitous gait. He was dressed in black: it was Armand Barbès. . . . He went to Paris, where already it was all over. The Reaction had killed the Republic in its cradle.[130]

In Doullens, Martin-Bernard heard only tantalizing fragments, the news from Paris delayed and interrupted. On 25 February—after the revolution was in fact over—the wife of one of his fellow prisoners brought back word that battle was engaged: "In the middle of the day we learn that a Provisional Government has just been proclaimed. But the greatest uncertainty reigns in regard to the names of those who compose it. Toward 6 P.M. the name of Ledru-Rollin is cited as figuring on the list of this government. No further doubt is possible: we can only be in a Republic." That evening the director of the prison came to Martin-Bernard with a letter formally announcing the new government's intention to liberate all political prisoners. The director was a realist; he hoped Martin-Bernard would put in a word for him with those who were now in power. Martin-Bernard took the letter and crumpled it convulsively in his hand.[131]

PART V

✦✦✦✦✦✦

DEFEAT

CHAPTER 13

RESTAGING THE REVOLUTION: FEBRUARY 1848

ONCE AGAIN, AS IN 1830, IT WAS A THREE-DAY REVOLUTION. But the February weather, in contrast to the excessive heat of July, was cold and inclement; on Wednesday, the middle day, the rain fell in torrents. The soldiers were sent out to stand and shiver, the demoralized symbols of failing governmental power. The insurgents kept warm by moving—ripping up paving stones, building barricades; they thawed their hands over the braziers they set up in the streets to melt lead for bullets. "One heard only the hatchet blows and the noise of the tree branches breaking as they fell," later recalled Marc Caussidière; "sometimes, the sound of weapons clashing and detonations lost in the shadows; almost always, as a monotonous accompaniment, the sound of the *tocsin*."[1]

As before the July Revolution, there was an economic recession. The cost of living had risen steadily throughout the regime, but wages had mostly failed to keep pace or even declined. Two bad harvests, in 1845 and 1846, had raised the price of grain; bread riots had occurred throughout much of the countryside. By 1847, there was a Europe-wide industrial depression and an accompanying increase in strikes, with textiles and the building trades particularly hard hit. Paris, by now a city of close to one million, was full of the jobless. The high unemployment rate before the revolution would be catastrophically increased by the revolution itself, rising in the spring of 1848 to 56 percent of all Parisian workers, and even higher in the furniture, metal working, and building trades that would dominate the June Days.[2]

Statistics compiled after the revolution revealed an estimated 1,512 barricades; with each figured at 845 paving stones, that meant 1,277,640 stones
pried up, most of them on Wednesday night. In addition, 4,013 trees were cut
down, 890 lanterns demolished, and 53 *corps de garde*, 41 sentry boxes, and 104
kiosks burned or destroyed. The casualties were fewer than in 1830: dead were
50 Line troops and 22 municipals on the government side, and 289 from the
ranks of the people, including 14 women.[3] According to a study by Mark
Traugott, the typical February insurgents were male, married, in their mid-
30s, and likely to have been born in the provinces. They represented, in numbers disproportionately high in comparison to their totals in Paris, the
construction and printing trades, the clothing and textile sectors, and workers
in both base and precious metals—the usual suspects, again.[4] And as in 1830,
the streets were filled with the liquid but unyielding masses of Paris, creating a
human topography quite unlike the swift, fleeting presence of the *émeute*. The
duc de Nemours, Louis-Philippe's second son, was disquieted as he watched
from his palace window, noting (though he did not realize it) the same kind of
glutinous persistence that had concerned Gendarmerie colonel Foucauld in
1830: dense crowds that opened for the troops and cavalry, then seamlessly
closed behind them as they passed. Nemours had witnessed the fierce but limited attempts of 1834 and 1839: "Here, on the contrary, [the insurrection] did
not show itself as aggressive and audacious anywhere, but it covered all the
quartiers of the capital with inert masses acting on the troops by surrounding
them, enveloping them, tightening its grip around them, without violence but
with an irresistible force."[5] But this time republican activists, with nearly 18
years of experience behind them, were ready to seize the initiative.

The revolution began with the banquet campaign to expand the suffrage.
The first banquet was held in Paris in July 1847. The movement spread to the
rest of the country, gaining momentum as it moved steadily leftward: the republican Ledru-Rollin at the Lille banquet, the socialist Louis Blanc at Dijon.
These orderly bourgeois protests also spilled dangerously out of doors, as
workers listened outside the halls and provided festive escorts for the speakers.[6] François Guizot made the mistake of believing that the demanded reforms were a mere pretext for gaining power by a jealous opposition, a means
to "unmake the majority"; the repetitious refrain throughout his memoirs that
the reforms were "inopportune," that they were "not necessary," his fear that
such changes would bring in "new elements of unknown effect," was a virtual
admission that the "majority" could not withstand an expanded electorate.[7]

The divisions on the left, though more profound than those on the right,
were temporarily masked by the campaign. The dynastic opposition was led by

Deputy Odilon Barrot (Adolphe Thiers held himself aloof from the reform banquets, the better perhaps to maintain his future viability as a minister); their demands (exclusions from the chamber only of certain types of *fonction-naires*, a limited change in the suffrage) were relatively modest. The Radicals, the deputies of the "democratic left"—Garnier-Pagès the younger, the famous defense attorney A. T. Marie, Hippolyte Carnot, son of Lazare—wanted more profound changes, but within constitutional limits. Their program was articulated in Carnot's influential pamphlet *Les Radicaux et la Charte*, an explicit revival of the old *programme de l'Hôtel de Ville*, in which he argued that the Charter was compatible with an expanded suffrage, liberty of the press, and the parliamentary responsibility of ministers.[8]

The republicans insisted upon an end to the monarchy. *La Réforme* was critical of Carnot's belief in a throne "surrounded by republican institutions": "Let God grant Lafayette and Laffitte the pardon they asked for! But who could pardon those who come in 1847?"[9] Yet there were only a handful of avowed republicans in the chambers on the eve of the Second Republic, including the attorney Ledru-Rollin in the deputies (elected to the seat held by the elder Garnier-Pagès upon his death in 1841) and the recent convert, the Comte d'Alton-Shée, in the peers.[10] And there were divisions even among republicans. The men of the increasingly moderate *National*, edited by Armand Marrast, wished to ally with the Radicals and were willing to support Thiers and Barrot. Those of the more energetic *Réforme*, linked with Ledru-Rollin, believed that such an alliance was an "abdication of principles."[11]

The banquet that finally brought down the regime was organized by the national guards and electors of the twelfth *arrondissement* in Paris, a student and working-class area that included the faubourg Saint-Marcel, the boulevard Saint-Jacques, and the Panthéon.[12] Reformist deputies were invited but declined, on the grounds that the chambers were in session.[13] The organizers nevertheless pressed forward. Lepelletier-Roinville, one of the leaders, was dissatisfied in any case with the dynastic opposition's narrow vision, suspecting them (in an ironic echo of Guizot) of desiring only "to arrive at a change in Ministry"—to the benefit of themselves—rather than serious structural reform.[14] With the tentative date of 19 January, the organizers decided to hold the banquet in a working-class district, and they opened it to the public; the ticket price, fixed at three francs, was not out of the question even for a working man. On 14 January, they were informed that Minister of the Interior Charles Duchatel had refused his authorization.[15]

The blunt prohibition changed everything. The opposition deputies who had earlier declined now decided that they had to defend the *droit de réunion*.[16]

In the early 1830s, moderate republicans had lost the battle for freedom of association; now the government was expanding its own authority, in a way that
threatened the reform campaign. The deputies hijacked the organizing commission (installing Barrot as president) and made several changes: the invitations were restricted to electors; the ticket price was doubled to six francs; and
the whole affair was moved to a location on the relatively unsettled Champs-
Élysées in the west, and to a weekday (ultimately Tuesday) rather than a Sunday or holiday. The republican Ledru-Rollin was disinvited.[17] And the
deputies also agreed, in backdoor negotiations with the government, to limit
the event. They would gather for the banquet, a police *commissaire* would
order them to disband, and the matter would go before the courts—likely, as
Guizot noted, to be friendly territory for the government.[18]

The original plans had also called for a procession before the banquet,
and on Monday, 21 February, Marrast printed in the *National* an order of
march for deputies, workers, and students, with a summons to sympathetic national guards to present themselves in uniform.[19] Louis-Philippe's council, effectively headed since 1840 by the unpopular Guizot—and worried by rumors
that twenty to thirty thousand national guards would participate, in a stunning
repudiation of the ministry—decided on Monday night, the eve of the procession, to forbid it. If the attendees wished to make their way individually, the
original judicial script would be followed; but government forces would be deployed against any demonstration in the streets. Under the leadership of Barrot, the deputies decided to cancel. As a cover for their withdrawal, they voted
instead to draft a meaningless "indictment" of the ministry.[20]

On that same evening (the twenty-first), editor Ferdinand Flocon had invited all interested subscribers to the offices of the *Réforme*. The meeting,
which began at 7 P.M., included close to 100 student delegates, working-class
activists, five police spies, and republican and socialist notables: Ledru-Rollin,
Louis Blanc, Albert, Étienne Arago (a founder of *La Réforme*, brother of
François), and Lyon veterans Caussidière, Eugène Beaune, and Charles Lagrange. They were generally agreed on the dangers of bowing to the government prohibition, and news that the deputies had backed down led to such an
angry backlash that there was a strong sentiment for trying "the fortunes of
the day." But there were a surprising number of voices, even here, on the side
of caution. Louis Blanc urged withdrawal; the government obviously wanted a
collision to "decapitate" the Left. Caussidière, in contrast, argued for a republican *prise d'armes*, to save from slaughter those who would unwittingly turn
out for the procession. The enthusiasm stirred by his speech was tempered
once again by Ledru-Rollin, who suggested a compromise: the republican
party would "wait and observe, before pushing the people into a manifesta-

tion"; if an insurrection did occur, it would be the duty of the leaders to join them.[21] But the proposal was sufficiently vague to satisfy even the activists. Caussidière's memory was that they had agreed to go in small groups, unarmed, "hands in pockets," "to observe things and lead public opinion against the Monarchy." If disturbances occurred, they would meet at the *Réforme* offices to "coordinate" and give the demonstration a "republican character."[22]

Tuesday, 22 February, was a day of skirmishes, especially on the Champs Elysées, which was to have been the procession route. A group composed largely of students and workers gathered in the morning on the Place du Panthéon to march to the banquet, many of them still unaware of the last-minute cancellation. Student activist Philippe Faure was part of the group of "five thousand" (his estimate), determined upon a clash: "We were going to get ourselves massacred; perhaps that would awaken the People."[23] An elderly woman was knocked down by the movement of the crowd, an event that soon metamorphosed into the assertion that women and children were being trampled under the feet of municipal guard horses.[24]

That evening the dynastic opposition gathered again at Barrot's to discuss their course of action if the scuffles of the day should lead to the overturning of the ministry—the limits, thus far, of their imagination.[25] About 20 of the *Réforme* activists, including Caussidière, Albert, and Flocon, met as agreed under the columns of the Palais-Royal that evening. The multiple exits provided insurance against capture, and they took the additional precautions of strolling about, breaking and reforming into different groups—pointless safeguards, since the police spies Chenu and Delahodde were both present. But they were unable to agree on the meaning of the day's events, and finished with a dramatically split decision. Some would continue merely to hold themselves in readiness; others would convoke the secret societies for the following day, at noon, in the faubourg Saint-Martin.[26]

At the Tuesday night meeting of the king's council, those in power were still confident of their course. They had reason to believe themselves secure, with 31,000 troops at their immediate disposal in Paris (the army could act in the capital only if required by the prefect of police).[27] There were also 3,900 municipal guards, a military policing organization directly under the prefect. This group would be the most aggressive for, unlike the regular troops, they did not require the formal requisition of the civil authorities to act; unfortunately, the municipals would be virtually abandoned on the third day, cut off from the prefecture and largely forgotten by the military commanders.[28] And there were, of course,

the national guards, some 85,000 of them in the greater Paris region, who were
the backbone of the regime.[29] Everyone present praised the conduct of the
troops on this first day; General Tiburce Sebastiani, commander of the First
military division, had ordered his senior officers to act with "moderation" and
"prudence" (almost every officer used both words), to remain on the "defensive," to shoot only after an unspecified but considerable amount of fire, and
only after legal *sommations*.[30] Within hours this restraint would come to be seen
in a different light, to be regarded as a "fatal hesitation," a "demoralizing uncertainty."[31] And there were two disquieting signs, for those who cared to read
them: the attitude of the National Guard, and the raids on the gunshops.

Several days before the events, Louis-Philippe had decided to replace
General Jean-François Jacqueminot as commander of the Paris National
Guard; but he was the father-in-law of Interior Minister Duchatel, who indicated that he would resign as well. Rather than shatter the ministry, Louis-
Philippe had left in place the ineffective, frequently ill commandant, who
assured the council that the Guard would defend the regime.[32] On the twenty-
second, the *rappel* ordered the legions to their strategic zones with the Line
troops, according to the Gérard Plan of 1839. The 1st Legion remained on
patrol until 11 P.M., troubled by no disorders.[33] After that the reports were
considerably more grim. In the conservative 2nd Legion, Colonel François
Talabot reported "shouts of *Vive la réforme!* that they shouted even in the
ranks, in spite of my efforts and those of many of my officers." By 1 P.M. he
had gathered only 150 men.[34] The third *arrondissement* had only about 150;
the 4th Legion, which included the troubled Saint-Martin area, had gathered
so few men that they were unable to occupy their zones.[35]

In the fifth *arrondissement* there appeared only ten national guards, who
gamely joined themselves to the Line troops in the vicinity.[36] The *rappel* gathered only 80 guards each in the 6th and 7th Legions.[37] Colonel Jacques
Beudin of the 8th, whose zone included the symbolic Place de la Bastille, gathered only a few men who were "little disposed to sustain the Ministry."[38]
Colonel François Boutarel of the 9th had about 150 national guards by
evening, and he was able to occupy the Hôtel de Ville with the Line; but one
of his men asserted that they had responded for the sole purpose of "guaran-
teeing property and preventing the spilling of blood," and not out of loyalty to
the regime.[39] The 10th and 11th Legions, few in number, at least had the
virtue of being less openly disruptive than the others.[40] The men of the 12th
Legion had organized the banquet, in opposition to the wishes of their colonel
(and Fieschi's patron) Gustave Ladvocat. Only about 100 to 150 men responded to the *rappel*, shouting *"Vive la Réforme! à bas Guizot!"* Ladvocat dis-

missed them at 10 P.M., reporting that they had been in a great state of "exasperation," their patrols the major cause of disorder in the area.[41]

The other disquieting sign of trouble was the raiding of the gunshops. Most owners reported that they had been hit first during the late afternoon or evening of 22 February in brief, violent attacks by large, unarmed bands. They had been left alone on the twenty-third, until the very end of the day, and then raided again on the twenty-fourth.[42] Charles Rozoy on the rue de Clichy was attacked between 8 and 9 P.M. on the twenty-second; the looters became angry when he had no gunpowder, striking his wife and putting a knife to his assistant's throat. Antoine Grandineau on the rue de la Ville-Levesque was attacked in the late afternoon of the twenty-second by about 30 men, some armed with iron bars; they took his guns, his wife's shawl, and 230 francs. Jean-Baptiste Baudoin, who sold sabers, was visited at 1 P.M. on the twenty-second by a polite band of several hundred, according to his estimate. A small delegation entered; a careful inspection of his wares, including "deluxe" weapons, had led to the decision that his goods were too insubstantial to battle the Municipal Guard. On the twenty-fourth a more threatening and less discriminating group made off with a number of épées. Louis Devisme (who had given Alibaud his *canne-fusil*) had two shops on the boulevard des Italiens, where he had recently bought out a competitor. Both were emptied, and he estimated his losses at between sixty and seventy thousand francs.[43] And finally, there was the Lepage shop on the rue Bourg l'Abbé, central supplier of Blanqui's May insurrection. In the early evening of the twenty-second approximately 100 unarmed men, undeterred by the massive post-1839 fortifications, stopped a passing omnibus, unhitched the horses, and used the shaft as a battering ram to break into the store.[44]

On Wednesday afternoon, the second day of the revolt, the National Guard continued to be disruptive, turning out in small numbers and increasingly ill-humor. The king had long regarded the National Guard as his "living symbol," his bourgeois defenders the very embodiment of his bourgeois monarchy. Nemours stated that their apparent defection had convinced the king, on Wednesday afternoon, to replace the hated Guizot with the veteran Comte Mathieu Molé. Molé was unable to form a government and resigned at about midnight. Louis-Philippe then called the unthinkable Adolphe Thiers, who was replaced at mid-morning on Thursday by the even more impossibly liberal Odilon Barrot, in vain attempts to pacify the crowds, who either heard nothing of the ministerial changes or were not satisfied with them.[45]

Nevertheless, the king seemed to be regaining control of his capital by Wednesday evening, as word of Guizot's dismissal spread through the city. To be sure, many of the activists were angry at such a tame resolution. Republican

attorney Emmanuel Arago (son of François) harangued the crowds outside the
offices of the *National*, saying "that the change in Ministry was no longer sufficient."[46] Ledru-Rollin, in a speech to those outside the *Réforme* office, urged
his supporters to hold out for amnesty for those arrested in the fighting, the
liberation of all political prisoners, the *droit de réunion*, and universal manhood
suffrage.[47] But hostile responses were atypical. Many commanders reported
"fraternization" between their troops and the people.[48] And most were inclined to celebrate; with nightfall, residents spontaneously lit up the city, putting lamps and candles in all their windows, attracting strollers outside in spite
of the weather to observe the unaccustomed illumination.

Two events then propelled the dying disorders into revolution: the massacre of
the boulevard des Capucines late Wednesday evening, and the retreat of General Bedeau's column through the city on Thursday morning. Both were vivid
symbols of the loss of legitimacy and power.

The boulevard des Capucines massacre was a matter of chance, transformed instantly into familiar ritual: the procession of corpses, the violation of
women, the "betrayal" of the people by their king.[49] The incident began when
troops outside Guizot's ministry of foreign affairs suddenly fired without
warning into a crowd of mostly unarmed marchers, killing over sixty men and
women. Some of the bodies were immediately placed on a cart and paraded
through the streets, accompanied by torchbearers who illuminated the grisly
cargo. By the following morning, Paris was thick with barricades.

Afterward, supporters of the fallen monarchy became convinced that this
fusillade had been provoked by republicans, the suspiciously convenient
wagon prepared in advance so that the lives so cynically sacrificed would
arouse a dying insurgency.[50] But the official investigation did not support the
conspiracy theory, laying out instead a series of unfortunate mischances. One
of the key witnesses to the event was the mechanic Jean Nicolas Schumacher,
an officer in the 8th Legion of the National Guard and a member of the suffrage reform group. He had not been satisfied with the fall of Guizot; that
evening, when he had found his local *mairie* under siege by men demanding
weapons and ammunition, he had suggested a march through the faubourg
Saint Antoine with himself at their head, along with lieutenants Hubert
Launette and Blot. Along the way they decided to go to the offices of the *National* on the rue Lepelletier, to urge the newspaper to make clear "that a Molé
and Thiers ministry would not satisfy [the people]."[51] As they marched the

column grew, though only a few were armed—Schumacher believed 10 or 12, others estimated as many as 50—along with several men with flags, perhaps "four or five" with torches. They sang the *Marseillaise* and the *Chant du départ*, shouted *Vive la réforme!* and, at Schumacher's insistence, *à bas le système!*[52] At the *National* Marrast spoke to them from the window; according to one of the observers, he "told us that the Ministry was going to be indicted," that there would be electoral and parliamentary reforms, "that it was necessary to keep our weapons until they had obtained all they wanted." Another marcher recalled the statement that "we had carried off a victory and we could not allow it to be snatched away [*escamotée*] as in 1830."[53]

The various troop detachments had allowed them to pass without difficulty, even with signs of approval. Their route led them eventually to the boulevard des Capucines, which was completely blocked by three companies of the 14th regiment of the Line. The soldiers here, guarding Guizot's ministry, had strict orders to allow no one through. Moreover, there were no national guards to negotiate the situation. Colonel Talabot of the 2nd Legion, assigned to the area as a buffer between people and troops, had just taken his men to put out a fire at the nearby Chancellery. The blaze, confined to a sentry box, was easily extinguished; Talabot's national guards had been dispersing the last few demonstrators when they heard the fusillade only a short distance away.[54]

The marching column were nearly upon the troops before they were told to turn back. Schumacher urged Lieutenant Colonel Jean Courand of the 14th, on horseback and slightly in front of his men, to open his ranks; those at the head of the column, now at least one thousand strong, were being pushed by the momentum of those behind. Suddenly the lieutenant colonel turned back into his ranks "and immediately the soldiers lowered their weapons and fired on us."[55] The gunfire sent the crowd into frantic flight. It also stampeded two nearby squads of *cuirassiers* and dragoons; exhausted men and horses were both "suddenly awakened from their somnolence," according to the colonel, and their uncontrolled gallop added to the confusion and injury.[56]

Two issues would be hotly debated by the survivors. The first was whether the commanding officer had ordered his men to shoot; the second was the matter of who had fired the initial shot. Several men, including Schumacher, believed they had heard a distinct order to fire; among the national guards, only Lieutenant Jean Neveau, very close to Courand, insisted that there had been no such command. At the same time, most believed that the soldiers had fired quickly and unevenly, and from the "present bayonet" position. In Schumacher's words, "the first discharge began with several detached shots," followed by a "badly-executed platoon fire," then a second "well-executed platoon fire." Neveau, who had heard the same pattern, added that the first isolated shots came from the platoon's left.[57]

The soldiers, in contrast, were convinced that they had been attacked first. Lieutenant Colonel Courand asserted that one of the demonstrators had grabbed his bridle and several had shaken their fists in his face; he had backed behind his line and ordered his men to present bayonets: "Immediately a gunshot was fired, I cannot tell you from [right or left]; and the same instant, and without orders, the platoon fired, in whole or in part." He believed that the first gunshot had killed one of his soldiers, and thus had come from the crowd. He adamantly denied having given an order to fire.[58]

The front rank agreed with Courand's version and stressed the militance of the advancing column. They had shouted that they wanted to "burn Guizot in his hôtel," that they wanted his "hide." They had agitated their torches in the faces of the soldiers, causing the line to buckle: "In spite of the efforts of the Lieutenant Colonel, these individuals arrived so close to us that they were chest to chest with the first ranks."[59] Captain Joseph Leroi suggested that the national guards, far from serving as a restraining force, had actually escalated the confrontation; Courand had ordered his men to present bayonets only when one of them had raised his saber in a threatening manner. The soldiers also agreed, unanimously, that there had been no order to fire, Lieutenant Alexandre Guillot adding that he was "certain that [the soldiers] fired without taking aim, and in the present-bayonet position."[60]

Many of the rank and file believed that the fusillade had been triggered by the sudden death of the soldier Henry at the extreme left of the line, shot in the face and knocked flat on his back. "The majority of our soldiers were young and not accustomed to gunfire," recalled one of the officers. Noël Mathurin had been pushing back stragglers at the edge of the crowd when he heard a single shot, then the multiple rounds: "In turning to rejoin my company, I saw behind me my comrade Henry who fell dead." Reported Jean Collignon, who had been right beside him: "Like all my comrades I fired, seeing Henry fall." Lieutenant Édouard Baillet, while not a direct witness, reported that the version "adopted by almost everyone" in his regiment was that the first fatal shot had come from the people and had killed the soldier.[61] Others also blamed the people but described a different sequence of events. When the marchers tried to grab the soldiers' muskets, recalled Sergeant Antoine Giacomoni, they "fired and struck a great number of people," without taking aim and without being ordered.[62]

The testimony thus suggested at least two causes for the fusillade into the crowd: the death of Henry, and the scuffling between the front ranks. The evidence also suggested that Lieutenant Colonel Courand had not given the order. While this discrepancy was not publicly explained, Courand later claimed, privately, that several *gamins* had agitated their torches in the face of a soldier who shot into the air. At the same moment, an officer who arrived "inopportunely at this point of the line, and believing combat engaged," had given the order to fire[63]—an explanation that might have accounted for the distinctly heard *en joue! feu!*

As soon as it was possible to get up, Schumacher looked around him for his son and his friends. Lieutenant Neveau, who stumbled over the body of their colleague Lieutenant Blot, escorted the injured Schumacher back home. Lieutenant Launette headed straight for the offices of the *Réforme*.[64]

The *Moniteur* reported that 52 people fell dead or wounded in the fusillade.[65] A more accurate count was made by Commissaire Charles Loyeux, stationed that night at the foreign affairs ministry, who had found 36 dead and 64 wounded on the pavements or in neighboring shops and cafés, of whom 7 died later (thus, 43 killed). The man who drove the famous cart had taken away an additional 16 bodies. Subsequent investigations by Loyeux had turned up 3 dead and 21 wounded, all of them brought directly by others to the Hôtel-Dieu or to their homes. Commissaire Alexandre Vassal listed an additional 3 wounded who had been brought to his district, and Commissaire Antoine Basset in the second *arrondissement* reported that "several" bodies from the Ministry of Foreign Affairs had been carried separately into his neighborhood to rouse the populace.[66] Thus the number of the dead was in the mid-60s, with a total of 81 wounded.

For Orléanists, the most suspicious aspect of the night was that all-too-convenient cart. In fact, the wagon that allowed for the famous procession through the city had arrived fortuitously; the driver, Pierre Junieau, had left the *Messageries générales* at 10 P.M. with three travelers, en route to the railroad station. Ten minutes later, having arrived at the corner of the boulevard, he was greeted by an officer who asked if he had come to take away the bodies (those in charge had urgently sent for someone to remove the corpses and wash down the area).[67] The obliging Junieau unloaded his passengers. Sixteen bodies were placed on his conveyance, including National Guard Blot, the soldier Henry, and fourteen civilians. The cart, and Junieau, were then appropriated by angry marchers, who had initially fled to the side streets. Men with torches took up stations alongside; three of them climbed atop the pile to illuminate the dead. They stopped at the offices of the *National* on the rue Lepelletier, addressed in the absence of Marrast by Garnier-Pagès, and then at the *Réforme*, on the rue Coq-Héron. Flocon, after a silent tour of the wagon, delivered an emotional speech, telling the crowd "that the moment to conquer or die for liberty had arrived, and that a terrible justice would be given to the murderers." They then made a restricted circuit of the eastern right bank, the barricades forcing them to turn back before they reached the Place de la Bastille. Those who accompanied the cortège attempted to stir the neighborhoods to revolt ("Down with Louis-Philippe! Vengeance! They are killing our brothers, to arms!"). At about 1:30 A.M. Junieau finally left the bodies at the *mairie* in the fourth *arrondissement*. The journey had lasted approximately three hours; only 30 of the original 200 marchers were still with the procession.[68]

The cortège echoed a famous event, and founding legend, of the July Revolution:

> On 27 July a woman had just been killed by the bullet of a Swiss or a Royal Guard; a citizen seized this bloodied body, carried it through the streets of Paris, showed it to his fellow citizens: "Vengeance! vengeance!" he told them, and the crowd repeated "Vengeance!" Finally he stopped before a barracks, and throwing this body at the feet of the soldiers, he shouted: "Soldiers! You are armed to protect your fellow citizens and not to massacre them; see this body, it is one of our women murdered by men who were also wearing epaulettes. The cowards have nothing of French soldiers in them except the name, but you have the courage, you have the sentiment of your duties and humanity, join with us, march against the tyrants!"[69]

Junieau claimed that all the bodies were male; the one woman placed on the cart had been removed when it was discovered that she was still breathing. Nevertheless, lithographs and descriptions after the event prominently included a woman, the stereotypical victim in republican ideology.[70]

Word of the massacre spread swiftly through the city. The *tocsin* began to sound from Saint-Sulpice on the Left Bank and Saint-Méry on the Right.[71] Barricades went up throughout the rue Saint-Martin, with working-class sentinels posted on the street corners.[72] The faubourg Saint Antoine had already been stirred by the rumor that heavy artillery was on the way from Vincennes; barricades were constructed during the evening and night to stop reinforcements from reaching the city.[73] Many of the troops, recalled to the center, spent an overcrowded night at the Place du Carrousel at the Tuileries, contending with rain, high winds, and the smoke from campfires; they could hear Saint-Sulpice tolling in the distance.[74]

The republicans, meeting in the *Réforme* offices under the chairmanship of Ledru-Rollin and Caussidière, decided to aim for the republic; verbal orders were sent out to the *hommes d'action*. They were especially concerned that the chamber might attempt to establish a new government on their own authority, as they had in 1830. Thus it was decided that the "armed sections of

the secret societies," led by Lagrange and Caussidière, would expel the legislators and also seize the nearby Tuileries.[75] The republicans of the Hôtel de
Ville had lost, in 1830, to the deputies of the Palais-Bourbon: this time there
would be no dual sovereignty.

On the following morning Paris was transformed. Alexis de Tocqueville
first heard of the massacre from his cook: "This good woman was beside herself
and told me I don't know what sort of tearful gibberish of which I understood
nothing, if not that the government had slaughtered the poor people." He went
to the streets and "breathed for the first time the atmosphere of revolution."[76]
Most Parisians probably knew as little as Tocqueville's cook, and the wealthy
neighborhoods were quiet. Indeed, the Comte d'Alton-Shée, on his way to join
the fighting, felt some embarrassment in walking armed through his tranquil
quartier (with an ornate hunting rifle, the only weapon he possessed).[77] But the
emotional excitement of revolution—the sight of the barricades, the smell of
the gunpowder, the sound of the *tocsin*—had been stirred too deeply to be resolved by a sudden change of ministry, especially one that could appear as yet
another *escamotage*. Moreover, the massacre had been transformed from the accident that it was to a more familiar narrative of betrayal. The *Courrier français*
distributed a placard on the morning of the twenty-fourth: "People of Paris!
Do not disarm! Maintain your barricades! 24 February will be a great day for
French liberty, for the freedom of the world!"[78]

Louis-Philippe had summoned Thiers in the middle of the night, shortly
after learning of the disaster; at the same time he called General Thomas
Bugeaud, the premier commander in France and fresh from the conquest of
Algeria. Bugeaud, unfairly burdened since 1834 with a reputation as the
"butcher of the rue Transnonain" (the culprits had not been his troops) had
been thinking seriously about the problem of public order since the early July
Monarchy. He had drawn up his suggestions in a small pamphlet, *La Guerre
des rues*, in which he had suggested the importance of "concentrating" all the
troops immediately, in order to send them out in strong columns for a military
conquest of the city—the strategy that would be followed in a few months by
General Eugène Cavaignac, in his victory in the June Days.[79]

Now Bugeaud had the opportunity to put his ideas into practice. The first
of his columns, of about 2,000 men under General Alphonse Bedeau, was to
go to the Place de la Bastille. The second, of 3,500 men under General
Tiburce Sébastiani (whom Bugeaud had just replaced), was to go to the Hôtel
de Ville; a third, smaller group was sent out under Colonel Jean Brunet, to
join General Pierre Renault at the Panthéon. Bugeaud kept a reserve of 7,000
to 8,000 men under his own command at the headquarters at the Tuileries, to

be used in mopping-up operations. His commanders, who left at dawn, were ordered to try persuasion and conciliation first, to inform the people of the new ministry; if that failed, they were to attack.[80]

But the orders soon changed. Thiers wanted to end the offensive, which had barely started, and to bring all the troops back to the Tuileries, leaving Paris to the National Guard. Between 8 and 9 A.M., Bugeaud ordered a cease-fire and recalled his columns.[81] By his own subsequent account, Bugeaud had protested this change until Nemours brought him a direct order from the king. A number of historians have suggested that Bugeaud had in fact already ordered a ceasefire, perhaps of his own accord, or perhaps, as Henri Guillemin has suggested, because of a verbal order from the king, at around 7 A.M.[82] Bugeaud certainly knew the difficulties of his troops, through a series of increasingly frantic messages from the field; later, embarrassed by defeat, he had attempted to rewrite history.

Odilon Barrot, part of Thiers' new ministry, left the Tuileries between 9 and 10 A.M., having heard the flattering report that Parisians thought news of his appointment too good to be true. He and his political allies encountered the first barricade only a few hundred feet from the Tuileries gate: "We advanced toward the barricade; my friends named me, shouting *Vive la Réforme!* Then the armed men who guarded this barricade came to us in turn shouting *Vive la Réforme!* and we passed through. This first success was a good augury"—virtually the last good one, as they soon encountered numerous soldiers in a "painful uncertainty," having received orders to cease fire but left standing in the streets, where the crowds subjected them to increasingly rough "fraternization." Near the boulevard Poissonnière, Barrot and his supporters sensed "a greater exaltation" among the masses, a growing number of "fanatics" who clearly desired to push things further. Finally he halted his procession at the Porte Saint-Denis, where he found a tall, imposing, red-flagged barricade, obviously the product of veteran *sectionnaires:* "Those who guarded it responded only with the silence of death to the acclamations of the crowd that surrounded me." When they did not come forward to shake his hand, Barrot decided to turn around.[83]

The troops had been on the streets almost continuously since Tuesday. Most soldiers were exhausted, confused by orders that seemed to change almost hourly. They were uncertain whether they should allow the crowds to take over posts, if stopping them would mean bloodshed—to say nothing of whether or not to intervene in lesser actions, including the cutting of trees, the breaking of street lamps, and the burning of abandoned guardhouses.[84] At the Place du Panthéon, General Renault received word of the ceasefire but no further orders. He told his men, marooned in the midst of an increasingly hostile crowd, to remain passive. "Our presence seemed to irritate the population," he recalled; "this mass was armed, and very exalted." Hours later, at 3 P.M., he was approached by the mayor's deputy and the lieutenant colonel of the 12th National Guard Legion, "who made known to me that the government no longer existed, that all the troops had gone back to their barracks." With some difficulty, and after surrendering their weapons ("which they did with tears in their eyes"), he and his men managed to get safely out of town.[85] Similarly, the thicket of barricades had forced Sébastiani to stop all patrols through his area by mid-morning; even as he left, the Place de l'Hôtel de Ville was filling up with combatants determined to seize this center of power.[86]

But the most striking portent of defeat was the disastrous, highly public retreat of Bedeau's column: a visual collapse, indeed an emasculation of royal power, that put the activism of the republicans in bold relief. Bedeau had set off at dawn for the Place de la Bastille, where he was to join forces with General Louis Duhot. Unfortunately the Bastille soon fell; the local mayor's attempts that morning to publicize the new ministry (received with "a type of enthusiasm," he reported) had led to an altercation, then to a fusillade in which Duhot had lost 12 men and 2 *cantinières* (canteen women). Duhot had believed it "prudent" to withdraw, and he and his men had headed off in the direction of Vincennes, away from Bedeau.[87] Duhot's retreat had led to the collapse of the smaller posts and barracks throughout the southeastern part of the city.

Bedeau, in the meantime, had encountered only slight resistance until the Porte Saint Denis—at the same formidable barricade that had stopped Barrot. He now faced a serious dilemma, for it was clear that if he wanted to go forward he would have to fight his way through. He kept his men stationary for what turned out to be two long hours, as he unsuccessfully attempted to obtain local national guard support from several bourgeois who approached his troops: "They answered me in complaining sharply of the event of the boulevard des Capucines, adding that the night before, [the government] had deceived them in announcing the change in ministry."[88] Nevertheless, two men volunteered to carry Bedeau's messages to headquarters, and one of them managed to return with the order to withdraw—to cease fire, "if it had commenced" (according to Nemours), and to remain "passive," attempting conciliation as he withdrew back to the Tuileries.[89]

Bedeau asked the local national guards to march at the head of his column, in order to negotiate a passage through the barricades they encountered; at one point they crossed paths with Barrot's procession.[90] But the troops were increasingly pressed, their ranks infiltrated by insurgents who grabbed at their weapons. Bedeau's route took him past the foreign affairs ministry, the site of the previous night's massacre, and once again surrounded by an angry crowd. An inspired national guard officer had chalked "The Peoples' Building, national

property!" on the wall and placed working-class sentinels at the door. The
harried troops on duty, their situation precarious, hitched themselves to Bedeau's column as it passed through.[91] National Guard Amédée Achard noticed
their "morose air," the "lassitude" as well as "irritation" on their faces; as they
approached the Place de la Concorde, they suddenly "were assailed and as if
devoured alive by eddies of men in *blouses* who penetrated and broke their
ranks. . . . The column fell into pieces."[92] Thiers later was critical of Bedeau:
"As it was, the people reduced his soldiers in detail: they broke into their
ranks; they shook them by the hand; they kissed them; they entreated them
not to fire on the people; they promised to take care of their artillery for them;
in short, they made them worse than useless. In an *émeute* the troops are lost if
they allow the mob to come into contact with them. The only wise order is to
shoot if they approach"—easier said than done, of course, especially coming
from the man who had demanded the ceasefire.[93]

Bedeau arrived at the Place de la Concorde at approximately 11 A.M.; the
Tuileries, close by, was chaotic. As the morning passed, the duc de Nemours
had found himself frequently called outside by new assaults against the palace.
Eventually even the steady 1st Legion, backed against the railings, was shouting
for reform. He was unable to travel the short distance to Bugeaud's headquarters, now under heavy sniper fire, and when he reentered the palace he was
promptly collared by *La Presse* editor Émile de Girardin, who shoved a piece of
paper in his hand: "Abdication of the king. Regency of the Duchesse d'Orléans.
Dissolution of the Chamber of Deputies. General Amnesty." Nemours took
the list to the king and Thiers, who uttered his famously ineffectual "The tide
is rising, rising." (Thiers later complained that he had been quoted out of context.)[94] Deputy Adolphe Crémieux, within hours to be part of the provisional
government, told the royal family that matters had gone beyond Thiers; he
suggested Barrot as the head of a frankly left council, with Marshal Maurice-
Étienne Gérard—elderly, ailing, blind in one eye, but popular—to replace
Bugeaud. Barrot was still in the streets, announcing the Thiers ministry. Louis-
Philippe asked Gérard, who had come to volunteer his services, to spread the
news of Barrot's ministry and his own appointment. Shortly after this last, futile
gesture, the king abdicated on behalf of his grandson, the little Comte de Paris.
The duchesse d'Orléans, widow of Louis-Philippe's beloved oldest son, was
tacitly regarded as the only possible regent, even though a law of 1842 had
named the conservative, unpopular Nemours.[95] Bugeaud, who had just been
removed, came inside and tried to stop the king: "I said it was too late; that it
would have no effect, except demoralizing the soldiers; they were ready to act,
and to fight it out was the only thing left to us."[96] But Louis-Philippe finished

writing out his abdication. The now ex-king, who suddenly looked his age, walked out to the carriage with his wife, who held her head high.[97] He found refuge in Great Britain, a brief twilight before he died in August 1850.

After the abdication Bugeaud had nothing more to do. He descended into the courtyard where he saw Marshal Gérard attempting to take command: "I observed for a moment what was happening . . . I judged that everything was finished and the chateau would soon be invaded." He strode out of the palace grounds, soon recognized and surrounded by an angry mob who accused him of slaughtering civilians in the rue Transnonain: "'That is not true,' I answered; 'I was not there, nor the troops I commanded, but the newspapers said it; the newspapers slandered me; that often happens.'" Then he boldly counterattacked, reminding them of his military exploits as the "conqueror of Abdel-Kader" in Algeria: "Down with the man who has subdued the Arabs and conquered Africa? Down with the man you will want to lead you against the Germans and the Russians?" The crowd began to cheer.[98] He would die in bed the following year, victim of a new cholera epidemic.

After the king's departure, the Tuileries was invaded. The throne was wrenched from its platform, dragged through the streets, and burned at the foot of the July column. There was, indeed, something of a race between sightseeing and vengeance; the stonemason Martin Nadaud recalled a terrible shoving match to get inside, the crowd "so tightly packed we were unable to breathe," moving from chamber to chamber almost as a block, until finally expelled back onto the Carrousel.[99] The code of *mort aux voleurs* (death to thieves) was observed, scrawled on the walls in big letters; a student saw two men dead in a corner, shot because they had tried to make off with some silverware.[100] Not all agreed with this fixation on property rights. Norbert Truquin, then only 14, recalled that an elderly man had made valiant efforts, at the risk of his own life, to save from summary execution a young thief caught absconding with a trifle from the palace.[101] And there were apparently no scruples about simple destruction, as many of the combatants fired their guns in celebration. Later it was reported that twenty-five thousand kilograms of shattered windows and crystal had been picked out of the wreckage; it required ten carts to carry away the shards of porcelain.[102]

Several hours before the abdication, it was clear that Louis-Philippe was on his way out, and the lessons of 1830 were explicitly invoked. An *affiche* posted on the barricade at the Collège de France warned of another *escamotage:* "As in

1830, the People are victorious; but this time they will not lay down their arms."[103] The same sentiment appeared in an anonymous placard on the rue de Richelieu: "Citizens! By your heroism, you have once more forced despotism into its last retrenchments. But you conquered on 14 July 1789, 10 August 1792, 29 July 1830, and each time you were robbed of the benefits of your victory. . . . Let these examples instruct you at last!"[104] The *Réforme* placard was relatively economical: "Citizens, Louis-Philippe has caused us to be murdered, as Charles X did; let him rejoin Charles X."[105]

The offices of the *National* had been crowded from early morning on. It was the oldest, most respected republican newspaper; its editor, Armand Marrast, was a veteran of prison and exile. Deputy Garnier-Pagès sent an emissary to urge him to rally to Barrot; Merruau of the *Constitutionnel*, Thiers's man, came on the same errand. Marrast told both of them that Louis-Philippe was no longer possible, though even he still expected a regency.[106] But the situation was fluid and rapidly evolving, as the regency steadily lost ground to the republic.[107] Between eleven o'clock and noon, the newspaper offices were the site of a meeting over which Benjamin Sarrans presided—the rooms completely filled, spilling into the hall and onto the stairway—to form a list for a provisional government.[108]

The names accepted unanimously were François Arago from *La Réforme*, a distinguished scientist and member of the Academy; Lamartine, a deputy, aristocrat, poet, author of the popular recent *Histoire des Girondins*; Marie, deputy and frequent attorney for republicans; Garnier-Pagès, deputy and younger brother of a republican martyr; and Marrast. Carnot and Crémieux were both voted down but Barrot was included to reassure the bourgeoisie, despite much criticism of his desertion of the banquet and his new role as Louis-Philippe's minister. The group was arguing over Ledru-Rollin—still considered too extremist, too "compromising"—when Louis Blanc arrived to insist upon his own name; he was offended when told bluntly that he was impossible. The choices were read from the window to the crowd outside, and each, except for Barrot, received applause.[109]

The list was then brought to the *Réforme*, its offices filled with a steady stream of activists, including a considerable number of workers and *sectionnaires*. This more radical group balked at Barrot but accepted the others, also adding several more: Dupont (de l'Eure), the veteran of 1789, Ledru-Rollin, Louis Blanc, and editor Ferdinand Flocon. Eugène Beaune of Lyon demanded a worker; Albert was the obvious choice, associated with the newspaper and a long-time activist.[110] A copy of this revised list was returned to the *National*, and hastily scrawled sheets were taken in all directions to the *chefs des barricades*.[111]

President Sauzet convened the Chamber of Deputies at 12:30 P.M., two hours earlier than scheduled; they would meet to the sound of the Chateau d'Eau gunfire close by, the site of the largest pitched battle of the revolution. The Palais-Bourbon was vulnerable to invasion, and as soon as the session opened Deputy François de Corcelles asked Sauzet's permission to call for protection from Bedeau, who had brought his bedraggled column to a halt just outside. Even by his own account Sauzet hedged, authorizing Corcelles only to tell Bedeau to bar the Pont de la Concorde, "that one was not asking him to take the initiative in a bloody conflict," but merely to block the crowd. Bedeau "asked to reflect and confer with his officers"; then he stated "that in view of the facts, he could not take on himself such a responsibility."[112]

Shortly thereafter, the first wave of "citizens" invaded the hall. The chief usher managed to direct this group into the public tribunes, but their presence created an atmosphere of noise and confusion from the beginning. Sauzet recalled the arrival of successive deputies, "out of breath, minute by minute," bringing news of the abdication and then departure of the king. He was soon astonished to learn that the duchesse d'Orléans, her two small sons, and the duc de Nemours were outside. Chairs were hurriedly brought into the lower hemicycle; with them, remembered the chief usher, came "an enormous mass of men of all types, armed and unarmed," who infiltrated the hall itself.[113] (Tocqueville described the deputies as relentlessly forced into the upper rows, "like those unfortunate ones, surprised by the rising tide, who withdraw from rock to rock, constantly pursued by the sea."[114]) Deputy André Dupin, who had escorted the royal party, announced the king's abdication and the regency of the duchesse, and reported that the National Guard had cheered her on their passage. His attempt to establish the regency by acclamation was drowned out by the strangers in the hall.[115] The royals soon emigrated to the top tier of seats, from which they viewed the proceedings.[116]

Deputy Alexandre Marie took the podium and proposed a provisional government, thus speaking the words for the first time.[117] The *Moniteur* reported that the crowd cheered; Sarrans suggested a more nuanced response from the audience, who liked the first part but not his subsequent suggestion that the new government "will advise; it will advise *concurrently with the Chambers*, it will have authority over the country."[118] Crémieux, who spoke next, reported the king's departure. Then he deliberately invoked history: "In 1830 we were very rushed, and here we are obliged, in 1848, to begin again. The Provisional Government that you name will not only be charged to maintain order, but to bring about some institutions that protect all parts of the population."[119] His statement met with tumultuous applause; the new little king was observed to join in.[120] Then came Barrot, who had arrived too late; his attempt to salvage a regency was regarded as embarrassed and unconvincing, a verdict with which he himself agreed.[121]

Bedeau, in the meantime, was still outside with his demoralized men, a witness to successive invasions, unwilling to act on his own but all too aware that there were also consequences to doing nothing. He did not believe he could fire on the invaders, for his last order from Bugeaud had called for a ceasefire. He attempted to send a messenger inside to consult with Barrot, then to offer protection to the royal family; but there was too much confusion.[122] Eventually, Bedeau simply led his troops back to barracks. Marshal MacMahon saw him just after these events, in tears because he believed his career was over. But the actions of Bedeau (a ten-year Algeria veteran, made general in 1841 at only 38), so humiliating from a military standpoint, had made him politically viable in the new order. Within hours, he would assume supreme command of all the forces of Paris.[123]

After Barrot's failed speech, a column composed of court employees and national guards of the wealthy 1st Legion attempted to save the regency by popular ovation. Marrast, on the journalists' bank, shouted that these were "*faux peuple*," and he rushed outside to get the "true" people.[124] As he left, the chamber was invaded by another wave, this one composed of the conquerors of the Tuileries, whose leader announced that the throne had just been broken and "thrown out the windows!"[125] The legitimist Rochejaquelein shouted to the deputies that "You are nothing here!" Barrot directly challenged him, more effectively this time; but as Barrot was speaking, a new column of armed men led by Charles Lagrange (veteran of Lyon, 1834) entered the hall, demanding a republic.[126] The president put on his hat, thus officially suspending the session; many deputies left altogether, while others clustered around the royal family to protect their departure.[127]

Ledru-Rollin spoke next, treating the audience to an apparently ill-timed review of history—the first revolution, the constitution of 1791—to the point that legitimist Antoine Berryer shouted at him to get on with it. Finally he called for a provisional government named by the "people."[128] According to Sarrans Ledru-Rollin was deliberately stalling, looking for Caussidière's expected column from the Tuileries—his own "true people" (and not the same as those of Marrast, for the rivalry between the two newspapers was serious). He concluded his remarks only when he saw Lamartine, who had already declared himself against the regency, heading for the tribune.[129] In his history of the February revolution, Lamartine presented his own speech as the dramatic climax of the session. He was convinced that he could have carried off a regency by his eloquence, in evoking pity for the unfortunate young widow and her sons; but it would have led sooner or later to a bloody conclusion, and "He [Lamartine wrote of himself in the third person] did not believe he had the right . . . to play a handsome role of the moment in the effeminate drama of a politics of sentiment." Thus Lamartine too called for a provisional government.[130] He was interrupted by a salvo of gunfire and the sound of muskets breaking down doors that opened to a new group of about three hundred armed men, hands black with powder—the most menacing and militant thus far, and the group for which Ledru-Rollin had been waiting.[131]

In the chamber, or what was left of it, the elderly Dupont de l'Eure was called to preside. Barrot left the hall, unable to watch.[132] Lamartine and Dupont each named the members of the Provisional Government for the crowd's approval, reading from the lists that were handed up to the podium; both deliberately omitted Blanc, Albert, Flocon, and Marrast.[133] After the acceptance of the group, Lamartine and the others left immediately for the Hôtel de Ville, while Ledru-Rollin stayed behind, ostensibly to ensure that the names were recorded accurately by the *Moniteur*. But the other two had named slightly different groups of five, and Ledru-Rollin confirmed seven: Dupont de l'Eure, Lamartine, Arago, Marie, Garnier-Pagès, Crémieux, and Ledru-Rollin.[134] A voice in the crowd insisted that those named be forced to shout *Vive la République* as a condition of their selection, a demand that went unheeded. After it was over, a student of the École Polytechnique exploded in anger: "You see that none of the members of your Provisional Government wants the Republic! We will be betrayed as in 1830!"[135]—very nearly the last statement made in the last chamber of the July Monarchy. A few non-sequiturs followed as the crowd straggled out. A worker began to fire at a portrait of the king, shouting with stupid glee that he was going to kill Louis-Philippe; stopping him, another worker delivered a fiery improvisation in favor of respecting art, to considerable applause. The chamber was finally emptied at 4:08 P.M.[136]

Caussidière walked into the prefecture of police late that afternoon to take up his appointment as prefect, conferred upon him in the offices of the *Réforme*. The courtyard was littered with the discarded helmets and saddles of the municipals, now in flight, and was full of excited people shouting *Vive la République!* and singing the *Marseillaise*. Caussidière rallied a small group of national guards; he also found some office clerks inside, still doggedly at their desks, and put them to work on a proclamation: "It is expressly recommended

to the people not to give up their weapons, their positions, or their revolutionary attitude. [The People] have been too often deceived by treason." He ordered all bakers and grocers to remain open, announced the release of political
prisoners, and urged the families of the killed and wounded to report to their
local authorities for assistance.[137]

Lamartine hurried to the Hôtel de Ville to prevent the proclamation of a
competing provisional government. The Place de l'Hôtel de Ville in front of
the building had become a magnet for the combatants, some of whom took up
temporary residence; Louis Blanc recalled people shouting *Vive la République*
continuously, others singing the *Marseillaise* in a "menacing frenzy," still others wildly haranguing those around them. Many of the city's casualties, some
still barely alive, were brought as a lesson and a warning to the new government.[138] (The *gamins* dragged dead horses there as well.[139]) The corpses, many
unidentified, were laid out on tables in one of the lower halls and guarded by
student volunteers from Saint-Cyr. They had to be embalmed because the
crowd would not allow them to be buried hastily and anonymously.[140]

Lamartine's prose in describing the early hours is as dense, as repetitive, as
exhausting, as the next few days must have been. The Provisional Government
was forced to explain itself repeatedly to new waves of suspicious, overexcited
"citizens," to submit itself frequently to popular approbation, to receive interminable deputations. They had difficulty in finding a place to meet, for each
room was full, resounding with improvised orations by combatants standing
on the furniture or window sills.[141] There was some difficulty over the four excluded members. But Marie supported the entry of Marrast into the Provisional Government, Ledru-Rollin wanted Flocon, and Blanc bullied his way in
and carried Albert with him. It was Garnier-Pagès, according to Blanc, who
hit upon the compromise of calling them "secretaries," a designation that fell
away within a few days: the Provisional Government would have eleven members. To keep their sanctuary from being invaded they piled up furniture
against the door; they heard shouts, occasionally even the sound of fighting, in
the hall outside their room.[142]

The people were, in this moment of victory, in a state of fury. Finally
Lamartine went out to face a large group who called themselves "delegates"
from the Place de l'Hôtel-de-Ville. They wanted to know what gave him the
right to govern; they wondered, belligerently, "if we are dealing with traitors,
tyrants, or citizens worthy of the conscience of the revolution." By his own account, Lamartine answered with a polished extemporaneous speech (he provided the text in his *History*). They were not satisfied, announcing their intention
to "install ourselves *en permanence*" in order to watch what the government

did.[143] Another group of combatants named Charles Lagrange as "governor" of the Hôtel de Ville; Lamartine recalled him, with saber in hand, haranguing his way through the masses, the years of imprisonment etched on his face.[144] The decrees of the next several days were passed through the crowd, read aloud, and subjected to criticism from the self-styled representatives of the popular will.[145]

On the morning of Friday the twenty-fifth, the members of the new government were confronted with another delegation of workers, led by the unknown Marche, who accented his statements by striking the butt of his musket on the floor. He demanded that a surveillance council composed of workers be admitted to observe the Provisional Government in action, and with the mission of bringing its decisions immediately to the people for their ratification.[146] He also demanded—immediately—the right to work and the red flag. Lamartine tried to swamp him with eloquence; Marche rudely told him to be quiet: "We want an accounting of the hours you have already lost, or employed in lulling the population to sleep and adjourning the revolution." In a famous moment Lamartine defended the old flag; the compromise reached was the tricolor, with the (easily detachable) red rosette on the flagpole.[147] And in the meantime Blanc, off in the corner, wrote a declaration that marked the origin of the National Workshops: "The Provisional Government of the French Republic engages itself to guarantee the existence of the laborer by work; it engages itself to guarantee work to all citizens; it recognizes that workers should associate in order to enjoy the benefits of their labor."[148]

There was indeed some trouble about proclaiming a republic, as the Provisional Government rapidly split into the minority left (Ledru-Rollin, Flocon, Blanc, Albert) and the moderates. Ironically, those against it argued precisely on the basis of 1830, when "deputies without mandate" had taken it upon themselves to make a new government. Lamartine hastily drew up a proclamation: "In the name of the French People! A retrograde and oligarchic government has just been overthrown by the heroism of the people of Paris." They listed their own names, then the key statement, inserted by Crémieux: "The Provisional Government prefers the Republic, provided it is ratified by the people, who will immediately be consulted."[149] Growing suspicion finally required something more definite. Thus: "The Provisional Government declares that the current government of France is the republican government, and that the nation will be called immediately to ratify by its vote the resolution of the Provisional Government and the people of Paris." This last was posted on the walls, but did not appear in the *Moniteur*.[150] Also unpublished was a proclamation handed about on the Place de l'Hôtel de Ville, and headed *République française:* "The Provisional Government of the Republic invites the citizens of Paris to distrust all the rumors put about by ill-intentioned individuals. The Republic is proclaimed."[151]

Under intense pressure, the Provisional Government issued a flurry of extraordinary decrees, not all of them realizable: the end to the hated *marchandage*, the ten-hour day, the lifting of restrictions on the press, the right of association, the right to work, universal manhood suffrage, the opening of the National Guard to all citizens.[152] On 25 February, Crémieux as justice minister ordered the *procureur-général* to prepare an indictment against the ministers of Louis-Philippe, an order resulting in the hundreds of depositions that now reside in the archives.[153] He also annulled all political and press convictions from the previous regime and abandoned all current cases, ordering also that all political prisoners be released immediately. The Tuileries was declared, by a decree of the same day, to be an asylum for *invalides du travail*, or workers incapacitated by labor.[154] The Mobile Guard was founded on 26 February as the "avant-garde" of the National Guard, to be composed of men under 30; with its provision of a salary, a place to live, and a uniform, it became a haven for the youthful unemployed.[155] The *Commission de Gouvernement pour les travailleurs*, the so-called Luxembourg Commission, was announced on 1 March, a powerless substitute for a ministry of labor.[156] Within a few days, a committee was set up under the presidency of Albert and including Martin-Bernard, Joseph Sobrier, and the novelist Eugène Sue, to provide financial recompense for those who, from 1830 to 1848, had "fought or suffered for the republican or socialist cause."[157]

The responses to the new republic were marked, from the first, with wariness verging on distrust. The *Société républicaine centrale*, soon to be known as the Club Blanqui—attended by Javelot, Flotte, Fombertaux, Boggio, Lagrange, Dézamy, Lacambre, and other names from the dark corners of 1840s republicanism—opened its first session of 26 February in an atmosphere of gloom and foreboding. The "impotent eunuchs" of the *National* had seized control of the government, and they would ruin it; one speaker insisted upon the necessity for another revolution and a capture of the Hôtel de Ville, to purge the faint-hearted and establish a true republic. His words met with strong approval. But it was Blanqui, this night, who called for patience: "Abandon the men of the Hôtel de Ville to their impotence; their weakness is a certain presage of their fall. . . . If we were to seize power by an audacious *coup de main*, like thieves in the night, how long would our power last? Below us, would there not be energetic and ambitious men who would burn to replace us by similar means?"[158]

CHAPTER 14

LIVING THE REPUBLIC: THE PROVISIONAL GOVERNMENT

A MONTH AFTER THE REVOLUTION, National Guard Melchior Guibert wrote to the newspapers to describe his actions in the Chamber of Deputies on 24 February:

> I finally penetrated to the foot of the tribune with the flag-bearer, I alone was armed, I struck the parquet with the butt of my weapon, shouting, "Gentlemen, there are no more Deputies, we are the masters!" I shouldered my weapon and I held myself facing the center left ready to fire. I cast my eyes slowly over the stupefied Deputies; I was very heated by my expeditions of the morning and by the importance of my position . . . my face was pale although streaming with sweat, I was foaming at the mouth, my eyes were sparkling and haggard, because I was powerfully overexcited, finally my whole appearance had something so menacing that none of the guards on duty dared employ force.

He was writing because all of the newspapers had inexplicably omitted him in their accounts of that day, thus ignoring "this episode, so dramatic, of my violent entry into the Chamber, in uniform, with my loaded gun."[1] The Republic had many fathers after 24 February.

The Provisional Government, the long-awaited revolutionary dictatorship, lasted until 4 May, the first day of the newly elected assembly. Its members repeatedly stressed that this was not to be the exalted republic of montagnard dreams: in a proclamation of 16 March, they declared it "a government of necessity. . . . One cannot go back to impossible monarchies. One cannot descend into unknown anarchies; one will be republican by force of reason." President of the National Assembly Jules Senard, speaking for the moderate bourgeoisie, later described it in much the same terms: "The truth, at least according to my understanding, is that one had neither love nor passion for the Republic; one felt it to be indispensable."[2] But the montagnards believed themselves on the verge of a new society: clubs sprang up in every neighborhood, newspapers—*Le Monde républicain, La Vraie république, Le Tocsin des Travailleurs*—published anything they wished, and *Le National* and *La Réforme* incredibly became the new "ministerial" journals. There were even some enthusiasts, stirred by the revolts in Poland, Italy, and Germany, who believed that the world was entering another revolutionary age.

The style of the provisional period was characterized by comradeship and fraternity, by male clubs, by men housed together in temporary quarters as they flocked to Paris from the prisons, the provinces, and exile. They were armed, for they had seized their weapons from the troops in February, obtained them as new national guards, or profited by the irregular distribution, mostly through the prefecture of police, of some eight to nine thousand army muskets to the men informally organized out of the February combatants.[3] Many of the militants were segregated by accident or design, cut off from regular life by unemployment or their own activism; focused entirely on revolution, they contributed to the overexcited atmosphere in those first few months. For some men, the revolution quickly turned into an occupation. Cabinetmaker Adrien Delaire, for example, became a professional *clubiste* for five francs a day, a delegate to the city-wide *Club des Clubs*, and liaison to Ledru-Rollin's ministry of the interior.[4] Both the interior ministry and the *Club des Clubs* sent paid emissaries into the provinces, most of them young men or old republicans, to agitate for republican votes.[5]

The most prominent of these organizations—the mobile guards, the clubs, the National Workshops—have been the subject of individual studies.[6] But many of these all-male groups were unofficial. (Garnier-Pagès complained of the great "quantity of armed corps which are recognized by no law, paid out of I don't know what budget."[7]) Claude Considère, convicted in 1832 for attempting to torch Notre Dame and acquitted in the Darmès case, had his own band of 60 men, who got "45 sous a day and tobacco." They worked for Ledru-Rollin at the ministry of the interior, and according to the police report, "every evening they spread out in groups or in clubs according to the orders that they received from Considère who himself received them from a certain Higonnet [convicted for possession of gunpowder, 1841] who received them directly from the Minister."[8] A band of squatters set up living quarters in the Tuileries and refused to leave; negotiations finally resulted in a triumphal exit in the form of a march to the Hôtel de Ville, where they were given a banquet.[9] At the Hôtel de Ville itself, there was a group of about four hundred *Gardes républicaines*, a semi-official new police organization, established at the post of the Salle des Morts (where the revolutionary dead had been displayed). They served under staunch Barbès partisan Colonel Rey, and received 1.50 francs per day and a well-provided kitchen.[10] They were soon infiltrated by *blanquistes*; the unemployed jeweler Joseph Delpech, one of the non-*blanquistes*, complained that many of the men were "very exalted and entirely devoted to Blanqui; they used the most frightful words, they spoke only of killing and burning."[11]

Marc Caussidière, prefect of police during the provisional period, created a new force called the *Montagnards*, composed of "unemployed workers" who had given "proofs of citizenship and courage on the barricades." They numbered about 600 men, later expanded by the similarly constituted *Garde républicaine* to a total of 2,700. Their uniform was a red belt and cravat and a blue *blouse*; Caussidière recalled that many of them lacked decent shoes and boots, which they now received from the government, along with 2.25 francs per day, regardless of rank.[12] They were armed with guns from the depot at Vincennes (a total of a thousand were delivered, along with sixty thousand cartridges).[13] They slept in the prefecture on stone floors or campbeds, turning the fortress-like building into a revolutionary barracks.[14] A small post of *Montagnards* was also established in wealthy republican activist Joseph Sobrier's building on the rue de Rivoli, where they were vividly remembered by the concierge. "The old *Montagnards* particularly frightened me," she reported. "One heard them say: 'I was in prison 11 years'; the other, 'I'd been there 12 years and still had some time to do.' They continually loaded their muskets, saying, 'Someone's coming to attack us.'"[15]

The *Montagnards* had been formed too casually, as Caussidière later agreed—they had allowed in some schismatic *blanquistes*, as well as many of the former squatters from the Tuileries—and after a bizarre midnight battle within the prefecture, Caussidière ordered a purge. At the end of two days they had expelled 80 of their number. The new National Assembly, understandably uneasy about this organization, ordered its dissolution after 15 May.[16] The ex-*Montagnards* issued a protest, defining themselves as those who had fought the "Girondin reaction"; who had "protested continually and courageously" against Napoleon's dictatorship; who had won the revolution of 1830 before the "hypocrite" had seized power; and finally, who had suffered in the dungeons of Mont-Saint-Michel: "Incessantly massacred, hunted down, imprisoned and exiled, these proud martyrs were never beaten. . . . They form a sacred and incorruptible battalion, which takes its true and only title: THE MOUNTAIN [*Montagne*]."[17]

The provisional authorities focused most of their anxiety on the new clubs—203 of them at the height of the movement, according to Peter Amann.[18] It was in this arena that women, largely excluded from republicanism before this, gained their first opportunities to speak out. Most men's clubs allowed women in the audience, and a few clubs devoted some time to the "women's" issues of divorce and prostitution. In its session of 13 April, the *Club lyonnais* allowed a *simple prolétaire* and *femme d'un honnête républicain* to take the floor, and she made the most of it. She linked the prevalence of prostitution to women's low salaries: women should no longer be the "slaves" of men, they should be elected to the chamber, they should be allowed to run their homes and have a consulting voice in the "commercial affairs" of their family. There was no reported reaction to her speech.[19] Early in May, Barbès' *Club de la Révolution*, which included many leaders of the old underground movement, received a proposition to admit women to membership. It was greeted with "warm sympathy," then immediately shuffled off to committee for decent burial.[20] In the 9 April session of the revived *Société des Droits de l'Homme et du Citoyen*, a certain Citizen Baudin spoke strongly in favor of the freeing of women, "civilly, morally, and intellectually," noting that "she [woman] has no civil rights; we deprive her of the benefits of education; we have made for her such a position that she cannot live by her labor." But his ideas seemed to stem from his distrust of the bourgeois family and his montagnard faith in the transformative power of government, and he spun off into an extravagant direction: "The state should take hold of the child, even in the womb of the mother."[21]

There was a women's club, the *Société de la Voix des Femmes*, named after the newspaper edited by Eugénie Niboyet (and called simply the *Club des Femmes* by the government, when they dissolved it after the June Days as dangerous to public order).[22] The group included many veterans of the Saint-Simonian movement: Eugénie Niboyet (president), Desirée Gay, Suzanne Voilquin, Jeanne Deroin.[23] The reports of their meetings suggested an explosion of ideas: association of labor in order to avoid the middle-managing *maîtresses* and *entrepreneuses*, who took so much of the profit; national washhouses and communal restaurants, along with public libraries and meeting halls; public crêches for children.[24] *La Voix des Femmes* also put forward the name of novelist George Sand as candidate for the National Assembly, and were famously snubbed by her.[25]

In mid-May, *Le Monde républicain* reported that the women's hall had been invaded by a group of men who stampeded the door; the women's appeals for order had met with "the grossest, even indecent pleasantries."[26] Their problems with hecklers grew worse in subsequent meetings. Niboyet vainly asserted that the members were not asking for the right to divorce, the most common accusation against them.[27] On 6 June, they doubled the price of admission for men (to 50 centimes, with 25 centimes for women). Soon they decided that no man would be admitted unless accompanied by a respectable woman.[28] But their newspaper showed evidence of continuing difficulties: "How to discuss, under noisy bursts of laughter? How to reason, when no argument can be followed? We are convinced, those who rail at us and trouble order are not republicans"—but sadly, they probably were, the republican movement having long ignored women's rights in order to stress masculine virtues and paternal dominance.[29] In mid-May, *La Voix des Femmes* had to suspend publication for lack of funds; the paper died on 10 June, to be followed by Gay's short-lived *La Politique des Femmes*.[30] Among the other newspapers, only *Le Tocsin des Travailleurs* (1 to 24 June), co-edited by the *crieur* Delente of the old SDHC, supported women's emancipation.[31]

The infusion of socialist ideas into 1840s republicanism had created some limited tolerance for issues involving sexuality and family life. But for most republicans, the "social question" remained linked with implicitly male visions of associated labor. And as the social republic itself came under increasing pressure, many of the old republicans turned back to business as usual. The new SDHC was militarily organized in *sections*, each now 50 men strong. In one of their mass meetings, on 9 May, they had decided that "each citizen should be armed, it is for each a right and a duty."[32] The leaders of the new SDHC, including President Joseph Vilain from the *Procès d'avril*, Napoléon Lebon from the old Propaganda Commission, and several others, shared bachelor quarters together in the Palais National (formerly Royal). They kept an open table at government expense, feeding some 30 to 40 old fighters every day. Mme. de Hai, one of the palace's long-time housekeepers, had finally concluded that they were "dangerous men" because they made cartridges (she had to clean up their spilled gunpowder) and kept loaded guns. Another servant had seen several hundred bullets on a table in Vilain's room, along with muskets, rifles and pistols, and a dagger in the pocket of a jacket draped over a chair.[33]

But the real organization for future combat was not in the clubs or the ad hoc groups but in the Paris National Guard, which expanded within weeks to a little over 190,000 in the city, and to 237,000 in the greater Paris region. The ranks were swollen by an influx of workingmen, many of them veterans of the barricades—and with the regular troops temporarily banished, they were the only real source of power.[34] The editors of *L'Atelier* advised their readers to "keep their weapons"—those they had acquired in February—and "democratize the National Guard." They urged the government to abolish the *coteries aristocratiques* in certain companies.[35] National Guard Henri Marin, one of the "old" guards from the July Monarchy, soon came to the conclusion that the "*droit au fusil* [right to the musket]for all is as impossible, but even more dangerous, than the *droit au travail* [right to work]."[36]

Much would depend on the election of officers, eventually set for 5 April. Controversies arose almost immediately. There were rumors that the old guards of Louis-Philippe were already "concerting" together "to exclude the proletariat from all the ranks, on the pretext that these *prolétaires* did not have the means to equip themselves"; it was said that they would attempt to prevent *prolétaires* from taking part in the officer elections. In mid-March, the radical *Club de la Sorbonne* sent a delegation to Paris mayor Armand Marrast to complain that the new working class guards were refused muskets when they presented themselves at the mayoralty offices.[37] Unhappy with his response, the Sorbonne club also sent a representative to Blanqui's *Société centrale républicaine* to discuss the "conspiracies" among the former guards, who all professed themselves to be republicans, despite the fact that they had fought republicans during the previous regime. Real republicans, in contrast, were treated with suspicion: "But a long-time democrat, a proletarian, wants to take the floor, one summons him to repeat his name, profession, residence, history; one searches in his intimate life, one makes him submit to humiliating interrogations . . . if after so many unpleasantnesses he is finally allowed to approach the tribune, there are shouts and continual interruptions." As for weapons, the new guards were put off by the local mayors with various pretexts: "They have not been able to obtain [weapons], whatever they do. Only the shopkeepers have them! But the *prolétaires* . . ."[38]

On 16 March, the *Commune de Paris* sounded a similar warning about the inscribing of workers on national guard registers, which was marked by "a slowness, an inertia," that could be taken as "ill will": "The workers are obliged to return to inscribe themselves; sometimes one puts their names on loose sheets, instead of a register; finally, when they are inscribed, one does not arm them."[39] As the elections neared, the SDHC heard further disturbing reports about the conduct of national guard meetings. Citizen Benoît had tried to object to "a man well known for his anti-republican opinions" as a candidate, but "his voice was stifled by a strong cabal." Citizen Gonnor had encountered the same maneuvers, and had even been threatened with expulsion from the meeting because he did not have the old uniform.[40] There were numerous complaints that the local *mairies* were ignoring the provisional government's order to remain open until midnight for the enlistment of new guards.[41] Nevertheless, something of an electoral campaign took place in the last few weeks before the elections, as candidates for the various officer ranks published *professions de foi*, or statements of principle, and even appeared in person before the clubs.

The SDHC occupied many of its sessions with these testimonials. Charles Lagrange, who ran unsuccessfully for colonel of the 6th Legion, required only a sort of shorthand: "My political life: 1830 and 1834; the streets of Lyon, the Chamber of Peers and the Dungeons of Doullens."[42] Armand Barbès, running for colonel of the 12th Legion, also did not suffer from a lack of name recognition. But he had been formally convicted of the murder of Lieutenant Drouineau in 1839; to combat this, he published a series of extracts from the courtroom testimony, alluding obliquely to the subsequent discovery of the "real killer," whom the government had hustled off to England.[43] To the horror of many moderates, he won the election.

Even relative unknowns found the details of their past challenged by listeners with long memories. The *Comité électoral du XIe arrondissement*, in their session of 20 March, heard an accusation against a certain Citizen D———, a candidate for *chef de bataillon*, that he had served in the Restoration police and taken "reactionary measures" against patriots; they formed a committee to investigate.[44] The *Club républicain de Montmartre* broke into loud argument when a candidate for colonel of the 1st Legion was accused of having fired on workers—in November 1831.[45] But the old national guards were all likely to have suppressed *émeutes;* thus attention became fixed on the issue of what they would do if the Constituent Assembly attempted to restore the monarchy. The radical *Club Popincourt* decided that they would support no candidate who did not take an oath in favor of Robespierre's Declaration of the Rights of Man, which became a common touchstone.[46]

In the end, the national guard elections were disappointing. Old montagnards such as Lagrange and Kersausie were edged out by moderates, and aside from Barbès, there were relatively few victories.[47] There were also charges of electoral manipulation. Citizen Bouillet claimed that in the 6th Legion, approximately two hundred voters had been told there were no more ballots; moreover, the voting period conflicted with the time when many workers received their pay.[48] The obviously dejected SDHC President Vilain commented that these were among "the thousand little means employed by the aristocrats to prevent the people from voting." And he added, revealing the anxiety underlying this issue, "the elections of the National Guard give us an idea of what the general elections will be."[49]

The elections for the Constituent Assembly were scheduled for 23 April. Activists formed several organizations to coordinate the selection of candidates and the voting drive; the most famous was the woefully ineffective *Club des Clubs*, a

superclub with delegates from clubs throughout the city.[50] The immediate task
was to establish a list of candidates for the 34 Paris seats, though the *Club des
Clubs* dissipated its energies in also trying to influence the provinces. Blanc, who
urged the Luxembourg to form its own committee, suggested 20 workers and 14
bourgeois republicans, which became the commonly accepted ratio.[51]

Candidates once again began to make the rounds and, as in the national
guard elections, attempted to craft republican pasts. Dr. Lesseré, one of the
founders of *La Réforme* and still bedridden from the Chateau d'Eau battle in
February, followed Lagrange's example of brevity: "July 1830; June 1832; July
1840 [the Belleville banquet]; and 24 February 1848."[52] Citizen Petel was a
printer, a *décoré de juillet* and a *condamné* for 5–6 June; he was endorsed by J.-J.
Pinson, ex-political prisoner, and H. Stévenot, wounded on 12 May 1839.[53]
Philippe Le Bas, an archaeologist, ran on the heritage of his grandfather: an
associate of Robespierre, representative on mission to the glorious army of the
Sambre-et-Meuse, and victim of 9 Thermidor.[54] A certain Laffaille boasted of
a son, a captain in the 4th Light, who had been disciplined for preaching republicanism; his nephew was Jean-Jacques Vignerte, from the *Procès d'avril*.[55]
Etienne Arago (brother of François) had been a republican in 1820 and a
member of the *carbonari* leadership. For his activities in 1830, he referred his
listeners to Louis Blanc's *Histoire de Dix Ans*; as for his political principles, he
was one of the founders of *La Réforme*.[56]

Disputes arose in these sessions as well. The *Club pacifique des Droits de
l'Homme* (a schismatic offshoot of the SDHC) read a campaign missive from
Victor Hugo, who did not appear in person. Hugo claimed that there were
two sorts of republics: the moderate sort, among whose allies he counted himself, and "the one which will promenade heads on pikes, fill prisons on mere
suspicion and empty them by massacre; set Europe in flames and civilization in
cinders." His "diatribe" was so poorly received, as an untimely reminder of
"the terrible necessities of another epoch," that the circular was burned, to the
applause of the meeting.[57] Citizen Gonon announced that he wanted a constitution like that of the United States, traditionally scorned by montagnards as a
Girondin or "federalist" system. Upon sharp questioning he backed down,
"saying that apparently he was not sufficiently enlightened about this constitution."[58] The journalist Cauchois-Lemaire ran as a veteran of the democratic
press. But when he appeared before the SDHC, President Vilain questioned
his credentials; had he not been an Orléanist during the Restoration? He had,
but in order to overthrow the Bourbons, "and not out of devotion to the duc
d'Orléans." What of the social question? Cauchois-Lemaire warned that private property could not be touched, "that the smallest peasant, though he pos-

sesses only a few *perches* of terrain, would kill himself rather than abandon his rights as a proprietor." Vilain insisted on the needs of the suffering proletariat, who should be provided for "by the most prompt and energetic measures." Cauchois-Lemaire answered "that such words seemed to him an appeal to civil war," causing such an enormous agitation that he lost the floor.[59]

The *professions de foi* of workers—an indication, in themselves, of the sense of possibility of the provisional era—revealed a variety of ideas about restructuring the social system and ending poverty. Jouy, cabinetmaker, had taken part in the July Revolution when he was 15 and had participated in every subsequent "demonstration [and] protest against tyranny." His program was to end "the exploitation of man by man," by means of worker association.[60] Savary, cobbler and long-time activist (and one of the workers on the *Club des Clubs'* final list), claimed that he brought with him "the practical knowledge of the physical and moral misery, of the *servitudes* that weigh upon the laborious classes."[61] L. Héronville was a worker-poet and shoemaker; his "*muse populaire*" had led him to write oppositional poetry under Louis-Philippe's regime.[62] Rozier, *coiffeur* and prominent speaker at the 1840 Belleville banquet, described his qualifications as 15 years of suffering for the republic, including three arrests: "I was dragged from dungeon to dungeon."[63] The gilder Collard was an *enfant de Paris* who had fought in July. As a soldier he had spent two years in Africa, returning to fight in the 1834 insurrection; he had spent many months in prison before charges were dropped. He supported equal education for all, a government bureaucracy open to merit, and a taxation system that was fairer to the poor.[64] Citizen Galland, weaver and writer for *L'Atelier*, was an orphan "raised in the school of misfortune." His program called for the right to work, the guarantee of existence for those unable to work because of old age or misfortune, and public education.[65] Less successful was a certain Citizen Rischmann, a self-described *prolétaire*, "a subaltern charged with a numerous family, a man who knows misery. . . ." After much study of the phalansterian and other communist systems, he had created out of them "the eclectic social system," a description of which he began to read until forced, by the interruptions and noisy impatience of his audience, to stop. Thus they disposed of the "système social éclectique," the product, or so he said, of twelve years of study.[66]

The *Club des Clubs* announced that the sessions of 13, 14, and 15 April would be devoted to the development of the "definitive list" of candidates to the National Assembly; in the end, they announced their candidates only on 22 April, the day before the elections, and thus had no time to publicize them. Moreover, there were several competing though overlapping lists, differing according to the inclusion of various socialists and Blanqui.[67] On 22 April, the

SDHC heard disturbing evidence that false voting lists were being distributed to the National Workshops. Two of the workers brought a copy, and after a brief examination President Vilain stated that it was "completely contrary to the list from the *comité révolutionnaire,*" for it included Cauchois-Lemaire, "of whom everybody recalled the *profession de foi,*" and other unacceptable choices.[68]

Out of the 851 deputies of the new Constituent Assembly, which convened on 4 May, only 285 had been republicans "of the day before" (the revolution), including only 55 radicals and socialists; 231 represented the dynastic opposition of the previous regime. The rest, including 56 legitimists, were conservative, their "republicanism" suspect.[69] All the members of the Provisional Government were elected, but only 6 of the 34 candidates chosen by the *Club des Clubs*—Albert, Blanc, Flocon, Ledru-Rollin, Caussidière, and the famous joiner Agricol Perdiguier, author of a defense of the *compagnonnages.*[70] Many republicans blamed the unpopular 45-centimes tax increase, approved by the Provisional Government on 16 March, for the electoral disaster. Throughout republican ranks there was a sense of failure and loss, a desire to do it all again and to profit from the lessons learned in the past few months. Joseph Vilain had already voiced what was in many minds: "If the retrograde party carries off the elections there always remains to true democrats a last argument whose power is not contestable"—the resort, in other words, to the barricades.[71]

Before the elections there were two major demonstrations, ostensibly in support of the Provisional Government, but each one embodying an implicit threat of purging it. On 17 March, an estimated group of a hundred thousand had gathered in protest against the previous day's manifestation by the *bonnets à poil,* the elite national guards whose companies were to be dissolved. (François Arago later recalled that one of the "bearskins," whom he recognized as a lawyer at the *Cour de Cassation,* had begun to shout "*A bas Ledru-Rollin!*" Arago had hurried to shut him up: "Here, I said to him, is the place where Foulon was murdered at the beginning of the first revolution; your words could incite a misfortune of the same nature"[72]—an indication of the precipice with which even the liberal bourgeoisie felt threatened.) The clubs on this day had three specific demands: postponement of both the National Guard and National Assembly elections, which were granted (though only for two weeks), and the permanent removal of all troops from Paris, which was not—though the planned military garrison of four to six regiments, announced on 14 March, had to be scrapped for the moment.[73] (A provisional government, according to *blanquiste* theory, had the task of enlightening the population, which took time; many old republicans hoped to maintain a purified and more radical dictatorship in power indefinitely, until the people understood their own interests.[74])

Between that day and the second demonstration of 16 April, the old republicans were roiled by the so-called Taschereau document, published on 31 March by journalist Jules Taschereau in his *Revue rétrospective*. The Taschereau document, found in the archives of the interior ministry, was an alleged confession and revelation to the police—a "betrayal" of comrades—made in late 1839 or early 1840 by a *Société des Saisons* leader.[75] Though the name was left out, it was clear from internal details that Blanqui was to be understood as the informant. Blanqui issued a brief public denial, soon followed by a more extensive denunciation of the text.

The contents of the Taschereau document mostly concerned the founding of the *Familles* and *Saisons*, the 1839 insurrection, and the reorganization of the *Saisons* afterward—events known, as Blanqui pointed out, by at least "1,500" old conspirators.[76] Such material, of course, could also easily have come from police spies, as well as from public trials. Nothing in the document was new. But the embittered Barbès thought the cynical personal criticisms of the inner circles, the cutting sarcasm of the piece as a whole, sounded like Blanqui, a man distinguished by his "irony." It was soon widely known that Barbès believed in Blanqui's guilt.[77] Since the Taschereau document played into the constant, familiar fear of treason and betrayal, it was given credence by others as well.

Blanqui attempted to fight back, asking Étienne Cabet, with whom he was at odds ideologically, to accompany him as a neutral observer in his own investigations. He boycotted an informal tribunal of old republicans, on the grounds that it was dominated by the allies of Barbès; the transcript of the proceedings revealed a depressing airing of ancient grievances, mostly to the effect that Blanqui had received special favors in prison, a charge that Dommanget has exhaustively disproved.[78] Blanqui's written defense finally appeared in mid-April, about two weeks after the initial revelations. It was published with a statement signed by 48 former members of the *Familles* and *Saisons*, who declared that everything included in the *Revue rétrospective* was a matter of common knowledge.[79]

Blanqui's response amounted mostly to an indictment of the previous two months. The revolution was already in danger when he had arrived in Paris on 24 February (meeting with only a "glacial reception"). The new *"programme de l'Hôtel-de-Ville"* had already been established; those who expected social as well as political changes were given "the exile of the Luxembourg"—in other words, were sidetracked into Louis Blanc's impotent labor commission. The government had attacked the only true republican (himself), a struggle waged at first with insidious rumors that he was "crazy," that he "wanted 200,000 heads." The massive demonstration of 17 March had terrified the Provisional

Government. (Without the Taschereau document the popular party would have been in control, he said, but now, "the Revolution is staggering.") Thus they had conspired against Blanqui through Taschereau, the "intimate friend" of the *National.* In the end, of course, Blanqui had no definitive way to disprove his authorship, as he himself realized. He warned his fellow republicans, "old soldiers of the old cause," to be on guard: "Today me, tomorrow you."[80]

The episode was a distraction, and momentarily weakened Blanqui. But it did not destroy him. Barbès, in prison in 1850, was told gently but bluntly by an outside correspondent that Blanqui could not be cast out from their ranks because the revolutionary cause still needed him.[81] Indeed, the tide would even turn, as *blanquistes* would begin to compare Barbès' relative comfort in Nîmes, his transfer there in a private carriage, to the dying Blanqui's 1844 trip to a prison hospital in the notoriously comfortless "cellular coach"; Blanqui's uncompromising revolutionary stance was to be contrasted to the "servile" conduct of Barbès as colonel of the 12th Legion—particularly on the disastrous *journée* of 16 April.[82]

The manifestation of 16 April unfolded against this disharmony. The organizers insisted that it was meant to be peaceful. The various workers' corporations were gathered to choose 14 officers for the national guard general staff, in compensation for the disappointing election results; they followed the meeting with an unarmed march. But the government and many others regarded this demonstration as an attempt by the extremists—by whom was meant the wounded Blanqui—to purge the Provisional Government of its moderate members.[83] Ledru-Rollin controversially ordered the beating of the *rappel* throughout Paris, and an immense turnout of national guards overwhelmed the marchers, even shouted "Down with the Communists!" at them.[84]

Blanqui was on the scene—by his own account, simply to distribute his response to the Taschereau document—but the other major clubs had discouraged their members from participation.[85] President Vilain of the SDHC, fearful that a few *malintentionnés* could stir up trouble, ordered *permanences*, established in 22 different spots in Paris, to keep his own men off the streets.[86] Barbès's divided *Club de la Révolution* finally settled on an "investigation" of the event, always a sure means to dampen any activity.[87] On the following day, Barbès rather apologetically announced that as colonel of the 12th, he had marched at the head of his legion because of the rumor that a "handful of men and more *perhaps*" would hijack the peaceful demonstration—in other words, he had marched against Blanqui.[88] But many old republicans regarded the day with great concern. *Le Représentant du peuple* warned its readers that the 1848 revolution could be *escamotée* as in 1830, that the old republicans were already being treated "as *fac-*

tieux, agitators, anarchists."[89] Blanqui regarded the day as the victory of the counterrevolution, more tragic because of the presence of proletarian "brothers" in the ranks of the National Guard. Another speaker at his club drew the lesson that "the people should never again descend into the streets without weapons."[90]

The final *journée* of 15 May, just days after the Provisional Government had ended and the new, conservative Constituent Assembly had begun, was the culmination of the provisional government period. It had a devastating effect on the Left, for it removed many of the old leaders (including Barbès, Blanqui, Raspail, Albert, Huber, Sobrier, Caussidière, Blanc), either by arrest, flight, or intimidation, from the coming June Days. But its real significance was more subtle, for the events of 15 May showed the chasm between the Second Republic and the montagnard dream.

The stated purpose of the 15 May demonstration (and for some, the genuine purpose as well) was to petition the new assembly to take immediate action on behalf of Poland, which was in the process of being crushed once more. The dedication to the cause of the Poles was long-standing: the doomed Polish insurrection of 1830–31 had led to the flight of approximately ten thousand exiles to France, many of them articulate intellectuals.[91] Blanqui later recalled that the news just before 15 May had been very bad, with reports of massacres in the Grand Duchy of Posen.[92] Many republicans saw the first reactionary boot step of the Holy Alliance; Sobrier believed that "if Poland is conquered, we will see 1815."[93] But there was a strong minority view against intervention, in the belief that conservatives would like nothing better than to export the most "exalted" Paris republicans to a doomed foreign adventure.[94]

The demonstration also occurred in the context of profound dissatisfaction: the recent bloody repression of rioters in Rouen, the continuing economic recession, the conservative new assembly, and the removal of Blanc and Albert from power when the five-man Executive Commission had been created. The National Assembly had decided, on 10 May, to order an "inquiry" into the situation of labor, a move universally seen as the beginning of the end for the Luxembourg Commission (which held its last session on 13 May), as well as a threat to the National Workshops.[95] The "fête of the so-called Concorde," planned by the government for 14 May, had to be cancelled because of the announced intention of significant groups of workers and activists to boycott it.

The decision to petition the assembly on behalf of Poland had originated in the *Comité centralisateur* (successor to the *Club des Clubs*) on 8 or 9 May.[96]

Several days before the march, the assembly prohibited the direct presentation of petitions, to avert the fate of the intimidated governments of the first revolution.[97] Nevertheless, the petition-march planners held an organizational meeting on 12 May, to which were invited only *chefs de barricades* and the "presidents, officers, or delegates" of the democratic clubs.[98] Aloysius Huber (a former political prisoner and president of the *Club des Clubs*) presided, and the meeting resolved to make an unarmed demonstration that would stop outside the assembly at a respectful distance.[99]

The clubs of Blanqui and Raspail were dissolved after the demonstration, but both men denied responsibility.[100] Blanqui claimed to have learned of the demonstration only on 13 May; by the accounts of many witnesses, he attempted to discourage his club's participation, on the grounds that the manifestations of March and April had caused public opinion to "retrograde." He had acceded only when he realized that his membership was overwhelmingly in favor.[101] Raspail's story was similar, but he was later singled out for punishment because of his inflammatory proclamation on Rouen and Poland—so violent, in fact, that the organizers of the demonstration had refused to use it, drafting a considerably more moderate one.[102]

On 15 May, the crowds gathered on the Place de la Bastille by 11 A.M.—about ten thousand, according to the police report—and began their march toward the National Assembly, Huber at their head.[103] Huber suddenly realized, to his embarrassment, that no one had the petition. He hastily sent for Raspail and his more radical document; Raspail took a coach down side streets to the head of the lines, thus drafted into a prominent role.[104] The *clubistes* marched in disciplined fashion until they neared the assembly, meeting with little resistance. The column did not halt at a safe distance as it was supposed to, and Blanqui later blamed the invasion of the chamber on the inexorable pressure of too many bodies.[105]

The building and grounds were soon packed with demonstrators. Representative Albert, who had this day worn worker's garb, was in the courtyard surrounded by a group of young activists who became embroiled in an argument with Lamartine.[106] A legislative stenographer who happened to be outside took down the heated conversation. "Lamartine: Citizens, the sentiment which has driven you to come here to express your wishes in regard to Poland is a noble sentiment, the more generous in that you forget your own miseries to think of those of your Polish brothers." But the young men were not having it: "Vote for Poland, or you're lost." They threatened to enter the assembly. Lamartine suggested they would have to go in over his dead body, and was finally informed that, "we're the masters here; we belong to the sovereign people; you're only our clerks."[107]

The military forces allowed the invasion of the assembly to occur, as the subsequent investigation revealed, because of complete confusion. Cavaignac would be appointed minister of war on 20 May to bring order to the situation. On the day of the *journée*, except for four battalions at the assembly itself, the mobile guards were confined to barracks; the small numbers of regular troops were mostly posted at the École militaire.[108] As for the National Guard (whose commandant, General Courtais, in overall command for the day, was later put on trial), one example perhaps will suffice. Joseph Guinard, Courtais' second at headquarters, received orders to beat the *rappel* at 2:45, 3:30, and 5:00 P.M., orders not to beat the *rappel* at 2:47 and 4:00 P.M., and an order to secure all the principle points only at 5:30 P.M., after the invasion of the assembly was over; the various orders were signed by Garnier-Pagès, Pagnerre, Courtais, Recurt, Buchez, Arago, and Marie, all holding positions of authority.[109] Among the legion commanders, Colonel Yautier of the 9th Legion had beaten the *rappel* on his own authority when he learned of the invasion of the assembly, but he had received no orders at all. Moreover, he had not prevented a large crowd from entering the Hôtel de Ville: "I thought of Bailly, who had ordered the firing on the people at the Champ-de-Mars [in 1791]. Two or three years later, this brave man was tried and convicted for this fact. If things had turned out differently on 15 May, one would have said: 'It's M. Yautier who made them fire on the people.'"[110] Ironically, and perhaps because of the military confusion, the day was entirely bloodless.

Inside the assembly hall there was chaos; several of the demonstration's leaders attempted to bring order. Raspail read his proclamation at the tribune—heard by virtually no one, because of the great noise—and then made serious efforts to clear the hall, denouncing those who remained as "traitors to the republic."[111] After the petition was read, Blanqui appeared (beside Barbès, also at the speakers' podium), and demanded that Poland be reconstituted according to its 1772 borders. Representative Antony Thouret believed that Blanqui, his old comrade in the *Amis*, then tried to leave, "but many men with sinister faces who were beside him . . . struck him violently with their fists, shouting '*Rouen! Rouen!* Speak of Rouen!'" It was then, said Thouret, that his discourse became violent.[112]

Speaking after Blanqui, Barbès asked that the petitioners be allowed to file before their representatives—one way of getting them out, of course—but then he went considerably further: "The assembly must vote immediately, and in the current session, the departure of an army for Poland, a tax of a billion [francs] on the rich; [the assembly must] prohibit the beating of the *rappel*; it must force the troops to leave Paris: if not, the representatives will be declared traitors to the fatherland."[113] Most believed that Barbès had been carried away by the passion of the moment, that what had happened to Barbès "is what often happened to him," according to one representative; "he mounted to the tribune with the intention of speaking with moderation, and, by the animation of [his own] speech, he allowed himself to be pulled along further than he wanted."[114] Many believed he had been overcome by the desire to "subalternise" Blanqui.[115] Ledru-Rollin, in contrast, asserted that Barbès had genuinely thought himself in the midst of a new revolution: "He had been told that there were 300,000 men in the manifestation; it was the people, the sovereign people. Barbès has never seen beyond that."[116] And Barbès himself later compared this day to 31 May 1793 (the attack on the Girondins) when the people had forced their assembly "to return to its proper path." He had opposed the invasion of the building, but then had seen it as an opportunity "to obtain something for the cause of the people."[117]

As the leaders of the demonstration argued among themselves, an unknown person grabbed the podium to demand the firing of "the majority of the ministers," war on behalf of the Poles, and—most importantly—the formation of "a social committee to watch over the executive power."[118] At that point, the beating of the *rappel* could be heard outside; there were threats to kill President of the Assembly Buchez, unless he ordered the drums to stop. It was 3:30 P.M.; the *questeur* François Dégousée (in charge of the assembly's security) whispered to Buchez to stall. The overcrowded galleries visibly began to buckle, causing a new panic.[119]

At this moment Aloysius Huber returned to the hall, having been absent for about half an hour—by his own account, unconscious from the crowds and heat. He took the podium at the decisive moment of the day: "Citizens, listen; no one wants to make a decision; well I, in the name of the people, in the name of the people betrayed by its representatives, I declare that the National Assembly is dissolved." He shook his fist at President Buchez, and repeated the pronouncement several times.[120] Many wondered at the time why Huber had done it. The questions became more pointed the following year, when he was denounced as a longtime police spy. A number of his former friends would come to believe that he had dissolved the assembly on behalf of unspecified reactionary forces who wished to compromise the old montagnard leaders.

The Huber matter has never been entirely settled.[121] But while he was almost certainly not an *agent provocateur* or regular undercover agent, it is also likely that he made several "revelations" to the police in 1838, in a moment of weakness and panic at the beginning of his long captivity.[122] After a brief imprisonment, ended in 1851 by Louis Napoleon's clemency, he would live the rest of his life in estrangement from his former republican colleagues.[123] As for 15 May itself, Huber later gave several explanations. Several hours after the event, he told a friend "that he had to do it, because without it, blood would have flowed, and they would have been slaughtered in the chamber." In his trial in October 1849, he elaborated on this initial justification: "They [the other demonstrators] said to me that the *rappel* was beating in all the *arrondissements*, and that the National Guard, furious, threatened to massacre everyone," and that "'they want to do as in Rouen.'" They reminded him that he had been the one who had insisted on an unarmed demonstration, which left them defenseless. And at the end of a long, exhausting day of testimony, Huber let slip what was likely the truth: "I had put my name at the bottom of the convocation of the clubs, I saw that everything was going to fall back on me. All of that passed rapidly in my mind; I saw myself as lost and I divined what would happen to me . . . it was only in losing my head that I pronounced the dissolution of the Assembly."[124]

Louis Blanc and Marc Caussidière were also compromised—the latter, as prefect of police, for doing nothing, the former for doing too much. In the course of the afternoon, Blanc had been told that the invaders were calling for him in the courtyard outside. After some hesitation he emerged, to find himself in the company of Albert and Barbès. Much of the effect of their joint appearance was pure theatrics: they clasped hands and draped themselves in the flag (as had Lafayette and Louis-Philippe in 1830), holding this pose for about ten minutes. Albert, as usual, said nothing. Barbès made a speech, followed by Blanc: "Workers, my friends, I say my friends, because between you and me, you know, it's to the death!"[125] According to a number of witnesses Blanc's delivery was fiery, and one man who was not sympathetic to the demonstration nevertheless had found himself swept up: "The speech of M. Louis Blanc transported the audience, I myself was moved."[126]

In his published defense, Louis Blanc reported a considerably more sedate performance on his part. In attempting to make his way back inside he had been captured by another group, who had forced him onto a chair to make another speech of much the same kind. Finally, he had found himself literally carried by the crowd up to the extreme end of the amphitheater, and it was there that he heard the assembly was dissolved: "Everybody rushed toward the doors, the torrent pulled me outside, and I left [the assembly] so lost in the heart of the surrounding multitude that I do not know by which door and by which street I arrived at the esplanade of the Invalides." Fortuitously, however, he washed ashore at the side of his brother, who commandeered a passing cabriolet and carried him to safety.[127]

Inside the chamber, an unidentified *factieux* read a list for a new provisional government: Barbès, Blanc, Ledru-Rollin, Blanqui, Huber, Raspail, Caussidière,

Étienne Arago, Albert, Lagrange. This list was immediately contested by another unknown *factieux*, who proclaimed a "good list": "Cabet, Blanc, Pierre
Leroux, Raspail, Considérant, Barbès, Blanqui, Proudhon." There developed a
general argument among those at the podium (one man warned the others not
to name too many socialists). There were also suggestions for a provisional "triumvirate," a nightmarish composition of Barbès, Blanqui, and Raspail (Barbès
and Blanqui were at odds, Raspail got along with no one.)[128]

    One of the most astonishing aspects of the day was the instant acceptance,
by so many, of a new revolution. Colonel Clément Thomas, on his way to the
National Assembly with his battalion, was told by another officer that they
might as well go home because the assembly was dissolved; there would be
placards to tell them who the new government was.[129] One of the most firmly
convinced was Barbès himself, who had believed "that there no longer existed
any other power than that of the crowd that surrounded me."[130] He left for the
Hôtel de Ville, taking the people with him. Within minutes the hall was empty
of demonstrators, and the assembly resumed in an excited, self-congratulatory
session. The young mobile guards on the steps outside, who had been laughing at the spectacle (their commandant admitted their mirth, "but you know
they're all *enfants de Paris*"), took possession of the hall at 4:45 P.M., shouting
Vive l'Assemblée nationale! They were followed by national guards, who finished
clearing it of all stragglers.[131]

    The action shifted to the Hôtel de Ville. Clerk Eugène Guyon saw Barbès
enter the canteen with three to four hundred men: "In this hall, Barbès
climbed on a scaffolding or table; he made a speech of which I remember the
following words: 'Citizens, the Assembly is dissolved, as on 24 February, by
the will of the people.'" He and Albert headed for the rooms occupied by the
old provisional government and began issuing decrees.[132] The first decree announced the new provisional government—Barbès, Ledru-Rollin, Albert,
Raspail, Pierre Leroux, Thoré (and not Blanqui)—and maintained Caussidière
at the prefecture of police. Their followers threw hastily scribbled lists out the
windows to inform the people, scraps as evanescent as the new regime itself.
Another decree, also tossed out the window, ordered Russia and Prussia to re-
constitute Poland or face war.[133]

    Finally, the national guards took control of the building. One of the first to
enter the room recalled that the seated Barbès had turned to him in great irritation, "having the air of complaining that he was being importuned." The guard
asked him who he was, and Barbès, still delusional, stated that he was a "member
of the provisional government."[134] He and Albert were taken immediately to the
old fortress of Vincennes, outside Paris. His guards reported that Barbès, con-

cerned that there was no fighting in the city, seemed to perk up when he heard a single gunshot that night, straightening his tie and pacing back and forth in his cell.[135] But the *journée* was now over: all that remained was repression.

The assembly's attention turned to the workshops. The *ateliers nationaux* had been established by decree on 27 February, in response to the blunt demand of the worker Marche. It was thought at first that excavation and filling projects for ten thousand workers would be sufficient to meet the demand, but by 15 June the number of enrollments had swelled to 117,300, with many provincials attracted to Paris by the promise of a job.[136] The workshops had been given a military division, into squads, brigades, lieutenancies, and companies, each company to be composed of nine hundred men.[137] Ironically, as Minister of Finance Duclerc later noted, the National Workshops originally had been regarded as "the only element of order that the government possessed," as a "counterweight to the Luxembourg." Their increasingly radical tone, as well as their expense, had made the government eager to get rid of them.[138]

Working-class newspapers published the list of proposed measures as early as 31 May. Single workers from ages 18 to 25 were to enroll in the army; workers who could not justify a six-months' residence in Paris were to be expelled. Private employers were to be given the right to request workers of certain specialties (with no controls, of course, on wages or conditions), and those workers who refused such offers were to be removed from the rolls. Finally, brigades of workers were to be directed to the departments, away from Paris. The announcement of payment by the piece seemed a further mockery, because of the scarcity of actual work provided.[139]

What would save the republic? *Le Tocsin des Travailleurs*, lamenting that "crowned eunuchs" had merely been replaced with "eunuchs in phrygian caps," decried the republic's lack of "virility."[140] The *Club des Montagnards* of Belleville began making bullets on 16 May.[141] The *Club de la Montagne* of Montmartre promoted a Peoples' Banquet. Other clubs, fearful of another 15 May disaster, pressured them to postpone it; the plans were ultimately overtaken by events.[142] Thoughts also turned to war. The 9 May meeting of the SDHC had been dominated by a stormy debate over Poland, and one speaker claimed that sending men to Poland was "the best means of having a foreign war" because, he added, "we must have war, and we will have it, and instead of waiting for it, it is better to go looking for it. We are strong enough to sustain it, let it be short, but good, and"—the sound of the montagnard rush to excess—"let us finish with all the rabble of kings, princes, and princelings that infect Europe and the rest of the civilized world!"[143]

CHAPTER 15

"*UNE MÂLE ET SOMBRE RÉSIGNATION*": THE JUNE DAYS

"ONE CANNOT IMAGINE, FAR FROM OUR DESOLATE CITY, what the women's lives have been for two days," wrote the editors of *La Démocratie pacifique* shortly after the bloody revolt known as the June Days; "everywhere you see them at the windows, on the doorsills, with disquieted tearful faces. Rich, poor, all are in the same anguish. They don't know what has become of their brothers, husbands, sons, friends, and the wind brings to their ears the distant sound of the artillery."[1] In February, women had moved freely among the soldiers, offering them food, asking them not to shoot their menfolk; there was nothing like this in June. On the contrary, women served as the messengers of the insurrection, transporting information as well as cartridges, and they were seen courageously caring for the wounded, even at close proximity to the barricades.[2] Against these images was a competing one, of the blood-drunk harpy eager for prey. Newspapers began to recount stories of female atrocity alongside those of male generosity; as the enormity of the conflict became apparent, its horror was displaced onto women. The reality of the class struggle was too terrifying: far better to define the June days as a product of chaos and irrationality, for which women traditionally served as the chief emblems.[3]

The images of male insurgency were also fluid. Former prefect of police Caussidière described the motivations of the combatants as "misery," and despair over the nature of the new republic; but also, "one had played with guns for too long"—a vision of a masculine subculture that resorted too easily to violence.[4] The government's official investigation took a more traditional line, blaming the insurrection on a "conspiracy" hatched in the National Work-shops, where the delegates from the Luxembourg, that other hated institution, "had spread the poison of their theories."[5] But soon the June Days came to be described, by moderates, as a defense of family; this argument was repeated in various forms, and it paved the way for the Second Republic's ideological and emotional assimilation of the events. Panisse, chief of the *Sûreté Générale*, de-scribed the participants as unemployed workers, "who saw their hungry women and children; men exalted and honest, but ignorant and easy to lead astray."[6] This last interpretation left the republic's legitimacy intact and reestablished its moral authority.

But for the insurgents, the June Days were different from all previous up-risings. This battle was not waged out of a montagnard confidence that they carried the future with them; it was, rather, a hopeless defense they had to un-dertake, in order to remain men and not victims of another stolen revolution. *Le Tocsin des Travailleurs* blamed the government for pursuing a more destruc-tive social and economic policy than that of Louis-Philippe: "According to all the reports that have come to us, the workers entrenched behind the barri-cades did not have the *élan* of February, but *une mâle et sombre résignation*. Bet-ter to die by gunfire, they said, than hunger."[7]

Only a few months after the February revolution, most had come to believe that a battle between the new conservative bourgeois government and the workers was inevitable, and that it would be decisive; the only uncertainty was the timing. The month before the June Days showed an ebbing and flowing of unrest, motivated by anxiety over diminishing revolutionary gains. The distur-bances began in earnest on 27 May with the firing of Émile Thomas, head of the National Workshops, which many saw as a prelude to the end of the work-shops themselves. "Several said that they had arms and ammunition, and that they would overthrow the government if the National Workshops were sup-pressed," according to a police report.[8] On 29 May, the crowds gathered "at the usual places"; on 30 May, the police reported large groups at the Porte Saint-Denis and the Porte Saint-Martin. On 31 May, there were several small gather-ings around the city, including approximately a hundred men on the Place de l'Hôtel de Ville, who appeared to be *Montagnards* and said that "they would do what they had already done in February."[9] On the eighth, ninth, and eleventh of June, there were reports of large crowds shouting *Vive Barbès* and threaten-ing another February; on 12 June, another large group on the Place de l'Hôtel de Ville appeared "discontented" with their situation, and "said that it wasn't over, that within a short time they would take up their muskets again."[10]

The demonstrators were by this time openly in defiance of the new law of 7 June on *attroupements*. An *attroupement* became armed and illegal when "several" of those in it were armed, whether the weapon was hidden or in full view, or when a single individual with a weapon in view was not immediately expelled. Even unarmed *attroupements* could be forcibly dispersed if they threatened "public tranquillity," after the usual three *sommations*.[11] *Le Représentant du peuple* referred to this new law, more stringent than any previous legislation on the subject, as the "first step on the path of counterrevolution." *La Commune de Paris* reported government spies in the clubs, in preparation for closing them down and arresting their members. *Le Monde républicain* blamed police provocateurs, acting in the manner of the previous regime, for the demonstrations.[12] By 22 June, a total of 1,427 men, including 130 for the *journée* of 15 May, had been taken into custody.[13]

On 20 June, *Le Représentant du peuple* reported that the government had made the final decision to send the workers either into the army or to the new public works project in Sologne: "They [workers] would sleep jumbled together on canvas hammocks, without mattresses. . . . During the entire duration of the engagement, no worker could absent himself without a special authorization." Moreover, they were to be paid *à la tâche*, or by the piece, such that (they wrote to anxious, status-conscious craftsmen) "ditchdiggers [*terrassiers*] would become the aristocracy of this association." But the implications were even worse than they appeared, for the authorities would undoubtedly use the workers' forced departure from Paris as a "pretext" to take away their national guard muskets: "One should understand that this entire plan has been conceived with no other goal than that of arriving at this double result: to send away, and to disarm, the 100,000 workers of the National Workshops."[14] On the evening of Thursday, 22 June, only 56 workers out of an expected 300 turned up to go to Angers, on Friday another 36.[15] *Ateliers* worker and hatter Louis Boquet testified later that they had resolved to defy the departure orders, "that no man would leave because one man gone is one fewer musket and one more exploited man."[16]

The news of the dissolution of the workshops was published on Thursday, 22 June, and quickly spread through Paris.[17] Crowds gathered throughout the city, singing, chanting, and carrying workshop banners. The *National*, in an ironic echo of the ministerial rhetoric of the previous regime, reported that "honest" workers had refused to be provoked by *agitateurs* and simply wanted to continue about their business.[18] At noon, there was a large group on the place de l'Hôtel de Ville: "They are speaking of Sologne," reported the police agent; "it is said that the country is unhealthy; that the workers should refuse to leave, and the government has taken this measure only to be rid of them." A group of about 150 workers marched through the center of the city, announcing a meeting that night at the Place du Panthéon.[19] There were rumors that workshop officers were actively promoting the battle; one of the *brigadiers* was supposed to have told his men "that they should go fight; that if not, they'd have no more money, they'd eat dirt and be deported to an island."[20]

Several thousand men were on the Place du Panthéon at the appointed time to hear a speech by workshop militant Louis Pujol. The crowd sang an improvised anthem, *"Du travail ou du plomb"* (Work or Lead), and they took an oath to meet the following day at 6 A.M. They had dispersed by midnight. Early the next morning, on Friday, 23 June, *Commissaire* Michel Yon at the Panthéon reported large and growing crowds of armed men. The group divided, its members going off in several directions, shouting, "To the barricades! To arms!"[21] Thus began the worst insurrection Paris had yet seen.

This first day witnessed a fierce disagreement between War Minister Eugène Cavaignac and the five-man Executive Commission. The commission wanted to attack the barricades as they went up; civil authorities were acutely aware of the political fallout from heavy casualties and pitched battles in the streets.[22] But in the person of Cavaignac, they were confronting a professional soldier eager to rebuild the army's confidence. Thus he was determined upon an anti-February: instead of sending men into the streets early, in small detachments, he wanted to concentrate them first and then send them out in overwhelming force.

Afterward, the popular view was that Cavaignac had allowed the barricades to become too formidable, that he had left the national guards without support in their neighborhoods. (He was in fact distrustful of the expanded worker presence in the guard, and had based his plans on the mobiles and regular troops.[23]) Cavaignac's deposition, summarized in the third person in the official report, seemed to bear out the common perception: "The system of defense adopted by the general in the June Days reposed on this conviction, that there was a danger in disseminating the troops. The experiences of July 1830 and February 1848 demonstrated to him the necessity of not engaging the troops in the streets and of gathering the *corps* in sufficient number so that the insurrection would always be forced to give way before it." According to the angry Executive Commission member Ledru-Rollin, besieged by national guards requesting troop support on Friday afternoon, it was also personal. Cavaignac had asserted to him that "the honor of the army requires that I per-

sist in my system," adding that if even a single one of his companies were disarmed, "I would blow my brains out."[24] But the legend of the June Days was
different from the reality.

Cavaignac, age 46 and the younger brother of the late Godefroy
Cavaignac, had become minister of war on 17 May, as a skilled professional officer and the bearer of a trusted republican name.[25] He and the Executive Commission had decided, not without disagreement, that Paris could be adequately
defended with 45,000 men, composed of 25,000 regular troops, 15,000 mobile
guards, and 5,000 municipal forces, including Caussidière's *Garde républicaine*.[26]
Cavaignac later asserted that he had had about 30,000 troops in the vicinity of
Paris, but a hasty census on 26 June showed a total of 24,047 men, as well as
12,000 mobiles, and perhaps only about 18,000 national guards (out of a theoretical national guard force, in Paris and the suburbs, of 237,000; the rest remained home or joined the insurgency).[27] It was normally the case that national
guards protected their own neighborhoods, and rare for these men—who were
not professional troops, but shopkeepers, professional men and, since February,
workers—to go beyond their *arrondissements*. Because of the need to assign soldiers to the National Assembly and other critical points, there were only about
11,500 Line troops and 13,000 mobile guards available to go on the attack.[28]

On Friday, 23 June, at about 8 A.M., Cavaignac was given supreme command of all Paris forces. He immediately called up the National Guard, and had
the mobile guards and troops already moving to their concentration points by
late morning; in order to gather as quickly as possible, they crossed barricades
without dismantling them.[29] The battle had been joined, in several locations, before noon on Friday. Cavaignac later noted that on 23 June, only "two-thirds" of
a day as far as the insurrection was concerned, the army had suffered 195 casualties (35 killed, 160 wounded) out of a total of 708 casualties for the entire battle.
On Friday afternoon and evening, Cavaignac himself commanded an unsuccessful assault on a major barricade in the faubourg du Temple.[30]

Despite evidence of fierce fighting on Friday, it nevertheless came to be
widely believed in Paris that Cavaignac had deliberately withheld the troops at
first in order to crush the insurgents more completely later, to "finish with the
workers" once and for all.[31] This perception was not limited to the Left. Louis
Napoléon's prefect of police, Émile de Maupas, encountered the after effects
of the June Days during the coup d'état of 2 December 1851, when he urged
the generals to combat the initial resistance in Paris before it became serious.
He found them instead determined to imitate the same massive deployment of
force that Cavaignac had used, perhaps indeed to recapture the same thrill of
victory: "The military authorities judged that the ardor of the insurgents could

only be finally extinguished by the infliction of a vigorous lesson. . . . They wished to crush them with one blow."[32]

Though the insurrection at first seemed to be everywhere, it was soon apparent that there were three main centers. The first was in the north and east of Paris, in the region between the boulevards and the *barrières* of Clichy, La Chapelle, and La Villette, to which General Lamoricière was sent. The second was on the eastern Right Bank and closer to the river, in the area of the Hôtel de Ville and the uprisings of 1834 and 1839; General Bedeau, soon taken out of combat by a leg wound, was ordered here. Finally, the third, unexpected stronghold of the insurgency was in the Latin Quarter on the Left Bank; General Damesme took command of this area, and was killed at the Panthéon.[33]

There was no grand strategy to the insurrection, no leadership except that provided by local, self-appointed *chefs de barricades;* nevertheless, Friday the twenty-third was their day of victory. At 11 A.M. the prefect reported an enormous barricade at the Porte Saint-Denis, where combat was begun by the local national guards. Women and children fought "in the ranks of the People," and two of the women had fallen.[34] Women and children were also seen building barricades in the eighth *arrondissement* and at the end of the Pont Saint-Michel,[35] but for the most part the participants were working-class men united by shared membership in the National Workshops or as newly enrolled national guards. They convinced themselves that they were backed by immense forces led by Caussidière; the passwords, at least in some circles, were *Caussidière et République,* or *Caen et Caussidière.*[36] (Caussidière himself later denied any involvement: "I was bored, disgusted, fatigued, and dreamed only of reentering private life, after having combated during twenty years for the Republic."[37]) In the faubourg Saint-Antoine, Louis Racary (a former Egalitarian Worker) was convinced that Caussidière would soon be arriving with six pieces of artillery and pumps to spray the Hôtel de Ville with explosive chemicals—the story reminiscent of the pyrotechnical fantasies of the 1840s, of small groups convincing themselves that they controlled forces beyond measure.[38]

One of the earliest clashes was near the Panthéon, where the insurgents had been summoned for early Friday morning. Most of the twenty thousand guards in the *arrondissement*'s legion remained at home or joined the rebels; only five hundred responded to the *rappel,* most of them out of uniform. It was still early enough—there had as yet been no bloodshed, nothing irrevocable—for conversation. Local mayor Dr. Félix Pinel-Grandchamps, floundering in a well-meant attempt to keep the peace, climbed atop the tallest barricade and urged the builders to regard their work as merely a "pacific demonstration" of discontent, a silent protest against the way things had gone; the government had made mistakes, he said, but "brothers do not fire upon brothers." The effect of this speech on the defenders of order, according to a witness, had been "deplorable"; when Pinel shook hands with the insurgents he occasioned "a great confusion" in the ranks, and national guards on the scene reported themselves "demoralized." Later, François Arago of the Executive Commission, summoned by distraught national guard officers, tried to negotiate with the insurgents; but, he recalled, it was impossible ("they demanded the liberation of Barbès, of Blanqui, and other inadmissible things"). He ordered the *sommations;* the main barricade was taken without resistance, the combatants close enough to shake their fists in Arago's face—too close indeed to shoot.[39]

In the same general area, *chef de bataillon* Cottu of the 11th Legion found the barricade at the Sorbonne commanded by a certain Jacob, in a red vest and armed with a sabre: "I spoke with this man, and declared that if anyone crossed a line of paving stones that I had marked, I would give the order to fire. Jacob said the workers were ready to die."[40] *Chef de bataillon* Renaud, also of the 11th, retook the Cluny Museum, then lost two men in an attack on a neighboring barricade. After this, he and his men held their positions; they received no support from the Line, "and the insurgents, masters of the windows, were an obstacle that [we] could not overcome."[41] Yet another *chef de bataillon* of the 11th Legion, Captain François Masson, was killed by gunfire at the barricade of the rue Saint-Sévérin. He had walked in front of his troop, his shako on the point of his sabre. "What do you want?" he had asked; "Is it gold, is it money to give bread to your wives and children, here is some" (putting his hand in his pocket); "what do you want? Is it universal suffrage? You have it." According to one of his men, his last words, spoken as he stood on the barricade, were "Don't fire, my friends, I beg you; don't begin the civil war!"[42]

The worst battle of the first day, according to many accounts, was at the Place Lafayette in the faubourg Poissonnière, where 20 national guards were killed or wounded.[43] Journalist Amédée Achard was ordered there as part of the wealthy 2nd Legion. A stretcher went by with the body of one of their *chefs de bataillon,* killed by a shot to the head. As they passed cross streets they could see insurgents in flight, firing at them and mostly missing; they also saw dead bodies, unmoving and unreal. Finally they reached their destination, the intersection of the rue Lafayette and the rue du faubourg Saint-Denis, and turned toward the massive barricade. Achard felt disembodied, a witness to the events in which he was an "actor," and abnormally aware of the smallest details. Suddenly they began to take casualties: the drummer was shot in the knee; a guard who had turned to look at him was shot in the elbow and ran, holding his wounded arm, to shelter in a corner; another guard jerked his arms into the air and then collapsed, motionless.[44] Three representatives from the National Assembly sent back to Cavaignac a hastily pencilled note: "The faubourg Poissonnière is in peril, if reinforcements are not sent immediately. Only the artillery can flush out the insurgents from the positions they have taken. Blood is flowing to no purpose. It's urgent! urgent!"[45]

The government did have some successes on Friday. The mobile guards were young workers of Paris (by law, aged 16–30), recruited after February to protect the city and government. In the few months since the revolution they had been trained and quartered at government expense, and had developed a considerable esprit de corps.[46] They were sent out in force on Friday, and displayed an *élan* that was notably absent elsewhere. At a barricade in the faubourg Saint-Denis, a joint attack by national guards and mobiles was met with "a terrible fire," and they were forced back by losses and lack of ammunition. General Lamoricière ordered another assault late that afternoon; they took the first two barricades by bayonet and "the [Mobile] commandant rallied his battalion and in spite of the most murderous fire coming from all directions, he immediately attacked the third barricade, which was taken very promptly, like the others. He thus pursued the insurgents to the fourth, then to the fifth barricade where he had to stop, having no more ammunition and finding himself supported by no [other] troops." Their supplies and reinforcements, including artillery, came in about an hour. They took the sixth barricade, and after two artillery blasts, the seventh barricade as well. The mobile guard commander reported that his men were "covered with glory."[47]

As this report indicated, the artillery was also deployed as early as Friday. National Guard Étienne Blancq, captured by insurgents and forced to work on the barricades, found himself on the wrong side of a barrage: "I saw an adjudant [of the *chef de barricade*] fall, a woman had her head carried off. I flattened myself against a boundary marker, and I thus awaited the Mobile Guard which advanced." He took a chance and ran toward the mobiles, who accepted him into their ranks: "As we were pressed one against the other, we could scarcely load our weapons; there were some mobiles who shot above my shoulder. At the moment when I had my hand in the air to withdraw the ramrod from my musket, a mobile guard shot me in the right hand." He rushed into a building and up to the third floor, heard shooting in the stairwell, and realized that several mobiles were following his blood trail. "Then I was afraid, I climbed to the highest floor, and from there to the roof." But the mobiles had seized the roof of the building across the street; he tried to hide in a chimney, but was shot twice in the chest before he was able to throw himself on the mercy of an officer—the officers taken from among the professional army—who protected him.[48]

Saturday the twenty-fourth was much like Friday—intense fighting in some places, peace in others—but with little sense of who was winning the battle. Combat remained concentrated in the eastern working-class districts. At 10 A.M. Paris was officially placed in a state of siege, with "all executive powers," as well as the unified military command, invested in General Cavaignac.[49] Once again on the twenty-fourth, the mobiles were the main story, their impulsiveness rapidly becoming legend. The rue Saint-Jacques on the Left Bank was attacked by the mobiles and Line troops; after a dozen men dead, they adopted insurgent techniques, posting snipers in the first and second floors of the buildings on the street, "in such a manner as to make a plunging fire on the insurgents who were thus flushed out in less than an hour from all their positions to the Place Maubert." But when they arrived at the Place Maubert, "about 50 men threw themselves with an imprudent courage, and in spite of my orders," reported the mobile commander, "into the rue Saint-Victor, defended throughout its length by monstrous barricades. This temerity was crowned with success, and in the face of strong fire they succeeded from barricade to barricade."[50] The commander of the 20th battalion reported a similar incident against a barricade in the rue Bichat; unable to contain his men, some of whom had advanced dangerously far ahead, he had decided to take the barricades of the entire *quartier*.[51]

The 2nd battalion of the mobiles was sent to the rue Saint-Jacques later that day, to take the remaining six barricades in the opposite direction, as far as the Pont Saint-Michel, and was "received by a terrible fusillade from all the windows and from the barricades." According to their commander, all action was "suspended until the arrival of the artillery."[52] A national guard described the sensation of the artillery attack: "Bullets crossed through the air above our heads, and about every five minutes we saw pass by some pale and unsteady casualty, supported or carried by his comrades. Emotions began." Suddenly the order was given to retreat, and they withdrew into an area near Notre Dame cathedral. "The street was evacuated; the cannon rumbled. The first shot was followed by the noise of broken glass falling on the pavement; at the second shot, the same music. I raised my eyes; the majority of windows no longer had anything but their frames." They pulled the artillery out of the way and attacked again, this time meeting with no resistance. After the battle, the national guards searched the buildings and found entire families flat on the floor under tables and beds, "almost crazy with terror" and convinced that they were about to be massacred. They had captured about 20 insurgents: "In the midst of the threats and cries for death that resounded in their ears, these men showed a firmness, a silent courage, that disarmed all of our legitimate anger."[53]

On the Right Bank, one commander was told simply to "cannon indefinitely the rue Saint-Martin" (he estimated about 60 rounds were fired). The mobiles retook the Saint-Martin barracks, sending most of the insurgents fleeing into nearby gardens, but—reported the *Gazette des Tribunaux*, during the fighting—"the others, in great number, were killed weapons in hand."[54] Several men taken on the rue Geoffroy-l'Asnier were shot on the spot, by soldiers in tears, according to the *National*, over the death of General Regnault, who had just been killed.[55] Representative Lebreton reported to the assembly on 27 June that he had "used all his influence on the National Guard to prevent prisoners taken weapons in hand from being shot without judgment."[56] (Soldiers justified these executions by the random killings on the other side: for example, Charles Vappreaux from the *barrière* Fontainebleau boasted that he had shot a mobile who had become separated from his unit, adding that his victim had staggered some distance before falling dead, leaving a long train of blood: "He bled like a boar."[57])

Sunday was the beginning of the end. Aside from the eastern suburbs and a few isolated pockets, the only remaining insurgent strongholds were the faubourg Saint-Marcel, on the Left Bank, and the faubourgs du Temple and Saint-Antoine, on the Right Bank.[58] The streets of Saint-Denis, Saint-Martin, and Transnonain, as well as the Place Maubert, were finally retaken.[59] The combatants, exhausted by two days of fighting, were beginning to flag, particularly in the face of increasingly serious assaults. The Sunday edition of *Le National* reported the arrival of fresh troops from the provinces.[60]

Theatrical gestures continued to be appropriated by the undisciplined mobiles, the "martial children" who might easily have been on the other side, "sons of workers, that one sent to the massacre of their fathers."[61] By Sunday, the Palais de Justice was in the hands of the 8th Mobiles, and they had nothing to do but patrol: "But the men of the battalion, exalted by the combat of the day before and knowing that there was fighting near the rue Saint-Antoine and the Place de la Bastille, asked me for permission to go there," reported their commandant; "I refused . . . [but] the desire to fight carried them away and half the men of my battalion, at least, ran to glory and danger . . . the results of this lack of discipline are magnificent and glorious for the 8th battalion."[62]

The mechanic Emmanuel Barthélemy, a *Saisons* veteran imprisoned in 1839 for firing at a *sergent de ville*, was a new national guard of the suburbs. He had rushed to Paris when the fighting began, taking command of the rue Grange aux Belles near the faubourg du Temple. In an article written two years later for a refugee newspaper in London, Barthélemy emphasized the traditional montagnard themes: the "fraternal" treatment of their national and mobile guard prisoners; the order they had imposed on the neighborhood, to prevent looting; the respect shown to mobile guard personal property when they took the local barracks ("nothing was taken in this barracks beyond the weapons, ammunition, and provisions"); and, above all, their gallant, hopelessly outnumbered cause. On Sunday, their barricades were pounded by artillery, in a battle that dragged on inconclusively for six hours. The barricade defenders scattered when the military commander attacked from a side street, leaving only Barthélemy and several others behind:

> We remained as five only to repel the combined efforts of the Line, the Mobile Guard, and the National Guard. This moment was terrible, we heard only the noise of the gunfire and the whistling of bullets past our heads. At the end of about a quarter of an hour, we were only two combatants, two of our comrades were killed and another wounded. . . . We remained thus for more than two hours and it was only after having entirely used up our ammunition and that of our dead comrades that we withdrew, carrying our wounded; we left the dead on the field of battle.

Barthélemy fell back into the faubourg du Temple, "stepped down" as commandant, and fought on as an individual. He was arrested and convicted; he managed to escape to London.[63]

Barthélemy's opponent in the faubourg du Temple, General Lamoricière, wrote to Cavaignac on Sunday as he was launching his attack: "We are fighting by the buildings [shooting from the windows] and we're nevertheless losing some people. . . . We will work all night."[64] At 6:30 P.M., the prefect of police reported that there was shooting at the entry of the faubourg du Temple, "and the insurgents established in the buildings or on the roofs defend their barricades with energy. However the troop is gaining terrain over the insurrection."[65]

By late Sunday afternoon, many of the insurgents had taken flight; the troops advanced against deserted barricades. But while some areas collapsed, elsewhere Sunday became the worst day of fighting. The 4th battalion of the

Mobile Guard, with Line troops of the 14th Light and two artillery pieces, attacked the streets Planche-Mibray, Maubuée, and others nearby: "I took all these barricades and inflicted cruel losses on the enemy," reported the commander of the mobiles, adding that they had captured 750 insurgents in all.[66] One detachment of mobiles had taken considerable fire as they attacked a large barricade at the junction of the streets Maubuée and Saint-Martin. According to their commander, "We hesitated a moment, but suddenly reanimated with courage and ardor for *la république en danger*, we knew nothing but conquest, we launched ourselves forward with a magnificent ardor, we climbed the barricade." Now it was their opponents who were on the defensive: "The insurgents fled, we shot several, the rest found safety in the buildings on the rue Maubuée, which received them, and from which they still shot at us from the windows." At the end of this street there was another huge barricade; they took it and the buildings that overlooked it: "We took several insurgents, weapons in hand, whom we shot immediately and without stopping."[67] They had killed the prisoners, casually and without hesitation about doing it or reporting it; but it was also noteworthy that the local buildings had received those in flight, despite the memories of Transnonain.

Bertrand Lacrosse, vice-president of the National Assembly, witnessed the taking of the faubourg Poissonnière on Sunday; he experienced "much difficulty in preventing the insurgents from being massacred."[68] But elsewhere men were shot, the actions multiplying in the last hours, as exhaustion and rage began to cloud judgment. The official investigation uncovered many reports of disarmed prisoners who were killed—isolated depositions which they scattered throughout the first two bulky volumes of the official report, effectively burying them in the surrounding material.[69] One of Cavaignac's proclamations to the soldiers urged his men to leave only "victors and vanquished" on the field, and not "victims"—a warning perhaps too oblique to be effective.[70]

The most widely publicized single event of the June Days was the death of General Jean de Bréa. A number of prominent generals were killed in battle—including Damesme, who died after a painful amputation of his shattered leg; Colonel Regnault (field-promoted to general) and Négrier, who both died on the spot; and Duvivier, who died later of an apparently slight wound that festered—but General de Bréa was murdered.[71] The trial of the 25 defendants indicted as accomplices became the central judicial event of the uprising, as Charles Jeanne's trial had been in 1832. But while Jeanne's case had involved a dramatic story with constant forward momentum and a genuine hero, the Bréa case was a violation of traditional montagnard narratives; as an insurrectional act it went nowhere, led to nothing. Women were not to blame for it, but retellings of the event nevertheless soon implicated them as the chief cause, and thus relegated the incident to the realm of the savage and inexplicable. In the subsequent trial all context was adamantly expunged, with no mention of mass arrests, or house-to-house searches, or the screams and gunfire in the holding areas for prisoners.

The episode began on Sunday, 25 June, at approximately 2:30 in the afternoon. Despite fierce resistance, the Left Bank had been largely recaptured. In the north and east, a series of *barrières* had yielded without bloodshed to Bréa in the course of the morning, their surrender facilitated by his announcement of the assembly's vote of three million francs for the unemployed.[72] Captain Charles Gobert of the troubled 12th Legion of the National Guard had gone ahead of Bréa's troops as *parlementaire*. The barrières Saint-Jacques, d'Enfer, and de la Glacière had given way.

The atmosphere was different behind the barrière Fontainebleau, which had become a refuge as other strongholds had capitulated. Bréa made his announcement about the three million francs and heard enough cheering, he thought, to justify crossing the barricade with Captain Mangin, his aide-de-camp, and with Lieutenant Colonel E. Desmarets of the 24th Light Infantry and *chef de bataillon* Gobert (both of whom survived). Gobert, the spokesman, advised Bréa not to go forward. But the general had faith in the sheer force of his gesture; he was "full of confidence," Gobert said, "and certain of succeeding there as he had succeeded at the other *barrières*."[73]

Once Bréa was beyond the reach of his troops, he and his party were taken hostage. Immediately his captors began to quarrel, with those determined to kill him held precariously at bay by those who wanted to save him; the general's supporters appealed on the basis of his age and generation, his status as *un vieux brave* of the Napoleonic Wars.[74] In the uneasy standoff, the captives were moved from one place to another, first to the small duty post and then, for about 45 minutes, to a building called the Grand Salon, owned by the local mayor. National Guard Gobert, briefly separated from the others, was beaten by his captors, who pulled his hair and beard and ripped the insignias from his uniform; Florent Dugas punched him repeatedly in the face. Gobert escaped into the Grand Salon, where Bréa was being pressured, by those trying to save him, to write an order to withdraw.[75] Bréa had finally written a proclamation, but only about the three million for the "necessitous class"; it was not well-received.[76] As they discovered later, a group of women had just arrived from the Panthéon with the news that troops were killing prisoners.[77] Growing pressure from the tenants of the Grand Salon, fearful of a massacre, led to the decision to move the hostages to the local national guard post.

During their passage, Colonel Desmarets became separated from the others: "Then [defendant] Pierre Gautron came to me: he sized me up from head to foot, and said to me: 'You're in the Mobiles?' 'No,' I said to him. And immediately he shouted, 'Death! Death! This is a traitor!' This cry of death flew from mouth to mouth, and I would have been done for without MM. [Pierre] Dumont and Gerard, who took me by the arm, telling me, 'We're going to save you, or at least do all that we can.'" The crowd then threw itself upon him, tearing away his epaulettes and ripping his tunic; he fought unsuccessfully to break his sabre across his knee before it was taken. His arm was grabbed roughly by Martin Nuens, a 35-year-old watchmaker who later received a sentence of hard labor for life. Gautron (also hard labor in perpetuity), armed with a paving stone and threatening to bludgeon him with it, "leaped" around him, crying, "We've got to kill him! He's a villain!" Desmarets remembered an elderly man who insisted that he be taken immediately into an alley and shot. A working woman threw herself on her knees before his captors, imploring them to spare him: "'Mercy, he's a father of a family; don't do him any harm!'—'We also,' said these *furieux*, 'We're fathers of families! Death! Death!'" To Desmaret's astonishment he recognized the woman as his laundress. His ally Dumont had kept hold of him, shouting that Desmarets was his prisoner in order to keep the killers at bay. Though badly beaten, he was aware that he had to stay on his feet and keep moving; otherwise, "I would have been pierced with a thousand bayonet blows."[78]

The Maison Blanche (or Grande) post was manned by a small contingent of national guards who supported the government but were hopelessly outnumbered. Lieutenant Louis Constant, in nominal command of the post, had been forced by the insurgents to take custody of a "little mobile" whom they were planning to shoot. One of those on duty recalled that Desmarets, who arrived just before the others, "was overcome, torn to shreds. He recovered his senses and told us that the assembly had voted 3 million for the working class." Constant appealed to the rules of war and the protection owed to *parlementaires*: "This is a brave officer who comes here with words of peace, he must be respected."[79] After Desmarets came Gobert, Mangin, and Bréa, "his arms crossed over his chest" like a condemned man.[80] The small post became crowded with both friends and foes. A secret attempt to break through the guardpost wall from an alleyway was discovered by Charles Choppart, who shouted that they had been betrayed. He began to beat post commander Constant's head with his musket.[81]

The four men and their captors would remain in the post for nearly two indecisive hours. General de Bréa asked for a drink but refused to use the common glass passed around the room. Gobert admitted to feelings of anger, for he had told Bréa not to go beyond the barricade. When the general noted that it was his birthday, "I recall that I answered him: 'It's my head too, General.'" Desmarets gamely attempted to find some common ground: "I drank with the insurgents. I sought to strike up a conversation with some Germans who were there, because my wife is from Strasbourg. No one was from this city." Nicolas Lahr was remembered by Gobert as in a state of unfocused agitation; though "not precisely" hostile to the general, "he walked up and down in the post, his carbine in his hand. He was very exalted."[82] Also present was Henri-Joseph Daix, who with Lahr would be executed; eventually Daix expelled all those friendly to the general's party, forcing those who stayed inside to swear that the captives would not leave the post alive.[83]

But the remaining insurgents did not seem to know what to do. "An individual even arrived at the post," recalled Gobert, "shouting, 'What! It's not finished yet? In a revolution, one must be quick!'"[84] At one point they turned on Gobert: "He's from the 11th [Légion]; he fired on our brothers; he must be shot!" He was saved by a certain Pâris: "No, you can see he's from the 12th [formerly Barbès' legion]."[85] Captain Mangin bore the tension least well, finally ripping open his tunic: "If you want to shoot us, here is my breast: shoot!"[86] General de Bréa also became frustrated; he unsheathed his sword and showed the inscription to Daix, saying, "See, *misérable*, read this and say whether one shoots a man like me!"[87] Despite repeated threats, Bréa refused to order the troops away, saying, according to a witness, "I'm an old soldier; I have no fear of death; shoot us; I'll not sign this order."[88] (Defendant Choppart produced an order he did sign, later given to the general's family and read in court, where it caused a sensation: "I am in the power of the insurgents; they want us to lay down our weapons; but I order you not to."[89])

The post was surrounded by a hostile crowd, shouting "Death! Death! Finish it!" The peddler Traideler, who had just arrived in Paris that afternoon, found himself standing next to a woman who kept shouting "Shoot! shoot!" Traideler told her to stop and she turned on him; he kicked her, and was then attacked by several others who decided to kill him. Fortunately, a man in the crowd, hearing his strong accent, urged caution on the grounds that he might be from Poland. "Was he Polish?" he was asked; and the German Traideler had replied: "Yes, I'm Polish! *Vive la Pologne!*"[90]

Finally it was decided to empty the post of all but the four captives; the "little mobile" took off his uniform jacket and slipped out the door with the rest. The four officers, now alone in the room, found themselves in the sights of armed men at all the doors and windows, muskets aimed; still they did not fire. The cries from outside intensified, then came shouts—women's shouts—

of "We're lost! Treason! There come the mobiles!"[91] A single shot was fired, then many; Gobert provided the fullest account of the final seconds:

> There was a moment of terrifying silence . . . then I heard the cry: "Shoot! Shoot! There come the Mobile Guards!" The muskets were lowered. A first shot was fired, and the general fell. I threw myself to the floor to avoid the discharge that was going to follow, and finding myself beside the camp bed, I slid underneath. The fusillade continued. Poor Mangin got a bullet in the cheek; he fell to his knees and uttered a frightful cry, bringing his hands to his head. The insurgents entered the post. One of them shouted: "There's one under the bed."—"Shoot him," called the others. And I saw the muskets lowered on me. Others entered, and I heard the blows of the butts of muskets fall on the General and on Mr. Mangin. . . . Fortunately for me, the crowd erupted into the post. A cry of horror was raised at the sight of the two cadavers that were extended on the ground. The insurgents fled; the post was evacuated and the door closed.[92]

Desmarets, crouched in a corner, was also missed. He had already experienced a mysterious intervention even before the gunfire, when someone from outside had whispered to him to get away from the window. He saw the general collapse, his head hitting the table: "Mangin was knocked down. The poor young man raised himself up an instant on his feet, and taking his head in his hands, in falling he gave a last cry of agony and despair." For a few moments there was dead silence. Dumont and Auguste Viel, among the first to reenter the post, took charge of Desmarets; they gave him a *blouse*, hastily shaved off his mustache, showed him the ladder over the garden wall and, "from ladder to ladder, and from garden to garden," he escaped. Gobert was rescued by Antoine Guimbal, an "honest worker" who gave him the shirt off his back, pushed him over a wall, and, recalled Gobert, "I thus found myself in the country."[93]

The autopsy revealed that Bréa had been bruised about the face and head, wounded by gunshots (especially to the chest) and finished off by bayonet thrusts. The numerous different wounds from different directions indicated multiple attackers. Mangin's body was the more appalling, his skull bones "shattered," his brain cavity empty, his left eye gone. The examining physician stated that his wounds were consistent with having been shot in the head at close range or bludgeoned to death with the butt of a musket or a hammer. The testimony of the two survivors indicated that many of the wounds had occurred just after death when the insurgents had entered the post.[94] The local curé, by his own uninspiring account cowering behind his shutters during the terrible period of uncertainty, finally came down to provide last rites.[95] In the meantime, Colonel Clement Thomas with the 11th Light Infantry, part of Bréa's command, ordered an immediate attack and was soon in possession of the neighborhood.[96]

The murders apparently were precipitated by two impatient young men. Jean Nourry, age 18, and François Lebelleguy, age 17, were together at one of the windows, urging each other on. Nourry was accused by several witnesses of having fired the first shot, which he denied.[97] His friend Lebelleguy confirmed that Nourry had indeed fired the first shot that triggered the fusillade. The witness Viel testified that Nourry had entered the post "and repeatedly plunged his bayonet into the body of the general."[98] Lebelleguy had also behaved with childish savagery, remarking that the general still "wriggled," and plunging Bréa's own sword into his chest; then he had waved it above his head, crying "whoever wants this, must earn it." "He left the post showing to the public the sword that he held high," confirmed another witness; "he brandished it, uttering cries of joy." In the courtroom Lebelleguy was considerably more subdued, denying that he had struck the general but admitting that he had bragged of having done so: "I did not want to pass for having done nothing; I believed it was a good action."[99]

The sword soon passed into the hands of Nourry, who boastfully showed it to a friend:

> I saw Jean Nourry arrive in the building where I live crying, "Look, Friend Favre, here it is, I've killed a General!" "What—you, you *misérable*," I said to him, "you've killed a General!" "Yes; here's his sword." He gave it to me, and I read on this sword: "Given to the brave de Bréa by General Carpentier, in memory of the battle of Waterloo." I said to him, "You've killed one of the brave officers of France—what have you done, my friend?"

Nourry had begun to cry, denying that he had killed the general, that it had been his "vertigo" that caused him to say it.[100] Before they made their final judgment, the court heard an evaluation of his mental condition, carried out by Dr. Ulysse Trélat. He and his colleagues determined that Nourry was unable to read or write, despite having been to school for several years; that he was plagued with a "spider in his head," as he called it, that led to migraines, loss of consciousness, and what he referred to as his "vertigo"; that he was the product of hereditary insanity, his father, paternal uncle, older brother, and cousin having lost their minds; and that, with the onset of puberty and the simultaneous death of his father at Bicêtre, Nourry had become markedly worse.[101]

Of the two men who would be executed for the murders,[102] one was 29-year-old Nicolas Lahr, according to fellow stonemason Martin Nadaud "a man of great energy and herculean strength." He had shouted *Vive Napoléon!*

as he fought (his political allegiance did not emerge during the trial, which oc-curred after the election of Louis Napoléon as president).[103] He had fled the city until 20 July, living off the land outside Paris, until hunger forced him back. On the thirtieth, he was spotted and taken into custody. Lahr had been one of the first inside the post, and one of the most vocal about killing the cap-tives; he had used his national guard uniform as a source of authority over the others, and he had fired through the window.[104]

The other man executed was Henri-Joseph Daix, age 40, a janitor at Bicêtre hospital. He denied any role in the insurrection, even claiming that he had attempted to save the general.[105] But a witness suggested that Daix, and not Nourry, might even have been the first to fire; certainly he was outside, shouting, "They must be shot! They must be shot!" Another observer claimed that Daix had savagely beaten Captain Mangin's body with the butt of his mus-ket.[106] There were also witnesses to Daix's conduct after the shooting: Daix as he swaggered away, bragging to a national guard lieutenant who was worried that the general was going to be shot, "No, he won't *be* shot, he's *been* shot"; or Daix boasting to a neighbor, waving Mangin's sword: "I've just killed a gen-eral; see, there's his sabre."[107]

To the shock of many of the defendants, the trial converted the hazy ambi-guity of the world behind the barricades into the sharply defined terrain of ac-cused and accusers, wrong and right. Several defendants seemed genuinely confused about their own status—surely to be interpreted differently, they thought, because of the republican victory in February. Jean Bussières was a new national guard whose uniform, in his own eyes, had conferred legitimacy on his actions: "It was thus that I proceeded toward the construction of barricades that I considered useful to my locality."[108] Quintin, another defendant, was asked if he had been with the insurgents on the barricades, and responded, "What do you call insurgents?"[109] Others were angry at being singled out. Defendant Mar-tin Nuens complained of the inactivity of all the witnesses, who had bestirred themselves only to testify: "If only ten [of these witnesses] had had the courage to take up a musket and protect the unfortunate officers, I would not have failed to be in their ranks."[110] "All the barrière Fontainebleau was in insurrection," claimed Charles Choppart, "and those who will come to testify against us did as much as we did." He had spent most of the insurrection fighting elsewhere in Paris. On Sunday, with defeat looming, he and his friend Duval had returned home to the barrière Fontainebleau, and Duval had shot himself in the head to avoid arrest; this act had surely affected Choppart's state of mind.[111]

As the barrière Fontainebleau fell, so did the remaining strongholds: the barrière Rochechouart, Montmartre, most of the Left Bank, the Ile de la Cité and the Ile Saint-Louis, as well as the Hôtel de Ville on the Right Bank, were secure by late afternoon. The defenders of the heavily manned barrière du Trône did not understand that the battle was essentially over, even though an army was visibly approaching from the direction of Vincennes. A government *parlementaire*, Representative Galy-Cazalat, convinced them that the rest of the city had fallen, and "the muskets disappeared gradually." An old soldier was sent as emissary to ask the approaching army not to shoot, and General Lebreton peacefully assumed control of the area.[112] The Place du Panthéon was the site of a great battle that lasted more than 15 hours and ended with a massacre of the prisoners; the government's victory there was followed by a series of minor skirmishes in surrounding streets.[113]

The last place to yield was the faubourg Saint-Antoine, by Sunday surrounded and cut off from the rest of the city. Newspapers reported a placard, a call to arms that ended on a note of desperation: "If a blind obstinacy finds you indifferent before all this bloodshed, we will all die under the burned-out rubble of the faubourg Saint-Antoine. Think of your wives, your children, you will join us!"[114] There were several efforts to negotiate with the authorities—freelance attempts, for the most part, and with no coordination among them. A man calling himself the "insurrectional commandant" of the eighth *arrondissement* told a national guard officer that they had fought for *la république démocratique et sociale*, which he explained as "the right accorded to workers to unite among themselves."[115] Representative Dahirel forwarded a letter written by the self-styled "delegates" of the insurgents of the faubourg Saint-Antoine to President Senard: "If we would agree not to pursue the bloody revolution now in progress, we would wish also to conserve our title as citizens, in continuing all our rights and all our duties as French citizens." It was a desire, though expressed in convoluted fashion, for amnesty. The president's response was unyielding.[116]

An "old" national guard, Reymond des Ménars, was pressed into service as *parlementaire* by another group; he was a moderate who believed the government had handled the workshop situation badly. The insurgents bound him to present their conditions, which he described only as "so exaggerated, that they were truly inadmissible."[117] (One of the more violent placards circulating through the faubourg called for a surtax on the rich, the dissolution of the National Assembly, and the execution of all its members, save for a few to be named later; an alternate proclamation issued by the men holding the eighth mayoralty merely called for the indictment of the assembly. Yet another called for the restoration of the workshops, the removal of the army from the city, and the release of Barbès and Blanqui.[118]) Des Ménars returned with

General Perrot's response: the immediate dismantling of the barricades, the entry of troops into the area, and the disarming of the neighborhood—as impossible, in their way, as the insurgent demands.[119]

Among those who came to the faubourg on Sunday—unofficial negotiators, representatives attempting to rally citizens to the government—was Archbishop Affre of Paris, who hoped to persuade the combatants to lay down their arms. Representative Charles Beslay, an eyewitness, stated that the archbishop had been shot from behind as he faced the rebels; Beslay believed that the bullets came from a balcony occupied by soldiers who were shooting into the interior of the barricade.[120] The archbishop's sudden collapse, mortally wounded, had led to a panicked fusillade and the seizure of three representatives, including Denis Larabit, as hostages.[121]

Des Ménars, who had just returned, proposed that Larabit escort him to assembly president Jules Senard or to Cavaignac, and the two set off immediately. The crowd "undulated" before them; they crossed successive barricades only with difficulty, and at least once were threatened with immediate execution. They finally reached Cavaignac at 1 A.M. on Monday, and he drew up the formula for submission: the inhabitants would destroy the barricades; no prisoners would be taken immediately, though the government would act later; and—perhaps most importantly—the insurgents' muskets would not be seized "militarily" by the troops, but disarmament would instead be carried out later by the local National Guard. But events overtook Des Ménars's efforts.[122] The government's final attack began a little after 10 A.M. on Monday. General Perrot was soon joined by Lamoricière, who had finally reduced the faubourg du Temple.[123]

Many of the men of the faubourg Saint-Antoine, as elsewhere, had already fled to the countryside around Paris; troops searched the area, periodically bringing in groups of prisoners.[124] "The men seemed beaten," recalled an observer who would also live through the Commune; "the women retained the animation of the struggle . . . they well foreshadowed those who would later stimulate the *fédérés* [the pro-Commune national guards] to combat! The same faces! The same passions!"[125]

The insurrection had been fought entirely in the working-class eastern half of the city—unlike the February Revolution, when barricades had appeared even around the palaces and government buildings in the wealthy western *arrondissements*. Brutal house-to-house searches followed the battle; the soldiers were ordered to look for hands and lips visibly blackened, for grains of gunpowder that might be found in the "wrinkles or crevices of callused hands" or under the nails. Moreover, the directive continued, "the thumb that cocked the gun sometimes has a scratch, more often a bruise"; the thumb and the tops of the hands would show scratches from the burst of the percussion caps; there would likely be bruises or contusions on the shoulder from the recoil of the weapon. Arresting officers were to check the pockets for traces of gunpowder, the clothing for bullet holes; the ear next to the musket "should, it is said, smell of gunpowder for eight days after the shooting."[126] Norbert Truquin recalled the courteous older officer who had commanded the search of his own building, reining in the excitement of his young soldiers and reassuring the women that he was there merely "to inspect your weapons." But the neighboring building was searched by a different group, and "almost all the men were killed on the spot or deported without judgment."[127] Troops patrolled the roads, railroads, and coach stations to capture those who attempted to flee and those who attempted to return.[128]

Among the insurgents, according to the study by Charles Tilly and Lynn H. Lees, there were clear connections between economic distress and participation. The workshops had been supporting approximately 113,000 men and their families; while many had found odd days or weeks of regular work, in the continuing crisis of depression and unemployment they had used the workshops as a fallback.[129] The industries hardest hit were the furniture, building, and metal trades, and all three contributed more than their share to the insurrection; the small leather and retail sales forces were also disproportionately active.[130] The average insurgent was married, from the provinces, and between the ages of 20 and 40. He was likely to be a member of the National Guard or the National Workshops, or both; each institution provided an organizational framework for the insurrection.[131] Largely absent from the June Days were students and middle-class republican leaders—traditional participants, even if in small numbers, in earlier uprisings. Untypically among the insurgents were small-scale employers and merchants, many of them in the National Guard, who saw their fragile businesses falling apart.[132] The maximum estimates, undoubtedly much too high, were that there were forty to fifty thousand insurgents; Tilly and Lees suggest a more reasonable number, based on arrests and convictions, of ten to fifteen thousand active combatants.[133]

Government casualty reports remained indefinite. Cavaignac reported the figures for the regular army at 708 casualties (killed and wounded), including six generals killed.[134] The figures for the Mobile Guard, according to a 19 July report, were 118 killed, 493 wounded, 175 missing; but this was not certain, for in several battalions that lost commanding officers there was no firm count.[135] In mid-July, the *Gazette des Tribunaux* reported that the number of deaths had been greatly exaggerated, that the total number of those killed or mortally wounded was no higher than 1,400—an astounding figure for an urban insurrection, despite the *Gazette*'s efforts to downplay it. The prefect's figures for about the same period stood at nearly 1,800 dead, with 500 still in the hospital.[136] Insurgents mostly avoided the hospitals; those forced into them—often too late, after gangrene had set in—found themselves next to their former opponents.

The government began to expel the new post-February national guards. At best they had failed to report for duty; at worst they had been on the other side, their uniforms a sign of command in the insurrection. The tailor Jean-Désiré Lévêque, lieutenant of the 12th Legion, had worn the "dress adopted by the insurgent officers of the 12th Legion," his képi and tunic but no epaulettes, and had led a group to the rue Mouffetard, where they built barricades.[137] Narcisse Dubois, the drummer of the 12th, had used his drums to summon the rebels to battle.[138] Pierre Bisson, a lieutenant in the 11th, had reported for duty but then threw down his sword in the presence of his company, saying that he did not wish to fire on his brothers.[139]

With the purging of the National Guard, the monopoly of force was soon retaken by the state and the bourgeoisie. A total of 66,929 muskets had been distributed to the 12 *arrondissements* between February and June, and 11,546 to the *banlieue*, along with 50,000 and 57,170 cartridges respectively.[140] Men were now told to turn in their weapons within 24 hours; the old guards also made house-to-house searches.[141] In Belleville, one of the centers of the insurrection, 7,000 muskets were retrieved. The commander noted that not 200 men, including officers, had answered the *rappel*: "to form a National Guard useful to Belleville, it would be necessary to bring back the cadres of before 24 February and not go beyond them."[142] The former commandant of Montmartre wrote to protest that 300 of his men had done their duty; nevertheless, they accepted the humiliating disarmament because "the majority, by halfheartedness perhaps, rather than from any culpable motive, were not at their posts."[143] By the end of June, it was reported that disarmament was proceeding very actively in the 8th, 9th, and 12th Legions, less so in others.[144] In the 12th, 27,000 muskets had come back, either voluntarily or as a result of house searches. Of these, only 17,000 had been delivered by the mayoralty since the revolution; others had likely been seized from the troops in February.[145] In La Chapelle, 2,800 muskets were taken back; the local *commissaire* remarked that the National Guard included 5,000 men, of whom only 1,000 to 1,200 "are good."[146] In a single company, the 3rd Legion had found 300 new national guards who had fought for the insurrection.[147] The disarming of the 11th Legion stalled because of the refusal of Colonel Edgar Quinet to take the necessary steps.[148] Despite such local resistance, however, by 7 July the prefecture of police had taken away more than 100,000 weapons.[149]

During the assembly session of 27 June, the representatives began to discuss the law calling for the transportation from France of "individuals currently detained who took part in the insurrection of 22 June and the following days." After a brief discussion, they rejected all amendments that would have required some sort of trial judgment before expulsion.[150] On 6 August came the first departure from Le Havre: "Several protested their innocence," according to a journalist on the scene, "but one saw a great number affect the most complete impassiveness and in a sense glorify their situation." They were being sent to Ile d'Ouessant, or to Belle Isle, until a final destination was determined; about 450 were transported that day.[151] As of mid-August, 8,258 individuals were still detained in the forts or prisons; the statistics of the military commissions showed that they had thus far examined 4,000 cases, that 150 of the indicted were to be brought before military tribunals, 1,700 were designated for transportation, and 2,000 had been liberated.[152]

Shortly after the battle, there were terrifying rumors of vengeance. Diehard insurgents were going to blow up the catacombs under the rue Saint-Jacques.[153] The mayor of the sixth *arrondissement*, writing in early July, believed that combat would be revived, but the next time it would be more destructive: "Barricades did not suffice for their triumph, fire will come to their aid. They still have hidden weapons, gunpowder and bullets. Many of their clandestine factories have been discovered; but not all, and they will know how to create new ones."[154] The police in early July investigated a conspiracy to burn Paris: "Several men would rent small lodgings in 12 or 15 quarters in Paris, fill them with straw, hose down this straw with turpentine, set fire to it, and escape."[155]

One way of deflecting the social anxiety borne of the June Days was to displace it onto women. Women became, as they would be in the Commune, the chief symbols of terror, simultaneously more monstrous and less potent than men. In the Saint-Lazare prison were more than two hundred women taken on the barricades or at the moment when they were bringing ammunition to the insurgents—few in total numbers, but disproportionately powerful in the image they conveyed to contemporaries.[156] Daniel Stern reported that women had thrown themselves in "frenzy" into the battle: "They were ingenious in inventing a thousand ruses by which to carry food and ammunition to the combatants. They surprised the projects of the enemy, spied the movements of the troops."[157] Hippolyte Castille's history, written shortly after the event, placed women prominently on the scene, first as powerless witnesses, then as "birds of prey":

Little by little these despairing widows, mothers, and sisters formed a band. As the troops advanced, as new fusillades occurred, this band grew. These unfortunate women circled around the column of General de Bréa, like a troop of wolves corrupted by blood. Sometimes they preceded the troop, sowing alarm at the barricades; sometimes they kept to the sides and behind, spying out its movements with a mixture of terror and hatred and also a vague hope of witnessing some unexpected vengeance.[158]

The newspapers were full of such stories of "viragos," of women who took on, in perverted form, the masculine violence of the defeated men of Paris; the tales of female prodigies made the June Days seem "unnatural," a barbarous eruption that would not come again. It was widely reported that women had sold poisoned *eau-de-vie* to the troops, a rumor so persistent that it prompted an investigation (which revealed that indeed they had—not deliberately, but simply by purveying a liquor so adulterated and noxious that it made the soldiers sick.)[159] At the barricades of the faubourg du Temple, the neighbors reported a certain widow Henry, a 77-year-old woman who "incited the people to engage in pillage and to set fire to the buildings." The local butcher described her at the head of an entire band of insurgent women, and claimed that she had threatened to gut him with her knife.[160] There was a persistent rumor of a woman dressed as a man seen on the barricade with a razor, trying to cut off the head of a wounded national guard.[161] A certain Thérèse, a "great and strong virago" known to the police already for her indecent behavior at public dances, was rumored to have fought in male costume, to have built barricades and sounded the tocsin at the Saint-Séverin church.[162] The *Gazette des Tribunaux* reported the rumor of a woman who boasted of having cut off the heads of three mobiles; on several barricades there had indeed been mobile heads, with their képis, on stakes.[163] Simonne Chignon, a 50-year-old varnisher, was arrested on the morning of 26 June as she bent over the body of a wounded mobile, her hands covered with blood; near her was a dead mobile with his head nearly severed from his body. She said that she hated the mobile guards and had cut off eight heads; she admitted that she had been drinking *eau-de-vie* all night, and was sentenced to ten years of hard labor for murder.[164]

Men, in contrast, were frequently described as objects of pathos. Jean-Baptiste Cornu was a 36-year-old worker in the furnishing trade, a recent widower with two small children; he was also a new sublieutenant of the 9th Legion. He had reported for duty, but found only a handful of his fellow guards. Saturday afternoon he had joined the insurgency; afterward he turned himself in. At his trial he stated that he had been overcome by the "misery" that had claimed his wife's life; that he had found it difficult to make ends meet even though he was a squad leader in the National Workshops; and that on 21 June, he had been unable to feed his son. The military court deliberated for 30 minutes, then sentenced him to ten years of hard labor.[165] Paul Saintard, a 29-year-old mechanic and *chef de barricade*, had been spotted by his neighbor whose window was just across from his, "seated at a table, his head supported in his two hands." She asked if he was sick: "'Oh madame,' he said, 'how can one be well, when people are killing each other?'" Before the June Days he had applied for a position as a *gardien de Paris*; his defender was able to build upon his obvious remorse, describing him as "only a miserable instrument, who had dreamed of a better future for himself, and whose entire ambition was to become a guardian of Paris." Even the prosecutor described him as an "obscure centurion" of the riot. Saintard was given ten years of hard labor.[166] Many of the early cases sounded like those of Saintard and Cornu, and *Le Représentant du peuple* soon began to urge mercy for the footsoldiers of the revolt: the men "dominated by local influences," the ignorant who had been deceived by rumors, the poor in despair. The magnitude of the uprising had had the inadvertent effect of creating isolated pockets in which combatants, believing themselves on the winning side, compromised themselves more than they otherwise might have.[167] The newspaper's plea for clemency was strengthened by the sight of exhausted prisoners chained together, most in the *blouse* and *casquette* that was the uniform of the poor, who began to be led through Paris.[168]

Norbert Truquin, in 1848 a fifteen-year-old *gamin*, later recalled that he had eaten almost nothing during the fighting, nor had most of the insurgents: "Everyone had the fever of combat."[169] A national guard who wrote an account of his battles to the *National* ended on a pensive note: "The excitement of combat is real. One forgets, in the midst of the tumult, why and on whom one is firing. The odor of gunpowder goes to one's head, the sentiment of peril exalts and intoxicates. But, returned to oneself, what remains of these triumphs, too dearly obtained, if it is not an afterthought full of bitterness and involuntary remorse?"[170] Garnier-Pagès had witnessed both riots and revolutions: "The war of the streets is only a series of incidents," he concluded, "by turns audacious, timid, humane, cruel. . . ."[171] As were those who fought it.

CHAPTER 16

EPILOGUE:
LA PROSCRIPTION

THIS STUDY BEGAN TO TAKE SHAPE AFTER I READ the following passage
from the memoirs of Jean Allemane, typographer and prominent Communard, describing one of the last stands of Bloody Week:

> . . . I am informed that the Versaillais are advancing by the rue d'Ulm; I run
> there with four or five veterans who mean to fight to the death. Among these
> old militants is a typographer, the Citizen Faure, better known in our typo-
> graphic workshops by the nickname of Navet, due to the whiteness of his hair
> and beard. Faure had known numerous proletarian defeats and did not want
> to know any others. He had fought with Barbès, combated on the streets in
> June 1848 and December 1851, and he believed that the hour of death had
> come for him. . . .
>
> "If you escape death, my young friend, don't forget to tell the brothers
> who will talk to you of Navet that he died fighting like an old revolutionary."
> And he smiled as he said this, the good old plebeian.
>
> "Bah! Maybe I'm the one who will die first; age doesn't count here."
>
> A few more shots, then a torrent of fire destroys the barricade. Half-
> blinded, I look for my poor comrade; his body is cut to pieces, three-quarters
> of his head is carried off. The old *barricadier*, the proletarian hero, the *com-
> pagnon* of labor with neither fear nor reproach, had been torn apart, and
> shreds of his flesh had been thrown in all directions.
>
> "Avenge the old man!" shout the survivors, and the combat resumes with
> even greater violence.[1]

But the cycle of vengeance had finally exhausted itself; the bourgeois republican consensus of the Third Republic would soon take hold. The copious memoirs of the Commune have quite a few stories of elderly men, veterans of the old battles who had marched with Barbès (who himself died just before the Commune, in exile in The Hague): men who knew everybody, and whom everybody knew, their names now forgotten. The Commune probably finished off most of them; between the June Days and Bloody Week lay the long, wasted years of exile, prison, or intimidated quiescence under the Second Empire. It seems fitting to conclude with a few last traces of the individuals, both great and obscure, who represented this doomed branch of republicanism.

The *journée* of 15 May 1848 led to the flight of Caussidière and Blanc and the imprisonment of Barbès, Blanqui, Raspail, Albert, and Flotte. The *journée* of 13 June 1849 sent into exile, in Britain or Belgium, Landolphe, Kersausie, Delescluze, Ribeyrolles, Ledru-Rollin, Martin-Bernard, Étienne Arago, Considérant, Boichot, Thoré, Guinard, and Lebon.[2] Those exiled after the *coup d'état* in 1851 included Beaune, Amédée Bruys, Antoine Fombertaux, Victor Hugo, Lagrange, Martin Nadaud, Agricol Perdiguier, Noël Parfait, Benjamin Raspail, Thouret, Dufraisse, Jules and Pierre Leroux, and Mathieu d'Épinal.[3] Léonce Fraisse and Eugène Sue went to Switzerland,[4] as did Ferdinand Flocon of the *Réforme*, who lived there humbly as a translator until his failing health and eyesight left him dependent on a pension supplied by friends. He died in 1866; in 1901 his godson, Ferdinand Scheurer-Kestner, brought his remains to Père Lachaise cemetery, thus fulfilling his dying wish: to be buried on the "republican soil" of France.[5]

Félix Mathé, from the old SDHC, eventually went to Barcelona, where he manufactured agricultural steam dredges.[6] Dr. Lacambre married Blanqui's niece and took up his profession in Valencia, among a small colony of exiles. Xavier Durrieu, former editor of the *Courier français*, went to Madrid, where he obtained an administrative position with a railroad company.[7] Charles Lagrange lived in ill-health in Holland, earning his living as a wine salesman until his death in Leyden in 1857.[8] Marc Caussidière in London also supported himself by selling wines; he remained active in refugee politics, and died in 1861.[9] The one-legged Bernard Pornin, a *commissaire de quartier* of the SDHC, was exiled to Guiana after the 1851 coup, for having distributed ammunition to the combatants.[10] Emmanuel Barthélemy, one of the barricade commanders in the faubourg du Temple, killed a fellow London exile in a duel over the relative merits of Blanc and Ledru-Rollin.[11] Louis Auguste Racary, a member of the *Travailleurs Égalitaires*, was wounded in the June Days and sentenced to hard labor for life; after a few years he threw himself off a parapet at Mont-Saint-Michel.[12]

François-Vincent Raspail practiced veterinary medicine in Belgium, then returned to France where he was elected to the Chamber of Deputies in the Third Republic. In 1872, in an essay about the early July Monarchy, Raspail plaintively wondered what had become of his old friend Kersausie: "Is he in America or in the tomb? Does he live somewhere, prey to the lassitude of old age, to this long agony of death?"[13] Kersausie, born to wealth and nobility, had indeed largely dropped from sight. In 1848, he went to Naples for the struggle against the Bourbons; Proudhon saw him in 1860 in Brussels, and described him as still "an impenitent revolutionary." He died in 1874.[14]

Alexandre Thomas, an amateur bombmaker and one of the accessories in the attempted escape from Mont-Saint-Michel, was forced to flee after 2 December 1851, and died in exile.[15] The ex-hatter Pottier, who escaped after being imprisoned for the June Days, established a tavern on Fitzroy Square in London, a haven for new refugees.[16] The provisional government member Albert was in prison (for the *journée* of 15 May) until the amnesty of 1859. He returned to Paris and worked at the *Compagnie du Gaz* until 1894, when he retired at the age of 79; he died the following year.[17] In 1869, in a letter to Barbès, he expressed his belief that the Empire was shaky, the atmosphere similar to the days of the banquet campaign in 1847. What was needed was a revolution of the entire people; the days of the old *émeutes* were past: "What can a few men do, no matter how devoted or brave, without weapons, faced with *chassepots*, rifled gunbarrels, *mitrailleuses?*"[18]

Former SDHC secretary Camille Berryer-Fontaine practiced medicine and belonged to refugee groups in London. In 1846 he made the acquaintance of fellow exile Louis Napoleon Bonaparte, who had just escaped from the prison of Ham; later he became the personal physician of Napoleon III.[19] Albert Laponneraye died in Marseilles in 1849; at the time of his death, the government had him under surveillance as a member of the new *Solidarité républicaine*.[20] Marc Dufraisse, elected to the Legislative Assembly in 1849 and forced into exile after the *coup*, taught comparative law in Zurich. He returned in the fall of 1870 and was elected to the National Assembly in 1871.[21] Antoine Amédée Bruys, arrested in 1836 in a gunpowder case and as a member of the *Familles*, was elected to both the Constituent and Legislative Assemblies. He went to Belgium with the *coup*, returned in 1859 with the amnesty, and died in 1878.[22]

J.-J. Pillot, author of *Ni châteaux ni chaumières*, spent the 1840s in Brazil studying homeopathic medicine. In 1848, he ran unsuccessfully for the assembly. He resurfaced during the Commune and became involved in the demolition of the Vendôme Column. In 1872, he was convicted for having attempted to burn down the Louvre, and was sentenced to hard labor for life; he soon died.[23] Antoine Fombertaux *père*, who took to the streets to resist the *coup*, managed to reach Jersey, where he joined the circle around Victor Hugo.[24] Sebastien Commissaire, finally released from prison in March 1859, borrowed money to start a small business in his native Lyon. He married a virtuous woman who proved to be fanatically pious: "I do not believe there is, for a *républicain libre penseur*, any greater misfortune than that of being condemned to live with a person who shares neither his political opinions nor his philosophical beliefs."[25]

The cook Benjamin Flotte, a Blanqui disciple and fellow inmate of Mont-Saint-Michel, was sentenced to five years for the *journée* of 15 May. After serving his sentence, he went to San Francisco and opened a restaurant. He returned for the Franco-Prussian War, and during the Commune attempted to negotiate Blanqui's release from the Versailles government.[26] Journalist Victor Pilhes wrote for Dupoty's *Journal du Peuple* as well as the *Réforme*. At first a disciple of Proudhon, he switched to Blanqui, and was actively involved in the February revolution; one of his brothers fought in Garibaldi's army. After the demonstration of 13 June 1849, Pilhes served time in Doullens, Mazas, and Belle-Ile; in August 1870 he was Blanqui's lieutenant in the *affaire de la Villette*, an abortive insurrection just days before the overthrow of the Second Empire.[27]

As for Blanqui himself, he lived long enough to see the disappointing Third Republic, and even to become an institution, of sorts. In 1879 he campaigned for amnesty for the communards and in 1880 went on a speaking tour, cheered as the grand old man of republicanism. His funeral on 5 January 1881 attracted an international crowd of two hundred thousand, for a ceremony that lasted most of the day.[28]

NOTES

CHAPTER 1

1. For a brief survey, see Tim Chapman, *The Congress of Vienna* (London: Routledge, 1998).
2. Alan B. Spitzer, *Old Hatreds and Young Hopes: The French Carbonari against the Bourbon Restoration* (Cambridge, MA: Harvard University Press, 1971); and also Sylvia Neely, *Lafayette and the Liberal Ideal, 1814–1824* (Carbondale: Southern Illinois University Press, 1991), 117, 124.
3. Sudhir Hazareesingh, *From Subject to Citizen: the Second Empire and the Emergence of Modern French Democracy* (Princeton University Press: Princeton, New Jersey, 1998); Stanley Hoffman, "The Republican Synthesis," in Hoffman, et al., *In Search of France* (New York: Harper and Row, 1963); Judith F. Stone, *Sons of the Revolution: Radical Democrats in France, 1862–1914* (Baton Rouge: Louisiana State University Press, 1996).
4. Philip Nord, *The Republican Moment* (Cambridge, MA: Harvard University Press, 1995); Katherine Auspitz, *The Radical Bourgeoisie: The Ligue de l'enseignement and the origins of the Third Republic, 1866–1885* (Cambridge, MA: Cambridge University Press, 1982).
5. For a classic Marxist approach, see Sanford Elwitt, *The Making of the Third Republic: Class and Politics in France, 1868–1884* (Baton Rouge: Louisiana State University Press, 1975); and also Sanford Elwitt, *The Third Republic Defended: Bourgeois Reform in France, 1880–1914* (Baton Rouge: Louisiana State University Press, 1986).
6. Maurice Agulhon, *The Republic in the Village*, trans. by Janet Lloyd (Cambridge, MA: Cambridge University Press, 1982); Ronald Aminzade, *Ballots and Barricades: Class Formation and Republican Politics in France, 1830–1871* (Princeton: Princeton University Press, 1993); Edward Berenson, *Populist Religion and Left-Wing Politics in France, 1830–1852* (Princeton: Princeton University Press, 1984); Ted W. Margadant, *French Peasants in Revolt: The Insurrection of 1851* (Princeton: Princeton University Press, 1979); John W. Merriman, *The Agony of the Republic: The Repression of the Left in Revolutionary France* (New Haven: Yale University Press, 1978).
7. François Furet, *La Gauche et la Révolution française au milieu du XIXe siècle: Edgar Quinet et la question du Jacobinisme* (Paris: Hachette, 1986), 12, 14. See also Claude Nicolet, *L'Idée républicaine en France* (Paris: Gallimard, 1982), especially 91–96.
8. Georges Weill, *Histoire du parti républicain en France 1814–1870* (Paris: Ressources, 1980; reprint ed. of 1928 edition), 28.

9. Maurice Agulhon, *Le Cercle dans la France bourgeoise 1810–1848* (Paris: Librairie Armand Colin, 1977); Pamela M. Pilbeam, *Republicanism in Nineteenth-Century France, 1814–1871* (New York: St. Martin's Press, 1995).

10. For Blanqui's belief in the importance of bourgeois leaders of working-class groups, see Alan B. Spitzer, *The Revolutionary Theories of Louis Auguste Blanqui* (New York: AMS Press, 1970), 163.

11. For labor movements, see William H. Sewell, Jr., *Work and Revolution in France: The Language of Labor from the Old Regime to 1848* (Cambridge, MA: Cambridge University Press, 1980); Bernard H. Moss, *The Origins of the French Labor Movement, 1830–1914* (Berkeley: University of California Press, 1976); Christopher H. Johnson, *Utopian Communism in France: Cabet and the Icarians, 1839–1851* (Ithaca: Cornell University Press, 1974); Jacques Rancière, *The Nights of Labor: the Workers' Dream in Nineteenth-Century France*, trans. by John Drury (Philadelphia: Temple University Press, 1989).

12. Patrice Higonnet, *Goodness Beyond Virtue* (Cambridge, MA: Harvard University Press, 1998), 3.

13. *Le Moniteur universel*, 18 December 1839, "Mérilhou's Report," 2154.

14. *L'Égalitaire*, June 1840, 56–57; reprinted in *Les Révolutions du XIXe siècle*, (Paris: EDHIS, 1979), 2nd ser., v. 6. For a classic interpretation of democracy and coercion, J. L. Talmon, *The Origins of Totalitarian Democracy* (New York: Penguin, 1952).

15. David Riches, "The Phenomenon of Violence," in David Riches, ed., *The Anthropology of Violence* (Oxford: Basil Blackwell, 1986), 25.

16. Louis-Auguste Blanqui, "Avis au peuple, 24 February 1851," ms., cited in Suzanne Wassermann, *Les Clubs de Barbès et de Blanqui en 1848* (Geneva: Megariotis Reprints, 1978), 32.

17. *Procès politique des Dix-Neuf Patriotes* (Paris: Prévot, 1831), "Défense de l'accusé Cavaignac," 217; reprinted in *Les Révolutions du XIXe siècle*, 1st ser., v. 11 (Paris: EDHIS, 1974).

18. For example, see Linda J. Nicholson, *Gender and History: the Limits of Social Theory in the Age of the Family* (New York: Columbia University Press, 1986), and Pat Caplan, ed., *The Cultural Construction of Sexuality* (London: Tavistock Publications, 1987).

19. Mark C. Carnes and Clyde Griffen, eds., *Meanings for Manhood: Constructions of Masculinity in Victorian America* (Chicago: University of Chicago Press, 1990), 3.

20. For example: Madelyn Gutwirth, *The Twilight of the Goddesses: Women and Representation in the French Revolutionary Era* (New Brunswick, NJ: Rutgers University Press, 1992); Joan B. Landes, *Women and the Public Sphere in the Age of the French Revolution* (Ithaca, NY: Cornell University Press, 1988); Darline Gay Levy, Harriet Branson Applewhite, and Mary Durham Johnson, *Women in Revolutionary Paris, 1789–1795* (Urbana: University of Illinois Press, 1979); Sara E. Melzer and Leslie W. Rabine, eds., *Rebel Daughters: Women and the French Revolution* (New York: Oxford University Press, 1992); Dorinda Outram, *The Body and the French Revolution: Sex, Class and Political Culture* (New Haven: Yale University Press, 1989). One of the few such studies for the later period is Elinor A. Accampo, Rachel G. Fuchs, and Mary Lynn Stewart, eds., *Gender and the Politics of Social Reform in France, 1870–1914* (Baltimore: Johns Hopkins University Press, 1995).

21. Peter N. Stearns, *Be A Man! Males in Modern Society* (New York: Holmes and Meier, 1979), 59–78.

22. E. Anthony Rotundo, "Learning about Manhood: Gender Ideals and the Middle Class Family in Nineteenth-Century America," in J. A. Mangan and James Walvin, eds., *Manliness and Morality: Middle-Class Masculinity in Britain and America, 1800–1940* (New York: St. Martin's Press, 1987), esp. 36–37.

23. For studies of British and American masculinity, see particularly the recent full-length studies by John Tosh, *A Man's Place: Masculinity and the Middle-Class Home in Victorian England* (New Haven: Yale University Press, 1999); E. Anthony Rotundo, *American Manhood: Transformations in Masculinity from the Revolution to the Modern Era* (New York: Basic Books, 1993).

24. Robert A. Nye, *Masculinity and Male Codes of Honor in Modern France* (New York: Oxford University Press, 1993), 42; see also 31–46.

25. Robert Nye, "The End of the Modern French Duel," in Pieter Spierenburg, ed., *Men and Violence* (Columbus, OH: Ohio State University Press, 1998), 82–95.

26. William M. Reddy, *Money and Liberty in Modern Europe: A critique of Historical Understanding* (Cambridge, MA: Cambridge University Press, 1987),163.

27. Joan Wallach Scott, *Gender and the Politics of History* (New York: Columbia University Press, 1988), 61–67.

28. For an excellent survey of this argument, see William H. Sewell, Jr., "Artisans, Factory Workers, and the Formation of the French Working Class, 1789–1848," in Ira Katznelson and Aristide R. Zolberg, eds., *Working-Class Formation: Nineteenth-Century Patterns in Western Europe and the United States* (Princeton, NJ: Princeton University Press, 1986), 46–70; Alain Cottereau, "Working-Class Cultures, 1848–1900," in Ibid., 111–156.

29. Lenard R. Berlanstein, "The Distinctiveness of the Nineteenth-Century French Labor Movement," *The Journal of Modern History* 64:4 (December 1992),660–685.

30. Tony Judt, *Marxism and the French Left* (Oxford: Oxford University Press, 1986), 73.

31. Gérard Noiriel, *Workers in French Society in the 19th and 20th Centuries* (New York: Berg, 1990), xii.

32. For 1830, see David H. Pinkney, "The Crowd in the French Revolution of 1830," *The American Historical Review*, LXX:1 (October 1964),1–17; for 1832, Alain Faure, "Mouvements populaires et Mouvement ouvrier à Paris (1830–1834)," *Annales. E. S. C.* (1974), 51–92; for May 1839, Claude Latta, "L'Insurrection de 1839," *Blanqui et les Blanquistes: Société d'Histoire de la Révolution de 1848 et des Révolutions du XIXe siècle* (Paris: Sedes, 1986), 69–85; for February, 1848, Mark Traugott, "The Crowd in the French Revolution of February, 1848," *The American Historical Review* 93:3 (June 1988), 638–652; for June 1848, Charles Tilly and Lynn H. Lees, "The People of June, 1848," Roger Price, ed., *Revolution and Reaction: 1848 and the Second French Republic* (London: Croom Helm, 1975), 170–209.

33. See this point about rural influence in Judt, *Marxism and the French Left*, 33.

34. Jacques Rougerie, "Remarques sur l'histoire des salaires à Paris au XIXe siècle," *Le Mouvement social* 63 (1968), 97.

35. See Martin J. Wiener, "The Victorian Criminalization of Men," in Pieter Spierenburg, ed., *Men and Violence*, 197–212.

36. Cour des Pairs, *Attentat du 15 Octobre 1840* (Paris: Imprimerie royale, 1841),119–120.

37. Fulgence Girard, "Le Premier pas de la réaction," *Les Veillées du peuple, Journal mensuel de la Démocratie-socialiste* (November 1849), 45; reprinted in *Les Révolutions du XIXe siècle*, 3rd ser., v. 2 (Paris: EDHIS, 1984).

38. *Gazette des Tribunaux*, 25 April 1836, IIe Conseil de Guerre, Affaire Pesquy.

39. Michael Paul Driskel, "The Proletarian's Body: Charlet's Representations of Social Class during the July Monarchy," in Petra Ten-Doesschate Chu and Gabriel P. Weisberg, eds., *The Popularization of Images: Visual Culture under the July Monarchy* (Princeton, NJ: Princeton University Press, 1994), 58–89. See also the discussion of the proletarian "Hercules" figure during the French Revolution, in Lynn Hunt, *Politics, Culture, and Class in the French Revolution* (Berkeley: University of California Press, 1984), 94–119.

40. For translations of Saint-Simonian women, including Tristan and Voilquin, as well as insightful essays on this group, see Claire Goldberg Moses and Leslie Wahl Rabine, *Feminism, Socialism, and French Romanticism* (Bloomington: Indiana University Press, 1993). See also Claire Goldberg Moses, *French Feminism in the Nineteenth Century* (Albany: State University of New York Press, 1984).

41. *Le Populaire*, 13 November 1842, cited and translated in Johnson, *Utopian Communism in France*, 173.

42. Judith F. Stone, "The Republican Brotherhood: Gender and Ideology," in Accampo, Fuchs, and Stewart, *Gender and the Politics of Social Reform*, 35.

43. For emulation as a male-centered concept, Thomas Crow, *Emulation: Making Artists for Revolutionary France* (New Haven: Yale University Press, 1995).

44. Elizabeth Eisenstein, *The First Professional Revolutionist: Filippo Michele Buonarroti* (Cambridge, MA: Harvard University Press, 1959), 98.

45. Hayden White, *Metahistory: The Historical Imagination in Nineteenth-Century Europe* (Baltimore: The Johns Hopkins University Press, 1973), 8.

46. "Du Peuple," *Le Travail*, No. 3, September 1841, 22–23; reprinted in *Les Révolutions du XIXe siècle*, 1st ser., vol. 12.

47. Mary Jo Maynes, *Taking the Hard Road* (Chapel Hill, NC: University of North Carolina Press, 1995). The Fall, 1992 issue of *Social Science History* was devoted to this subject, most notably William H. Sewell, Jr., "Introduction: Narratives and Social Identities," *Social Science History* 16:3 (Fall 1992), 479–488; and George Steinmetz, "Reflections on the Role of Social Narratives in Working-Class Formation: Narrative Theory in the Social Sciences," *Social Science History* 16:3 (Fall 1992), 489–516.

48. *Le Populaire*, 20 June 1841, "Revue judiciaire: Exécution de Darmès"; see also *Le National*, 2 June 1841.

49. From BN, n.a.f. 9582, cited in Auguste Blanqui, *Instructions pour une prise d'armes*, ed. by Miguel Abensour and Valentin Pelosse (Paris: Société encyclopédique française, 1973), 59n.

50. Lawrence Stone, "The Revival of Narrative: Reflections on a New Old History," in *The Past and the Present* (Boston: Routledge and Kegan Paul, 1981), 74.

51. Keith Jenkins, "Introduction: On Being Open about our Closures," in *The Postmodern History Reader* (London: Routledge, 1997), 6–7.

52. Robert F. Berkhofer, Jr., *Beyond the Great Story* (Cambridge, MA: Harvard University Press, 1995), 37.

53. Hayden White, *The Content of the Form: Narrative Discourse and Historical Representation* (Baltimore: The Johns Hopkins University Press, 1987), ix.

54. Louis O. Mink, "Narrative Form as a Cognitive Instrument," in Robert H. Canary and Henry Kozicki, *The Writing of History* (Madison, WI: The University of Wisconsin Press, 1978), 144–145.

55. Lynn Hunt, "History as Gesture; or, The Scandal of History," in Jonathan Arac and Barbara Johnson, eds., *Consequences of Theory* (Baltimore: Johns Hopkins University Press, 1991), 103.

56. *Obsèques de Godefroy Cavaignac* (Paris: Lange Lévy, 1845), 10–11, reprinted in *Les Révolutions du XIX siècle*, 2nd ser., v. 4 (Paris: EDHIS, 1979).

CHAPTER 2

1. Cour des Pairs, *Attentat du 29 juillet 1846* (Paris: Imprimerie royale, 1846), 131. All subsequent judicial references, including the *Lettre* and the *Préméditation*, are from this printed source (cited as *1846*) unless otherwise noted.

2. Jacques Rancière, *The Nights of Labor: the Workers' Dream in Nineteenth-Century France*, translated from the French by John Drury (Philadelphia: Temple University Press, 1989); see also Edgar Leon Newman, "Sounds in the Desert: the Socialist Worker Poets of the Bourgeois Monarchy, 1830–1848," in *Proceedings of the Third Annual Meeting of the Western Society for French History* (1975), 269–299.

3. Adolphe Boyer, *De l'État des ouvriers et de son amélioration par l'organisation du travail*, 2nd ed. (Paris: Mme. Veuve Boyer, 1841); Paul Chauvet, *Les Ouvriers du livre en France* (Paris: Marcel Rivière, 1964), 165–168. For contemporary reviews, see *Le Populaire*, 10 October 1841, and "Suicide d'Adolphe Boyer," in Ibid., 13 November 1841.

4. Jacques Rancière, "Ronds de fumée: les poètes ouvriers dans la France de Louis Philippe," *Revue des sciences humaines* LXI:190 (April–June 1983), 31–37.

5. *Préméditation*, 155; *Lettre*, 83.

6. *Préméditation*, 97. The neighbors observed this habit; see *1846*, dep[osition] Cercleron, 86, Leroux, 84.

7. *1846*, 5th dep. Henry, 28. For the dates of composition, see *Lettre*, 37, 101.

8. *1846*, 2nd dep. Henry, 16; *Le Moniteur universel*, 21 August 1846, 2181.

9. *Lettre*, 16.

10. *Lettre*, 48.

11. *Le Moniteur universel*, 21 August 1846, "Rapport . . . par Laplagne-Barris," 2182.

12. *Préméditation*, 198–199.

13. Ibid.

14. Ibid., 184.

15. *Lettre*, 17.

16. *1846*, dep. Somiliana, 100.

17. *1846*, dep. Chevalier, 62–63.

18. Ibid., 62–64. For Henry's view of her (she was "accoutumé au vice" and became a drunk), see *Préméditation*, 176–177, 188–189; see also *La Démocratie pacifique*, 1 August 1846, "Nouveaux détails sur Joseph Henry."

19. *Préméditation*, 188–189.

20. *Lettre*, 18.

21. Ibid., 18–19.

22. Ibid., 20.

23. *Le Moniteur universel*, 27 August 1846, 2255.

24. *Lettre*, 20–21. Henry's foreman shared his view of Lemaury; *1846*, dep. Mercier, 71.

25. *Lettre*, 20.

26. Ibid., 23–24.

27. *Préméditation*, 189, 151–152; see also *1846*, dep. Louise Henry, 60–61.

28. *1846*, 3rd dep. Henry, 17.

29. Ibid.

30. *Préméditation*, 132, 152; and *1846*, dep. Frédéric Henry, 61.

31. *1846*, deps. Lamaury, femme Bacquet, 67, 68; and *Lettre*, 25.

32. *Lettre*, 21.

33. Ibid., 27–28.

34. Ibid., 28.

35. Ibid., 30.

36. Ibid., 31, 72.

37. *1846*, 5th dep. Henry, 26–27. He saw his first hunchback in the Tuileries garden; see *Lettre*, 42–43. A friend mentioned his own "repugnance" for Henry's preferences; *1846*, dep. Guérin, 86–87.

38. *Lettre*, 31–32, 34; see also *1846*, dep. Aymes, 91.

39. *Lettre*, 32–33.

40. Ibid., 33; the investigation confirmed Henry's account of their agreement. See *Le Moniteur universel*, 21 August 1846, "Rapport . . . par M. Laplagne-Barris," 2182.

41. *Lettre*, 93.

42. Henry's employees: *1846*, dep. Mocquet, 77; dep. Fonssard, 68; dep. Delaforêt, 69; dep. L'Hotel, 70; dep. Mercier, 71; dep. Philippe, 76; dep. Bernard, 81.

43. *1846*, dep. Petit, 80.

44. Ibid., dep. Péregaux, 76.

45. Tilly and Lees, "The People of June 1848," 175. His factory was medium-sized; the two largest factories in Paris during the 1820s were both in the faubourg Saint-Antoine, occupying 110 and 90 workers. Maurice Moissonnier, "Des origines à 1871," in *La France ouvrière et du mouvement ouvrier français*, v. 1: *Des origines à 1920*, ed. Claude Willard (Paris: Éditions sociales, 1993), 63–64.

46. *1846*, dep. Chatenoud, 79.

47. Jean Tulard, *Les Révolutions* (Paris: Fayard, 1985), 362–363, 365–366.

48. *La Démocratie pacifique*, 2 August 1846, "Lettres de Joseph Henry."

49. See Michael Sonenscher, "Journeymen's Migrations and Workshop Organization in Eighteenth-Century France," in Steven Laurence Kaplan and Cynthia J. Koepp, eds., *Work in France: Representations, Meaning, Organization, and Practice* (Ithaca: Cornell University Press, 1986), 76, 93.

50. See the discussions in William H. Sewell, Jr., "Artisans, Factory Workers, and the Formation of the French Working Class, 1789–1848," in Ira Katznelson and Aristide R. Zolberg, eds., *Working Class Formation: Nineteenth-Century Patterns in Western Europe and the United States* (Princeton, NJ: Princeton University Press, 1986), 45–70, which discusses this process and political consciousness in detail.

51. Victor Considérant, *Principes du Socialisme manifeste de la Démocratie au XIXe siècle* (Paris: Librairie Phalanstérienne, 1847), 6–11, 23–24; reprinted in *Les Révolutions du XIXe siècle*, 2nd series, v. 4 (Paris: EDHIS, 1979); Étienne Cabet, *Douze Lettres d'un Communiste* (Paris, 1841), 41–44; reprinted in *Les Révolutions du XIXe siècle*, 2nd ser., v. 5; Louis Blanc, *Organisation du Travail*, in J. A. R. Marriott, ed., *The French Revolution of 1848* (Oxford: the Clarendon Press, 1913), I:61, 77, 85–88; A. Ott, *Des Associations des ouvriers* (Paris: Poussin, 1838[?]), 3, 6 (a disciple of Buchez). For the Caillard and Laffitte case, see Blanc, *Organisation du travail*, 79–80.

52. Considérant, *Principes du Socialisme*, 9.

53. Jules Leroux, "Aux ouvriers typographes," 1833, in Alain Faure and Jacques Rancière, eds., *La Parole ouvrière, 1830–1851*, (Paris: Union générale d'Éditions, 1976), 93–94.

54. *Lettre*, 46; also Charles Noiret, "Deuxième Lettre aux Travailleurs," in Faure and Rancière, *La Parole ouvrière*, 132–133.

55. *Le Moniteur universel*, 26 August 1846, dep. Fontaine, 2244. Marie-Hyacinthe Chartron, a *quincaillier* [ironmonger], had lent Henry 1,600 francs, its repayment long overdue ("Je ne le pressais pas parce que je le savais gêné"). *1846*, dep. Chartron, 90.

56. *Préméditation*, 178.

57. *L'Atelier*, July 1841, 87; Ibid., 28 February 1843, "De la discipline des ateliers," 44.

58. *Préméditation*, 154; see also 192–193.

59. Ibid., 167.

60. His letters to philanthropist Victor Richard, another member, were published in *La Démocratie pacifique*, 2 August 1846, "Lettres de Joseph Henry."

61. *1846*, dep. Debucourt, 82–83.

62. Alain Cottereau, "Étude préalable" to Denis Poulot, *Question sociale: Le sublime, ou le travailleur comme il est en 1870 et ce qu'il peut être* (Paris: François Maspero, 1980), 46–48. For a discussion of Poulot, see Jacques Rancière, "The Myth of the Artisan," in Kaplan and Koepp, eds., *Work in France*, 330.

63. *La Démocratie pacifique*, 1 August 1846, "Nouveaux détails sur Joseph Henry"; Ibid., 2 August 1846, "Lettres de Joseph Henry"; *1846*, dep. Somiliana, 101.

64. *La Démocratie pacifique*, 1 July 1848, "Leçons pour tous et à tous!" by Victor Considérant; Blanc, *Organisation du Travail*, 114; Bernard H. Moss, *The Origins of the French Labor Movement, 1830–1914* (Berkeley: University of California Press, 1976),43–44.

65. David Landes, *The Unbound Prometheus* (Cambridge, MA: Cambridge University Press, 1969), 155.

66. Philip T. Hoffman, Gilles Postel-Vinay, and Jean-Laurent Rosenthal, *Priceless Markets: The Political Economy of Credit in Paris* (Chicago: University of Chicago Press, 2000), 256.

67. *Lettre*, 49–50.

68. Ibid., 53.

69. *Jacques Étienne Bédé, Un Ouvrier en 1820*, Rémi Gossez, ed. (Paris: PUF, 1984), 21, 23–24.

70. *1846*, dep. Montjoye, femme Guérin, 88.

71. *Lettre*, 47.

72. *1846, Réquisitoire et réplique prononcés par M. Hébert, Procureur-Général du Roi*, 17.

73. *1846*, 11th dep. Henry, 68. See also *Le Moniteur universel*, 26 August 1846, dep. Henry, 2239.

74. Martin Nadaud, *Mémoires de Léonard, ancien garçon maçon*, Maurice Agulhon, ed. (Paris: Hachette, 1976), 100. The militant Norbert Truquin noted "qu'on refusait du travail aux hommes de cinquante ans." Norbert Truquin, *Mémoires et aventures d'un prolétaire à travers la révolution* (Paris: François Maspero, 1977), 52.

75. *Le Moniteur universel*, 27 August 1846, *Réquisitoire* of Procureur-Général Hébert, 2255.

76. *1846*, dep. Debucourt, 82–83.

77. *Le Moniteur universel*, 28 May 1846, "Rapport . . . par M. Franck Carré," 1539.

78. *Le Moniteur universel*, 30 May 1846, letter from Lecomte of 15 January 1844, cited in *Acte d'accusation*, 1568; and Ibid., 5 June 1846, deps. Bois d'Hyver (Lecomte's superior) and Lecomte, 1655.

79. He was given 388 francs per year. *Le Moniteur universel*, 30 May 1846, *Acte d'accusation*, 1568; see also Ibid., 5 June 1846, dep. Montalivet (*intendant général de la liste civile*), 1652.

80. *Le Moniteur universel*, 28 May 1846, "Rapport . . . par M. Franck Carré, 1540, including letter from Lecomte to Louis Philippe on 20 October 1844.

81. *Le Moniteur universel*, 28 May 1846, "Rapport . . . par M. Franck-Carré," 1537; Ibid., 5 June 1846, dep. Lecomte, 1651.

82. *Le Moniteur universel*, 6 June 1846, 1671. See also *La Démocratie pacifique*, 8–9 June 1846, "Exécution de Lecomte."

83. *Préméditation*, 159.

84. *1846*, 2nd dep. Henry, 13, 14.

85. *Préméditation*, 159.

86. *Le Moniteur universel*, 26 August 1846, dep. Henry, 2239–2240, 2242.

87. *Préméditation*, 160–161.

88. *Lettre*, 82–83.

89. Ibid., 83. Henry felt the departure of his workers as a desertion, but some left because they needed regular work; *1846*, dep. Milcent, 78. By the writing of the *Préméditation*, the loss of workers had become a more rapid drain: "ils s'ap- perçoivent de ma misère et petit à petit ils s'en vont"). *Préméditation*, 155.

90. See Peter Temin, "Entrepreneurs and Managers," in Patrice Higonnet, David S. Landes, and Henry Rosovsky, eds., *Favorites of Fortune* (Cambridge, MA: Harvard University Press, 1991), 339–355.

91. *Préméditation*, 156.

92. Ibid., 163, 177–187.

93. "Discours du citoyen Agricol Perdiguier" (Paris: Durand, 1848), 7; reprinted in *Les Révolutions du XIXe siècle*, 3rd ser., v. 2(Paris: EDHIS, 1984).

94. *Préméditation*, 215.

95. Ibid., 187.

96. *Lettre*, 93–94.

97. *1846*, dep. Roussel, *officier de paix*, 7; dep. Villers, 34; dep. Legros, *sergent de ville*, 7–8; dep. Ingouf, 27; dep. Ulm, 18; and the depositions of seven other men, either in the police or in the armed forces, who had assisted in the capture, 7–11. See also *Le Moniteur universel*, 26 August 1846, Cour des Pairs, 2240; and for the witnesses, 2242–2243.

98. Abbé Grivel, *La Prison du Luxembourg sous la règne de Louis-Philippe* (Paris: Auguste Vaton, 1862), 300; Lucien Delahodde, *Histoire des sociétés secrètes et du parti républicain de 1830 à 1848* (Paris: Julien, Lanier, et cie, 1850), 505.

99. Michael Sonenscher, "Mythical Work: Workshop Production and the Compagnonnages of Eighteenth-Century France," in Patrick Joyce, ed., *The Historical Meanings of Work* (Cambridge, MA: Cambridge University Press, 1987), 53.

CHAPTER 3

1. For accounts of the revolution, see David H. Pinkney, *The French Revolution of 1830* (Princeton: Princeton University Press, 1972); Jean-Louis Bory, *La Révolution de Juillet* (Paris: Gallimard, 1972); John M. Merriman, ed., *1830 in France*

(New York: Franklin Watts, 1975); Guillaume Bertier de Sauvigny, *Au Soir de la Monarchie: histoire de la Restauration* (Paris: Flammarion, 1955).

2. Prosper Duvergier de Hauranne, *Histoire du gouvernement parlementaire en France* (Paris: Michel Lévy frères, 1871), X:651–652.

3. Pinkney, *The French Revolution*, 59–66; André Jardin and André-Jean Tudesq, *Restoration and Reaction, 1815–1848*, trans. Elborg Forster (Cambridge, MA: Cambridge University Press, 1983), 93–94.

4. Achille de Vaulabelle, *Histoire des deux Restaurations* (Paris: Perrotin, 1857), VIII:92, 94; Pamela Pilbeam, "The Growth of Liberalism and the Crisis of the Bourbon Restoration, 1827–1830," *The Historical Journal* 25:2 (1982), 351.

5. *Procès des ex-ministres*, 2nd ed., 3 vols. (Paris: Librairie Roret, [1831]), II:17–20.

6. Pinkney, "The Crowd in the French Revolution of 1830," *The American Historical Review* 70:1 (October, 1964), 3–8, 15; Pinkney, *The French Revolution*, 121, 252–257, 269–271; F. L. Poumiès de la Siboutie, *Souvenirs d'un médecin dans les journées immortelles des 26, 27, 28, et 29 juillet 1830* (Paris: Guyot, 1830), 207–208.

7. Edgar Leon Newman, "The Blouse and Frock Coat," *Journal of Modern History* 46:1 (March 1974), esp. 27, 43–49. See also R. S. Alexander, "Restoration Republicanism Reconsidered," *French History* 8:4 (December 1994), 443–447.

8. Armand Carrel, *Oeuvres politiques et littéraires d'Armand Carrel*, 5 vols. (Paris: Librairie de F. Chamerot, 1857), I:141–142.

9. Ferdinand-Philippe d'Orléans, *Souvenirs*, Hervé Robert, ed. (Geneva: Droz, 1993), 320.

10. Jacques Laffitte, *Mémoires de Laffitte 1767–1844*, ed. by Paul Duchon (Paris: Firmin-Didot, n.d.), 143; R.-G. Nobécourt, *La Vie d'Armand Carrel* (Paris: Librairie Gallimard, 1930), 38ff, 64–65, 74–76; Daniel L. Rader, *The Journalists and the July Revolution in France* (The Hague: Martinus Niijhoff, 1973), 112–116.

11. Cited in Louis Blanc, *The History of Ten Years, 1830–1840*, 2 vols., trans. Walter K. Kelly (Philadelphia: Lea & Blanchard, 1848), I:185–186.

12. Blanc, *History of Ten Years*, I:186.

13. Odilon Barrot, *Mémoires posthumes de Odilon Barrot*, 2nd ed., 4 vols. (Paris: Charpentier et cie, 1875), I:104.

14. Guy Antonetti, *Louis-Philippe* (Paris: Arthème Fayard, 1994), esp. 13–31.

15. Rodolphe Apponyi, *Journal du Comte Rodolphe Apponyi*, 4 vols. (Paris: Plon, 1913), I:259–261.

16. Étienne-Denis Pasquier, *Mémoires du Chancelier Pasquier*, 6 vols. (Paris: Plon, 1895), VI:290, 307–309; Laffitte, *Mémoires*, 179.

17. Vaulabelle, *Histoire*, VIII:267–288, 336–337. For the *Amis du Peuple*, see "Manifeste de la Société des Amis du peuple" (Paris, 1830), and "Règlement de la Société des Amis du peuple" (Paris: David, 1830), both reprinted in *Les Révolutions du XIXe siècle*, 1st ser., vol. 2.

18. F. Rittiez, *Histoire du règne de Louis-Philippe Ier, 1830 à 1848*, 3 vols. (Paris: V. Lecou, 1855), I:33–34.

19. Pinkney, *The French Revolution of 1830*, 139–140n. For the *carbonari*, an underground group that included future liberal and republican middle-class leaders, see Alan B. Spitzer, *Old Hatreds and Young Hopes: The French Carbonari against the Bourbon Restoration* (Cambridge, MA: Harvard University Press, 1971).

20. Vaulabelle, *Histoire*, VIII:352–353.

21. Vaulabelle, *Histoire*, VIII:347–353; Barrot, *Mémoires*, I:110–111.

22. "No. 6, Pièces justificatives," in A. Bérard, *Souvenirs historiques sur la Révolution de 1830* (Paris: Perrotin, 1834), 489–490.

23. B. Sarrans, *Louis-Philippe et la Contre-Révolution de 1830*, 2 vols. (Paris: Thoisnier-Desplaces, 1834), I:274–275; Bérard, *Souvenirs*, 123–124.

24. "Pièces justificatives," in Bérard, *Souvenirs*, 494, 497; Duvergier de Hauranne, *Histoire*, X:616–621.

25. Sarrans, *Louis-Philippe*, I:24–25.

26. Guillaume Bertier de Sauvigny, ed., *La Révolution de 1830 en France* (Paris: Armand Colin, 1970), 190–191.

27. Bérard, *Souvenirs*, 128–131; Sarrans, *Louis-Philippe*, II:15.

28. Bérard, *Souvenirs*, 146; François-Pierre-Guillaume Guizot, *Mémoires pour servir à l'histoire de mon temps*, 8 vols. (Paris: Michel Lévy frères, 1872), II:29.

29. Laffitte, *Mémoires*, 195, 198–200; Blanc, *The History of Ten Years*, I:198.

30. Laffitte, *Mémoires*, 204–205.

31. Blanc, *History of Ten Years*, I:202–203; Rittiez, *Histoire du règne*, I:58–59.

32. Duvergier de Hauranne, *Histoire*, X:623–625; Vaulabelle, *Histoire*, VIII:592–593.

33. Armand Marrast, *Programme de l'Hôtel de Ville* (Paris: Rouant, 1831), cited in Étienne Charavay, *Le Général La Fayette* (Paris: Société de l'Histoire de la Révolution française, 1898), 476.

34. Duvergier de Hauranne, *Histoire*, X:674–675.

35. "Manifeste de la Société des amis du Peuple," 8.

36. Guizot, *Mémoires*, II:22–23.

37. Auguste Fabre, *La Révolution de 1830, et le véritable parti républicain*, 2 vols. (Paris: Thoisnier-Desplaces, 1833), I:v, lxviii-lxxvii, 141–143.

38. *Procès politique des Dix-Neuf Patriotes*, (Paris: Prévot, 1831), *Plaidoirie* of Rittiez, 173; reprinted in *Les Révolutions du XiXe siècle*, 1st ser., vol. 11.

39. Rittiez, *Histoire du règne*, I:123; Bérard, *Souvenirs*, 399; Pinkney, *The French Revolution*, 188; Maurice de la Fuye, *Rouget de Lisle Inconnu* (Paris: Hachette, 1943), 268–269.

40. Apponyi, *Journal*, I:302–303; I:296.

41. Archives nationales [AN], F9 682, letter to General Comte Gérard, from aide-de-camp Sougnier, 13 August 1830.

42. Louis Girard, *La Garde nationale, 1814–1871* (Paris: Librairie Plon, 1964), 196–201.

43. François Furet, *Revolutionary France, 1770–1880* (Oxford: Blackwell, 1988), 361.

44. Girard, *La Garde nationale*, 201.

45. Jean Tulard, *Les Révolutions* (Paris: Fayard, 1985), 336.

46. Christophe Charle, *A Social History of France in the 19th Century* (Oxford: Berg, 1994), 29; for 1846, Pamela Pilbeam, "Republicanism in Early Nineteenth-Century France, 1814–1835," *French History* 5:1 (March 1991), 40.

47. Jean Touchard, *Histoire des idées politiques*, 2 vols. (Paris: Presses universitaires de France, 1967), II:523–525. See also Pamela Pilbeam, "The 'Liberal' Revolution of 1830," *Historical Research* LXIII (1990), 162–163, 171–173.

48. Victor de Nouvion, *Histoire du règne de Louis-Philippe Ier*, 4 vols. (Paris: Didier et cie, 1857), III:166–169; Rittiez, *Histoire du règne*, I:241–243, 371. For *l'Association libre*, its "Réglement" (Paris: 1833); reprinted in *Les Révolutions du XIXe siècle*, 1st ser., vol. 1.

49. Armand Cuvillier, *P.-J.-B. Buchez et les origines du socialisme chrétien* (Paris: Presses universitaires de France, 1948), 10–19, 28–34; *Le Globe*, 10 October 1830, letter from Buchez, et al.

50. Newman, "The Blouse and the Frock Coat," 44–45; I. Tchernoff, *Le Parti républicain sous la Monarchie de Juillet* (Paris: A. Pedone, 1901), 248–250.

51. Dora B. Weiner, "François-Vincent Raspail: Doctor and Champion of the Poor," *French Historical Studies* I:2 (1959), 151–161.

52. Georges Weill, "Philippe Buonarroti," *Revue historique* 76 (1901), 255–275; Alessandro Galante Garrone, *Philippe Buonarroti et les révolutionnaires du XIXe siècle* (Paris: Éditions Champ Libre, 1975), 14–27, 40–63; Blanc, *History of Ten Years*, II:186–187 (for Jean-Baptiste).

53. *Le Globe*, 22 and 25 January 1831.

54. Rittiez, *Histoire du règne*, I:147.

55. Cited in André-Jacques Dupin, *Mémoires de M. Dupin*, 4 vols. (Paris: Henri Plon, 1855), II:237, 238–239; Guizot, *Mémoires*, II:111–115.

56. Nouvion, *Histoire du règne*, II:70; "Procès-verbal de la Séance du 25 Septembre 1830," in *Les Révolutions du XIXe siècle*, 1st ser., vol. 2; Rittiez, *Histoire du règne*, I:150–151; *Le National*, 30 September 1830.

57. See Benjamin F. Martin, *Crime and Criminal Justice Under the Third Republic* (Baton Rouge, LA: Louisiana State University Press, 1990), 125–156 for an historical survey.

58. Adhémar Esmein, *A History of Continental Criminal Procedure with Special Reference to France*, trans. John Simpson (Boston: Little, Brown, and Company, 1913), 507–508.

59. *Procès politique des Dix-Neuf Patriotes* (Paris: Prévot, 1831), reprinted in *Les Révolutions du XiXe siècle*, 1st ser., vol. 11 (Paris: EDHIS 1974), 108–109; the *Familles* rule in *Le Moniteur universel*, 15 June 1839, 973.

60. *La Propagande*, October 1839, "Des arrestations et des détentions préventives"; reprinted in *Les Révolutions du XIXe siècle*, 1st ser., vol. 12; Adolphe Chauveau and Faustin Hélie, *Théorie du code pénal*, 2nd ed., 6 vols. (Paris: Édouard Legrand, 1843), I:274–276.

61. AN BB18 1335, "Interior to Justice," 4 May 1833, cited in Gabriel Perreux, *Aux Temps des Sociétés Secrètes* (Paris: Rieder, 1931), 307.

62. Gordon Wright, *Between the Guillotine and Liberty* (New York: Oxford University Press, 1983), 27, 39–40; Esmein, *A History*, 498–499, 509–511.

63. Bernard Schnapper, "Le jury français aux XIX et XXème siècles," in *The Trial Jury in England, France, Germany 1700–1900*, ed. Dr. Antonio Padoa Schioppa (Berlin: Duncker et Humblot, 1987), 180–187. For contemporary complaints, see *Le National*, 10 July 1832, "De l'influence du gouvernement dans la composition des listes des jurés"; and 11 November 1833, "Le jury attaqué par les hommes du 7 août."

64. Esmein, *A History*, 514, 535, 484.

65. Schnapper, "Le jury français," 177–178.

66. Esmein, *A History*, 534; and see Schnapper, "Le jury français," 177–178.

67. Martin, *Crime and Criminal Justice*, 194, 195.

68. Jules Sambuc, "Aux Étudiants" (Paris: C. F. Benoist, 1 December 1830), 6; reprinted in *Les Révolutions du XIXe siècle*, 1st ser., vol. 7.

69. *Gazette des Tribunaux*, 13 April 1831; *Procès politique des Dix-Neuf*, 133, 5.

70. *Gazette des Tribunaux*, 6 April 1831, *Acte d'accusation*.

71. *Gazette des Tribunaux*, 6 April 1831, *Acte d'accusation*.

72. *Gazette des Tribunaux*, 6 April 1831, *Acte d'accusation; Procès politique des Dix-Neuf*, 7.

73. *Gazette des Tribunaux*, 11 April 1831, deps. Fourchon, Leclere.

74. *Gazette des Tribunaux*, 8 April 1831, dep. Danton.

75. *Gazette des Tribunaux*, 6 April 1831, *Acte d'accusation; Procès politique des Dix-Neuf*, 45–49.

76. *Procès politique des Dix-Neuf*, 50.

77. Ibid., 115–116.

78. *Gazette des Tribunaux*, 12 April 1831, dep. Boirot; *Procès politique des Dix-Neuf*, 117.

79. *Gazette des Tribunaux*, 12 April 1831, dep. Joly.

80. Rittiez, *Histoire du règne*, I:241.

81. "Exposé des motifs de la Délibération du 2 février 1831" (Paris: Prévot, 1831), 5, 10–15; reprinted in *Les Révolutions du XIX siècle*, 1st ser., vol. 2, which also includes several of the brochures.

82. *Procès politique de la sixième brochure des Amis du Peuple* (Paris: David, [1831]), 4, reprinted in *Les Révolutions du XIXe siècle*, 1st ser., vol. 2.

83. Rittiez, *Histoire du règne*, I:328.

84. *Gazette des Tribunaux*, 18 June 1831, "Chronique"; and 19 June 1831, "Chronique." The full brochure in *Les Révolutions du XIXe siècle*, 1st ser., vol. 2.

85. *Procès des Quinze* (Paris: Levasseur, 1832), 11–12; reprinted in *Les Révolutions du XIXe siècle*, 1st ser., vol. 2.

86. *Procès des Quinze*, 145, 149; see also Guizot, *Mémoires*, II:205–206.

87. For example, *Gazette des Tribunaux*, 15 December 1831, and 24 February 1832.

88. Henri-Joseph Gisquet, *Mémoires de M. Gisquet*, 4 vols. (Paris: Marchant, 1840), II:168–169. Gisquet was the controversial prefect of police through the most volatile period of the reign, from 26 November 1831 to 10 September 1836; Gabriel Delessert served until the end of the regime. Jean Tulard, *La Préfecture de police sous la monarchie de juillet* (Paris: Imprimerie municipale, 1964), 40–47.

89. *Procès du droit d'association* (Paris: Auguste Mie, 1833), reprinted in *Les Révolutions du XIXe siècle*, 1st ser., vol. 2. For the other case, *Gazette des Tribunaux*, 12 August 1832; Rittiez, *Histoire du règne*, I:366, II:8–10.

90. See Fernand Rudé, *C'est nous les canuts* (Paris: François Maspero, 1977).

91. See Jo Burr Margadant, "The Duchesse de Berry and Royalist Political Culture in Postrevolutionary France," *History Workshop Journal* 43 (Spring 1997), 39–43.

92. William Coleman, *Death is a Social Disease: Public Health and Political Economy in Early Industrial France* (Madison: University of Wisconsin, 1982), 172–180.

93. Gisquet, *Mémoires*, I:465–466; Nouvion, *Histoire*, II:566–567.

94. Poumiès de la Siboutie, *Souvenirs*, 236–237.

95. For Périer, see Carrel's unflattering eulogy in *Le National*, 17 May 1832; for Lamarque, see Rittiez, *Histoire du règne*, I:211–212; *Le National*, 3 June 1832, letter of J. V. Lavallée (Lamarque's secretary).

96. *Le National*, 5 June 1832, "Funérailles du Général Lamarque."

97. Blanc, *History of Ten Years*, II:42–44; see also Rittiez, *Histoire du règne*, II:12.

98. Gisquet, *Mémoires*, II:205–207; Rittiez, *Histoire du règne*, II:12–14; B. Sarrans, *Lafayette et la Révolution de 1830*, 2 vols. (Paris: Thoisnier Desplaces, 1833), II:373–375.

99. Rittiez, *Histoire du règne*, II:13–14 (1st quotation); Gisquet, *Mémoires*, II:207–209 (2nd); Blanc, *History of Ten Years*, II:45.

100. Rittiez, *Histoire du règne*, II:14; Sarrans, *Lafayette*, II:377; Gisquet, *Mémoires*, II:207–209.

101. *Gazette des Tribunaux*, 18–19 June 1832, *Affaire du sieur Geoffroy*.

102. Blanc, *History of Ten Years*, II:47; Gisquet, *Mémoires*, II:210–211.

103. Rittiez, *Histoire du règne*, II:15–16; Gisquet, *Mémoires*, II:211–212.

104. For 1830, Pinkney estimates 10,300 to 11,500 soldiers (*The French* Revolution, 102).

105. Gisquet, *Mémoires*, II:213–217; Rittiez, *Histoire du règne*, II:16.

106. Gisquet, *Mémoires*, II:222–223; Antonetti, *Louis-Philippe*, 693.

107. *Gazette des Tribunaux*, 3–4 September 1832.

108. Gisquet, *Mémoires*, II:224–231; *Gazette des Tribunaux*, 16 June 1832, Rapport de M. le Général Schramm; Girard, *La Garde nationale*, 239.

109. Apponyi, *Journal*, II:215.

110. *Gazette des Tribunaux*, 16 June 1832, Rapport de M. le Général Tiburce Sébastiani.

111. Gisquet, *Mémoires*, II:237–238 (military figures); Rittiez, *Histoire du règne*, II:20; Girard, *La Garde nationale*, 239n; *Le National*, 21 June 1832, "Nouveau bulletin sur les affaires des 5 et 6 juin."

112. Faure, "Mouvements populaires," 78. (The construction, metal, leather, and clothing trades.)

113. Gisquet, *Mémoires*, II:238–239, 241.

114. Ibid., II:260–266; Paul Thureau-Dangin, *Histoire de la Monarchie de Juillet*, 3rd. ed., 7 vols. (Paris: Plon, 1902), II:137–139.

115. *Gazette des Tribunaux*, 10 June 1832; Ibid., 1 August 1832.

116. *Gazette des Tribunaux*, 22 September 1832.

117. Gisquet, *Mémoires*, II:281–283; Chauveau and Hélie, *Theorie du Code pénal*, I:109–110.

118. *Gazette des Tribunaux*, 24 August 1832; *La Réforme*, 16 November 1843.

119. *Gazette des Tribunaux*, 24 August 1832, *Affaire Cuny*; *Le National*, 1 October 1832, "La Tribune"; S. Posener, *Adolphe Crémieux*, 2 vols. (Paris: Félix Alcan, 1933), I:146.

120. *Gazette des Tribunaux*, 7 October 1832.

121. *Gazette des Tribunaux*, 18 October 1832, and 9 November 1832, and 29 December 1834.

122. *Gazette des Tribunaux*, 22 November 1832; *Prospert (ouvrier tailleur) devant ses juges* (Paris: Rouannet, 1832), reprinted in *Les révolutions du XIX siècle*, 1st ser., v. 11.

123. *Gazette des Tribunaux*, 29 September 1832, *Affaire du passage du Saumon*.

124. Blanc, *History of Ten Years*, II:61, 64. The Paris population was 785,000 in 1831; see H. A. C. Collingham, *The July Monarchy* (London: Longman, 1988), 332.

125. *Procès des Vingt-Deux Accusés du Cloître Saint-Méry* (Paris: Rouanet, 1832), 12–13; reprinted in *Les Révolutions du XIXe siècle*, 1st ser., vol. 11.

126. Gisquet, *Mémoires*, II:277–278. See also *Gazette des Tribunaux*, 24 October 1832.

127. *Procès des Vingt-Deux Accusés*, 39, 19.

128. *Procès des Vingt-Deux Accusés*, deps. Claris, 47, and others, 44–45; Gisquet, *Mémoires*, II:276–277.

129. *Procès des Vingt-Deux Accusés*, dep. Gravelle, 43.

130. *Procès des Vingt-Deux Accusés*, 47, 59.

131. Carrel, *Oeuvres*, III:142.

132. *Procès des Vingt-Deux Accusés*, 58.

133. *Procès des Vingt-Deux Accusés*, deps. Delair, Liembert, Thibaudot, 60–63; *Gazette des Tribunaux*, 27 October 1832.

134. *Procès des Vingt-Deux Accusés*, dep. Dessolliers, 74–77; *Gazette des Tribunaux*, 29–30 October 1832.

135. *Gazette des Tribunaux*, 1 November 1832.
136. *Le National*, 9 August 1833, letter to the minister of commerce and public works.
137. *Le National*, 4 May 1834, letter from Charles Jeanne.
138. *La Tribune*, 9 September 1834; letter of Olivier Dufresne, in *le Moniteur universel*, 9 September 1834, 1804. For his death, see *Le National*, 16 June 1844.

CHAPTER 4

1. CC586, doss. *Faits généraux*, nos. 18 and 19, letters of Gallay.
2. A small SDHC had existed in 1830, affiliated with the *Amis;* the name was co-opted. Henri-Joseph Gisquet, *Mémoires de M. Gisquet*, 4 vols. (Paris: Marchant, 1840), III:64; see the August 1830 "Déclaration de principes de la Société des droits de l'homme et du citoyen," in *Les Révolutions du XIXe siècle*, 1st. ser., v. 1. See also F. Rittiez, *Histoire du règne*, 3 vols. (Paris: V. Lecou, 1855), I:366–367. The first trial of this group also describes its history, in *Gazette des Tribunaux*, 14 April 1833, *Affaire de la Société des Droits de l'Homme et du Citoyen, Réquisitoire*. See also Gisquet, *Mémoires*, III:64; Rittiez, *Histoire du règne*, I:366–367.
3. *Le Moniteur universel*, 11 May 1835, *Acte d'accusation*, 1111; Gisquet, *Mémoires*, III:66, 204.
4. The other founders are disputed. See Rittiez, *Histoire du règne*, I:367–368; *Gazette des Tribunaux*, 14 April 1833, *Réquisitoire;* and "Procès politique et républicain du citoyen Auguste Caunes" (Paris, 1831), 5–13; reprinted in *Les Révolutions du XIXe siècle*, 1st ser., v. 11.
5. Rittiez, *Histoire du règne*, I:368–369. For the text of Robespierre's Declaration, see Lucien Jaume, ed., *Les Déclarations des Droits de l'Homme* (Paris: Flammarion, 1989), 254–261.
6. "Réglement" (Paris: Auguste Mie, n.d.), 9–15; reprinted in *Les Révolutions du XIXe siècle*, 1st ser., v. 3.
7. *Le Moniteur universel*, 11 May 1835, *Acte d'accusation*, 1113.
8. *Gazette des Tribunaux*, 11 April 1833, *Acte d'accusation;* Gisquet, *Mémoires*, III:69–70.
9. *Gazette des Tribunaux*, 14 April 1833, *Réquisitoire*.
10. *Le Moniteur universel*, 11 May 1835, *Acte d'accusation*, 1114.
11. *Le Moniteur universel*, 11 May 1835, *Acte d'accusation*, 1115.
12. Gabriel Perreux, *Aux Temps des Sociétés Secrètes* (Paris: Rieder, 1931), 236.
13. Rittiez, *Histoire du règne*, II:77; Guizot, *Mémoires*, III:228.
14. See Adolphe Chauveau and Faustin Hélie, *Théorie du Code pénal*, 2nd ed., 6 vols. (Paris: Edouard Legrand, 1843), II:81–89.
15. *Procès des Vingt-Sept ou de la Société des Droits de l'Homme* (Paris: Adolphe Riou, 1834), 39–40, 103–113; reprinted in *Les Révolutions du XIXe siècle*, 1st ser., v. 3.
16. *Procès des Vingt-Sept, Acte d'accusation*, 8. See also the *Comité Lebon* circular cited in Gisquet, *Mémoires*, III:118; Victor de Nouvion, *Histoire du règne de Louis-Philippe*, 4 vols. (Paris: Didier et cie, 1857), III:279–280.
17. *Procès des Vingt-Sept*, 8–9, and "Plaidoirie de M. Dupont," 71.
18. For the text, *Le Moniteur universel*, 19 January 1836, 107; Gisquet, *Mémoires*, III:106.
19. *Procès des Vingt-Sept*, 9, and Raspail's "Ordre du jour," cited in "Plaidoirie de M. Dupont," 70–71.

20. *Procès des Vingt-Sept*, "Discours de Raspail," 53. The *Gazette des Tribunaux*, 20 December 1833, more correctly quoted him as saying he had quit the society entirely.

21. *Gazette des Tribunaux*, 13 December 1833.

22. The earlier structure is discussed in *Gazette des Tribunaux*, 11 April 1833, *Acte d'accusation*, and *Le Moniteur universel*, 11 May 1835, 1112. For *des Victoires*, *Procès des Vingt-Sept*, 83–84.

23. Douglas Porch, *Army and Revolution: France, 1815–1848* (London: Routledge and Kegan Paul, 1974), 95–96 (for Lunéville); Robert J. Bezucha, *The Lyon Uprising of 1834: Social and Political Conflict in the Early July Monarchy* (Cambridge, MA: Harvard University Press, 1974), 80–88 (for Lyon); see also *Le Moniteur universel*, 13 May 1835, *Acte d'accusation*, 1147.

24. *Le Moniteur universel*, 11 May 1835, 1112, for the manifesto and critique; see also *Le National*, 27 October 1833, "Politique intérieure: Du Nouveau Procès entre la République et le Tiers-Parti."

25. *Le National*, 27 October 1833, "Politique intérieure."

26. *Le Moniteur universel*, 11 May 1835, 1113. See also Gisquet, *Mémoires*, III:197.

27. *Le Journal des Débats*, 29 October 1833.

28. Armand Carrel, "Dossier d'un prévenu," in *Oeuvres politiques et littéraires*, 5 vols. (Paris: Librairie de F. Chamerot, 1857), V:390–457.

29. *Le Messager*, quoted in *Le National*, 27 October 1833, "Politique intérieure."

30. Carrel, "Dossier d'un prévenu," V:434–435, 452–453.

31. Albert Laponneraye, *Déclaration des Droits de l'Homme, avec des commentaires par le Citoyen Laponneraye*, 3–4; reprinted in *Les Révolutions du XIXe siècle*, 1st ser., v. 3.

32. Jean-Jacques Vignerte, *Procès des Citoyens Vignerte et Pagnerre* (Paris: L. E. Herhand, 1834), 4–6; reprinted in *Les Révolutions du XIXe siècle*, 1st ser., v. 3.

33. Nouvion, *Histoire*, III:287; Rittiez, *Histoire du règne*, II:85.

34. *Gazette des Tribunaux*, 30 November 1833. See Georges Bourgin, "La Crise ouvrière à Paris dans la seconde moitié de 1830," *Revue historique* (1947), 203–214.

35. *Le Moniteur universel*, 11 May 1835, *Acte d'accusation*, 1113.

36. *Procès des citoyens Voyer d'Argenson, Charles Teste, et Auguste Mie* (Paris, [1833?]), 3; reprinted in *Les Révolutions du XIXe siècle*, 1st ser., v. 7; *Gazette des Tribunaux*, 26 April 1834.

37. *Le National*, 28 April 1834, "D'un nouveau moyen d'éluder la juridiction du jury."

38. Efrahem, "De l'association des ouvriers de tous les corps d'état," in *Les Révolutions du XIXe siècle*, 1st ser., v. 4. In the controversy over whether Efrahem's brochure was written by Marc Dufraisse, Dolléans argues convincingly that there were two brochures with two different styles, one by Dufraisse and the other by Efrahem. Edouard Dolléans, *Histoire du Mouvement ouvrier*, 2 vols. (Paris: Librairie Armand Colin, 1936), I:86–88; see also Lynn Hunt and George Sheridan, "Corporatism, Association, and the Language of Labor in France," *Journal of Modern History* 58:4 (December 1986), 832–833.

39. Grignon, "Réflexions d'un ouvrier tailleur," in Alain Faure and Jacques Rancière, eds., *La Parole ouvrière, 1830–1851* (Paris: Union générale d'Editions, 1976), 80–81.

40. *Gazette des Tribunaux*, 2–3 December 1833, *coalition des ouvriers tailleurs*.

41. Théophile Thoré, *La Vérité sur le parti démocratique* (Paris: Dessessart, 1840), 21–22; reprinted in *Les Révolutions du XIXe siècle*, 2nd ser., v. 4.

42. CC590. no. 17, letter from Prefect Gisquet, 6 May 1834. See the congratulatory *ordre du jour*, in *Gazette des Tribunaux*, 13 December 1833.

43. Comte H. d'Ideville, *Le Maréchal Bugeaud, d'après sa correspondance intime et des documents inédits, 1784–1849*, 2 vols. (Paris: Firmin-Didot, 1881), I:22, 395–396; see also Robert A. Nye, *Masculinity and Male Codes*, 138.

44. *Le National*, 30 January 1834, and 1 February 1834, letter from Armand Carrel to General de Rumigny; Odilon Barrot, *Mémoires posthumes*, 2nd ed., 4 vols. (Paris: Charpentier et cie, 1875), I:275.

45. *Le Moniteur universel*, 12 January 1836, 58; *Le National*, 2 February 1834, "Convoi de M. Dulong."

46. Irene Collins, *The Government and the Newspaper Press in France, 1814–1881* (Oxford: Oxford University Press, 1959), 80; Chauveau and Hélie, *Théorie du Code pénal*, III:372, 382–383.

47. *Le National*, 15 August 1833, letter from Delente; *Gazette des Tribunaux*, 23 November 1833.

48. *Le National*, 23 September 1833, "Les crieurs publics et le préfet de police."

49. Rittiez, *Histoire du règne*, II:106, 112; Gisquet, *Mémoires*, III:222–223.

50. *Le National*, 24 February 1834, "Scènes de la place de la Bourse," 25 February 1834, and 27 February 1834. See also Gisquet, *Mémoires*, III:253–265.

51. Gisquet, *Mémoires*, III:257.

52. CC590. no. 17, letter from Prefect of Police Gisquet to procureur-général, 6 May 1834.

53. CC590, doss. *Kersosie* (sic), no. 20: "Causes de la démission de Kersosi: Ses projets," 13 March 1834. In preparation for the trial that followed the 1834 insurrection, the police and judiciary compiled dossiers on all the defendants.

54. Cited in *Le Moniteur universel*, 11 May 1835, 1113.

55. CC590, doss. *Kersosie*, no. 38, dep. Kersosie; no. 20: "Causes de la démission de Kersosi."

56. CC590, doss. *Kersosie*, no. 20: "Causes de la démission de Kersosi."

57. CC590, doss. *Cavaignac*, no. 14, Unsigned note or réglement, 3 February 1834.

58. *Le Moniteur universel*, 14 January 1836, dep. Recurt, 77.

59. Alain Faure, "Mouvements populaires," *Le Mouvement social* 88 (1974), 80–81 (based on 685 members in 7 arrondissements).

60. Gisquet, *Mémoires*, III:414–415. These dossiers are in CC587–589, which include interviews with 298 rank and file members. There are many additional interviews filed in the dossiers of the leaders.

61. CC593, no. 20, dep. Quetin; CC589, doss. *Cordeliers*, dep. Mazlard.

62. CC589, doss. *Jacobins*, dep. Borovast; CC587, doss. *Lebas*, dep. Gaesmann.

63. CC593, doss. *Fournier*, no. 5, dep. Fournier.

64. CC593, doss. *Travailleurs*, no. 40, dep. Duplain.

65. CC593, doss. *Bernard Pornin*, no. 31, dep. David.

66. CC593, doss. *Travailleurs*, no. 16, dep. Testanier.

67. CC587, doss. *Marcus Brutus*, dep. Grevin.

68. CC593, no. 19, dep. Pommery.

69. CC589, doss. *Dévouement social*, dep. Latour.

70. CC587, doss. *Marcus Brutus*, dep. Leclerc.

71. CC587, doss. *Vengeurs/Socrates*, dep. Lepreux.

72. CC587, doss. *Torrijos*, dep. Vaux.

73. CC587, doss. *Torrijos*, dep. Gardinal.

74. CC587, doss. *Mucius Scaevola*, dep. Bignon; doss. *Vengeurs/Socrates*, dep. Beaumont; doss. *Torrijos*, dep. Pitard; doss. *Barricades*, dep. Moulin.

75. CC587, doss. *Vengeurs*, dep. Bardot.

76. CC587, doss. *Barricades*, dep. Lefevre.

77. *Le Moniteur universel*, 11 January 1836, 59.

78. CC587, doss. *Marcus Brutus*, dep. Leclerc. See also CC589, doss. *Cordeliers*, dep. Comagny.

79. CC587, doss. *Torrijos*, dep. Gardinal.

80. CC590, doss. *Kersosie*, dep. Peux.

81. CC588, 4e dossier, dep. Bach; CC593, doss. *Bernard Pornin*, no. 22, dep. Delangle; no. 23, dep. Budinger; no. 24, dep. Touzé.

82. CC593, doss. *Fournier*, no. 5, dep. Fournier.

83. CC593, doss. *Bernard Pornin*, no. 40, dep. Duplain.

84. CC587, doss. *Mort aux Tyrans*, dep. Reusse.

85. CC587, doss. *Marcus Brutus*, dep. Dumesnil.

86. CC587, doss. *Cimber*, dep. Bonnet.

87. *Le Moniteur universel*, 11 January 1836, 58; Ibid., 12 January 1836, dep. Grevin, 58.

88. CC588, doss. *5e arrondissement*, dep Chapuis; CC597, doss. *Mugnier*, dep. Mugnier; CC591, doss. *Billon*, dep. Billon.

89. Gisquet, *Mémoires*, III:296–297.

90. Gisquet, *Mémoires*, III:285; Rittiez, *Histoire du règne*, II:120; for Kersausie's comment, see *Le Moniteur universel*, 11 January 1836, dep. Cagnard (Cogniard).

91. Gisquet, *Mémoires*, III:296–297, 302–303.

92. *Le Moniteur universel*, 14 May 1835, *Acte d'accusation* (Paris), 1169–1170.

93. *Le Moniteur universel*, 14 May 1835, 1170; CC593, doss. *Tassin*, no. 25, dep. Tassin.

94. CC592, doss. *Yvon*, no. 1, *Procès-verbal*; *Le Moniteur universel*, 14 May 1835, 1170.

95. *Le National*, 13 May 1834; J. P. T. Bury and Robert Tombs, *Thiers 1797–1877* (London: 1986), 52.

96. Gisquet, *Mémoires*, II:89, III:305–308; see also Rittiez, *Histoire du règne*, II:123.

97. *Le Moniteur universel*, 16 May 1835, *Acte d'accusation*, 1201; Gisquet, *Mémoires*, III:301–302.

98. *Gazette des Tribunaux*, 8 June 1836.

99. CC590, doss. *Guinard*, no. 10, dep. Berryer-Fontaine; doss. *Marrast*; doss. *Cavaignac, Mandat d'amener*, 24 April 1834.

100. Bezucha, *The Lyon Uprising in 1834*, esp. 123–155.

101. Rittiez, *Histoire du règne*, II:135–136; Bezucha, *The Lyon Uprising*, 154.

102. *La Tribune*, cited in *Le Moniteur universel*, 14 May 1835, *Acte d'accusation* (Paris), 1171.

103. CC590, no. 12, report from Gisquet, 20 April 1834; Gisquet, *Mémoires*, III:285–288.

104. CC593, doss. *Fournier*.

105. *Le Moniteur universel*, 14 May 1835, *Acte d'accusation*, 1170.

106. *Le Moniteur universel*, 14 May 1835, 1170; and 11 January 1836, dep. Pouchin, 60.

107. CC593, doss. *Fournier*.

108. Ibid.; CC594, doss. *Sauriac*, no. 21, from prefect of police, 19 June 1834.

109. CC590, no. 12, report from Gisquet, 20 April 1834.

110. Gisquet, *Mémoires*, III:381–382; CC590, no. 12, report from Gisquet, 20 April 1834.
111. Gisquet, *Mémoires*, III:382–383.
112. *Le Moniteur universel*, 13 January 1836, dep. Tranchard, 67.
113. CC590, no. 52, dep. Viannet; and Gisquet, *Mémoires*, III:382–384.
114. CC590, doss. *Kersausie*, no. 21, dep. Fabre; see also no. 15, dep. Kersausie.
115. CC590, no. 12, report from Gisquet, 20 April 1834.

CHAPTER 5

1. *Le Moniteur universel*, 17 July 1835, 1722; Robert J Bezucha, *The Lyon Uprising of 1834* (Cambridge, MA: Harvard University Press, 1974), 154–155, 161–162; Bezucha notes that, as in Paris, there was no "master list."
2. Of the 53 dead civilians, 30 were noncombatants; 11 could not be categorized; and 12 were insurgents. Of the military, 10 soldiers, 3 municipal guards, and 3 national guards were killed. These reports were drawn from CC586, doss. *Faits généraux [Faits]*, *liasse* 4, especially Gisquet's letter to M. le Procureur-Général, 6 August 1834; and from F9 1162, for the military forces. For civilians, CC586, doss. *rive droite [rive dr.]*, no. 13, *Procès Verbal and Rapport of the Commissaire of Sainte-Avoie*, 14 April 1834.
3. Roger Passeron, *Daumier* (Secaucus, NJ: Poplar, 1981), 102.
4. Alexandre-Auguste Ledru-Rollin, *Mémoire sur les évènements de la rue Transnonain dans les journées des 13 et 14 avril 1834* (Paris: Guillaumin, 1834); reprinted in *Les Révolutions du XIXe siècle*, 1st ser., v. 7. The *National* devoted most of their 28 July issue to selections.
5. CC586, doss. *rue Transnonain [Trans.]*, no. 46, dep. Colas; for the estimate of 150, see CC 586, doss. *rive dr.*, no. 18, dep. Donval.
6. CC586, doss. *rive dr.*, no. 80, dep. Guetté; no. 73, dep. Durant; no. 88, dep. Conci, femme Ponat.
7. CC586, doss. *rive dr.*, no. 72, deps. Collet, Dreux, and Ramond.
8. CC586, doss. *rive dr.*, no. 136, report to M. le Procureur-Général, from the *commissaires* of Sainte-Avoye, Lombards, Saint Martin des Champs, Mont-de-piété, and Marché St. Jean, undated.
9. CC586, doss. *rive dr.*, no. 49, dep. Delpêche.
10. CC 585, *liasse* 3, dep. Laselve.
11. CC586, doss. *Trans.*, no. 13, dep. Rolot.
12. CC586, doss. *rive dr.*, no. 92, letter from Jean-Baptiste Dupont; see also no. 99, dep. Dupont.
13. CC586, doss. *rive dr.*, no. 42, dep. Brunet; and no. 18, dep. Donval.
14. Henri-Joseph Gisquet, *Mémoires de M. Gisquet* (Paris: Marchant, 1840), III:386–387, 401; Louis Girard, *La Garde nationale* (Paris: Librairie Plon, 1964), 253.
15. CC586, doss. *rive dr.*, no. 60, dep. Cendrier; no. 76, dep. Cohar; no. 89, dep. Remé.
16. CC586, doss. *Trans.*, no. 17, dep. Gauthier.
17. CC585, 3rd *liasse*, dep. Lesouef.
18. See CC586, doss. *rive dr.*, no. 77, dep. Lemoine femme Cohar; no. 76, dep. Cohar.
19. CC586, doss. *rive dr.*, no. 89, dep. Remé.
20. CC586, doss. *rive dr.*, no. 136, report to M. le Procureur-Général.
21. CC586, doss. *rive dr.*, no. 73, dep. Roussel.

22. CC586, doss. *rive dr.*, no. 136, report to M. le Procureur-Général.
23. *Gazette des Tribunaux*, 16 May 1835, *Acte d'accusation*, Paris section.
24. CC586, doss. *Faits*, no. 5, *Procès-verbal* of Commissaires Louis Gourlet and Pierre Henchard.
25. CC586, doss. *Faits*, no. 18, dep. Hersant.
26. CC586, doss. *Faits*, no. 10, dep. Dethuy.
27. CC586, doss. *Faits*, no. 12, *Procès-verbal* of Commissaire Louis Dyonnet.
28. CC586, doss. *Faits*, no. 24, dep. Henrion.
29. CC586, doss. *Faits*, no. 6, dep. Orset; no. 18, dep. Dorsay (sic).
30. CC585, doss. *Faits*, dep. Leroux.
31. CC586, doss. *Faits*, no. 7, report of Quartier Saint-Jacques.
32. CC586, doss. *rive dr.*, no. 136, report to M. le Procureur-Général.
33. CC586, doss. *Trans.*, no. 7, dep. Béranger.
34. CC586, doss. *Trans.*, no. 27, dep. Ponce.
35. CC593, doss. *Fournier*, dep. Fournier.
36. "Bulletin officiel," quoted in *Le National*, 15 April 1834; see also Gisquet, *Mémoires*, III:396–397.
37. For the minimal investigation of Beaubourg, see CC586, doss. *rive dr.*, *Enquête* of Commissaires Alexandre Dourlens and Charles Goujer, 22 April 1834. The timing was determined by two depositions that placed Beaubourg clearly before Transnonain; CC586, doss. *Trans.*, no. 14, dep. Monnier; no. 11, dep. Roguet.
38. CC586, doss. *rive dr.*, no. 136, report to M. le Procureur-Général.
39. CC586, doss. *rive dr.*, no. 73, deps. N. Blondeau and J. Blondeau.
40. CC586, doss. *rive dr.*, no. 73, dep. Lelievre.
41. CC586, *liasse* 4, *Procès-verbal*, commissaires of Mont de piété and Marché Saint-Jean, 16 April 1834; CC591, doss. *Charles Caillet*, no. 13, dep. Bremont; no. 12, dep. femme Bremont. (Breliniat also listed as Bertrinka.)
42. CC586, doss. *rive dr.*, no. 73, deps. Lelievre, N. Blondeau.
43. CC586, doss. *rive dr.*, no. 73, dep. J. Blondeau.
44. CC586, doss. *rive dr.*, no. 136, letter to M. le Procureur-Général. Those killed included Étienne Gallay, quoted at the beginning of chapter 4. See CC586, *liasse* 4, for the casualties.
45. *Le Moniteur universel*, 14 May 1835, *Acte d'accusation*, 1172.
46. CC586, doss. *Trans.*, no. 1, *Extrait d'un Procès-verbal*, dep. Lemire; no. 2, *Procès-verbal* of Commissaire Jean Palluy.
47. CC586, doss. *Trans.*, dep. Montigny; doss. *rive dr.*, no. 136, report to the procureur-général.
48. CC586, doss. *Trans.*, dep. Lemire.
49. *Gazette des Tribunaux*, 16 May 1835, *Acte d'accusation* (Paris).
50. CC594, doss. *Adolphe Buzelin*, no. 28, dep. Voisin.
51. Captain DuPont deGault survived; see F9 1162, *État nominatif* of 26 May 1834.
52. CC586, doss. *Trans.*, dep. Aufray; CC586, doss. *Trans.*, from the Civil Tribunal of Compeigne (Oise), dep. de Tarlé; CC586, doss. *Trans.*, no. 10, dep. de Gibon.
53. CC586, doss. *Trans.*, no. 59, dep. Brunaux.
54. CC586, doss. *Trans.*, no. 54, dep. Roblin, Veuve Daubigny.
55. CC586, doss. *Trans.*, nos. 106 and 54, dep. Roblin, Veuve Daubigny.
56. CC586, doss. *Trans.*, no. 25, dep. Lamy; and no. 54, dep. Roblin, Veuve Daubigny.
57. CC586, doss. *Trans.*, *Procès-verbal*, commissaires Dourlens and Loyeux, dep. Planche; Ledru-Rollin, *Mémoire*, 41–43.

58. CC586, doss. *Trans.*, no. 58, dep. Bonneville.

59. Ibid.; Ledru-Rollin, *Mémoire*, 18.

60. Ledru-Rollin, *Mémoire*, 17–18 (from autopsy reports); see also CC586, doss. *Trans.*, no. 13, dep. Planté; no. 10, dep. de Gibon.

61. CC586, doss. *Trans.*, no. 58, dep. Bonneville.

62. CC586, doss. *Trans.*, no. 31, dep. A. Hordesseaux; no. 76, dep. L. Hordesseaux.

63. CC586, doss. *Trans.*, no. 55, dep. femme Lamy; no. 90, dep. Doyen, Veuve Roblin.

64. CC586, doss. *Trans.*, no. 25, dep. Lamy; and no. 78, dep. Closmenil.

65. CC586, doss. *Trans.*, no. 73, dep. Rivière, Veuve Leperre.

66. CC586, doss. *Trans.*, *Procès-verbal* of Dourlens and Loyeux, 14 April 1834; and no. 77, dep. Couban.

67. CC586, doss. *Trans.*, no. 73, dep. Rivière, Veuve Lepère.

68. CC586, doss. *Trans.*, no. 42, dep. Dumont femme Nicaise.

69. Ledru-Rollin, *Mémoire*, 47.

70. Ibid., 19–21.

71. CC586, doss. *Trans.*, no. 48, dep. Julienne, Veuve Pajot.

72. CC586 doss. *Trans.*, no. 52, dep. Alliaud, Veuve Hû.

73. CC586, doss. *Trans.*, no. 48, dep. Julienne, Veuve Pajot.

74. CC586, doss. *Trans.*, no. 52, dep. Alliaud, veuve Hû.

75. CC586, doss. *Trans.*, no. 79, dep. Certeaux.

76. Mme. Godefroy was taken in by Mme. Closmenil in time to see the husband flee. CC586, doss. *Trans.*, no. 75, dep. Emelienne femme Godefroy.

77. CC586, doss. *Trans.*, no. 52, dep. Alliaud, Veuve Hû; see also no. 48, dep. Julienne, Veuve Pajot.

78. CC586, doss. *Trans.*, no. 59, dep. Brunaux; and no. 79, dep. Certeaux.

79. C586, doss. *Trans.*, no. 52, dep. Alliaud, Veuve Hû; Ledru-Rollin, *Mémoire*, 23.

80. CC586, doss. *Trans.*, no. 48, dep. Julienne, Veuve Pajot; for her background, see Ibid., letter from President of the *Cour des Pairs*, 7 October 1834, and letter from Ministry of Interior, 28 February 1835.

81. The dead were: François (or Victor) Loisillon, hat maker, age 20; Edme Daubigny, painter and glass maker, age 36; Adolphe Guittard, clerk, age 28; Louis Marin Hû, furniture seller, age 46; Annette Besson, clerk, age 49; Charles Breffort, manufacturer of decorative papers, age 58; Louis Delarivière, law clerk, age 20–22; Pierre Robiquet, bronze worker, age 29; Jean Lepère, gilder (of paper), age 30; Louis Breffort, artist, age 22; Antoine Pierre Bouton, painter, age 52; Pierre Thierry, jeweler, age 20. CC586, doss. *Trans.*, no. 2, *Procès-verbal* of Commissaires Alexandre Dourlens and Charles Loyeux, 14 April 1834.

82. CC586, doss. *Trans.*, no. 113bis, dep. Lamy; no. 7, deps. Béranger and Bernand; no. 13, dep. Planté; no. 12, dep. Redel; no. 18, dep. Simon; no. 5, dep. Kerner; no. 8, deps. Enard and Gaillard; no. 19, dep. Planche; no. 20, dep. Lanquetin; no. 21, dep. Arnould; no. 44, dep. de Paquis; no. 24, dep. Breton; no. 23, dep. Desprez; no. 26, dep. Leridais; no. 30, dep. Haulard; no. 29, dep. Richer; no. 41, dep. Aufray.

83. CC586, doss. *Trans.*, no. 18, dep. Simon; no. 25, dep. L. Lamy; no. 98, dep. Remond.

84. CC586, doss. *Trans.*, no. 84, *Procès-verbal* by Commissaire Vassal; no. 104, *mairie du 7e arrondissement*; no. 65, dep. J Hû.

85. CC586, doss. *Trans.*, no. 26, dep. Leridais.

86. CC586, doss. *Trans.*, letter from Ledru-Rollin to Léon de la Chauvinière, *greffier en chef de la Cour des Pairs*, 1 September 1834.

87. CC586, doss. *Trans.*, no. 72, dep. Raoul.
88. CC586, doss. *Trans.*, no. 93, dep. Mestre; no. 20, dep. Lanquetin; no. 12, dep. Redel.
89. CC586, doss. *Trans.*, *Procès-verbal* of Commissaire Dourlens, dep. Lemire.
90. CC586, doss. *Trans.*, no. 2, *Procès-verbal*, commissaire from quartier Ste. Avoye.
91. CC586, doss. *Trans.*, no. 82, dep. Fredricy.
92. CC586, doss. *Trans.*, no. 85, dep. Bourgeot
93. CC586, doss. *Trans.*, no. 98, dep. Remond.
94. CC586, doss. *Trans.*, no. 6, *Procès-verbal* Dourlens, dep. Mabille; and witnesses in no. 10, dep. Gibon; no. 44, dep. Depaquit; no. 15, dep. Matheaude; no. 109, dep. Raimbault; no. 25, dep. Chaumery; no. 12, dep. Redel.
95. CC586, doss. *Trans.*, no. 7, dep. Bernand.
96. CC586, doss. *Trans.*, no. 18, dep. Simon; this was Séraphine Brunaux, who also described the episode; see no. 80, dep. Brunaux.
97. CC586 doss. *Trans.*, no. 4, dep. Simon.
98. CC586, doss. *Trans.*, no. 101, dep. de Gibon.
99. Gisquet, *Mémoires*, III:399.
100. Ledru-Rollin, *Mémoire*, 34. General Thomas Bugeaud was blamed for this, as the "butcher of Transnonain," though the offending troops were under General de Lascours. *La Commune de Paris*, 20 April 1848, letter from Bugeaud. The *Journal des Débats* identified Lascours as commander, 15 April 1834; see also François-Pierre-Guillaume Guizot, *Mémoires*, 8 vols. (Paris: Michel Lévy, 1872), III:248.
101. CC586, doss. *rive dr.*, no. 73, dep. J. Blondeau.
102. *Le National*, 11 May 1834.
103. CC586, doss. *Trans.*, dep. Hernu.
104. *Le National*, 20 April 1834, letter from Charles Breffort; Ibid., 12 August 1834, letter from Charles Breffort, *frère de Louis Breffort* (sic), *massacré*, to M. de Lascours, *pair de France*.
105. Gisquet, *Mémoires*, III:400; Ferdinand Philippe, duc d'Orléans, *Lettres* (Paris: Calmann Lévy, 1889), 130.
106. CC586, doss. *rive dr.*, no. 7, *Procès-verbal* of Commissaire of the Marchés, 14 April 1834; Ibid., no. 3, *Procès-verbal* of Commissaire Michel Cabuchet, 14 April 1834.
107. CC592, doss. *Nicolas Augustin Pruvost*, no. 42, dep. Pruvost; no. 9, dep. Pruvost; *Le National*, 4 June 1834, letter from Provost, *invalide, décoré de juillet*; *La Commune de Paris*, 6 June 1848.
108. *Le Moniteur universel*, 16 May 1835, *Acte d'accusation*, 1200.
109. *Le Moniteur universel*, 12 January 1836, dep. Beaudot, 58.
110. *Le Messager*, cited in *Le National*, 16 April 1834; Gisquet, *Mémoires*, IV:248.
111. CC586, doss. *Faits*, no. 36, *Procès-verbal* of Commissaire Charles Gabet; no. 37, *Procès-verbal* of Commissaires Vassal and Loyeux, undated.
112. CC586, doss. *Faits*, no. 39, *Procès-verbal* of Commissaires Vassal and Loyeux, 17 April 1834.
113. CC586, doss. *Faits*, no. 50, *Procès-verbal* of Commissaire Louis Gourlet, 27 April 1834; no. 49, *Procès-verbal* of Commissaires Blavier and Demontmort, 19 April 1834.
114. CC586, doss. *rive dr.*, no. 140, dep. Crétigny; no. 141, letter from municipal guard colonel, 13 September 1834.

115. *Le National,* 3 September 1834, "La Cour des Pairs et le complot d'avril," and 23 June 1834, "Nouvelles diverses." See Jeannine Charon-Bordas, ed., *Cour des Pairs: Procès politiques,* 3 vols. (Paris: Archives nationales, 1984), II:122–146.

116. Armand Carrel, *Oeuvres politiques et littéraires,* 5 vols. (Paris: Librairie F. Chamerot, 1857), IV:114–124.

117. *Le Journal des Débats,* 27 May 1834, letter from Benjamin and J.-J. Vignerte, cited from *Le Journal de Paris;* Ibid., 12 June 1834, letter from the 86, from *Le Journal de Paris.*

118. *La Tribune,* cited in Émile Gigault, *Vie politique de Marie-Paul-Jean-Roch-Yves-Gilbert de Motié, Marquis de Lafayette* (Paris: A. Pinard, 1833), 6–7 (for critiques); reprinted in *Les Révolutions du XIXe siècle,* 1st. ser., v. 7. For Gigault and the authorship of this book, see Alessandro Galante Garrone, *Philippe Buonarroti et les révolutionnaires du XIXe siècle,* trans. by Anne and Claude Manceron (Paris: Editions Champ Libre, 1975), 30, 326fn; James H. Billington, *Fire in the Minds of Men: Origins of the Revolutionary Faith* (New York: Basic Books, 1980), 194; Elizabeth L. Eisenstein, *The First Professional Revolutionist* (Cambridge, MA: Harvard University Press, 1957), 116.

119. Carrel, *Oeuvres,* IV:201, 202–203n.

120. *Le National,* 1 October 1834, letter from Dr. Gervais (de Caen); *Gazette des Tribunaux,* 25 February and 27 February 1835; Gisquet, *Mémoires,* III:428–432.

121. *Le National,* 3 October 1834, letter from Sainte-Pélagie; see also 2 September 1834, letter from Durdan, (father of the children).

122. *Le National,* 24 October 1834, letter from 48 prisoners in the Force.

123. *Le National,* 6 November 1834, letter from 46 prisoners in the Force.

124. *Le National,* 5 October 1834, and 14 December 1834, letter from Imbert.

125. Gisquet, *Mémoires,* III:452.

126. *Le Moniteur universel,* 6 May 1835, Cour des Pairs, 1062. The cities were Lyon, Saint-Étienne, Grenoble, Arbois, Besançon, Marseille, Paris, Lunéville, and Épinal. Cour des Pairs, *Affaire du mois d'avril, 1834* (Paris: Imprimerie Crapelet, 1835), 406–459, and 502–509.

127. For the Cour des Pairs, see E. Cauchy, *Les Précédents de la Cour des Pairs* (Paris: Imprimerie royale, 1839).

128. Cour des Pairs, *Affaire,* 785–787. See also *Le National,* 21 April 1835.

129. *Le Bon Sens,* 31 May 1835, cited in [Pagnerre], *Procès des Accusés d'avril,* 2 vols. (Paris: Pagnerre, 1835), I:39–40; reprinted in Gisquet, *Mémoires,* III:463–465.

130. Gisquet, *Mémoires,* III:477; for the list of escapees, see Cour des Pairs, *Affaire,* 1082–1083.

131. Gisquet, *Mémoires,* III:482–484 (Gisquet denied involvement); *Le National,* 14 July 1835; 15 July 1835, letter from Landolphe; 16 July 1835, letter from Kersausie, Beaumont, Recurt, Pruvost, et al.; 17 July 1835, letter from Parfait, Stevenot, et al.; *Le Moniteur universel,* 16 July 1835, 1711.

132. *Le Moniteur universel,* 12 January 1836, 58; Rittiez, *Histoire du règne,* II:181.

133. *Le Moniteur universel,* 12 January 1836, 58.

134. *Le Moniteur universel,* 13 January 1836, 67; Cour des Pairs, Affaire, 1566.

135. *Gazette des Tribunaux,* 16 January 1836; *Le Moniteur universel,* 16 January 1836, dep. Bolle, 91.

136. *Le Moniteur universel,* 13 January 1836, deps. Hérisson, Michel, Brunel, 68.

137. *Le Moniteur universel,* 20 January 1836, *Plaidoirie* Bavoux, 110.

138. Cour des Pairs, *Affaire,* 1618–1623.

139. Ibid., 1645–1647, 1658–1660, 1662–1665; Gisquet, *Mémoires*, III:486.
140. It was a barrier duel; see Robert A. Nye, *Masculinity and Male Codes of Honor in Modern France* (New York: Oxford University Press, 1993), 139.
141. *Le National*, 25 July 1836.
142. Odilon Barrot, *Mémoires posthumes*, 2nd ed. (Paris: Charpentier et cie, 1875), II:79; Hippolyte Castille, *Histoire de la Seconde République française*, 4 vols. (Paris: Victor Lecou, 1854), II:138.

CHAPTER 6

1. *Gazette des Tribunaux*, 3 August 1836.
2. Victor de Nouvion, *Histoire du règne de Louis-Philippe Ier Roi des Français 1830–1848*, 4 vols. (Paris: Didier et cie, 1857), III:317–319; Adolphe Chauveau and Faustin Hélie, *Théorie du Code pénal*, 2nd ed., 6 vols. (Paris: Edouard Legrand, 1843), III:392–400.
3. E. Cauchy, *Les Précédents de la Cour des Pairs* (Paris: Imprimerie royale, Oct. 1839), 534–535; Nouvion, *Histoire*, III:522–526; André-Jacques Dupin, *Mémoires de M. Dupin*, 4 vols. (Paris: Henri Plon, 1855), III:166–167.
4. Dupin, *Mémoires*, III:164, 169–175; Odilon Barrot, *Mémoires posthumes*, 2nd ed., 4 vols. (Paris: Charpentier et cie, 1875), I:281–282.
5. Irene Collins, *The Government and the Newspaper Press* (Oxford: Oxford University Press, 1959), 73; see also Chauveau and Hélie, *Théorie du Code pénal*, III:367–368.
6. "Procès du *National* au sujet des arrestations préventives pour délits de la presse" (Paris: Auguste Mie, 1832), 11–12; reprinted in *Les Révolutions du XIXe siècle*, 1st. ser., v. 10.
7. For Articles 86, 87, and 88, see Chauveau and Hélie, *Théorie du Code pénal*, II:104.
8. Collins, *The Government and the Newspaper Press*, 82–83; Robert Justin Goldstein, "Censorship of Caricature in France, 1815–1914," *French History* 3:1 (March 1989), 71–73.
9. Collins, *The Government and the Newspaper Press*, 82–84.
10. *Le National*, 15 April 1834, letter from Armand Marrast; Henri-Joseph Gisquet, *Mémoires de M. Gisquet*, 4 vols. (Paris: Marchant, 1840), III:394–395.
11. *Le National* issues, from 1834, of 21 April; 27 April; 4 May; 8 May; 10 May; 20 May; and 25 May 1834, letter from Germain Sarrut, et. al; 16 July 1834, letter from Marrast and Sarrut.
12. Nouvion, *Histoire*, III:460; Gisquet, *Mémoires*, III:421.
13. Gisquet, *Mémoires*, III:489; Collins, *The Government and the Newspaper Press*, 76–77, 85.
14. F. Rittiez, *Histoire du règne*, 3 vols. (Paris: V. Lecou, 1855), II:140; Nouvion, *Histoire*, III:362.
15. Chauveau and Hélie, *Théorie du Code pénal*, II:118–130; see also the explanation by *garde-des-sceaux* Persil, in *Le Moniteur universel*, 15 May 1834, 1253.
16. Chauveau and Hélie, *Théorie du Code pénal*, II:96–100, 132.
17. Chauveau and Hélie, *Theorie du Code pénal*, I:138–139; *Collection officielle des ordonnances de police, depuis 1800 jusqu'à 1844* (Paris: Librairie administrative de Paul Dupont, 1845), I:156–157.
18. *Le Moniteur universel*, 15 May 1834, 1250–1253; Chauveau and Hélie, *Théorie du Code pénal*, IV:88.

19. *Le Moniteur universel*, 15 May 1834, 1250–1253.

20. Louis Girard, *La Garde nationale* (Paris: Librairie Plon, 1964), 217–218. See F9 682, letter of 14 May 1833 from the prefect of the Seine to the minister of the interior.

21. *Le Moniteur universel*, 15 May 1834, 1245, 1246.

22. *Le Représentant du peuple*, 14 April 1848, "Réponse du citoyen Blanqui"; Maurice Dommanget, *Auguste Blanqui: Des Origines à la Révolution de 1848* (Paris: Mouton, 1969), 147.

23. *Le National*, 22 February 1836, Pepin's confession; Ibid., letter of L.-Aug. Blanqui.

24. The so-called Spira letter was mentioned in many cases; see *Gazette des Tribunaux*, 6 August 1836; Ibid., 16 March 1837; *Le Moniteur universel*, 11 August 1836, 1730.

25. *Le Moniteur universel*, 15 June 1839, Mérilhou Report, 973.

26. Lucien Delahodde, *Histoire des sociétés secrètes* (Paris: Julien, Lanier, et cie, 1850), 207–209; I. Tchernoff, *Le Parti républicain* (Paris: A. Pedone, 1901), 380–386; Dommanget, *Des Origines*, 163–164, 181.

27. Delahodde, *Histoire des sociétés secrètes*, 205–206; Gisquet, *Mémoires*, IV:188.

28. Gustave Geffroy, *L'Enfermé* (Paris: Bibliothèque-Charpentier, 1897), 14, 59; CC725, doss. Blanqui, letter from the prefect of police, 16 May 1839.

29. Amédée Achard, *Souvenirs personnels d'émeutes et de révolutions* (Paris: Michel Lévy, 1872), 83.

30. J. F. Jeanjean, "L'Éternel Révolté," *La Révolution de 1848*, 5 (1908–1909), 348.

31. Dommanget, *Des Origines*, 165; Daniel Stern, *Histoire de la Révolution de 1848* (Paris: Éditions Balland, 1985), 341–342.

32. Martin-Bernard, *Dix Ans de Prison au Mont-Saint-Michel et à la Citadelle de Doullens, 1839 à 1848*, 2nd ed. (Paris: Pagnerre, 1861), 190–201; Paul Chauvet, *Les Ouvriers du livre en France* (Paris: Librairie Marcel Rivière et cie, 1964), 155–156; Dommanget, *Des Origines*, 166, 182–183.

33. *Le Moniteur universel*, 6 July 1839, *Réquisitoire*, 1252.

34. Cour des Pairs, *Attentat du 27 December 1836* (Paris: Imprimerie royale, 1837), dep. Grison, 172–173 (quotations), 174–178 (hereafter *1837*).

35. *Gazette des Tribunaux*, 3 August 1836; *Le Moniteur universel*, 15 June 1839, Mérilhou Report, 973.

36. *Le Moniteur universel*, 15 June 1839, Mérilhou Report, 973, 977; a slightly different version in CC725, letter from prefect of police to the procureur-général, 20 May 1839.

37. "Rapport sur les mesures à prendre" (London: Thompson, 1840), 9, 6, 7; reprinted in *Les Révolutions du XIXe siècle*, 2nd ser., v. 7; see Arthur Lehning, *From Buonarroti to Bakunin* (Leiden: E.J. Brill, 1970), 126–128.

38. *Le Moniteur universel*, 15 June 1839, Mérilhou Report, 973; *Gazette des Tribunaux*, 14–15 March 1836, "Chronique"; Ibid., 16 March 1836. See also Gisquet, *Mémoires*, IV:175–194.

39. *Gazette des Tribunaux*, 4 June 1836; Ibid., 30 September 1836; Gisquet, *Mémoires*, IV:189.

40. *Gazette des Tribunaux*, 3 August 1836, dep. Yon; Ibid., 6 August 1836, *Réquisitoire*.

41. *Le Moniteur universel*, 15 June 1839, Mérilhou Report, 973.

42. *Gazette des Tribunaux*, 6 August 1836, dep. Raisant.

43. *Le Moniteur universel*, 21 October 1836, 2010.

44. *Gazette des Tribunaux*, 3 August 1836.

45. *Gazette des Tribunaux*, 20 October 1836; for amnesty, see Paul Thureau-Dangin, *Histoire de la Monarchie de Juillet*, 3rd ed., 7 vols. (Paris: Librairie Plon, 1902), IV:143.
46. *Gazette des Tribunaux*, 14 December 1836, *Acte d'accusation*.
47. *1837*, dep. Grison, 175–176.
48. *Gazette des Tribunaux*, 28 December 1836, deps. Dubos, Yon; Ibid.,14 December 1836, *Acte d'accusation;* 29 Ibid., January 1837, dep. Yon; Ibid., 15 March 1837, dep. Tranchard.
49. *Gazette des Tribunaux*, 15 March 1837, deps. Duthé, Senier, Bruneau-Viteau, Talon, Dupré.
50. *Gazette des Tribunaux*, 26–27 December 1836, dep. Dubocage; Jean Maitron, *Dictionnaire biographique du Mouvement ouvrier français: 1789–1864*, 3 vols. (Paris: Les Éditions ouvrières, 1964), II:497.
51. *Gazette des Tribunaux*, 2 February 1837, *Plaidoirie* Plocque.
52. *Gazette des Tribunaux*, 14 December 1836, *Acte d'accusation*. Grimault, Hennin, and Perrodin were also sentenced; see Ibid., 15 March 1837.
53. Cour des Pairs, *Attentat des 12 et 13 Mai 1839* (Paris: Imprimerie royale, 1839), *Réquisitoire*, 33, for the numerous arrests (hereafter *1839*).
54. Delahodde, *Histoire des sociétés secrètes*, 219, 231–233; Dommanget, *Des Origines*, 194.
55. *Gazette des Tribunaux*, 16 March 1837; Ibid., 19 March 1837; see also *Le National*, 1 August 1838. For Flotte, see also CC587, doss. Phocion, dep. Flotte.
56. *Gazette des Tribunaux*, 13 October 1838; Ibid., 18 October 1838; *Le National*, 19 October 1838.
57. Jules Taschereau, *Revue Rétrospective* (Paris: Paulin, 1848), 6–8; Gabriel Perreux, *Aux Temps des Sociétés secrètes* (Paris: Rieder, 1931), 363; Tchernoff, *Le Parti républicain*, 380; Dommanget, *Des Origines*, 167, 180–181.
58. CC725, no. 1, *Rapport* from the prefect of police to the procureur-général, 16 May 1839; *1839*, *Acte d'accusation*, 56–57; Ibid., 1st ser., 4th dep. Nouguès, 20–21.
59. *1839*, 2nd ser., dep. Viot, 31–34.
60. Ibid., 33–34.
61. *1839*, 2nd ser., no. 74, dep. Nibaut, 78.
62. *1839*, 2nd ser., no. 29, dep. Pons, 27–30.
63. *1839*, 2nd ser., deps. Quarré, 9–12; Delahodde, *Histoire des sociétés secrètes*, 217–219.
64. CC725, doss. Blanqui, Extrait des fiches communiqués par M. le Préfet, 11 June 1839, reports of 2 January 1839 and 23 April 1839; *1839*, 2nd ser., no. 5, dep. Launois, 7 (villager).
65. Delahodde, *Histoire des sociétés secrètes*, 237; *1839*, *Acte d'accusation*, 61.
66. CC725, "Renseignemens confidentiels sur les menées des principaux membres de la Société des Saisons et de celle des Montagnards, depuis le 1er avril, jusqu'au jour de l'insurrection."
67. CC725, "Renseignemens confidentiels . . ."; see also *1839*, 2nd ser., 3rd dep. Quarré, 9–10.
68. *1839*, 2nd ser., no. 29, deps. Pons, 28–29, 31.
69. CC725, "Renseignemens confidentiels . . ."
70. *1839*, 2nd ser., no. 3, deps. Léchaudé and Lemit, 8.
71. *Le Moniteur universel*, 15 June 1839, Mérilhou Report, 978.

72. J. Tripier-Lefranc, *M. Gabriel Delessert* (Paris: E. Dentu, 1859), 293–295; CC725, no. 1, *Rapport* from the prefect of police.

73. *1839*, 1st ser., no. 123, dep. Lecuze, 114; Ibid., nos. 89–90, deps. Bernier, 78–79; Ibid., no. 281, dep. Regnard, 275–277.

74. Tripier-Lefranc, *M. Gabriel Delessert*, 294–295; Dommanget, *Des Origines*, 222.

CHAPTER 7

1. Cour des Pairs de France, *Attentat des 12 et 13 Mai 1839* (Paris: Imprimerie royale, 1839), *Acte d'Accusation*, 68–74. The judicial materials on which this chapter is based are either from the Archives Nationales (the CC series) or from the documents printed by the *Cour des Pairs*, listed henceforward as *1839* (1st and 2nd series).

2. *Le Moniteur universel*, 15 June 1839, "Rapport fait à la cour par M. Mérilhou," 979 (henceforth cited as Mérilhou Report); *1839*, 1st ser., no. 7, deps. Lepage and Lepage, 8–12.

3. *1839*, 1st ser., no. 1., dep[osition] Rouchon, Veuve Roux, 1–2; for neighborhood witnesses, dep. Bertrand, 3; dep. Renault, 239; dep. Bourg, 280.

4. L. Nouguès, *Une Condamnation de Mai* (Paris: J. Bry aîné, 1850), 245–246; *Le Moniteur universel*, 1 July 1839, dep. Bonnet, 1172.

5. Lucien Delahodde, *Histoire des sociétés secretes* (Paris: Julien, Lanier, et cie, 1850), 240, 242–243; Maurice Dommanget, *Auguste Blanqui: Des Origines à la Révolution de 1848* (Paris: Mouton, 1969), 196–198.

6. *1839*, 2nd ser., 3rd dep. Quarré, 10.

7. *1839*, 1st ser., 3rd dep. Nouguès, 13–14.

8. CC724, doss. *[I]nformation [G]énérale*, letter from General de Rumigny to Lieutenant-General Pajol, 13 May 1839.

9. CC724, doss. *I.G.*, État nominatif des sous-officiers et gardes partis en détachement; and Lieutenant-General Comte Pajol, *Rapport Général sur les évènements*; see also CC725, no. 1, *Rapport* from the prefect of police to the procureur-général, 16 May 1839.

10. CC723, doss. *Châtelet*, dep. Baylac; Ibid., doss. *I.G.*, dep. Luiset; CC723, État des décès occasionnés par suite des Évènements des 12 et 13 Mai 1839, 31 May 1839.

11. For the Municipal Guards: CC723, doss. *I.G.*, dep. Luiset; dep. Ladroite; CC723, doss. *6e et 7e arrondissements*, dep. Servant; dep. Post. For Fournier, *Le National*, 19 May 1839.

12. *1839*, 1st ser., no. 244, dep. Grossmann, 234; no. 245, dep. Meunier, 237.

13. *1839*, 1st ser., no. 16, dep. Huignard, 20–21. See also 1st ser., no. 14, dep. Grossmann, 19; no. 18, dep. Gervaisi, 22; no. 20, dep. Paulhan, 23.

14. *1839*, 1st ser., no. 31, dep. Michelan, 31–32.

15. *1839*, 2nd ser., no. 78, dep. Bonnardet, 81; no. 79, dep. Aloffe, 82.

16. CC724, doss. *I. G.*, dep. Bisson.

17. *Le Moniteur universel*, 1 July 1839, dep. Vassal, 1171.

18. CC723, doss. *Marché Saint-Jean*, dep. Drouot; CC723, doss. *Commissaires, Procès-verbal* (Commissaire, Hôtel-de-Ville), 2 June 1839.

19. CC723, doss. *Marché Saint-Jean*, dep. Patissier; dep. Saugrin.

20. CC723, doss. *Marché Saint-Jean*, deps. Farjas, Leroy, Saugrin, Thomas, Devignon, Drouot, Sadoul.

21. *Acte d'accusation*, 62–63, reprinted in *Les Révolutions du XIXe siècle*, 2nd ser., v. 9.

22. See *1839*, 1st. ser., no. 251, dep. Voyer d'Argenson, 244–245; no. 252, dep. Lamennais, 245; no. 250, dep. Dubosc, 244; Mérilhou Report, 28, reprinted in *Les Révolutions du XIXe siècle*, 2nd series, v. 9. For Netré as exile, see Gustave Lefrançais, *Souvenirs d'un révolutionnaire* (Bruxelles: Administration, n.d.), 218, 223.

23. CC723, doss. *Marché Saint-Jean*, dep. Farjas.

24. CC723, doss. *Commissaires, Procès-verbal* (Commissaire Hôtel de Ville), 2 June 1839; CC724, doss. *I. G.*, Garde municipale de Paris, *Rapport général du 12 au 13 mai 1839*.

25. See Ferrari listed as *Saisons* chef in Jules Taschereau, *Revue Rétrospective* (Paris: Paulin, 1848), 7–8.

26. 221 AP 4 (d'Arriule papers), Tableau indiquant . . . les postes que par leur isolement ou leur faiblesse, ne sont pas susceptibles de défense; CC724, doss. *I. G.*, General d'Arriule, *Rapport sur les évènements*, 15 May 1839.

27. CC723, doss. *Marché St. Jean*, dep. Girard; dep. Morsaline; dep. Henriet; dep. Moreau; dep. Josset; *1839*, 1st ser., dep. Amy, 52–53.

28. CC723, doss. *Marché St. Jean*, dep. Riquier; dep. Henriet.

29. *1839*, 1st ser., *Procès-verbal relatif à l'attaque du poste du Marché Saint-Jean*, 41–42.

30. *1839*, 1st ser., dep. Girard, 47–50; CC723, doss. *Marché Saint Jean*, dep. Josset.

31. CC724, doss. *7e arrondissement*, dep. Morsaline.

32. CC723, doss. *Marché Saint-Jean*, dep. Amy.

33. *1839*, 1st ser., 1st dep. Nouguès, 11.

34. CC723, doss. *Marché Saint Jean*, dep. Buhrel; dep. Levasseur.

35. *1839*, 1st ser., *Procès-verbal relatif à l'attaque du poste du Marché Saint-Jean*, 41–42.

36. CC724, doss. *7e arrondissement*, dep. Moreau.

37. CC724, doss. *7e arrondissement*, dep. Levillain; dep. Thibault.

38. CC724, doss. *7e arrondissement*, dep. Moreau; dep. Levillain.

39. CC723, doss. *6e et 7e arrondissements, Procès-verbal* of Commissaire Loyeux, dep. Levasseur.

40. CC724, doss. *7e arrondissement*, dep. Lamy; and see deps Mille, Rafin, Moreau.

41. CC724, doss. *7e arrondissement*, dep. Chanu.

42. CC723, doss. *Commissaires, Procès-verbal* of Commissaire Cabuchet; CC723, doss. *6e et 7e arrondissements*, dep. Vallois; CC724, *I.G.*, dep. Vedie; dep. Hellonis (description).

43. *1839*, 1st ser., no. 174, dep. Samson, 165–166; no. 126, dep. Duval, 117.

44. *1839*, 1st ser., no. 174, dep. Samson, 165–166; CC723, doss. *Commissaires, Procès-verbal* of Commissaire Haymonet (quotation).

45. *1839*, 1st ser., no. 253, dep. Leblond, 245–246; no. 120, dep. Deldine, 110.

46. *1839*, 1st ser., no. 118, dep Tisserand, 106; no. 125, dep. Pelletier, 116; no. 187, dep. Cauche, 175–176.

47. CC724, doss. *I.G.*, Lieutenant Émile Tisserand, *Faits relatifs à l'enlèvement des barricades*.

48. J. F. Dupont, in *Revue du Progrès politique, social et littéraire*, 99, in CC725; published as *Blanqui devant les Révélations historiques*, par R*** (Brussels: la veuve Verteneuil, 1859), 10.

49. *1839*, 1st ser., no. 253, dep. Leblond, 246–247; no. 11, dep. Godquin, 17.

50. *1839*, 1st ser., nos. 116–117, *Procès-verbaux*, 105; 1st–3rd deps. Austen, 65–68; Arthur Lehning, *From Buonarroti to Bakunin* (Leiden: E. J. Brill, 1970), 161–162.

51. *Le Moniteur universel*, 19 December 1839, Mérilhou Report, 2158. (The letters were in German.)

52. *Le Moniteur universel*, 3 July 1839, dep. Tisserand, 1205.

53. *1839*, 2nd ser., 1st dep. Moulines, 22–23; see also 2nd dep. Moulines, 26, 28.

54. *1839*, 2nd ser., 1st dep. Moulines, 21; no. 455, letter, 393.

55. CC723, *Procès-verbal* of Zangiacomi on Émile Maréchal; CC723, *I.G.*, no. 90, dep. Tisserand.

56. *1839*, 2nd ser., nos. 47, 48, deps. femme Varin, 62–64; no. 44, dep. Mennesson, 56–57.

57. CC725, doss. *Maréchal*, Note from prefect of police, 29 May 1839; letter from prefect of police to procureur-général, 23 May 1839.

58. CC723, doss. *I.G.*, no. 53, dep. Brulé.

59. *1839*, 2nd ser., nos. 274 and 275, deps. Venant, 241–242; no. 277, dep. Caron, 244.

60. *1839*, 2nd ser., no. 306, dep. Deschamps, 267–268.

61. CC723, *Procès-verbal* of Zangiacomi on Louis-François Dantan, 13 May 1839.

62. *1839*, 2nd ser., no. 243, dep. Boyer, 212–13.

63. *1839*, 1st ser., no. 166, dep. Devilliers, 155–156; no. 167, dep. Deneveu, 157–158; CC723, no. 28, dep. Uhrich.

64. *1839*, 1st ser., no. 167, dep. Deneveu, 158; CC724, doss. *7e arrondissement*, dep. Alexandre.

65. Amédée Achard, *Souvenirs personnels d'émeutes et de revolutions* (Paris: Lévy frères, 1872), 20.

66. *1839*, 1st ser., no. 167, dep. Deneveu, 157–158; CC723, doss. *Marché des Inno-cents*, no. 29, dep. Dussenti; no. 27, dep. Devilliers.

67. CC723, doss. *des tués et blessés* (Lionnet); CC724, doss. *I.G.*, dep. Guillateaux; dep. Leproust.

68. CC724, doss. *I.G.*, dep. Robertet; *Le Moniteur universel*, 16 January 1840, dep. Robertet, 113.

69. *1839*, 1st ser., no. 124, dep. Garnot, 115.

70. *1839*, 2nd ser., no. 173, dep. Hébert, 147–49.

71. Paul Thureau-Dangin, *Histoire de la Monarchie de Juillet*, 3rd ed., 7 vols. (Paris: Librairie Plon, 1902), III:360–361, 391.

72. CC724, doss. *I.G.*, Lieutenant-Général Comte Pajol, *Rapport Général sur les évènements;* and letter of Lieutenant-General Trézel, 13 May 1839; *Le Journal des Débats*, 14 May 1839.

73. Louis Girard, *La Garde nationale* (Paris: Librairie Plon, 1964), 266–267; for a copy of the plan, see Louis Garnier-Pagès, *Histoire de la Révolution de 1848*, 2nd ed., 4 vols. (Paris: Pagnerre, 1866), II:358–364.

74. Claude Latta, "L'Insurrection de 1839," *Blanqui et les Blanquistes: Société d'His-toire de la Révolution* (Paris: Sedes, 1986), 75. See also CC723, prefect of the Seine Rambuteau, État des décès occasionnés par suite des Évènements des 12 et 13 May 1839, 31 May 1839, who reported 85 deaths; *Le Moniteur universel*, 15 June 1839, Mérilhou Report, 980. For their status, see CC723, doss. *des tués et blessés*.

75. The luxury trades contributed the largest numbers, followed by the familiar trades of textiles and clothing, iron-work, carpentry and wood-work, building, and finally leather. Latta does not calculate according to their proportions in the overall work force. Latta, "L'Insurrection de 1839," 78–79.

76. CC723, doss. *des tués et blessés*, *Procès-verbal* of Commissaire Prosper Truy, 13 May 1839.
77. CC723, doss. *des tués et blessés*, *Procès-verbaux* of Commissaire Blavier, 13 May 1839.
78. CC723, doss. *des tués et blessés*, *Procès-verbal* of Commissaire Aimé Chauvin, 12 May 1839.
79. CC723, doss. *des tués et blessés* (Demoiselle Wolff).
80. CC725, letter from prefect of police to procureur-général, 27 August 1839.
81. CC725, *Procès-verbal* of Commissaire Louis Gille, dep. Aubry, veuve Sépot.
82. CC725, letter from L. Millot to prefect of police, 15 November 1839.
83. CC725, report from prefect of police, 3 June 1839.
84. CC725, undated, unsigned, unaddressed note from the prefecture of police.
85. For prisons, see Sébastien Commissaire, *Mémoires et Souvenirs*, 2 vols. (Lyon: Meton, 1888), I:371, 377.
86. An approximation of 645, calculated from the *Cour des Pairs: Procès Politiques*, ed. Jeannine Charon-Bordas, 3 vols. (Paris: Archives nationales, 1984), III:61–92; Latta found a list of 692 names. Latta, "L'Insurrection de 1839," 76.
87. *1839*, 2nd ser., no. 442, *Procès-verbal d'arrestation de Blanqui*, 14 October 1839, 375–377.
88. *Procès-verbal constatant l'arrestation de l'accusé Bernard (Martin)*, 21 June 1839, 157, in *Les Révolutions du XIXe siècle*, 2nd series, v. 9; CC725, From the prefecture of police, *Extrait des sommiers*, 21 June 1839.
89. *Le Moniteur universel*, 28 June 1839, *Acte d'accusation*, 1136–1137.
90. *1839*, 2nd ser., 1st dep. Gérard, 177.
91. *Le Moniteur universel*, 30 June 1839, statement by Barbès, 1162.
92. J. F. Jeanjean, *Armand Barbès* (Paris: Édouard Cornély, 1909), 73–80.
93. Henri Eugène Philippe Louis d'Orléans, duc d'Aumale, *Le Roi Louis-Philippe et le droit de grâce* (Paris: Calmann Lévy, 1897), 8; Jeanjean, *Armand Barbès*, 74.
94. *Le Moniteur universel*, 14 January 1839, statement by Blanqui, 85.
95. Dupont, *Revue du Progrès politique, social et littéraire*, 98, in CC725.
96. *Réquisitoire de M. Franck-Carré, Procureur-Général du Roi*, 17–18; reprinted in *Les Révolutions du XIXe siècle*, 2nd ser., v. 9.
97. *Le Moniteur universel*, 22 January 1840, 155; Dupont, *Revue du Progrès politique, social et littéraire*, 98–99, in CC725.
98. The sentences listed in *Le Moniteur universel*, 1 February 1840, 208.
99. *La Commune sociale*, May 1849, Excerpts from *Blanqui et Barbès*, by *"plusieurs anciens détenus politiques"*; reprinted in *Les Révolutions du XIXe siècle*, 3rd ser., v. 9.
100. Blanqui MSS, 9584 (part 1), 116–117, cited in Alan B. Spitzer, *The Revolutionary Theories of Louis-Auguste Blanqui* (New York: Columbia University Press, 1957; reprint ed., AMS Press, 1970), 175.
101. Louis-Auguste Blanqui, *Instructions pour une prise d'armes*, ed. Miguel Abensour and Valentin Pelosse (Paris: Société encyclopédique française, 1973), 31 (quotation), 33–35.
102. Ibid., 41.
103. Ibid., 71–75.
104. Ibid., 45–47.
105. Ibid., 47.
106. Ibid., 49–53.
107. Ibid., 65, 61.

108. *Le National,* 30 June 1848, "Paris, 29 juin."

109. Blanqui, *Instructions pour une prise d'armes,* 55–69.

110. Ibid., 67–69.

111. Ibid., 22–23.

112. Ibid., 23.

113. Norbert Truquin, *Mémoires et aventures d'un prolétaire à travers la révolution* (Paris: François Maspero, 1977), 75.

114. Blanqui, *Instructions pour une prise d'armes,* 24–25.

CHAPTER 8

1. Cour des Pairs, *Attentat du 28 Juillet 1835* (Paris: Imprimerie royale, 1836), 2–3 (hereafter *1835*); *Le Moniteur universel,* 11 December 1835, Rapport fait à la cour par M. le comte Portalis, 2455–2457 (hereafter Portalis Report).

2. *1835,* dep[osition] Vaillant, 239.

3. *1835,* dep. Pelissier, 39.

4. *1835,* dep. Ragon, 265; dep. Laimbourg, 241–242; dep. Ferlay, 270; dep. Barfety, 102; dep. Besson, 26; Marie-Théodore, Comte Gueulluy de Rumigny, *Souvenirs du général comte de Rumigny* (Paris: Émile-Paul frères, 1921), 269; Comte Rudolphe Apponyi, *Journal,* 4 vols. (Paris: Plon, 1913), III:111.

5. Joinville, *Vieux Souvenirs de Monseigneur le Prince de Joinville 1818–1848,* ed. Daniel Meyer (Paris: Mercure de France, 1986), 71–72; Ferdinand-Philippe, duc d'Orléans, *Lettres, 1825–1842* (Paris: Calmann Lévy, 1889), 153–154; Rumigny, *Souvenirs,* 266.

6. Apponyi, *Journal,* III:109; Joinville, *Vieux Souvenirs,* 71; Alfred-Auguste Cuvillier-Fleury, *Journal intime de Cuvillier-Fleury,* 2 vols. (Paris: Plon, 1900), II:145.

7. *Le Moniteur universel,* 29 July 1835, 1783. See also André-Jacques Dupin, *Mémoires,* 4 vols. (Paris: Henri Plon, 1855), III:164, who reported that the king finally broke down, sobbing.

8. *1835, Procès-verbal de transport,* 20.

9. *1835,* dep. Boucharet, 268; dep. Dautrepe, 255. See also Henri-Joseph Gisquet, *Mémoires de M. Gisquet* (Paris: Marchant, 1840), IV:28.

10. *1835, Procès verbal de perquisition,* 12–13; see also dep. Laimbourg, 241–242.

11. *1835,* dep. Renniau, 234–235; dep. Berranger, 275; dep. Doreille, 244.

12. *1835,* dep. Drauguet, 38; dep. Boguet, 232.

13. *1835,* dep. Boillot, 20–21; dep. Ferlet, 40; dep. Villers, 249; dep. Mongin, 261; dep. Membré, 260.

14. *1835,* dep. Nonès, veuve Gommès, 88.

15. Portalis Report, 2461, 2457; *1835,* Rapports des médecins, 296–300.

16. Portalis Rapport, 2457; Gisquet, *Mémoires,* IV:29–30.

17. Gisquet, *Mémoires,* IV:33; see also *Le Moniteur universel,* 5 February 1836, dep. Ladvocat, 214.

18. J. Davis, *People of the Mediterranean: An Essay in Comparative Social Anthropology* (London: Routledge and Kegan Paul, 1977), 89–101.

19. Portalis Report, 2462; for brother Antoine, see *L'insulaire français,* cited in *Le National,* 28 September 1835; and also Eric Hobsbawm, *Bandits* (New York: Pantheon Books, 1981).

20. Portalis Report, 2462; Gisquet, *Mémoires,* IV:36–37.

21. Portalis Report, 2462; *1835,* dep. Petit, 417.

22. Portalis Report, 2463.

23. *1835*, dep. Petit, 413; Portalis Report, 2460.

24. *1835*, dep. Naulin, 230; dep. Petit, 420.

25. *1835*, *Procès-verbal*, 154; dep. Petit, 415; *Le Moniteur universel*, 1 February 1836, dep. Fieschi, 174.

26. Portalis Report, 2463; *Le Moniteur universel*, 5 February 1836, dep. Ladvocat, 214; *1835*, dep. de Caunes, 434.

27. *Le Moniteur universel*, 10 February 1836, 247. For Grenoble, André Jardin and André-Jean Tudesq, *Restoration and Reaction*, trans. Elborg Foster (Cambridge, MA: Cambridge University Press, 1983), 289; R. S. Alexander, "Restoration Republicanism Reconsidered," *French History* 8:4 (December 1994), 456.

28. *1835*, dep. Ladvocat, 430–33. See also *Le National*, 4 August 1835, "Détails relatifs à l'attentat."

29. Portalis Report, 2463; *Le Moniteur universel*, 10 February 1836, dep. Corréard, 248.

30. *1835*, dep. Petit, 414–415; Ibid., *Procès-verbal*, 139–40; *Procès de Fieschi et de ses complices*, 3 vols. (Paris: A. Ernest Bourdin, 1836), I:215.

31. *Le Moniteur universel*, 9 February 1836, deps. Briant, Fieschi, 245; *1835*, dep. Petit, 418.

32. Portalis Report, 2460.

33. Portalis Report, 2455; Gisquet, *Mémoires*, IV:41–42.

34. *1835*, deps. de Caunes, 433–38.

35. Canler, *Mémoires de Canler* (Paris: Mercure de France, 1968), 212–213.

36. Portalis Report, 2463–2464.

37. *Procès de Fieschi*, I:48–49, I:117–118; *1835*, dep. Petit, 420.

38. *1835*, deps. Petit, 414–415, 418.

39. *1835*, deps. Petit, 415, 419–420; *Le Moniteur universel*, 2 February 1836, 192.

40. *Procès de Fieschi*, I:288.

41. *Le Moniteur universel*, 5 February 1836, dep. Renaudin, 216.

42. Portalis Report, 2464–2465; *Le Moniteur universel*, 31 January 1836, dep. Fieschi, 171–172.

43. *Le Moniteur universel*, 12 February 1836, *plaidoyer* of Dupont, 261–62.

44. Portalis Report, 2472; *Le Moniteur universel*, 31 January 1836, dep. Fieschi, 171.

45. *Procès de Fieschi*, II:32; also *Le Moniteur universel*, 31 January 1836, dep. Fieschi, 171.

46. *Procès de Fieschi*, II:35–37; III:46; see also *Le Moniteur universel*, 31 January 1836, dep. Fieschi, 171; Ibid., 7 February 1836, dep. Fieschi, 232.

47. *Le Moniteur universel*, 1 February 1836, dep. Fieschi, 174.

48. *Procès de Fieschi*, I:320; II:101.

49. Portalis Report, 2475.

50. *Le Moniteur universel*, 1 February 1836, dep. Fieschi, 174; Ibid., 2 February 1836, dep. Pepin, 192.

51. Jean Bossu, "De l'Épicerie aux Barricades," *1848 et les révolutions du XIXe siècle* 38 (Summer 1947), 177–178.

52. *Procès de Fieschi*, II:114, 119, 138; *Le Moniteur universel*, 2 February 1836, 187, 189; Ibid., 3 February 1836, 194.

53. *Procès de Fieschi*, II:114, 116.

54. *Procès de Fieschi*, II:159–63; I:234. See also Portalis Report, 2469.

55. *Le Moniteur universel*, 2 February 1836, dep. Pepin, 191.

56. *Procès de Fieschi*, II:36, 45, 159 (quotation).

57. *Procès de Fieschi*, II:160.

58. *Le Moniteur universel*, 3 February 1836, 194; Ibid., 7 February 1836, 232; Ibid., 2 February 1836, 187–188.

59. *Procès de Fieschi*, Pepin's confession of 17 February, III:410–411.

60. *Le Moniteur universel*, 2 February 1836, 188.

61. *Le Moniteur universel*, 1 February 1836, 174–175. See also Ibid., 20 January 1836 (supplément), IV.

62. *Le Moniteur universel*, 2 February 1836, dep. Pepin, 187; Ibid., 9 February 1836, 244.

63. *Procès de Fieschi*, II:46, 153 (quotation).

64. Pepin's confessions of 17 February and 19 February in *Procès de Fieschi*, III:405–406, 413–416.

65. Portalis Report, 2467; see also Gisquet, *Mémoires*, II:231–232, 274.

66. *Gazette des Tribunaux*, 17 June 1832, 1er Conseil de Guerre.

67. *Le Moniteur universel*, 15 February 1836, *plaidoyer* of Marie, 271.

68. Adolphe Chenu, *Les Conspirateurs* (Paris: Garnier frères, 1850), 15–16.

69. *1835, Procès-verbal de perquisition*, 14–15.

70. *Le Moniteur universel*, 1 February 1836, dep. Fieschi, 174; *1835*, dep. femme Salmon, 45.

71. *Le Moniteur universel*, 4 February 1836, 203.

72. *1835*, dep. Bury, 354–55; *Le Moniteur universel*, 1 February 1836, dep. Fieschi, 175.

73. *Le Moniteur universel*, 1 February 1836, dep. Fieschi, 175; Ibid., 9 February 1836, 244.

74. *1835*, dep. femme Salmon, 45; dep. Travault, 116.

75. *1835*, dep. Salmon, 47; dep. E. Paul, 63–64; dep. F. Paul, 91–92.

76. *1835*, dep. femme Salmon, 45; dep. Andrener, 59; dep. femme Baudon, 65.

77. *1835*, dep. femme Salmon, 44; dep. S. Salmon, 42; dep. Andrener, 55–56; dep. veuve Robert, 66.

78. *1835*, deps. Daurat, 221–229.

79. *1835*, deps. Bocquin, 211–220; *Le Moniteur universel*, 1 February 1836, dep. Fieschi, 174.

80. *1835*, dep. S. Salmon, 42; dep. Travault, 114.

81. *1835, Procès-verbal*, 151; *Le Moniteur universel*, 4 February 1836, dep. Lassave, 203.

82. *Le Moniteur universel*, 1 February 1836, dep. Fieschi, 175.

83. Morey went bankrupt in 1826, and the bankruptcy official blamed his mistress. Portalis Report, 2471–2472; and *Le Moniteur universel*, 31 January 1836, dep. Fieschi, 171.

84. *Procès de Fieschi*, III:51; *Le Moniteur universel*, 7 February 1836, 232; and Ibid., 1 February 1836, 176.

85. *1835*, dep. Lassave, 195–201 (Nina heard the details from Morey); *Le Moniteur universel*, 1 February 1836, dep. Fieschi, 174–179.

86. *Le Moniteur universel*, 1 February 1836, dep. Fieschi, 176.

87. *1835*, dep. femme Salmon, 45; and dep. S. Salmon, 42–43.

88. *1835*, dep. S. Salmon, 77–78.

89. Joinville, *Vieux Souvenirs*, 71; *Le Moniteur universel*, 3 February 1836, dep. Boireau, 196.

90. *Le Moniteur universel*, 4 February 1836, dep. Fieschi, 201.

91. *Le Moniteur universel*, 4 February 1836, dep. Fieschi, 201.
92. *Le Moniteur universel*, 3 February 1836, dep. veuve Boilot, 197.
93. *Le Moniteur universel*, 4 February 1836, dep. Fieschi, 201.
94. *1835*, dep. N. Lassave, 186; *nouvelles déclarations*, 192–93.
95. *1835*, dep. Beauvillers, 153; dep. Lassave, 195–196; *nouvelles déclarations*, 193–194.
96. *1835*, deps. Lassave, 197–199; *nouvelles déclarations*, 193–194.
97. Morey denied that he had referred to Mortier as *canaille*. *Procès de Fieschi*, II:101–105 (1st quotation); *Le Moniteur universel*, 6 February 1836, dep. Dambreville, 226.
98. *1835*, dep. Lassave, 199–202; *nouvelles déclarations*, 194.
99. Portalis Report, 2458, 2460; *1835*, *Procès-verbaux de transport, de perquisition*, 161–167.
100. Gisquet, *Mémoires*, IV:31–32. See arrest list of those rounded up as known political dissidents in *Procès de Fieschi*, I:90–97; for arrests of Morey and Pepin, see Ibid., I:105–117.
101. *Le Moniteur universel*, 8 February 1836, deps. Suireau, Dyonnet, 237, 240.
102. Gisquet, *Mémoires*, IV:30–31; *Le Moniteur universel*, 6 February 1836, dep. Boireau, 228.
103. *1835*, dep. Meunier, 120; dep. Vienot, 121; dep. Momon, 122.
104. *1835*, *Procès-verbaux de recherche*, 126–129; *Procès-verbal de perquisition*, 134–135.
105. *1835*, *Procès-verbaux*, 126–129, 134–140, 539–544; Ibid., dep. Morey, 132–133.
106. *1835*, *Procès-verbal de recherche*, 141–143; dep. Dubromet, 144–145.
107. *1835*, *Procès-verbal de transport*, 156–57; Portalis Report, 2458.
108. *1835*, *Procès-verbal d'arrestation*, 561–563; Gisquet, *Mémoires*, IV:53–55.
109. *1835*, dep. femme Pepin, 597–600, 603–604.
110. Gisquet, *Mémoires*, IV:60–67; *1835*, *Procès-verbal d'arrestation*, 567; Portalis Report, 2473.
111. Abbé Grivel, *La Prison du Luxembourg sous la règne de Louis-Philippe* (Paris: Auguste Vaton, 1862), 18; *Journal des Débats*, 20 February 1836, letter from Fieschi; *Le National*, 20 January 1836, letter from Fieschi.
112. *Le Moniteur universel*, 3 February 1836, dep. Boireau, 194.
113. *Le Moniteur universel*, 1 February 1836, 177.
114. *Le Moniteur universel*, 4 February 1836, 203; Ibid., 7 February 1836, 234; *1835*, 1re Rapport d'experts, 34; dep. Sidrac, 251.
115. *Le Moniteur universel*, 4 February 1836, dep. Lassave, 203.
116. *Le Moniteur universel*, 1 February 1836, dep. Fieschi, 177.
117. *Le Moniteur universel*, 5 February 1836, 214.
118. *Le Moniteur universel*, 7 February 1836, 234.
119. *Le Moniteur universel*, 9 February 1836, deps. Bonnet, Bouvier, Baude, 244–245.
120. *Le Moniteur universel*, 9 February 1836, 245–246.
121. *Le Moniteur universel*, 10 February 1836, 248.
122. *Le Moniteur universel*, 10 February 1836, dep. Petit, 249.
123. *Le Moniteur universel*, 11 February 1836, *plaidoyer* Patorni, 257–258; Ibid., 12 February 1836, *plaidoyer* Dupont, 263–264; Ibid., 14 February 1836, *plaidoyer* Parquin, 280; Ibid., 14 February 1836, *plaidoyer* Dupin, 285–286; and Ibid., 15 February 1836, *plaidoyer* Chaix-d'Est-Ange, 288.
124. *Le Moniteur universel*, 15 February 1836, 289.
125. Gisquet, *Mémoires*, IV:88, 86.

126. *Journal des Débats*, 18 February 1836.

127. *Journal des Débats*, 20 February 1836, letter from Fieschi.

128. From *Le Bon Sens*, cited in *Le National*, 22 February 1836.

129. Gisquet, *Mémoires*, IV:85–87.

130. J. Lucas-Dubreton, *Louis-Philippe et la machine infernale 1830–1835* (Paris: Amiot-Dumont, 1951), 321, 352.

131. Paul Thureau-Dangin, *Histoire de la Monarchie de Juillet*, 3rd ed., 7 vols. (Paris: Plon, 1902), VII:400–401.

132. *Gazette des Tribunaux*, 20–21 February 1837, "Projet d'attentat contre la vie du Roi"; Ibid., 22 February 1837, "Chronique"; Ibid., 23 February 1837, "Chronique."

133. *Le National*, 13 December 1835; Canler, *Mémoires*, 220.

134. *Le Messager*, cited in *Le National*, 20 February 1836.

135. *Gazette des Tribunaux*, 23 February 1837, "Chronique."

136. Bossu, "De l'Épicerie aux Barricades," 61–64.

CHAPTER 9

1. J. Lucas-Dubreton, *L'Affaire Alibaud ou Louis-Philippe traqué* (1836) (Paris: Perrin et cie, 1927), 217. It was Lucas-Dubreton who used the term "cult."

2. *Procès d'Alibaud devant la Cour des Pairs* (Paris: Pagnerre, 1836), 24; *Le Moniteur universel*, 9 July 1836, dep. Delaborde, 1596.

3. Cour des Pairs de France, *Attentat du 27 décembre 1836* (Paris: Imprimerie royale, 1837), 3–4, hereafter cited as *1836*. See also *Le Journal des Débats*, 26 June 1836.

4. *Gazette des Tribunaux*, 28 June 1836; *Journal du Commerce*, cited in *Procès d'Alibaud*, 14–16, 26. See also the "Attentat contre la vie du Roi," and "Exécution d'Alibaud," two popular broadsheets; reprinted in *Les Révolutions du XIXe siècle*, 1st ser., vol. 12.

5. Letter from Alibaud, printed in *Procès d'Alibaud*, 52–53.

6. *1836*, "Rapport fait à la Cour par M. le Comte de Bastard," 5–7 (Bastard Report); *Le Moniteur universel*, 9 July 1836, 1595.

7. *Le Moniteur universel*, 9 July 1836, 1595.

8. *1836*, Bastard Report, 8–9; on Barcelona, see Armand Carrel, "De la guerre d'Espagne en 1823," *Oeuvres politiques et littéraires*, 5 vols. (Paris: Librairie de F. Chamerot, 1857), V:124–125.

9. *1836*, Bastard Report, 8–10; *Le Moniteur universel*, 9 July 1836, 1595; John Coverdale, *The Basque Phase of Spain's First Carlist War* (Princeton: Princeton University Press, 1984), esp. 205–225, 286–294.

10. *1836*, Bastard Report, 10–11; *Le Moniteur universel*, 9 July 1836, dep[osition] Maurice, 1596–1597.

11. *Gazette des Tribunaux*, 9 July 1836, dep. Fraisse; *1836*, Bastard Report, 13–18.

12. *1836*, Bastard Report, 12–14; *Gazette des Tribunaux*, 9 July 1836, dep. Manoury.

13. *Le Moniteur universel*, 9 July 1836, dep. Alibaud, 1596.

14. *1836*, Bastard Report, 15–16.

15. *1836*, Bastard Report, 17–18; *Le Moniteur universel*, 9 July 1836, dep. Alibaud, 1596.

16. Henri-Joseph Gisquet, *Mémoires de M. Gisquet*, 4 vols. (Paris: Marchant, 1840), IV:154–156; *Procès d'Alibaud, Acte d'accusation*, 25–26.

17. *Procès d'Alibaud*, 58–64; E. Cauchy, *Les Précédents de la Cour des Pairs* (Paris: Imprimerie Royale, October 1839), 443–445.
18. *Le Moniteur universel*, 9 July 1836, deps. Dubois and Fraisse, 1598; Corbières, 1599.
19. *Le Moniteur universel*, 9 July 1836, dep. Alibaud, 1595; *Procès d'Alibaud*, 57.
20. *Procès d'Alibaud*, 149–150.
21. Ibid., 147–148.
22. *Le Moniteur universel*, 10 July 1836, *Plaidoyer* Ledru, 1605.
23. *Procès d'Alibaud*, 145; Henri Eugène Philippe Louis d'Orléans, duc d'Aumale, *Le Roi Louis-Philippe et le droit de grace* (Paris: Calmann Lévy, 1897), 15.
24. *Le National*, 13 July 1836.
25. *Procès d'Alibaud*, 154–56; also *Le National*, 13 July 1836; *Journal des Débats*, 12 July 1836. Karl Sand assassinated the conservative Austrian playwright Auguste Kotzebue in 1819.
26. *Procès d'Alibaud*, 156–158.
27. *Gazette des Tribunaux*, 1 December 1836; Gisquet, *Mémoires*, IV:169–171.
28. *Gazette des Tribunaux*, 1 December 1836, *Acte d'accusation;* and 16 December 1836. For *Le Bon Sens*, subtitled *Tribune des prolétaires*, see R. Gossez, "Presse Parisienne à destination des ouvriers (1848–1851)," *La Presse ouvrière 1819–1850* (Paris: Bibliothèque de la Révolution de 1848, 1966), 23:128.
29. *Gazette des Tribunaux*, 16 December 1836.
30. Ibid.
31. Cour des Pairs, *Attentat du 27 décembre 1836* (Paris: Imprimerie royale, 1837; henceforth cited as *1837*), deps. Mézières, 21; Cardon, 12; and Soher, 12 (who heard the king shout "don't kill him!" as Meunier was seized); *Journal des Débats*, 28 December 1836.
32. *1837*, deps. Raynouard, 17–18; Germain, 8; Marix, 47–48 (quotation).
33. *1837*, *Acte d'accusation*, 19–20; dep. Barré, 30–31.
34. *1837*, *Acte d'accusation*, 18; 1st dep. Meunier, 9.
35. *1837*, dep. Marut de l'Ombre, 165–166; see also dep. Doignies, 167.
36. *1837*, "Rapport fait à la cour par M. Barthe," 37 (Barthe Report).
37. In the *coup de pistolet* assassination attempt in 1832, 19-year-old Prosper Hess revealed to the authorities in Melun "qu'il connaissait des jeunes gens qui avaient fait le serment de commettre un régicide" ("that he knew of some young men who had taken the oath to commit a regicide"). *Gazette des Tribunaux*, 28–29 January 1833. The would-be assassin Darmès also boasted of such a society; *Le Moniteur universel*, 26 May 1841, dep. Martin, femme Grébin, 1486. See also the several obscure young workers of the regicidal *Légions révolutionnaires*, in *Le Journal des Débats*, 28 August 1835; and I. Tchernoff, *Le Parti républicain sous la Monarchie de Juillet* (Paris: A Pedone, 1901), 378–380; Gisquet, *Mémoires*, IV:194–198.
38. *1837*, Barthe Report, 82–84; Gisquet, *Mémoires*, IV:159.
39. *Procès d'Alibaud*, 141–142; 144.
40. *1837*, dep. Grisier, 50–51.
41. *1837*, dep. Champion, 32–33; dep. Barré, 27–28.
42. *1837*, dep. Simonet, 34–35.
43. *1837*, dep. Barré, 27–28.
44. *1837*, dep. Husson, 40–41; dep. Muller, femme Henraux, 42; dep. Cauvin, 43.
45. *1837*, *Procès-verbal constatant le transport, à l'hospice Beaujon*, 60–62.
46. *1837*, 1st dep. Meunier, 3.

47. *1837*, dep. Desenclos, 121–122.
48. *1837*, dep. Breteuil, 157 (quotation); see also deps. Belliot, 158; Girard, 138–139; Perrot, 152.
49. *1837*, *Réquisitoire*, 57–58. The ministerial *Journal des Débats* first described him as a brutish and self-motivated assassin; by the next day he was portrayed as a weak character who could be "pushed" into committing a crime. *Journal des Débats*, 28 December 1836; and 29 December 1836. See also François-Pierre-Guillaume Guizot, *Mémoires*, 8 vols. (Paris: Michel Lévy frères, 1872), IV:208
50. *1837*, dep. Bollot, 40.
51. *1837*, dep. Dupont, 49; dep. Grisier, 51–52.
52. *1837*, dep. femme Jacquet, 71–72.
53. *1837*, dep. femme Jacquet, 72; dep. Salbat, 77; dep. femme Duchêne, 58; dep. Dupont, 49; dep. Jacquillon, 45.
54. For Meunier's last few days, see *1837*, Barthe Report, 16; dep. Girard, 137; dep. Jacquet, 68.
55. *1837*, 6th dep. Meunier, 46.
56. *1837*, 10th dep. Meunier, 59–60.
57. *1837*, 10th dep. Meunier, 60.
58. *1837*, 13th dep. Meunier, 67–68.
59. *1837*, 14th dep. Meunier, 69–71.
60. *1837*, 14th dep. Meunier, 74.
61. *1837*, 15th dep. Meunier, 76–77.
62. *1837*, 16th dep. Meunier, 83.
63. *Le Moniteur universel*, 25 April 1837, 997.
64. *Le Moniteur universel*, 23 April 1837, deps. Desenclos, Dumont, 971–972.
65. *1837*, 3rd dep. Lacaze, 187.
66. *Le Moniteur universel*, 29 April 1837, 1034; *Le National*, 28 April 1837. Meunier's fate was discussed in the Darmès case, in *Le Moniteur universel*, 28 May 1841, *Réquisitoire*, 1522.
67. See the *Procès du coup de pistolet* (Paris: P. Dupont and Laguionie, 1833); reprinted in *Les Révolutions du XIXe siècle*, 1st ser., vol. 3.
68. Guizot, *Mémoires*, III:304.
69. Gisquet, *Mémoires*, IV:147, 203. Paul Thureau-Dangin, *Histoire de la Monarchie de Juillet*, 3rd ed., 7 vols. (Paris: Librairie Plon, 1902), III:122, notes that Gisquet was forced out by questions about his business dealings.
70. Letter to President of the Chamber of Deputies Dupin, 23 July 1836, cited in André-Jacques Dupin, *Mémoires*, 4 vols. (Paris: Henri Plon, 1855), III:218.
71. *Le Globe*, 19 June 1831, unsigned letter to the editor.
72. *Le Moniteur universel*, 12 February 1836, *plaidoyer* Dupont, 263.
73. *Gazette des Tribunaux*, 26 April 1834; *Le Moniteur universel*, 15 June 1839, Mérilhou Report, 973.
74. *Gazette des Tribunaux*, 7 August 1836; see also Thureau-Dangin, *Histoire*, II:317–318.
75. "Au Roi," reprinted in Maxime Du Camp, *L'Attentat Fieschi* (Paris: G. Charpentier, 1877), 297–300. See also abbreviated form in *Le Moniteur universel*, 15 June 1839, Mérilhou Report, 975.
76. Henri Dourille, *Histoire de la Conspiration du Général Malet, 1812* (Paris: Bureau du Journal du Peuple, 1840); see also Malet, *Le National*, 25 August 1834; and 3 August 1840.

77. For complete versions of Nos. 1, 3, 6, and 8 of the *Moniteur républicain*, see *Les Révolutions du XIXe siècle*, 1st ser., v. 12.

78. *Gazette des Tribunaux*, 31 October 1841.

79. *Gazette des Tribunaux*, 26 May 1839, *Acte d'accusation*.

80. *Le Moniteur universel*, 15 June 1839, Mérilhou Report, 975.

81. Ibid.

82. *Le Moniteur universel*, 6 July 1839, *Réquisitoire*, 1250–1251; and 15 June 1839, Mérilhou Report, 975.

83. *Le Moniteur universel*, 15 June 1839, Mérilhou Report, 975.

84. Ibid.

85. Ibid., 976.

86. Ibid.; aphorisms printed in *Gazette des Tribunaux*, 26 May 1836: "One does not judge a king, one kills him" ("On ne juge pas un roi, on le tue"), Billaud-Varennes; "One cannot reign innocently" ("On ne peut pas régner innocent(sic)"), Saint-Just; "Regicide is the right of the man who can only obtain justice by his own hand" ("Le régicide le droit de l'homme qui ne peut obtenir justice que par ses mains"), Alibaud.

87. *Gazette des Tribunaux*, 8 June 1839.

88. *Le Moniteur universel*, 15 June 1839, Mérilhou Report, 976; *Gazette des Tribunaux*, 26 May 1839.

89. *Le Moniteur universel*, 15 June 1839, Mérilhou Report, 976; Georges Sencier, *Le Babouvisme après Babeuf* (Geneva: Mégariotis Reprints; reprint of Paris ed., 1912), 96–97, 107–108.

90. Jean Bossu, "De l'Épicerie aux Barricades," *1848 et les Révolutions du XIXe siècle* 38:177–178 (Summer 1947), 61–62.

91. Jules Taschereau, *Revue Rétrospective* (Paris: Paulin, 1848), 9; Lucien Delahodde, *Histoire des sociétés secrètes* (Paris: Julien, Lanier et cie, 1850), 227–228; Tchernoff, *Le Parti républicain*, 375.

92. See *Le Moniteur universel*, 15 June 1839, Mérilhou Report, 975, 977; *Gazette des Tribunaux*, 26 May 1839, *Acte d'accusation*; 8 June 1839; and 9 June 1839.

93. *Gazette des Tribunaux*, 26 May 1839, *Acte d'accusation*; for the trial, Ibid., issues 8 to 12 June 1839.

94. *Gazette des Tribunaux*, 30 November 1839, *Acte d'accusation*; 1 December 1839.

95. *Gazette des Tribunaux*, 31 October 1841; Zephir-Zacharie Seigneurgens, "Affaire du *Moniteur républicain*" (Paris: Rouanet, 1841); reprinted in *Les Révolutions du XIXe siècle*, 1st ser., v. 12. See also Jacques Rancière, *The Nights of Labor*, trans. John Drury (Philadelphia: Temple University Press, 1989), 101.

96. *L'Atelier*, October 1840, 9–10.

97. *Gazette des Tribunaux*, 16 December 1836.

CHAPTER 10

1. *Le Moniteur universel*, 13 May 1841, "Rapport fait à la cour par M. le baron Girod (de l'Ain)," 1300–1301 (subsequently cited as Girod Report).

2. Cour des Pairs de France, *Attentat du 15 Octobre 1840* (Paris: Imprimerie royale, 1841), 121. (All subsequent references to the Darmès case, aside from the trial references, come from this printed source, cited as *1840*.)

3. Girod Report, 1300–1301.

4. *1840*, depositions of witnesses, 22–33.

5. *1840*, dep. Devaux, 16; see also dep. Bachelier, 11.

6. *Le Moniteur universel*, 25 May 1841, *Acte d'accusation*, 1465.

7. *Le Populaire*, 20 May 1841, "Rapport sur l'Affaire Darmès." Cabet correctly reported that about sixty had been arrested. *Cour des Pairs: Procès Politiques*, ed. Jeannine Charon-Bordas, 3 vols. (Paris: Archives nationales, 1984), III:113–116.

8. *Le Moniteur universel*, 25 May 1841, *Acte d'accusation*, 1462.

9. *1840*, 1st dep. Darmès, 1–2.

10. *1840*, *Procès-verbaux* by Commissaire François Monvalle, 412–419; *Le Moniteur universel*, 25 May 1841, *Acte d'accusation*, 1462.

11. *Gazette des Tribunaux*, 3 July 1841; and Ibid., 9–11 July 1841, *Cour royale de Paris*.

12. Girod Report, 1299; *1840*, dep. Simard, 514–515.

13. *Gazette des Tribunaux*, 7 March 1832, and 16–22 March 1832, *Affaire des Tours de Notre-Dame; Le Moniteur universel*, 25 May 1841, dep. Considère, 1467–1468.

14. Girod Report, 1299; *Le Moniteur universel*, 28 May 1841, dep. Pannié, 1518. For Laffitte's letter, see *Gazette des Tribunaux*, 29 May 1841; see also Laffitte, *Mémoires*, 340–341.

15. *1840*, dep. Troquet, 208; *4e perquisition*, 100–103.

16. *1840*, dep. Mirault, 202–204; dep. Joly, 291–292, also dep. Pagès, 299 (employers).

17. *1840*, deps. Dubois and Veuve Petit, 185–87.

18. *1840*, deps. Joly, 293, 297; *Procès-verbal de perquisition*, 110. See also Girod Report, 1272.

19. *1840*, dep. femme Billoret, 187.

20. *1840*, deps. Billoret; Vve Courcier; Sinet, 188–90.

21. *1840*, deps. Vanderbroeck, 284; femme Grébin, 193; femme Marchand, 251. "Monomania" was briefly a faddish diagnosis; see Jan Goldstein, *Console and Classify: The French Psychiatric Profession in the Nineteenth Century* (Cambridge, MA: Cambridge University Press, 1987), 152–196.

22. *1840*, *Procès-verbaux* of Commissaire Alphonse Colin, 99; of Commissaire Gille, 283–286.

23. *1840*, dep. Ballefin, 196.

24. For the evolution of service, see Cissie Fairchilds, *Domestic Enemies: Servants and their Masters in Old Regime France* (Baltimore: The Johns Hopkins Press, 1984), esp. 13–20; Sara Maza, *Servants and Masters in Eighteenth-Century France* (Princeton: Princeton University Press, 1983).

25. *1840*, dep. Fassola, 215.

26. Ibid., 218–219.

27. *1840*, dep. Brisedou, 239.

28. *1840*, dep. Bergeret, 206; dep. Raulet, 295.

29. *1840*, dep. Reybaud, 301–302; for the *National* remark, dep. Sauzet, 241.

30. *1840*, dep. Estienne, 207.

31. *1840*, dep. femme Sinet, 249.

32. *1840*, *Procès-verbal* by Commissaire Pierre Masson, 106; dep. Fassola, 218; *3e perquisition*, 99.

33. *Le Moniteur universel*, 25 May 1841, *Acte d'accusation*, 1462. For Judith, see Franklin Ford, *Political Murder: From Tyrannicide to Terrorism* (Cambridge, MA: Harvard University Press, 1985), 9–11. For Lycurgus, see for example Etienne Cabet, *Le Populaire*, 20 May 1841, "Rapport sur l'Affaire Darmès." His third engraving was *la première confidence d'une jeune fille*.

34. *1840, Perquisitions*, 96–100. The ad for the medallion, advertised as in the style of Jacques-Louis David, was in *Le National*, 9 July 1837.
35. *1840, Procès-verbal d'ouverture de la malle*, 104–108.
36. *1840, Procès-verbal d'ouverture de la malle*, 105–106.
37. *1840, Perquisitions*, 134ff; 4th dep. Darmès, 8.
38. *1840*, dep. Tournier, 195; see also dep. Chauvière, 198. The poem was found in his papers, 170–177.
39. *1840, Perquisitions*, "Discour d'un homme du peuple," 148–152.
40. *Le Moniteur universel*, 25 May 1841, *Acte d'accusation*, 1462.
41. *1840*, 3rd dep. Darmès, 4–6.
42. *1840, Perquisitions et pièces saisies*, 136.
43. For a full discussion, see Paul Thureau-Dangin, *Histoire de la Monarchie de Juillet*, 3rd ed., 7 vols. (Paris: Librairie Plon, 1902), IV:198ff, esp. 222–228. See the lengthy article in *Le National*, 30 August 1840; and 12 September 1840. For the popular impact of the treaty of 15 July, Michael Paul Driskel, "Singing 'The Marseillaise' in 1840: the Case of Charlet's Censored Prints," *The Art Bulletin* LXIX:4 (December 1987), 604–625, esp. 607–615.
44. *Le Moniteur universel*, 25 May 1841, *Acte d'accusation*, 1462.
45. *1840*, dep. L'Hoste, 285.
46. *1840*, dep. Petit, 281.
47. For Darmès' attendence, see *1840*, dep. Mirault, 203; dep. Grébin, 191; dep. Estienne, 207; dep. Lefort, 244; for the banquet, *Le National*, 1 September 1840, "Manifestation réformiste."
48. There were 130 cases brought against coalitions, compared to 64 in 1839; see Octave Festy, "Le mouvement ouvrier à Paris en 1840," *Revue des sciences politiques* (July–November 1913):67–79; 221–240; 333–361.
49. *1840*, dep. Bickel, 201–205.
50. *1840*, dep. Fassola, 216–217.
51. *1840*, dep. Petit, 206.
52. Girod Report, 1272, 1286.
53. *1840*, dep. Lefort, 275.
54. *1840*, dep. Grébin, 192.
55. *Le Moniteur universel*, 25 May 1841, *Acte d'accusation*, 1462; Girod Report, 1299.
56. *Le Moniteur universel*, 25 May 1841, dep. Darmès, 1466; and 26 May 1841, dep. Darmès, 1486.
57. *Le Moniteur universel*, 25 May 1841, dep. Darmès, 1465; Ibid., 26 May 1841, 1487.
58. *Le Moniteur universel*, 28 May 1841, *Réquisitoire*, 1519.
59. *Le Populaire*, 20 June 1841, "Revue judiciaire: Exécution de Darmès"; *Le National*, 2 June 1841.
60. *1840*, 3rd dep. Darmès, 5.
61. Cited by H. A. C. Collingham, *The July Monarchy: A Political History of France, 1830–1848* (London: Longman, 1988), 294–95. See also *Journal des Débats*, 14 September 1841.
62. Cour des Pairs de France, *Attentat du 13 Septembre 1841* (Paris: Imprimerie royale, 1841), dep. Bignon, 46; see also dep. Mantel, 63–64. (Henceforth cited as *1841*).
63. *Journal des Débats*, 14 September 1841; *1841, Procès-verbal* of Commissaire Jean Noël, 20–23.

64. *Rapport fait à la Cour Par M. le Comte de Bastard* (Paris: Imprimerie royale, 1841), 5 (cited as Bastard Report); reprinted in *Les Révolutions du XIXe siècle*, 2nd series, v. 11.

65. *1841*, dep. Fournier, 56.

66. *1841*, dep. Élophe, 13.

67. *1841*, dep. Camusat, 203.

68. Bastard Report, 180.

69. *1841*, 2nd dep. Quenisset, 3; 3rd dep. Quenisset, 10; Bastard Report, 10.

70. *1841*, 4th dep. Quenisset, 23.

71. *1841*, 16th dep. Quenisset, 80. See also Jean Bossu, "Mathieu d'Épinal et son temps," 1848 et *Les Révolutions du XIXe siècle* 18 (Fall 1947):27–64.

72. *1841*, 16th dep. Quenisset, 81–83.

73. For Prioul, *Le National*, 4 November 1841.

74. *1841*, 4th dep. Quenisset, 14–17.

75. *1841*, 1st dep. Boucheron, 86.

76. *1841*, dep. Pradel, 193–94.

77. *1841*, 3rd dep. Mallet, 269; l6th dep. Petit, 197; 1st dep. Boggio dit Martin, 246; 2nd–3rd deps. Colombier, 98.

78. *1841*, 3rd dep. Quenisset, 10–11; dep. Riokotter, 102–103; dep. Martin, 102; dep. Maguier, 104; dep. fille Leplâtre, 97.

79. *1841*, 3rd dep. Quenisset, 10–11.

80. *1841*, 6th dep. Quenisset, 37; 5th dep. Quenisset, 27; 4th dep. Quenisset, 17.

81. *1841*, 3rd dep. Boggio, 250–251; *Gazette des Tribunaux*, 4 December 1841, dep. Petit.

82. *1841*, 5th dep. Quenisset, 30.

83. *1841*, 4th dep. Quenisset, 18; 5th dep. Quenisset, 30.

84. *1841*, 5th dep. Quenisset, 28–29; for Couturat, dep. Savelle dit Marin, 249. Cabet believed that Dufour had acted as an *agent provocateur,* in setting up mass arrests for possession; see *Le Populaire*, 30 January 1842, "La Vérité sur l'attentat Quenisset."

85. *1841*, 4th dep. Quenisset, 18–20.

86. *1841*, 6th dep. Quenisset, 40–41.

87. *1841*, 4th dep. Quenisset, 20–21.

88. *1841*, 6th dep. Quenisset, 43; 4th dep. Quenisset, 13.

89. *Gazette des Tribunaux*, 4 December 1841, dep. Boucheron; *1841*, 2nd dep. Colombier, 99.

90. *1841*, 5th and 6th deps. Petit dit Auguste, 192.

91. *1841*, dep. Hermann, 158–59.

92. *1841*, 3rd dep. Mallet, 269–270.

93. *1841*, 5th and 6th deps. Petit dit Auguste, 191–94.

94. *1841*, dep. Savelle, 105–106.

95. *1841*, 2nd dep. Colombier, 99.

96. *Journal des Débats*, 12 December 1841.

97. *1841*, 5th dep. Quenisset, 25–27; 5th and 6th deps. Petit dit Auguste, 197–98.

98. *1841*, dep. Duru, 153.

99. *1841*, *Réquisitoire prononcé par M. Hébert*, 76–77.

100. Adolphe Chauveau and Faustin Hélie, *Théorie du Code pénal*, 2nd ed., 6 vols. (Paris: Edouard Legrand, 1843), I:449–450; II:136–139; *Plaidoirie de M. Ledru-Rollin pour M. Dupoty* (Paris: Lange Lévy et cie, 1841); reprinted in *Les Révolutions du XIXe siècle*, 2nd ser., v. 7.

101. A. Gourvitch, "Le Mouvement pour la réforme, 1838–41," in *La Révolution de 1848*, vols. 12 (1915–1916), 13 (1916–1917), and 14 (1917–1918); see also Élias Regnault, *Histoire de Huit Ans, 1840–1848*, 5th ed., 3 vols. (Paris: Librairie Germer Baillière, 1882), I:167–184.
102. Gourvitch, "Le Mouvement," 12:99–100.
103. Ibid., 12:126.
104. Ibid., 12:128, 111–113.
105. Abbé Grivel, *La Prison du Luxembourg sous la règne de Louis Philippe* (Paris: Auguste Vaton, 1862), 189–190.
106. J. Tripier-Le Franc, *M. Gabriel Delessert* (Paris: E. Dentu, 1859), 175–176; Grivel, *La Prison du Luxembourg*, 192; *Le Populaire*, 11 December 1842, "Curieuse révélation sur Quenisset"; and Ibid., October 1844, "Revue judiciaire: Amnistie."
107. Suzanne Huart, *Journal de Marie-Amélie, Reine des Français, 1800–1866* (Paris: Libraire Académique Perrin, 1981), 512–513.
108. André-Jacques Dupin, *Mémoires*, 4 vols. (Paris: Henri Plon, 1855), IV:185–186; François-Pierre-Guillaume Guizot, *Mémoires*, 8 vols. (Paris: Michel Lévy frères, 1872), VII:34–38.
109. Michael Marrinan, *Painting Politics for Louis-Philippe: Art and Ideology in Orléanist France* (New Haven: Yale University Press, 1988), 17–19.

CHAPTER 11

1. *L'Atelier*, October 1844, 1–2.
2. Review of Louis Blanc, *Histoire de Dix Ans*, in *La Démocratie pacifique*, 23 November 1843; Victor Considérant, *Principes du socialisme de la démocratie au XIXe siècle* (Paris: Librairie Phalanstèrienne, 1847), 42–43; reprinted in *Les Révolutions du XIXe siècle*, 2nd ser., v. 4.
3. *Le National*, 28 December 1844.
4. Roger Magraw, *A History of the French Working Class*, vol. 1: *The Age of Artisan Revolution* (Oxford: Blackwell Publishers, 1992), I:36.
5. Magraw, *The Age of Artisan Revolution*, I:34–35; Adolphe Chauveau and Faustin Hélie, *Théorie du Code Pénal*, 2nd ed., 6 vols. (Paris: Edouard Legrand, 1843), V:509–511.
6. *Le National*, 21 September 1844; see also *Le Populaire*, 2 April 1842, "Revue judiciaire."
7. Chauveau and Hélie, *Théorie du Code Pénal*, V:516–517 (quotation), 512–513, 521.
8. G. Duchène, *Livrets et Prud'hommes* (Paris: Au bureau de la Société de l'Industrie fraternelle, 1847), 28–29; reprinted in *Les Révolutions du XIXe siècle*, 2nd ser., v. 2. (21 March 1827, art. 1701 of the Code.)
9. Chauveau and Hélie, *Théorie du Code Pénal*, V:521–522.
10. Speech of 9 November 1830, cited in André-Jacques Dupin, *Mémoires de M. Dupin*, 4 vols. (Paris: Henri Plon, 1855), II:257–258.
11. Alain Faure, "Mouvements populaires," *Le Mouvement social* 88 (1979), 53–67.
12. Octave Festy, "Le Mouvement ouvrier à Paris en 1840," *Revue des Sciences politiques* (July–November 1913), 67, for figures. See also Edouard Dolléans, *Histoire du Mouvement ouvrier*, 2 vols. (Paris: Librairie Armand Colin, 1936), I:182–184.
13. *Le National*, 4 September 1840, letter from Dominique, *ouvrier menuisier* (carpenter); *L'Atelier*, December 1843, "Les ouvriers charpentiers et leurs maîtres,"

43. For the eighteenth-century background of subcontracting, see Michael Sonenscher, *Work and Wages: Natural Law, Politics, and the Eighteenth-Century French Trades* (Cambridge, MA: Cambridge University Press, 1989), 33–41.

14. Cited in Bernard Mottez, *Systèmes de Salaire et politiques patronales* (Paris: Éditions du Centre Nationale de la Recherche Scientifique, 1966), 48.

15. Julien Blanc, *La Grève des Charpentiers en 1845* (Paris: Librairie sociétaire, 1845), letter to Master Carpenters from Vincent, 18; Ibid., "Manifeste des entrepreneurs," 52; see also Casey Harison, "An Organization of Labor: Laissez-Faire and *Marchandage* in the Paris Building Trades through 1848," *French Historical Studies* 20:3 (Summer 1997), 357–358.

16. *L'Atelier*, March 1845, "Projet de loi sur le livret, pétition des ouvriers de Paris," 84–88. See also *La Démocratie pacifique*, 25 February 1847, "Le Livret des ouvriers"; Ibid., 1–2 March 1847, "Le Livret des ouvriers"; Ibid., 3 March 1847, "Le Livret et la liberté d'association"; *Le Livret, c'est le servage* (Paris: Librairie sociétaire, 1847); reprinted in *Les Révolutions du XIXe siècle*, 2nd ser., v. 2.

17. For the articles from *La Démocratie pacifique*, which provided the fullest coverage, see J. Blanc, *La Grève des Charpentiers*.

18. Harison, "An Organization of Labor," 360–365.

19. William H. Sewell, Jr., *"Corporations républicaines:* The Revolutionary Idiom of Parisian Workers in 1848," *Comparative Studies in Society and History* 21:2 (April 1979), 197. For the 1833 strike see Faure, "Mouvements populaires," 68; F. Rittiez, *Histoire du règne*, 3 vols. (Paris: V. Lecou, 1855), III:267–269.

20. *La Démocratie pacifique*, 15 July 1845, letter from *ouvriers charpentiers* of Paris and the Seine, reprinted from *Journal des Débats;* J. Blanc, *La Grève des Charpentiers*, 1.

21. *La Démocratie pacifique*, 21 August 1845; Cynthia M. Truant, *The Rites of Labor: Brotherhoods of Compagnonnage in Old and New Regime France* (Ithaca: Cornell University Press, 1994), 39–44.

22. J. Blanc, *La Grève des Charpentiers*, 44.

23. *La Démocratie pacifique*, 19 July 1845, "Affaire des charpentiers."

24. *L'Atelier*, July 1845, "Luttes du travail contre le capital: les charpentiers de Paris," 149–150.

25. *La Démocratie pacifique*, 29 June 1845, letter from Eugène Sue.

26. *La Démocratie pacifique*, 17 June 1845, letter on behalf of the *ouvriers charpentiers* of Paris and the Seine, signed "Vincent"; see also *Le Populaire*, 13 July 1845, "Lettre des ouvriers charpentiers."

27. *La Démocratie pacifique*, 16 July 1845, letter to the *Constitutionnel* by the *chambre syndicale des entrepreneurs de charpente;* Ibid., 19 July 1845, "Affaire des charpentiers." For carpenters' wages, Jacques Rougerie, "Remarques sur l'histoire des salaires," *Le Mouvement social* 63 (1968),73–75.

28. Le National, 21 September 1833, letter from Auguste Ribot, carpenter.

29. *La Démocratie pacifique*, 13 August 1845, from Saint-Salvi; Ibid., 16 August 1845.

30. *La Démocratie pacifique*, 23 August 1845; Ibid., 21 August 1845; Ibid., 22 August 1845.

31. *La Démocratie pacifique*, 26 October 1845.

32. *La Démocratie pacifique*, 24 August 1845; Ibid., "Fin de la Grève des charpentiers de la Seine."

33. Greppo, *Catéchisme social ou exposé succinct de la doctrine de la solidarité* (Paris: Gustave Sandre, 1848), 5; reprinted in *Les Révolutions du XIXe siècle*, 3rd ser., v. 2.

34. William H. Sewell, Jr., *Work and Revolution in France* (Cambridge, MA: Cambridge University Press, 1980), 201–203; see also Georges Weill, "Les journaux ouvriers à Paris (1830–1870)," *Revue d'histoire moderne et contemporaine* 9 (1907–1908), 89–90, 92.

35. Bernard H. Moss, *The Origins of the French Labor Movement* (Berkeley: University of California Press, 1976), 37; Bernard H. Moss, "Producers' Associations and the Origins of French Socialism: Ideology from Below," *Journal of Modern History* 48:1 (March 1976), 72–73.

36. *Le Tocsin des Travailleurs*, 12 June 1848; reprinted in *Les Révolutions du XIXe siècle*, 3rd ser., v. 8.

37. Louis Blanc, *Organisation du Travail*, 5th ed. (Paris: Au bureau de la Société de l'industrie fraternelle, 1848), I:102–104.

38. Ibid., 105–106.

39. Louis Blanc, *La Révolution de Février au Luxembourg* (Paris: Michel Lévy, 1849), 70, 91–92; reprinted in *Les Révolutions du XIXe siècle*, 3rd ser., vol. 4.

40. See Ozouf, a comparison of utopians and republicans; Sewell, a comparison of the Babouvism of the 1790s and the socialism of Louis Blanc, as well as a more general discussion of socialism; and Lovell, on the differences between 1840s socialists and communists. Mona Ozouf, "La Révolution française au tribunal de l'utopie," in François Furet and Mona Ozouf, eds., *The French Revolution and the Creation of Modern Political Culture* (Oxford: Pergamon Press, 1989), especially 3:564–565; William H. Sewell, Jr., "Beyond 1793: Babeuf, Louis Blanc and the Genealogy of 'Social Revolution'," in Ibid., v. 3; William H. Sewell, Jr., "Artisans and Factory Workers, 1789–1848," in Ira Katznelson and Aristide R. Zolberg, eds., *Working-Class Formation* (Princeton: Princeton University Press, 1986), 64–65; David W. Lovell, "The French Revolution and the Origins of Socialism: The Case of Early French Socialism," *French History* 6:2 (June 1992), 186–199. See also Paul Bastid, *Doctrines et Institutions politiques de la Seconde République*, 2 vols. (Paris: Hachette, 1945), I:68–71, for a discussion of communism and socialism.

41. Lovell, "The French Revolution and the Origins of Socialism," 203.

42. *Le National*, 23 November 1841.

43. Théophile Thoré, *La Vérité sur le parti démocratique* (Paris: Dessessart, 1840), 37; reprinted in *Les Révolutions du XIXe siècle*, 2nd ser., v. 4; Sewell, "Beyond 1793," 518, 522.

44. Albert Laponneraye, "Notice historique sur Maximilien Robespierre," in *Oeuvres de Maximilien Robespierre* (Paris: n.p., 1840), I:5; *La Montagne*, 5 May 1848, "La Montagne,"; reprinted in *Les Révolutions du XIXe siècle*, 3rd ser., v. 7.

45. Irene Collins, *The Government and the Newspaper Press* (Oxford: Oxford University Press, 1959), 66–67, 75; Edward Berenson, "A New Religion of the Left: Christianity and Social Radicalism in France, 1815–1848," in François Furet and Mona Ozouf, eds., *The French Revolution and the Creation of Modern Political Culture*, 3:543–554.

46. Jules Thomas, *Le Procès de la Bible de la liberté* (Paris: Pilout, 1841), 8; reprinted in *Les Révolutions du XIXe siècle*, 2nd ser., v. 6.

47. Jean-Jacques Pillot, *Ni Chateaux ni Chaumières* (Paris: Bureaux de la Tribune du Peuple, 1840), 27; reprinted in *Les Révolutions du XIXe siècle*, 2nd ser., v. 6; see V. P. Volguine, "Jean-Jacques Pillot, Communiste utopique," *La Pensée* 84 (1959), 37–39, 53.

48. Cabet listed 36 works, both major and minor, that constituted the entire corpus of communism as of 1842, beginning with Buonarroti's *L'Histoire de la Conspiration de Babeuf*. Étienne Cabet, *Le Democrate devenu Communiste malgré lui* (Paris: 1842), 2–4; reprinted in *Les Révolutions du XIXe siècle*, 2nd ser., v. 5.

49. Étienne Cabet, *Credo communiste* (Paris: Prévot, 1841), 9, 6; reprinted in *Les Révolutions du XIXe siècle*, 2nd ser., v. 5.

50. Cabet, *Credo communiste*, 15.

51. Christopher Johnson, "Étienne Cabet and the Problem of Class Antagonism," *International Review of Social History* 11 (1966), 407–413; Étienne Cabet, *Le Cataclysme social, ou conjurons la tempête* (Paris: Au bureau du *Populaire*, 1845), 5; reprinted in *Les Révolutions du XIXe siècle*, 2nd ser., v. 5.

52. *Gazette des Tribunaux*, 11 November 1841, for *L'Humanitaire* case; "Prospectus" of *L'Humanitaire*, in Faure and Rancière, *La Parole ouvrière*, 268; and the two numbers of *L'Humanitaire* in *Les Révolutions du XIXe siècle*, 1st ser., v. 12. For criticism, see *La Fraternité*, August 1841, and Prospectus of *le Communautaire*, cited in Georges Sencier, *La Babouvisme après Babeuf* (Geneva: Mégariotis Reprints; reprint ed. of 1912 ed.), 187–188, 190–191; Zévaès, "L'agitation communiste de 1840 à 1848," *La Révolution de 1848* 24 (April–December 1926), 978–979; *L'Égalitaire*, June 1840, 52; reprinted in *Les Révolutions du XIXe siècle*, 2nd ser., v. 6.

53. Philippe Buonarroti, *La Conspiration pour l'Égalité*, 2 vols. (Paris: Editions socials, 1957), I:124, 149; *L'Égalitaire*, June 1840, 54–55; reprinted in *Les Révolutions du XIXe siècle*, 2nd ser., v. 6.

54. Cabet and Dézamy, briefly associated, had become enemies; see Théodore Dézamy, *Calomnies et politique de M. Cabet* (Paris: Prévost, n.d.); reprinted in *Les Révolutions du XIXe siècle*, 2nd ser., v. 8.

55. Théodore Dézamy, ed., *Almanach de la Communauté* (Paris: Prevost, 1843), 40; reprinted in *Les Révolutions du XIXe siècle*, 2nd ser., v. 8. See also Billington, *Fire in the Minds of Men*, 249–250.

56. Théodore Dézamy, *Code de la Communauté* (Paris: Prevost, 1842), 32–33; reprint ed. Paris: EDHIS, 1967.

57. Ibid., 37–39.

58. Ibid., 125–132; Dézamy, ed., *Almanach de la Communauté*, 40–41, 57.

59. Belleville was organized by Dézamy, Pillot, Dutilloy, and Hombert from *L'Humanitaire*. For the two latter, Jean Maitron, *Dictionnaire biographique*, 9 vols. (Paris: les Editions ouvrières, 1964), II:351 and II:146; for Guéret, Ibid., II:312; for Parent, *Gazette des Tribunaux*, 14 December 1835; for Couturat, Cour des Pairs, *Attentat du 13 Septembre 1841*, deps. Couturat, 348–353.

60. *Rapport fait à la Cour par M. le Comte de Bastard*, 153–155; reprinted in *Les Révolutions du XIXe siècle*, 2nd ser., v. 11.

61. Marc Caussidière, *Mémoires*, 2 vols. (Paris: Michel Lévy, 1849), I:149–153.

62. Lucien Delahodde, *La Naissance de la République*, 4th ed. (Paris: Chez l'Éditeur, 1850), 7.

63. *Gazette des Tribunaux*, 6 October 1832; Chenu, *Les Conspirateurs*, 9–17.

64. Chenu, *Les Conspirateurs*, 18–26; Caussidière, *Mémoires*, I:156–157.

65. Delahodde, *Histoire des sociétés secrètes*, 253.

66. Ibid., 257–258; 260.

67. Ibid., 293.

68. Ibid., 263–264.

69. *Gazette des Tribunaux*, 7 December 1841, Cour des Pairs, dep. Fougeray.

70. Zévaès, "L'agitation communiste de 1840 à 1848," 34–35. See also *Le National*, 21 March 1841, letter of Henri Dourille; *Gazette des Tribunaux*, 9 June 1841.

71. Delahodde, *Histoire des sociétés secrètes*, 320–321.

72. See *Le Moniteur universel*, 13 May 1841, *Rapport de M. Girod (de l'Ain)*, 1300.

73. Étienne Cabet, "Attaque et Défense des communistes, au sujet de l'attentat Quenisset" (Paris: C. Bajat, 1841), 90; reprinted in *Les Révolutions du XIXe siècle*, 2nd ser., v. 5.

74. Chenu, *Les Conspirateurs*, 30.

75. Ibid., 34–40; *Le Populaire*, 24 December 1843, "Affaire de la rue Pastourelle: Grandes Leçons"; *Gazette des Tribunaux*, 13 December 1843.

76. Chenu, *Les Conspirateurs*, 32–33.

77. Ibid., 40; Delahodde, *Histoire des sociétés secrètes*, 357–358.

78. Delahodde, *Histoire des sociétés secrètes*, 313–319.

79. Delahodde, *Histoire des sociétés secrètes*, 313–315, 358–359; F. Rittiez, *Histoire du Gouvernement provisoire en 1848*, 2 vols. (Paris: A. Lacroix, Verboeckhoven et cie, 1867), I:154.

80. Delahodde, *Histoire des sociétés secrètes*, 322–323, 354–355; *Gazette des Tribunaux*, 13 December 1843.

81. Chenu, *Les Conspirateurs*, 56–57; Delahodde, *Histoire des sociétés secrètes*, 355.

82. *Le Moniteur universel*, 13 May 1841, Girod Report, 1299; Charles de Rémusat, *Mémoires de ma vie*, ed. by Charles Pouthas (Paris: Plon, 1958), III:423.

83. Chenu, *Les Conspirateurs*, 47–48; Delahodde, *Histoire des sociétés secrètes*, 356–357, 369.

84. Information about the case can be found in *Gazette des Tribunaux*, 12 June 1847, to 17 June 1847, Affair of the *communistes matérialistes;* Ibid., 14 July 1847, 15 July 1847, 17 July 1847.

85. Chenu, *Les Conspirateurs*, 49.

86. *Gazette des Tribunaux*, 12 June 1847.

87. *Gazette des Tribunaux*, 14 July 1847.

88. *Gazette des Tribunaux*, 14 July 1847; Ibid., 15 July 1847; Javelot's dossier in CC742, no. 246, in *Cour des Pairs: Procès politiques*, III:80.

89. *Gazette des Tribunaux*, 15 July 1847; *Le Représentant du peuple*, 15 May 1848, letter from Coffineau, ex-détenu politique.

90. *Gazette des Tribunaux*, 14 July 1847, *acte d'accusation*.

91. *Gazette des Tribunaux*, 12 June 1847.

92. Ibid.

93. *Gazette des Tribunaux*, 15 July 1847.

94. *La Réforme*, 18 July 1847; Thureau-Dangin, *Histoire de la Monarchie de Juillet*, VII:52–68.

95. Caussidière, *Mémoires*, I:34–35.

96. Chenu, *Les Conspirateurs*, 53–55.

97. For the *Procès des bombes*, see *Gazette des Tribunaux*, 8 October 1847, and 10 October 1847; Chenu, *Les Conspirateurs*, 55–56; for Delahodde's unmasking, Delahodde, *Histoire des sociétés secrètes*, 372, 492–494; Caussidière, *Mémoires*, I:145–149; *Le Moniteur universel*, 12 October 1849, dep. Monnier, 3061; *Gazette des Tribunaux*, 15 October 1849, letter from Lucien de la Hodde.

CHAPTER 12

1. *Le Moniteur universel*, 18 December 1839, *Affaire de la rue Montpensier*, 2161.

3. Gustave Geffroy's term for Blanqui, in *L'Enfermé* (Paris: Bibliothèque Charpentier, 1897).

2. SDHC *Ordre du jour*, 5 June 1833, cited in Henri-Joseph Gisquet, *Mémoires de M. Gisquet*, 4 vols. (Paris: Marchant, 1840), II:291.

4. L. Nouguès, *Une Condamnation de Mai* (Paris: J. Bry ainé, 1850), 18–21.

5. *La Réforme*, 26 February 1847.

6. *Gazette des Tribunaux*, 26 February 1832.

7. *Le National*, 16 September 1833, "Le Régime des prisons politiques"; Georges Weill, *Histoire du parti républicain en France* (Paris: Ressources, 1980; reprint of 1928 ed.), 72–74.

8. *Le National*, 14 February 1831, letter from Louis-Auguste Blanqui.

9. See the work of Erving Goffman, *Asylums: Essays on the Social Situation of Mental Patients and Other Inmates* (Chicago, 1961), for the concept of the total institution; Michel Foucault, *Discipline and Punish* (New York: Random House, 1979); for a discussion of Foucault see Patricia O'Brien, *The Promise of Punishment: Prisons in Nineteenth-Century France* (Princeton, NJ: Princeton University Press, 1982), 19ff; and Gordon Wright, *Between the Guillotine and Liberty* (New York: Oxford University Press, 1983), 21–22, 52.

10. Michael Ignatieff, *A Just Measure of Pain* (London: Peregrine, 1989), 3–11.

11. Wright, *Between the Guillotine and Liberty*, 72–73.

12. Ibid., 62, 67–68, 70.

13. Ibid., 68–69.

14. *La Réforme*, 6 May 1844, "Du régime cellulaire et des prisonniers politiques"; cited in Maurice Dommanget, *Auguste Blanqui: Des Origines à la Révolution de 1848* (Paris: Mouton, 1969), 273–274.

15. Michelle Perrot, "1848: Révolution et prisons," in Michelle Perrot, ed., *L'Impossible Prison* (Paris: Éditions du seuil, 1980), 281. See also Robert A. Nye, *Crime, Madness, and Politics in Modern France* (Princeton, NJ: Princeton University Press, 1984), 37.

16. See *détention* and *pénitentiaire* in the moderate republican compilation, E. Duclerc, ed., *Dictionnaire politique: Encyclopédie de langage et de la science politique*, 2nd. ed. (Paris: E. Duclerc and Pagnerre, 1843), 318, 706–707.

17. Victor Brombert, *The Romantic Prison* (Princeton: Princeton University Press, 1978), 14.

18. *Le National*, 15 September 1841, "Silvio Pellico"; and 1 October 1841, for Pellico's response.

19. Silvio Pellico, *My Imprisonments: Memoirs of Silvio Pellico de Saluzzo*, trans. Thomas Roscoe (New York: J. and J. Harper, 1833), 174–175.

20. Pellico, *My Imprisonments*, 186–187.

21. Ibid., 155–156.

22. Alexandre Andryane, *Souvenirs de Genève*, 2 vols. (Paris: W. Coquebert, 1839), II:141.

23. Andryane, *Souvenirs de Genève*, II:306–308, 328–329.

24. Alexandre Andryane, *Mémoires d'un prisonnier d'État*, 2 vols., 5th ed. (Paris: Gaume et cie, 1879), I:53.

25. Andryane, *Mémoires*, II:66.

26. Ibid., II:32–33, 161.

27. Ibid., II:200.

28. Ibid., II:212–230.

29. Ibid., II:414, 430–432 (quotation).

30. Ibid., II:425, 441.

31. Martin-Bernard, *Dix Ans de Prison au Mont-Saint-Michel et à la Citadelle de Doullens*, 2nd ed. (Paris: Pagnerre, 1861), 62–65.

32. Brombert, *The Romantic Prison*, 9.

33. Sébastien Commissaire, *Mémoires et Souvenirs*, 2 vols. (Lyon: Meton, 1888), I:69.

34. Adolphe Blanqui, "Souvenirs d'un étudiant sous la Restauration," *La Revue de Paris* 148 (15 October 1918), 149 (1 November 1918), 161.

35. Bernard, *Dix Ans de Prison*, 214.

36. Commissaire, *Mémoires*, II:97.

37. Bernard, *Dix Ans de Prison*, 18–20.

38. Ibid., 37–38.

39. Ibid., 76.

40. Ibid., 67–68.

41. Ibid., 58.

42. Ibid., 58–59.

43. Ibid., 75–81, 90; Fulgence Girard, *Histoire du Mont-Saint-Michel comme prison d'état* (Paris: Paul Permain et cie, 1849), 159.

44. Girard, *Histoire du Mont-Saint-Michel*, 130; Dommanget, *Des Origines*, 255–256.

45. Ibid., 130 (Barbès), 181 (Blanqui).

46. Bernard, *Dix Ans de Prison*, 83.

47. Cour des Pairs, *Attentat des 12 et 13 Mai 1839* (Paris: Imprimerie royale, 1839), 1st ser., 2nd dep. Martin, 142–143 (cited hereafter as *1839*).

48. *1839*, 1st ser., deps. Roudil, 27–29; *Le Moniteur universel*, 2 July 1839, dep. Roudil, 1186–1187.

49. Nouguès, *Une Condamnation de Mai*, 98–113; Bernard, *Dix Ans de Prison*, 84–87.

50. Girard, *Histoire du Mont-Saint-Michel*, 138–139.

51. Bernard, *Dix Ans de Prison*, 88–89.

52. J. B. Boichot, *Souvenirs d'un prisonnier d'État 1854–1859* (Paris: Librairie du progrès, n.d.), 46–47.

53. Bernard, *Dix Ans de Prison*, 90; Girard, *Histoire du Mont-Saint-Michel*, 173.

54. Girard, *Histoire du Mont-Saint-Michel*, 194–196.

55. Commissaire, *Mémoires*, II:143–144.

56. Marc Caussidière, *Mémoires de Caussidière*, 2 vols. (Paris: Michel Lévy, 1849), II:171.

57. Dommanget, *Des Origines*, 264–265; Geffroy, *L'Enfermé*, 95.

58. Dommanget, *Des Origines*, 264–265.

59. For Flotte, see *Gazette des Tribunaux*, 4 April 1840; CC725, Judicial *Rapport* on Mathieu d'Épinal, Béraud, Thomas, et al.; Dommanget, *Des Origines*, 227, 265–266.

60. Bernard, *Dix Ans de Prison*, 113–114; Dommanget, *Des Origines*, 269.

61. Girard, *Histoire du Mont-Saint-Michel*, 223; Dommanget, *Des Origines*, 267; *Le National*, 30 April 1841, letter of Fulgence Gérard (sic).

62. Dommanget, *Des Origines*, 266–269.

63. Bernard, *Dix Ans de Prison*, 114–122; Girard, *Histoire du Mont-Saint-Michel*, 224–228.

64. Bernard, *Dix Ans de Prison*, 128–129; also Girard, *Histoire du Mont-Saint-Michel*, 229–239.

65. Bernard, *Dix Ans de Prison*, 130–131. See also "Les Détenus politiques au Mont Saint-Michel," *Les Révolutions du XIXe siècle*, 2nd ser., v. 4.

66. Bernard, *Dix Ans de Prison*, 132–135.

67. *La Réforme*, 16 November 1843, "Le Mont-Saint-Michel"; *Le National*, 30 April 1841, letter of Fulgence Gérard; Bernard, *Dix Ans de Prison*, 134–136.

68. "Les Détenus politiques au Mont Saint-Michel," 12; Bernard, *Dix Ans de Prison*, 136–137.

69. "Les Détenus politiques au Mont Saint-Michel," 12; Girard, *Histoire du Mont-Saint-Michel*, 242–243.

70. Girard, *Histoire du Mont-Saint-Michel*, 246–247, 249.

71. Ibid., 250.

72. *1839*, 2nd ser., no. 208, dep. Hoffer, 171–172; deps. Bordon, 100–102.

73. Girard, *Histoire du Mont-Saint-Michel*, 251; "Les Détenus politiques au Mont Saint-Michel" 13, 14.

74. Bernard, *Dix Ans de Prison*, 137–138, 140 (quotation).

75. Girard, *Histoire du Mont-Saint-Michel*, 256–257; Bernard, *Dix Ans de Prison*, 117–118.

76. Girard, *Histoire du Mont-Saint-Michel*, 278.

77. Dommanget, *Des Origines*, 277–279; Girard, *Histoire du Mont-Saint-Michel*, 262–264, 278–280.

78. Girard, *Histoire du Mont-Saint-Michel*, 302–303.

79. *Le National*, 12 November 1841, "Consultation"; see also Ibid., 26 August 1839, "Les condamnés politiques de Doullens et du Mont-Saint-Michel"; Adolphe Chauveau and Faustin Hélie, *Theorie du Code pénal*, 2nd ed., 6 vols. (Paris: Edouard Legrand, 1843), I:122–123.

80. See Charles Lucas, *Exposé de l'État de la Question pénitentiaire en Europe et aux États-Unis* (Paris: Panckoucke, 1844), 3; Girard, *Histoire du Mont-Saint-Michel*, 288–291, 298.

81. Bernard, *Dix Ans de Prison*, 163.

82. Ibid., 240.

83. Girard, *Histoire du Mont-Saint-Michel*, 310–311. (Jarrasse, Dufour, Petit, and Launois.)

84. Bernard, *Dix Ans de Prison*, 163–165; Dommanget, *Des Origines*, 279.

85. Dommanget, *Des Origines*, 281–284; Bernard, *Dix Ans de Prison*, 167–175; Girard, *Histoire du Mont-Saint-Michel*, 314–315.

86. Dommanget, *Des Origines*, 281.

87. Bernard, *Dix Ans de Prison*, 175–176.

88. Bernard, *Dix Ans de Prison*, 177 (quotation); Dommanget, *Des Origines*, 286–287.

89. Bernard, *Dix Ans de Prison*, 178; Dommanget, *Des Origines*, 286–290; *Le National*, 21 February 1842, "Tentative d'évasion au Mont-Saint-Michel," reprinted from *Journal du Peuple*.

90. Girard, *Histoire*, 104–111; Jules Antoine Cauvain, *Les Prisonniers du Mont-Saint-Michel* (Paris: Au bureau de l'Éclipse, 1872), 48–58. For Colombat, see *Gazette des Tribunaux*, 13–14 August 1832.

91. Letter of Marc Caussidière, in *Le Censeur de Lyon*, cited in *Le National*, 30 October 1836.

92. Nouguès, *Une Condamnation de Mai*, 173–184; *Le National*, 28 September 1840, "Evasion de Doullens."

93. Commissaire, *Mémoires*, II:94–95.

94. Dommanget, *Des Origines*, 289–292.

95. Bernard, *Dix Ans de Prison*, 182–184.

96. Ibid., 184–185.

97. Ibid., 187–188, 189 (quotation).

98. Commissaire, *Mémoires*, II:96–97.

99. Girard, *Histoire du Mont-Saint-Michel*, 336; Bernard, *Dix Ans de Prison*, 208–212.

100. Girard, *Histoire du Mont-Saint-Michel*, 342; also Bernard, *Dix Ans de Prison*, 211–212.

101. *La Réforme*, 18 July 1847, letter from Armand Barbès. He was right; Nîmes was used against him. See *La Commune sociale*, May 1849; reprinted in *Les Révolutions du XIXe siècle*, 3rd ser., v. 9.

102. Maurice Dommanget, "Les 'faveurs' de Blanqui," *1848: Revue des révolutions contemporaines*, 43 (July 1950), 142–149.

103. *Le National*, 26 August 1839, "Les condamnés politiques de Doullens et du Mont-Saint-Michel"; Ibid., 16 September 1839; Ibid., 2 October 1839.

104. *Journal du Peuple*, cited in *Le National*, 2 October 1839.

105. *Le National*, 8 July 1840.

106. *Le National*, 12 October 1840.

107. *La Réforme*, 5 September 1843; Ibid., 1 October 1843.

108. *Le National*, 6 November 1843, "Un autre épisode du Mont-Saint-Michel."

109. *La Réforme*, 21 November 1843; *Le National*, 23 November 1843.

110. *Le National*, 23 November 1843; Ibid., 16 December 1843; *La Réforme*, 23 November 1843; Ibid., 25 December 1843, from the *Courrier de Loir-et-Cher*.

111. *Le National*, 17 November 1843; *La Réforme*, 16 November 1843, "Le Mont-Saint-Michel."

112. *La Réforme*, 18 November 1843, "Le Mont-Saint-Michel."

113. *Le Moniteur universel*, 27 April 1844, cited in *Le National*, 2 May 1844; for a criticism of Tocqueville, see *La Réforme*, 6 May 1844, "Du régime cellulaire et des prisonniers politiques."

114. Alexis de Tocqueville, "Projet de loi," May 1844, in *Oeuvres complètes*, v. 4: *Écrits sur le système pénitentiaire en France et à l'étranger*, ed. Michelle Perrot (Paris: Gallimard, 1984), 179.

115. Tocqueville, *Rapport fait au nom de la Commission*, in *Écrits sur le système pénitentiaire*, 121–151. See also L. M. Moreau-Christophe, *De la Mortalité et de la Folie dans le régime pénitentiaire* (Paris: Paul Renouard, 1839).

116. Tocqueville, "Interventions d'Alexis de Tocqueville en qualité de rapporteur de la loi," 26 April 1844, in *Écrits sur le système pénitentiaire*, 232–233.

117. Tocqueville, *Rapport fait au nom de la Commission*, in *Écrits sur le système pénitentiaire*, 145–146.

118. *La Réforme*, 6 May 1844, "Du régime cellulaire et des prisonniers politiques."

119. *Le National*, 2 May 1844, "Les Prisonniers politiques: le Mont-Saint-Michel." See also *La Démocratie pacifique*, 6 May 1844, "De la réforme pénitentiaire."

120. *La Réforme*, 11 June 1844; Ibid., 15 June 1844, "Mort d'un prisonnier politique."

121. *Le National*, 16 June 1844. See also *La Réforme*, 21 July 1844; Ibid., 25 July 1844.

122. Etienne Cabet, "Réflexion sur cet écrit d'Huber," introduction to Aloysius Huber, *L'esclavage du riche, par un prolétaire, Aloysius Huber, détenu politique* (Paris: Au bureau du Populaire, 1845), 22–23; reprinted in *Les Révolutions du XIXe siècle*, 2nd ser., v. 5.

123. *Le National*, 9 October 1844, "Faits divers"; *La Réforme*, 9 October 1844.

124. *La Réforme*, 21 October 1844, "L'amnistie"; Chauveau and Hélie, *Théorie du Code pénal*, I:328–329.

125. See "Les Détenus politiques au Mont-Saint-Michel."

126. Bernard, *Dix Ans de Prison*, 238–240.

127. Ibid., 257–263.

128. See H. Monin, "Blanqui et la Police (1847–1848), *La Révolution de 1848*, 12 (March 1914–February 1916), 32–35.

129. *Le Représentant du peuple*, 14 April 1848, "Réponse du citoyen Blanqui."

130. Letter from Gaillard *père*, *détenu politique* from Sainte-Pélagie, 13 May 1869, cited J.F. Jeanjean, *Armand Barbès* (Paris: Édouard Cornély, 1909), 259.

131. Bernard, *Dix Ans de Prison*, 278–279.

CHAPTER 13

1. Marc Caussidière, *Mémoires de Caussidière*, 2 vols. (Paris: Michel Lévy, 1849), I:47–49.

2. André Jardin and André-Jean Tudesq, *Restoration and Reaction*, tr. Elborg Forster (Cambridge, MA: Cambridge University Press, 1983), 192–197; Roger Price, ed., "Introduction," *Revolution and Reaction: 1848 and the Second French Revolution* (London: Croom Helm, 1975), 23.

3. *Le Représentation du Peuple*, 13 April 1848; *Bulletin de la République*, 11 April 1848, cited in Henri Guillemin, *La première résurrection de la République* (Paris: Éditions Gallimard, 1967), 127.

4. Mark Traugott, "The Crowd in the French Revolution of February, 1848," *The American Historical Review* 93:3 (June 1988), 644, 647.

5. Louis d'Orléans, duc de Nemours, "Sur les événements dont j'ai été témoin," reprinted in René Bazin, *Le Duc de Nemours* (Paris: Émile Paul, 1907), 274, 296–297; Jacques Jean, Vicomte de Foucauld, *Mémoires sur les événements de juillet 1839* (Paris: E. Dentu, 1851), 41–44.

6. B. Sarrans, *Histoire de la Révolution de Février 1848*, 2 vols. (Paris: Administration de Librairie, 1851), I:132, 149, 151; Odilon Barrot, *Mémoires posthumes*, 2nd ed., 4 vols. (Paris: Charpentier et cie, 1875), I:462–465; Alphonse de Lamartine, *Histoire de la Révolution de 1848*, 2 vols. (Bruxelles: Méline, Cans et cie, 1849), I:34.

7. François-Pierre-Guillaume, *Mémoires pour servir à l'histoire de mon temps*, 8 vols. (Paris: Michel Lévy frères, 1872), VIII:531–532, 524–525.

8. Sarrans, *Histoire*, I:129–135

9. *La Réforme*, 26 February 1847.

10. Comte d'Alton-Shée, *Souvenirs de 1847 et de 1848* (Paris: Maurice Dreyfous, n.d.), 8–9 (republican as of May 1847).

11. Sarrans, *Histoire*, I:129–132.

12. BB30 296, no. 4, dep[osition] Boissel.

13. BB30 297, no. 457, dep. Duvergier de Hauranne; BB30 296, no. 4, dep. Boissel.

14. BB30 296, no. 10, dep. Lepelletier Roinville.

15. BB30 296, no. 7, dep. d'Heurle; no. 8, dep. Delestre; no. 10, dep. Lepelletier Roinville; no. 4, dep. Boissel; Guizot, *Mémoires*, VIII:554.

16. BB30 297, no. 458, dep. Léon de Malleville; no. 455, dep. Larabit; no. 457, dep. Duvergier de Hauranne.

17. BB30 297, no. 448, dep. Barrot; Barrot, *Mémoires posthumes*, I:506–507; Sarrans, *Histoire*, I:252; Hippolyte Castille, *Histoire de la Seconde République française*, 4 vols. (Paris: Victor Lecou, 1854), I:113.

18. Guizot, *Mémoires*, VIII:554–559; Sarrans, *Histoire*, I:253–256; Louis Garnier-Pagès, *Histoire de la revolution de 1848*, 2nd ed., 4 vols. (Paris: Pagnerre, 1866), I:196–197; see also Robert L. Koepke, "The Short Unhappy History of Progressive Conservatism in France, 1846–1848," *Canadian Journal of History* XVIII:2 (August 1983), 187–216.

19. *La Réforme*, 21 February 1848, "Manifestation réformiste."

20. Barrot, *Mémoires posthumes*, I:506–510; BB30 297, no. 448, dep. Barrot; BB30 298, no. 1090, dep. Berger. The text was in *Le National*, 23 February 1848.

21. Lucien Delahodde, *Histoire des sociétés secrètes*, (Paris: Julien, Lanier et cie, 1850), 421–430; J. Tripier-Lefranc, *M. Gabriel Delessert* (Paris: E. Dentu, 1859), 332; Sarrans, *Histoire*, I:282–285; d'Alton-Shée, *Souvenirs*, 224–226.

22. Caussidière, *Mémoires*, I:36–37.

23. BB30 296, no. 1, Report from Delessert, 22 February 1848; Philippe Faure, *Journal d'un combattant de février* (Jersey: Auguste Desmoulins, 1859), 132–135.

24. BB30 298, no. 1178, dep Mazure (the woman); Amédée Achard, *Souvenirs personnels d'émeutes et de révolutions* (Paris: Michel Lévy frères, 1872), 34.

25. Sarrans, *Histoire*, I:320–321.

26. Sarrans, *Histoire*, I:318–319; Adolphe Chenu, *Les Conspirateurs* (Paris: Garnier frères, 1850), 71–72; Delahodde, *Histoire des sociétés secrètes*, 439.

27. Roger Price, "Techniques of Repression: The Control of Popular Protest in Mid-Nineteenth-Century France," *Historical Journal* 25:4 (1982), 871.

28. General Tiburce Sébastiani, "Rapport sur les journées de Février," *La Révolution de 1848*, v. 8 (1911–1912), 323–324. House reported 33,400 regulars in Paris and Versailles; House, "Civil-Military Relations in Paris, 1848," in Roger Price, ed., *Revolution and Reaction*, 153.

29. Guizot, *Mémoires*, VIII:575, 575–576n; Henri Guillemin, *La première résurrection de la République* (Paris: Editions Gallimard, 1967), 82.

30. For his senior officers, see BB30 297, nos. 546, 548–552, 575, 691, 747, 784, 859.

31. Paul Sauzet, *La Chambre des Députés et la Révolution de Février* (Paris: Perisse frères, 1851), 259–260.

32. Robert Koepke, "Charles Tanneguy Duchatel and the Revolution of 1848," *French Historical Studies* VII:2 (Fall 1973), 253.

33. BB30 297, no. 514, dep. David; Garnier-Pagès, *Histoire*, I:303.

34. BB30 297, no. 483, dep. Talabot; no. 508, dep. Baignères.

35. BB30 297, no. 484, dep. Besson; no. 549, dep. Friant; no. 506, dep. Thirion.

36. BB30 297, no. 519, dep. Aubert-Roche; BB30, 296, no. 139, *Procès-verbal* of Commissaire Nusse.

37. BB30 297, no. 467, dep. Husson; no. 490, dep. Corbeau; no. 492, dep. Siredery.

38. BB30 297, no. 493, dep. Beudin; no. 491, dep. Besson.

39. BB30 297, no. 496, dep. Boutarel; BB30 296, no. 201, *Procès-verbal* of Commissaire Lapic-Lasage.

40. BB30 297, no. 497, dep. Dequevauvilliers; Garnier-Pagès, *Histoire*, I:316.

41. BB30 297, dep. Ladvocat; BB30 296, no. 10, dep. Lepelletier Roinville.

42. For depositions of gunshop owners, see BB30 298, nos. 1111, 1112, 1114, 1117–1120.

43. BB30 298, no. 1110, dep. Rozoy; no. 1116, dep. Grandineau; no. 1108, dep. Devisme; BB30 296, no. 118, *Procès-verbal* of Commissaire Deroste, for Baudoin.

44. BB30 298, no. 1109, dep. Lepage Moutier; no. 1190, dep. Lepage; no. 984, dep. Bouvier.

45. Guizot, *Mémoires*, VIII:578–579; Nemours, "Sur les évènements," 283; BB30 297, no. 449, dep. Molé; Barrot, *Mémoires posthumes*, I:517.

46. BB30 297, no. 483, dep. Talabot.

47. D'Alton-Shée, *Souvenirs*, 253–254; Sarrans, *Histoire*, I:364–365.

48. BB30 297, no. 784, dep. Puech; dep. Duval; Marthe-Camille Bachasson, comte de Montalivet, *Fragments et Souvenirs*, 2 vols. (Paris: Calmann Lévy, 1899), II:120–121.

49. See these themes in the account by *Le National*, 24 February 1848.

50. Jean Pons Guillaume Viennet, *Journal de Viennet: Pair de France, témoin de trois règnes, 1817–1848* (Paris: Amiot-Dumont, n.d.), 294–295; Nemours, "Sur les évènements," 287–288; Guizot, *Mémoires*, VIII:590–591. Crémieux traced the origin of this story; see Albert Crémieux, "La Fusillade du boulevard des Capucines," *La Révolution de 1848: Bulletin de la Société d'histoire de la Révolution de 1848*, 5 (1908–1909), 101–103.

51. BB30 297, nos. 472 and 475, deps. Schumacher; no. 473, dep. Launette.

52. BB30 297, no. 475, dep. Schumacher; no. 473, dep. Launette.

53. BB30 297, no. 474, dep. Neveaux; BB30 296, no. 106, dep. Collier; no. 61, dep. Benoist.

54. BB30 297, no. 483, dep. Talabot; no. 585, dep. Dumetz; no. 859, dep. Courand.

55. BB30 297, no. 475, dep. Schumacher.

56. BB30 297, no. 583, dep. Carrière.

57. BB30 297, no. 475, dep. Schumacher; no. 473, dep. Launette; no. 474, dep. Neveaux.

58. BB30 297, no. 859, dep. Courand.

59. BB30 297, no. 862, dep. Dard; no. 861, dep. St. Ouen.

60. BB30 297, no. 922, dep. Leroi; no. 894, dep. Thurninger; no. 864, dep. Guillot.

61. BB30 297, no. 860, dep. de Brotonne; no. 898, dep. Mathurin; no. 897, dep. Collignon; no. 866, dep. Baillet.

62. BB30 297, no. 863, dep. Giacomoni; see also no. 920, dep. Demauton; nos. 923–925.

63. Sarrans, *Histoire*, I:372.

64. BB30 297, no. 473, dep. Launette.

65. *Compte-rendu: 24 Février et 15 Mai 1848, ou compte-rendu exact et complèt des deux mémorables séances* (Paris: chez l'éditeur, 1848), 8; see also Albert Crémieux, *La Révolution de février* (Paris: Edouard Cornély, 1912), 195–196n.

66. BB30 296, no. 106, *Procès-verbal* of Commissaire Loyeux; no. 60, dep. Junieau; no. 120, *Procès-verbal* of Commissaire Vassal; no. 122, *Procès-verbal* of Commissaire Basset.

67. BB30 296, no. 60, dep. Junieau; no. 63, dep. Avelini; see also BB30 297, no. 475, dep. Schumacher.

68. BB30 296, no. 60, dep. Junieau; Sarrans, *Histoire*, I:376.

69. *Procès politique des Dix-Neuf*, "Défense de M. Pierre Grand pour l'accusé Lenoble," 258. The attorney seems to have taken the story from the reports of Dartaing, the editor of the *Gazette des Tribunaux*, 26 July–1 August 1830; see also Marie-Théodore Gueulluy de Rumigny, *Souvenirs du général comte de Rumigny*

(Paris: Emile-Paul frères, 1921), 302. "On se propose de répéter ce qui s'est passé lors de la tragique promenade du cadavre d'une femme en juillet 1830" ("One proposed to repeat what had happened at the time of the tragic promenade of the body of a woman in July 1830").

70. Contemporary accounts also mentioned a woman; see, for example, Daniel Stern, *Histoire de la Révolution de 1848* (Paris: Editions Ballard, 1985), 124, who provides a quite vivid account; and see a similar passage in Lamartine, *Histoire*, I:74–75. Garnier-Pagès, who actually saw the wagon, wrote of "all ages," and "both sexes," though his description seems to be less descriptive than an attempt to invoke the universality of victimhood. Garnier-Pagès, *Histoire*, I:376. Eyewitness Amédée Achard, who correctly identified the cart as from the Messageries, described the national guard officer as the most striking figure; Achard, *Souvenirs personnels*, 43.

71. For Saint-Méry, see F. Rittiez, *Histoire du Gouvernement provisoire*, 2 vols. (Paris: A. Lacroix, Verboeckhover et cie, 1867), I:34; for Saint-Sulpice, BB30 296, no. 211, *Procès-verbal* of Commissaire Cabuchet; BB30 298, no. 943, dep. Tisserand.

72. BB30 298, no. 1205, dep. Charon; see also no. 1206, dep. Pères.

73. BB30 298, no. 1122, dep. Tiger.

74. BB30 297, no. 784, deps. Puech, Duval.

75. Sarrans, *Histoire*, I:409. Regnault puts this meeting in the morning; Elias Regnault, *Histoire du Gouvernement provisoire*, 2nd ed. (Paris: Victor Lecou, 1850), 55–56.

76. Alexis de Tocqueville, *Souvenirs* (Paris: Gallimard, 1942), 50.

77. D'Alton-Shée, *Souvenirs*, 269.

78. Cited in Crémieux, *La Révolution de février*, 289.

79. D'Ideville, *Le Maréchal Bugeaud, d'après sa correspondance intime*, 2 vols. (Paris: Firmin-Didot, 1881), I:275–279.

80. Crémieux, *La Révolution de février*, 217–218; Sarrans, *Histoire*, I:397–398. See also BB30 297, no. 575, dep. Rolin; Nemours, "Sur les événements," 295–297.

81. Nassau Senior, *Conversations with M. Thiers, M. Guizot, and Other Distinguished Persons, during the Second Empire*, 2 vols. (London: Hurst and Blackett, 1878), I:11–12; BB30 297, no. 450, dep. Thiers. See also Tiburce Sébastiani, "Rapport sur les journées de février," *La Révolution de 1848*, 8 1911–1912), 328.

82. Letter from Bugeaud, cited in Senior, *Conversations*, I:23n; Garnier-Pagès, *Histoire*, II:54–55n; Guillemin, *La première résurrection*, 103.

83. BB30 297, no. 448, dep. Barrot; Barrot, *Mémoires posthumes*, I:528–531.

84. Letter from Bugeaud, cited in Senior, *Conversations*, I:22–23n.

85. BB30 297, no. 553, dep. Renault; no. 879. See also B30 297, no. 786, dep. Lemaire; no. 784, dep. Puech; no. 683, dep. Brunet; BB30 296, no. 8, dep. Delestre, who arranged Renaud's retreat.

86. Crémieux, *La Révolution de février*, 272, 274; BB30 297, no. 753, dep. d'Hugues.

87. BB30 297, no. 554, dep. Duhot; see also no. 848, dep. Baligaud.

88. BB30 297, no. 564, dep. Bedeau; see also no. 699, dep. Sauvan; no. 670, dep. Burot.

89. BB30 298, no. 1187, dep. Avisse; no. 1186, dep. Fauvelle-Delabarre; Nemours, "Sur les évènements," 299–300.

90. BB30 297, no. 518, dep. Labelonge; Crémieux, *La Révolution de février*, 265–266.

91. BB30 297, no. 595, dep. Dumor.

92. Achard, *Souvenirs personnels*, 55–56. See also d'Alton-Shée, *Souvenirs*, 269–270; G. Vauthier, ed., "Notes de Villemain sur les journées de Février 1848," *La Révolution de 1848*, 9(1912–1913), 252.

93. Senior, *Conversations*, I:21, 13.

94. Nemours, "Sur les évènements," 307–309; Senior, *Conversations*, I:14–15.

95. Senior, *Conversations*, I:15–16; Nemours, "Sur les évènements," 310–313; "Récit de l'abdication par le Roi Louis-Philippe," in René Bazin, *Le Duc de Nemours* (Paris: Emile Paul, 1907), 241; BB30 297, no. 450, dep. Thiers; no. 451, dep. Gérard.

96. Letter from Bugeaud, cited in Senior, *Conversations*, I:24–25n; BB30 297, no. 559, dep. Bugeaud.

97. Dupin, *Mémoires*, IV:456–457; Villemain, "Notes," 255; BB30 297, no. 831, dep. Capoul.

98. BB30 297, no. 559, dep. Bugeaud; letter from Bugeaud, cited in Senior, *Conversations*, I:24–25n.

99. Martin Nadaud, *Mémoires de Léonard, ancien garçon maçon*, ed. Maurice Agulhon (Paris: Hachette, 1976), 337.

100. F. Rittiez, *Histoire du Gouvernement provisoire*, 2 vols. (Paris: A. Lacroix, Verboeckhoven et cie, 1867), I:160; Paul Guichonnet, ed., "William de la Rive," *Société d'histoire de la Révolution de 1848, Études* (1956), 154.

101. Norbert Truquin, *Mémoires et aventures* (Paris: François Maspero, 1977), 63.

102. Louis Tirel, *La République dans les Carrosses du Roi*, 2nd ed. (Paris: Comptoir des Imprimeurs, 1850), 75.

103. Alfred Delvau, *Les Murailles révolutionnaires de 1848*, 17th ed., 2 vols. (Paris: F. Picard, 1868), I:21.

104. Crémieux, *La Révolution de février*, 289.

105. Ibid., 287.

106. Sarrans, *Histoire*, I:411.

107. Garnier-Pagès, *Histoire*, II:191.

108. Guillemin, *La première résurrection*, 112.

109. Rittiez, *Histoire*, I:53–55; Sarrans, *Histoire*, I:412–417.

110. Louis Blanc, *1848: Historical Revelations* (New York: Howard Fertig, 1971), 98.

111. Sarrans, *Histoire*, I:416, 422–423; Rittiez, *Gouvernement provisoire*, I:54–55, 152–153. For a list of those present, about 40 men, see Chenu, *Les Conspirateurs*, 77–78; Delahodde, *Histoire des sociétés secrètes*, 476–478.

112. Sauzet, *La Chambre des Députés*, 286–290, 316 (for Bedeau's response).

113. Ibid., 291–294, 298; BB30 298, no. 1164, dep. Duponceau.

114. Tocqueville, *Souvenirs*, 61–62.

115. Nemours, "Sur les événements," 323; Sauzet, *La Chambre des Députés*, 299–300.

116. *Compte-rendu*, 17–18; Lamartine, *Histoire*, I:136–137. See also Nemours, "Sur les événements," 324.

117. *Compte-rendu*, 17–18; Barrot, *Mémoires posthumes*, I:545.

118. Sarrans, *Histoire*, II:8–9.

119. *Compte-rendu*, 18.

120. Lamartine, *Histoire*, I:140.

121. *Compte-rendu*, 20; Sarrans, *Histoire*, I:457–462; Barrot, *Mémoires posthumes*, I:546–548.

122. BB30 297, no. 576, dep. Fabar; see also no. 456, dep. Courtais.

123. Maréchal de MacMahon, *Mémoires du Maréchal de MacMahon, Duc de Magenta* (Paris: Plon, 1932), 237–238.

124. *Compte-rendu*, 22; Sarrans, *Histoire*, II:12–15; Lamartine, *Histoire*, I:148–149.

125. Barrot, *Mémoires posthumes*, I:550–551.

126. Ibid., I:548–549.
127. *Compte-rendu*, 21–22; Sauzet, *La Chambre des Députés*, 310–313.
128. *Compte-rendu*, 23–25.
129. Sarrans, *Histoire*, II:17; Barrot, *Mémoires posthumes*, I:550–551; Rittiez, *Gouvernement provisoire*, I:57.
130. Lamartine, *Histoire*, I:154; 155–157.
131. Ibid., I:158; Sarrans, *Histoire*, II:20–21.
132. *Compte-rendu*, 27–30; Barrot, *Mémoires posthumes*, I:553, 555.
133. Castille, *Histoire*, I:294; Sarrans, *Histoire*, II:30; Guillemin, *La première résurrection*, 119–120.
134. *Compte-rendu*, 27–30.
135. Ibid., 29–31.
136. Ibid., 32–33; Barrot, *Mémoires posthumes*, I:553.
137. (Sobrier was co-prefect for several days before resigning.) Caussidière, *Mémoires*, I:66–68, 71–73; Rittiez, *Gouvernement provisoire*, I:155–156. For an assessment of Caussidière's tenure, see Patricia O'Brien, "The Revolutionary Police of 1848," in Roger Price, ed., *Revolution and Reaction*, 133–149.
138. Lamartine, *Histoire*, I:174–175, 276–277; Blanc, *1848: Historical Revelations*, 15; Castille, *Histoire*, I:316.
139. Castille, *Histoire*, I:329.
140. Théodore Fix, *Souvenirs d'un officier d'État-Major* (Paris: Juven, n.d.), 8; Castille, *Histoire*, I:341. The mass burial was held on 4 March. Rittiez, *Gouvernement provisoire*, I:172.
141. Lamartine, *Histoire*, I:178.
142. Blanc, *1848: Historical Revelations*, 20; Assemblée nationale (Quentin-Bauchart, rapporteur), *Rapport de la Commission d'enquête*, 2 vols. (Paris: Imprimerie nationale, n.d.), dep. Cremieux, I:266; Lamartine, *Histoire*, I:223; Sarrans, *Histoire*, II:43–44; Rittiez, *Gouvernement provisoire*, I:75–76.
143. Lamartine, *Histoire*, I:225–230.
144. Ibid., I:217.
145. Castille, *Histoire*, I:311.
146. Delahodde, *Histoire des sociétés secrètes*, 488; Sarrans, *Histoire*, II:155.
147. Castille, *Histoire*, I:332–334; see also Sarrans, *Histoire*, II:139–155; Lamartine, *Histoire*, I:280–288, 295–297; and *La Réforme*, 26 March 1848, letter from Marche, *ouvrier mécanicien*.
148. *Rapport de la Commission d'enquête*, II:38.
149. Sarrans, *Histoire*, II:53–59; Blanc, *1848: Historical Revelations*, 29–32.
150. Sarrans, *Histoire*, II:69–70.
151. Castille, *Histoire*, I:410.
152. *Rapport de la Commission d'enquête*, II:29–30.
153. S. Posener, *Adolphe Crémieux*, 2 vols. (Paris: Félix Alcan, 1933), II:70.
154. Delvau, *Les Murailles révolutionnaires*, I:31, 178; *Rapport de la Commission d'enquête*, II:39.
155. F9 1072, *Rapport* from the minister of the interior, 24 January 1849; for a full discussion, see Mark Traugott, *Armies of the Poor* (Princeton: Princeton University Press, 1985).
156. *Rapport de la Commission d'enquête*, II:29; Blanc, *1848: Historical Revelations*, 90–93.
157. *La Réforme*, 14 March 1848, Commission des récompenses nationales.

158.   Alphonse Lucas, *Les Clubs et les Clubistes* (Paris: E. Dentu, 1851), 211–215.

CHAPTER 14

1.   *Le Populaire*, 23 March 1848, "Nouveau Récit historique de la fameuse séance du 24 février 1848."

2.   Assemblée nationale, *Rapport de la Commission d'Enquête*, 2 vols. (Paris: Imprimerie nationale, n.d.), II:33; Ibid., dep. Senard, I:349.

3.   C934, doss. 3, "Commissaire en service spécial du Palais de l'assemblée nationale," to Cavaignac, 28 June 1848.

4.   *Gazette des Tribunaux*, 1 November 1848; see his letter to *La Réforme*, 7 March 1848.

5.   *Rapport de la Commission d'Enquête*, circular of the Ministry of Interior, 12 March 1848, II:68.

6.   For the Mobile Guard, see Mark Traugott, *Armies of the Poor* (Princeton, NJ: Princeton University Press, 1985); for the clubs, Peter H. Amann, *Revolution and Mass Democracy: the Paris Club Movement in 1848* (Princeton, NJ: Princeton University Press, 1975); for the National Workshops, Donald Cope McKay, *The National Workshops: A Study in the French Revolution of 1848* (Cambridge, MA: Harvard University Press, 1933).

7.   *Le Moniteur universel*, 17 May 1848, National Assembly, 1062.

8.   C934, doss. 8, report to the prefect of police, 13 June 1848.

9.   Marc Caussidière, *Mémoires*, 2 vols. (Paris: Michel Lévy, 1849), I:136–137, 140; Daniel Stern, *Histoire de la Révolution de 1848* (Paris: Éditions Balland, 1985), 355–356.

10.   Caussidière, *Mémoires*, I:223; he believed there were eight hundred men in this group.

11.   *Le Moniteur universel*, 15 March 1849, dep. Delpech, 860.

12.   Caussidière, *Mémoires*, I:99–100. Rittiez criticized the name as an "anachronism" from the old republicans of the SDHC. F. Rittiez, *Histoire du Gouvernement provisoire*, 2 vols. (Paris: A. Lacroix, Verboeckhoven et cie, 1867), I:156; see also Patricia O'Brien, "The Revolutionary Police of 1848," in Roger Price., ed. *Revolution and Reaction: 1848 and the Second French Republic* (London: Croom Helm, 1975), 138–140.

13.   *Le Moniteur universel*, 21 May 1848, "Intérieur."

14.   *Rapport de la Commission d'Enquête*, Protestation des Montagnards, II:288.

15.   Ibid., dep. Huet, I:295. See also Caussidière, *Mémoires*, II:180–181.

16.   Caussidière, *Mémoires*, II:53–54; 136–137, for dissolution.

17.   *Rapport de la Commission d'Enquête*, Protestation des Montagnards, II:287–288.

18.   Amann, *Revolution and Mass Democracy*, 33.

19.   *La Voix des Femmes*, 14 April 1848, "Club lyonnais."

20.   *Le Monde républicain*, 6 May 1848.

21.   *La Commune de Paris*, 11 April 1848, "Société des droits de l'homme."

22.   *La Voix des Femmes*, 6–8 June 1848, "Le Club des Femmes"; reprinted in *La Révolution du XIXe siècle*, 3rd ser., v. 8.

23.   Claire Goldberg Moses, *French Feminism in the Nineteenth Century* (Albany, NY: State University of New York Press, 1984), 130.

24.   *La Voix des Femmes*, 3 April 1848; Ibid., 22 March 1848, letter of 2 March; Ibid., 31 March 1848, "A Messieurs les membres du Gouvernement provisoire," from

P.G., *ouvrière*; Ibid., 3 April 1848. See also *Le Tocsin des Travailleurs*, 23 June 1848, "Misère des femmes," and Désirée Gay's letter on women's workshops, in *Journal des Travailleurs*, 15–18 June 1848, both reprinted in *Les Révolutions du XIXe siècle*, 3rd ser., v. 8.

25. *La Voix des Femmes*, 6 April 1848; Ibid., 10 April 1848. Sand's response in *La Réforme*, 9 April 1848. See Evelyne Sullerot, "Journaux féminins et lutte ouvrière, 1848–1849," in *La Presse ouvrière, 1819–1850* (Paris: Bibliothèque de la Révolution de 1848, 1966), 23:104.

26. *Le Monde républicain*, 13 May 1848, "Les Clubs."

27. Sullerot, "Journaux féminins," 106.

28. *La Voix des Femmes*, 6–8 June 1848; Ibid., 8–10 June 1848, "La Liberté et la Légalité."

29. *La Voix des Femmes*, 8–10 June 1848, "La Liberté et la Légalité."

30. *La Démocratie pacifique*, 15 May 1848, letter from Eugénie Niboyet. (It had lasted from 20 March to 10 June; see Sullerot, "Journaux Féminins," 101). *La Politique des Femmes*, 18–24 June 1848, suffered from bad timing; reprinted in *Les Révolutions du XIXe siècle*, 3rd ser., v. 10.

31. R. Gossez, "Presse Parisienne à destination des ouvriers, 1848–1851," in *La Presse ouvrière, 1819–1850* (Paris: Bibliothèque de la Révolution de 1848, 1966), 151–154. See also Eugène Fombertaux and Gabriel Charavay, *La Commune sociale*, May 1849, "Droits politiques et civils des femmes"; reprinted in *Les Révolutions du XIXe siècle*, 3rd ser., v. 9.

32. *Le Moniteur universel*, 23 March 1849, 991; *Rapport de la Commission d'Enquête*, II:114 (quotation).

33. *Rapport de la Commission d'Enquête*, dep. Gayot de Montfleury, II:91; dep. de Hai, I:293 and II:80; dep. Peuvrier, II:88.

34. *Rapport de la Commission d'Enquête*, II:34; Louis Girard, *La Garde nationale* (Librairie Plon, 1964), 294.

35. *L'Atelier*, 12 March 1848, "La Question du travail," 85; Ibid., "De la garde nationale," 85–86.

36. Henri Marin, "Réflexions d'un homme de rien sur la Garde nationale en général," *La Révolution de 1848*, 7 (1910–1911), 231.

37. *La Commune de Paris*, 11 March 1848.

38. *La Commune de Paris*, 14 March 1848, "Compte rendu des Clubs."

39. *La Commune de Paris*, 16 March 1848.

40. *La Commune de Paris*, 16 March 1848, "Compte rendu des Clubs."

41. Ibid.

42. Alfred Delvau, *Les Murailles révolutionnaires de 1848*, 17th ed., 2 vols. (Paris: E. Picard, 1868), II:287; *La Commune de Paris*, 15 March 1848, "Compte rendu des clubs."

43. Delvau, *Les Murailles*, I:468–470, "Candidature du citoyen Armand Barbès."

44. *La Commune de Paris*, 25 March 1848, "Compte rendu des Clubs."

45. *La Commune de Paris*, 2 April 1848, "Club républicain de Montmartre."

46. *La Commune de Paris*, 18 March 1848, "Compte rendu des Clubs."

47. Girard, *La Garde nationale*, 297.

48. *La Commune de Paris*, 11 April 1848, "Société des Droits de l'homme."

49. Ibid.

50. Amann, *Revolution and Mass Democracy*, 124–143.

51. *Rapport de la Commission d'Enquête*, "Discours de M. Louis Blanc," I:119, 121.

52. *La Réforme*, 22 April 1848.

53. *La Commune de Paris*, 31 March 1848.

54. Delvau, *Les Murailles*, "Philippe Le Bas à ses concitoyens," I:436.

55. Delvau, *Les Murailles*, II:524.

56. Delvau, *Les Murailles*, "Aux électeurs de la Seine," I:460–461.

57. *La Commune de Paris*, 1 June 1848, "Club pacifique des Droits de l'Homme."

58. *La Commune de Paris*, 7 April 1848, "Société des Droits de l'Homme."

59. *La Commune de Paris*, 1 April 1848, "Société des Droits de l'Homme."

60. *La Réforme*, 30 March 1848, "Adresse d'un ouvrier à ses frères ouvriers de tous les corps d'état."

61. *La Démocratie pacifique*, 29 May 1848, letter from Savary, *ouvrier cordonnier*.

62. Delvau, *Les Murailles*, "Aux Électeurs du département de la Seine," I:476–477.

63. *Le Représentant du Peuple*, 5 April 1848.

64. *La Commune de Paris*, 11 April 1848; *La Réforme*, 14 April 1848.

65. *La Commune de Paris*, 3 June 1848.

66. *La Commune de Paris*, 20 April 1848, "Société des Droits de l'Homme."

67. *La Commune de Paris*, 13 April 1848; for additional lists, *Le Monde républicain*, 21 April 1848; *L'Atelier*, 12 March 1848, 84; *La Réforme*, 23 April 1848.

68. *La Commune de Paris*, 25 April 1848. It excluded Albert, Flocon, Ledru-Rollin, and Blanc; there was also a phony Luxembourg list. Louis Blanc, *1848: Historical Revelations* (New York: Howard Fertig, 1971), 369, 377.

69. Roger Price, "Introduction," in *Revolution and Reaction*, 29; see also George W. Fasel, "The French Election of April 23, 1848," *French Historical Studies* 5:3 (Spring 1968), 289–290.

70. Amann, *Revolution and Mass Democracy*, 187–188.

71. *La Commune de Paris*, 11 April 1848, "Société des Droits de l'homme."

72. Ernest Duquai, ed., *Les Accusés du 15 Mai 1848* (Paris: Armand Le Chevalier, 1869), dep. Arago, 164.

73. Amann, *Revolution and Mass Democracy*, 93; for the garrison, House, "Civil-Military Relations in Paris, 1848," in Price, ed., *Revolution and Reaction*, 156.

74. Alan B. Spitzer, *The Revolutionary Theories of Louis-Auguste Blanqui* (New York: Columbia University Press, 1957; reprint AMS Press, 1970),138–139; and Louis-Auguste Blanqui, *Écrits sur la révolution: Oeuvres complètes*, I, ed. Arno Münster (Paris: Éditions Galilée, 1977), 162–164.

75. See Jules Taschereau, *Revue Rétrospective* (Paris: Paulin, 1848), 290–292, for the inconclusive results on the origin of the document, generated by the lawsuit Taschereau brought against Blanqui (for defamation).

76. *Le Représentant du peuple*, 14 April 1848, "Réponse du citoyen Blanqui."

77. Duquai, *Les Accusés du 15 mai 1848*, dep. Barbès, 198–199; *Le Monde républicain*, 5 April 1848; and see Georges Renard, "Une lettre relative au document Taschereau," in *La Révolution de 1848* 7 (1910–1911):7–15; and J. F. Jeanjean, "L'Éternel Révolté," in *La Révolution de 1848*, vol. 5 (1908–1909), 533–552.

78. *Le Populaire*, 12 April 1848, "Mes Rapports avec Blanqui"; Maurice Dommanget, "Les 'Faveurs' de Blanqui," *1848: Revue des révolutions contemporaines* 43 (July 1950), 137–166.

79. For the signers in Blanqui's defense, see *Le Représentant du peuple*, 13 April 1848, no. 13.

80. *Le Monde républicain*, 15 April 1848, "Réponse du citoyen Auguste Blanqui."

81. Cited in J. F. Jeanjean, "Barbès et Blanqui," in *La Révolution de 1848*, vol. 8 (1911–1912), 204.

82. *La Commune sociale*, May 1849, Excerpts from "Blanqui et Barbès"; reprinted in *Les Révolutions du XIXe siècle*, 3rd. ser., v. 9.

83. See Spitzer, *The Revolutionary Theories*, 149, who finds no direct evidence of his involvement.

84. For differing opinions of the day, see *Rapport de la Commission d'Enquête*, dep. Carteret, I:250; dep. Favre, I:279; II:321; Caussidière, *Mémoires*, II:20; Hippolyte Castille, *Histoire de la Seconde République française*, 4 vols. (Paris: Victor Lecou, 1854), II:221–228; B. Sarrans, *Histoire de la Révolution de Février 1848*, 2 vols. (Paris: Administration de Librairie, 1851), II:472–477; Blanc, *1848: Historical Revelations*, 314–338; Amann, *Revolution and Mass Democracy*, 184; Alvin P. Calman, *Ledru-Rollin and the Second French Republic* (New York: Columbia University Press, 1922), 149–158.

85. Suzanne Wassermann, *Les Clubs de Barbès et de Blanqui en 1848* (Geneva: Megariotis Reprints, 1978), 127–128.

86. *La Commune de Paris*, 29 April 1848, "Société des Droits de l'Homme," session of 19 April 1848.

87. *Rapport de la Commission d'Enquête*, II:104; Wassermann, *Les Clubs*, 125–127.

88. *Rapport de la Commission d'Enquête*, II:104–105.

89. *Le Représentant du peuple*, 19 April 1848, "Où allons nous?"

90. *La Commune de Paris*, 19 April 1848; Wassermann, *Les Clubs*, 133–134.

91. Lloyd S. Kramer, "Exile and European Thought: Heine, Marx and Mickiewicz in July Monarchy Paris," *Historical Reflections/Réflexions historiques* 11 (1984), 65–67.

92. *Le Moniteur universel*, 15 March 1849, dep. Blanqui, 859.

93. *Gazette des Tribunaux*, 16 March 1849, dep. Lebreton.

94. *Le Représentant du peuple*, 15 May 1848.

95. The Executive Commission included Arago, Garnier-Pagès, Marie, Lamartine, and Ledru-Rollin; Marrast remained mayor of Paris, Crémieux minister of justice, Flocon was given commerce, and the elderly Dupont retired. Blanc and Albert were excluded.

96. *Le Moniteur universel*, 11 March 1849, Haute-Cour de Justice, dep. Dandurand, 823.

97. *Le Moniteur universel*, 13 March 1849, dep. Buchez, 829.

98. *Gazette des Tribunaux*, 11 October 1849, Haute-Cour de Justice.

99. *Le Moniteur universel*, 11 March 1849, dep. Dandurand, 823; see also *La Réforme*, 15 May 1848, letter from Aloysius Huber, promising a peaceful demonstration.

100. *La Commune de Paris*, 24 May 1848, "Actes officiels."

101. *Le Moniteur universel*, 16 March 1849, dep. Trinité, 872; Ibid., 15 March 1849, dep. Blanqui, 859.

102. Duquai, *Les Accusés*, dep. Raspail, 92–93; *Gazette des Tribunaux*, 13 October 1849; *Le Moniteur universel*, 11 March 1849, dep. Dandurand, 823.

103. *Rapport de la Commission d'Enquête*, II:225.

104. *Le Moniteur universel*, 11 March 1849, dep. Dandurand, 823; *Gazette des Tribunaux*, 11 October 1849, dep. Huber; Duquai, *Les Accusés*, 43–44.

105. *Le Moniteur universel*, 15 March 1849, dep. Blanqui, 860.

106. Duquai, *Les Accusés*, 24.

107. *Le Moniteur universel*, 17 March 1849, dep. Sklower, 889.
108. House, "Civil-Military Relations in Paris, 1848," in Price, ed., *Revolution and Reaction*, 162.
109. *Le Moniteur universel*, 25 March 1849, dep. Guinard, 1030. See also *Rapport de la Commission d'Enquête*, II:40, and Girard, *La Garde nationale*, 307–308.
110. *Le Moniteur universel*, 15 March 1849, dep. Yautier, 858.
111. *Compte-rendu* (of the session), 38–39.
112. *Le Moniteur universel*, 24 March 1849, deps. Pensée, 1010; Thouret, 1011; *Compte-rendu*, 42–44.
113. *Compte-rendu*, 48.
114. *Le Moniteur universel*, 17 March 1849, dep. Degousée, 890.
115. *Le Moniteur universel*, 13 March 1849, dep. Buchez, 829.
116. *Rapport de la Commission d'Enquête*, dep. Ledru-Rollin, I:311.
117. Duquai, *Les Accusés*, dep. Barbès, 200–201.
118. *Compte-rendu*, 49.
119. Ibid., 50–54; *Le Moniteur universel*, 17 March 1849, dep. Degousée, 890.
120. *Compte-rendu*, 52.
121. Peter Amann makes a strong case against Huber as *agent provocateur* on 15 May 1848, suggesting that he had "buckled under the strain" of his harsh imprisonment; see Peter Amann, "The Huber Enigma: Revolutionary or Police-Spy," *International Review of Social History* XII:2 (1967), 190–203. Blaisdell describes Huber as an hysterical personality, unstable and dependent on approval of authority figures. Lowell L. Blaisdell, "Aloysius Huber and May 15, 1848: New Insights into an Old Mystery," *International Review of Social History*, XXIX:1 (1984), esp. 40–43.
122. For the testimony in his cases, see *Le Moniteur universel*, 10 May 1838–24 May 1838; Ibid., 11 October 1849–13 October 1849.
123. Blaisdell, "Aloysius Huber," 60; Amann, "The Huber Enigma," 203.
124. *Gazette des Tribunaux*, 11 October 1849, Haute Cour de Justice, dep Huber; Ibid., 12 October 1849.
125. *Rapport de la Commission d'enquête*, dep. Levasseur, 80 (quotation); see also dep. Pecontal, 78.
126. *Rapport de la Commission d'Enquête*, deps. Verdun, Levasseur, Dautriche, Benafort, I:79–82; *Le Moniteur universel*, 11 March 1849, dep. Dautriche, 823 (quotation).
127. *La Commune de Paris*, 4 June 1848 and 5 June 1848, Louis Blanc, "A l'Opinion publique." See also *Rapport de la Commission d'Enquête*, deps. Blanc, Artique, Persoz, I:105, 84–85, 83.
128. *Compte-rendu*, 54; *Gazette des Tribunaux*, 22 June 1848, *Tribunal correctionnel* (for *triumvirate* remark).
129. *Le Moniteur universel*, 23 March 1849, dep. Joanne, 987.
130. *La Commune de Paris*, 31 May 1848, letter from A. Barbès, Donjon de Vincennes.
131. *Le Moniteur universel*, 17 March 1849, dep. Bassac, 889 (quotation); *Compte-rendu*, 55.
132. *Le Moniteur universel*, 15 March 1849, dep. Guyon, 858; Ibid., 14 March 1849, dep. Adam, 847; Ibid., 19 May 1848, "Rapport du maire de Paris," 1086.
133. *Rapport de la Commission d'enquête*, I:64.
134. *Le Moniteur universel*, 18 March 1849, dep. Pichinat, 907.
135. *La Réforme*, 17 May 1848; Duquai, *Les Accusés*, 35.

136. McKay, *The National Workshops*, 13–14. See also the reports of Léon Lalanne, "Lettres sur les Ateliers Nationaux," in *Le National*, in a series beginning 14 July 1848 and ending 26 August 1848.

137. *Rapport de la Commission d'enquête*, II:142; see also McKay, *The National Workshops*, 21.

138. *Rapport de la Commission d'enquête*, dep. Duclerc, I:276.

139. *La Commune de Paris*, 31 May 1848, "Affaire Émile Thomas."

140. *Le Tocsin des Travailleurs*, 17 June 1848; reprinted in *Les Révolutions du XIXe siècle*, 3rd.ser., v. 8.

141. Castille, *Histoire*, III:69.

142. See Peter Amann, "Prelude to Insurrection: The Banquet of the People," *French Historical Studies* 1:4 (December, 1960), 436–444; for the announcement, *La Réforme*, 29 May 1848; for fears, *Le Travail*, 4–6 June 1848, and 8–11 June 1848, "Club de la Révolution"; reprinted in *Les Révolutions du XIXe siècle*, 3rd ser., v. 8.

143. *Rapport de la Commission d'enquête*, II:113.

CHAPTER 15

1. *La Démocratie pacifique*, 26 June 1848, "Les Femmes."

2. Amédée Achard, *Souvenirs personnels d'émeutes et de révolutions* (Paris: Michel Lévy frères, 1872), 140–141; Norbert Truquin, *Mémoires et aventures d'un prolétaire à travers la révolution* (Paris: François Maspero, 1977), 76.

3. For class and gender tensions, see Judith A. DeGroat, "The Public Nature of Women's Work," *French Historical Studies* 20:1 (Winter 1997), 31–48; and William H. Sewell Jr., "Social and Cultural Perspectives on Women's Work," *French Historical Studies* 20:1 (Winter 1997), 53–54; and for the Commune, Gay L. Gullickson, *Unruly Women of Paris* (Ithaca: Cornell University Press, 1996).

4. Assemblée nationale, *Rapport de la Commission d'Enquête*, 2 vols. (Paris: Imprimerie nationale, n.d.), dep. Caussidière, I:255–256.

5. Ibid., I:41.

6. *Gazette des Tribunaux*, 21–22 August 1848, "Notes sur les principales causes," by Panisse.

7. *Le Tocsin des Travailleurs*, 24 June 1848, "Le Sang"; reprinted in *Les Révolutions du XIXe siècle*, 3rd ser., v. 8.

8. *Rapport de la Commission d'Enquête*, II:186. See also Mark Traugott, *Armies of the Poor* (Princeton: Princeton University Press, 1985), 134–144.

9. *Rapport de la Commission d'Enquête*, II:190–194, 196.

10. Ibid., II:201–202, 204, 206.

11. Maurice Hauriou, *Précis de droit constitutionnel* (Paris: Librairie du recueil Sirey, 1929), 668.

12. *Le Représentant du peuple*, 10 June 1848; *La Commune de Paris*, 5 June 1848, "Le terrorisme contre les clubs"; *Le Monde républicain*, 10 June 1848.

13. C934, doss. 8, "Etat des principales arrestations politiques du 15 mai au 22 juin 1848."

14. *Le Représentant du peuple*, 20 June 1848, "Mesure relative aux ouvriers des Ateliers nationaux."

15. *Rapport de la Commission d'Enquête*, dep. Lalanne, I:303.

16. BB18 1465A, doss. 5964A, letter from the Procureur-Général Cornu, 23 June 1848.

17. *Le Moniteur universel*, 31 May 1848, Assembly session, 1217, for text of decree.
18. *Rapport de la Commission d'Enquête*, II:212; *Le National*, 23 June 1848.
19. *Rapport de la Commission d'Enquête*, II:212–213.
20. Ibid., dep. Hainguerlot, I:293.
21. BB18 1465A, doss. 5964A, letter from Cadet Gassicourt to the minister of justice, 2 July 1848; C934, doss. 8, Report from prefecture of police, 5 July 1848.
22. *Rapport de la Commission d'Enquête*, dep. Garnier-Pagès, I:285; dep. Marie, I:320; dep. Lamartine, I:306.
23. House, "Civil-Military Relations in Paris, 1848," in Roger Price, ed., *Revolution and Reaction: 1848 and the Second French Republic* (London: Croom Helm, 1975), 164–165.
24. *Rapport de la Commission d'Enquête*, dep. Cavaignac, I:258; dep. Ledru-Rollin, I:312–313.
25. Doumenc, "L'Armée et les journées de juin," *Actes du Congrès historique du centenaire de la Révolution de 1848* (Paris: PUF, 1948), 256.
26. Doumenc, "L'Armée et les journées de juin," 257; see also House, "Civil-Military Relations in Paris, 1848," in Price, ed., *Revolution and Reaction*, 157.
27. *Rapport de la Commission d'Enquête*, deps. Cavaignac, I:258, II:46–48; see also Frederick A. de Luna, *The French Republic under Cavaignac* (Princeton: Princeton University Press, 1969), 134; Girard, *La Garde nationale*, 309–310.
28. De Luna, *The French Republic*, 168.
29. Doumenc, "L'Armée et les journées de juin," 261–262. See the late General Regnault's comment about crossing barricades, in *Le Moniteur universel*, 26 November 1848, *Assemblée nationale*, 3363.
30. *Le Moniteur universel*, 26 November 1848, 3358; De Luna, *The French Republic*, 140–141.
31. Étienne Cabet, *Insurrection du 23 juin* (Paris: Au bureau du *Populaire*, 1848), 3; reprinted in *Les Révolutions du XIXe siècle*, 3rd. ser., v. 1.
32. Charlemagne-Émile de Maupas, *The Story of the Coup d'État*, trans. from the French by Albert D. Vandam (New York: D. Appleton and Co., 1884), 339.
33. Doumenc, "L'Armée et les journées de juin," 264–265; De Luna, *The French Republic*, 162–170.
34. *Rapport de la Commission d'Enquête*, II:232; for women, see Louis Ménard, *Prologue d'une Révolution: Février–Juin 1848* (Paris: Au bureau du peuple, 1849), 210.
35. C934, doss. 4, letter from mayor Moreau of the eighth; Ibid., doss. 12, letter from Dupin.
36. *Rapport de la Commission d'Enquête*, dep. Bertrand, I:237.
37. Ibid., dep. Caussidière, I:256; also Marc Caussidière, *Mémoires* (Paris: Michel Lévy, 1849), II:226.
38. Ibid., dep. Berg, I:157.
39. *Gazette des Tribunaux*, 11–12 September 1848, 1er Conseil de guerre; Ibid., 14 September 1848.
40. *Rapport de la Commission d'Enquête*, dep. Cottu, I:263.
41. C934, doss. 12, letter from Fraysse, 11th Legion, to the Assemblée nationale, 14 July 1848.
42. *Gazette des Tribunaux*, 1 October 1848, IIe Conseil de Guerre, deps. Giles, Réaume.
43. Daniel Stern, *Histoire de la Révolution de 1848* (Paris: Editions Balland, 1985), 622–623.

44. Achard, *Souvenirs personnels*, 145–167.

45. C934, doss. 3, note from Terrier, Laussedat, Girard; undated.

46. Traugott, in *Armies of the Poor*, stresses the development of an esprit de corps through training, the uniform, and isolation; Girard, *La Garde nationale*, 291.

47. F1 15, 5th Bataillon, *Rapport* de M. le chef de Bataillon Bassac.

48. *Gazette des Tribunaux*, 21 February 1849, IIe Conseil de guerre de Paris.

49. *Gazette des Tribunaux*, 25 June 1848; De Luna, *The French Republic*, 145.

50. F1 15, 1st Bataillon, Report to Colonel Thomas; see also Alphonse Balleydier, *Histoire de la Garde Mobile* (Paris: Pillet fils aîné, 1848), 56.

51. F1 15, 20th Bataillon, Chef de bataillion Huet, *Rapport*.

52. F1 15, 2nd Bataillon, letter to Colonel Thomas from commandant of 2nd bat.

53. *Le National*, 25 June 1848, "Evénéments de la Journée."

54. F1 15, 15th Bataillon, Chef de bataillon Moutariot, *Rapport;* Xd 386, *Rapport* du Lieutenant Moulin (artillery); *Gazette des Tribunaux*, 25 June 1848.

55. *Le National*, 28 June 1848.

56. *Gazette des Tribunaux*, 26–27 June 1848, Assemblée Nationale.

57. *Gazette des Tribunaux*, 29–30 January 1849, IIe Conseil de guerre, dep. Acker.

58. De Luna, *The Second Republic*, 146.

59. C 934, doss. 6, letter from Prefect of Police Trouvé-Chauvel; F1 15, 3rd Bataillon, from chef du 3rd Bataillon, Résumé; Ibid., 15th Bataillon, chef de bataillon Moutariot, *Rapport*.

60. *Le National*, 25 June 1848, "Evenements de la Journée."

61. Louis Blanc, *1848: Historical Revelations* (New York: Howard Fertig, 1971), 266 (1st quote); Truquin, *Mémoires et aventures*, 72.

62. F1 15, 8th Bataillon, letter from Commandant Couchot.

63. Emmanuel Barthélemy, "L'insurrection de Juin au faubourg du Temple," in *Les Veillées du peuple* (March 1850), 93, 94–95 (quotation); reprinted in *Les Révolutions du XIXe siècle*, 3rd ser., v. 2.

64. C 934, doss. 6, dispatch from General Lamoricière to the minister of war, 25 June 1848.

65. C 934, doss. 6, letter from Prefect of Police Trouvé-Chauvel to Cavaignac, 25 June 1848, 6:30 P.M.

66. F1 15, 4th Bataillon, *Rapport* . . . from chef du 4e bataillon.

67. F1 15, 17th Bataillon, *Rapport* de M. Denard.

68. *Rapport de la Commission d'Enquête*, dep. Lacrosse, I:299.

69. Reports combined in Hippolyte Castille, *Histoire de la Seconde République française*, 4 vols. (Paris: Victor Lecou, 1854), III:331–335.

70. For the proclamation and its interpretation, see Cabet, *Insurrection du 23 juin*, 14.

71. *Le National*, 28 June 1848; Balleydier, *Histoire de la Garde Mobile*, 73.

72. The general outline of the events is presented in *Gazette des Tribunaux*, 15 and 16 January 1849, a fuller account than *Le Moniteur*'s rather cursory coverage.

73. *Gazette des Tribunaux*, 21 January 1849, dep. Gobert.

74. Ibid.

75. Ibid.; Ibid., 24 January 1849, dep. Mercier.

76. *Gazette des Tribunaux*, 22–23 January 1849, dep. Dordelin.

77. Stern, *Histoire*, 664.

78. *Gazette des Tribunaux*, 20 January 1849, deps. Desmarets, Dumont.

79. *Gazette des Tribunaux*, 27 January 1849, dep. Constant; Ibid., 22–23 January 1849, dep. Baudot; Ibid., 20 January 1849, dep. Desmarets.

80. *Gazette des Tribunaux*, 22–23 January 1849, dep. Mercier.
81. *Gazette des Tribunaux*, 27 January 1849, deps. Dubois, Constant.
82. *Gazette des Tribunaux*, 20 January 1849, dep. Desmarets; Ibid., 21 January 1849, dep. Gobert.
83. *Gazette des Tribunaux*, 27 January 1849, dep. Armagnac; Ibid., 21 January 1849, dep. Gobert.
84. *Gazette des Tribunaux*, 21 January 1849, dep. Gobert.
85. Ibid., dep. Gobert.
86. Ibid., dep. Viel.
87. *Gazette des Tribunaux*, 24 January 1849, dep. Fillette.
88. *Gazette des Tribunaux*, 21 January 1849, dep. Viel.
89. *Gazette des Tribunaux*, 19 January 1849, dep. Goué. Bréa finally wrote an order to the troops to withdraw the way they had come, which was not emphasized in the trial. Castille, *Histoire*, III:202.
90. *Gazette des Tribunaux*, 24 January 1849, dep. Traideler.
91. *Gazette des Tribunaux*, 26 January 1849, dep. Nuens; Ibid., 19 January 1849, dep. Gautron.
92. *Gazette des Tribunaux*, 21 January 1849, dep. Gobert.
93. *Gazette des Tribunaux*, 20 January 1849, dep. Desmarets; Ibid., 21 January 1849, dep. Gobert.
94. *Gazette des Tribunaux*. 15–16 January 1849, Autopsy report of Boys de Loury.
95. *Gazette des Tribunaux*, 24 January 1849. dep. Genriel, curé.
96. *Gazette des Tribunaux*, 25 January 1849, dep. Colonel Thomas.
97. *Gazette des Tribunaux*, 15–16 January 1849, dep. Nourrit (sic).
98. *Gazette des Tribunaux*, 19 January 1849, dep. Lebelleguy; Ibid., 21 January 1849, dep. Viel.
99. Ibid., dep. Lebelleguy; Ibid., 21 January 1849, dep. Le Main.
100. *Gazette des Tribunaux*, 21 January 1849, dep. Favre.
101. *Gazette des Tribunaux*, 4 February 1849, Report from Trélat, Baillarger, and Lélut.
102. Four out of the 25 were convicted of murder (others of lesser charges): Lahr, Daix, Vappereaux, and Choppart. Stern, *Histoire*, 668n.
103. Martin Nadaud, *Mémoires de Léonard, ancien garçon maçon*, ed. Maurice Agulhon (Paris: Hachette, 1976), 352. See also Blanc, *1848: Historical Revelations*, 430–431.
104. *Gazette des Tribunaux*, 20 January 1849, dep. Lahr; Ibid., 21 January 1849, deps. Viel, Dutoit.
105. *Gazette des Tribunaux*, 15–16 January 1849, dep. Daix.
106. *Gazette des Tribunaux*, 26 January 1849, deps. Marion, Deschamps.
107. Ibid., deps. Voiturier, Pichenot.
108. *Gazette des Tribunaux*, 20 January 1849, dep. Bussières.
109. *Gazette des Tribunaux*, 19 January 1849, dep. Quintin.
110. *Gazette des Tribunaux*, 26 January 1849, dep. Nuens.
111. *Gazette des Tribunaux*, 20 January 1849, dep. Choppart.
112. *Rapport de la Commission d'Enquête*, dep. Galy-Cazalat, II:250.
113. *Le National*, 26 June 1848, "Evénèments de la journée (25 Juin)"; see also Stern, *Histoire*, 650–654.
114. See in *Le Représentant du peuple*, 30 June 1848; *Le National*, 30 June 1848; *Rapport de la Commission d'Enquête*, Rapport, II:290.

115. C934, doss. 6, from Rondot, chef du 5e bataillon de la 4e Légion (*banlieue*) to Cavaignac.
116. C934, doss. 3, undirected, undated note from Dahirel, representative.
117. Reymond des Ménars, "Le Faubourg Saint-Antoine du 23 au 27 juin 1848," (Paris: Imp. Bonaventure, s.d.), 10–11; reprinted in *Les Révolutions du XIXe siècle*, 3rd. ser., v. 1.
118. C934, doss. 6, Report from the prefect of police to the minister of war; *Rapport de la Commission d'Enquête*, II:290; Stern, *Histoire*, 679.
119. Des Ménars, "Le Faubourg Saint-Antoine du 23 au 27 juin 1848," 10–11.
120. C934, doss. 3, no. 2865, letter from Rolland du Lot; Charles Beslay, *Mes souvenirs 1830–1848–1870* (Geneva: Slatkine, 1979), 189–190. See also E. Terson, "Documents sur la mort de Mgr. Affre," *1848 et les Révolutions du XIXe siècle*, v. 39 (March 1949), 42–52.
121. *Rapport de la Commission d'Enquête*, deps. Galy-Cazalat, I:247, Larabit, I:309.
122. Des Ménars, "Le Faubourg Saint-Antoine," 12–15; see also Stern, *Histoire*, 678–681.
123. De Luna, *The French Republic*, 148; Stern, *Histoire*, 682.
124. *Le National*, 28 June 1848.
125. Achard, *Souvenirs personnels*, 190–191.
126. "Pièces justificatives, no. 7," in Castille, *Histoire*, III:326.
127. Truquin, *Mémoires et aventures*, 80.
128. *Le National*, 1 July 1848.
129. Tilly and Lees, "The People of June, 1848," in Price, ed., *Revolution and Reaction*, 176–177.
130. Tilly and Lees, "The People of June, 1848," 189. Metal workers were 11.8 percent of the insurgents, and represented only 2.9 percent of the labor force; construction workers, 18.4 percent and 6.6 percent, respectively; furniture and wood crafts, 6.0 percent and 4.0 percent; leather, 1.5 percent and 0.6 percent; transport, 4.7 percent and 2.1 percent; retail trade, 7.1 percent and 4.7 percent.
131. Tilly and Lees, "The People of June, 1848," 190, 194.
132. Price, "Introduction," *Revolution and Reaction*, 30.
133. Tilly and Lees, "The People of June, 1848," 185–186.
134. Tilly and Lees, "The People of June, 1848," 186; Guillemin, *La Première résurrection*, 445; de Luna, *The French Republic*, 149.
135. *Gazette des Tribunaux*, 19 July 1848 (and a slightly different count from the F15 series); Balleydier reported 90 killed and 584 wounded. Balleydier, *Histoire de la Garde mobile*, 115–128.
136. *Rapport de la Commission d'Enquête*, dep. Trouvé-Chauvel, I:363; *Gazette des Tribunaux*, 16 July 1848; C934, doss. 8, Etat numerique des Citoyens blessés ou morts reçues dans les hôpitaux et hospices et à la Morgue du 23 au 27 juin.
137. *Gazette des Tribunaux*, 22 August 1849, "Chronique." He was sentenced to five years.
138. *Gazette des Tribunaux*, 28 September 1848, Ier Conseil de Guerre.
139. *Gazette des Tribunaux*, 23 September 1848, Ier Conseil de guerre; 2 years.
140. C934, doss. 6, Etat des armes et munitions sorties de Vincennes du 25 février au 19 juin . . . ; Girard's figure is 106,000 to the Paris Guards, by the last half of April. Girard, *La Garde nationale*, 298.
141. *Gazette des Tribunaux*, 28 June 1848.

142.   *Rapport de la Commission d'Enquête*, dep. Vilain, I:369; BB18 1465A doss. 5964A, letter from Commission militaire d'enquête, 22 August 1848.
143.   *Le National*, 2 July 1848, letter from ex-commandant Brédy, Montmartre.
144.   *Gazette des Tribunaux*, 30 June 1848.
145.   *Gazette des Tribunaux*, 2 July 1848.
146.   *Rapport de la Commission d'Enquête*, dep. Winter, I:369.
147.   BB18 1465A 5964A, letter from procureur-général to the minister of justice, 1 July 1848.
148.   C934, doss. 5, no. 2913, 11th Legion.
149.   *Rapport de la Commission d'Enquête*, dep. Trouvé-Chauvel, I:362.
150.   *Gazette des Tribunaux*, 26–27 June 1848, Assemblée Nationale; *Le National*, 1 July 1848.
151.   *Gazette des Tribunaux*, 7–8 August 1848, "Transportation des insurgés: Premier Départ."
152.   *Gazette des Tribunaux*, 14–15 August 1848, *Chronique*.
153.   *Rapport de la Commission d'Enquête*, dep. Rousseau, I:345.
154.   C934, doss. 4, letter from Mayor of the 6th *arrondissement* to Odilon Barrot, 7 July 1848.
155.   *Rapport de la Commission d'Enquête*, dep. Panisse, I:332.
156.   *Gazette des Tribunaux*, 24–25 July 1848.
157.   Stern, *Histoire*, 659.
158.   Castille, *Histoire*, III:193; see also Jacques Arago, *Histoire de Paris: ses révolutions, ses gouvernements et ses évènements de 1841 à 1852* (Paris: Dion Lambert, 1855), 333.
159.   *Gazette des Tribunaux*, 30 June 1848; Ibid., 5 July 1848.
160.   *Gazette des Tribunaux*, 27 October 1848, IIe Conseil de Guerre.
161.   *Gazette des Tribunaux*, 26–27 June 1848, *Chronique*.
162.   *Gazette des Tribunaux*, 16 July 1848, *Chronique*.
163.   *Gazette des Tribunaux*, 29 June 1848.
164.   *Gazette des Tribunaux*, 28 March 1849, IIe Conseil de Guerre.
165.   *Gazette des Tribunaux*, 4–5 September 1848, Ie Conseil de Guerre; see also *L'Atelier*, 7 October 1848, "Circonstances atténuantes," 232, which highlighted this case.
166.   *Gazette des Tribunaux*, 21–22 August 1848, Ie Conseil de Guerre; the *gardiens* were a new unarmed police force, created in late March. House, "Civil Military Relations in Paris," 157.
167.   *Le Représentant du peuple*, 5 July 1848, letter from B. Carrière, ex-sublieutenant, 12th Legion.
168.   *Le Représentant du peuple*, 2 July 1848; Achard, *Souvenirs personnels*, 191.
169.   Truquin, *Mémoires et aventures*, 74.
170.   *Le National*, 25 June 1848, "Evénèments de la journée."
171.   Louis Garnier-Pagès, *Histoire de la Révolution de 1848*, 4 vols., 2nd ed. (Paris: Pagnerre, 1866), I:296.

CHAPTER 16

1.   For Allemane, see Jean Maitron, *Dictionnaire biographique du mouvement ouvrier français* (Paris: Les Éditions ouvrières, 1964), IV:103–106. Jean Allemane, *Mémoires d'un communard* (Paris: n.d.), 124–125. I have been unable to trace Faure, or Navet; Maitron has only this listing taken from Allemane.

2. Amédée Saint-Ferréol, *Les Proscrits français en Belgique*, 2 vols. (Paris: Armand Le Chevalier, 1871), I:47, 65–66; for the last three, see *Gazette des Tribunaux*, 11 November 1849.
3. Saint-Ferréol, *Les Proscrits*, I:58–59, 65–66.
4. Ibid., II:20.
5. Adam-Flocon, "Ferdinand Flocon (1800–1866)," *1848 et les Révolutions du XIXe siècle* (Autumn 1947), v. 38, n. 178: 56–57; 62.
6. Saint-Ferréol, *Les Proscrits*, II:21.
7. Ibid., II:21.
8. Ibid., I:20–21; Maitron, *Dictionnaire biographique*, II:415–416.
9. Maitron, *Dictionnaire biographique*, I:365–366.
10. Ibid., III:243–244.
11. Alexandre Zévaès, "Les Proscrits français de 1848 et de 1851," in *Les Rèvolution de 1848 et les Rèvolutions du XIXe siècle* 21 (1924), 96–99; Jacques Rancière, *The Nights of Labor*, tr. John Drury (Philadelphia: Temple University Press, 1989), 93.
12. Maitron, *Dictionnaire biographique*, III:274. See his trial, connected with the Darmès case, in *Gazette des Tribunaux*, 24 July 1841.
13. Dora B. Weiner, "François-Vincent Raspail: Doctor and Champion of the Poor," *French Historical Studies* I:2 (1959), 158; Maitron, *Dictionnaire biographique*, III:283; François-Vincent Raspail, "Fondation du Réformateur," in Daniel Ligou, ed., *François-Vincent Raspail ou l'usage de la prison* (Paris: Jérôme Martineau, 1968), 235.
14. Saint-Ferréol, *Les Proscrits*, II:57; Maitron, *Dictionnaire biographique*, II:319.
15. Martin Bernard, *Dix Ans de Prison*, 2nd ed. (Paris: Pagnerre, 1861), 175.
16. Alexandre Zévaès, "Les Proscrits français en 1848 et 1851 à Londres," *La Révolution de 1848 et les révolutions du XIXe siècle* 20 (March 1923–February 1924), 351.
17. Maitron, *Dictionnaire biographique*, I:84–85.
18. Letter from Albert to Barbès, 20 October 1869, cited in "Quelques Lettres inédites reçues par Armand Barbès," *La Révolution de 1848* 5 (1908–1909), 830–831.
19. Maitron, *Dictionnaire biographique*, I:207–208; Arthur Lehning, *From Buonarroti to Bakunin* (Leiden: E. J. Brill, 1970), 128–130.
20. Maitron, *Dictionnaire biographique*, II:436.
21. Ibid., II:119–121.
22. Ibid., I:317–318.
23. V. P. Volguine, "Jean-Jacques Pillot," in *La Pensée* 84 (1959), 37, 39, 53.
24. Maitron, *Dictionnaire biographique*, II:197.
25. Sébastien Commissaire, *Mémoires et Souvenirs*, 2 vols. (Lyon: Meton, 1888), II:149, 178, 180–181.
26. Maxime Vuillaume, *Mes Cahiers rouges au Temps de la Commune* (Paris: Albin Michel, 1971; reprint of 1909 edition), 231–232; Patrick H. Hutton, *The Cult of the Revolutionary Tradition: The Blanquists in French Politics, 1864–1893* (Berkeley: University of California Press, 1981), 124.
27. Philippe Morère, "Un Révolutionnaire ariégeois Victor Pilhes," *La Revolution de 1848 et les Révolutions du XIXe siècle* 19 (1922–1923).
28. Hutton, *The Cult of the Revolutionary Tradition*, 119–122.

Selected Bibliography

ARCHIVAL SOURCES

ARCHIVES NATIONALES

Military and National Guard Records

221 AP 4: Papers of General Darriule, Lieutenant Général commandant, la Place de Paris
F9 682: National Guards
F9 684: National Guards
F9 686: National Guards
F9 1072: Mobile Guards
F9 1162: Personnel Records

April 1834

CC585-CC586: General Information
CC587-CC589: Police and Judicial Dossiers (Suspects Arrested, Dismissed without Charges)
CC590-CC594: Police and Judicial Dossiers (Defendants Convicted for Conspiracy and Insurrection)
CC595: Police and Judicial Dossiers (Defendants Acquitted)
CC596-CC599: Police and Judicial Dossiers (Suspects Arrested, Dismissed without Charges)

May 1839

CC723-CC724: General Information
CC725: Judicial Correspondence
F9 683: Victims of May 1839

February and June 1848

BB18 1463: Judicial Correspondence
BB18 1465A: Judicial Correspondence
BB30 296: Depositions of Politicians, Administrators (February 1848)
BB30 297: Depositions of Army Officers and Soldiers (February 1848)

BB30 298: Depositions of Municipal Guards, Paris mayors, insurgents, and others (February 1848)

C934: *Commission d'Enquête* documents (15 May and June Days)

ARCHIVES DE LA PRÉFECTURE DE POLICE

116 AP 1: Letters and Reports of Carlier, Prefect of Police

ARCHIVES HISTORIQUES DE LA GUERRE (VINCENNES)

F1 15: 1st–24th *bataillons, Garde Mobile* (15 May and June Days, 1848)

Xd 386: Artillery, 1848

PRINTED DOCUMENTS

Assemblée nationale. Quentin-Bauchart, rapporteur. *Rapport de la Commission d'Enquête,* 2 vols. Paris: Imprimerie nationale, n.d.

Bertier de Sauvigny, G. de., ed. *La Révolution de 1830 en France.* Paris: Armand Colin, 1970.

Charon-Bordas, Jeannine, ed. *Cour des Pairs: Procès politiques,* 3 vols. Paris: Archives nationales, 1984.

Collection officielle des ordonnances de police, depuis 1800 jusqu'à 1844. Paris: Librairie administrative de Paul Dupont, 1845.

Compte-rendu: 24 Février et 15 Mai 1848, ou compte-rendu exact et complèt des deux mémorables séances. Paris: chez l'éditeur, 1848.

Cour des Pairs de France. *Affaire du mois d'avril, 1834: Procès-verbal des séances relatives au jugement de cette affaire.* Paris: Imprimerie Crapelet, 1835.

Cour des Pairs de France. *Attentat du 28 Juillet 1835.* Paris: Imprimerie royale, 1835.

Cour des Pairs de France. *Attentat du 25 Juin 1836.* Paris: Imprimerie royale, 1836.

Cour des Pairs de France. *Attentat du 27 Decembre 1836.* Paris: Imprimerie royale, 1837.

Cour des Pairs de France. *Attentat des 12 et 13 Mai 1839.* Paris: Imprimerie royale, 1839.

Cour des Pairs de France. *Attentat du 15 Octobre 1840.* Paris: Imprimerie royale, 1841.

Cour des Pairs de France. *Attentat du 13 Septembre 1841.* Paris: Imprimerie royale, 1841.

Cour des Pairs de France. *Attentat du 16 Avril 1846.* Paris: Imprimerie royale, 1846.

Cour des Pairs de France. *Attentat du 29 Juillet 1846.* Paris: Imprimerie royale, 1846.

Delvau, Alfred. *Les Murailles révolutionnaires de 1848,* 17th ed. 2 vols. Paris: E. Picard, 1868.

Duquai, Ernest, ed. *Les Accusés du 15 Mai 1848.* Paris: Armand Le Chevalier, 1869.

Faure, Alain, and Rancière, Jacques, eds. *La Parole ouvrière, 1830–1851.* Paris: Union générale d'Editions, 1976.

Procès d'Alibaud devant la Cour des Pairs. Paris: Pagnerre, 1836.

Procès de Fieschi et de ses complices, devant la cour des Pairs, précédé des faits préliminaires et de l'acte d'accusation. 3 vols. Paris: A. Ernest Bourdin, 1836.

Procès des Accusés d'avril devant la Cour des Pairs, 2 vols. Paris: Pagnerre, 1835.

Procès des Ex-Ministres, 2nd. ed., 3 vols. Paris: Librairie Roret, [1831].

Les Révolutions du XIXe siècle, 1st. series. Paris: EDHIS, 1974.
    Vol. 1: *Les Associations Républicaines 1830–1834*
    Vol. 2: *La Société des Amis du Peuple 1830–1832*
    Vol. 3: *La Société des Droits de l'Homme et du Citoyen 1832–1834*
    Vol. 4: *Naissance du Mouvement ouvrier, 1830–1834*
    Vol. 7: *Écrits de Philippe Buonarroti—Voyer d'Argenson—L.-A. Blanqui—de Potter— Ch. Teste—U. Trélat-Laponneraye et autres révolutionnaires 1830–1834*
    Vol. 8: *Cabet et les publications du Populaire*
    Vol. 10: *La Presse républicaine devant les Tribunaux 1831–1834*
    Vol. 11: *Les Républicains devant les Tribunaux, 1831–1834*
    Vol. 12: *Feuilles Populaires et Documents divers, 1835–1847*
Les Révolutions du XIXe siècle, 2nd series. Paris: EDHIS, 1979.
    Vol. 2: *Le Mouvement ouvrier de 1835 à 1848*
    Vol. 4: *La Propagande socialiste de 1835 à 1848*
    Vol. 5: *Cabet, le communisme icarien de 1840 à 1847*
    Vol. 6: *Révolutionnaires et Néo-babouvistes de 1835 à 1847*
    Vol. 9: *L'Insurrection des 12 et 13 Mai 1839*
    Vol. 11: *L'Attentat Quenisset, 13 Septembre 1841*
Les Révolution du XIXe siècle, 3rd series: *La Révolution démocratique et sociale*. Paris: EDHIS, 1984.

NEWSPAPERS

L'Atelier
La Commune de Paris
La Démocratie pacifique
La Gazette des Tribunaux
Le Globe
Le Monde républicain
Le Moniteur universel
Le National
Le Populaire
La Réforme
Le Représentant du peuple

MEMOIRS

Achard, Amédée. *Souvenirs personnels d'émeutes et de révolutions.* Paris: Michel Lévy frères, 1872.

Allemane, Jean. *Mémoires d'un communard.* Paris: n.d.

Alton-Shée, Comte d'. *Souvenirs de 1847 et de 1848.* Paris: Maurice Dreyfous, n.d.

Andryane, Alexandre. *Mémoires d'un prisonnier d'État.* 2 vols. 5th edition. Paris: Gaume et cie, 1879.

———. *Souvenirs de Genève.* 2 vols. Paris: W. Coquebert, 1839.

Apponyi, Rodolphe Comte. *Journal du Comte Rodolphe Apponyi.* 4 vols. Paris: Plon, 1913.

Barrot, Odilon. *Mémoires posthumes de Odilon Barrot,* 2nd ed. 4 vols. Paris: Charpentier et cie, 1875.

Bédé, Jacques Étienne. *Un ouvrier en 1820: Manuscrit inédit de Jacques Étienne Bédé.* Introduction and notes by Rémi Gossez. Paris: Presses Universitaires de France, 1984.

Bérard, A. *Souvenirs historiques sur la Révolution de 1830*. Paris: Perrotin, 1834.

Bernard, Martin. *Dix Ans de Prison au Mont-Saint-Michel et à la Citadelle de Doullens, 1839 à 1848*. 2nd edition. Paris: Pagnerre, 1861.

Beslay, Charles. *Mes souvenirs 1830–1848–1870*. Geneva: Slatkine reprints, 1979.

Boichot, J. B. *Souvenirs d'un prisonnier d'état (1854–1859)*. Paris: Librairie du progrès, n.d.

Canler, Paul-Louis-Alphonse. *Mémoires de Canler*. Paris: Mercure de France, 1968.

Caussidière, Marc. *Mémoires de Caussidière*. 2 vols. Paris: Michel Lévy, 1849.

Commissaire, Sébastien. *Mémoires et Souvenirs*. 2 vols. Lyon: Meton, 1888.

Cuvillier-Fleury, Alfred-Auguste. *Journal intime de Cuvillier-Fleury*. 2 vols. Paris: Plon, 1900.

Dupin, André-Jacques. *Mémoires de M. Dupin*. 4 vols. Paris: Henri Plon, 1855.

Faure, Philippe. *Journal d'un combattant de février*. Jersey: Auguste Desmoulins, 1859.

Fix, Théodore. *Souvenirs d'un officier d'État-Major*. Paris: Juven, n.d.

Foucauld, Jacques-Jean, Vicomte de. *Mémoires sur les événements de juillet 1830*. Paris: E. Dentu, 1851.

Gisquet, Henri-Joseph. *Mémoires de M. Gisquet, ancien Préfet de police, écrits par lui-même*. 4 vols. Paris: Marchant, 1840.

Grivel, Abbé. *La Prison du Luxembourg sous la règne de Louis-Philippe*. Paris: Auguste Vaton, 1862.

Gueulluy de Rumigny, Marie-Théodore, Comte de. *Souvenirs du général comte de Rumigny*. Paris: Émile-Paul frères, 1921.

Guizot, François-Pierre-Guillaume. *Mémoires pour servir à l'histoire de mon temps*. 8 vols. Paris: Michel Lévy frères, 1872.

Huart, Suzanne d', ed. *Journal de Marie-Amélie, Reine des Français, 1800–1866*. Paris: Librairie Académique Perrin, 1981.

Ideville, Comte H. d'. *Le Maréchal Bugeaud, d'après sa correspondance intime et des documents inédits, 1784–1849*. 2 vols. Paris: Firmin-Didot, 1881.

Joinville, Prince de. *Vieux Souvenirs de Monseigneur le Prince de Joinville, 1818–1848*. Edited by Daniel Meyer. Paris: Mercure de France, 1986.

Laffitte, Jacques. *Mémoires de Laffitte (1767–1844)*. Edited by Paul Duchon. Paris: Firmin-Didot, n.d.

Lefrançais, Gustave. *Souvenirs d'un révolutionnaire*. Bruxelles: Administration, n.d.

MacMahon, Maréchal de. *Mémoires du Maréchal de MacMahon, Duc de Magenta: Souvenirs d'Algérie, publiés par le Comte Guy de Miribel*. Paris: Plon, 1932.

Maupas, Charlemagne Émile. *The Story of the Coup d'Etat*. Trans. from the French by Albert D. Vandam. New York: D. Appleton and Co., 1884.

Montalivet, Marthe-Camille Bachasson, comte de. *Fragments et Souvenirs*. 2 vols. Paris: Calmann Lévy, 1899.

Nadaud, Martin. *Mémoires de Léonard, ancien garçon maçon*. Edited by Maurice Agulhon. Paris: Hachette, 1976.

Nemours, Louis d'Orléans, duc de. "Sur les événements dont j'ai été témoin pendant les journées des 22, 23, et 24 février 1848." Reprinted in René Bazin, *Le Duc de Nemours*. Paris: Émile-Paul, 1907.

Orléans, Ferdinand-Philippe, duc d'. *Lettres, 1825–1842*. Paris: Calmann Lévy, 1889.

———. *Souvenirs*. Edited and annotated by Hervé Robert. Geneva: Droz, 1993.

Pasquier, Étienne-Denis. *Mémoires du Chancelier Pasquier*. 6 vols. Paris: Plon, 1895.

Pellico, Silvio. *My Imprisonments: Memoirs of Silvio Pellico de Saluzzo*. Trans. from the Italian by Thomas Roscoe. New York: J. and J. Harper, 1833.

Périer, Casimir. *Opinions et Discours de M. Casimir Périer*. 4 vols. Edited by M. A. Lesieur. Paris: Paulin, n.d.

Poncet de Bermond, Hippolyte. *La Garde Royale pendant les évènements du 26 Juillet au 5 Août 1830.* 2nd ed. Paris: G. A. Dentu, 1830.

Poumiès de la Siboutie, F. L. *Souvenirs d'un médecin dans les journées immortelles des 26, 27, 28, et 29 juillet 1830.* Paris: Guyot, 1830.

Rambuteau, Comte Claude Philibert de. *Memoirs of the Comte de Rambuteau.* Trans. from the French by J. C. Brogan. New York: G. P. Putnam's Sons, 1908.

Rémusat, Charles de. *Mémoires de Ma Vie.* Edited by Charles Pouthas. Paris: Plon, 1958.

Rive, William de la. "William de la Rive: un témoin genevois de la Révolution de 1848." Paul Guichonnet, ed. *Société d'histoire de la Révolution de 1848: Études,* vol. xv (Nancy: Imp. Georges Thomas, 1956): 143–63.

Sébastiani, Tiburce. "Rapport sur les journées de Février, adressé à Villemain par le général Sébastiani." G. Vauthier, ed. *La Révolution de 1848,* vol. 8 (1911–1912): 320–330.

Tocqueville, Alexis de. *Souvenirs d'Alexis de Tocqueville.* Paris: Gallimard, 1942.

Truquin, Norbert. *Mémoires et aventures d'un prolétaire à travers la révolution.* Paris: François Maspero, 1977.

Vendôme, duchesse de. *La Jeunesse de Marie-Amélie.* Paris: Plon, 1935.

Viennet, Jean Pons Guillaume. *Journal de Viennet: Pair de France, témoin de trois règnes, 1817–1848.* Paris: Amiot-Dumont, n.d.

Vitrolles, Baron de [Eugène d'Arnauld]. *Mémoires et relations politiques.* 3 vols. Paris: G. Charpentier et cie., 1884.

Vuillaume, Maxime. *Mes Cahiers rouges au Temps de la Commune.* Paris: Albin Michel, 1971; reprint of original 1909 edition.

PRIMARY SOURCES

Anon. "Les Détenus politiques au Mont Saint-Michel." Paris: A. René, 1845. Reprinted in *Les Révolutions du XIXe siècle,* 2nd series, IV: Vol. 4: *La Propagande socialiste de 1835 à 1848.*

[Anon.] "Quelques Lettres inédites reçues par Armand Barbès." *La Révolution de 1848* V (1908–1909): 826–831.

Arago, Jacques. *Histoire de Paris: ses révolutions, ses gouvernements et ses évènements de 1841 à 1852.* Paris: Dion Lambert, 1855.

Aumale, Henri Eugène Philippe Louis d'Orléans, duc d'. *Le Roi Louis-Philippe et le droit de grâce, 1830–1848.* Paris: Calmann Lévy, 1897.

Balleydier, Alphonse. *Histoire de la Garde mobile depuis les barricades de février.* Paris: Pillet fils ainé, 1848.

Blanc, Julien. *La Grève des Charpentiers en 1845; épisode de la crise sociale de l'époque.* Paris: Librairie sociétaire, 1845.

Blanc, Louis. *1848: Historical Revelations.* New York: Howard Fertig, 1971.

———. *The History of Ten Years, 1830–1840; or, France under Louis Philippe.* Trans. from the French by Walter K. Kelly. 2 vols. Philadelphia: Lea & Blanchard, 1848.

———. *Organisation du Travail.* 5th ed. Paris: Au bureau de la Société de l'industrie fraternelle, 1848. Reprinted in J.A.R. Marriott, ed. *The French Revolution of 1848,* vol. 1. Oxford: The Clarendon Press, 1913.

———. *La Révolution de Février au Luxembourg.* Paris: Michel Lévy, 1849. Reprinted in *Les Révolutions du XIX siècle,* 3rd series, vol. 4: *La Révolution démocratique et sociale.* Paris: EDHIS, 1984.

Blanqui, Adolphe. "Souvenirs d'un étudiant sous la Restauration." *La Revue de Paris* 148:15 (October 1918): 776–796; 149:1 (November 1918): 158–176.999.

Blanqui, Auguste. *Instructions pour un prise d'armes . . . et autres textes.* Edited by Miguel Abensour and Valentin Pelosse. Paris: Société encyclopédique française, 1973.

Blanqui, Louis Auguste. *Écrits sur la Révolution: Oeuvres complètes I, textes politiques et lettres de prison.* Edited by Arno Münster. Paris: Éditions Galilée, 1977.

Boyer, Adolphe. *De l'État des ouvriers et de son amélioration par l'organisation du travail.* 2nd. éd. Paris: Mme. veuve Boyer, 1841.

Buonarroti, Philippe. *La Conspiration pour l'Égalité dite de Babeuf.* 2 vols. Preface by Georges Lefebvre. Paris: Éditions sociales, 1957.

Carrel, Armand. *Oeuvres politiques et littéraires d'Armand Carrel.* 5 vols. Paris: Librairie de F. Chamerot, 1857.

Castille, Hippolyte. *Histoire de la Seconde République française.* 4 vols. Paris: Victor Lecou, 1854.

Cauchy, E. *Les Précédents de la Cour des Pairs.* Paris: Imprimerie royale, October 1839.

Cavaignac, Godefroy. "La Force révolutionnaire." *Paris révolutionnaire,* vol. 1:vii-lxxxiv. Paris: Pagnerre, 1838.

Chauveau, Adolphe, and Faustin Hélie. *Théorie du Code pénal,* 2nd ed. 6 vols. Paris: Édouard Legrand, 1843.

Chenu, Adolphe. *Les Conspirateurs.* Paris: Garnier frères, 1850.

Delahodde, Lucien. *Histoire des sociétés secrètes et du parti républicain de 1830 à 1848.* Paris: Julien, Lanier et cie, 1850.

———. *La Naissance de la République,* 4th ed. Paris: Chez l'Éditeur, 1850.

Dézamy, Théodore. *Code de la Communauté.* Paris: Prévost, 1842. Reprint ed. Paris: EDHIS, 1967.

Dourille, Henri. *Histoire de la Conspiration du Général Malet, 1812* Paris: Bureau du *Journal du Peuple,* 1840.

Duclerc, E., ed. *Dictionnaire politique: Encyclopédie de langage et de la science politiques.* 2nd ed. Paris: Duclerc and Pagnerre, 1843.

Duvergier de Hauranne, Prosper. *Histoire du Gouvernement parlementaire en France,* vol. 10. Paris: Michel Lévy frères, 1871.

Fabre, Auguste. *La Révolution de 1830, et le véritable parti républicain.* 2 vols. Paris: Thoisnier-Desplaces, 1833.

Garnier-Pagès, Louis. *Histoire de la Révolution de 1848,* 2nd ed. 4 vols. Paris: Pagnerre, 1866.

Girard, Fulgence. *Histoire du Mont-Saint-Michel comme prison d'état.* Paris: Paul Permain et cie, 1849.

Huber, Aloysius. *Nuit de Veille d'un Prisonnier d'État.* Paris: E. Dentu, 1862.

———. *Quelques Paroles d'un Proscrit.* Paris: Rouanet, 1848.

Lamartine, Alphonse de. *Histoire de la Révolution de 1848.* 2 vols. Bruxelles: Méline, Cans et cie, 1849.

Lucas, Alphonse. *Les Clubs et les Clubistes.* Paris: E. Dentu, 1851.

Lucas, Charles. *Exposé de l'État de la Question pénitentiaire en Europe et aux États-Unis.* Paris: Panckoucke, 1844.

Marin, Henri. "Les Réflexions d'un homme de rien sur la Garde nationale en général. . . ." *La Révolution de 1848,* VII (1910–1911): 224–241; 326–340; 367–390.

Marrast, Armand. "La Presse révolutionnaire." *Paris révolutionnaire,* vol. 2:3–128. Paris: Pagnerre, 1838.

———. *Vingt Jours de Secret.* Paris: Guillaumin, 1834.

Menard, Louis. *Prologue d'une Révolution: Février-Juin 1848.* Paris: Au bureau du peuple, 1849.

Moreau-Christophe, L. M. *De la Mortalité et de la Folie dans le régime pénitentiaire.* Paris: Paul Renouard, 1839.

Noiret, Charles, *Mémoires d'un ouvrier rouennais* Rouen: François, 1836; reprint ed. Jean-Pierre Chaline, *L'Affaire Noiret.* Rouen: Société de l'Histoire de Normandie, 1986.

Nouguès, L. *Une Condamnation de Mai, 1839.* Paris: J. Bry aîné, 1850.

Nouvion, Victor de. *Histoire du règne de Louis-Philippe Ier Roi des Français 1830–1848,* 4 vols. Paris: Didier et cie, 1857.

Ott, A. *Des Associations d'ouvriers.* Paris: Poussin, 1838[?].

[Pepin, Albert]. *La Royauté de Juillet et la Révolution,* 2 vols. Paris: Dezauche, 1837.

Poulot, Denis. *Question sociale: Le sublime, ou le travailleur comme il est en 1870 et ce qu'il peut être.* Étude préalable by Alain Cottereau. Paris: François Maspero, 1980.

Raspail, François-Vincent. *François-Vincent Raspail ou le bon usage de la prison.* Edited by Daniel Ligou. Paris: Jérôme Martineau, 1968.

Raspail, François-Vincent. *Réforme pénitentiaire: Lettres sur les Prisons de Paris.* 2 vols. Paris: Tamisey et Champion, 1839.

Regnault, Élias. *Histoire de Huit Ans, 1840–1848,* 5th ed. 3 vols. Paris: Librairie Germer Baillière, 1882.

Renouvier, Charles. *Manuel Républicain de l'homme et du citoyen: 1848.* Edited by Maurice Agulhon. Paris: Éditions Garnier frères, 1981.

Rittiez, F. *Histoire du Gouvernement provisoire en 1848.* 2 vols. Paris: A. Lacroix, Verboeckhoven et cie., 1867.

———. *Histoire du règne de Louis-Philippe I, 1830 à 1848.* 3 vols. Paris: V. Lecou, 1855.

Robespierre, Maximilien. *Oeuvres de Maximilien Robespierre,* 3 vols. Editor, Albert Lapponeraye. Preface by Armand Carrel. Paris: n.p., 1840.

Saint-Ferréol, Amédée. *Les Proscrits français en Belgique.* 2 vols. Paris: Armand Le Chevalier, 1871.

Sarrans, B. *Histoire de la Révolution de Février 1848.* 2 vols. Paris: Administration de Librairie, 1851.

———. *Louis-Philippe et la Contre-Révolution de 1830.* 2 vols. Paris: Thoisnier-Desplaces, 1834.

———. *Lafayette et la Révolution de 1830, Histoire des choses et des hommes de Juillet,* 2 vols. 2nd. ed. Paris: Thoisnier Desplaces, 1833.

Sauzet, Paul. *La Chambre des Députés et la Révolution de Février.* Paris: Perisse frères, 1851.

Senior, Nassau. *Conversations with M. Thiers, M. Guizot, and Other Distinguished Persons, during the Second Empire.* 2 vols. London: Hurst and Blackett, 1878.

———. *Journals kept in France and Italy from 1848 to 1852,* 2 vols. Edited by M.C.M. Simpson. London: Henry S. King and Co., 1871.

Stern, Daniel [Comtesse Marie d'Agoult]. *Histoire de la Révolution de 1848.* Paris: Éditions Balland, 1985.

Taschereau, Jules. *Revue Rétrospective.* Paris: Paulin, 1848.

Tirel, Louis. *La République dans les carosses du roi.* 2nd ed. Paris: Comptoir des Imprimeurs, 1850.

Tocqueville, Alexis de. *Oeuvres complètes,* vol. IV: *Écrits sur le système pénitentiaire en France et à l'étranger.* Edited by Michelle Perrot. Paris: Gallimard, 1984.

Tripier Le Franc, J. *M. Gabriel Delessert.* Paris: E. Dentu, 1859.

Tristan, Flora. *The Workers' Union.* Trans. and with an Introduction by Beverly Livingston. Urbana: University of Illinois Press, 1983.

Truquin, Norbert. *Mémoires et aventures d'un prolétaire à travers la révolution.* Paris: François Maspero, 1977.

Vaulabelle, Achille de. *Histoire des Deux Restaurations.* Vol. 8. Paris: Perrotin, 1857.

Vauthier, G., ed. "Notes de Villemain sur les journées de Février 1848." *La Revolution de 1848*, vol. 9 (1912–1913): 241–265.

SECONDARY SOURCES

Accampo, Elinor A., Fuchs, Rachel G., and Stewart, Mary Lynn, eds. *Gender and the Politics of Social Reform in France, 1870–1914.* Baltimore: The Johns Hopkins University Press, 1995.

Adam-Flocon. "Ferdinand Flocon (1800–1866)." *1848 et les Révolutions du XIXe siècle* (autumn 1947), vol. 38, n. 178: 56–62.

Agulhon, Maurice. *The Republican Experiment, 1848–1852.* Translated from the French by Janet Lloyd. Cambridge, MA: Cambridge University Press, 1983.

———. *The Republic in the Village: The People of the Var from the French Revolution to the Second Republic.* Translated from the French by Janet Lloyd. Cambridge, MA: Cambridge University Press, 1982.

———. *Le Cercle dans la France bourgeoise 1810–1848.* Paris: Libraire Armand Colin, 1977.

Alexander, R. S. "Restoration Republicanism Reconsidered." *French History* 8:4 (December 1994): 442–469.

Amann, Peter. "The Huber Enigma: Revolutionary or Police-Spy." *International Review of Social History* XII:2 (1967): 190–203.

———. "Prelude to Insurrection: The Banquet of the People." *French Historical Studies* 1:4 (December, 1960): 436–444.

———. *Revolution and Mass Democracy: the Paris Club Movement in 1848.* Princeton: Princeton University Press, 1975.

Aminzade, Ronald. *Ballots and Barricades: Class Formation and Republican Politics in France, 1830–1871.* Princeton: Princeton University Press, 1993.

———. *Class, Politics, and Early Industrial Capitalism: A Study of Mid-Nineteenth-Century Toulouse, France.* Albany: State University of New York Press, 1981.

Antonetti, Guy. *Louis-Philippe.* Paris: Arthème Fayard, 1994.

Arac, Jonathan, and Johnson, Barbara, eds. *Consequences of Theory.* Baltimore: The Johns Hopkins University Press, 1991.

Auspitz, Katherine. *The Radical Bourgeoisie: the Ligue de l'enseignement and the Origins of the Third Republic, 1866–1885.* Cambridge, MA: Cambridge University Press, 1982.

Bastid, Paul. *Doctrines et Institutions politiques de la Seconde République.* 2 vols. Paris: Hachette, 1945.

Bazin, René. *Le Duc de Nemours.* Paris: Émile-Paul, 1907.

Berenson, Edward. *Populist Religion and Left-Wing Politics in France, 1830–1852.* Princeton: Princeton University Press, 1984.

Berlanstein, Lenard R. "The Distinctiveness of the Nineteenth-Century French Labor Movement." *The Journal of Modern History* 64/4 (December 1992): 660–685.

Berkhofer, Jr., Robert F. *Beyond the Great Story.* Cambridge, MA: Harvard University Press, 1995.

Bernstein, Samuel. *The Beginnings of Marxian Socialism in France.* New York: Social Science Studies, 1933.

———. *Auguste Blanqui and the Art of Insurrection.* London: Lawrence and Wishart, 1971.

Bertier de Sauvigny, Guillaume. *Au Soir de la Monarchie: histoire de la Restauration.* Paris: Flammarion, 1955.

Bezucha, Robert J. *The Lyon Uprising of 1834: Social and Political Conflict in the Early July Monarchy.* Cambridge, MA: Harvard University Press, 1974.

Billington, James H. *Fire in the Minds of Men: Origins of the Revolutionary Faith.* New York: Basic Books, 1980.

Blaisdell, Lowell L. "Aloysius Huber and May 15, 1848: New Insights into an Old Mystery." *International Review of Social History* 29:1 (1984): 34–61.

Bory, Jean-Louis. *La Révolution de Juillet.* Paris: Gallimard, 1972.

Bossu, Jean. "De l'Épicerie aux Barricades." *1848 et les révolutions du XIXe siècle* (Summer 1947), vol. 38, no. 177–178: 60–64.

———. "Mathieu d'Epinal et son temps." *1848 et les Révolutions du XIXe siècle* 18 (Fall 1947): 27–64.

Bourgin, Georges. "La Crise ouvrière à Paris dans la seconde moitié de 1830." *Revue historique* (1947): 203–214.

Bowman, Frank Paul. *Le Christ des Barricades, 1789–1848.* Paris: Les Éditions du Cerf, 1987.

Brombert, Victor. *The Romantic Prison.* Princeton: Princeton University Press, 1978.

Bury, J. P. T., and Robert Tombs. *Thiers 1797–1877.* London: 1986.

Calman, Alvin R. *Ledru-Rollin and the Second French Republic.* New York: Columbia, 1922.

Canary, Robert H., and Kozicki, Henry. *The Writing of History.* Madison, WI: The University of Wisconsin Press, 1978.

Caplan, Pat, ed. *The Cultural Construction of Sexuality.* London: Tavistock Publications, 1987.

Carnes, Mark C. and Griffen, Clyde, eds. *Meanings for Manhood: Constructions of Masculinity in Victorian America.* Chicago: The University of Chicago Press, 1990.

Cauvain, Jules Antoine. *Les Prisonniers du Mont-Saint-Michel.* Paris: Au bureau de l'Éclipse, 1872.

Chapman, Tim. *The Congress of Vienna.* London: Routledge, 1998.

Charavay, Étienne. *Le Général La Fayette.* Paris: Société de l'Histoire de la Révolution française, 1898.

Charle, Christophe. *A Social History of France in the Nineteenth Century.* Translated from the French by Miriam Kochan. Oxford: Berg, 1994.

Chauvet, Paul. *Les Ouvriers du livre en France.* Paris: Librairie Marcel Rivière et cie, 1964.

Cherest, Aimé. *La Vie et les oeuvres de A.-T. Marie.* Paris: Durand et Pedone Lauriel, 1873.

Chevalier, Louis. *Laboring Classes and Dangerous Classes in Paris during the First Half of the Nineteenth Century.* Trans. from the French by Frank Jellinek. Princeton, NJ: Princeton University Press, 1973.

———. *La Formation de la population parisienne aux XIXe siècle.* Paris: Presses universitaires de France, 1950.

Chu, Petra Ten-Soesschate, and Gabriel P. Weisberg, eds. *The Popularization of Images: Visual Culture under the July Monarchy* (Princeton, NJ: Princeton University Press, 1994).

Coleman, William. *Death is a Social Disease: Public Health and Political Economy in Early Industrial France.* Madison, WI: University of Wisconsin Press, 1982.

Collingham, H. A. C. *The July Monarchy: A Political History of France, 1830–1848.* London: Longman, 1988.

Collins, Irene. *The Government and the Newspaper Press in France, 1814–1881.* Oxford: Oxford University Press, 1959.

Coverdale, John. F. *The Basque Phase of Spain's First Carlist War.* Princeton: Princeton University Press, 1984.

Crémieux, Albert. "La Fusillade du boulevard des Capucines." *La Révolution de 1848: Bulletin de la Société d'histoire de la Révolution de 1848,* 5 (1908–1909): 99–116.

———. *La Révolution de février: Étude critique sur les journées des 21, 22, 23, et 24 février 1848.* Paris: Édouard Cornély, 1912.

Crow, Thomas. *Emulation: Making Artists for Revolutionary France.* New Haven: Yale University Press, 1995.

Cuvillier, Armand. *Un journal d'Ouvriers: "L'Atelier" (1840–1850).* Paris: Les Éditions ouvrières, 1954.

———. *P.-J.-B. Buchez et les origines du socialisme chrétien.* Paris: Presses universitaires de France, 1948.

Daumard, Adeline. *Les Bourgeois de Paris au XIXe siècle.* Paris: Flammarion, 1970.

Davis, J. *People of the Mediterranean: An Essay in Comparative Social Anthropology.* London: Routledge and Kegan Paul, 1977.

DeGroat, Judith A. "The Public Nature of Women's Work: Definitions and Debates during the Revolution of 1848." *French Historical Studies* 20:1 (Winter 1997): 31–48.

De la Fuye, Maurice. *Rouget de Lisle Inconnu.* Paris: Hachette, 1943.

De Luna, Frederick A. *The French Republic Under Cavaignac.* Princeton: Princeton University Press, 1969.

Dolléans, Édouard. *Histoire du Mouvement ouvrier,* 2 vols. Paris: Librairie Armand Colin, 1936.

Dommanget, Maurice. "Auguste Blanqui à la citadelle de Doullens." *Société d'histoire de la Révolution de 1848: Études* 16 (1954): 43–78.

———. "Les 'Faveurs' de Blanqui." *1848: Revue des révolutions contemporaines* 43 (July 1950): 137–166.

———. *Auguste Blanqui: Des Origines à la Révolution de 1848.* Paris: Mouton, 1969.

Doumenc, [General]. "L'Armée et les journées de juin." *Actes du congrès historique du centenaire de la Révolution de 1848.* Paris: PUF, 1948: 255–263.

Driskel, Michael Paul. "Singing 'The Marseillaise' in 1840: the Case of Charlet's Censored Prints." *The Art Bulletin* 69:4 (December 1987): 604–625.

Du Camp, Maxime. *L'Attentat Fieschi.* Paris: G. Charpentier, 1877.

Eisenstein, Elizabeth L. *The First Professional Revolutionist: Filippo Michele Buonarroti.* Cambridge, MA: Harvard University Press, 1959.

———. *The Evolution of the Jacobin Tradition in France: The Survival and Revival of the Ethos of 1793 under the Bourbon and Orleanist Regimes.* Ph.D. diss., Radcliffe College, 1952.

Elwitt, Sanford. *Third Republic Defended: Bourgeois Reform in France, 1880–1914.* Baton Rouge, LA: Louisiana University Press, 1986.

———. *The Making of the Third Republic: Class and Politics in France, 1868–1884.* Baton Rouge: Louisiana State University Press, 1975.

Esmein, Adhémar. *A History of Continental Criminal Procedure, with Special Reference to France.* Translated from the French by John Simpson. Boston: Little, Brown, and Company, 1913.

Fairchilds, Cissie. *Domestic Enemies: Servants and their Masters in Old Regime France.* Baltimore, MD: The Johns Hopkins Press, 1984.

Fasel, George W. "The French Election of April 23, 1848: Suggestions for a Revision." *French Historical Studies* 5/3 (Spring 1968): 285–298.

Faure, Alain. "Mouvements populaires et mouvement ouvrier à Paris (1830–1834)." *Le Mouvement social* 88 (1974): 51–92.

Festy, Octave. "Le mouvement ouvrier à Paris en 1840." *Revue des Sciences politiques* (July–November 1913): 67–79; 226–240; 333–361.

———. *Le Mouvement ouvrier au début de la monarchie de juillet.* Paris: Édouard Cornély, 1908.

Ford, Franklin. *Political Murder: From Tyrannicide to Terrorism.* Cambridge, MA: Harvard University Press, 1985.

Foucault, Michel. *Discipline and Punish.* New York: Random House, 1979.

Furet, François, and Ozouf, Mona, eds., *The French Revolution and the Creation of Modern Political Culture.* 3 vols. Oxford: Pergamon Press, 1989.

Furet, François. *Revolutionary France, 1770–1880.* Translated from the French by Antonia Nevill. Oxford: Blackwell, 1988.

———. *La Gauche et la Révolution française au milieu du XIXe siècle: Edgar Quinet et la question du Jacobinisme.* Paris: Hachette, 1986.

Galante Garrone, Alessandro. *Philippe Buonarroti et les révolutionnaires du XIXe siècle.* Translated from the Italian by Anne and Claude Manceron. Paris: Éditions Champ Libre, 1975.

Gallaher, John G. *The Students of Paris and the Revolution of 1848.* Carbondale: Southern Illinois University Press, 1980.

Geffroy, Gustave. *L'Enfermé.* Paris: Bibliothèque-Charpentier, 1897.

Girard, Louis. *La Garde Nationale, 1814–1871.* Paris: Librairie Plon, 1964.

Goffman, Erving. *Asylums: Essays on the Social Situation of Mental Patients and other Inmates.* Chicago, 1961.

Goldstein, Jan. *Console and Classify: The French Psychiatric Profession in the Nineteenth Century.* Cambridge, MA: Cambridge University Press, 1987.

Goldstein, Robert Justin. "Censorship of Caricature in France, 1815–1914." *French History* 3:1 (March, 1989): 71–107.

Gossez, Remi. "Presse Parisienne à destination des ouvriers, 1848–1851." *La Presse ouvrière 1819–1850.* Paris: Bibliothèque de la Révolution de 1848 (1966), vol. 23: 123–189.

———. "Diversité des antagonismes sociaux vers le milieu du XIXe siècle." *Revue economique.* (1956): 439–458.

———. "Notes sur la composition et l'attitude politique de la troupe." *Société d'histoire de la Révolution de 1848.* 18 (1955): 77–110.

Gourvitch, A. "Le Mouvement pour la réforme, 1838–41." *La Révolution de 1848,* 12 (1915–1916): 93–131, 185–211, 265–88, 345–59, 397–417; 13 (1916–1917): 37–44, 95–115, 173–92, 256–71; 14 (1917–1918): 62–81.

Guillemin, Henri. *La première résurrection de la République.* Paris: Éditions Gallimard, 1967.

Gullickson, Gay L. *Unruly Women of Paris.* Ithaca: Cornell University Press, 1996.

Gutwirth, Madelyn. *The Twilight of the Goddesses: Women and Representation in the French Revolutionary Era.* New Brunswick, NJ: Rutgers University Press, 1992.

Haine, W. Scott. *The World of the Paris Café: Sociability Among the French Working Class, 1789–1914.* Baltimore: The Johns Hopkins University Press, 1996.

Halévy, Daniel. "L'Attentat de Fieschi." *La Revue de Paris* 42:9 (1935): 91–118.

Harison, Casey. "An Organization of Labor: Laissez-Faire and *Marchandage* in the Paris Building Trades through 1848." *French Historical Studies* 20:3 (Summer 1997): 357–380.

Hauriou, Maurice. *Précis de droit constitutionnel.* Paris: Librairie du recueil Sirey, 1929.

Hazareesingh, Sudhir. *From Subject to Citizen: the Second Empire and the Emergence of Modern French Democracy.* Princeton, NJ: Princeton University Press, 1998.

Higonnet, Patrice, David S. Landes, and Henry Rosovsky, eds. *Favorites of Fortune.* Cambridge, MA: Harvard University Press, 1991.

Higonnet, Patrice. *Goodness beyond Virtue: Jacobins during the French Revolution.* Cambridge, MA: Harvard University Press, 1998.

Hiver, M., *Histoire critique des institutions judiciaires de la France de 1789 à 1848.* Paris: Auguste Durand, 1851.

Hobsbawm, Eric. *Bandits.* New York: Pantheon Books, 1981.

Hobsbawm, E. J., and Joan Wallach Scott. "Political Shoemakers." *Past and Present* 89 (November 1980): 86–114.

Hoffman, Philip T., Gilles Postel-Vinay, and Jean-Laurent Rosenthal. *Priceless Markets: The Political Economy of Credit in Paris.* Chicago: University of Chicago Press, 2000.

Hoffman, Stanley. *In Search of France.* New York: Harper and Row, 1963.

Hunt, Lynn, and George Sheridan. "Corporations, Association, and the Language of Labor in France, 1750–1850." *The Journal of Modern History* 58/4 (December 1986): 813–844.

Hunt, Lynn. *Politics, Culture and Class in the French Revolution.* Berkeley: University of California Press, 1984.

Hutton, Patrick H. *The Cult of the Revolutionary Tradition: The Blanquists in French Politics, 1864–1893.* Berkeley: University of California Press, 1981.

Ignatieff, Michael. *A Just Measure of Pain: The Penitentiary in the Industrial Revolution 1750–1850.* New York: Penguin, 1989.

Jardin, André, and André-Jean Tudesq. *Restoration and Reaction, 1815–1848.* Translated from the French by Elborg Forster. Cambridge, MA: Cambridge University Press, 1983.

Jaume, Lucien, ed. *Les Déclarations des Droits de l'Homme, 1789–1793–1848–1946.* Paris: Flammarion, 1989.

Jeanjean, J. F. "Barbès et Blanqui." *La Révolution de 1848,* vol. 8 (1911–1912): 187–207.

———. "L'Éternel Révolté," *La Révolution de 1848,* vol. 5 (1908–1909).

———. *Armand Barbès.* Paris: Édouard Cornély, 1909.

Jenkins, Keith, ed. *The Postmodern History Reader.* London: Routledge, 1997.

Johnson, Christopher H. "Etienne Cabet and the Problem of Class Antagonism." *International Review of Social History* 11 (1966): 403–443.

———. *Utopian Communism in France: Cabet and the Icarians, 1839–1851.* Ithaca: Cornell University Press, 1974.

Jordan, David P. *Transforming Paris: The Life and Labors of Baron Haussmann.* Chicago: University of Chicago Press, 1995.

Joyce, Patrick, ed. *The Historical Meanings of Work.* Cambridge, MA: Cambridge University Press, 1987.

Judt, Tony. *Marxism and the French Left: Studies in Labour and Politics in France, 1830–1981.* Oxford: Clarendon Press, 1986.

Kaplan, Steven Laurence, and Cynthia J. Koepp, eds. *Work in France: Representations, Meaning, Organization, and Practice.* Ithaca: Cornell University Press, 1986.

Katznelson, Ira, and Aristide R. Zolberg, eds. *Working-Class Formation: Nineteenth-Century Patterns in Western Europe and the United States.* Princeton: Princeton University Press, 1986.

Koepke, Robert. "Charles Tanneguy Duchatel and the Revolution of 1848." *French Historical Studies* 8:2 (Fall 1973): 236–254.

Koepke, Robert L. "The Short, Unhappy History of Progressive Conservatism in France, 1846–1848." *Canadian Journal of History* XVIII:2 (August 1983): 187–216.

Kramer, Lloyd S. "Exile and European Thought: Heine, Marx and Mickiewicz in July Monarchy Paris." *Historical Reflections/Réflexions historiques* 11 (1984): 45–70.

———. *Lafayette in Two Worlds.* Chapel Hill: University of North Carolina Press, 1996.

Landes, David. *The Unbound Prometheus.* Cambridge, MA: Cambridge University Press, 1969.

Landes, Joan B. *Women and the Public Sphere in the Age of the French Revolution.* Ithaca, NY: Cornell University Press, 1988.

Latta, Claude. "L'Insurrection de 1839." *Blanqui et les Blanquistes: Société d'Histoire de la Révolution de 1848 et des Révolutions du XIXe siècle.* Paris: Sedes, 1986: 69–85.

Lehning, Arthur. "Buonarroti's Ideas on Communism and Dictatorship." *International Review of Social History* (1957): 266–87.

———. "Buonarroti and his International Secret Societies." *International Review of Social History* 1:1 (1956): 112–130.

———. "Buonarroti et la révolution belge de 1830." *Société des études robespierristes: Babeuf, Buonarroti.* Nancy: Georges Thomas, n.d.: 212–218.

———. *From Buonarroti to Bakunin: Studies in International Socialism.* Leiden: E. J. Brill, 1970.

Lenotre, G. *Vieilles maisons, vieux papiers,* 5th série. Paris: Librairie Académique Perrin, 1935.

Levy, Darline Gay, Harriet Applewhite, and Mary Johnson. *Women in Revolutionary Paris, 1789–1795.* Urbana: University of Illinois Press, 1979.

Lovell, David W. "The French Revolution and the Origins of Socialism: The Case of Early French Socialism." *French History* 6:2 (June 1992): 185–205.

Lucas-Dubreton, J. *Louis-Philippe et la machine infernale (1830–1835).* Paris: Amiot-Dumont, 1951.

———. *La Manière forte: Casimir Perier et la Révolution de 1830.* Paris: Bernard Grasset, 1929.

———. *L'Affaire Alibaud ou Louis-Philippe traqué (1836).* Paris: Perrin et cie, 1927.

Magraw, Roger. *A History of the French Working Class,* vol. I: *The Age of Artisan Revolution, 1815–1871.* Oxford: Blackwell Publishers, 1992.

Maitron, Jean. *Dictionnaire biographique du Mouvement ouvrier français,* 9 vols. Paris: Les Éditions ouvrières, 1964.

Mangan, J. A., and James Walvin, eds. *Manliness and Morality: Middle-Class Masculinity in Britain and America, 1800–1940.* New York: St. Martin's Press, 1987.

Mansel, Philip. *The Court of France 1789–1830.* Cambridge, MA: Cambridge University Press, 1988.

Margadant, Jo Burr. "The Duchesse de Berry and Royalist Political Culture in Postrevolutionary France." *History Workshop Journal* 43 (Spring 1997): 23–52.

Margadant, Ted. *French Peasants in Revolt: the Insurrection of 1851.* Princeton, NJ: Princeton University Press, 1979.

Marrinan, Michael. *Painting Politics for Louis-Philippe: Art and Ideology in Orléanist France, 1830–1848.* New Haven: Yale University Press, 1988.

Martin, Benjamin F. *Crime and Criminal Justice Under the Third Republic.* Baton Rouge, LA: Louisiana State University Press, 1990.

Maynes, Mary Jo. *Taking the Hard Road.* Chapel Hill: University of North Carolina Press, 1995.

Maza, Sarah. *Servants and Masters in Eighteenth-Century France.* Princeton: Princeton University Press, 1983.

McKay, Donald Cope. *The National Workshops: A Study in the French Revolution of 1848.* Cambridge, MA: Harvard University Press, 1933.

Mellon, Stanley. *The Political Uses of History.* Stanford, CA: Stanford University Press, 1958.

Melzer, Sara E., and Leslie W. Rabine, eds. *Rebel Daughters: Women and the French Revolution.* New York: Oxford University Press, 1992.

Merriman, John W. *The Agony of the Republic: The Repression of the Left in Revolutionary France.* New Haven: Yale University Press, 1978.

———, ed. *Consciousness and Class Experience in Nineteenth-Century Europe.* New York: Holmes and Meier, 1979.

———, ed. *1830 in France.* New York: Franklin Watts, 1975.

Moissonnier, Maurice. "Des origines à 1871." *La France ouvrière et du mouvement ouvrier français,* vol. 1: *Des origines à 1920,* ed. Claude Willard. Paris: Éditions sociales, 1993: 13–220.

Monin, H. "Blanqui et la Police." *La Révolution de 1848,* 12 (March 1914–February 1916): 26–38.

Morère, Philippe. "Un Révolutionnaire ariégeois Victor Pilhes." *La Révolution de 1848 et les Révolutions du XIXe siècle* 19 (1922–1923): 53–54.

Moses, Claire Goldberg, and Leslie Wahl Rabine. *Feminism, Socialism, and French Romanticism.* Bloomington, IN: Indiana University Press, 1993.

Moses, Claire Goldberg. *French Feminism in the Nineteenth Century.* Albany, NY: State University of New York Press, 1984.

Moss, Bernard H. "Producers' Associations and the Origins of French Socialism: Ideology from Below." *Journal of Modern History* 48:1 (March 1976): 69–89.

———. *The Origins of the French Labor Mouvement, 1830–1914.* Berkeley: University of California Press, 1976.

Mottez, Bernard, *Systèmes de Salaire et Politiques patronales: Essai sur l'évolution des pratiques et des ideologies patronales.* Paris: Éditions du Centre Nationale de la Recherche Scientifique, 1966.

Neely, Sylvia, *Lafayette and the Liberal Ideal, 1814–1824.* Carbondale: Southern Illinois University Press, 1991.

Newman, Edgar Leon. "Sounds in the Desert: The Socialist Worker Poets of the Bourgeois Monarchy, 1830–1848." *Proceedings of the Third Annual Meeting of the Western Society for French History,* 1975: 269–299.

———. "The Blouse and the Frock Coat: The Alliance of the Common People of Paris with the Liberal Leadership and the Middle Class during the Last Years of the Bourbon Restoration." *Journal of Modern History* 46:1 (March 1974): 26–59.

Nicholson, Linda J. *Gender and History: the Limits of Social Theory in the Age of the Family.* New York: Columbia University Press, 1986.

Nicolet, Claude. *L'Idée républicaine en France (1789–1924).* Paris: Gallimard, 1982.

Nobécourt, R.-G. *La Vie d'Armand Carrel.* Paris: Librairie Gallimard, 1930.

Noiriel, Gérard. *Workers in French Society in the 19th and 20th Centuries.* Translated from the French by Helen McPhail. New York: Berg, 1990.

Nord, Philip. *The Republican Moment: Struggles for Democracy in Nineteenth-Century France.* Cambridge, MA: Harvard University Press, 1995.

Nye, Robert A. *Masculinity and Male Codes of Honor in Modern France.* New York: Oxford University Press, 1993.

———. *Crime, Madness, and Politics in Modern France.* Princeton: Princeton University Press, 1984.

O'Brien, Patricia. *The Promise of Punishment: Prisons in Nineteenth- Century France.* Princeton: Princeton University Press, 1982.

Outram, Dorinda. *The Body and the French Revolution: Sex, Class, and Political Culture.* New Haven: Yale University Press, 1989.

Papayanis, Nicholas. *The Coachmen of Nineteenth-Century Paris: Service Workers and Class Consciousness.* Baton Rouge: Louisiana State University Press, 1993.

Passeron, Roger. *Daumier.* Secaucus, NJ: Poplar, 1981.

Perreux, Gabriel. *Aux Temps des Sociétés Secrètes: La Propagande républicaine au début de la Monarchie de Juillet (1830–1835).* Paris: Rieder, 1931.

———. *Les Origines du drapeau rouge en France.* Paris: PUF, 1930.

Perrot, Michelle, ed. *L'Impossible Prison.* Paris: Éditions du Seuil, 1980.

Pilbeam, Pamela. "Republicanism in Early Nineteenth-Century France, 1814–1835." *French History* 5:1 (March 1991): 30–47.

———. "The 'Liberal' Revolution of 1830." *Historical Research* 63 (1990): 162–177.

———. "The Growth of Liberalism and the Crisis of the Bourbon Restoration, 1827–1830." *The Historical Journal* 25:2 (1982): 351–366.

———. "The Emergence of Opposition to the Orleanist Monarchy, August 1830–April 1831." *English Historical Review* 85 (1970): 12–28.

———. *Republicanism in Nineteenth-Century France.* New York: St. Martin's Press, 1995.

Pinkney, David H. "The Crowd in the French Revolution of 1830." *The American Historical Review,* 70:1 (October 1964): 1–17.

———. *Decisive Years in France, 1840–1847.* Princeton: Princeton University Press, 1986.

———. *The French Revolution of 1830.* Princeton: Princeton University Press, 1972.

Porch, Douglas. *Army and Revolution: France, 1815–1848.* London: Routledge and Kegan Paul, 1974. Posener, S. *Adolphe Crémieux,* 2 vols. Paris: Félix Alcan, 1933.

Price, Roger. "Techniques of Repression: the Control of Popular Protest in Mid-Nineteenth-Century France." *Historical Journal* 25:4 (1982): 859–887.

Price, Roger, ed. *Revolution and Reaction: 1848 and the Second French Republic.* London: Croom Helm, 1975.

Rader, Daniel L. *The Journalists and the July Revolution in France.* The Hague: Martinus Nijhoff, 1973.

Rancière, Jacques. "Ronds de fumée: les poètes ouvriers dans la France de Louis-Philippe." *Revue des sciences humaines* 61:190 (April–June 1983): 31–47.

———. *The Nights of Labor: the Workers' Dream in Nineteenth-Century France.* Translated from the French by John Drury. Philadelphia: Temple University Press, 1989.

Reddy, William M. *Money and Liberty in Modern Europe: A Critique of Historical Understanding.* Cambridge, MA: Cambridge University Press, 1987.

Reid, Donald. "In the Name of the Father: a Language of Labour Relations in Nineteenth-Century France." *History Workshop* 38 (Autumn 1994): 1–22.

Renard, Georges. "Une lettre relative au document Taschereau." *La Révolution de 1848* 7 (1910–1911): 7–15.

Reynolds, Siân, ed. *Women, State and Revolution: Essays on Power and Gender in Europe since 1789.* Amherst: University of Massachusetts Press, 1987.

Riches, David, ed. *The Anthropology of Violence.* Oxford: Basil Blackwell, 1986.

Rotundo, E. Anthony. *American Manhood: Transformations in Masculinity from the Revolution to the Modern Era.* New York: Basic Books, 1993.

Rougerie, Jacques. "Remarques sur l'histoire des salaires à Paris au XIXe siècle." *Le Mouvement social* 63 (1968): 71–108.

Rudé, Fernand. *C'est nous les canuts.* Paris: François Maspero, 1977.

Schnapper, Bernard. "Le jury français aux XIX et XXème siècles." *The Trial Jury in England, France, Germany 1700–1900,* ed. by Dr. Antonio Padoa Schioppa. Berlin: Duncker et Humblot, 1987: 165–240.

Scott, Joan Wallach. *Gender and the Politics of History.* New York: Columbia University Press, 1988.

Sencier, Georges. *Le Babouvisme après Babeuf.* Geneva: Mégariotis Reprints; reprint ed. of Paris, 1912.

Sewell, Jr., William H. "Social and Cultural Perspectives on Women's Work." *French Historical Studies* 20:1 (Winter 1997): 49–54.

———. "Introduction: Narratives and Social Identities." *Social Science History* 16:3 (Fall 1992): 479–488.

———."La Confraternité des Prolétaires: Conscience de classe sous la monarchie de juillet." *Annales, E. S. C.* (1981): 650–671.

———. "*Corporations Républicaines:* The Revolutionary Idiom of Parisian Workers in 1848." *Comparative Studies in Society and History* 21:2 (April 1979): 195–203.

———. *Work and Revolution in France: The Language of Labor from the Old Regime to 1848.* Cambridge, MA: Cambridge University Press, 1980.

Sibalis, Michael David. "The Mutual Aid Societies of Paris, 1789–1848." *French History* 3:1 (March 1989): 1–30.

Sonenscher, Michael. *Work and Wages: Natural Law, Politics, and the Eighteenth-Century French Trades.* Cambridge, MA: Cambridge University Press, 1989.

Spierenburg, Pieter, ed. *Men and Violence.* Columbus, OH: Ohio State University Press, 1998.

Spitzer, Alan B. "The Historical Problem of Generations." *American Historical Review* 78:5 (December 1973):1353–1385.

———. *Old Hatreds and Young Hopes: The French Carbonari against the Bourbon Restoration.* Cambridge, MA: Harvard University Press, 1971.

———. *The Revolutionary Theories of Louis-Auguste Blanqui.* New York: Columbia University Press, 1957; reprint ed., AMS Press, 1970.

Stearns, Peter N. *Be a Man! Males in Modern Society.* New York: Holmes and Meier, 1979.

Steinmetz, George. "Reflections on the Role of Social Narratives in Working-Class Formation: Narrative Theory In the Social Sciences." *Social Science History* 16:3 (Fall 1992): 489–516.

Stone, Judith F. *Sons of the Revolution: Radical Democrats in France, 1862–1914.* Baton Rouge: Louisiana State University Press, 1996.

Stone, Lawrence. "The Revival of Narrative: Reflections on a New Old History." *The Past and the Present.* Boston: Routledge and Kegan Paul, 1981.

Sullerot, Evelyne. "Journaux féminins et lutte ouvrière, 1848–1849." *La Presse Ouvrière 1819–1850.* Paris: Bibliothèque de la Révolution de 1848 (1966), vol. 23: 88–121.

Talmon, J. L. *Romanticism and Revolt: Europe 1815–1848.* New York: W. W. Norton, 1967.

———. *The Origins of Totalitarian Democracy.* New York: Penguin, 1952.

Tchernoff, I. *Associations et sociétés secrètes sous la deuxième République, 1848–1851, d'après des documents inédits.* Paris: Félix Alcan, 1905.

———. *Le Parti républicain sous la Monarchie de Juillet: Formation et évolution de la doctrine républicaine.* Paris: A. Pedone, 1901.

Terson, E. "Documents sur la mort de Mgr. Affre." *1848 et les Révolutions du XIXe siècle* 39 (March 1949): 42–52.

Thureau-Dangin, Paul. *Histoire de la Monarchie de Juillet*, 3rd. ed. 7 vols. Paris: Librairie Plon, 1902.

———. *Le Parti Libéral sous la Restauration*. 2nd edition. Paris: Plon, 1888.

Tosh, John. *A Man's Place: Masculinity and the Middle-Class Home in Victorian England.* New Haven: Yale University Press, 1999.

Touchard, Jean. *Histoire des Idées politiques.* 2 vols. Paris: Presses Universitaires de France, 1967.

Traugott, Mark. "The Crowd in the French Revolution of February, 1848." *The American Historical Review* 93:3 (June 1988): 638–652.

———. *Armies of the Poor: Determinants of Working-Class Participation in the Parisian Insurrection of June 1848.* Princeton: Princeton University Press, 1985.

Trognon, Auguste. *Vie de Marie-Amélie, Reine des Français.* 2nd ed. Paris: Michel Lévy frères, 1872.

Truant, Cynthia Maria. *The Rites of Labor: Brotherhoods of Compagnonnage in Old and New Regime France.* Ithaca: Cornell University Press, 1994.

Tulard, Jean. *Les Révolutions.* Paris: Fayard, 1985.

———. *La Préfecture de police sous la monarchie de juillet.* Paris: Imprimerie municipale, 1964.

Volguine, V. P. "Jean-Jacques Pillot, Communiste utopique." *La Pensée* 84 (1959): 37–53.

Wassermann, Suzanne. "Le Club de Raspail en 1848." *La Révolution de 1848: Bulletin de la Société d'histoire de la Révolution de 1848* (1908–1909): 589–605; 655–674; 748–762.

———. *Les Clubs de Barbès et de Blanqui en 1848.* Geneva: Megariotis Reprints, 1978.

Weill, Georges. "Les journaux ouvriers à Paris (1830–1870)." *Revue d'histoire moderne et contemporaine* 9 (1907–1908): 89–103.

———. "Philippe Buonarroti." Revue historique 76 (1901): 241–275.

———. *Histoire du parti républicain en France 1814–1870.* Paris: Ressources, 1980; reprint of 1928 edition.

Weiner, Dora B. "François-Vincent Raspail: Doctor and Champion of the Poor," *French Historical Studies* I, no. 2 (1959): 149–171.

White, Hayden. *The Content of the Form: Narrative Discourse and Historical Representation.* Baltimore: The Johns Hopkins University Press, 1987.

———. *Metahistory: the Historical Imagination in Nineteenth-Century Europe.* Baltimore: The Johns Hopkins University Press, 1973.

Willard, Claude. *Socialisme et communisme français.* Paris: Armand Colin, 1978.

Wright, Gordon. *Between the Guillotine and Liberty.* New York: Oxford University Press, 1983.

Zévaès, Alexandre. "L'agitation communiste de 1840 à 1848," *La Révolution de 1848 et les révolutions du XIXe siècle*, 24 (April–December 1926): 971–981; 26 (June 1926):1035–1044.

———. "Les Proscrits français en 1848 et 1851 à Londres." *La Révolution de 1848 et les Révolutions du XIXe siècle*, 20 (March 1923–February 1924): 345–375; 21 (March–April 1924): 94–114.

———. *Une Révolution manquée (l'insurrection du 12 mai 1839).* Paris: Nouvelle Revue critique, 1933.

INDEX

agents révolutionnaires   111, 119
Albert   36, 223, 224, 254, 255, 268, 271,
  272, 273, 274, 284, 320, 321
  journée of 15 May 287–292
Algeria   40, 95, 263, 267, 270
Alibaud, Louis   117, 168–172, 175, 183,
  186, 187, 194
Allemane, Jean   319
Alton-Shée, Comte d'   253, 263
amnesty
  March 1859   321, 322
  May 1837   116
  October 1844   223, 246
Andryane, Alexandre   232–233
April 1834   79–96, 101–102
    Beaubourg massacre   89–90, 99
  see also Transnonain, rue, massacre
Arago, Emmanuel   213
Arago, Étienne   254, 282, 292, 320
Arago, François   254, 258, 268, 271,
  284, 289, 300
Artisan, L'   216
assassination
    early attempts   181
    Fontelle and Oursel   172–173, 187
    justifications of   181–183
    lottery   174, 175
association (right of)   7, 50, 57, 107,
  253–254
  law of   65
Association gauloise   58–59
Association libre pour l'éducation du peuple
  49
*Association républicaine de la liberté de la
  presse*   70
Atelier, L'   28, 29, 49, 186, 211, 214,
  215, 279, 283

ateliers nationaux   *see* National
  Workshops
attentats à la sûreté de l'État   107
  see also September Laws
attroupement   296
Audry de Puyraveau   75, 80, 82, 83,
Aumale, duc d'   198
Austen, Florentz (Fritz)   133–134, 225,
  229, 235, 236–237

Babeuf, Gracchus   8, 50, 111, 114, 217,
  219
banquet campaign   252–254; *see also*
  suffrage reform
Barbès, Armand   111, 112, 115, 116, 118,
  128, 185, 281, 300, 319, 320, 321
  journée of 15 May   287, 289–293
  May 1839   121, 125, 127, 131–132,
    133, 139–140
  Mont-Saint-Michel   235–244, 246,
    247
  quarrel with Blanqui   138, 285, 286
barricades (law) 109
  Blanqui's ideal   142–143
Barrot, Odilon   42, 44, 61, 74, 107, 255,
  257, 264, 266, 268, 270
  suffrage reform   253, 254
Barthélemy, Emmanuel   304, 320
Bastide, Jules   44
Baude (Prefect of Police)   151, 164
Bazin, Napoléon   138, 200
Beaumont, Dr. Arthur   70, 104
Beaumont, Gustave de   230
Beaune, Eugène   254, 268, 320
Bédé, J. F.   31
Bedeau, General Alphonse   258, 263,
  265–266, 267, 270, 299

Belleville banquet, 220, 282, 283
Bérard, Auguste   45
Bergeron, Louis   181
Bernard, Martin, *see* Martin-Bernard
Berry, duc de   5, 180
   duchesse de Berry   57, 73
Berryer, Antoine   215, 270
Berryer-Fontaine, Camille   70, 72, 76,
   80, 321
Bescher, Tell   154, 163, 165
Beslay, Charles   313
Billaud-Varennes, Nicolas   184
Blanc, Louis   28, 30, 42, 58, 59, 62, 71,
   216–217, 252, 254, 268, 271,
   272–273, 282, 284, 285, 320
   journée of 15 May   287, 291, 292
Blanqui, Louis-Auguste   8, 17, 50, 51,
   52, 56, 73, 74, 110–112, 115,
   116, 120–121, 128, 141, 230, 234,
   274, 283, 285, 287, 300, 320,
   321, 322
   Instructions pour une prise d'armes
   141–144
   journée of 15 May   287–292
   May 1839   120–121, 122, 125, 132,
   133, 135, 139, 140–141
   Mont-Saint-Michel   235–240,
   241–242, 243, 244, 246, 247
   quarrel with Barbès   138, 285
   Taschereau document   285–286
Bloody Week   319, 320   *see also*
   Commune
Boireau, Victor (Fieschi attempt)   154,
   157, 159, 161, 162, 163, 165
Bonaparte, Louis Napoléon, Bonapartism
   70, 190, 194, 196, 246, 247, 290,
   298, 321
Bon Sens, Le   74, 102, 104, 173
Bourseau, Claude-Maurice   153, 165
Boyer, Adolphe   21
Bréa, General Jean de   305–311, 317
Brutus (assassin)   172, 175, 181, 183,
   184, 185, 186
Bruys, Amédée   320, 321
Buchez, Philippe   28, 49, 216, 289,
   290
Bugeaud, General Thomas   73–74, 263,
   264–266, 267, 270
Buonarroti, Philippe   50, 217, 232

Cabet, Étienne   15, 28, 65, 76, 77, 101,
   218–219, 223, 225, 246, 285
carbonari   5, 44, 49, 282
Carnot, Hippolyte   253, 268
carpenters' strike   72, 214–216   *see also*
   coalitions; labor
Carrel, Armand   41, 42, 63, 70–71, 102,
   103, 105, 194, 218
casualties
   April 1834   84
   February 1848   252
   Infernal machine   147
   July Revolution   41
   June 1832   60
   June Days   314–315, 298
   May 1839   137
Cauchois-Lemaire   282, 283, 284
Caunes, Auguste de   66, 151
Caunes, Jacques de   151, 152
Caussidière, Marc   221, 224, 228, 237,
   251, 254, 255, 262, 263, 284, 287,
   291, 292, 298, 299, 320
   prefect of police   270, 271, 277
Cavaignac, Eugène   50, 263, 289, 301,
   302, 304, 305, 313, 314
   June Days strategy   297–298
Cavaignac, Godefroy   9, 18, 39, 50, 52,
   53, 54, 70, 75, 81, 103, 155, 156,
   223, 298
Chaix d'Est-Ange, L.-A. (Fieschi's
   attorney)   163, 165
chambre syndicale   215
Charles X   3, 5, 39, 40, 53, 55, 57, 59,
   61
Charter (*Charte*)   39, 40, 47, 61, 198
Châtel, abbé   134
Châtillon banquet   196, 207
Chenu, Adolphe   157, 221–223, 224,
   225, 228, 255
cholera   57–58
Christian socialism   49, 218
clubs
   *club Blanqui   see Société républicaine
   centrale*
   club de la Montagne   293
   club de la révolution (club Barbès)   278,
   286
   club de la Sorbonne   280
   club des Montagnards   293

club lyonnais   278

club pacifique des droits de l'homme   282

club popincourt   281

club républicain de Montmartre   281

Club des Clubs   276, 281–282, 283, 284, 287, 288

coalitions   72, 197, 212, 213

Collot d'Herbois   184

Comité centralisateur   287

Commissaire, Sebastien   234, 237, 242, 243, 322

Commission de Gouvernement pour les travailleurs   *see* Luxembourg Commission

Commune (1871)   313, 316, 319, 320, 321, 322

Commune de Paris, La   280, 296

communism, varieties of   188–189, 217–218

Communistes matérialistes   224–228

compagnonnage   8, 12, 72, 212, 214, 215

Considérant, Victor   28, 30, 211, 292, 320

Considère, Claude   191, 197, 276

Constant, Alphonse Louis (abbé)   218

Constant, Benjamin   48, 105, 225

Constituent Assembly (1848)   *see* National Assembly

Convention   6, 43, 50, 66

Corday, Charlotte   134

Cour des Pairs   32, 33

April 1834 trial   88, 100–101, 103–104

May 1839 trial   139–140

Crémieux, Adolphe   61, 266, 268, 269, 271, 273, 274

Crevat, Victor   104, 111

Damas, Comte Gustave de   150, 151

Damesme, General   299, 305

Dantan, Louis-François   135

Danton, Georges   4

Darmès, Ennemond Marius   13, 16, 189–191, 193–196, 197, 198, 207, 218, 222

background   190, 192–193

interrogation   195–196

Daumier, Honoré   84

death tolls, *see* casualties

Decazes, duc Élie   178–179, 180

Delahodde, Lucien (police spy)   111, 125, 185, 221–222, 224, 228, 255

Delaire, Adrien   276

Delente, François   70, 74, 81, 225, 279

Delescluze, Charles   320

Delessert, Gabriel (prefect of police)   122, 181, 207, 221, 225

Delsade, Louis   235, 236, 237, 238, 240, 246

Démocratie pacifique, La   27, 30, 215, 216, 294

deportation   61, 64, 107, 316

Deroin, Jeanne   278

Dézamy, Théodore   219–220, 225–226, 274

Doullens   *see* prisons

Dourille, Henri   182–183, 195–196, 222, 224

Dubosc, Prosper Richard   129

Duchatel, Charles (Minister of Interior)   253, 256

Dufraisse, Marc   72, 182, 320, 321

Dufresne, Olivier   149

Dupin, André   47, 107, 213, 269

Dupin, Philippe (Pepin's attorney)   163, 165

Dupont de l'Eure, Jacques   73–74, 268, 271

Dupont, J.-F. (republican attorney)   56, 69, 133, 140, 153, 156, 163, 165, 181

Dupoty, Auguste   206, 207

Durrieu, Xavier   320

Dutertre, Frédéric   224

Duvivier, General Franciade Fleurus   305

École polytechnique   58, 271

Efrahem   72

Égalitaire, L'   8, 219

Egalitarian Workers, *see* Travailleurs Égalitaires

Égalité, Philippe   43

Église française   167, 248

electoral reform, *see* suffrage

escamotage   47, 183, 259, 267–268, 286

Fabre, Auguste   47

February 1848 revolution 251–255, 257, 262, 264, 265, 266–268, 299
    Capucines, boulevard des 212, 258–262, 265
    casualties 252
    insurgents 252
    proclamation of republic 273–274
    troops 255, 256
Ferrari, Benoît 121, 129–131, 135–136
Ficschi, Joseph 104, 148–149, 157–165, 168–169, 182–183, 187
    background 149–153
    Lassave, Virginie (Nina) 150–151, 153, 158, 160, 161, 162–163, 166
    Petit, Laurence 150–151, 152, 153, 155, 164–165, 166
Flocon, Ferdinand 223, 254, 255, 261, 268, 271, 272, 273, 284, 320
Flotte, Benjamin 118, 237, 239, 241, 243, 274, 322
Fombertaux, Antoine 136, 185, 274, 320, 322
Fombertaux, Eugène 185
Foucauld, Vicomte Jean de 252
Fourierists 10, 15
    see also Victor Considérant
Fraisse, Léonce 170, 171, 320
Franck-Carré (prosecutor) 32, 140, 177, 180, 190, 196, 198
Franco-Prussian War 10, 322
Fraternité, La 226

garde républicaine 277, 298
Garnier-Pagès, Étienne (the elder) 53, 253
Garnier-Pagès, Louis (the younger) 53, 253, 261, 268, 271, 272, 276, 289, 318
Gasparin, Adrien de 230, 231
Gay, Désirée 278–279
Gazette des Tribunaux 104, 173, 186, 221, 228, 303, 314, 315, 317
Gérard, Maurice-Étienne 137, 266, 267
    Gérard Plan 137, 256; see also National Guard
Girard, Fulgence 112, 236, 237, 239, 240, 243, 244
Girardin, Émile de 105, 266

Girod de l'Ain 222
Gironde, Girondins 17, 66, 68, 76
Gisquet, Henri-Joseph (prefect of police) 57, 58, 59, 63, 74, 75, 79, 80, 80, 83, 99, 108, 149, 163, 181
    infernal machine 160, 162, 165
Globe, Le 28, 50
Grignon 72–73
Grivel, abbé 33, 163, 172, 207
Guéret, Louis 220, 223, 224
Guillemin, Jean-Baptiste 185, 235–236, 237, 238
Guinard, Joseph 44, 53, 54, 70, 81, 101, 103, 156, 289, 320
Guizot, François 45, 47, 50, 58, 63, 190, 206, 252, 253, 254, 257, 258, 259, 260

Hadot-Desages 110
Hébert, Michel 31
Henry, Joseph 21, 33–34
    attempt 35–36
    background 21–27
Holy Alliance 196, 287
Homme libre, L' 185
hommes d'action 65–66, 85, 262
honor 9, 10–11, 13–14
Hôtel de Ville (in insurrection) 127–128, 265, 277, 289, 292
    Provisional Government 272, 273
Huber, Aloysius 237, 239–240, 242–243, 244–245, 246
    journée of 15 May 287–288, 290–291
Hubert, Jean-Louis 44
Hugo, Victor 57, 139–140, 282, 322
Humanitaire, L' 219, 223, 225, 226

Icarians 10, 15
    see also Cabet, Étienne
industrialization 11–12
infernal machine
    Fieschi 148, 153–154, 157–159, 161–162
    Champion 166
insurgents
    February 1848 252
    July 1830 41
    June Days 314

June 1832   60
   May 1839   125
   occupations of   12–13
insurrections   see April 1834, June Days
   (1848), June 1832, May 1839

Jacqueminot, Jean-François   256
Janot, Isidore   154, 158
Jeanne, Charles   59, 62–64, 85, 305
Jesus Christ   55, 218
   see Christian socialism
Joinville, prince de   137, 147–148, 174
Journal de Paris, Le   102
Journal des Débats   70, 205
Journal du Peuple   206, 220, 222, 322
journées
   17 March 1848   284
   16 April 1848   286, 287
   15 May 1848   287–293
   13 June 1849   320, 322
Jubelin, Étienne-Martial   126, 127,
   135
July Monarchy
   ended   269–271
   philosophy of 48–49
July 1830 revolution   39–41
   economy   27–29, 30, 31, 40
   philosophy of   48–49
   republicans   39, 43–44, 45, 47
   settlement   42–43, 46–48
   woman killed   262
June Days   251, 263, 287, 298, 299–312,
   320
   casualties   298, 314–315
   faubourg Saint-Antoine   312–313
   insurgents   300, 303, 305, 312,
   313–314, 316
   Mobile Guards   301–303
   women   294, 299, 305–306, 308,
   313, 316–317
June 1832   14, 39, 50, 57–60, 61–64,
   156, 230
   Saint-Mery   60, 62–64, 229
jury, legislation   51–52, 107
   see also trials

Kersausie, Théophile Guillard de
   68–69, 70, 73, 75, 80, 81, 82–83,
   104, 105, 281, 320, 321

labor
   carpenters' strike   214–215
   laws   212–213
   livret   213, 214
Lacambre, Dr. Louis   125, 274, 320
Ladvocat, Colonel Gustave   149, 151,
   164, 256
Lafayette   44, 45, 46, 47, 58, 74, 102,
   110, 253, 294
Laffitte, Jacques   41, 42, 43, 45, 47, 48,
   191, 253
Lagrange, Charles   254, 263, 270, 273,
   274, 281, 282, 292, 320
Lamarque, General Maximilien   58–59,
   63, 221
Lamartine, Alphonse de   21, 268,
   270–271, 272, 273, 288
Lamennais, Felicité de   128–129, 134,
   218
Lamieussens, Eugène   116
Lamoricière, General Christophe   299,
   301, 304, 313,
Laponneraye, Albert   71, 129, 134, 218,
   321
Lebon, Napoléon   68, 69, 70, 72, 73, 80,
   103, 279, 320
Lecomte, Pierre   21, 32–33
Leconte, Henri   80, 156
Leconte, Minor Christophe   166–167
Ledru, Charles   171–172, 191
Ledru-Rollin, Alexandre   180, 219, 224,
   248, 297, 320
   February revolution   252–254, 258,
   262, 268, 270–273
   rue Transnonain affair   84–85, 92,
   94, 97, 99, 100
   Provisional Government   276, 284,
   286, 290–292
Legitimism   57
   see also Berry, duc de
Leroux, Jules 28, 320
Leroux, Pierre   28, 223, 292, 320
Lobau, Marshal   60
Louis XVI   43, 103, 184
Louis XVIII   5
Louis-Philippe   3, 5, 20, 23, 27, 35,
   39–45, 46–49, 58, 59, 60, 61,
   74, 137, 139–140, 198, 291,
   295

abdication   266–267, 269
assassination attempts against   32,
    168–169, 172, 189–190, 147–148,
    160, 172–174
    February revolution   254–257, 263,
        264
    Orléans, death of duc d'   207–208
Louvel   180
Lucas, Charles   240, 241
Luxembourg Commission   274, 282,
    285, 287, 293, 295
Lyon   57, 70, 81, 83, 84, 102

MacMahon, Maréchal   270
Malet, General   182–183
Marat, Jean-Paul   5, 15, 49, 55, 134,
    173, 186
marchandage, marchandeur   27–28,
    213–214, 274
Marche (worker)   273, 293
Marie, Alexandre   63–64, 157, 163, 253,
    268, 269, 271, 272, 289
Marie-Amélie, queen   43, 207
Marie-Antoinette   43
Marie-Caroline (Naples)   43
Maroncelli, Pietro   232
Marrast, Armand   46, 81, 102, 105, 108,
    224, 253, 254, 259, 268, 270, 271,
    280
Marseillaise, La   17, 35, 47, 197, 227,
    230, 240, 259, 271–272
Martin, Alexandre   see Albert
Martin-Bernard   112, 115, 119, 120,
    128–129, 243, 244, 246, 247–248,
    274, 320
    May 1839   126, 128, 132, 135, 139
    Mont-Saint-Michel   234–237,
        241–242
Martin du Nord, Nicolas   154, 155, 171
Marx, Karl   6
masculinity   9–11, 14–15   see also honor
Materialist Communists   see communiste
    matérialiste
Mathé, Félix   320
Mathieu d'Épinal, Joseph   200, 237, 320
Maupas, Émile de   298
May 1839   120–121, 126–127, 129–130,
    135
    Greneta, battle of   132–134, 229

Messager, Le   71, 99, 101
Meunier, François   168, 174–175, 180
    background   176–178
    interrogations   178–180
Mignet, François   41
Mobile Guard   301–304
    founded   271
Molé, Comte Mathieu   257, 258
Monde républicain, Le   276, 278
Moniteur, Le   273
Moniteur républicain, Le   181, 183–186,
    235
montagnardism   6–19, 282, 295, 304
    ideals of   304
Montagnards (underground group)   121,
    130, 138, 276–277
Montagne, La   218
Mont-Saint-Michel   61, 62, 64, 231,
    233, 239–243, 246–247, 277, 321,
    322
    brutality   238–239, 244–245
    cachots and loges   231, 236, 238–239,
        240, 243
    see also prisons
Moreau-Christophe, Louis   243
Morey, Pierre   153–154, 157, 159,
    161–166, 187
    praised, 182–183
mort aux voleurs   14, 267
Mortier, Maréchal   147, 161
Murat, Joachim   150

Nadaud, Martin   12, 32, 267, 310, 320
Napoléon I   4, 150
narrative   18–19
National Assembly
    elections 281–284
    Executive Commission   287, 197,
        300
National, Le   41, 45, 58, 61, 63, 64, 70,
    73, 99, 100, 101, 102, 105, 173,
    193, 196, 211–212, 218, 223, 224,
    231, 244–245, 253, 254, 258–259,
    261, 268, 274, 276, 286, 296, 303,
    318
National Guard   48, 110, 274, 279, 315
    elections   280–281, 284, 286
    February 1848   253–254, 256–257
    reviews   166, 172, 181

suffrage reform   206–207
National Workshops   273, 277, 284,
     287, 293, 295, 299, 314, 318
     dissolution   293, 296–297
     size   293
Négrier   305
Nemours, duc de   100, 137, 147–148,
     174, 198, 207–208, 252, 257, 264,
     265, 266, 269
     newspapers, *see* press
Niboyet, Eugenie   278
Nouguès, Pierre   119, 125, 126, 130,
     229, 237, 242–243
Nouvelles Saisons   220, 221–223

ordre du jour   66, 69, 72, 75, 222, 224,
     229
     see also Société des Droits de l'Homme
Orléans, duc d'   (son of Louis-Philippe)
     100, 137, 147–148, 174, 198, 207,
     223
     duchesse d'Orléans   208, 266, 269
     Paris, comte de   207, 266
Oursine, rue de l'   115–116

Pasquier, Étienne-Denis (Chancellor)
     103, 155, 178–179
Pellico, Silvio   231–232, 233
Pepin, Théodore   153, 154–157, 159,
     163, 164, 165–166, 182, 183, 187
     Mme. Pepin   161, 163, 166–167
     Société des Familles   110–111
Perdiguier, Agricole   35, 213, 284, 320
Père Duchêne, Le   17
Périer, Casimir   48, 58, 107
permanence, en permanence   17, 69,
     73–74, 78–79, 88, 104, 286
     see also Société des Droits de l'Homme et
          du Citoyen
Phalanges démocratiques   183–184
Pillot, Jean-Jacques, abbé   194, 218,
     220, 321–322
Plocque, J.-A. (attorney)   117
Poland   4, 287–289, 293
Polignac, Jules de   40, 53
Politique des Femmes, La   279
Populaire, Le   65, 74, 76, 207, 225, 226, 246
Pornin, Bernard   67, 320
Poulot, Denis   29–30

Prefect of Police   110, 121   *see also*
     Gisquet; Delessert
press   7, 108
     crieurs publics   74
     September Laws   107
Presse, La   105
prisons   230–231
     Conciergerie   83
     Doullens   235, 236, 237, 242, 249,
          322
     Force   103
     Nîmes   243, 247
     Sainte-Pélagie   76, 102–103, 153,
          155–156, 221, 230, 316
     Salpêtrière   150
     Spielberg   231–233, 240
     see also Mont-Saint-Michel
Procès d'avril, des Dix-Neuf, etc.   *see* trials
programme de l'Hôtel de Ville   46, 76, 198,
     253, 285
Proudhon, Pierre-Joseph   30, 216, 225,
     292, 321, 322
Provisional Government (1848)   8, 36,
     61, 63, 223, 228, 268, 269–270,
     271–276, 284, 286–287
     concept of   8, 114, 115, 217, 219
     early decrees   273–274
     journées (17 March, 16 April, 15 May)
          284, 286–287, 287–293
Pruvost, Nicolas (*Invalide*)   85, 100
Pujol, Louis   297

Quadruple Alliance   4, 5
Quenisset, François   199, 204–205, 207,
     222, 223
     confession   199–201, 202–203
Quignot, Louis   7, 128–129, 188, 237,
     240, 247
Quinet, Edgar   5, 315

Racary, Louis-Auguste   320–321
Radicals   253
Raisant, Alexandre   112, 116, 118, 120
Raspail, François-Vincent   49, 52, 56,
     68, 69, 108, 320
     journée of 15 May   287–292
Recurt, Dr. Adrien   70, 104, 289
Réforme, La   18, 50, 61, 73, 219, 223,
     224, 227, 228, 230, 244–245, 246,

253, 254, 255, 258, 261, 262, 268,
    276, 282, 320–322
regency   207–208, 268–271
Reign of Terror   4, 6
Renault, General Pierre   263, 264
Représentant du peuple, Le   286, 296, 318
republicans   48
    and communism, socialism   211,
        216–217, 218
    July revolution   3, 5, 39, 47
revolution   *see* February 1848; July 1830
revolutionary dictatorship   *see*
        provisional government
right to bear arms   109
    see also weapons
Robespierre, Maximilien   4, 5, 8, 15, 17,
    55, 61, 77, 173, 184, 186, 194, 218,
    281, 282
    Declaration of the Rights of Man
        66, 70–72
romantic, romanticism   15–16
Rouen, repression   287, 288, 289, 291
Rouget de l'Isle   47
Rousseau, Jean-Jacques   190, 218
Royer-Collard, Pierre   107
Rumigny, General Marie-Theodore   74,
    126

Sainte-Pélagie, *see* prisons
Saint-Just, Louis   15, 118, 163, 170,
    173, 184, 194
Saint-Simonians   10, 15, 49, 50, 278
Sambuc, Jules   53–54
Sand, George   278
Sarrans, Benjamin   268, 269, 270
Sauzet, Paul   269
Sebastiani, Tiburce   60, 256, 263, 265
Senard, Jules   276, 313
September Laws   107, 206
    see also press
Sobrier, Joseph   274, 277, 287
Société d'Action   75, 79, 80, 81, 82
Société de la Voix des Femmes   278–279
Société démocratique française   115
Société des Amis du Peuple   7, 39, 43–44,
    49–51, 54, 55–57, 58, 65, 66, 67,
    68, 69, 70, 72, 75
*Société des Droits de l'Homme et du
    Citoyen*   9, 17, 50, 65–69, 72, 75,

84, 86, 154–155, 190, 225, 278,
    320, 321
Central Committee and manifesto
    69–71, 73–74, 75, 104
divisions within   68–72
labor, relations with   72–73
membership   75–79
permanence, en permanence   73–74,
    78–79
Propaganda Commission   72–73,
    113, 216, 279
revived in 1848   281–184, 279–281,
    286, 293
sections   65, 66–67, 70, 76–79, 80,
    86, 87, 88, 89, 100–101, 154
Société des Familles   9, 51, 110–112,
    115–118, 185–186, 220, 225, 321
    rules and initiation   106, 111,
        113–114
Société des Saisons   7, 9, 119, 120,
    184–185, 188, 225, 285
    rules and initiation   111, 114–115
*Société pour la Défense de la Liberté de la
    Presse patriote*   49
Société pour l'Instruction du Peuple   154
Société républicaine centrale   274, 280
Solidarité républicaine   321
solitary confinement   240
    see also prisons
Soult, Marshal   137, 150, 190
Spielberg, *see* prisons
strikes   *see* coalitions
Sue, Eugène   215, 274, 320
suffrage   48, 274
    Châtillon banquet   196, 207
    reform   196–197, 206–207, 220,
        252–253

Taschereau, Jules   285
Taschereau document   119, 185,
    285–286
Teste, Charles   44, 50
Teste, Jean-Baptiste   50, 228
Teste-Cubières affair   50, 228
Thiers, Adolphe   41, 45, 80, 253, 257,
    258, 263–264, 266, 268
Thomas, Colonel Clément   252, 310
Thomas, Émile   295
    see also National Workshops

Thoré, Théophile   73, 218, 292, 320
Thouret, Antony   56, 289, 320
Tocqueville, Alexis de   230, 245, 263, 269
Tocsin des Travailleurs, Le   276, 279, 293, 295
Torrijos, General José   77
Transnonain, massacre   9, 84, 85, 86, 88, 90–100, 109, 218, 263, 267, 303, 305
transportation   *see* deportation
Travail, Le   16
Travailleurs Égalitaires   199, 202, 203–204, 205, 206, 220, 223, 225, 226, 299, 320
    Nouvelles Saisons   222–223
    origin and rules   188–189, 200–201
Treaty of 15 July (1840)   195–196
Trélat, Dr. Ulysse   44, 49, 51, 53, 310
trials   53–57
    June 1832   61–62
    procedures   51–53, 107
    Procès d'avril   103–105, 107
    Procès des Dix Neuf   39, 51, 53–55
    Procès des Quinze   56
    Procès des Ministres   53

Procès des Vingt-Sept   68, 73
Tribune, La   47, 55, 62, 81, 102, 105, 108
Tristan, Flora   15, 216
Truquin, Norbert   143, 267, 314, 318

Union de Juillet, l'   154

Vernet, Horace   208
Vignerte, Jean-Jacques   68, 70, 71, 72, 73, 80, 102, 282
Vilain, Joseph   279, 281, 282, 283, 284, 286
Vilcoq, Henri Stanislaus   186, 237, 246
Voilquin, Suzanne   15, 278
Voix des Femme, La   278, 279
Voyer d'Argenson, René   50, 70, 72, 75, 80, 82, 83, 128–129
Vraie République, La   276

weapons   60, 75, 77–78, 86, 115–119
    law   7, 108–110
    Lepage shop   125, 257
women (and republican movement)   15
    1848   278–279
workers   *see* labor